The Ultimate Encyclopedia of

BOXING

DEDICATION

To Miguel Matthews, Seamus Casey and their blood brothers: journeymen fighters who will never feature in any encyclopedia of boxing, but without whose honest professionalism the game could not flourish.

THIS IS A CARLTON BOOK

This edition published in 1996 by Chartwell Books, an imprint of Book Sales Inc., 114 Northfield Avenue, Edison, N.J.

10 9 8 7 6 5 4 3 2 1

Produced by Carlton Books Limited, 20 St Anne's Court, Wardour Street, London W1V 3AW

Catalog-in-Publication Data for this book is available upon request

ISBN 0 7858 0641 5

Printed and bound in Dubai

Project Editor: Martin Corteel
Project art direction: Paul Messam
Production: Sarah Schuman
Picture research: Charlotte Bush
Designer: Paul Cooper

LIST OF ABBREVIATIONS

Alg Algeria
Arg Argentina
Aus Australia
Aut Austria
Bah Bahamas
Bel Belgium
Bop Bophuthatswana
Bra Brazil
Cam Cambodia
Can Canada
Ch China
Col Colombia
Cub Cuba
Den Denmark
DR Dominican Republic
Ecu Ecuador
Eng England
Fra France
Ger Germany
Gha Ghana
Guad Guadaloupe
Hol Holland
Hun Hungary
IC Ivory Coast
Indo Indonesia
Ire Ireland
Is Israel
Ita Italy
Jam Jamaica
Jap Japan
Kaz Kazakhstan

Ken Kenya
Kor South Korea
Ku Kuwait
Mex Mexico
Mon Monaco
N. Ire Northern Ireland
Neth Ant Netherlands Antilles
Nic Nicaragua
Nig Nigeria
Nor Norway
NZ New Zealand
Pan Panama
Par Paraguay
Phil Philippines
Por Portugal
PR Puerto Rico
SA South Africa
Sco Scotland
Sp Spain
Swe Sweden
Swi Switzerland
Thai Thailand
Tr Trinidad
Tun Tunisia
Ug Uganda
Ur Uruguay
US United States
Ven Venezuela
Wal Wales
Yug Yugoslavia
Zam Zambia

CHAMPIONSHIP WEIGHT LIMITS

Category	American	British	Metric
Strawweight	105 lb	7st 7 lb	47.627 kg
Light-flyweight	108 lb	7st 10 lb	48.988 kg
Flyweight	112 lb	8st	50.802 kg
Super-flyweight	115 lb	8st 3 lb	52.163 kg
Bantamweight	118 lb	8st 6 lb	53.524 kg
Super-bantamweight	122 lb	8st 10 lb	55.338 kg
Featherweight	126 lb	9st	57.153 kg
Super-featherweight	130 lb	9st 4 lb	58.967 kg
Lightweight	135 lb	9st 9 lb	61.235 kg
Light-welterweight	140 lb	10st	63.503 kg
Welterweight	147 lb	10st 7 lb	66.678 kg
Light-middleweight	154 lb	11st	69.853 kg
Middleweight	160 lb	11st 6 lb	72.575 kg
Super-middleweight	168 lb	12st	76.203 kg
Light-heavyweight	175 lb	12st 7 lb	79.379 ks
Cruiserweight	190 lb	13st 8 lb	86.183 kg
Heavyweight	*any weight above the cruiserweight limit*		

(OPPOSITE) SHORT BUT SWEET *Mike Tyson ends Frank Bruno's brief reign as WBC heavyweight champion*
(FACING CONTENTS) READY TO RUMBLE *An opponent's-eye view of Prince Naseem Hamed*
(PAGES 6 AND 7) LENNOX LEWIS *(left) wins a tough 10-rounder against Ray Mercer*

The Ultimate Encyclopedia of

BOXING

The definitive illustrated guide to world boxing

Harry Mullan

CHARTWELL
BOOKS, INC.

CONTENTS

CLOWN PRINCE *Max Baer*

GOLDEN BOY *Oscar De La Hoya*

SILK-SMOOTH *Superstar Roy Jones*

INTRODUCTION

Boxing changes. Records are broken, new standards are set, championships fragment and sub-divide again as yet another self-appointed "governing body" tries to grab its share of the big money with which the business, at the top level, is awash. Even in the period since my late friend and mentor Gilbert Odd issued the last major encyclopedia of boxing in 1983 (updated in 1990) the sport has moved on, hence the need for this volume.

Gilbert's book did not, for example, recognize the World Boxing Organization or list its champions, which given the fact that in 1990 the WBO regarded Francesco Damiani as heavyweight champion of the world was probably a reasonable decision at the time. (On much the same basis, I have not included the champions of bodies like the International Boxing Organization or the World Boxing Union.) But in the years since then the WBO has grown in stature and can now claim champions of the quality of Marco Antonio Barrera, Oscar De La Hoya and Naseem Hamed, which makes them a serious force in boxing. If the IBO and WBU make similar strides, they may well find their way into any revised edition of this book.

The purist in me wishes that things were different, that we could go back to the way the game was when I was young and there were just eight

weight divisions, each with (usually) a single champion. Realistically, though, it will not happen: commercial interests dictate that championships should not be unified, save in the case of the heavyweight championship where the rest of the field could probably earn more as Mike Tyson's challenger than they could for defending whichever splinter of the divided title they held. Like them or not, the groups for whom former *Ring* editor Bert Sugar coined the phrase "The Alphabet Boys" are here to stay. So, too, are poverty, hunger and war: we don't want them either, but it would be unrealistic to pretend they do not exist.

Rather than do a straightforward chronological list of title fights in each division, littering the page with all kinds of symbols and footnotes to explain which version of the title was at stake in any given fight, I have tried to disentangle the various strands of the title and follow them through from inauguration to reunification.

It was a difficult but worthwhile exercise, and the result emphasizes how much of a misnomer the term "world champion" has become. In most cases, modern title-holders are not world champions in the sense that Sugar Ray Robinson, Joe Louis or Henry Armstrong understood the term: they are merely WBC, WBA, IBF or WBO champions.

In compiling the world title list I have drawn heavily on standard sources like the *Ring Record Book* (which ceased publication in 1987), the *Boxing News Annual* (now also extinct) and the invaluable Italian annual *Pugilato*, whose founder and compiler Giuseppe Ballarati, an avid historian and statistician, is much missed since his death in 1995.

The principal reference, though, has been the extraordinarily detailed work done by Barry Hugman and his associates for the *British Boxing Yearbook* 1995 and 1996 editions. Hugman and the others spent much time in America combing newspaper libraries and microfilmed records in a bid to ascertain, once and for all, which were genuine title fights and which were not. A surprising number of fights which the previously mentioned volumes had recorded as title fights turned out to have been overweight matches or, in several instances, not to have taken place at all!

I do not, however, accept Hugman's argument that a champion's No Decision fights should be included as title defences; his position is that, since the champion would have lost the title if (a) he was knocked out and (b) both were inside the championship weight, the title was automatically at stake. Similarly, he includes modern-era non-title fights involving champions like the Argentine flyweight Pascual Perez, where both champion and opponent were inside the weight. My view is that a match can only properly be considered a title fight when full championship conditions are observed: when it is over the recognized championship distance, with both inside the weight, and the contest is billed and announced as a title fight.

But that disagreement on interpretation does nothing to diminish my respect for a superb (and on-going) work of research, and I am grateful for his permission to draw on his findings here.

The other principal section in this encyclopedia is The Great Boxers, brief pen-pictures of 200 of the game's top names. If your particular favourite is not here or in the Legends of the Ring section, my apologies. With unlimited space, I could easily have stretched that figure to 500, but restraints applied and a final selection had to be made on the basis of

their achievements and their significance in the overall development and history of the sport. Some of my own personal favourites did not make the final cut: there was no room for Joey Giambra, Joe Becerra, Bennie Briscoe, Jim Watt, Alan Rudkin, Danny Lopez or many others whose careers I have followed and, in some cases, reported on over the last 30 years. Maybe a future volume will do them all justice.

The list of 15 Great Fights was also difficult to compile, since they had to meet the twin criteria of being an outstanding contest which was also of lasting importance to the sport's history. Here again, I have reluctantly had to omit epics like Marvin Hagler vs. John Mugabi, Danny Lopez vs. Juan Malvarez, Barry McGuigan vs. Steve Cruz and, at British title level, Clinton McKenzie vs. Colin Power, Des Morrison vs. Joe Tetteh or Tom Collins vs. John Moody, all of which I covered from ringside. In fact, I only reported on four of the final 15, so can safely plead not guilty to any charge of personal bias. For the rest, I have relied on films or contemporary accounts, and in some instances on the biographies or autobiographies of the men involved.

Where boxers' records are quoted, they are complete up to the end of 1995,

although in a few exceptional cases (Mike Tyson's and Frank Bruno's, for example) we had time to incorporate their 1996 meeting before the printers' deadline was enforced.

The names of some weight divisions vary according to which authority is involved, but where possible I have used the British names: cruiserweight, not junior-heavyweight; light-middleweight rather than junior-middleweight; light-welterweight, not junior-welterweight or super-lightweight; super-featherweight rather than junior-lightweight; super-bantamweight, not junior featherweight; super-flyweight rather than junior-bantamweight, and light-flyweight rather than mini-flyweight.

I am grateful to Bob Mee, compiler of the invaluable annual *British Boxing Records*, for contributing the chapters on the sport's origins and its leading promoters.

This book could not have been compiled without access to the archives of *Boxing News*, the world's oldest boxing publication, which it has been my privilege to edit for almost 20 years. I am grateful to publisher Peter Kravitz for his co-opera-

tion, which included extensive use of photographs from the paper's files, and to my editorial colleagues Daniel Herbert, Claude Abrams, Mark Butcher and Konrad Manning for their help and support. I must also acknowledge the assistance of my wife, Jessie, who read the first drafts and was, as ever, my severest critic.

Any errors you spot – and despite the best efforts of myself and copy editor Peter Arnold, there are bound to be a couple – are my responsibility. But I trust they are minor, and not enough to detract from your enjoyment of a work of reference which was, for me, a labour of love.

HARRY MULLAN
Bridge, Kent
July 1996

THE ORIGINS OF BOXING

Prizefighting reached its peak in eighteenth and nineteenth-century England, when champions were recognized and kings, poets and statesmen patronized a sport which the law nevertheless prohibited. By the time modern boxing began to take over from bare-knuckle savagery, the centre of activity was switching to America.

Perhaps the one incontrovertible piece of evidence boxing's abolitionists can never deny is that it has been with us for as long as man can remember. Fist-fighting, as sporting competition, has been a part of us for thousands of years. It was certainly practised during the original Olympic Games in ancient Greece. Homer refers to it in the *Iliad*. It was a regular entertainment in Roman times too, and possibly existed in Britain during the centuries of Roman occupation. However, the first vague references do not emerge until the late seventeenth century. In January 1681, the *Protestant Mercury* recorded "a match of boxing before His Grace, the Duke of Albemarle, between the Duke's footman and a butcher". The latter, apparently, was a small but experienced boxer, and he won. How and where, we know not.

The first English champion of record was James Figg, from Thame in Oxfordshire, who was brought to London by a patron who saw him performing on the village green and set him up in a boxing "academy". Figg was illiterate, but a cunning businessman and the most celebrated teacher of the 1720s. Boxing was so popular King George I ordered a ring to be erected in Hyde Park for public use. Figg taught the use of sword, broadsword, cudgel and fist in premises at the Adam And Eve pub between what is now Tottenham Court Road and Oxford Street.

Boxing was only loosely related to the art we see today, but then so were other fledgling sports – cricket, for example, bore only rough comparison to the complicated game now laid before us. Wrestling was accepted as a proper part of boxing, and so were blatant fouls like gouging and "purring" – the raking of the spiked boot across a fallen man. These were outlawed only by the rules introduced in 1743 by Figg's successor, John Broughton, which laid the broad foundation for the way boxing was run for almost 100 years until the establishment of the London Prize Ring Rules in 1838.

But it took the first major ring tragedy for the atmosphere to be created whereby such regulations could be enforced. Broughton beat the inexperienced George Stevenson of Hull in his own booth, close to Figg's old premises, in February 1741. It was a brutal bout which lasted almost 40 minutes before Broughton drove in a punch beneath the heart that forced Stevenson's collapse. He recovered consciousness, only to linger a few weeks in the Adam and Eve before dying in Broughton's arms. The champion was so affected that he used his influence and status to

JAMES FIGG *Prize fighter, swordsman and bear baiter*

BROOME VS HANNAR *was for a £1,000 purse and took place at New Farm Park, near Bicester, in England's South Midlands*

introduce this first attempt to regulate boxing and to lessen the possibility of tragedy in the ring.

Royal Patronage

Aside from his rules, Broughton made boxing acceptable to the gentry, providing lessons and sparring sessions with "mufflers" to minimize the risk of damage to a man's looks. His career was enhanced by the patronage of the Duke of Cumberland, the notorious Butcher of Culloden, whom he beat in a "small sword" match held at the academy, which Cumberland had visited as an exercise.

This victory was important in that it persuaded the gentry and aristocracy that there was something to be learned from "academies" where "the science of defence" was taught. It also helped enormously that John Broughton's personality was unusually cultured for a man who made his living in the way that he did. This enabled him to make influential friends who helped him

even when Cumberland's patronage ended, following his shock defeat by Jack Slack in 1750. Cumberland made a crazy bet of £10,000 to win £400 from a lesser crony, then blamed Broughton when a surprise punch from Slack blinded him temporarily and rendered him unable to fight.

The undiluted anguish of Broughton's plaintive: "By God, I'm done!" passes down the centuries, but Cumberland was unimpressed, claimed he had been double-crossed and promptly closed down the academy and had boxing outlawed from civilized society. Broughton, however, knew enough people to survive, turned his academy into what amounts now to a furniture warehouse, made a fortune on the stock market and lived to the age of 84. He was buried in Lambeth and a tablet was erected in his memory in Westminster Abbey.

Slack is largely blamed for pugilism's demise in the middle years of the eighteenth century, but then he lacked Broughton's tower-

ing personality, his business acumen – and royal patronage. He was a butcher by trade, who travelled to London from Norwich to find his fortune. He did draw some fame from a victory over a 6ft 4in Frenchman known only as "Petit", presumably a nickname, at Harleston in Norfolk in July 1751. A

THE FIRST PRIZE RING RULES *were drawn up in London in 1743*

defeat of a foreigner always went down well. Slack based himself in London where he gave lessons. But he was a rugged fighter with a huge heart and big punch ... and that doesn't necessarily make for a good teacher.

John Broughton opened the "Tennis Court" in London's Haymarket, which housed a fight between Slack and William Stevens of Birmingham in 1760. Cumberland, by now a man of declining fortunes, returned to his old habits and gambled on this fight again ... on Slack, who lost the championship when Stevens landed his "chopper blow" and threw him heavily, his head smacking on the wooden boards. This time Cumberland broke all ties with pugilism. Within nine months Stevens had taken a dive against one George Meggs of Bristol and the decline of boxing was set.

After a run of ordinary champions, boxing was effectively rescued by a former corn porter from Derby, Thomas Jackling, who took the ring name Johnson. He drew crowds on a regular basis, and eventually royal interest returned – most notably the young Prince of Wales, the future George IV. Peers of the realm began to sponsor fighters and once more boxing became an activity on which large sums could be won and lost. By using his fists a man could escape poverty and, while he could never traverse the boundaries of class, he could at least appear to do so by association.

The greatest star to emerge since Broughton was Daniel Mendoza, born in Aldgate in the east end of

London of Jewish descent. Mendoza was one of the cleverest boxers in history, who had a celebrated series of bouts with Richard "The Gentleman" Humphries between 1788 and 1790, which captured the imagination of the nation. Humphries won the first, after which he sent a message to his patron that read simply: "Sir, I have done the Jew and am in good health", but Mendoza won the second and third battles.

Their third encounter was in Doncaster and was important enough to persuade men to travel nearly 200 miles from London to see it – no easy journey when roads were often no more than mudtracks. Humphries was beaten after 73 minutes, retired and made good money as a coal merchant, while Mendoza lived on his wits, touring with a circus, mixing with royalty, giving public sparring tours, and even writing his autobiography. He also found himself in debtors' prison more than once, but his friends usually bailed him out.

John Jackson

Mendoza was beaten by a formidably intelligent man named John Jack-

son, who was known as "Gentleman", and who was perhaps the most complete "heir" to Broughton. Like the old hero he was a tremendous technical boxer, a thinking man, and a genius in business. He thrashed the smaller Mendoza in little more than 10 minutes near Hornchurch in Essex in April 1795. He had worked hard for his success – the only bout he lost was when he broke an ankle and yet he still offered to fight on if he could be strapped to a chair! – and after defeating Mendoza he cashed in, retiring to open what became a busy and thriving business at 13 Old Bond Street in the centre of London. It was there that the rich and famous flocked to be taught the "noble art" and Jackson became one of the most celebrated figures of his day. Lord Byron was a pupil and once grandly labelled Jackson "The Emperor of Pugilism". Through Jackson's influence, boxing became fashionable once more, and moved into perhaps its grandest age. Jackson himself lived on into old age in comfort, dying in 1845 at the age of 76.

The supremacy of the Bristol "school" of pugilism reached its height at the turn of the nineteenth century with the arrival of Jem Belcher, a precocious young man who astonished London society with his brilliance and who was called "Napoleon of the Ring". He was barely 19 when he beat Jack Bartholomew, a man who laid good claim to be champion. Belcher was acknowledged beyond dispute as the champion when he defeated Andrew Gamble, a stonemason who was the Irish champion, on Wimbledon Common in December 1800. It is said that the roar of the crowd could be heard 10 miles away, and pigeons carrying news of his victory were sent back to Bristol, where church bells were rung in celebration.

After that Belcher defeated a tough Shropshireman named Joe Berks three times and then Jack Fearby. Still only 22, Belcher had the world at his feet. But in July 1803, he was struck in the eye by a ball while playing racquets and maimed permanently. He retired to run a pub in

Wardour Street in Soho, inviting another Bristol man, Henry Pearce, to London to assume his championship status. Pearce did so well enough, beating Jack Fearby in a 10-foot square taproom in a pub in Windmill Street so badly that a woman had to be hired to clean the blood from the walls.

Pearce quickly established his supremacy but then had the unpleasant task of dealing with a challenge from the one-eyed and by now bitter Belcher, who had lost his money and was old before his time. They drew a crowd of 25,000 people to Blyth, south of Doncaster, on December 6, 1805. Belcher boxed well for a time before Pearce took over. After 35 minutes Belcher was tottering pathetically, unable to see, and with one arm hanging uselessly by his side. Pearce called out: "I'll take no advantage of thee, Jem. I'll not strike thee, lest I hurt thy other eye."

As astonishing as it seems to us now, Belcher fought twice more, losing to a new champion, Tom Cribb, in 1807 and 1809. He lost all his money, and with it his health, eventually dying in July 1811 at the age of 30. Henry Pearce, who was called "The Game Chicken", also died young. After beating Belcher, he lost his way, giving exhibitions in various towns and living on his wits and what was left of the fortune he had amassed and somehow blown. By 1808 he had tuberculosis. And after watching Belcher fight Tom Cribb for the second time, he was taken ill on the way back to London and died, aged 32, in April 1809.

The most gruelling fight Pearce had was a remarkable encounter with John Gully, whom he had known in his youth in Bristol, and whom he found languishing in the debtors' prison at Fleet. These were wild times in which men could lose everything and find themselves rotting away in jail, in the vague hope that somehow their debts could be cleared. Gambling, not only on boxing, was a national habit. The Duchess of Bedford was once forced to admit to her husband that she had lost a little matter of £176,000 playing cards!

DANIEL MENDOZA *was one of the first boxers to bring science to the prize ring*

TOM CRIBB *(of England, left) beat American Tom Molineaux in the first international contest of note at Copthall Common, south of London*

Because of the readiness of the people who travelled miles in often appalling conditions to witness and gamble large sums of money on their fights, the rewards for pugilists increased dramatically. And because of that, Pearce was able to entice young, wretched Gully into a prize fight after a "sporting gentleman" named Fletcher Reid had cleared the debts that had put him inside. Gully could fight – and proved it by extending Pearce for 64 rounds at Hailsham in Sussex in October 1805. Pearce eventually knocked him out with a blow to the throat.

Upon Pearce's retirement Gully was considered the best man in the country, purely because of that single epic battle. He proved his ability when he defeated a Lancastrian rogue named Bob Gregson in front of a crowd that included dukes, marquises and lords, at Six Mile Bottom near Newmarket in 1807. They were matched again the

following year and once more Gully triumphed, in 28 rounds lasting an hour and a quarter in front of a crowd of more than 20,000 near Woburn. Gully had the good sense to announce his retirement and unlike so many stuck to his decision. He took over a pub, ran with a disreputable crowd and made more money from bookmaking, and eventually won a £40,000 fortune by betting on horses he owned. He built himself a house in Yorkshire, owned three Derby winners and became MP for Pontefract in 1832! He lived to be 80 years old.

An American Challenge

Tom Cribb, from Hanham near Bristol, succeeded Gully and became one of the greatest sporting heroes England has ever known. He was not particularly skilful, but his courage – known then as "bottom" – was magnificent, and he was a man of the people. He had charisma. He beat Gregson, Belcher twice (as he

should have done) and the 42-year-old American Bill Richmond, who was the first black fighter of note. But it was Richmond's acquaintance and protégé, Tom Molineaux, another black American and a former slave, who made Cribb into a national star. Molineaux was a talented fighter, but Cribb beat him in a vicious fight that lasted 55 minutes on Copthall Common south of London in December 1810. Molineaux seemed on the way to victory when Cribb's second, Joe Ward, accused the American of carrying bullets in his hands. The ensuing row bought Cribb time – and the freezing English winter did the rest. Cribb recovered and slowly broke Molineaux down, fouling as he pleased without restraint from the referee. In the end, frozen stiff and thoroughly discouraged, Molineaux quit.

Cribb retired but returned when Molineaux claimed the championship. England consid-

ered this an affront – and Cribb fought him again at Thistleton Gap, Rutland, in September 1811. Molineaux wasn't the brightest man boxing has ever embraced – he devoured a whole chicken, an apple pie and four pints of beer before the fight! He managed to close Cribb's eye, but couldn't fight for long and Cribb prolonged it into the 11th round because he was enjoying himself.

Cribb's successor was the more talented Tom Spring from Townhope near Hereford. Like so many who follow great sporting heroes, he was overshadowed. Nevertheless, his fights drew enormous crowds as pugilism's popularity soared. More than 30,000 saw him beat Bill Neat near Andover in Hampshire in 1823 and a similar number turned up at Worcester racecourse to watch his incredible, 149-minute epic with the Irishman, Jack Langan, in 1824. Before the Langan fight, part of the grandstand collapsed under the weight of humanity – one person was killed and several injured. A return with Langan five months later lasted a mere 76 rounds and 108 minutes! By the end Langan was so exhausted he went down from a push and couldn't get up.

Prizefighting in Decline

Both men retired to run pubs, their fortunes intact, and with their exit boxing began to fade. Tom Cannon, nicknamed The Great Gun of Windsor, followed Spring, but lost to Jem Ward at Warwick in 1825. Ward was a rogue, brilliantly gifted as an artist and musician as well as a fighter, but was also known to throw the odd fight or two. Ward somehow lost to Peter Crawley, who was suffering from a hernia at the time of the fight, and who retired immediately afterwards to invest his £530 purse in a butcher's shop, leaving Ward to continue his reign as champion.

England was changing. George IV died, to be followed by the colourless William and, in 1837, Queen Victoria. The new morality of the Victorian era is often considered a product of the lady herself, but this is probably unfair: the influence of the new evangelical movement, the new Protestantism of the Wesleyans and Baptists, was already set when Victoria took the throne. However, it must be admitted that she did fit the mood perfectly. Disapproval was rife. Boxing declined, just as other sports and pastimes did.

James "Deaf 'Un" Burke claimed the championship, but killed a man, Simon Byrne, at Ascot in 1833 and subsequently became the first English pugilist to try his luck in America. He didn't have much. He was beating Sam O'Rourke in New Orleans when the mob, O'Rourke's fans to a man, broke up the ring, Burke very narrowly escaped being lynched.

Bendigo, alias William Thompson, was a southpaw from Nottingham who conceded 5in in height and more than three stones to Ben Caunt in 1835 yet beat him after 22 rounds in which he had sensibly refused to stand and trade punches with the big man. Finally Caunt lost his temper, ran over to Bendigo's corner and hit him as he sat enjoying his rest. Caunt was disqualified.

Disqualifications were a common result as men toiled for hours, often manipulating the rules by dropping when tapped or cuffed, simply to get out of tough situations or when they wanted a rest. In the first rematch, Caunt beat Bendigo on a foul in 75 rounds, a decision which caused a riot. A third fight, in 1845, saw the third disqualification result between them – Bendigo winning this time in the 93rd round for a purse of £400.

Bendigo was a larger than life figure who was converted to the ministry when in prison for what was described as his "28th breach of the peace". Apparently he gave well-attended sermons on the evils of drink. This sort of thing was popular entertainment in its own right. Bendigo died at the age of 68 in August 1880 after a fall at his Nottingham home.

Boxing has a way of surviving, but by the middle years of the century was in steep decline. Old men remembered its glory days, but fights were now poorly attended and not especially well paid. One of the better-known champions was William Perry, the "Tipton Slasher." He had fought Ben Caunt's giant American protégé Charles Freeman in a marathon that spread over three days before Freeman was given the verdict on a foul. Perry beat Tom Paddock, but lost to Harry Broome of Birmingham. And in 1857 the poor old Slasher gambled every penny he had on himself against the young, rising Tom Sayers, who beat him in 10 rounds that lasted 102 minutes on a boat moored on the Thames.

Sayers, a cobbler's son from Brighton, stood only 5ft 8in and scaled 147lb … a welterweight by modern standards … yet was one of the greatest boxers Britain has ever produced. He learned the hard way, inevitably giving away weight to stronger, bigger men, but progressed to become the best in England.

Sayers vs Heenan

Then on April 17, 1860 Sayers fought John Heenan from West Troy, New York at Farnborough in Hampshire. Historians hail this as the last great prizefight staged in Britain and through this single meeting boxing had a sudden resurgence. The police virtually stood aside to let it happen – they didn't really have much choice in the matter as hordes left on trains out of London clutching tickets with "To Nowhere" printed on them. Included in the throng were Members of Parliament and writers Charles Dickens and William Thackeray.

Sayers found the big man easy to hit, and cut him in the opening round, but Heenan got on top and in the sixth landed a heavy punch on Sayers' right arm, rendering it useless. Sayers boxed one-handed from then on, chipping away at Heenan's face and closing his right eye in the seventh. Heenan hurt his left hand, which was swollen and puffy … and so it went on, round after round, with Sayers "weak but cheerful" by the 25th round. Heenan was suddenly tiring in the 29th and his left eye seemed to be closing too. By the 36th his face was in a terrible mess, but he still had the strength to pin Sayers against the ropes and put all his weight on the little man's throat. He applied the same tactic in round 37, at which point the police finally closed in to stop the fight, only to find the crowd close in even further.

The ring was now only a few feet wide, but the two men fought on for five more so-called rounds before the officials finally had their way and called a halt. Heenan ran away but within minutes was unable to see, while Sayers, his arm feared broken, and desperately tired, was helped to his carriage. Both received commemorative belts and Sayers also had a payout of £3,000, raised by the public in appreciation of his effort, on the promise that he never boxed again. He didn't, but the combined effects of alcohol and tuberculosis drove him into an early grave, at the age of 39, in November 1865. Heenan returned to England to fight Tom King but lost in 24 rounds and was himself only 38 when he died penniless in Wyoming in 1873.

After Sayers came a string of unremarkable men, punctuated only by Jem Mace, who allowed himself to be called the Swaffham Gypsy even though he had no gypsy blood. Mace was a man of marvellous skill, like Sayers, small and tough, who happily took on opponents weighing dozens of pounds more. He was an innovator, a ring artist completely at home when involved in the toughest of fights. But the pickings for a pugilist were becoming so poor in England that he took his craft abroad, first to the USA, then to Australia and New Zealand, where he taught from his own booth. Among his pupils were the

Sayers and Heenan in a Great Fight for the Championship

They fought like lions in the ring,
Both men did boldly stand,
They two hours and six minutes fought,
And neither beat his man.

POPULAR BALLAD OF 1860

early glove heroes Bob Fitzsimmons and Peter Jackson.

When Mace retired, the title was claimed by Tom Allen, Birmingham-born but by now an American citizen. He lost to the 37-year-old, Northampton-born Joe Goss in 1876. By now the boxing scene had well and truly shifted to the USA.

Queensberry Rules

Bare-knuckle fighting was declining rapidly in Britain as, with the introduction of the Queensberry Rules in 1867, amateur and glove fighting was generally thought to be more in keeping with the times. The Queensberry Rules banned wrestling, changed the length of rounds to three minutes with a one-minute rest in between, and ruled that the contestants had to wear "fair-sized boxing gloves of the best quality and new".

The old habits still died hard. There were still fights to a finish, but gradually promoters saw the commercial sense in using a maximum number of rounds and, if no knockout had been achieved, having a points verdict based on which man had done the better work over the whole of the fight.

For some time the bare knuckle and gloved codes existed side by side, but it was boxing with gloves which prevailed. The title in America passed from Goss to Paddy Ryan, a raw, unskilled Irishman, in 1880 … and on to the last and one of the greatest of all bareknuckle legends, the immortal John L. Sullivan, who thrashed Ryan in nine rounds, lasting only 10½ minutes, in Mississippi City in February 1882.

Sullivan, the Boston Strong Boy, was only 23 and as good as anybody had been for years. Sullivan, who would walk into a bar and boast "My name is John L. Sullivan and I can lick any son-of-a-bitch in this house", was adored by the multitudes and loathed by the moralists.

But he walked his own path for 10 long years, his supremacy only rarely challenged.

Emotionally Sullivan was the heir of James Figg, not Jack Broughton. There was nothing cerebral or slick about him, but his attraction was that he could fight and loved to do so.

Sullivan took part in the last bare-knuckle championship contest in history when he outlasted Jake Kilrain for a stoppage in the 75th round at Richburg, Mississippi, in July 1889. Afterwards, he vowed he would never take a bare-knuckle fight again.

However, in September 1892, in New Orleans, Sullivan fitted his new-fangled gloves and was thoroughly beaten in 21 one-sided rounds by the princely, pompadoured artist of the ring James J. Corbett otherwise known as "Gentleman Jim".

Corbett belonged to a new era, a new world where practiced skill, physical conditioning and well-drilled technique would always overcome heart, toughness and desire. Those privileged few who saw John L. fall into the resin saw the passing, not just of a great champion, but of a way of life.

TOM SAYERS *and John Heenan were the combatants in the last great prizefight to be staged in England, at Farnborough, Hampshire, in 1860*

THE GREAT BOXERS

Boxing has had more than its share of heroes, and it is not an easy task to whittle them down to the 200 who were the most outstanding performers in the history of the modern, gloved game. These are the men who created their own legends, and whose memories are cherished by fans around the world. They are, by any definition, the game's greats.

Muhammad Ali

see Legends of the Ring (pp 66–67)

Lou Ambers

Real name: *Louis D'Ambrosio*
Born: *Herkimer, New York, November 8, 1913*
Titles: *World lightweight champion 1936–38 and 1939–40*
Record: *100 contests, 86 wins, 6 draws, 8 defeats*

Ambers, inevitably nicknamed the "Herkimer Hurricane", was part of an exciting generation of lightweights which included Henry Armstrong, Tony Canzoneri, Baby Arizmendi and Jimmy McLarnin. The Italian-American turned pro in 1932, and lost only once in his first 48 fights before Canzoneri outscored him for the vacant world title in May 1935.

He took revenge in September 1936, and retained the championship twice, against Canzoneri and Pedro Montanez. Armstrong took the title from him on points in August 1938, but Ambers reversed the decision almost exactly a year later. He was finally dethroned by Lew Jenkins in May 1940, and after being knocked out again by Jenkins in a non-title match in February 1941 he retired to join the US Coast Guard.

His hard-punching, highly aggressive style brought him 27 inside-schedule wins, but despite his fine record he is seldom accorded the recognition given to his old rivals Canzoneri and Armstrong. Apart from that distinguished pair, he also defeated sometime world champions Johnny Jadick, Fritzie Zivic, Frankie Klick and Arizmendi. He died on April 25, 1995.

Dennis Andries

Born: *Georgetown, Guyana, November 5, 1953*
Titles: *WBC light-heavyweight champion 1986–1987, 1989, 1990–91; British light-heavyweight champion 1984–86; WBC Continental Americas champion 1990; British cruiserweight champion 1995*
Record: *62 contests, 48 wins, 2 draws, 12 defeats*

The date of birth is debatable, since Andries has always claimed to be considerably older, but whatever the truth, he is a remarkable character. From the most unpromising raw material, he became WBC light-heavyweight champion three times, and won the British cruiserweight title when he was officially past 40.

After an undistinguished amateur

DENNIS ANDRIES *celebrates his second British title, aged 41*

career he turned pro in May 1976, and his crude but powerful style quickly made him a man to avoid. He was jeered from the ring after his first British title fight, a points loss to Bunny Johnson in 1980, but ignored the jibes and worked his way back. Tom Collins outpointed him for the British title in 1982, but he finally claimed it two years later, winning a Lonsdale Belt outright.

In April 1986 he became an improbable WBC champion, beating J.B. Williamson in London, but lost the title on his first defence to Thomas Hearns. He promptly joined the Hearns camp and, basing himself in Detroit, won the title twice more, including a memorable three-fight series with the Australian, Jeff Harding, before moving up to win and lose the British cruiserweight crown in 1995.

Yuri Arbachakov

Born: *Kenerova, Armenia, October 22, 1966*
Titles: *WBC flyweight champion 1992–*
Record: *21 contests, 21 wins*

The long-serving WBC flyweight champion has been one of the most successful of the amateur stars who turned professional in the wake of the break-up of the Russian Federation. He had represented Russia in international competition, winning the world and European championships and losing only 21 of 186 fights, with 53 wins inside the distance.

He opted to launch his professional career in Japan, reasoning that progress would be quicker in a country where the lighter weights are much more popular than in the West. Using the ring name of Ebihara in honour of the former flyweight champion, he stopped his first six opponents and then took the Japanese title in his seventh outing with a first-round blitz of Takahiro Mizuno.

Arbachakov became WBC champion in his 13th fight, coming off the floor in the third to stop Muangchai Kittikasem in the eighth. By the end of 1995 he had made seven successful defences,

A JUBILANT *Alexis Arguello, after claiming his third world title*

including a ninth-round stoppage of Kittikasem in a controversial rematch which saw one round cut short when the Thai was in trouble. At that point, he had won all 21 of his fights, 15 inside the distance.

Alexis Arguello

Born: *Managua, Nicaragua, April 19, 1952*
Titles: *WBA featherweight champion 1974–77, WBC super-featherweight champion 1978–80, WBC lightweight champion 1981–82*
Record: *87 contests, 80 wins, 7 defeats*

The stylish, handsome Arguello was a major star in the 1970s and early 1980s, winning titles at three weights and becoming a favourite with American TV viewers, who were enjoying a glut of live networked boxing during that period. Like so many of the great Latin fighters, he started young: he was a pro at 16, and was beaten only twice in his first five years.

Ernesto Marcel outpointed him in his first bid for the WBA featherweight title in 1974, but nine months later he knocked out Marcel's successor Ruben Olivares in 13 rounds. Increasing weight forced him to relinquish the title two years later, and he promptly won the WBC super-featherweight championship, retaining it eight times.

British fans saw him in action in

June 1981 when he took the WBC lightweight title from Scotland's Jim Watt. He came close to a fourth title in July 1982, when he battled Aaron Pryor for 14 unforgettable rounds for the WBA light-welterweight title, but retired after Pryor knocked him out in a rematch. He lost most of his money in the Nicaraguan Civil War, and made a short-lived comeback in 1995.

Henry Armstrong

see Legends of the Ring (pp 68–69)

Abe Attell

Born: *San Francisco, California, February 22, 1884*
Titles: *World featherweight title claimant 1904–12*
Record: *(approx.) 171 contests, 91 wins, 18 draws, 2 No Contests, 51 No Decisions, 9 defeats*

The clever Californian became accepted as the best man in the featherweight division after the champion, Young Corbett II, announced that he could no longer make the weight. Attell – still only 17 – had drawn with and beaten the great George Dixon in 1901, and on that basis proclaimed himself champion.

He consolidated his position with an unbeaten run of 18, against the era's outstanding featherweights. Owen Moran from Birmingham held him to a draw in 1908, and was given a rematch eight months later. Attell wanted 20 rounds, the Englishman 25, so they compromised and, for the only time in history, a championship was contested over 23 rounds. Again, they drew.

Jim Driscoll easily outboxed Attell in New York in February 1909, but because it was a "No Decision" contest the American continued to claim the title until he was outpointed by Johnny Kilbane in 1912. His career virtually ended in 1913, as he boxed only twice between then and his farewell appearance in 1917. He was later involved in a notorious baseball betting scandal. Attell died at New Paltz, New York on February 7, 1970.

Max Baer

Born: *Omaha, Nebraska, February 11, 1909*
Titles: *World heavyweight champion 1934–35*
Record: *83 contests, 70 wins, 13 defeats*

Had Max Baer been able to take boxing seriously, his ferocious hitting could have made him an outstanding heavyweight champion. Instead, he lost the title in his first defence against James J. Braddock, in what remained the biggest upset in history until Buster Douglas dethroned Mike Tyson in 1990. Baer loved to clown and wisecrack, which while it endeared him to the fans prevented him achieving his full potential.

But he could fight when he chose to, and wins over contenders Tom Heeney, King Levinsky and ex-champion Max Schmeling earned him a title fight with the Italian giant Primo Carnera in June 1934. The unfortunate Carnera took a brutal beating, being

PLAYBOY CHAMPION *Max Baer*

floored 12 times in 11 rounds.

Baer was humiliated in four rounds by Joe Louis in his first fight after losing to Braddock, a defeat which removed him from the title picture. He fought on until 1941, but retired after Lou Nova knocked him out. He died in a Hollywood hotel room on November 21, 1959: his last words, to the hotel operator who asked if he wanted the house doctor, were "No – I need a people doctor."

Marco Antonio Barrera

Born: *Mexico City, Mexico, January 17, 1974*
Titles: *NABF super-flyweight champion 1993, WBO super-bantamweight champion 1995–*
Record: *40 contests, 40 wins*

As Julio Cesar Chavez's star waned, Mexico found a possible replacement in Barrera, whose methodical ring style and destructive body punches invite comparison with the country's best-loved sporting hero. The youngster was still only 21 when he outpointed Daniel Jiminez to become WBO super-bantamweight champion in March 1995, but was already a veteran of six years in the professional ring. By the time 1995 was over, he had retained the title four times, setting a pace which could make him one of the sport's busiest champions, and had yet to be beaten in 39 fights, 28 of them won by knockout or stoppage.

Barrera crashed the world ratings in 1992 when he outpointed Josefino Suarez for the vacant Mexican super-flyweight title, which he defended five times in two years. He added the NABF championship in August 1993 by outpointing Eduardo Ramirez, but then failed to make the weight for a WBC final eliminator against Carlos Salazar and immediately moved up two divisions to super-bantam.

A second-round blowout of the former WBA bantamweight champion Eddie Cook in December 1994 set up the challenge for Jiminez's WBO title.

Barrera opened his 1996 account with a thrilling 12th round stoppage of the former Olympic and IBF champion Kennedy McKinney, which greatly enhanced his standing with the American boxing public.

Carmen Basilio

Born: *Canastota, New York, April 2, 1927*
Titles: *World welterweight champion 1955–56, 1956–57, world middleweight champion 1957–58*
Record: *79 contests, 56 wins, 7 draws, 16 defeats*

Carmen Basilio's rugged fighting philosophy was shaped in the onion fields around Canastota, where he worked alongside his nine brothers and sisters. After that, he reckoned, boxing was easy. He learned the business as he went along, and his early record was littered with defeats and draws. But through sheer hard work and persistence he developed into a contender for the welterweight title, losing to Kid Gavilan in his first title bid in 1953.

Two years later he knocked out Tony DeMarco in the 12th round of a wildly exciting championship battle, and repeated the result in a rematch before losing to Johnny Saxton on a shockingly bad verdict. He took no chances in the rematch, knocking Saxton out in nine rounds. In September 1957 he scored his most famous victory, taking the middleweight title from Ray Robinson after 15 thrilling rounds. The rematch was just as exciting, though Robinson won this time.

Basilio tried three times to regain the title, being stopped twice by Gene Fullmer and, in his last fight, losing on points to Paul Pender in April 1961.

Hogan Bassey

Real name: *Okon Bassey Asuguo*
Born: *Calibar, Nigeria, June 3, 1932*
Titles: *British Empire featherweight champion 1955–57, world featherweight champion 1957–59*
Record: *74 contests, 59 wins, 2 draws, 13 defeats*

Bassey's first three pro fights were for championships: he won and lost the Nigerian flyweight title, and boxed a draw for the West African title. By the time he came to Britain in late 1951 he had won the Nigerian and West African bantamweight titles, but found the going harder against the higher standard of competition.

It took him four years and 43 fights to become a champion again, knocking out Billy Kelly – who had previously beaten him – for the Empire featherweight title. When Sandy Saddler relinquished the world title, Bassey became Nigeria's first world champion by stopping Cherif Hamia for the vacant title in Paris on June 24, 1957.

He retained it with a stunning knockout of Ricardo Moreno, a fierce-hitting Mexican who had been widely expected to dethrone him, but then found the stylish Davey Moore too good for him. Moore took his title in 13 rounds in March 1959, and when he repeated the result in a rematch, Bassey quit the ring. He later trained the Nigerian Olympic boxing team.

Wilfred Benitez

Born: *Bronx, New York, September 12, 1958*
Titles: *WBA light-welterweight champion 1976–77, WBC welterweight champion 1979, WBC light-middleweight champion 1981–82*
Record: *62 contests, 53 wins, 1 draw, 8 defeats*

The flashy Benitez, of Puerto Rican parentage, was a true prodigy of the ring. Managed by his volatile father Gregorio, he became the youngest-ever world champion when, on March 6, 1976, he ended Antonio Cervantes's long reign as WBA light-welterweight champion. The WBA stripped him of the title after two defences when he refused to give Cervantes a rematch, so he moved up to welterweight and took that title from Carlos Palomino.

He defended it against Harold Weston, but in November 1979 Ray Leonard stopped him in the 15th and final round. Still only 22, Benitez won his third title in May 1981, knocking out Britain's Maurice Hope with a crushing right in the 12th round in Las Vegas for the WBC light-middleweight belt. He retained it against Carlos Santos and Roberto Duran, but after Thomas Hearns outpointed him in December 1982, Benitez's career went into abrupt and steep decline.

A combination of management problems, ill-discipline and high living soon took care of the substantial fortune he had earned, and the career which had once promised so much petered out in a sad series of unsuccessful comebacks.

Nigel Benn

Born: *Ilford, England, January 26, 1964*
Titles: *Commonwealth middleweight champion 1988–89, WBO middleweight champion 1990, WBC super-middleweight champion 1992–96*
Record: *46 fights, 42 wins, 1 draw, 3 defeats*

The former soldier, nicknamed "The Dark Destroyer", became one of Britain's most successful and popular champions with a style based on relentless aggression, hard punching and an indomitable will to win. He won the ABA middleweight title in 1986, and turned pro in disgust when Rod Douglas, whom he had eliminated in the London championships, was preferred for the Commonwealth Games team.

He was an instant sensation, and flattened his first 21 opponents, 11 in the opening round, winning the vacant Commonwealth title in April 1988. Michael Watson brought him

PENSIVE *Nigel Benn faces the press*

down to earth by knocking him out in six rounds in May 1989, but Benn re-established himself in America where he won the WBO title from Doug DeWitt and retained it sensationally against Iran Barkley.

Arch-rival Chris Eubank stopped him in a nine-rounds thriller in November 1990, but Benn stepped up to super-middleweight and won the WBC version of the title, which he still held at the end of 1995. His knockout of Gerald McClellan in 1995 deserves to be remembered as a classic of the British ring, despite its tragic aftermath which saw the American suffer permanent damage

A hot favourite to retain his crown against the South African Sugar Boy Malinga in March 1996, Benn lost on points to a challenger he had already beaten in a non-title fight in 1992.

Nino Benvenuti

Born: *Trieste, Italy, April 26, 1938*
Titles: *European middleweight champion 1965–66, world light-middleweight champion 1965–66, world middleweight champion 1967, 1968–70*
Record: *90 contests, 82 wins, 1 draw, 7 defeats*

Benvenuti was always a winner. He was a gold medallist at the Rome Olympics in 1960 – beating Cassius Clay in the voting for the Val Barker trophy as the Games' best stylist – and went undefeated in his first 65 fights, winning the Italian middleweight title in 1963. By 1965 he was a contender for the world middleweight title, but instead dropped down a division to knock out his compatriot Sandro Mazzinghi for the light-middleweight championship.

He lost it in his first defence to Ki-Soo Kim of Korea, who became his country's first world champion by out-pointing the elegant Italian in Seoul in June 1966, but Benvenuti came back as a middleweight to beat Emile Griffith in two of their three clashes for the 160-lb title. He retained it four times before Carlos Monzon stopped him in 12 rounds, and retired after Monzon knocked him out in three in a rematch.

He entered politics, and built a

successful business career before, in 1995, he turned his back on material rewards to become a volunteer in Mother Teresa's hospice in Calcutta.

Jack "Kid" Berg

Real name: *Judah Bergman*
Born: *London, England, June 28, 1909*
Titles: *World light-welterweight champion 1930–31, British lightweight champion 1934–36*
Record: *(approx.) 192 contests, 157 wins, 9 draws, 26 defeats*

Berg, a product of the East London Jewish community, was boxing professionally at 14, his all-action style earning him the nickname "The Whitechapel Whirlwind". He boxed all-comers in a hectic few years between 1924 and 1927 before moving to New York, where he became hugely popular. He returned briefly in February 1930 to beat Mushy Callahan for the junior-welterweight title at the Albert Hall in London, an event notable for the pre-fight intervention of Lord Lonsdale who, waving his walking stick, announced that no such title existed.

Nevertheless, Berg made a career out of defending the championship throughout 1930 and 1931, and even after Tony Canzoneri knocked him out in April 1931 he continued to claim the title on the grounds that their fight had involved Canzoneri's lightweight championship rather than his own crown.

He boxed in top class for another five years, but his busy career eventually wound down to the eight-rounds class. He returned to England in 1939, and boxed sporadically until 1945, enjoying a second career as a film stuntman. He died on April 22, 1991.

Riddick Bowe

Born: *New York, NY, August 10, 1967*
Titles: *WBC, WBA and IBF heavyweight champion 1992, WBA and IBF champion 1993, WBO champion 1995*
Record: *41 contests, 39 wins, 1 No Contest, 1 defeat*

The amiable Bowe, nicknamed "Big Daddy", was the dominant figure in world heavyweight boxing during the years of Mike Tyson's absence. Bowe, from the same Brownsville district as Tyson, was beaten by Lennox Lewis in the 1988 Olympic final, one of only eight defeats he sustained in 112 amateur fights. He turned pro after the Games and, guided by the independent-minded Rock Newman, made rapid progress with wins over the likes of Pinklon Thomas, Bruce Seldon and Tony Tubbs.

By 1992 he was the leading contender for Evander Holyfield's championship, which he won in November 1992 in the first of their three epic meetings. Their second fight, a year later in the same outdoor arena at Caesars Palace, Las Vegas, featured a truly bizarre incident when the action was interrupted by the arrival in the ring of a publicity-seeking paraglider. Bowe lost the decision in this exciting contest, but was a champion again by 1995, beating Britain's Herbie Hide to capture the WBO title.

He retained that title against the dangerous Cuban Jorge Luis Gonzalez, and then survived the first knockdown of his career to stop Holyfield in the final instalment of their memorable series.

Cornelius Boza-Edwards

Born: *Kampala, Uganda, May 27, 1956*
Titles: *WBC super-featherweight champion 1981, European super-featherweight champion 1982*
Record: *51 contests, 44 wins, 1 draw, 6 defeats*

The Ugandan southpaw was brought to England as a boy by a Londoner, Jack Edwards, and adopted his surname in appreciation. He was an outstanding amateur before turning professional in December 1976, and served an exotic apprenticeship with fights in Italy, Zambia and Monte Carlo.

But his career did not take off until he faced WBC super-featherweight champion Alexis Arguello in a non-title match in his American debut in 1980. He lost, but performed so well that he was rewarded seven months later with a crack at Arguello's successor, Rafael Limon. Boza won a thriller on points, and retained the title in another epic against Bobby Chacon before he was surprisingly knocked out by Rolando Navarette in August 1981.

He came back to win the European title, but was outpointed by

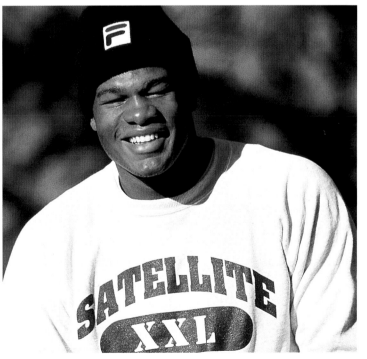

BIG DADDY *Riddick Bowe in training at this camp on Big Bear Mountain*

Chacon when he tried to regain his WBC title. His popularity with American TV viewers ensured other opportunities, and he made two losing bids for the WBC lightweight title before retiring in 1987. His first wife died tragically, but he remarried and now lives in Las Vegas where he trains fighters.

James J. Braddock

Born: *New York, NY, June 7, 1906*
Titles: *World heavyweight champion 1935–37*
Record: *86 contests, 46 wins, 4 draws, 11 No Decisions, 2 No Contests, 23 defeats*

Braddock's late-career success is one of the ring's heart-warming stories. He had been a mediocre light-heavyweight, whose career highlight was a points defeat by Tommy Loughran for the world title in 1929. Losses were as numerous as wins after that, and by 1933 Braddock was so down on his luck that he had to apply for welfare payments to keep his family together.

In June 1934 he was engaged as an "opponent" for Corn Griffin, a bright young heavyweight prospect, but upset the script by winning in three rounds. When he outpointed future

BRADDOCK *prepares for Louis*

light-heavyweight champion John Henry Lewis – who had beaten him in 1932 – the business began to take note of him, but even so he was regarded as a soft touch for Max Baer when they met for Baer's heavyweight title in June 1935. It was said an ambulance waited discreetly outside the arena ready to take Braddock away. Instead Braddock boxed steadily to outpoint the erratic champion, and earn himself the nickname of "The Cinderella Man". In his only defence, Braddock had the satisfaction of flooring Joe Louis before Louis took his title on an eighth-round knockout two years later.

Jack Britton

Real name: *William J. Breslin*
Born: *Clinton, New York, October 14, 1885*
Titles: *World welterweight champion 1915, 1916–17, 1919–22*
Record: *(approx.) 339 contests, 100 wins, 20 draws, 2 No Contests, 190 No Decisions, 27 defeats*

Britton enjoyed one of the longest careers of any world champion: he had his first pro fight in 1904 and his last in 1930, when he was almost 45. He was already a veteran when he won the welterweight title in 1915, and he and arch-rival Ted "Kid" Lewis alternated the title between them until 1921. They met at least 20 times – records of the time are incomplete – of which Britton won four, Lewis three, one was drawn and the other 12 were No Decision affairs.

He featured in a controversial defence against lightweight champion Benny Leonard, who was well on the way to victory when he floored Britton and then deliberately hit him while he was down, earning instant disqualification. His reign was finally ended by Mickey Walker, who beat him on points in November 1921. Walker was 20, Britton 36, but the cagey Irish-American made Walker work hard for his win.

Britton boxed on for another eight years, and finished his career on a downbeat note by winning only three of his final 12 fights.

"Panama" Al Brown

Born: *Panama, July 5, 1902*
Titles: *World bantamweight champion 1929–35*
Record: *155 contests, 123 wins, 10 draws, 4 No Decisions, 18 defeats*

Brown was exceptionally tall for a bantamweight at 5ft 11 in, and he used his freakish build to maximum effect during a career which extended from 1919 to 1942. He won the vacant world title by outpointing Vidal Gregorio in 1929, and thereafter became a popular performer in Europe, beating many of the era's leading bantams and featherweights.

His extravagant personal style made him a major personality in the sport: he was a homosexual, at a time when such things were not even whispered about in society at large, never mind boxing circles. The conservative American establishment in the form of the NBA were glad to find a reason to strip him of the title, ostensibly for his failure to defend against Baby Casanova, and he spared them further embarrassment by losing his New York and IBU versions of the title to Baltazar Sangchilli of Spain in 1935.

Brown boxed on until December 1942, ending with a victory in his native Panama. He died in New York on April 11, 1951, and was buried in Panama City.

Joe Brown

Born: *New Orleans, Louisiana, May 18, 1926*
Titles: *World lightweight champion 1956–62*
Record: *161 contests, 104 wins, 13 draws, 2 No Contests, 42 defeats*

One of the great ring mechanics of the post-war era, Brown started boxing in the army and won the All-Services title before turning pro in January 1946. He boxed top-class lightweights and welterweights for a decade before finally winning the lightweight title in August 1956. He was 30 by then, known as "Old Bones", but proved a fine champion, holding on to his title 11 times against outstanding contenders like Kenny Lane, Ralph Dupas, Dave Charnley (twice) and

Cisco Andrade before losing on points to Carlos Ortiz in Las Vegas in April 1962.

His career went into a steady decline after that, and he won only 20 of his remaining 45 fights before finally retiring, aged 44, in 1970. Brown had been a real globe-trotter, performing in Australia, Cuba, England, Italy, the Philippines, Mexico, Argentina, Venezuela, South Africa and Finland, and his smooth skills were appreciated wherever he went.

Like so many former champions, his money soon disappeared and he was reported to be driving a cab for a living in New Orleans.

Frank Bruno

Born: *London, England, November 16, 1961*
Titles: *WBC heavyweight champion 1995–96, European champion 1985*
Record: *45 contests, 40 wins, 5 defeats*

Bruno's career has been a model of persistence and hard work. He took up boxing as an outlet for the energy which had made him a difficult boy to handle, and responded so well to its disciplines that he became, in 1980, the youngest-ever ABA heavyweight champion. He had to wait almost two years before launching his pro career, because of managerial disputes and an eye problem which necessitated surgery, but his rise was meteoric.

Managed by Terry Lawless and promoted by Mickey Duff and his associates, he scored 21 straight knockouts before Bonecrusher Smith, then unknown, knocked him out in 10 rounds at Wembley in May 1984. He was re-established via the European championship, but failed in 11 rounds against Tim Witherspoon for the WBA title in 1986.

Astonishingly, he secured two more title fights, losing in five rounds to Mike Tyson in 1989 and in seven to Lennox Lewis in 1993, but just when his career looked to be virtually over his new promoter Frank Warren got him one last chance and this time Bruno outpointed Oliver McCall to win the WBC title at Wembley in September 1995. His glory lasted bare-

PERSISTENCE PAID *for Frank Bruno, world champion at the fourth attempt*

ly six months, however, as Tyson stopped him in three one-sided rounds in March 1996 in Las Vegas.

Ken Buchanan

Born: *Edinburgh, Scotland, January 28, 1945*
Titles: *WBA lightweight champion 1970, world champion 1971–72, European champion 1974–75, British champion 1968–70, 1973–74*
Record: *69 contests, 62 wins, 7 defeats*

Buchanan was probably Britain's best-ever lightweight, but this one-time carpenter was always more respected in America than at home. Most of his early fights were in sporting clubs, so that by the time he became British champion in 1968 he was barely known outside the game's hard-core followers.

Manager Eddie Thomas manoeuvred him into a challenge for Ismael Laguna's WBA title in September 1970. Few gave him a

chance, but he boxed brilliantly to take the title. He became undisputed champion in February 1971, but was then stripped by the WBC for meeting Laguna in a rematch.

In June 1972 he lost the title to Roberto Duran in 13 brutal rounds, and Duran always refused to face him again. Wins over Jim Watt (which won him a Lonsdale Belt outright) for the British title and Antonio Puddu for the European championship brought a crack at Guts Ishimatsu's WBC title in 1975, but the Scot lost on points. He boxed on with limited success until November 1981.

His money gone, he made a brief and regrettable comeback on the unlicensed circuit.

Tommy Burns

Real name: *Noah Brusso*
Born: *Chesley, Canada, June 17, 1881*
Titles: *World heavyweight champion 1906–08*
Record: *60 contests, 46 wins, 9 draws, 5 defeats*

Burns was the smallest of all the heavyweight champions, standing only 5ft 7in, but he compensated for his lack of height with a remarkably long reach and a decent punch, which brought him 36 knockouts in his 60 recorded fights.

He became champion by out-pointing Marvin Hart in February 1906, but the fact that Burns had won only three of his previous nine fights did little to enhance his credibility as champion. He took the title "on the road" for the first time, defending it in England, Ireland and France before moving on to Australia in 1908. Jack Johnson was widely regarded as uncrowned champion, and he followed Burns to Australia to force a showdown.

They boxed at Rushcutter's Bay, Sydney on December 26, when Burns – outweighed by 20 lb – fought bravely before being stopped in the 14th. He boxed only six times in the next 12 years, and retired after being knocked out by Joe Beckett in a bid for the Empire title in London in 1920, when he was 39. He later became a minister of religion, and died in Vancouver on May 10, 1955.

Hector Camacho

Born: *Bayamon, Puerto Rico, May 24, 1962*
Titles: *WBC super-featherweight champion 1983, WBC light-weight champion 1985, WBO light-welterweight champion 1989–91, 1991–92*
Record: *61 contests, 58 wins, 3 defeats*

As 1995 ended, the outrageous but so-gifted "Macho" Camacho was boxing better than ever and poised to challenge for his fourth title, at welter-

weight. The flashy youngster of a decade ago had matured into a cagey and seasoned campaigner.

The ring attire was as daft as it had always been: Camacho cornered the market in frills, skirts and loin-cloths, and his capacity to shock extended far beyond the ring. But he could really fight, for all the corny showmanship, and when he took a painful beating from Julio Cesar Chavez in a losing bid for the WBC light-welterweight title in 1992, he proved that he had heart to match his gimmickry.

Weight problems caused him to relinquish the super-featherweight title after one defence, and the light-weight championship after two. He took the WBO light-welterweight title by beating Ray Mancini in 1989, lost it to Greg Haugen in 1991 and regained it from him in May, but was stripped in 1992 for failure to defend it.

Orlando Canizales

Born: *Laredo, Texas, November 25, 1965*
Titles: *NABF flyweight champion 1987, USBA super-flyweight champion 1988, IBF bantam-weight champion 1988–94*
Record: *45 contests, 42 wins, 1 draw, 2 defeats*

This busy performer was an outstanding bantamweight champion between July 1988, when he stopped Kelvin Seabrooks in the 15th and final round of a rare all-American bantam-weight title fight to win the IBF version, and December 1994, when he relinquished it because of weight-making problems.

In between, he made 16 defences which included a two-rounds stoppage of the only man to have beaten him, the former Olympic champion Paul Gonzalez. That loss came in a 1986 challenge for the NABF flyweight title, which he eventually won by stopping Armando Velasquez for the vacant title a year later. He moved up to super-flyweight, winning the USBA title in 1988 in his last fight before beating Seabrooks on his bantamweight debut.

He defended his IBF title in England, France and South Africa, and at one time shared the bantamweight championship with his elder brother Gaby, the former WBA champion, whose brief three-month reign as WBO champion coincided with his brother's IBF tenure. Wilfredo Vasquez beat Orlando in a WBA super-bantamweight title bid in January 1995, but the tough Texan still ended the year as a highly ranked contender.

Tony Canzoneri

Born: *Slidell, Louisiana, November 6, 1908.*
Titles: *World featherweight champion 1928, world light-weight champion 1930–33, 1935–36, world light-welter-weight champion 1931–32, 1933*
Record: *175 contests, 141 wins, 10 draws, 24 defeats*

In the days when there were only ten weight divisions and (usually) one champion per division, Canzoneri achieved the astonishing feat of con-testing four titles and winning three of them. He turned pro at 16 in 1925, and lost only once in 39 fights before being matched with Bud Taylor for the vacant NBA title in March 1927. They drew, and Taylor won the rematch.

Canzoneri moved up to feather-weight, beating Benny Bass for the title in February 1928. Andre Routis took his championship seven months later, but Canzoneri stepped up again to beat Sammy Mandell for the lightweight title in August 1929. His win over Jack "Kid' Berg in 1931, although officially a lightweight match, also gave him the Englishman's junior-welter title since both were inside that division's limit, and Canzoneri continued to defend both titles. He lost the 140 lb title to Johnny Jadick and regained it from Battling Shaw before losing both titles to Barney Ross in June 1933.

He enjoyed one last spell as light-weight champion in 1935–36, retiring in November 1939 to become an actor and restaurateur. He died in New York on December 9, 1959.

Primo Carnera

Born: *Sequals, Italy, October 26, 1906*
Titles: *World heavyweight champion 1933–34*
Record: *103 contests, 88 wins, 1 No Decision, 14 defeats*

The exploitation of the giant Carnera, who stood 6ft 5¾in and weighed 270lb, says much about the way boxing operated in the 1930s. He was discovered working as a circus strongman, and his manager, Leon See, launched him as a professional in September 1928.

Virtually all his early fights were fixed, although Carnera may have been unaware of this. When See took him to America in 1930 the manager was quickly pushed aside by much more sinister figures, who provided Carnera with a long series of "knockovers" on the way to a title fight. Occasionally, they made mis-takes, but by June 1933 he was judged ready to challenge Sharkey for the title.

The American succumbed in six rounds, a result which remains unconvincing, and although Carnera managed two successful defences he was then badly beaten by Max Baer in June 1934. The Mob did get one more payday out of him, feeding him to Joe Louis in June 1935, but that beating effectively ended his career. He retired in December 1937, making a brief comeback in 1945–46.

He later enjoyed a second lucra-tive career as a wrestler in America, and died in his home town of Sequals on June 29, 1967.

GEORGES CARPENTIER *in classic pose*

Georges Carpentier

Born: *Lens, France, January 12, 1894*
Titles: *European welterweight champion 1911, middleweight champion 1912, light-heavyweight champion 1913, heavyweight champion 1913–19, world light-heavyweight cham-pion 1920–22*
Record: *109 contests, 88 wins, 6 draws, 1 No Decision, 14 defeats*

Carpentier boxed professionally in each of the (then) eight weight divi-sions, starting as a 13-year-old fly-weight in 1908. He won the French lightweight title at 15, and was wel-terweight champion of France and Europe at 17. His combination of styl-ish boxing, heavy hitting and good looks made him a major attraction, and for the first time women began to attend fights in significant numbers.

He progressed through the divi-sions, winning European titles at welterweight (1911), middleweight (1912) light-heavyweight and heavy-weight (both in 1913), knocking out the English star Bombardier Billy Wells twice in heavyweight title fights. When the First World War broke out he joined the French Air Force, and was awarded the Croix De

PRIMO CARNERA *(left) and trainer Maurice Eudeline do their roadwork in St James's Park, London, in 1932*

Guerre and the Medaille Militaire. He resumed his career in 1917, and by 1919 was world light-heavyweight champion.

He used that title as a stepping stone to a heavyweight title clash with Jack Dempsey in 1921, but was knocked out in four rounds. Battling Siki took his light-heavyweight title in 1922, and he boxed infrequently from then until his retirement in 1927. He remained immensely popular until his death in Paris on October 28, 1975.

Jimmy Carruthers

Born: *Paddington, Australia, July 5, 1929*
Titles: *World bantamweight champion 1952–54*
Record: *25 contests, 21 wins, 4 defeats*

This hard-punching southpaw was Australia's first undisputed world champion, knocking out the South African Vic Toweel in the first round in November 1952, and again in the 10th round four months later. Ironically, he had been inspired to turn pro by the success of Toweel, whom he had watched in the 1948 Olympic Games in London, in which they both competed.

He took the national title from Elley Bennett in his ninth fight, but despite being unbeaten in 14 fights he had no international pedigree to speak of when he challenged Toweel, and his win was a major upset. He retained the title against Henry "Pappy" Gault of America and the Thai, Chamrern Songkitrat in a match which was remarkable for two reasons: they fought in bare feet, during a rain storm in the open-air arena, and the fight was over the then-unusual distance of 12 rounds.

Carruthers retired after that to run a pub and become a referee, but was tempted into an ill-advised comeback in 1961 and lost four of his six fights before retiring for good in 1962.

Marcel Cerdan

Born: *Sidi Bel-Abbes, Algeria, July 22, 1916*
Titles: *European welterweight champion 1939–42, middleweight champion 1947–48, world middleweight champion 1948–49*
Record: *123 contests, 119 wins, 4 defeats*

Two of Cerdan's four defeats were on disqualification, one on a bitterly disputed decision, and the last on injury. He was never beaten on merit. That is a true measure of the ability of this extraordinary fighter, who won French and European welterweight titles before moving up to middleweight and doing the same again. Had the Second World War not retarded his career he would surely have won world titles in both divisions, but instead he had to wait until 1946, when he made his American debut, to be taken seriously as a contender.

Cyrille Delannoit looked to have wrecked his dream when he out-pointed him for the European title in May 1948, but the handsome Algerian reversed the result two months later and then, in September that year, battered Tony Zale into a 12th-round defeat to become world middleweight champion.

He lost the title to Jake LaMotta on a shoulder injury in June 1949, and was killed on October 27, 1949 when the plane carrying him back to America for the LaMotta rematch crashed in the Azores. Cerdan's place in the romantic affections of the French was cemented by his long-running affair with the singing star Edith Piaf.

Bobby Chacon

Born: *Los Angeles, California, November 28, 1951*
Titles: *WBC featherweight champion 1974–75, WBC super-featherweight champion 1982–83*
Record: *65 contests, 57 wins, 1 draw, 7 defeats*

Chacon's explosive style made him a huge drawing card in Los Angeles. Only two of his 26 fights on the way to his first world title went the distance, with the solitary loss being a ninth-round knockout by Ruben Olivares in June 1973.

He knocked out Alfredo Marcano to win the WBC featherweight title in September 1974, but lost it in his second defence to Olivares, this time in two rounds. He finally beat

ILL-FATED *Maurice Cerdan died en route to a world title rematch*

Olivares in a 10-rounder in August 1977, and then moved up to super-feather. Alexis Arguello turned back his first title bid, and Cornelius Boza-Edwards stopped him in a 13-round thriller in May 1981, but he won the WBC belt at the third attempt, outpointing Rafael Limon in December 1982.

The WBC stripped him six months later when he refused to fight Hector Camacho on a Don King promotion for $450,000 when he had been offered $1m by another promoter for the same fight. He was stopped in three rounds by Ray Mancini in a WBA lightweight challenge in 1984, and retired in 1985.

Jeff Chandler

Born: *Philadelphia, Pennsylvania, September 3, 1956*
Titles: *USBA champion 1979–80, NABF champion 1980, WBA bantamweight champion 1980–84*
Record: *37 contests, 33 wins, 2 draws, 2 defeats*

Until Chandler took the WBA title from Julian Solis in November 1980, no American had been bantamweight champion since Harold Dade reigned for just two months in 1947. The classy Philadelphian proved rather more durable: he turned back nine challengers in over three years before losing to fellow-American Richard Sandoval.

Chandler was not the usual Philadelphia fighter, all left hooks and snarling aggression *à la* Joe Frazier. He was a stylish boxer and an excellent counter-puncher, and achieved a respectable 18 inside-the-distance wins in his 33 victories.

There has never been a great market for bantamweights on the Eastern side of America, since they are considered more the province of the Mexican border states like Texas and California. Consequently Chandler managed only 15 fights in three years, and the first six were four-rounders. But by 1979 he had moved up to main-event status, winning the USBA title and adding the NABF championship the following February, before taking the WBA belt from Solis in November. His 10 challengers included four Americans, clear evidence of the division's growing popularity there. Chandler retired after losing to Sandoval in April 1984.

Ezzard Charles

Born: *Lawrenceville, Georgia, July 7, 1921*
Titles: *NBA heavyweight champion 1949–50, world heavyweight champion 1950–51*
Record: *122 contests, 96 wins, 1 draw, 25 defeats*

Many of those who saw him in action maintain that Charles was a better middleweight and light-heavyweight than he was a heavyweight. He beat Joey Maxim and Archie Moore three times apiece, knocked out former light-heavyweight champion Anton Christoforodis, beat Teddy Yarosz, and drew with Ken Overlin, both ex-middleweight champions.

But he could not secure a title chance, and so moved up to heavyweight where, despite weighing no more than the modern cruiserweight limit of 190 lb, he scored a string of wins which culminated in him beating Jersey Joe Walcott for the NBA title left vacant by Joe Louis's retirement. He retained that three times before beating Louis (on a comeback) in September 1950 to earn undisputed recognition, and made a further four defences before Walcott knocked him out in July 1951.

He made two heroic efforts to regain the title from Rocky Marciano in 1954, but then disappointingly had only 10 wins in 23 fights. He retired in 1959, and died from multiple sclerosis in Chicago on May 27, 1975.

Julio Cesar Chavez

Born: *Sonora, Mexico, July 12, 1962*
Titles: *WBC super-featherweight champion 1984–87, WBA lightweight 1987–89, WBC lightweight champion 1988–89, WBC light-welterweight champion 1989–94, 1995–, IBF light-welterweight champion 1990–91*
Record: *97 contests, 95 wins, 1 draw, 1 defeat*

HANDSOME *Julio's three world titles make him Mexico's greatest champion*

Chavez wanted to go 100 fights without a loss, and he almost made it: his first defeat, by Frankie Randall for the WBC light-welterweight title in January 1994, came after 91 fights in 13 years. He is generally accepted as the greatest fighter of his generation: even Mike Tyson acknowledged Chavez as a major influence and inspiration.

His methodical style, featuring explosive short hooks and body punches, brought him the WBC super-featherweight crown in September 1984, and he retained it nine times before moving up to lightweight in 1987. He completed the WBA/WBC double there, then stepped up to light-welterweight, where he achieved his greatest fame. He won the WBC title in May 1989, and added the IBF championship in the most dramatic ending imaginable when, trailing on points, he produced a blistering attack to stop Meldrick Taylor with just two seconds left in the final round.

His reputation was dented when he was given a fortunate draw in a challenge for Pernell Whitaker's WBC welterweight title in 1993, but he regained his light-welterweight title from Randall in May 1994 and continues to defend it regularly.

Kid Chocolate

Real name: *Eligio Sardinias*
Born: *Cerro, Cuba, January 6, 1910*
Titles: *World junior-lightweight (super-featherweight) champion 1931–33, NY-recognised world featherweight champion 1932–34*
Record: *148 contests, 132 wins, 6 draws, 10 defeats*

The hard-punching "Cuban Bon Bon" knocked out 86 of his 100 amateur opponents, and all 21 as a pro in Cuba before trying his luck in America in 1928. He was unbeaten in a further 45 fights, mainly in New York, before his record was spoilt by Jack "Kid" Berg, who outpointed him over 10 rounds in August 1930.

It was the first of three defeats that year, including a points loss to Bat Battalino for the featherweight title. Seven months later, in July 1931, he knocked out Benny Bass for the junior-lightweight championship, but was outscored by Tony Canzoneri in November 1931 when he tried for the lightweight title. He dropped down to featherweight and won the New York version of the world title in October 1932, defending it twice before outgrowing the division.

Frankie Klick took his junior-lightweight title in December 1933, and despite losing only three of his subsequent 50 fights he was unable to land another title chance. The Cuban government awarded him a pension when he retired in 1938, in recognition of his services to country and sport.

Steve Collins

Born: *Dublin, July 21, 1964*
Titles: *WBO middleweight champion 1994–95, WBO super-middleweight champion 1995–*
Record: *33 contests, 30 wins, 3 defeats*

The tough Dubliner made his name in America, but enjoyed his greatest success when he returned home to become the first Irishman to win versions of the world title at two weights. It was a deserved late-career bonus for a single-minded professional who never lost faith in his own ability, despite setbacks in the ring and managerial disputes outside it.

Collins had a good amateur career, reaching three Irish finals and winning the middleweight championship in 1986. He emigrated to Boston later that year and joined the Petronelli brothers' gym, winning the Irish and USBA titles in an unbeaten 16-fight run before being outpointed by Mike McCallum in a gallant bid for the WBA title.

It was a good learning experience for the Irishman, as were his only other defeats, close points losses to Reggie Johnson for the vacant WBA title and Sumbu Kalambay for the European title, both in 1992. He stopped Chris Pyatt for the WBO middleweight title in May 1994, relinquishing it after taking the WBO super-middleweight title from the previously unbeaten Chris Eubank in March 1995.

THE END *of the line nears for Billy Conn as he prepares for his last fight, in 1948*

Billy Conn

Born: *East Liberty, Pennsylvania, October 8, 1917*
Titles: *World light-heavyweight champion 1939–41*
Record: *76 contests, 63 wins, 1 draw, 12 defeats*

Billy Conn gained immortality for a fight he lost, his bid for Joe Louis's world heavyweight title in June 1941. He was ahead on points after 12 rounds, boxing brilliantly and staying away from Louis's powerful punches, but in the 13th he had a rush of blood to the head and decided to go for the big finish and was flattened. His defeat fulfilled Louis's prediction: "He can run, but he can't hide."

Conn, an Irish-American, started as a welterweight in 1935. He was hardly an overnight sensation, losing six of his first 14 fights, but he persevered and was soon a contender for the middleweight title, beating champions like Fritzie Zivic, Vince Dundee, Teddy Yarosz, Solly Krieger and Fred Apostoli. But his chance came at light-heavyweight, when he beat Melio Bettina for the vacant championship in 1939.

He made three defences, then relinquished the title to challenge Louis. Like Louis, he joined the US Army in 1942, and was inactive from then until June 1946, when Louis knocked him out in eight one-sided rounds. He retired in 1948, and died on May 29, 1993.

John Conteh

Born: *Liverpool, England, May 27, 1951*
Titles: *European light-heavyweight champion 1973–74, British and Commonwealth champion 1973–74, WBC world champion 1974–77*
Record: *39 contests, 34 wins, 1 draw, 4 defeats*

Had it not been for managerial disputes and injury problems, Conteh would surely have earned a place with Britain's all-time greats. As it was, he compiled a record of which he could be proud and won every championship open to him.

A brilliant amateur, he took the European title in his 19th fight and the British and Commonwealth in his 20th, beating his arch-rival Chris Finnegan for the latter two. When Bob Foster was stripped by the WBC in August 1974 for failing to defend against either Conteh or Jorge Ahumada of Argentina, Conteh outpointed Ahumada in London for the vacant championship.

He made three successful defences, but a serious hand injury restricted his activity. He gave up the title on a point of principle a couple of days before he was due to defend against Miguel Cuello, and then failed in three bids to regain it, losing to Mate Parlov in Belgrade and being beaten twice by Matthew Saad Muhammad in Atlantic City. The first

Muhammad fight was desperately close, but he lost badly in the second and retired after just one more fight.

Henry Cooper

Born: *Bellingham, England, May 3, 1934*
Titles: *British and Empire (later Commonwealth) heavyweight champion 1959–69 and 1970–71, European champion 1964, 1968–69, 1970–71*
Record: *55 contests, 40 wins, 1 draw, 14 defeats*

Cooper's amiable disposition and sportsmanship earned him a unique place in the affections of the British public, based largely on his two most famous defeats, by Cassius Clay in 1963 and Joe Bugner in 1971. Cooper floored Clay with a perfect left hook at the end of the fourth round, and trainer Angelo Dundee gained his dazed man more invaluable recovery time between the rounds by drawing the referee's attention to Clay's burst glove.

Clay won on cuts in the next round, but the myth grew that somehow the gallant British loser had been given a raw deal. They met again for the title in 1966, but Cooper's vulnerable eyebrows let him down, as they often did.

He was European champion three times and was Britain's longest-serving heavyweight champion, reigning from 1959 to 1971 with only a short break when he relinquished the title because the British Board would not allow him to contest

HENRY COOPER *National hero, in 1966*

the WBA title. Cooper won three Lonsdale Belts outright, a record, and retired on a wave of sympathy after Bugner was given a controversial verdict over him. His charity work brought him a Papal knighthood, and he remains hugely popular.

James J. Corbett

Born: *San Francisco, California, September 1, 1866*
Titles: *World heavyweight champion 1892–97*
Record: *19 contests, 11 wins, 2 draws, 2 No Contests, 4 defeats*

The elegant Corbett rewrote the textbooks as well as the history books. He was the first heavyweight champion of the gloved era, and the first to utilize speed, accuracy of punch and deft footwork in preference to the raw strength personified by John L. Sullivan, from whom he took the title in September 1892.

Unusually for boxers then, he was an educated man who worked as a bank clerk in San Francisco before taking up boxing. He made his name in a famous battle with local rival Joe Choynski, staged on a barge in June 1889. Corbett won in 27 rounds, and earned his title chance by beating Jake Kilrain and fighting a 61-round "No Contest" with Peter Jackson.

Corbett outboxed Sullivan effortlessly before knocking him out in the 25th, sending the old champion into retirement. He defended the title only once in five years, against Charlie Mitchell, and was dethroned by Bob Fitzsimmons in March 1897. Corbett tried twice to regain the title from James J. Jeffries in 1900 and again in 1903, but was knocked out each time. He died in Bayside, New York on February 18, 1933.

Jose "Pipino" Cuevas

Born: *Mexico City, Mexico, December 27, 1957*
Titles: *WBA welterweight champion 1976–80*
Record: *50 contests, 35 wins, 15 defeats*

Cuevas was the archetypal Mexican fighter: an explosive puncher, particularly with the left hook, but short on defence. He turned pro at 14, and was outpointed in four of his first 11 fights. Naturally, he won the rest by knockout. When he was only 17 he won the Mexican welterweight title from world-ranked Jose Palacios.

That win brought him international attention, but when the clever American Andy Price outscored him two fights later, WBA champion Angel Espada was fooled into thinking that the Mexican, still five months away from his 19th birthday, would be an easy defence. He lasted less than two rounds, and Cuevas's spectacular reign was under way.

His fierce punching accounted for 11 challengers, many of them high-quality contenders, and only Randy Shields took him the distance. But, like an old-time gunfighter, Cuevas eventually met someone faster and harder than himself: Thomas Hearns, who knocked him out with one punch in August 1980. He boxed on until 1989, but a fourth-round stoppage by Roberto Duran in 1983 ended his hopes of regaining the title.

Les Darcy

Born: *Maitland, Australia,*
October 31, 1895
Titles: *Australian recognition as*
world middleweight champion,
1915–17
Record: *49 contests, 45 wins,*
4 defeats

Darcy was just 15, a blacksmith's apprentice, when he had his first pro fight in 1910. He made rapid progress and challenged for the Australian welterweight title in 1913, Bob Whitelaw ending his unbeaten record with a 20-rounds points win.

It was a minor setback, and by 1915 Darcy, now a middleweight,

PIN-UP BOY *Oscar De La Hoya could be boxing's biggest star of the '90s*

staked a strong claim to the disputed world title by beating leading men like Jeff Smith, Eddie McGoorty and Jimmy Clabby. Darcy was now so dominant a figure in Australian boxing that he even won the national heavyweight title, which he defended three times in 1916.

He wanted to go to America to pursue his claims, but because of the war men of military age were forbidden to leave the country. Darcy departed furtively on a cargo ship, but when he arrived in America he found himself labelled a draft-dodger and a coward. He could not get a fight, and a theatrical tour flopped. The unfortunate Darcy caught a fever and died in Memphis, Tennessee on May 27, 1917; romantics say he died of a broken heart.

Esteban DeJesus

Born: *Carolina, Puerto Rico,*
August 2, 1951
Titles: *WBC lightweight champion*
1976–78
Record: *62 contests, 57 wins,*
5 defeats

DeJesus claimed his own little piece of boxing history on November 17, 1972, when he became the first man to beat Roberto Duran, winning their non-title 10-round bout in New York on points. It had been a brave match for Duran to take: DeJesus had lost only once in 33 fights, and was clearly a rising star.

He won the NABF title in his next fight, but then lost to Duran in a lightweight championship bid, and to Antonio Cervantes for the WBA light-welterweight crown, before finally taking the WBC lightweight title from Guts Ishimatsu in May 1976. He made three successful defences, but was then knocked out in 12 by Duran in a championship unification match.

He boxed until 1980, being stopped in the 13th round by Jamaican Saoul Mamby for the WBC light-welterweight title in his last fight. Drugs took over his life after boxing, and while serving a jail sentence for a drug-related killing he contracted AIDS, from which he died on May 11, 1989. His old rival, Duran, visited him in hospital in the last week of his life.

Oscar De La Hoya

Born: *Montebello, California,*
February 4, 1973
Titles: *WBO super-featherweight*
champion 1994, WBO light-
weight champion 1994–, IBF
lightweight champion 1995
Record: *20 contests, 20 wins*

Boxing was in De La Hoya's blood, as his grandfather, father and brother had all been professionals. Oscar started boxing under his father's tuition when he was just six, and went on to win a host of championships and become America's darling when he was the country's only boxing gold medallist at the 1992 Olympics.

His boyish good looks and telegenic personality made him hugely marketable. He had been expected to turn professional with New York manager Shelley Finkel, who had been subsidizing him heavily during his amateur career, but instead he signed with Bob Mittleman and Steve Nelson in return for a large bonus. This calculating trait resurfaced later when he dumped them unceremoniously, but even his critics acknowledge that De La Hoya's performances in the ring have been flawless.

He won the WBO super-featherweight title from Jimmi Bredahl in March 1994, took the vacant WBO lightweight title four months later with a second-round knockout of former featherweight champion Jorge Paez, and added the IBF championship when he stopped Rafael Ruelas in dazzling style in a unification match in May 1995. He later relinquished the IBF belt.

"Nonpareil" Jack Dempsey

Real name: *John Kelly*
Born: *Kildare, Ireland,*
December 15, 1862
Titles: *World middleweight*
champion 1884–91
Record: *64 contests, 50 wins, 8*
draws, 3 No Contests, 3 defeats

The most impressive evidence of Dempsey's ability in the ring is the fact that William Harrison Dempsey chose to borrow his *nom du ring* from the Irishman. The original Jack Dempsey was known as "Nonpareil" because he was precisely that: without a peer amongst his contemporaries. He was unbeaten for the first six years of his career, and staked a claim to the middleweight championship in 1884, when he beat George Fulljames.

He was not generally accepted as champion, however, until his 27-rounds win over Jack Fogarty in 1886, and he defended the title twice before being knocked out in controversial circumstances by George LaBlanche, whom he had beaten in an 1886 title defence. LaBlanche used the so-called "pivot punch", a back-handed blow, to do the damage. The punch was subsequently declared illegal, and Dempsey continued as champion until Bob Fitzsimmons knocked him out in 1891.

He boxed only three more times, and in his last fight, in January 1895, was knocked out in three rounds by Tommy Ryan for the welterweight title. Dempsey died in Portland, Oregon that same year, on November 2.

Jack Dempsey

see Legends of the Ring (pp 70–71)

George Dixon

Born: *Halifax, Canada,*
July 29, 1870
Titles: *World featherweight title*
claimant 1890–96, 1897,
1898–1900
Record: *146 contests, 78 wins, 37*
draws, 3 No Contests, 3 No
Decisions, 25 defeats

The skilful Canadian, known as "Little Chocolate", was the first major star of the featherweight division. He established a claim to the disputed title in 1890, and was generally accepted as champion after beating the Englishman, Fred Johnson, in 1892. His first defence, against Jack Skelly in New Orleans, was remarkable in that Skelly was having his first professional fight.

Dixon lost the title to Frank Erne in November 1896, but regained it four months later. This time, he was champion for only seven months, losing on points to Solly Smith. The challenger was two pounds over the agreed limit of 118 lb, so Dixon continued to style himself world champion even though Smith was widely regarded as the rigilful holder.

He regained the title in 1898 from Dave Sullivan, who had defeated Smith, and held it for another two years until a bad beating from Terry McGovern finished his top-flight career. He boxed on until 1906, spending most of his time in England, but won only 10 of his remaining 53 fights.

James "Buster" Douglas

Born: *Columbus, Ohio,*
April 7, 1960
Titles: *WBC, WBA and IBF*
heavyweight champion 1990
Record: *36 contests, 30 wins, 1 draw,*
5 defeats

Douglas was on the road to obscurity when, on February 11, 1990, he scored the biggest upset in history by knocking out Mike Tyson for the world title in Tokyo. A huge outsider in the betting, Douglas made the most of his opportunity: he was superbly conditioned, for virtually the only time in his career, and he outboxed and outpunched the hitherto unbeatable Tyson, surviving an eighth-round knockdown to knock him out in the 10th.

Managed by his father Billy, a former pro middleweight, Douglas had his first fight in 1981. He possessed plenty of natural talent but little discipline, and when he flopped in the 10th round of a fight with Tony Tucker for the vacant IBF title, critics questioned his heart as well. But he had the last laugh in Tokyo, even if his reign was short and ended in a third-round humiliation by Evander Holyfield eight months later.

He retired with ring earnings of around $30m, and let his weight balloon from the 224 lb of his fighting peak to over 300 lb. By the end of 1995, though, he was reported to be training for a comeback.

Terry Downes

Born: *London, England,*
May 9, 1936.
Titles: *British middleweight*
champion 1958–59, 1959–62,
New York and European
recognition as world middle-
weight champion 1961–62
Record: *44 contests, 35 wins,*
9 defeats

Terry Downes learned his boxing – and acquired his extraordinary accent – in the US Marines. He won the All-Services title and qualified for the American team for the 1956 Olympics, before his true nationality was discovered. On his return to Britain he turned professional and, despite a tendency to cut, became British middleweight champion after only 17 months. A points wins over Joey Giardello earned him a challenge for Paul Pender's championship, but the Bostonian stopped him on cuts in seven rounds in January 1961.

There was a rematch at Wembley six months later, and this time the American retired in his corner at the end of the ninth round, claiming exhaustion. They met for the third time in Boston in April 1962, Pender winnning on points. Downes was already a wealthy man, having capitalized on the legalization of bookmaking by opening a string of betting shops, but he boxed on in the hope of another world title opportunity.

He beat the fading Sugar Ray Robinson in September 1962, and then moved up to light-heavyweight, making a brave bid for Willie Pastrano's world title in his last fight, in November 1964.

"Peerless" Jim Driscoll

Born: *Cardiff, Wales,*
December 15, 1881
Titles: *British featherweight*
champion 1906–1913, Empire
champion 1908–13, European
champion 1912–13, British and
IBU recognition as world
champion 1909–13
Record: *69 contests, 52 wins, 6*
draws, 8 No Decisions, 3 defeats

Driscoll was a classic exponent of the "British style" of boxing, built around a fast straight left and deft footwork. He took up the sport professionally in 1899: according to legend, he had taught himself to box using wastepaper wrapped around his hands.

By 1906 he was British featherweight champion, although that status was not officially recognized until 1910, when he won the first Lonsdale Belt contest at that division. He made the Belt his own property in

TERRY DOWNES *The Paddington Express*

MASTER BOXER *"Peerless" Jim Driscoll*

1911 and added the European title a year later. But his career peaked in 1909, when he faced Abe Attell, the world champion, in New York. Attell would only agree to a "No Decision" contest, but Driscoll won each of the 10 rounds and was accepted as world champion by Britain and the IBU.

He retired in 1913, after an epic 20-round draw with Owen Moran at the NSC. Six years later, he made a three-fight comeback aged 38, which ended when he outboxed the dangerous Frenchman Charles Ledoux for 16 rounds before being beaten by a body punch. He was already suffering from consumption, which finally killed him on January 31, 1925.

Johnny Dundee

Real name: *Joseph Corrara*
Born: *Shaikai, Italy,*
November 22, 1893
Titles: *World junior-lightweight*
champion 1921–23, 1923–24,
world featherweight champion
1923–24
Record: *(approx.) 337 contests, 88*
wins, 19 draws, 198 No
Decisions, 1 No Contest,
31 defeats

Dundee, whose mildly offensive nickname was "The Scotch Wop", had more pro fights than any other world champion: records vary between 322 and 337, and because so many of them

were No Decision contests and often went unreported, the exact total will never be known. Even more remarkably, the overwhelming majority went the full distance. He scored just 22 inside-schedule wins, and was knocked out only twice.

His career spanned 22 years, from 1910 to 1932, and his first title chance came in 1913 when he drew with Johnny Kilbane for the featherweight title. Despite meeting all the top featherweights and lightweights of the time, he had to wait until 1921 for a second chance, beating George Chaney on disqualification in the first-ever junior-lightweight title fight. After two defences he lost the championship to Jack Bernstein in May 1923, but two months later won the featherweight title from the French war hero Eugene Criqui and then, in December that year, regained the junior-lightweight title from Bernstein.

He never defended the featherweight title, and lost the junior-lightweight championship to Kid Sullivan in June 1924.

Roberto Duran

see Legends of the Ring (pp 72–73)

Gabriel "Flash" Elorde

Born: *Bogo, Philippines,*
March 22, 1935
Titles: *World junior-lightweight*
champion 1960–67
Record: *115 contests, 88 wins, 2*
draws, 25 defeats

The colourful Filipino deserves to be remembered as the man who, single-handedly, gave credibility to the super-featherweight (or junior-lightweight, as it was then known) division. He won the recently revived title from

Harold Gomes in March 1960, and his 10 successful defences, most of them against top-quality challengers from around the world, established the 130-lb division in the public mind.

Elorde was already a national hero in the Philippines before then, having won national and Oriental titles from bantamweight to lightweight and battled for 13 rounds with Sandy Saddler in a tremendous world featherweight title challenge in 1956. He also tried twice to become lightweight champion, but each time Carlos Ortiz turned him back in 14 rounds, in 1964 and 1966.

He finally lost his junior lightweight title to Yoshiaki Numata in June 1967, and retired after an unsuccessful comeback in 1969–71. He later became a leading promoter, working with his father-in-law Lope Sarreal (who had also been his manager), before his early death from cancer on January 2, 1985.

Alfredo Escalera

Born: *Carolina, Puerto Rico,*
March 21, 1952
Titles: *WBC super-featherweight*
champion 1975–78
Record: *69 contests, 52 wins,*
3 draws, 14 defeats

Few fighters have employed as colourful a gimmick as Alfredo "Snake Man" Escalera, who used to enter the ring with a serpent or two around his neck and limbs. He was a capable if unspectacular performer in the early years of a career which began in September 1970, and had won only two of the five fights which preceded his WBC super-featherweight title win over Kuniaki Shibata in July 1975.

His championship reign began equally uncertainly with a disputed 15-rounds draw with Leonel Hernandez in Caracas, but he settled down to become one of the better 130-lb champions, making 10 successful defences in five countries (Finland, Japan, America, Puerto Rico and Venezuela) before Alexis Arguello took his title in 13 rounds in January 1978. Escalera's points win over the flashy Philadelphian Tyrone Everett in November 1976 is remembered as an outrageously unjust verdict, and he was

careful not to give the American a second chance.

He had only a handful of fights after losing his title, and was beaten in 13 rounds again when he tried to regain the championship from the Nicaraguan in February 1979.

Sixto Escobar

Born: *Barcelona, Puerto Rico,*
March 23, 1913
Titles: *NBA bantamweight*
champion 1934–35, 1935, New
York champion 1935–36, world
champion 1936–37, 1938, 1939
Record: *72 contests, 45 wins,*
4 draws, 23 defeats

The host of champions who have come out of Puerto Rico in the last few decades owe a debt to Escobar, who won the bantamweight title three times and was one of that tiny country's early success stories in the ring.

Escobar came to America in 1934 via Canada and Venezuela, where he had most of his early fights. He won the vacant NBA title in Montreal by knocking out Baby Casanova, retained it against Eugene Huat in August 1934, then lost to Lou Salica in the first of their three championship meetings. Less than three months later he was champion again, and went on to become the undisputed title-holder in August 1936 by beating the ill-fated Tony Marino (who collapsed and died after a fight in January 1937.)

Escobar lost the title in his third defence, to Harry Jeffra, but regained it in February 1938. It was the only time in five fights that he got the better of Jeffra. He relinquished the title in October 1939 because of his inability to make the weight, and retired the following year after losing five of his last six fights.

Chris Eubank

Born: *London, England,*
August 8, 1966
Titles: *WBC International middle-*
weight champion 1990, WBO
middleweight champion 1990–
91, WBO super-middleweight
champion 1991–95
Record: *47 contests, 43 wins,*
2 draws, 2 defeats

The flamboyant and frequently outrageous Eubank professed to despise boxing, yet made a fortune from the sport and, with 21 WBO title fights (17 wins, two draws and two defeats) engaged in more so-called world title fights than any other British boxer.

A troubled and difficult youth, he was sent to New York to join his mother, and it was there that he took up amateur boxing seriously. He turned professional in October 1985, winning five four-rounders in Atlantic City before returning to Britain in 1987. His career really took off when he joined promoter Barry Hearn, who steered him to the WBO middleweight championship, won in a heroic battle from Nigel Benn.

He defended that three times, the last a disputed win over Michael Watson, then moved up to super-middleweight and captured the vacant WBO title in a dramatic and tragic rematch with Watson, who was left permanently disabled after being stopped in the final round. That experience seemed to affect Eubank, as he repeatedly settled for points decisions when he could have won by stoppage. He retired after a second loss to Steve Collins in September 1995.

Johnny Famechon

Born: *Paris, France, March 28, 1945*
Titles: *Empire (Commonwealth) featherweight champion 1967–69, WBC champion 1969–70*
Record: *67 contests, 56 wins, 6 draws, 5 defeats*

Famechon was born into the aristocracy of French boxing. His uncle Ray was an outstanding European feath-

erweight champion who fought for the world title, while his father Andre and uncle Emile were both French champions. When Andre divorced he moved to Australia, taking Johnny with him.

The youngster never boxed as an amateur, turning pro at 16 in June 1961. He won the Australian featherweight title after 22 fights and the Commonwealth championship in his 49th. In January 1969 he took the WBC title from Jose Legra in London, giving a dazzling display of quickfire boxing to outscore the Cuban. British fans liked his style, and he had a series of non-title fights there.

He retained his title twice, each time against former flyweight and bantamweight champion Fighting Harada of Japan. Famechon was floored three times in their first meeting, but knocked the Japanese out in the 14th round of their rematch in Tokyo. He lost the title to Vicente Saldivar in Rome in May 1970, and never fought again. In 1995 he was critically injured in a car accident, spending some time on a life support machine before making a good recovery.

Tommy Farr

Born: *Tonypandy, Wales, March 12, 1913*
Titles: *British heavyweight champion 1937–38*
Record: *107 contests, 71 wins, 11 draws, 25 defeats*

The rugged Welshman will always be remembered for his stirring 15-

BRAVE AND STUBBORN *Tommy Farr*

round challenge for Joe Louis's heavyweight title in August 1937. It was the American's first defence, and he was confidently expected to dismiss the little-known British champion without much difficulty. Instead Farr, fighting bravely and stubbornly, defied him for the full distance of a fight, which millions at home listened to on BBC radio.

Farr came from a tough school, having learned his boxing on the booths from the age of 13. He started as a middleweight in 1926 and progressed to the Welsh light-heavyweight title, which he won in 1933, but after a string of defeats he moved up to heavyweight and started a long winning run which carried him to the British title in March 1937. Victories over former champion Max Baer and the German star Walter Neusel earned him the fight with Louis.

He stayed on in America hoping for a second chance, but lost four bad verdicts, including a return with Baer, and came home to find that the Board had stripped him of the British title. Farr retired in 1940, but made a reasonably successful comeback 10 years later before quitting for good in 1953. He died in Brighton on March 1, 1986.

AUSSIE PRODIGY *Jeff Fenech was world champion after just seven fights*

Jeff Fenech

Born: *Sydney, Australia, May 28, 1964*
Titles: *IBF bantamweight champion 1985–87, WBC super-bantamweight champion 1987–88, WBC featherweight champion 1988–89*
Record: *30 contests, 27 wins, 1 draw, 2 defeats*

Fenech was a rough handful in or out of the ring, a delinquent tearaway who successfully channelled his aggression into boxing. The son of Maltese immigrants, he represented Australia in the 1984 Olympic Games and turned professional on his return, winning the national super-flyweight title in his third bout.

Just four fights later, after a grand total of 24 rounds as a professional, he was a world champion, having knocked out Satoshi Shingaki for the IBF bantamweight title in Sydney. He made three defences before moving up to super-bantamweight to win the WBC title from the Thai, Samart Payakarun, with a surprise fourth-round knockout in May 1987. He retained that against former world champions Greg Richardson and Carlos Zarate, then stepped up again to featherweight to become WBC champion by stopping Victor Callejas in March 1988.

After three defences he announced his retirement, but then returned as a super-featherweight to fight a draw with Azumah Nelson, a verdict he bitterly disputed. But Nelson beat him easily in the rematch, Fenech's first defeat, and he retired again ... only to launch yet another comeback in Atlantic City, late in 1995.

Bob Fitzsimmons

Born: *Helston, England,
    May 26, 1863*
Titles: *World middleweight
    champion 1891–94, heavy-
    weight champion 1897–99,
    light-heavyweight champion
    1903–05*
Record: *62 contests, 40 wins, 10 No
    Decisions, 1 No Contest,
    11 defeats*

The spindly, unathletic-looking Fitzsimmons, who never scaled more than 175 lb, was a true cosmopolitan. He was born in Cornwall, England, raised in New Zealand, spent the first seven years of his career in Australia, and won two of his three world titles as an American citizen. His career

BOB FITZSIMMONS *champion in 1891*

started when, as an apprentice black-smith, he won a competition organized by the old bare-knuckle champion Jem Mace.

He took the middleweight title from "Nonpareil" Jack Dempsey in 13 rounds in January 1891, retaining it twice before moving up to heavy-weight. Challenging James J. Corbett on St Patrick's Day, 1897, Fitzsimmons was comprehensively outboxed for 13 rounds before land-ing a left to the stomach which left Corbett on his knees, gasping for breath.

He lost in his first defence to James J. Jeffries, who outweighed him by 50 lb, and Jeffries knocked him out again in 1902. Fitzsimmons bounced back once more, this time in the newly created light-heavyweight division, and won his third world title by out-pointing George Gardner in 1903, holding it for two years. He finally retired in 1914, aged 52, and died in Chicago on October 22, 1917.

Tiger Flowers

Real name: *Theodore Flowers*
Born: *Camile, Georgia,
    August 5, 1895*
Titles: *World middleweight
    champion 1926*
Record: *157 contests, 116 wins,
    6 draws, 21 No Decisions,
    1 No Contest, 13 defeats*

Flowers was a thoughtful and religious man, a rarity in an era of hellraising middleweights like Harry Greb and Mickey Walker, so he was known as the "Georgia Deacon". A southpaw, he started boxing in 1918 and main-tained a prodigious work rate, having 36 fights in 1924 alone.

He was a cagey boxer with a stiff punch, but frequently had to fight out of his weight class, losing to light-heavy-weight champions Jack Delaney (twice), Mike McTigue and Maxie Rosenbloom. He finally got a world title chance in February 1926, and out-pointed Greb (who by then was blind in one eye) over 15 rounds to become the first black middleweight champion.

He fought Mickey Walker in Chicago in December that year, under the impression that it would be a No Decision affair, only to hear

GRANDAD *George Foreman became the oldest-ever heavyweight champion*

Walker proclaimed champion at the end of their 10-rounder. He cam-paigned for a rematch, and lost only one of his 18 fights in 1927. But on November 16, 1927, he died in New York following a routine eye operation.

George Foreman

Born: *Marshall, Texas,
    January 22, 1948*
Titles: *World heavyweight
    champion 1973–74, WBA and
    IBF champion 1994–95*
Record: *78 contests, 74 wins,
    4 defeats*

Foreman took up boxing as a rebel-lious teenager, winning the heavy-weight gold medal at the 1968 Olympics before launching a spec-tacular pro career. He had won 37 in a row, 34 by knockout, when he faced the formidable Joe Frazier for the title in Kingston, Jamaica on Foreman's 25th birthday.

Despite his KO record, Foreman was a big outsider, but he floored Frazier six times to force a second-round stoppage. Chilling defences against Joe Roman and Ken Norton made him seem invincible, and there were fears for Muhammad Ali's safety when the ex-champion chal-lenged him in Zaire in October 1974. Instead, Ali took everything Foreman had and then flattened the exhausted Texan in the eighth.

Foreman drifted away from box-ing, becoming a minister before, after a 10-year layoff, he started an improbable comeback. He worked his way into contention, and lost hon-ourably to Evander Holyfield in his first attempt to regain the title. In November 1994, he knocked out WBA and IBF champion Michael Moorer to become the oldest-ever heavyweight champion. The WBA later stripped him, and he relin-quished the IBF title after one unim-pressive defence in April 1995.

Joe Frazier

Born: *Beaufort, South Carolina, January 12, 1944.*
Titles: *New York recognition as heavyweight champion 1968–1970, world heavyweight champion 1970–73*
Record: *37 contests, 32 wins, 1 draw, 4 defeats*

Despite his Southern origins, "Smokin' Joe" came to personify the left-hooking, aggressive Philadelphia style of fighting. The family had moved north when Joe was a boy, and he turned professional in August 1965 after winning the 1964 Olympic gold medal, coming in as a late replacement for the injured Buster Mathis.

He was managed by a syndicate of mainly white businessmen, calling themselves Cloverlay Inc., but the training and match-making decisions were made first by Yank Durham and later by Eddie Futch. Frazier surged up the rankings with important wins over men like Oscar Bonavena, Doug Jones, Eddie Machen and George Chuvalo, and in 1968 he stopped his old amateur rival Mathis to win the New York version of the world title which had been stripped from Muhammad Ali. Two years later he stopped WBA champion Jimmy Ellis to unify the title, and removed all doubts about his right to be champion when he floored and out-pointed Ali in March 1971.

He lost the title to George Foreman in 1973, and failed in a magnificent effort to regain it from Ali in the "Thrilla in Manila" in October 1975, retiring a year later.

Gene Fullmer

Born: *West Jordan, Utah, July 21, 1931.*
Titles: *World middleweight champion 1957, NBA champion 1959–62*
Record: *64 contests, 55 wins, 3 draws, 6 defeats*

SMOKIN' JOE FRAZIER *left-hooked his way to boxing immortality*

One of a family of boxing brothers, the crude, brawling Fullmer had his first pro fight in June 1951 under the management of a Utah mink farmer, Marv Jensen, who guided him throughout his memorable career. He knocked out his first 11 opponents, six in the first round, and before the end of 1951 had established himself by beating the respected Garth Panter.

By 1957, having lost only three times in 40 fights, he was a leading contender and, on January 2, 1957, shocked Ray Robinson by outpointing him in New York. Robinson reclaimed the title four months later with a perfect, one-punch knockout, but Fullmer fought on and, in August 1959, stopped Carmen Basilio to win the vacant NBA title.

He retained it seven times, including a repeat stoppage of Basilio and a draw and points win in further meetings with Robinson. Dick Tiger outpointed him in October 1962, and although Fullmer held him to a draw in a rematch he was on borrowed time. Tiger stopped him in seven rounds in their third fight, and Fullmer, a shrewd man who had invested his money well, never fought again.

Victor Galindez

Born: *Buenos Aires, Argentina November 2, 1948*
Titles: *WBA light-heavyweight champion 1974–78, 1979*
Record: *70 contests, 55 wins, 4 draws, 2 No Contests, 9 defeats*

Although Victor Galindez held only the WBA version of the light-heavyweight title, he was good enough to have been a world champion in any era. Yet he made an indifferent start, winning only half of his first 22 fights.

After that, though, he never looked back. An unbeaten run of 23 brought him the Argentine title and a match with Len Hutchins of America for the WBA title, which had been stripped from Bob Foster.

Galindez won in 13 rounds and proved a busy champion, willing to go anywhere for a payday. He retained the title 10 times against outstanding challengers like Alvaro Lopez, Pierre Fourie, Jorge Ahumada, Richie Kates and Eddie Gregory. He was especially popular in Italy, where he defended four times, and in South Africa, where his four defences included a last-round knockout of Kates in a dramatic and bloody battle.

Mike Rossman took the title with a surprise 13th round stoppage in New Orleans in September 1978, but Galindez regained it in April 1979 before losing it Marvin Johnson seven months later. He boxed just once more, dying in a car accident on October 26, 1980.

Joe Gans

Real name: *Joseph Gaines*
Born: *Baltimore, Maryland, November 25, 1874*
Titles: *World lightweight champion 1902–04, 1906–08*
Record: *156 contests, 120 wins, 10 draws, 18 No Decisions, 8 defeats*

Gans, a classy counter-puncher, was one of the best lightweights in history, but the suspicion attaching to several of his defeats tainted his reputation. He began boxing in 1891, and was beaten only three times on the way to his first world title bid, against Frank Erne in 1900. He was comfortably ahead when, in the 12th round, he sustained a cut eye and suddenly quit.

In December of that year he performed so poorly in losing in two rounds to Terry McGovern that the fight could scarcely have been on the level, but despite these scandals he was given a rematch with Erne in May 1902 and this time won on a first-round knockout – which served only to strengthen the doubts about the previous result.

He retained the title six times

between 1902 and 1908, when he lost it to Battling Nelson, and fought a 20-rounds draw with Joe Walcott for the welterweight title in 1904. Nelson knocked him out in a rematch, and Gans boxed only once more, retiring in 1909. He died of tuberculosis in Baltimore on August 10, 1910.

Kid Gavilan

Real name: *Gerardo Gonzalez*
Born: *Camaguey, Cuba,*
January 6, 1926
Titles: *World welterweight*
champion 1951–54
Record: *143 contests, 107 wins,*
6 draws, 30 defeats

Known as the "Cuban Hawk", Gavilan's trademark was a whipping half-hook, half-uppercut called the bolo punch, which he claimed to have perfected during his years of using a machete in the sugar fields where he worked before becoming a pro fighter in 1943. He had lost only twice in 27 fights when he moved to America in 1946, where his all-action style proved immensely popular.

Although not a heavy puncher – only 27 of his 107 victories were inside the distance – he was never in a bad fight. Sugar Ray Robinson outpointed him in his first world title bid in 1949, but he became champion two years later when he outscored NBA champion Johnny Bratton for the vacant undisputed title. He held it for three years and seven successful defences, until Johnny Saxton outpointed him in October 1954.

KID GAVILAN *The "Cuban Hawk"*

He tried for the middleweight title in April 1954, losing to Carl "Bobo" Olson, and continued boxing in top class, though with scant success, right up to his retirement in September 1958. Sadly, his eyesight had been affected by his punishing 143-fight career, and he later went blind.

Joey Giardello

Real name: *Carmine Tilelli*
Born: *Brooklyn, New York,*
July 16, 1930
Titles: *World middleweight*
champion 1963–65
Record: *133 contests, 100 wins, 7*
draws, 1 No Decision, 25 defeats

Joey Giardello was already a veteran of 123 fights and 15 years in the business when he finally became world middleweight champion in December 1963, outsmarting Dick Tiger in a cagey 15-rounds tactical battle in Atlantic City. It was his second title challenge, having fought a bruising draw with Gene Fullmer for the NBA championship three years earlier.

Based in Philadelphia, Giardello had been boxing in top class from an early stage of his career, but he tended to win a series of important fights and then lose just when he was on the point of a title fight. He fought all the stars of the 1950s – the golden years of the middleweight division – and beat most of them, but his career looked to be winding down when Tiger gave him his chance.

It was their third meeting, having split a pair of 10-rounders in 1959. Giardello managed one defence, outpointing Rubin "Hurricane" Carter, but then lost the title back to Tiger in October 1965. He made a brief comeback as a light-heavyweight, having the last of his 133 fights in November 1967.

Wilfredo Gomez

Born: *Las Monjas, Puerto Rico,*
October 29, 1956
Titles: *WBC super-bantamweight*
champion 1977–83, WBC
featherweight champion 1984,
WBA junior-lightweight
champion 1985–86
Record: *48 contests, 44 wins, 1 draw,*
3 defeats

The hard-punching Gomez compiled a remarkable championship record. He drew his first pro fight, in November 1974, but won the next 32 inside the distance, including 14 for the WBC super-bantamweight title which he won in May 1977. He had been a brilliant amateur, and would almost certainly have taken a gold medal in the 1976 Olympics had he waited that long.

The highlights of his super-bantamweight reign were stoppages of the Mexican pair Carlos Zarate and Lupe Pintor, who had both been outstanding bantamweight champions. Gomez relinquished the title in April 1983 after 17 defences, all by knockout or stoppage, and won the WBC featherweight title in March 1984. It was his second attempt, having been stopped in eight rounds by Salvador Sanchez in August 1981.

Azumah Nelson knocked him out in 11 rounds in August 1984, but Gomez bounced back to win his third title, taking the WBA junior-lightweight championship from Rocky Lockridge in May 1985. Alfredo Layne ended his championship career with a ninth-round stoppage a year later, and Gomez retired in 1989. He was jailed for drug-related offences in 1994.

Alejandro Gonzalez

Born: *Guadalajara, Mexico,*
August 11, 1973
Titles: *WBC featherweight*
champion 1995
Record: *40 contests, 37 wins,*
3 defeats

Nicknamed "Littler Cobra", the lanky Gonzalez had the look of a major star in the making when he took the WBC featherweight title from the flashy New Yorker Kevin Kelley in January 1995 and then retained it against Louie Espinosa and Tony Green, but his third defence saw him dethroned by Manuel Medina in September. It was only Gonzalez's third defeat in 40 fights, and one of the losses came in his third fight, when he was just 14.

Gonzalez spent his early professional years in his home town of Guadalajara, and did not box in Mexico City until 1991. However, the

WBC hierarchy were sufficiently impressed by what they saw then to pair him with Harold Rhodes for the vacant International title (open to boxers ranked between 11 and 30) in February 1992. The Mexican forced Rhodes to retire after eight one-sided rounds, and a succession of impressive defences earned him a final eliminator for the title against Cesar Soto.

Gonzalez fought Soto, the no. 1 contender, in Soto's home town but still came away with a split decision, going on to take Kelley's title and spoil the American's unbeaten record.

Humberto Gonzalez

Born: *Mexico City, Mexico,*
March 25, 1966
Titles: *WBC light-flyweight*
champion 1989–90, 1991–93,
WBC and IBF champion
1994–95
Record: *44 contests, 41 wins,*
3 defeats

The explosive Gonzalez, known affectionately as "Chiquita", has been around the championship scene since 1989, when he took the WBC light-flyweight title from the Korean Yul-Woo Lee in Seoul. He held the title for five defences before losing in an upset to the Filipino Rolando Pascua in December 1990, but regained it from Pascua's conqueror Melchor Cob Castro in June 1991. This time, he managed a further four defences, then lost to IBF champion Michael Carbajal in March 1993 in a unification match.

It was a typical Gonzalez fight: he floored Carbajal twice, only to be knocked out himself in seven rounds. In the rematch in February 1994, Gonzalez opted to box rather than bang and survived a bad cut to win a split decision. They met for the third time in November 1994, when the Mexican confirmed his superiority with another points victory.

His championship reign ended in July 1995 when Saman Sorjaturong stopped him in seven rounds. It was only his third loss in 44 fights in a career which began in September 1984, as a stablemate of the former welterweight champion Pipino Cuevas, whose style he adopted.

Miguel Angel Gonzalez

Born: *Ensenada, Mexico,*
November 15, 1970
Titles: *WBC Internatiuonal light-*
weight champion 1992, WBC
lightweight champion 1992–
Record: *39 contests, 39 wins*

The tall, stylish Gonzalez defied tradition by coming from a comfortable
middle-class background rather
than the grinding poverty which has
spawned so many of the great
Mexican champions. He was educated
to university level, but after representing his country in the 1988
Olympics and losing only two of 65
bouts, he decided to put his natural talent to work in the ring and turned professional in January 1989.

In 1990 he moved to Japan
where, boxing as Santa Tokyo, he won
five in a row to earn himself a world
ranking. In 1992 he won the WBC
International lightweight title, a useful stepping stone to a major championship, and in August that year was
matched with Wilfredo Rocha of
Colombia for the vacant WBC title.
Rocha, who came in as a late
replacement for Darryl Tyson, gave
him an unexpectedly tough fight, even
flooring him, before being forced to
retire after nine rounds.

Gonzalez had defended his title 10
times up to the end of 1995, although
his points win over the American
Lamar Murphy in Las Vegas on the
undercard of Mike Tyson's comeback
was hotly disputed.

Rocky Graziano

Real name: *Thomas Rocco Barbella*
Born: *New York, NY,*
January 1, 1922
Titles: *World middleweight*
champion 1947–48
Record: *83 contests, 67 wins,*
6 draws, 10 defeats

Graziano, the son of an old fighter, was
in constant trouble with the law. He
was drafted into the US Army, but was
given a dishonourable discharge for
striking an officer and after serving
time in an Army prison he turned professional in March 1942.

His brawling style made him a

ROUGH, TOUGH *Rocky Graziano*

popular attraction, although his
crude technique meant that he could
often be outboxed: he lost six decisions
in his first three years. 1945 was his
breakthrough year, with big wins over
Al Davis, welterweight champion
Freddie Cochrane (twice), and
Harold Green, who had outpointed
him twice in 1944. A two-rounds
knockout of former welterweight
champion Marty Servo brought him
a crack at middleweight champion
Tony Zale in 1946, but Graziano was
knocked out in the sixth round of a
classic encounter.

The rematch a year later was a car-
bon copy, except this time Graziano
won, but Zale took the title back in
three rounds in 1948. Graziano compiled an unbeaten run of 21 as he
sought another chance, but when it
came Ray Robinson knocked him out
in three rounds. He retired in
September 1952 and died on May 22,
1990.

Harry Greb

Born: *Pittsburgh, Pennsylvania,*
June 6, 1894
Titles: *American light-heavy-*
weight champion 1922–23,
world middleweight champion
1923–26
Record: *299 contests, 105 wins,*
3 draws, 183 No Decisions,
8 defeats

Greb broke all the rules, in every
sense: he was a rough and dirty fighter, and his lifestyle was the antithesis
of a professional athlete's. He was a
drinker and a prodigious womanizer,
yet compiled an astonishing record of
almost 300 fights in a hectic 13-year
career. He scorned training, arguing
that fighting so often kept him fit
enough. He had a point: he boxed 32
times in 1917 alone, while his 26 fights
in 1918 included 10-rounders with
light-heavyweight champions Jack
Dillon, Mike McTigue and Battling
Levinsky.

His most famous victory came in
May 1922, when he battered Gene
Tunney over 15 rounds. It was
Tunney's sole defeat, and he
trounced Greb in a rematch in
February 1923. Greb won the middleweight title from Johnny Wilson in
his next fight, and his five successful
defences included a ferocious battle
with Mickey Walker which, reportedly,
was continued later that evening
when the pair met outside a nightclub.

He lost the title to Tiger Flowers
in February 1926, and Flowers beat
him again six months later. It was
Greb's last fight: he died on October
22, 1926 following an eye operation.

Emile Griffith

Born: *St Thomas, Virgin Islands,*
February 3, 1938
Titles: *World welterweight*
champion 1961, 1962–63,
1963–66, world middleweight
champion 1966–67, 1967–68
Record: *112 contests, 85 wins, 2*
draws, 1 No Contest, 24 defeats

The colourful Griffith worked in a
New York milliner's before turning
pro in June 1958, and by 1960 had
beaten top contenders like Gaspar
Ortega, Denny Moyer, Jorge and
Florentino Fernandez and Luis
Rodriguez to earn a crack at Benny
Paret's welterweight title. He
knocked Paret out in 13 rounds in
April 1961, but lost the title back to
him in September before stopping the
Cuban in 12 rounds in their rubber
match in March 1962. Paret never
regained consciousness.

Griffith was dethroned by Luis
Rodriguez in March 1963, but
regained the crown three months later
and then won their third meeting in
June 1964. In total, he won 10 and
lost two welterweight title
fights before taking the
middleweight title from
Dick Tiger in April 1966.
He retained it twice

CRAFTSMAN *Emile*
Griffith was five times a
world champion

against New York rival Joey Archer, then lost two out of three clashes with Nino Benvenuti.

Jose Napoles outpointed him when he tried to regain the welterweight title in 1969, and Carlos Monzon defeated him twice in middleweight title bids. Griffith also lost a 1976 challenge for the WBC light-middleweight title, and retired the following year after 112 fights.

Marvin Hagler

Born: *Newark, New Jersey, May 23, 1952*
Titles: *World middleweight champion 1980–87, WBA and IBF champion 1987*
Record: *67 contests, 62 wins, 2 draws, 3 defeats*

Marvin Hagler added the word "Marvelous" to his name by deed poll, and nobody argued. For the best part of a decade, he was the unbeatable king of the middleweights, who should have been champion for a couple of years before he eventually won it.

The shaven-skulled switch-hitter, equally at home in the southpaw or orthodox stance, moved with his family to Brockton, Mass. after the race riots in Newark in 1967, and turned professional after winning the AAU title in 1973. When he beat former Olympic champion Ray Seales in only his 15th fight, he became known as a man to avoid. Despite losing only two of his first 50 fights, he had to wait until 1979 for a title chance, when a draw allowed Vito Antuofermo to keep the title.

But he made no mistake next time, stopping Alan Minter in three rounds and going on to retain the title 12 times, including classic fights with Thomas Hearns and John Mugabi.

When Ray Leonard was given a controversial verdict over him, in April 1987, Hagler walked away from boxing to begin a new career in films.

Naseem Hamed

Born: *Sheffield, England, February 12, 1974*
Titles: *European bantamweight champion 1994, WBC International super-bantamweight champion 1994–95, WBO featherweight champion 1995–*
Record: *20 contests, 20 wins*

Hamed's precocious talent was nurtured by trainer Brendan Ingle, who discovered him as a seven-year-old and guided him from his first contest to the WBO featherweight title, won in breathtaking style from Steve

Robinson in September 1995. Of Yemeni parentage, Hamed's highly individualistic style did not endear him to the conservative amateur authori-

MARVELOUS MARVIN HAGLER *for once hides his famous shaven skull*

ties, who took a dim view of his backflips and gimmickry.

But there was no hiding his ability, and he won schools and junior ABA titles before turning pro in 1992 without ever boxing at senior level. His whole persona was geared to appeal to the mass market rather than merely boxing fans, but TV did not latch onto him until he joined the Frank Warren team after spells with rival promoters Mickey Duff and Barry Hearn. Warren tested him in May 1994 against the veteran European bantamweight champion Vincenzo Belcastro in Hamed's 12th fight, and the youngster won every round and the title.

He relinquished that after one defence because of increasing weight, and won the vacant WBC International super-bantamweight title in his first fight in the new division, using it as a springboard to the featherweight title.

Mashiko "Fighting" Harada

Born: *Tokyo, Japan, April 5, 1943*
Titles: *World flyweight champion 1962–63, world bantamweight champion 1965–68*
Record: *62 contests, 55 wins, 7 defeats*

The rugged Harada won world titles at flyweight and bantamweight and only narrowly failed to add the featherweight crown. He knocked out the Thai, Pone Kingpetch in 11 rounds for the flyweight title in October 1962, in his 28th pro fight, but Kingpetch regained it a few months later and Harada moved up to bantamweight.

A stoppage loss to the dangerous Mexican Joe Medel in September 1963 hindered his progress, but he came back strongly and, in May 1965, took the world title from the brilliant Brazilian Eder Jofre, who had not been beaten in 50 fights. He made four successful defences, including a revenge win over Medel, then lost it on points to Lionel Rose.

Harada was involved in a bizarre featherweight title fight in Sydney in July 1969 against Johnny Famechon, whom he floored three times and appeared to have outpointed. Referee Willie Pep, himself a former featherweight champion, at first declared it a draw but then said he had found an error in his arithmetic, and gave Famechon the decision. Famechon won a rematch decisively, and Harada retired. He is now a respected TV boxing commentator in Japan.

Marvin Hart

Born: *Jefferson County, Kentucky, September 16, 1876*
Titles: *World heavyweight champion 1905–06*
Record: *47 contests, 28 wins, 4 draws, 8 No Decisions, 7 defeats*

Nowadays if Marvin Hart is remembered at all it is usually as the other world heavyweight champion to come from Louisville, Kentucky, or else as an undeserving stop-gap champion who bridged the reigns of James J. Jeffries and Tommy Burns. While he certainly was not one of the better champions, Hart was not as bad a fighter as unkind historians have depicted: he outpointed Jack Johnson over 20 rounds in 1905, one of only two verdicts Johnson lost in 112 fights, and he also fought draws against George Gardner and Gus Ruhlin, both well-respected performers.

But he was basically a light-heavyweight, as was Jack Root, the man he beat to win the vacant heavyweight title at Reno in July 1905. Jeffries had retired, and acting as referee as well as promoter, the former champion staged the Hart vs Root match and "awarded" his title to the winner. Hart's short and undistinguished reign as champion was ended by Tommy Burns over 20 rounds in February 1906, and he never came close to another championship opportunity.

He had the last of his 47 fights in December 1910, and died at Fern Creek, Kentucky on September 17, 1931.

Len Harvey

Born: *Stoke Climsland, England, July 11, 1907*
Titles: *British middleweight champion 1929–33, light-heavyweight champion 1933–34, 1938–42, heavyweight champion 1933–34, 1938–42, Empire heavyweight champion 1934, 1939–42, Empire light-heavyweight champion 1939–42, British recognition as world light-heavyweight champion 1939–42*
Record: *133 contests, 111 wins, 9 draws, 13 defeats*

The Cornishman, a master tactician, collected championships like parking tickets. He fought a draw for the British welterweight title in 1926, won the middleweight and light-heavyweight titles in 1929, and completed a unique treble of British titles by winning the heavyweight championship in 1933. He also won the Empire heavyweight title and a version of the world light-heavyweight title which was only recognized in Britain, as well as challenging for the world middleweight title in 1932. Modern regulations mean that his feat will never be emulated.

Harvey started boxing professionally at 12, and the precise number of his contests is unknown. He claimed 418, but was surely including booth fights, as the most that record-compilers have been able to trace is 133, spread over 22 years.

His ring achievements and gentlemanly bearing made him a national idol, and it is significant that when he joined the forces on the outbreak of the Second World War he was given officer rank. He retired after losing his "world" title to Freddie Mills in June 1942, the only knockout defeat of his long career, and died in London on November 28, 1976.

Thomas Hearns

Born: *Memphis, Tennessee, October 18, 1958*
Titles: *WBA welterweight champion 1980–81, WBC light-middleweight champion 1982–86, WBC light-heavyweight champion 1987, WBC middleweight champion 1987–88, WBO super-middleweight champion 1988–91, WBA light-heavyweight champion 1991–92*
Record: *60 contests, 55 wins, 1 draw, 4 defeats*

Although born in Tennessee, Hearns will always be associated with his adopted hometown of Detroit, where he became the most famous product of Emanuel Steward's Kronk gym. He represented America as an amateur, but had a very low knockout percentage. Yet under Steward's coaching, Hearns developed into the most feared hitter of his era.

He became the first to win championships at five weights, starting with the WBA welterweight title which he took from Pipino Cuevas in 1980. That led to a unification match with Ray Leonard, which proved a modern classic. Leonard was trailing on points when he launched a desperate rally in

HEARNS *lifts the WBA belt in 1991*

the 14th round, flooring Hearns to force a stoppage.

Hearns also figured in perhaps the most thrilling middleweight title fight of all, when Marvin Hagler stopped him in three dramatic rounds in 1985. He took the WBC light-middleweight title from Wilfredo Benitez in 1982, the WBC light-heavyweight crown from Dennis Andries in 1987, the vacant WBC middleweight title later that year and then completed the five-timer by winning the vacant WBO super-middleweight title in 1988 – just three days before arch-rival Leonard duplicated the feat.

Pete Herman

Real name: *Peter Gulotta*
Born: *New Orleans, Louisiana, February 12, 1896*
Titles: *World bantamweight champion 1917–20, 1921*
Record: *144 contests, 66 wins, 8 draws, 57 No Decisions, 13 defeats*

Herman was a light puncher who won only 21 of his 144 recorded contests inside the distance, but he compensated with a shrewd tactical brain and accurate hitting. He started boxing professionally at 16, rarely venturing outside New Orleans, but by 1916 had

TRIPLE CHAMPION *Len Harvey prepares for another fight in 1938*

progressed to a world bantamweight title challenge against Kid Williams.

They drew, but in a return a year later Herman got the verdict. Curiously, he made only one defence in three years, outpointing Frankie Burns in November 1917; all but a handful of his fights during that period were No Decision affairs. He lost the title in December 1920 with a suspiciously lethargic performance against Joe Lynch. Barely three weeks later he knocked out flyweight champion Jimmy Wilde in London, and then in July 1921 he outclassed Lynch in a championship rematch.

Two months later he lost the title to Johnny Buff, and retired soon afterwards. He had suffered eye damage and later went blind, although that did not stop him from running a restaurant and serving as a member of the Louisiana State Athletic Commission. He died in New Orleans on April 13, 1973.

Herbie Hide

Born: *Nigeria, August 27, 1971*
Titles: *WBC International heavyweight champion 1992–94, PentaContinental champion 1993–94, British champion 1993, WBO champion 1994–95*
Record: *27 contests, 26 wins, 1 defeat*

Billed as "The Dancing Destroyer" by his manager Barry Hearn, Hide used his nimble footwork and fast hands to win the WBO and British heavyweight titles. He was raised by adoptive parents in Norwich, where he boxed for the local Lads Club and reached the ABA final at 17 in his first senior season, losing to Henry Akinwande.

Hearn matched him unambitiously, and he won all his first 21 fights inside the distance, seven in the first round. But at least he was accumulating titles, winning the vacant WBC International title and the Penta-Continental belt and then crushing the overweight and unmotivated Michael Murray in five rounds for the vacant British championship, a title which he never defended.

Everett Martin, a practised survivor, took him the full 10 rounds for

the first time, and after three more wins Hide faced Michael Bentt for the WBO title. Bentt, coming off a sensational first-round knockout of Tommy Morrison, was favoured to win but Hide handled him easily, knocking him out in seven rounds. He fought gamely against Riddick Bowe in his first defence in April 1995, but was beaten in five rounds and thereafter drifted away from boxing.

Virgil Hill

Born: *Clinton, Missouri, January 18, 1964*
Titles: *WBA light-heavyweight champion 1987–91, 1992–*
Record: *42 contests, 41 wins, 1 defeat*

The neat-boxing Hill, of Native American extraction, was beaten only once in 19 fights for the WBA light-heavyweight title between 1987, when he knocked out Leslie Stewart to become champion, and the end of 1995. Eleven of those were staged in Hill's adopted hometown of Bismark, North Dakota, where he regularly drew huge crowds. His cautious style, though, did not endear him to the American fans, who prefer their action a little more robust than that which Hill offered.

He had been an outstanding amateur, a converted southpaw who lost only 11 of 261 contests and crowned his career with a silver medal in the 1984 Olympic Games, turning professional later that year. Hill worked his way quietly up the rankings, but took the title in style when he floored Stewart twice to win in four rounds. He made 10 successful defences before Thomas Hearns outpointed him in Las Vegas in June 1991, the only defeat on Hill's impressive record up to the end of 1995.

He took a nine-month break, then returned to action in Australia and won the WBC International title before outscoring Frank Tate to reclaim the WBA championship, which had been vacated by Hearns' conqueror Iran Barkley.

Larry Holmes

Born: *Cuthbert, Georgia, November 3, 1949*
Titles: *WBC heavyweight champion 1978–83, IBF champion 1983–85*
Record: *67 contests, 62 wins, 5 defeats*

Like so many who succeed popular idols like Muhammad Ali, Larry Holmes was doomed to suffer by comparison with his predecessor. Yet the stylish Holmes, who once earned a living as Ali's sparring partner, was a fine fighter in his own right.

Although he had been a top-flight amateur, Holmes had to struggle for recognition when he turned professional in 1973, and found it difficult to get significant matches until he beat the fearsome-punching Earnie Shavers in March 1978. That brought him a fight with Ken Norton for the WBC title, which Holmes won after a superb 15-rounder. He retained the title 16 times, including a highly publicized encounter with "White Hope" Gerry Cooney, and then relinquished the

WBC belt in December 1983 to accept recognition from the newly formed IBF.

He lost the IBF belt in his fourth defence and 48th fight to Mike Spinks, a defeat which ruined his ambition to emulate Rocky Marciano's record of 49 unbeaten fights, and Spinks was given another dubious verdict in the rematch. Holmes tried unsuccessfully to regain the title from Mike Tyson (1988), Evander Holyfield (1992) and Oliver McCall (1995).

Evander Holyfield

Born: *Atmore, Alabama, October 19, 1962*
Titles: *WBA cruiserweight champion 1987–88, IBF cruiserweight champion 1987–88, WBC cruiserweight champion 1988, WBC, WBA and IBF champion 1990–1992, WBA and IBF heavyweight champion 1993–94*
Record: *34 contests, 31 wins, 3 defeats*

Evander Holyfield is the only man to have unified the cruiserweight title, but he will be best remembered for his exploits as a heavyweight. He also earned more than any other heavyweight champion, but not even his opponents could begrudge this brave and quiet-spoken man his rewards.

He turned professional after competing in the 1984 Olympic Games. It took him 11 fights to become a champion, outpointing Dwight Muhammad Qawi for the WBA cruiserweight title, and he added the IBF championship (beating Ricky Parkey in 1987) and the WBC title (knocking out Carlos DeLeon in 1988). But there was no serious money to be made, so he embarked on an elaborate diet and exercise regime which boosted his weight sufficiently to

LARRY HOLMES *lived in Muhammad Ali's shadow*

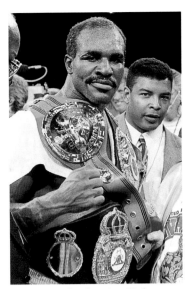

HOLYFIELD *after beating Holmes*

beat heavyweight contenders like Mike Dokes and Alex Stewart.

In October 1990 he won the championship from Tyson's conqueror Buster Douglas, and defended against George Foreman, Bert Cooper and Larry Holmes before losing to Bowe in the first of their three epics. He regained the WBA and IBF titles from Bowe in November 1993, but lost to Michael Moorer in April 1994 and, in November 1995, was knocked out by Bowe.

Lloyd Honeyghan

Born: *Jamaica, April 22, 1960*
Titles: *British welterweight
    champion 1983–86, European
    champion 1985–86,
    Commonwealth champion
    1985–86, world welterweight
    champion 1986, WBC and IBF
    champion 1986–87, WBC
    champion 1988–89,
    Commonwealth light-
    middleweight champion
    1993–94*
Record: *48 contests, 43 wins,
    5 defeats*

When Lloyd Honeyghan faced Don Curry for the undisputed welterweight title on September 27, 1986, virtually no-one apart from Honeyghan (who had backed himself to win $25,000) and his manager Mickey Duff gave the challenger a realistic chance. Yet six rounds later Honeyghan was world champion, as the demoralized

American, hitherto regarded as the world's best pound-for-pound fighter, retired. It was the summit of Honeyghan's career.

He learned his boxing in Bermondsey's Fisher Club, after the family had moved to London when he was a youngster. He represented England and won the London championship before turning professional under Terry Lawless, who guided him to the British and European titles before they split acrimoniously.

Honeyghan relinquished the WBA title in December 1986, and lost his WBC championship to Jorge Vaca on a technical decision in October 1987, when the IBF also stripped him. He regained the WBC title from Vaca in March 1988, holding it for a year until Marlon Starling stopped him in nine rounds. He was outclassed by Mark Breland for the WBA title, but made a moderately successful comeback, winning the Commonwealth light-middleweight title. He retired in 1995.

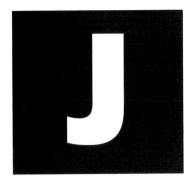

Beau Jack

Real name: *Sidney Walker*
Born: *Augusta, Georgia,
    April 1, 1921*
Titles: *New York recognition as
    world lightweight champion
    1942–43, 1943–44*
Record: *112 contests, 83 wins,
    5 draws, 24 defeats*

Beau Jack started his working life as a shoe-shine boy in a Miami hotel. The irony is that, after becoming one of America's most popular boxers, he

had to go back to shining shoes when he quit the ring in 1955.

He started boxing professionally in 1940, and his slam-bang style soon made him a major attraction. A third-round knockout of Allie Stolz in 1942 earned him a match with Tippy Larkin for New York's version of the vacant lightweight title, which Jack won on a third-round knockout in December 1942. Bob Montgomery dethroned him in May 1943, but Jack regained the title from him in November that year.

Montgomery outscored him again in March 1944, and although he boxed on for another 11 years Jack never got another title chance. But he always mixed in good company until he retired in August 1955. His victims included welterweight champions Fritzie Zivic, Henry Armstrong and Johnny Bratton, and lightweight champions Sammy Angott, Juan Zurita, Lew Jenkins and Ike Williams.

Julian Jackson

Born: *St Thomas, Virgin Islands,
    September 12, 1960*
Titles: *WBA light-middleweight
    champion 1987–90, WBC
    middleweight champion
    1990–93, 1995*
Record: *55 contests, 51 wins,
    4 defeats*

There have not been many harder hitters than Jackson, who could turn defeat into victory with a single punch – and did so many times in his long and explosive career. Yet away from business hours he was a gentle and religious man, so devoted to his children that he even paraded them in the ring before his fights.

The often-derided Continental Americas title brought him his first recognition; he won it in 1984 and defended it twice in Las Vegas, where his punching power impressed the right people. He had won 29 in a row, 27 inside the distance and 16 by clean countout, when he faced Mike McCallum in a thriller for the WBA light-middleweight title. McCallum was almost knocked out in the first, but rallied to stop Jackson in the second.

LLOYD HONEYGHAN *with his clean sweep of welterweight belts in 1986*

He won the vacant title the following year, and retained it with three stunning victories (including a second-round stoppage of Terry Norris) before moving up to middleweight. to win the vacant WBC title with a sensational knockout of Herol Graham Gerald McClellan stopped him in 1993, but Jackson briefly regained the championship in 1995.

James J. Jeffries

Born: *Carroll, Ohio, April 15, 1875*
Titles: *World heavyweight champion 1899–1905*
Record: *21 contests, 18 wins, 2 draws, 1 defeat*

By modern standards, Jeffries was not a big heavyweight, weighing around 220lb and standing 6ft 2½in tall, but in his time he was considered a giant. Because of his bulk and his ability to absorb punishment, he was a popular choice as sparring partner for the leading heavyweights, but he soon established his worth as a contender and, in 1899, knocked out Bob Fitzsimmons to become champion after only 13 fights.

He made seven defences, including a 23-round knockout of his former employer James J. Corbett. He retired in August 1910, undefeated in 20 fights of which he had won 15 by knockout and drawn two. But the eventual succession of Jack Johnson to the championship sparked a wave of racist feeling in America and Jeffries, by then a 35-year-old farmer, was persuaded to return to the ring in order, as novelist Jack London infamously phrased it, "to wipe the smile off the nigger's face".

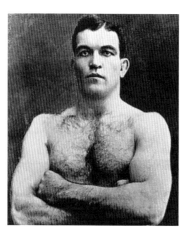

JEFFRIES *From sparmate to champion*

They met in Reno on July 4, 1910, and Johnson administered a painful beating before stopping him in the 15th round. Jeffries died in Burbank, California on March 3, 1953.

Eder Jofre

Born: *Sao Paulo, Brazil, March 26, 1936*
Titles: *NBA bantamweight champion 1960–62, world bantamweight champion 1962–65, WBC featherweight champion 1973–74*
Record: *78 contests, 72 wins, 4 draws, 2 defeats*

One of the few vegetarians ever to win a world boxing title, Jofre turned professional in March 1957. His heavy punching soon made him a championship contender, and wins over top men like Danny Kid, Ernesto Miranda (for the South American title) and Mexico's perennial contender Joe Medel brought him a match with Eloy Sanchez for the vacant NBA bantamweight title, Jofre winning in six rounds.

He defeated Europe's representative John Caldwell to become undisputed champion in January 1962, and went on to compile an undefeated record of 50 fights (including three draws) until the tough Japanese Fighting Harada took his title in May 1965. He retired after an unsuccessful attempt to regain the championship from Harada, but returned as a featherweight in 1969 after a three-year layoff and over the next three years fought his way to the WBC title, which he won from Jose Legra in May 1973.

The WBC stripped him in June 1974 for failing to meet their leading contender, and he retired for good after seven more fights. He later became a successful businessman and politician.

Ingemar Johansson

Born: *Gothenburg, Sweden, October 16, 1932*
Titles: *European heavyweight champion 1956–59, 1962–63, world champion 1959–60*
Record: *28 contests, 26 wins, 2 defeats*

POWER-PUNCHER *Ingemar Johansson tunes up for a 1962 European title bid*

The Swede had the unusual experience of going from national disgrace to national hero. He was disqualified for "not trying" against Ed Sanders in the 1952 Olympic final, but laid that ghost by knocking out Floyd Patterson for the heavyweight title in 1959. He had a stunning right-hand punch, which the press nicknamed "Ingo's Bingo" when he started to build a knockout record after turning pro in December 1952.

By 1956 he had taken the European title from Franco Cavicchi, and retained it with knockouts of British challengers Henry Cooper and Joe Erskine. But it was his first-round kayo of the classy American Eddie Machen which brought him his big chance. Patterson was floored seven times before the referee intervened in the third round, but Johansson was champion for less than a year before Patterson knocked him cold in the rematch and then flattened him again in their third meeting.

He rewon the European title from Dick Richardson, but retired after one more fight. Johansson settled in America after divorcing his second wife, and owned a Miami hotel for a while. He now works as a boxing summarizer for Swedish TV.

Harold Johnson

Born: *Manayunk, Pennsylvania, August 9, 1928*
Titles: *NBA light-heavyweight champion 1961–62, world champion 1962–63*
Record: *87 contests, 76 wins, 11 defeats*

The career of this craftsman light-heavyweight champion extended from 1946 to 1971. He alternated between light-heavyweight and heavyweight, beating stars like Archie Moore, Jimmy Bivins, Ezzard Charles and Nino Valdes. Moore's long reign as world champion held back his progress: he and Moore met five times, Johnson winning once, and after Moore stopped him in 14 rounds in a 1954 title fight he decided he had seen quite enough of the Philadelphian.

Johnson was the leading contender for years, but had to wait until 1961, when the NBA finally stripped Moore, for another chance. He halted Jesse Bowdrey in nine rounds for the vacant NBA title, retaining it twice before outscoring Doug Jones to gain universal recognition as champion. He was already past his best by then, and managed only one successful defence, against Gustav Scholz in Berlin, before Willie Pastrano dethroned him on a questionable decision in June 1963.

His subsequent appearances were infrequent, as he boxed only nine times in the next eight years, retiring after Herschel Jacobs stopped him in three rounds in March 1971.

Jack Johnson

see Legends of the Ring (pp 74–75)

Marvin Johnson

Born: *Indianapolis, Indiana, April 12, 1954*
Titles: *WBC light-heavyweight champion 1978–79, WBA light-heavyweight champion 1979–80, 1986–87*
Record: *49 contests, 43 wins, 6 defeats*

The balding Johnson became a byword for courage, featuring in some of the toughest light-heavyweight battles of recent times. He won the 1972 Golden Gloves and took a bronze medal in the same year's Munich Olympic Games, turning professional in 1973. His early progress was slow, managing only 13 fights in four years, but the turning point was his first defeat, a 12th round stoppage by Matthew Saad Muhammad (then boxing as Matt Franklin) in a titanic battle for the NABF title.

Wins over Billy Douglas (Buster's father), Eddie Davis and Jerry Celestine earned him a fight with Mate Parlov in December 1978 for the WBC title, and Johnson won in 10 rounds. Franklin dethroned him only four months later, but Johnson was a champion again before 1979 was out, stopping Victor Galindez in 11 rounds for the WBA belt. Once more, his reign was short: Eddie Gregory stopped him three months later, and then Mike Spinks knocked him out.

It looked like the end, but Johnson plodded on. His patience was rewarded in February 1986 when he stopped Leslie Stewart for the vacant WBA title, losing it in a rematch a year later

Roy Jones Jr

Born: *Pensacola, Florida, January 16, 1969*
Titles: *IBF middleweight champion 1993–94, IBF super-middleweight champion 1994–*
Record: *30 contests, 30 wins*

Jones was born for the ring. His father, Roy Sr, was a competent professional middleweight who fought Marvin Hagler in 1977, and he started Roy Jr boxing before the boy's seventh birthday. Jones won the National Golden Gloves at light-welterweight in 1986, aged 17, and at light-middleweight in 1987, going on to take a silver medal in the 1988 Olympics where a scandalously unjust verdict robbed him of victory.

He turned professional under his father's cautious management, but after three years of fighting low-grade opposition for poor rewards, he parted acrimoniously from Roy Sr to manage himself. By 1992 he was beating quality men like Jorge Castro, Jorge Vaca and Glenn Thomas, and when the IBF title became vacant he was matched with Bernard Hopkins for it, winning comfortably on points.

He was finding it hard to make the weight, and moved up to super-middleweight after defending the title only once. James Toney, the IBF champion, was regarded as the world's best fighter at the time, but Jones gave him a boxing lesson to win his second championship in November 1994, defending it impressively twice in 1995.

ROY JONES JR *superstar of the 1990s*

Peter Kane

Real name: *Peter Cain*
Born: *Golborne, England, February 28, 1918*
Titles: *World flyweight champion 1938–43, European bantamweight champion 1947–48*
Record: *108 contests, 98 wins, 2 draws, 1 No Contest, 7 defeats*

The saucer-eyed flyweight was a blacksmith's apprentice before becoming a professional fighter aged 16, and perhaps his extraordinary punching power was developed at the forge. His real name was Cain, but it was spelt wrongly on his debut, as a flyweight in 1934, and he kept the wrong spelling. He knocked out or stopped 33 of his first 41 opponents, including top-flight men like Jim Maharg and Jimmy Warnock, and his points victims were equally well-known names: Tiny Bostock, Joe Curran, Ernst Weiss and Valentin Angelmann.

In his 42nd fight he faced Benny Lynch for the world title in Glasgow on October 13, 1937, but was knocked out in the 13th round of a thrilling contest. They were rematched six months later, but Lynch failed to make the weight and the fight went ahead as a non-title affair, ending in a disappointing draw. Kane outpointed the American Jackie Jurich for the vacant title in September 1938 but did not defend it until June 1943, when Jackie Paterson knocked him out in 61 seconds.

He was inactive for nearly three years before returning as a bantamweight. He won the European title from Theo Medina in September 1947, but lost it to Guido Ferracin in February 1948 and retired after Ferracin beat him again. He died on July 23, 1991.

Stanley Ketchel

Real name: *Stanislaus Kiecal*
Born: *Grand Rapids, Michigan, September 14, 1886*
Titles: *World middleweight champion 1906–08, 1908–09*
Record: *64 contests, 52 wins, 4 draws, 4 No Decisions, 4 defeats*

The son of a Russian father and Polish mother, Ketchel's heavy punching and non-stop aggression soon gained him a reputation, and by 1906 he was already claiming the middleweight title vacated by Tommy Ryan. He beat all three rival claimants in 1908, but lost in bizarre circumstances in a rematch with one of them, Billy Papke, in September 1908. Papke punched him in the throat before the first bell, and Ketchel was so dazed that he took four counts in the first round before losing in the 12th.

He beat Papke mercilessly in the return, and then faced heavyweight champion Jack Johnson. Johnson had agreed to "carry" Ketchel, whom he outweighed by 35 lb, but in the 12th round Ketchel tried to double-cross the champion and scored a shock knockdown. Johnson got straight back up to flatten Ketchel with the next punch, hitting him so hard that several teeth were found embedded in his glove.

Ketchel stuck to the middleweights after that, and was still champion when he was shot dead in a dispute over a woman at Conway, Missouri on October 15, 1910.

Johnny Kilbane

Born: *Cleveland, Ohio, April 18, 1889*
Titles: *World featherweight champion 1912–23*
Record: *142 contests, 51 wins, 7 draws, 78 No Decisions, 2 No Contests, 4 defeats*

Kilbane, an Irish-American who worked as a clerk for the Pennsylvania Railways, had been obsessed with boxing long before he had his first fight in 1907, but became one of the most reluctant world champions in history. He won the featherweight title in 1912, but

RELUCTANT WARRIOR *Johnny Kilbane*

defended it only four times in 11 years.

An artful fighter, he scored only 21 inside the distance wins in a 16-year career but was as much at ease against top lightweights like Benny Leonard as against men his own size.

He dethroned Abe Attell in 1912, and drew with future champion Johnny Dundee in his first defence in 1913. But despite a busy schedule of No Decision contests he did not defend again for three years, or for a further five years after that. The New York Commission finally stripped him of their version of the title, but Kilbane was tempted out of semi-retirement to face French war hero Eugene Criqui, who finished his career with a sixth-round knockout. Kilbane later became a State Senator, and died in Cleveland on May 31, 1957.

Pone Kingpetch

Born: *Hui Hui Province, Thailand,*
February 12, 1936
Titles: *World flyweight champion*
1960–62, 1963, 1964–65
Record: *40 contests, 33 wins,*
7 defeats

Thailand's first world champion started boxing in 1955. He entered the world ratings when he took the Orient flyweight title from the tough Filipino Danny Kid in 1957, losing to Leo Espinosa in his first defence before regaining it from Hitoshi Misako.

His career seemed to falter in 1958–59, when he had only five

fights, but in April 1960 he was matched with Pascual Perez, who had been champion for over five years. The stocky champion could never get to grips with a challenger who was seven inches taller, and was soundly outpointed. Kingpetch went to Los Angeles for a rematch in September 1960, and stopped the Argentinean in eight rounds.

He retained the title twice, but then the Japanese Fighting Harada knocked him out in October 1962. Three months later, Kingpetch outscored Harada to become the first man to regain the flyweight title, but he lost it again on a first-round knockout to Hiroyuki Ebihara. He became champion for the third time by outpointing Ebihara in January 1964, but lost it finally to Salvatore Burruni the following year. He died of pneumonia at Ramanthi, Bangkok on May 31, 1982.

Jake LaMotta

Real name: *Giacobe LaMotta*
Born: *Bronx, New York,*
July 10, 1921
Titles: *World middleweight*
champion 1949–51
Record: *106 contests, 83 wins,*
4 draws, 19 defeats

LaMotta gloried in his well-deserved reputation as a tough guy, and indeed the crude but immensely strong New Yorker – immortalized in the film *Raging Bull* – had almost superhuman endurance in the ring.

He scored his most famous victory in February 1943 when he became the first man to beat Sugar Ray Robinson, but it was the only time he got the better of Robinson in six meetings. He also had a four-fight series with former welterweight

champion Fritzie Zivic, winning that three to one, but successive champions declined to give him a title shot. Finally, he did a deal with the gangsters who ran the sport at the time: he would take a dive against Blackjack Billy Fox, a light-heavyweight they were promoting, in return for a title fight.

LaMotta duly obliged against Fox, but had to wait two years to get his reward, when Marcel Cerdan retired with an injured shoulder after nine rounds of their title fight. He retained the championship with a last-gasp knockout of Laurent Dauthuille, but then lost it to Robinson in February 1951 and retired after a few more fights.

Sam Langford

Born: *Weymouth, Canada,*
February 12, 1880
Titles: *None*
Record: *291 contests, 167 wins,*
37 draws, 47 No Decisions,
3 No Contests, 37 defeats

Had Langford been white, he would have been one of the great champions of the early century at any weight from middleweight upwards, but in those days opportunities were rare for good black fighters and so he spent much of his career having long series of fights with others in the same predicament. He faced Harry Wills 18 times, Sam McVey 15, Joe Jeanette 14, Jeff Clark 13 and Jim Barry 12: a total of 72 fights against just five opponents. Known patronizingly as "The Boston Tar Baby", Langford was only 5ft 7in tall and rarely scaled more than the middleweight limit, but he routinely gave away chunks of weight to heavyweights in order to keep busy.

Despite his fine record of almost 300 fights, he was never given a crack at a world title, although he faced many men who were or became champions. His career lasted until 1924, when he was virtually blind. He later went completely blind and lived in obscure poverty until a newspaper highlighted his plight and raised enough to keep him in modest comfort until his death in Cambridge, Massachusetts, on January 12, 1956.

Jose Legra

Born: *Baracoa, Cuba,*
April 19, 1943
Titles: *European featherweight*
champion 1967–68, 1970–72,
WBC featherweight champion
1968–69, 1972–73
Record: *148 contests, 132 wins,*
4 draws, 12 defeats

The flashy, long-armed Legra, who favoured the "bolo punch" popularized by fellow-Cuban Kid Gavilan, was the busiest top-class fighter of his era, packing 148 fights into a 13-year career which began in Havana in 1960. He moved to Spain in 1963, and compiled an astonishing run of 83 fights with just one defeat, a 10-rounds points loss to Howard Winstone, between his European debut and his revenge win over Winstone for the WBC featherweight title in July 1968.

He had earlier knocked out Yves Desmarets to become European champion in December 1967, having taken out Spanish citizenship. He was surprisingly outpointed in his first WBC title defence by Johnny Famechon of Australia, and a later points loss to Vicente Saldivar seemed to rule him out of contention. But he carried on at European level, regaining and defending the continental title.

In December 1972 he finally got another world title chance, stopping Clemente Sanchez in 10 rounds in Monterrey, Mexico. Sanchez was overweight, but the WBC agreed to recognize Legra as the new champion. He was dethroned in his next fight by Eder Jofre, and retired shortly afterwards.

Benny Leonard

Real name: *Benjamin Leiner*
Born: *New York, NY, April 7, 1896*
Titles: *World lightweight champion*
1917–25
Record: *212 contests, 85 wins,*
1 draw, 121 No Decisions,
5 defeats

Leonard began and ended his career with knockout defeats, but in between compiled a remarkable record and reigned for seven years as

SLEEK AND STYLISH *Benny Leonard*

world lightweight champion. More than half his contests were No Decision affairs, but his inside-schedule victories over boxers of the quality of Freddie Welsh, Johnny Kilbane, Charlie White and Richie Mitchell show that he must have been an impressive performer.

He won the title in disputed circumstances from Welsh, after flooring him three times to force a ninth-round stoppage. The fight was a No Decision match and Welsh was over the championship weight anyway, but his protests went unheeded and the New Yorker was accepted as the new champion.

His reputation was tarnished by a curious disqualification in a welterweight championship bid against Jack Britton, when he deliberately struck Britton on the ground after flooring him. He retired as undefeated champion in 1924, but lost his savings in the Wall Street Crash of 1929 and returned to the ring, quitting for good in 1932. He died of a heart attack in New York on April 18, 1947, while refereeing a fight.

Sugar Ray Leonard

see Legends of the Ring (pp 76–77)

Gus Lesnevich

Born: *Cliffside Park, New Jersey, February 22, 1915*
Titles: *World light-heavyweight champion 1941–46*
Record: *79 contests, 60 wins, 5 draws, 14 defeats*

Lesnevich was one of those unfortunate champions who lost the best years of his career to the Second World War, which America joined shortly after he had won the light-heavyweight title in May 1941. He was out of the ring from March 1942 to January 1946.

Of Russian stock, he started boxing professionally in 1934 after winning the National Golden Gloves, and his only defeats in five years were to sometime world champions Freddie Steele and Young Corbett III, and to the talented Australian Ron Richards. He moved up to light-heavyweight after a four-fight trip to Australia in 1938–39, and lost twice in

BATTLE WORN *Gus Lesnevich, in 1948*

bids for Billy Conn's title before beating Anton Christoforodis to become champion at last.

Lesnevich made five defences, including a famous victory over Freddie Mills (whom Britain recognized as champion), but was outscored by Mills in a return fight in July 1948. Joey Maxim beat him for the American title in May 1949, and when Ezzard Charles knocked him out in his next fight, a challenge for Charles' NBA heavyweight crown, Lesnevich retired. He died at his Cliffside home on February 28, 1964.

John Henry Lewis

Born: *Los Angeles, California, May 1, 1914*
Titles: *World light-heavyweight champion 1935–39*
Record: *117 contests, 103 wins, 6 draws, 8 defeats*

Lewis dominated the light-heavyweight division from 1935 until his retirement as undefeated champion four years later. A stylish and hard-punching boxer, he lost only two of his first 56 fights, both to sometime world champions Maxie Rosenbloom and James J. Braddock, whom he had previously outscored.

Oddly, he lost both his fights immediately before challenging Bob Olin for the world title: Rosenbloom outpointed him to level their series at 2–2, and the relatively obscure Abe Feldman beat him on points. His win over Olin was a hard-fought affair, and when he boxed again only four weeks later against his perennial rival Rosenbloom, he lost their non-title fight on points.

Lewis defended the championship five times, and kept busy on the non-title circuit with a total of 51 appearances, which today's champions would find unthinkable. But he developed eye problems, and by late 1938 his sight was failing fast. Heavyweight king Joe Louis, a close friend, agreed to give him a title shot, and some welcome retirement money, on condition that Lewis never boxed again. Louis won in the first round, and Lewis kept his word.

Lennox Lewis

Born: *London, England, September 2, 1965*
Titles: *European heavyweight champion 1990–92, British champion 1991–92, Commonwealth champion 1992, WBC champion 1992–94*
Record: *29 contests, 28 wins, 1 defeat*

For British amateur boxing, Lewis was the one who got away – he won every honour open to him, but in a Canadian vest. He had been taken to Canada as a child, and started boxing there, with spectacular success. He won the world junior championships, a Commonwealth Games Gold medal, a World Cup championship, and an Olympic gold medal, stopping Riddick Bowe in the final.

But he came back to Britain to launch his pro career, reasoning that it was better to be a big star in England than one of a host of promising youngsters on the other side of the Atlantic. The move paid off, and he soon won the European, British and Commonwealth titles, earning a high world ranking. In October 1992 he scored a stunning two-rounds win over Razor Ruddock in a final eliminator for the WBC title, and when Bowe relinquished the title Lewis was declared champion retrospectively on the basis of the Ruddock win.

He made three successful defences, but then was knocked out in a big upset by Oliver McCall in

LENNOX LEWIS *Champion by default*

September 1994 and spent 1995 working his way back towards another chance.

Ted "Kid" Lewis

Real name: *Gershon Mendeloff*
Born: *London, England, October 24, 1894*
Titles: *British featherweight champion 1913, European featherweight champion 1914, world welterweight champion 1915–16, 1917–19, British and European welterweight champion 1920, British and European middleweight champion 1921–23, Empire middleweight champion 1922–23, Empire welterweight champion 1924*
Record: *282 contests, 173 wins, 14 draws, 65 No Decisions, 30 defeats*

The indefatigable Lewis had 48 fights in 1911 alone, more than Ray Leonard had in his entire career. Starting at 14 in 1909, he thought nothing of boxing three or four times a week, and by the time he won the British featherweight title in October 1913, three weeks before his 19th birthday, was already a veteran of 115 contests. He added the European title, then toured Australia

GLOBETROTTER *Lewis fought anywhere*

before heading for America where he twice won and lost the welterweight title in a famous 20-fight series with arch-rival Jack Britton.

He returned to Britain in 1919, and in five hectic years won British, Empire and European titles at welterweight and middleweight, claimed the British light-heavyweight title, and challenged for Georges Carpentier's world light-heavyweight title, being knocked out in the opening round.

The last of his titles went in 1924, but he carried on boxing until 1929 with appearances in America (where he remains the most popular British fighter ever to box in the country), Canada and South Africa. He died in London on October 20, 1970.

Charles "Sonny" Liston

Born: *St Francis, Arkansas, May 8, 1932*
Titles: *World heavyweight champion 1962–64*
Record: *54 contests, 50 wins, 4 defeats*

The brooding figure of Sonny Liston cast a shadow over the heavyweight division for years before he became champion in 1962. He deserved the chance much earlier, but his unsavoury background, which included jail terms and a spell as a strike-breaker, saddled him with a Bad Boy image which he was never able to shake off.

Cus D'Amato, who managed champion Floyd Patterson, refused to allow him to defend against Liston, but Patterson was a proud champion and took the match against D'Amato's advice. He was knocked out in two minutes six seconds, and lasted four seconds longer in the rematch.

Liston looked unbeatable, but Cassius Clay (as he then was) thought otherwise. He harrassed the champion into giving him a title fight, which took place in February 1964. Liston retired after six rounds, claiming a damaged shoulder. The return was even less satisfactory, Liston going down for the count in the first round from a "phantom" punch. He won 15 fights on a comeback, which ended when Leotis Martin knocked

him out. He was found dead in mysterious circumstances at his Las Vegas home on December 30, 1970.

Duilio Loi

Born: *Trieste, Italy, April 19, 1929*
Titles: *European lightweight champion 1954–58, European welterweight champion 1959–63, world light-welterweight champion 1960–62, 1962–63*
Record: *126 contests, 115 wins, 8 draws, 3 defeats*

Loi was a phenomenally successful performer. He was beaten only once in his first 110 fights, when the Dane Jorgen Johansen outscored him in his first attempt on the European lightweight title. Loi took revenge over Johansen in 1954, and went on to retain the championship eight times until he relinquished it four years later.

For some reason he was unable to land a world title chance, but moved up to welterweight and took the European title from fellow-Italian Emilio Marconi in 1959. The light-welterweight division had recently been resurrected, and Loi, never a natural welterweight, saw an opportunity to fulfil his world championship dream. Carlos Ortiz turned back his first challenge, in San Francisco in June 1960, but Loi finally made it by outpointing Ortiz three months later.

He defended both his world and European titles for two years. The stylish American Eddie Perkins, who had previously held him to a draw, took the light-welterweight belt with a points win in September 1962, but Loi regained it in December that year and, the following month, announced his retirement.

Eamonn Loughran

Born: *Ballymena, Ireland, June 5, 1970*
Titles: *Commonwealth welterweight champion 1992–1993, WBO welterweight champion 1993–*
Record: *29 contests, 26 wins, 1 draw, 1 No Contest, 1 defeat*

The aggressive Irishman enjoyed a fine amateur career with the All Saints ABC, coming back from the 1987

world junior championships with a silver medal and boxing for the full international side later that year before joining manager Barney Eastwood, who had also guided the careers of Ireland's recent world champions Barry McGuigan and Dave McAuley.

But progress proved slow, and he split from Eastwood in 1989, taking a year away from the ring before returning under Barry Hearn's promotion. With regular fights, he improved quickly and earned a British welterweight title eliminator against Tony Ekubia in March 1992, only to throw the chance away with a silly disqualification loss.

Hearn moved smartly to match him with the classy Canadian Donovan Boucher for the Commonwealth title. Boucher had impressed on previous visits to Britain, but Loughran took him apart with body punches in three rounds, his best performance, and was matched against Lorenzo Smith – a substitute opponent – for the vacant WBO title. Loughran won on points in October 1993, and to the end of 1995 retained the title five times. His career has been plagued by recurring hand injuries, a frequent problem for big punchers.

Tommy Loughran

Born: *Philadelphia, Pennsylvania, November 29, 1902*
Titles: *New York recognition as world light-heavyweight champion 1927, world champion 1927–29*
Record: *173 contests, 95 wins, 9 draws, 45 No Decisions, 1 No Contest, 23 defeats*

The career of this stylish Irish-American spanned 18 years, from 1919 to 1937, during which he won the world light-heavyweight title, challenged for the heavyweight championship, and fought 14 men who were, or became, world champions from welterweight to heavyweight. His victims included Harry Greb, Mickey Walker, Georges Carpentier, James J. Braddock and Max Baer, and he faced many other stars in no decision bouts.

He was a master boxer who worked behind a stinging left jab, but his lack of a telling punch meant that only 18 of his 173 fights ended inside the distance. Loughran started fighting for a living at 17, but despite being good enough to face Greb and Gene Tunney in successive bouts before his 20th birthday it took him 102 fights to become world champion, outpointing Mike McTigue in October 1927 for the New York version and then beating Jimmy Slattery to establish himself as undisputed champion.

He moved up to heavyweight in 1929 after five defences, but found title-holder Primo Carnera just too big for him (he was conceding a record 86lb) and lost on points in his only title bid at heavyweight. He died at Altoona, Pennsylvania on July 7, 1982.

Joe Louis

see Legends of the Ring (pp 78–79)

Benny Lynch

Born: *Clydesdale, Scotland, April 12, 1913*
Titles: *British flyweight champion 1935–38, NBA and IBU champion 1935–37, world champion 1937–38*
Record: *122 contests, 90 wins, 17 draws, 15 defeats*

Drink destroyed Benny Lynch, who went from being a brilliant world flyweight champion to the scrapheap in a year, and died of malnutrition at 33. Yet in his brief prime, Lynch was arguably the best flyweight in history, a stiff puncher who also had a shrewd tactical brain and the charisma which marks out the great champions.

He learned his trade on the booths and turned professional at 18, often boxing every week. He won the Scottish title in 1934, and the following year destroyed world and British champion Jackie Brown in two rounds at Manchester, flooring him 10 times. They had boxed a draw in a non-title match earlier in the year, and Lynch learned from the experience.

A points defeat of Small Montana made him undisputed champion, and he retained the title in an epic clash with Peter Kane, but his drinking was now

out of control and he was stripped of the championship when he weighed in almost seven pounds overweight for a defence against Jackie Jurich in June 1938. He retired later that year, after suffering his only knockout, and died in Glasgow on August 6, 1946.

Jock McAvoy

Real name: *Joseph Bamford*
Born: *Burnley, England, November 20, 1908*
Titles: *British and Empire middleweight champion 1933–39, British light-heavyweight champion 1937*
Record: *147 contests, 133 wins, 14 defeats*

McAvoy was a fierce-punching, extremely aggressive character. who started boxing in 1927 to help supplement the family income, adopting a *nom du ring* to keep his occupation a secret from his widowed mother.

His heavy hitting made him a big attraction, but competition was strong in those days and it took him five years to land a title chance, losing to Len Harvey for the British middleweight title. He reversed the result a year later, and won a Lonsdale Belt outright before going to America to knock out world title claimant Ed "Babe" Risko in an overweight match.

He was outpointed by the classy John Henry Lewis for the world light-heavyweight title, and by Jack Petersen when he tried for the British heavyweight title. But he won the British light-heavyweight championship, only to lose it to Harvey, who beat him again in 1939 in a fight recognized in Britain alone

as being for the vacant world title. He had his last fight in 1945 and later became a polio victim, spending 20 years confined to a wheelchair before his death in Rochdale on November 20, 1971.

Mike McCallum

Born: *Kingston, Jamaica, December 7, 1956*
Titles: *WBA light-middleweight champion 1984–87, WBA middleweight champion 1989–91, WBC light-heavyweight champion 1994–95*
Record: *52 contests, 48 wins, 1 draw, 3 defeats*

Known as "The Bodysnatcher" because of his ferocious body punching, McCallum was one of that rare breed who improve with age. He won a Commonwealth Games gold medal, turning pro in 1981 and winning 21 in a row, 19 inside schedule, to earn a match with the durable Irishman Sean Mannion for the vacant WBA light-middleweight title.

McCallum won a dour battle on points, and retained the title six times with some memorable performances like his stoppages of Julian Jackson and Milton McCrory, and his one-punch knockout of Don Curry. He relinquished it in September 1987 to go after the middleweight title, but failed in his first attempt when Sumbu Kalambay outpointed him for the WBA belt in 1988. He became WBA champion a year later, and his three defences included a revenge win over Kalambay.

He was stripped in December 1991 for agreeing to fight IBF champion James Toney, with whom he boxed a draw, and then stepped up to light-heavyweight to take the WBC title from Jeff Harding in July 1994. This time, he managed only one successful defence before losing to Fabrice Tiozzo in June 1995.

Al McCoy

Real name: *Al Rudolph*
Born: *Rosenhayn, New Jersey, October 23, 1894*
Titles: *World middleweight champion 1914–17*
Record: *156 contests, 43 wins, 13 draws, 92 No Decisions, 8 defeats*

McCoy became world middleweight champion almost by accident. He had been due to fight Joe Chip, the brother of George, who held the title at the time, but Joe pulled out and George, sniffing some easy money, agreed to substitute in a No Decision match in which his title could only change hands on a knockout. McCoy's father, a poultry farmer, bet 100 chickens to a cigar that his son would lose, but had to pay out when Chip was flattened in 111 seconds of the opening round on April 6, 1914.

His surprise win made him the first southpaw champion at any weight, and he held onto the title for over four years, fighting mainly No Decision contests in New York and Pennsylvania. His reluctance to make a "proper"

MIKE McCALLUM *"The Bodysnatcher"*

defence earned him the sneering nickname of "Cheese Champion", yet his title was always at risk – as Chip's had been – were he to be knocked out.

He stayed champion until Mike O'Dowd did just that in November 1917, and when O'Dowd beat him again in a rematch, McCoy retired. He died in Los Angeles on August 22, 1966.

Charles "Kid" McCoy

Real name: *Norman Selby*
Born: *Rush County, Indiana, October 13, 1872*
Titles: *World middleweight title claimant 1896–97*
Record: *107 contests, 86 wins, 6 draws, 6 No Decisions, 3 No Contests, 6 defeats*

The adjective "controversial" is barely adequate when applied to Kid McCoy, an extraordinary rascal who conned a champion out of his title, was involved in a fixed fight with James J. Corbett, became a film actor on retirement from the ring, murdered his seventh wife and committed suicide after his release from jail. As a role model, he left a lot to be desired.

His erratic performances led fans to wonder which McCoy would turn up … the fraudster or "the real McCoy", an accomplished fighter who won more than half his 107 fights by knockout. When he persuaded middleweight champion Tommy Ryan (who had formerly employed him as a sparring partner) that he was dying of consumption and needed cash to pay doctors' bills, the gullible Ryan did not even bother to train and was duly knocked out by a perfectly conditioned challenger in 15 rounds in March 1896.

He later moved up to heavyweight with mixed success, then lost on points to Jack Root for the light-heavyweight title in 1903. He had his last fight in 1916, and died in Detroit on April 18, 1940.

Wayne McCullough

Born: *Belfast, Ireland, July 7, 1970*
Titles: *WBC bantamweight champion 1995–*
Record: *18 contests, 18 wins*

Belfast's "Pocket Rocket" ignored conventional routes to professional success when he returned from the 1992 Olympic Games a national hero, having won a silver medal to go with his 1990 Commonwealth Games gold medal and a pair of Irish championships. He opted for a move to Las Vegas, under the management of Mat Tinley, a young TV executive who had no boxing experience or background. The attractions (apart from a sweet financial deal) were guaranteed TV exposure through Tinley's Prime Network channel, and the chance to work with trainer Eddie Futch, the game's most respected guru.

The move paid off when barely two years after his pro debut in February 1993, McCullough achieved a famous victory by travelling to Japan to take the WBC bantamweight title from Yasuei Yakashiji. It had been a brilliant campaign, plotted by master strategist Futch and superbly executed by a young fighter who improved with every outing and who proved his right to the title chance by beating former world champions Victor Rabanales and Fabrice Benichou.

McCullough retained his title on an emotional homecoming to Belfast in December 1995, stopping former WBO champion Johnny Bredahl in eight rounds.

Terry McGovern

Born: *Johnstown, Pennsylvania, March 9, 1880*
Titles: *World bantamweight champion 1899, world featherweight champion 1900–01*
Record: *78 contests, 60 wins, 4 draws, 10 No Decisions, 4 defeats*

The hard-punching Irish-American turned professional at 17 in 1897, and was not yet 20 when he flattened the Englishman Pedlar Palmer in 75 seconds to win the bantamweight title in September 1899. His solitary defeat in 35 fights had been on a disqualification, and he rattled off another nine wins (eight by knockout) in 1899 before moving up to featherweight.

The champion there was the redoubtable George Dixon, but McGovern gave him a fearful beating and won his second title on an eighth-round stoppage. He retained it three times in 1900, including a fifth-round knockout of Eddie Santry, who claimed the British version of the championship, and scored knockouts over Frank Erne and Joe Gans in three and two rounds respectively, although there was an unpleasant aroma attached to the Gans result.

Still only 21, McGovern seemed to have a dazzling future, yet it all turned sour when Young Corbett took his title in two rounds in November 1901. McGovern gave a feeble showing, and fared little better in a rematch two years later. His career ended in 1908, and he died in Brooklyn on February 26, 1918.

Barry McGuigan

Born: *Clones, Ireland, February 28, 1961*
Titles: *British and European featherweight champion 1983–85, WBA featherweight champion 1985–86*
Record: *35 contests, 32 wins, 3 defeats*

The charismatic McGuigan boxed for Ireland in the Olympic Games, won a Commonwealth Games gold medal for Northern Ireland, and took out naturalization papers in order to compete for the British title, which he won in April 1983. Under Barney Eastwood's management and promotion, he drew huge TV audiences

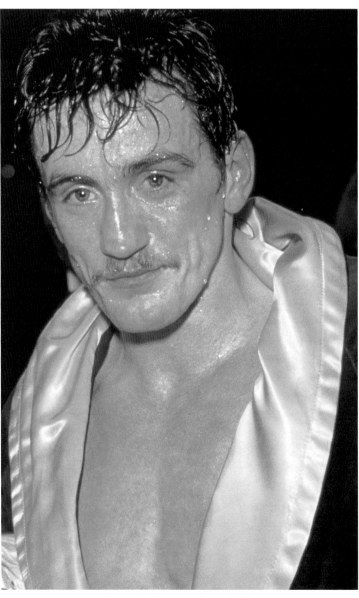

THE CLONES CYCLONE *Barry McGuigan, after a 1988 comeback victory*

and capacity crowds to Belfast's atmospheric Kings Hall.

He was projected as a symbol of unity in a divided society, helped by the fact that he was a Catholic married to a Protestant. He was an obsessive trainer, always working on refinements to his thrillingly aggressive style. McGuigan's body punching was, in all senses, breath-taking, and he looked irresistible as he moved towards a shot at Eusebio Pedroza's WBA featherweight title. He became European champion in 1983, and by 1985 was ready for the veteran Panamanian.

Their 15-rounder, watched by a crowd of 25,000 at QPR football ground in London, was utterly absorbing, but McGuigan won clearly. He made two defences, then surprisingly lost to Steve Cruz in 1986, in unbearable heat in Las Vegas. He returned at super-feather, but retired after losing on a cut to Jim McDonnell. He has became an accomplished TV performer, serving as commentator and summarizer, as well as fronting a weekly programme of classic fights on Sky Sports.

Duke McKenzie

Born: *Croydon, England, May 5, 1963*
Titles: *British flyweight champion 1985–86, European flyweight champion 1986–88, IBF flyweight champion 1988–89, WBO bantamweight champion 1991–92, WBO super-bantamweight champion 1992–93, British featherweight champion 1993–94*
Record: *41 contests, 36 wins, 5 defeats*

The McKenzies of Croydon are one of Britain's most famous fighting families, but none of them can match Duke's achievements. He started in 1985 with the British flyweight title, and in May 1986 added the European title by sending former WBC champion Charlie Magri into retirement.

The first of his three world titles came in October 1988, when he knocked out Rolando Bohol for the IBF title, which he retained once but lost to Dave McAuley in 1989. He moved up to bantamweight, and a

points defeat by Thierry Jacob in a European title bid proved only a temporary setback, as in June 1991 he outscored the respected Gaby Canizales to become WBO champion. Rafael del Valle knocked him out in a round in May 1992, his third defence, but before the year ended he had taken the WBO super-bantamweight crown from another top-flight American, Jesse Benavides.

He lost it in his next fight, but stepped up again to win the British featherweight title in December 1993. A knockout by Steve Robinson in October 1994, when he tried for the WBO featherweight title, ended his dreams of a fourth world title.

Jimmy McLarnin

Born: *Inchicore, Ireland, December 19, 1906*
Titles: *World welterweight champion 1933–34, 1934–35*
Record: *77 contests, 63 wins, 3 draws, 11 defeats*

McLarnin was one of the game's success stories, who had a brilliant ring career and kept his considerable fortune to the end of his life. He was taken to Canada as a child, and started boxing professionally as a 17-year-old bantamweight in 1923, soon acquiring the nickname of "Babyface". His manager throughout his career was "Pop" Foster, and the pair were so close that when Foster died in 1956 he left everything to his former fighter.

McLarnin soon reached top class, and challenged Sammy Mandell for the lightweight title in 1928, losing on points. Foster regarded that as merely a learning experience, and manoeuvred his man into a shot at the welterweight title, while avoiding promotional tie-ups. Considering the way boxing was run in those days, that was a considerable achievement.

In 1933, McLarnin knocked out Young Corbett III to become champion, and then engaged in a classic three-fight series with Barney Ross, winning one. He lost and won against Tony Canzoneri, and quit on a high note by beating another champion, Lou Ambers, in November 1936. In all, he beat 13 men who held world titles.

Sam McVey

Born: *Oxnard, California, May 17, 1885*
Titles: *none*
Record: *92 contests, 59 wins, 8 draws, 10 No Decisions, 2 No Contests, 13 defeats*

Like his famous contemporaries Joe Jeanette, Sam Langford and Jack Johnson, Sam McVey suffered cruel discrimination which prevented him achieving his full potential. He was restricted to meeting his fellow-blacks in endless round robins – for example, he fought Langford 15 times in nine years in France, Australia, America and Argentina. He met Jeanette four times, with their best-known being a brutal battle in Paris in April 1909.

Jeanette was floored 22 times in the first 37 rounds, but showed exceptional endurance to keep going and finally, in the 39th round, he put McVey down. But McVey could match him for courage, and although Sam was knocked down a further 18 times, he scored six more knockdowns himself. By the time the fight ended in the 49th round when the exhausted McVey got off his stool at the start of the round and collapsed without a punch being struck, the knockdown total was 46! They had been fighting for three hours and 12 minutes.

He boxed twice in England in 1911, beating the Boer George Rodel in a round and Alf Langford in seven. McVey died in New York in 1921.

Charlie Magri

Born: *Tunisia, July 20, 1956*
Titles: *British flyweight champion 1977–81, European champion 1979–82, 1984, 1985–86, WBC champion 1983*
Record: *35 contests, 30 wins, 5 defeats*

Magri can claim to have rescued the British flyweight division from extinction. Prior to his emergence after a dazzling amateur career which included three ABA titles and an Olympic vest, the division was virtually dormant and there were serious proposals for its abolition. But the colourful Magri, raised in London, was

a star from the start and won the British title in only his third fight.

He raced through 23 wins in a row, most of them won in short order, and outscored the former WBC light-flyweight champion Franco Udella to win the European title in 1979. But then the vulnerability which, combined with his own heavy punching made him such an exciting performer to watch, let him down. He was stopped twice, by Juan Diaz and Jose Torres, but somehow was steered back into the world title picture.

He finally became WBC champion on March 15, 1983, stopping Eleoncio Mercedes on a cut, but lost the title on his first defence to Frank Cedeno. He twice regained and relinquished the European title, and made a brave bid for Sot Chitalada's WBC title before retiring after losing his European crown to Duke McKenzie.

Saoul Mamby

Born: *Jamaica, June 4, 1947*
Titles: *WBC light-welterweight champion 1980–82*
Record: *79 contests, 42 wins, 6 draws, 31 defeats*

Mamby had his first pro fight in September 1969 and his 79th and last 24 years later, when he was 46. It is one of the longest careers of modern times. He spent most of it in top class, boxed in 14 countries and failed to go the distance only once, in his final fight.

He made his debut in Jamaica but moved to New York immediately afterwards, basing himself there for the rest of his busy career. His crafty style and durability earned him respect as "a good opponent", who could be relied on to lose on points to top names. He filled this role perfectly, proving his worth in 10-rounders against world champions Antonio Cervantes and Roberto Duran and, in 1977, giving Saensak Muangsurin a tough fight in his first WBC title bid.

He won the title at the second attempt, stopping Kim-Sang Hyun in 1980, and proved an efficient champion with five successful defences before Leroy Haley dethroned him in 1982. He failed to regain it from Billy Costello in 1984, and later became a high-quality journeyman, subsidizing his income by driving a yellow cab.

Sammy Mandell

Real name: *Samuel Mandella*
Born: *Rockford, Illinois,*
February 5, 1904
Titles: *World lightweight champion*
1926–30
Record: *187 contests, 82 wins,*
9 draws, 73 No Decisions,
2 No Contests, 21 defeats

It is one of history's ironies that, while Jimmy McLarnin and Tony Canzoneri are honoured as two of the greatest lightweights of all time, Sammy Mandell is known today only to the game's obsessives – yet he beat them both, in title fights. Perhaps because Mandell was not a big puncher – only 33 quick wins in 187 fights – he never captured the public's affections as the other two did, but he was a tough and competent battler who fought the best men of his era.

Of Italian-Albanian extraction, Mandell began boxing in 1920. He beat the popular Sid Terris in 1925 to earn a place in the elimination tournament to find a new champion following Benny Leonard's retirement. Mandell missed his chance, losing on a foul to Jimmy Goodrich, but stayed unbeaten to earn a crack at Rocky Kansas's title in July 1926 and this time made no mistake, winning on points.

He retained it against McLarnin and Canzoneri, then lost on a first-round knockout to Al Singer in July 1930. Mandell boxed for another four years, and died in Oak Park, Illinois on November 7, 1967.

Rocky Marciano

see Legends of the Ring
(pp 80–81)

Terry Marsh

Born: *London, England,*
February 7, 1958
Titles: *British light-*
welterweight champion
1984–86, European
champion 1985–86,
IBF champion 1987
Record: *27 contests, 26 wins,*
1 draw

UNBEATEN *Terry Marsh was Britain's first IBF world champion*

A former Marine with a gift for self-publicity, Marsh joined the Fire Brigade and served there throughout his professional boxing career. He remains the only British world champion to have gone through his entire pro career undefeated, although he was held to a draw in one of his early fights.

Marsh was a brilliant amateur, appearing in five ABA finals and winning three of them. He turned professional under Frank Warren's management in October 1981 and made steady progress through the domestic ranks, winning the British light-welterweight title from Clinton McKenzie in a magnificent contest in September 1984.

The European title followed a year later, and then in March 1987 he became Britain's first holder of an IBF championship belt when he stopped the American title-holder, Joe Manley, in 10 rounds on an emotional night in a specially erected marquee in his home town of Basildon in Essex.

He defended it only once, beating Japan's Akio Kameda in six rounds, and then retired in puzzling circumstances the day after he had signed contracts for his next fight. He was later tried and acquitted of the attempted murder of Warren, and took a Political Science degree at City University, London, with a view to a new career in politics.

Henry Maske

Born: *Trevenbrietzen, Germany,*
January 6, 1964
Titles: *IBF light-heavyweight*
champion 1993–
Record: *27 contests, 27 wins*

This tall (6ft 3 in) southpaw is one of the few men who have become world champion without needing to adapt the style learned as an amateur. In his case, as a product of the former East Germany, that meant a rigid concentration on the basic jab-and-cross routine, while utilizing his height and long reach to make himself an inaccessible target. It carried him to world, Olympic and European gold medals as an amateur, and made him unbeatable as a professional: he had won all 27 contests to the end of 1995, and the only man to have troubled him seriously – his compatriot Graciano Rocchigiani – was easily outscored in a rematch.

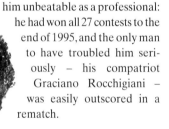

Although an undramatic performer, Maske is extremely popular in Germany, where he regularly draws huge crowds for his IBF light-heavyweight title defences. His emergence coincided with his country's reunification, and he has come to be seen as a symbol of the new Germany.

He won the title from a good champion, Prince Charles Williams, in March 1993 and retained it eight times, including those two clashes with Rocchigiani. Maske was badly hurt late in their first encounter, but dominated the return fight.

Joey Maxim

Real name: *Giuseppe Antonio*
Berardinelli
Born: *Cleveland, Ohio,*
March 28, 1922
Titles: *World light-heavyweight*
champion 1950–52
Record: *115 contests, 82 wins,*
4 draws, 29 defeats

The former light-heavyweight champion took his ring name from the Maxim gun, his hyperbolic manager Doc Kearns claiming that his boy could fire left jabs at machine-gun speed. A former Golden Gloves champion, Maxim competed in top class from virtually the start of his pro career in 1941. He was mixing with contenders like Jimmy Bivins and Ezzard Charles by 1942, and beat Jersey Joe Walcott in 1946, losing a rematch.

In May 1949 he outscored ex-champ Gus Lesnevich for the American title, and the following January trounced Britain's Freddie Mills to win the world title. Two years later he had the last of his four-fight series with Ezzard Charles, who won on points to retain the NBA heavyweight title.

Maxim scored a famous victory in a 1952 defence against Sugar Ray Robinson, who was overcome by heat exhaustion after 13 rounds. Long-time contender Archie Moore took Maxim's title in December 1952, but Kearns (who managed them both) secured him two unsuccessful rematches. But he had one more significant win, when he outpointed

Floyd Patterson in 1954, and he boxed on until 1958.

Freddie Miller

Born: *Cincinnati, Ohio,*
April 3, 1911
Titles: *NBA featherweight*
champion 1933–36
Record: *247 contests, 209 wins,*
6 draws, 4 No Decisions,
1 No Contest, 27 defeats

Miller, a prodigiously busy performer, crammed 247 fights into his 13-year career. He won the world title in his first fight of 1933, yet had a further 18 contests that year, followed by 28 in 1934 and a remarkable 35 in 1935.

His first title chance came against stablemate Bat Battalino in July 1931, Battalino winning on points. They were rematched in January 1932. The deal was that the title would change hands, but Battalino came in three pounds overweight and, when the fight went ahead as a non-title match, the champion went down in the third from a harmless-looking punch and the referee stopped it. The NBA and the New York Commission both ruled a "No Contest" and declared the title vacant.

Surprisingly, Miller got a second chance less than a year later, out-pointing Tommy Paul for the NBA version. He retained it 11 times, including trips to England and Spain as well as non-title appearances in France, Belgium and Cuba, but was finally dethroned by Petey Sarron, a veteran whom he had already beaten three times. Sarron won their rematch in 1937, and Miller retired in 1940. He died on May 8, 1962.

Freddie Mills

Born: *Parkstone, England,*
June 26, 1919
Titles: *British and Empire light-*
heavyweight champion 1942–
50, European champion 1947–
50, world champion 1948–50
Record: *97 contests, 74 wins,*
6 draws, 17 defeats

Mills's courage and dogged determination was legendary. He could absorb endless batterings yet come

BULLDOG BREED *Freddie Mills*

back to win, even if the unseen toll was heavy.

He learned his boxing in a West Country touring booth, turning professional at 16. His brawling style and heavy punching made him a crowd-puller, although he lost 10 times on the way up. By 1942 he was a contender from middleweight to heavyweight, but his big chance came at light-heavyweight, and he knocked out Len Harvey to win the British and Empire titles and the domestic version of the world title.

Jack London beat him in a brutal 15-rounder for the British and Empire heavyweight titles in 1944, and he took another pummelling from Gus Lesnevich for the world title in 1946. He also lost painfully to Bruce Woodcock, Joe Baksi and Lloyd Marshall, but rebounded to win the European title and take revenge over Lesnevich for the world title in

1948. Woodcock hammered him again in 1949, and he retired after losing his world title to Joey Maxim in 1950. He was found shot outside his London night-club on July 25, 1965, apparently a suicide.

Alan Minter

Born: *Crawley, England,*
August 17, 1951
Titles: *British middleweight*
champion 1975–77, 1977–78,
European champion 1977,
1978–79, world champion
1980
Record: *49 contests,*
39 wins, 1 No Contest,
9 defeats

An unfortunate tendency to cut caused six of the eight inside-schedule defeats on the otherwise impressive record of this rangy south-paw, Britain's most successful middleweight of the 1970s. He won a bronze medal at the Munich Olympics – appropriately, as his mother was German – and turned professional in October 1972.

Minter started well, then hit a disastrous spell in 1973–74 when he could win only three out of eight fights. But he kept his nerve, and in November 1975 took the vacant British title by outpointing arch-rival Kevin Finnegan in the first of their epic three-fight series. Minter won all three contests, each time by the minimum margin.

He gained a Lonsdale Belt outright, and won, lost and regained the European title which he relinquished in December 1979 to go after the world title. That meant a trip to Las Vegas in March 1980, where he scored a rare British "away" victory by outpointing Vito Antuofermo for the undisputed title. He retained it once, then was stopped in three by Marvin Hagler in a fight which provoked disgraceful scenes at Wembley. Minter retired after Tony Sibson knocked him out in September 1981.

Brian Mitchell

Born: *Johannesburg, South Africa,*
August 30, 1961
Titles: *WBA junior-lightweight*
champion 1986–91, IBF
champion 1991–92
Record: *48 contests, 44 wins,*
3 draws, 1 defeat

His country's loathsome apartheid policy meant that Mitchell could not defend his WBA junior-lightweight (super-featherweight) championship at home, which makes his achievement in retaining it 12 times all the more praise-worthy. He was the ultimate professional, unperturbed by risking his title in the challenger's country and ready to go wherever there was a payday.

Yet, ironically, almost all Mitchell's early opponents were black South Africans, and he boxed frequently in the townships around Durban and Johannesburg. He won the South African 130-lb title in 1983, and made seven successful defences before crossing the border into Bophutaswana to take the WBA championship from Alfredo Layne in September 1986. He defended it in Puerto Rico, Panama, France, Italy, Spain, England and America, and in March 1991 he drew with IBF champion Tony Lopez in a unification match staged, inevitably, in Lopez's hometown of Sacramento.

The verdict outraged Mitchell, and he gave up the WBA belt to force a rematch for the IBF title in September 1991. He was vindicated when the judges gave him the verdict this time, and announced his retirement. He made a winning comeback as a light-welterweight in 1994.

Bob Montgomery

Born: *Sumter, South Carolina,*
February 10, 1919
Titles: *New York recognition as*
world lightweight champion
1943, 1944–47
Record: *97 contests, 75 wins,*
3 draws, 19 defeats

Montgomery's big break came in May 1941 when he outpointed lightweight champion Lew Jenkins in a non-title 10-rounder. It was their second meeting, Jenkins having outscored him the previous year, but the result firmly established the hard-punching Southerner as a contender. He could never get the better of Sammy Angott, who outpointed him three times in as many meetings, but the only other men to beat him in 69 fights on his way to the title were Tommy Spiegel in 1939 and Maxie Shapiro in 1942, a result Montgomery reversed in his next fight.

He outpointed the colourful Beau Jack to win the New York version of the title in May 1943, but lost it back to him six months later. He went 2–1 ahead in their entertaining series in March 1944, and made two defences before NBA champion Ike Williams knocked him out to unify the title in August 1947.

Montgomery never won another fight, losing seven in a row and retiring in March 1950.

Carlos Monzon

Born: *Santa Fe, Argentina, August 7, 1942*
Titles: *World middleweight champion 1970–74, WBA champion 1974–77, world champion 1977*
Record: *101 contests, 89 wins, 8 draws, 1 No Contest, 3 defeats*

For 13 years between 1964 and 1977, Monzon was unbeatable. He compiled an astonishing undefeated run of 82 fights, and set a new record for the middleweight division by making 14 defences of the title he took from Nino Benvenuti in 1970.

The handsome Argentinean was as close to the perfect fighting machine as anyone has ever come. Tall and rangy, with a long reach and a rock-hard chin, his left jab would soften up his opponents for the heavy hooks and uppercuts which brought him 61 inside-schedule victories in 102 fights. He won the Argentine title in 1967, but did not attract international attention until he held Bennie Briscoe to a draw in 1967.

Despite his record Monzon was still the underdog when he challenged Benvenuti in November 1977. He knocked the Italian out in 12 rounds, stopped him in three rounds in a

return, and embarked on his spectacular reign. His contenders were all top-drawer, and when he ran out of opposition he retired in 1977. He was later jailed for killing his mistress, and died in a car crash on January 8, 1995, while on parole.

Archie Moore

Real name: *Archibald Lee Wright*
Born: *Benoit, Mississippi, December 13, 1913*
Titles: *World light-heavyweight champion 1952–62*
Record: *215 contests, 183 wins, 9 draws, 1 No Contest, 22 defeats*

It took Archie Moore 18 years to win the world light-heavyweight title, and ten years to lose it. Self-belief, and a stubborn streak of independence, kept him going during the scandalously long time he had to wait for his chance, despite being commonly accepted as the best man at the weight for years before making it official.

Moore was a comparatively late starter, having his first fight (against the gloriously named Piano Man Jones) when he was 22. He had extraordinary punching ability, which brought him a modern record of 129 knockouts in 215 fights, but he also acquired a reputation as a hard man to deal with, perhaps because he got through eight managers during his near-30 years in the ring.

He won the light-heavyweight title in his 175th fight, dethroning his stablemate Joey Maxim in 1952, and over the next 10 years he defended it nine times, including a modern classic against the Canadian Yvon Durelle in 1958. He challenged twice for the heavyweight title, losing to Rocky Marciano in nine rounds and Floyd Patterson in five, and retired in 1963.

Davey Moore

Born: *Lexington, Kentucky, November 1, 1933*
Titles: *World featherweight champion 1959–63*
Record: *67 contests, 59 wins, 1 draw, 7 defeats*

The ill-fated Moore, known as "The Springfield Rifle" in honour of his

adopted hometown, was a compact and precise boxer who won the 1952 AAU bantamweight title before turning professional the following year. He had some early setbacks, but then hit a 13-fight winning run which carried him all the way to the world featherweight championship.

A first-round blitz of the Mexican contender Ricardo Moreno brought him a match with champion Hogan Bassey in Los Angeles in March 1959, and Moore forced the Nigerian to retire after 13 rounds, his face a mess of cuts and swellings. He did the job in 11 rounds in the rematch, and then became a globe-trotter with appearances in England, Venezuela, Mexico, France, Spain, Italy, Japan and even Finland.

He notched up five successful defences, and his only defeat in 24 fights as champion was when Carlos Hernandez, a heavy hitter who later won the light-welterweight title, broke his jaw. But then the Cuban, Sugar Ramos, surprisingly took his title in 10 rounds in Los Angeles, on March 21, 1963. Tragically, Moore collapsed in the dressing room, and died two days later.

Michael Moorer

Born: *Monessen, Pennsylvania, November 12, 1967*
Titles: *WBO light-heavyweight champion 1988–91, WBO heavyweight champion 1992–93, WBA and IBF champion 1994*
Record: *37 contests, 36 wins, 1 defeat*

Moorer merits several footnotes in history, as the WBO's first light-heavyweight champion and, more significantly, as the first southpaw to win the heavyweight championship. He profited from the close association his then manager Emanuel Steward had with the WBO, and stopped Ramzi Hassan for their inaugural light-heavyweight title in December 1988, only seven months after turning professional. None of his 11 fights up to then had gone past four rounds.

Moorer made nine successful defences of his title, none of them lasting more than nine rounds, and then

relinquished it in April 1991 to box at heavyweight. Once more, Steward's connections paid off, as Moorer won a wildly exciting brawl with Bert Cooper for the vacant WBO title. He gave up his title in February 1993, however, on the grounds that it was "retarding his career".

He took the genuine heavyweight championship from Evander Holyfield on a points verdict in April 1994, a fight remembered for the inspirational corner work of his trainer Teddy Atlas, but then gave a disappointing performance to lose to the ancient George Foreman, who scored a surprise one-punch knockout in the 10th round in Las Vegas in November 1994.

Jose Napoles

Born: *Oriente, Cuba, April 13, 1940*
Titles: *World welterweight champion 1969–70, 1971–76*
Record: *84 contests, 77 wins, 7 defeats*

His nickname, *Mantequilla* (butter – he was said to be as smooth as butter) was particularly apt, as the sleek Cuban, who moved to Mexico in 1962, made boxing seem an effortless art. He was a venomous puncher, who won 54 of his 84 fights inside the distance, but was also a tactician who could out-think the best craftsmen of his era.

Napoles first came to notice as a light-welterweight in 1963, and commanded a high ranking in that division. His solitary loss in 33 fights between May 1963 and April 1969, when he stopped Curtis Cokes for the welterweight title, was a freak defeat by L.C. Morgan, which he quickly reversed.

He proved a fine champion, retaining his title 13 times. He ducked

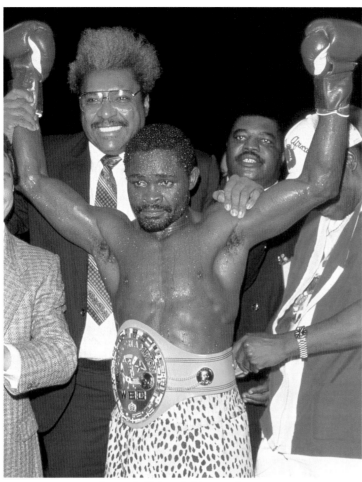

THE LION OF AFRICA *Azumah Nelson is king again*

nobody, defending in Mexico, America, England, Switzerland and Canada. There was a brief hiccup when Billy Backus – Carmen Basilio's nephew – stopped him on cuts in December 1970, but Napoles soon regained the title. He quit after six rounds of a middleweight challenge against Carlos Monzon in Paris in February 1974, relinquished the WBA title in May 1975, and lost the WBC belt to John H. Stracey in his final fight seven months later.

Azumah Nelson

Born: *Accra, Ghana, July 19, 1958*
Titles: *Commonwealth feather-
    weight champion 1981–83,
    WBC champion 1984–88, WBC
    super-featherweight champion
    1988–94, 1995–*
Record: *43 contests, 38 wins,
    2 draws, 3 defeats*

The ageless African ended 1995 by battering Gabriel Ruelas to defeat to regain the WBC super-feather-weight title, an astonishing perfor-mance by a man who had his first world title fight 13 years previously.

He won a gold medal at feather-weight in the 1978 Commonwealth Games and had a meteoric rise as a professional, lifting the Ghanaian title in his second fight, the African in his sixth, and the Commonwealth in his 10th. He came in as a late substi-tute against the magnificent WBC champion Salvador Sanchez in July 1982, and made his reputation by tak-ing Sanchez into the 15th round of a savage fight.

Two years later Nelson took the title, retaining it with six stunning vic-tories and then moving up to outpoint Mario Martinez for the vacant WBC super-featherweight title in 1988. His nine successful defences included appearances in Ghana, America, England, Australia and Mexico. Jesse James Leija, who had held him to a draw in a 1993 challenge, out-pointed him in May 1994, and when Nelson took 18 months out of the ring it was widely assumed he had retired … until that remarkable comeback against Leija's conqueror, Ruelas.

Terry Norris

Born: *Lubbock, Texas, June 17, 1967*
Titles: *WBC light-middleweight
    champion 1990–93, 1994,
    1995–*
Record: *47 contests, 41 wins,
    6 defeats*

The gifted but erratic Norris, whose older brother Orlin held the WBC cruiserweight title, is prone to lapses of concentration and self-control. In 1987 he was disqualified for hitting Joe Walker when he was down, and lost his WBC light-middleweight title in November 1994 for the second time in farcical circumstances. Luis Santana was declared the winner on a foul while he was lying on a stretcher, hav-ing been hit by a rabbit punch. In the rematch, incredibly, it happened again, Norris being disqualified this time for hitting after the bell.

But in August 1995 he finally got it right, stopping Santana to become a three-time champion. A pro since August 1986, he challenged Julian Jackson for the WBA title in July 1989, hurting Jackson badly before being stopped in the second round. He suc-ceeded at the second attempt, knocking out John Mugabi in a

ERRATIC BUT GIFTED *Terry Norris is a three-times champion*

round for the WBC title in March 1990, and made 10 defences – including a win over Ray Leonard – before Simon Brown knocked him out in December 1993.

He beat Brown in a return in May 1994, and then came his three-fight series with Santana.

Ken Norton

Born: *Jacksonville, Illinois, August 9, 1945*
Titles: *WBC heavyweight champion 1978*
Record: *50 contests, 42 wins, 1 draw, 7 defeats*

Even the great fighters have their bogeymen, opponents who, while technically inferior, will always give them trouble. In Muhammad Ali's case, the bogeyman was Norton. They fought three times, and even though Norton got the verdict only once, the other two were desperately close.

A former US Marine, Norton won his first 16 in a row, 15 inside schedule, before Jose Luis Garcia snapped his record in July 1970. He

KEN NORTON *The only champion who never won a world title fight*

put together another winning streak of 14, including breaking Ali's jaw in a points win for the NABF title in March 1973. Ali won the return six months later, and in his next outing, Norton was humiliated in two rounds in a bid for George Foreman's world title. He rebounded with seven straight knockouts, then looked unlucky to be outpointed by Ali in their 1976 title fight.

When Leon Spinks was stripped of the WBC title in 1978, Norton was proclaimed champion. He lost the title in his first defence to Larry Holmes, after a bitterly fought contest, and boxed only five more times before his retirement in 1981. He later suffered horrific injuries in a car accident, but made a remarkable recovery.

Michael Nunn

Born: *Sherman Oaks, California, April 14, 1963*
Titles: *IBF middleweight champion 1988–91, WBA super-middleweight champion 1992–93*
Record: *51 contests, 48 wins, 3 defeats*

For a while in the late 1980s, this tall southpaw looked to have the potential to become one of the great middleweight champions. He won 168 out of 174 as an amateur, having been inspired to take up the sport by watching Ray Leonard's gold medal success in the 1976 Olympics. He just missed out on an Olympic place himself in 1984 and turned pro in December that year, winning all 30 on the way to the IBF middleweight title which he took from Frank Tate in July 1988.

Nunn made five impressive defences, one a first-round knockout of Sumbu Kalambay, but then suffered a dramatic 11th round knockout by the aptly named James "Lights Out" Toney. He stepped up to win the NABF super-middleweight title, and took the WBA championship from the tough Panamanian Victor Cordoba in September 1992.

He made four successful defences to bring his record to 42 wins in 43 fights, 27 inside the distance, but then performed lethargically to lose the title on points to fellow American Steve Little in London in February 1994. Nunn scaled close to heavyweight in comeback fights in 1995.

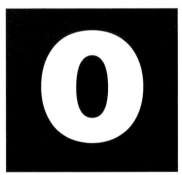

Philadelphia Jack O'Brien

Real name: *Joseph Francis Hagen (O'Hagan)*
Born: *Philadelphia, Pennsylvania, January 17, 1878*
Titles: *World light-heavyweight champion 1905–06*
Record: *179 contests, 100 wins, 16 draws, 57 No Decisions, 6 defeats*

O'Brien's parents came from a small townland in County Derry, Ireland. Their son, who started boxing for a living in 1896, was an incorrigible and

unrepentant rogue who figured in a host of fixed fights, including the one which made him world light-heavyweight champion. Only two years after he knocked out Bob Fitzsimmons to become champion in December 1905, O'Brien published a signed statement in a San Francisco newspaper revealing that the title fight, like the majority of his approximately 150 contests up to then, had been a fraud.

He fought Tommy Burns twice for the heavyweight title, drawing with him in November 1906 and losing on points in May 1907. Both were set-ups, he cheerfully acknowledged. Oddly, O'Brien scaled under the modern light-middleweight limit in the first Burns fight, weighing in at 153½ lbs, while Burns himself was only 170 lb.

O'Brien faced many champions and contenders in a career spanning 179 fights, 57 of them No Decision affairs, but his extraordinary admissions make it impossible to know from this distance in time whether he could really fight at all.

Ruben Olivares

Born: *Mexico City, Mexico, January 14, 1947*
Titles: *World bantamweight champion 1969–70, 1971–72, WBA featherweight champion 1974, WBC featherweight champion 1975*
Record: *102 contests, 87 wins, 3 draws, 12 defeats*

Genuine one-punch knockout hitters are rare, but Olivares had the knack. The Mexican, unusually, came from a prosperous background: his father was a successful businessman, and Ruben boxed simply because he liked it. He was unbeaten in his first 60 fights after turning professional in February 1964, and only four of them went the distance.

An eighth-round win over perennial contender Joe Medel in 1968 earned him a crack at Lionel Rose's bantamweight title, and the thunderous hitting challenger won it easily in three rounds. He retained it against respected opponents Alan Rudkin and Chuchu Castillo, but Castillo beat him on a 14th round cuts stoppage in October 1970, his first defeat. Olivares recaptured the title in 1971, losing it in his fourth defence to Rafael Herrera in March 1972.

He returned as a featherweight and fought his way to the WBA title, which he won in July 1974 but lost four months later to Alexis Arguello. Boxers as popular as Olivares never lack for opportunities, and he won the WBC version of the featherweight crown from Bobby Chacon in June 1975. Again, his reign was short, David Kotey outpointing him in a thriller in September of that year. He was stopped by Eusebio Pedroza for the WBA title in 1979, and retired shortly afterwards.

Carl "Bobo" Olson

Born: *Honolulu, Hawaii, July 11, 1928*
Titles: *World middleweight champion 1953–55*
Record: *116 contests, 98 wins, 2 draws, 16 defeats*

Tattooed and balding, Olson was a fixture in the world ratings from 1950 until his retirement in 1966, a real model of consistency. Olson, whose father was Swedish and mother Portuguese, was in such a hurry to box professionally that he lied about his age. When the authorities learned the truth he left for San Francisco, and had his first seven fights there before returning home in 1946.

He progressed to fight Ray Robinson for a version of the middleweight title, but was knocked out in 12 rounds in 1950. Robinson outpointed him in 1952 for the real title, but when he retired Olson beat Randy Turpin for the vacant championship in October 1953. He retained it against three tough challengers, but failed in a bid for Archie Moore's light-heavyweight title in 1955.

His old foe Robinson reclaimed the title from him with a second-round knockout in December that year, and beat him again, in four rounds, the following year. Olson then moved up to light-heavyweight permanently, occasionally even taking on heavyweights, but he continued to campaign in the top class to the end of his long career.

FAST AND FLASHY *Carlos Ortiz won two world titles*

Carlos Ortiz

Born: *Ponce, Puerto Rico, September 9, 1936*
Titles: *World light-welterweight champion 1959–60, world lightweight champion 1962–65, 1965–68*
Record: *70 contests, 61 wins, 1 draw, 1 No Contest, 7 defeats*

The smooth-boxing Ortiz, who moved to New York at nine and represented America as an amateur, was the first champion of the revived 140-lb division but made his mark as a two-time lightweight champion. He turned pro in 1955 and was a contender by 1958, but when the chance came to contest the vacant light-welterweight title against Kenny

Lane, he took it. The fight, in New York in June 1959, ended disappointingly when Lane was stopped on a cut in the second round.

Ortiz defended against Battling Torres and Duilio Loi, then lost his next two title fights with the Italian and came back down to lightweight, outscoring long-serving champion Joe Brown in April 1962. He defended his crown in Tokyo, Puerto Rico (twice) and the Philippines, losing to Ismael Laguna in Panama in April 1965. Ortiz won the rematch and made a further five successful defences before Carlos Teo Cruz ended his reign in Santo Domingo in June 1968.

Down on his luck, he launched a comeback in 1971 which brought him nine more wins but ended in defeat by Ken Buchanan in September 1972.

Manuel Ortiz

Born: *Corona, California, July 2, 1916*
Titles: *World bantamweght champion 1942–47, 1947–50*
Record: *127 contests, 95 wins, 3 draws, 29 defeats*

The son of Mexican immigrants, Manuel Ortiz is deservedly remembered as one of the finest of all bantamweight champions. Yet there was little hint of future greatness as he lost nine of his first 23 fights after turning pro in 1938, hardly surprising as he was facing world-class men like Richie Lemos, Small Montana and Lou Salica, all of whom won world titles of one kind or another.

Three wins out of four against Jackie Jurich earned him a flyweight rating in 1940, and in August 1942 he outscored bantamweight champion Lou Salica to launch his phenomenal reign. Apart from a two-month break in 1947, when he lost the title to Harold Dade in January and regained it in March, he was champion for eight years and made 19 successful defences. Yet he could be an indifferent performer in non-title matches, and lost nine of them.

He faced nine world champions, at every weight from flyweight to lightweight. Ortiz was finally beaten by Vic Toweel in Johannesburg in May 1950, and he never got another chance to regain the title he had graced for so long.

LONG SERVING *Manuel Ortiz*

Carlos Palomino

Born: *San Luis, Mexico,*
August 10, 1949
Titles: *WBC welterweight*
champion 1976–79
Record: *34 contests, 28 wins,*
3 draws, 3 defeats

The moustachioed Mexican, who did most of his fighting in Los Angeles, was a cool professional who was at his best when under pressure. He was a fine all-round technician with a particularly sharp left hook, equally effective to head or body, and he used the body punches to devastating effect when, after 22 fights (three draws, one defeat) he challenged John H. Stracey for the WBC welterweight title at Wembley in June 1976.

Stracey was rescued in the 12th round as he knelt on the ring canvas, gasping for breath. It was the start of Palomino's busy spell as champion. He stopped local rival Armando Muniz with 36 seconds remaining in the final round, when the points were exactly even, and had a desperate struggle with the fiery Englishman Dave Green, pulling out one magnificent left hook to knock Green cold in the 11th round.

He made five more successful defences, beating Muniz again in May 1978, but then lost the title to Wilfred Benitez in January 1979. Palomino boxed just once more, losing to Roberto Duran, and retired to pursue an acting career.

Billy Papke

Born: *Spring Valley, Illinois,*
September 17, 1886
Titles: *World middleweight*
champion 1908, 1910–13
Record: *62 contests, 37 wins, 6 draws,*
8 No Decisions, 11 defeats

Papke was an unscrupulous fighter who would do anything to gain an edge, as he demonstrated by smashing Stanley Ketchel in the throat as the referee was completing his instructions before their middleweight title fight in September 1908. He was allowed to get away with it, and Ketchel, who had not recovered from the foul, was knocked out in the 12th round. It was their second meeting, Ketchel having ruined Papke's 29-fight unbeaten record by outpointing him three months earlier.

In their third meeting Ketchel administered a savage beating, knocking him out in the 11th, and outpointed him again the following year. When Ketchel gave up the title in 1910 Papke regained it by knocking out Willie Lewis, but then Ketchel changed his mind and was once more regarded as champion until he was shot dead in October 1910.

Papke proclaimed himself champion again, and defended his version of the title three times, losing it, with poetic justice, on disqualification to Frank Klaus in 1913. He had just three more fights before his retirement in 1919. He murdered his wife and committed suicide at Newport, California, on November 26, 1936.

Laszlo Papp

Born: *Hungary, March 25, 1926*
Titles: *European middleweight*
champion 1962–65
Record: *29 contests, 26 wins, 3 draws*

Considering that he did not have his first professional fight until he was 31, Papp's record is impressive. A power-hitting southpaw, he won three Olympic Games gold medals at middleweight (1948) and light-middleweight (1952 and 1956), a hitherto unmatched feat, which the Hungarian Government rewarded by giving him permission to box for money. He was the only man to be given this concession until the collapse of the Communist system, decades after Papp's retirement.

They did not go so far as allowing him to box at home, so he fought mainly in Vienna against a string of Europeans and imported Americans. He moved steadily up the world ratings, but a recurring hand injury cost him vital time out of the ring and delayed a European title chance until May 1962, when he stopped the balding Dane Chris Christensen.

He defended the title six times around the continent, in Paris, Vienna (twice), Dortmund, Madrid and Copenhagen, and by 1965 negotiations were under way for a world title challenge against Joey Giardello. But the Government abruptly withdrew their permission for Papp to box for money and he was forced to retire undefeated. He later became the Hungarian team coach.

Willie Pastrano

Born: *New Orleans, Louisiana,*
November 27, 1935
Titles: *World light-heavyweight*
champion 1963–65
Record: *84 contests, 63 wins,*
8 draws, 13 defeats

The handsome Pastrano, an indefatigable womanizer, was never more than a natural light-heavyweight but he routinely fought full-blown heavyweights. His very "British" style of left-hand boxing was particularly appreciated in England, where he appeared five times between 1958 and 1959.

He was not a big puncher, scoring only 14 inside-schedule wins in 84 fights, but within two years of his pro debut aged 16 in 1951 Pastrano was meeting rated opposition. He entered the world heavyweight ratings in 1955 with wins over Joey Maxim and Rex Layne, but according to his exasperated trainer Angelo Dundee, he always preferred a pretty girl to a session in the gym. By the early 1960s, his ambition seemed to have evaporated. He could still box with the best, but defeats were becoming more frequent.

Pastrano won only once in three meetings with Wayne Thornton in 1963, but that proved a blessing in disguise. Light-heavyweight champion Harold Johnson decided that Pastrano would make a safe defence, but came unstuck as the challenger was given a controversial points decision. He retained the title twice, and retired after Jose Torres stopped him in March 1965.

Jackie Paterson

Born: *Springfield, Scotland,*
September 5, 1920
Titles: *British flyweight champion*
1939–48, Empire flyweight
champion 1940–48, world fly-
weight champion 1943–48,
Empire bantamweight champion
1945–49, European bantam-
weight champion 1946, British
bantamweight champion
1947–49
Record: *91 contests, 63 wins,*
3 draws, 25 defeats

Weight-making destroyed this hard-hitting southpaw, who struggled for years to make the flyweight limit. He had a meteoric rise, winning the vacant British and Empire titles at 19 but losing an early bantamweight foray when Jim Brady outpointed him in a thriller for the Empire title.

In June 1943 he flattened Peter Kane in 61 seconds to become world champion, but thereafter met bantams and even feathers. He reversed the Brady result in September 1945, adding the European bantamweight title by beating Theo Medina, and drew a Scottish record crowd of 50,000 for his first defence of the world title, a points win over Joe Curran in June 1946 (which levelled their series at 2–2).

Paterson promptly lost his European title to Medina, but took the British bantamweight championship from Johnny King in February 1947. Having already lost NBA recognition because of weight problems, he went through agonies to get down to 112 lb for a world flyweight title defence against Rinty Monaghan, who had beaten him once already. This time, Paterson was knocked out in seven rounds. His remaining titles soon went, and he retired in 1951. He emigrated to South Africa, where he was murdered on November 19, 1966.

Floyd Patterson

Born: *Waco, North Carolina,*
January 4, 1935
Titles: *World heavyweight*
champion 1956–59, 1960–62
Record: *64 contests, 55 wins, 1 draw,*
8 defeats

FLOYD PATTERSON *made history when he became the first man to regain the world heavyweight championship*

brittle hands, and had only five contests between March 1952 and November 1958, one of them a points defeat by future champion Gene Fullmer.

Pender returned to regular action late in 1958, and a winning run of nine earned him the shot at Robinson. The verdict in their first fight was close enough for argument, but Pender won the return convincingly and retained the championship against Terry Downes and Carmen Basilio before losing to Downes in a rematch. He regained the title from the Englishman in April 1962, and never boxed again.

Willie Pep

Real name: *Guglielmo Papaleo*
Born: *Middletown, Connecticut, September 19, 1922*
Titles: *New York recognition as world featherweight champion, 1942–46, world champion 1946–48, 1949–50*
Record: *242 contests, 230 wins, 1 draw, 11 defeats*

The cleverest featherweight of them all, Pep's defensive wizardry earned him the nickname "Will O' The Wisp". He was introduced to boxing when his father took him to watch the state's earlier featherweight idol, Bat Battalino, and one of his only two amateur defeats was to Ray Robinson. He turned pro at 17 and reeled off 62 straight wins before lightweight champion Sammy Angott outpointed him in March 1943, but then put together another amazing run of 73 victories.

He became the youngest world champion in 40 years by outpointing Chalky Wright for the New York title in November 1942, but the war restricted him to three defences between then and June 1946, when he knocked out NBA champion Sal Bartolo for the undisputed title.

He was dethroned in October 1948 by his great rival Sandy Saddler, but gave his finest display to outscore Saddler in a rematch in February 1949. He then made more three defences before Saddler took the title back in seven rounds and retained it in nine. Pep boxed on until 1959, and staged a brief comeback in 1965–66.

Boxing proved the making of Patterson. He was a disturbed youth who spent his days hiding in New York subway tunnels, but his life changed when he met trainer Cus D'Amato. He became D'Amato's star pupil, winning the 1952 Olympic middleweight title when he was just 17.

He turned pro under D'Amato's fiercely independent management, losing only to Joey Maxim in his first 36 fights. When Rocky Marciano retired, Patterson became the youngest-ever heavyweight champion, knocking out Archie Moore in November 1956. But he was never more than a cruiserweight (190 lb), and was always vulnerable against fully fledged heavyweights, taking a total of 17 counts in his championship reign.

D'Amato picked easy opponents (one, Pete Rademacher, was having his first professional fight!) but in his fifth defence Patterson was knocked down seven times by the Swede Ingemar Johansson, and lost on a stoppage in the third round. He regained the title a year later, the first to do so, but lost it in one round to Sonny Liston and failed in attempts to regain it from Liston, Muhammad Ali and Jimmy Ellis (for the WBA title). He retired in 1972, and served several terms as New York State Athletic Commissioner.

Eusebio Pedroza

Born: *Panama City, Panama, March 2, 1953*
Titles: *WBA featherweight champion 1978–85*
Record: *49 contests, 42 wins, 1 draw, 6 defeats*

The tall Panamanian was a true professional who faced every worthwhile contender and, in the course of a 20-defence tenure of the WBA featherweight title, gave new significance to the term "world champion". He risked his title in Puerto Rico, America, Japan, New Guinea, Korea, Venezuela, Italy, St Vincent and England, and proved unbeatable from 1978 until Ireland's Barry McGuigan outworked him in June 1985.

He began his career as a bantamweight, but was easily dismissed in two rounds by Alfonso Zamora when he tried for the WBA title in April 1978. That was his second knockout loss in 16 fights, and when it happened again two fights later Pedroza looked finished. Instead, he moved up to featherweight, his natural division given that he stood 5ft 9in, and was instantly successful.

He took the WBA title from a moderate champion, Cecilio Lastra of Spain, but quickly proved his worth by defeating a host of outstanding challengers. Pedroza acquired a reputation as a dirty fighter, but performed impeccably when losing to McGuigan in a superb contest. He retired after it, but made a short-lived and unsuccessful comeback as a lightweight.

Paul Pender

Born: *Brookline, Massachusetts, June 20, 1930*
Titles: *New York and European recognition as world middleweight champion 1960–61, 1962*
Record: *48 contests, 40 wins, 2 draws, 6 defeats*

Few fans outside Boston had heard of Paul Pender when the news came through on January 23, 1960 that the one-time fireman had ended Sugar Ray Robinson's reign as middleweight champion the previous night. The Irish-American with the distinctively crooked nose had done nothing to suggest he was capable of such an upset, barely scraping into the world ratings.

His career had started promisingly enough in January 1949, and he went undefeated in 21 fights before a run of bad form which saw him win only twice in seven attempts. He was consistently handicapped by injuries to his

Pascual Perez

Born: *Tupungate, Argentina,*
March 4, 1926
Titles: *World flyweight champion*
1954–60
Record: *91 contests, 83 wins, 1 draw,*
7 defeats

The diminutive Argentinean stood only 4ft 10$\frac{1}{2}$in, but is a giant in the history of the flyweight division. He won the 1948 Olympic gold medal but did not turn professional for another four years, by which time he was 26. Despite the late start he was an instant success, taking the Argentine title in only his seventh fight and winning the world championship from Yoshio Shirai in November 1954.

He built his unbeaten run to 51, including seven defences in Japan, Argentina, Uruguay, Venezuela and the Philippines before Sadao Yaoita outpointed him in a non-title match in Tokyo in January 1959. Perez knocked him out in a championship rematch in November 1959, but then lost the title to Pone Kingpetch in April 1960. It was only his second loss in 56 fights.

Kingpetch stopped him in eight rounds in a return in Los Angeles, the first time in 25 years that the flyweight title had been contested in America. Perez retired in 1964, and died in Argentina on January 22, 1977.

Lupe Pintor

Real name: *Jose Guadalupe Pintor*
Born: *Cuajimalpa, Mexico,*
April 13, 1955
Titles: *WBC bantamweight*
champion 1979–83, WBC super-
bantamweight champion
1985–86
Record: *72 contests, 56 wins,*
2 draws, 14 defeats

Pintor won the WBC bantamweight title on a highly debatable split decision from his stablemate Carlos Zarate in June 1979: two judges had Pintor ahead by a solitary point, 143–142, but the third gave it to Zarate by a huge margin, 145–133. It was an unconvincing start, but the hard-punching Mexican developed into a

solid champion, proving himself with eight successful defences. One, against the Welshman Johnny Owen, ended in tragedy. Owen was knocked out in the 12th round, and died, after weeks in a coma, on November 4, 1980.

Pintor tried for Wilfredo Gomez's WBC super-bantamweight title in December 1982, but the brilliant Puerto Rican was too big for him and stopped him in 14 rounds. In 1983, Pintor suffered serious injuries in a motorbike accident, and his title was declared vacant because of his inability to defend it.

He eventually returned to action as a super-bantamweight, and took the WBC title from Juan Meza in Mexico City in August 1985, but forfeited the title on the scales when he turned up three pounds overweight for his first defence, against Samart Payakarun.

Aaron Pryor

Born: *Cincinnati, Ohio,*
October 20, 1955
Titles: *WBA light-welterweight*
champion 1980–83, IBF light-
welterweight champion
1983–85
Record: *40 contests, 39 wins,*
1 defeat

Yet another victim of America's drug culture, Pryor could have become the greatest of all the light-welterweight champions. Known as "The Hawk" because of the speed and ferocity of his attacks, he even rated comparison with Henry Armstrong, one of the few champions who could have matched his prodigious work-rate.

He was unstoppable as an amateur, winning the AAU title and boxing for his country before turning professional in November 1976. He was very much a hometown boy, most of his fights taking place in Cincinnati, and his reluctance to move to more glamorous venues probably prevented him becoming champion earlier. His chance finally did come in Cincinnati in August 1980, when he ended the championship career of WBA title-holder Antonio Cervantes with a fourth-round knockout.

Pryor made eight defences, including two classic battles with the Mexican Alexis Arguello, before relinquishing the title to accept recognition by the newly formed IBF. But he was already hooked on drugs, and drifted away from the sport after two IBF defences. When Pryor first retired, he had a perfect 36–0 record, but, blind in one eye and financially ruined, he made a bizarre comeback attempt some years later and was knocked out.

Dwight Muhammad Qawi

Formerly known as Dwight Braxton
Born: *Baltimore, Maryland,*
January 5, 1953
Titles: *WBC light-heavyweight*
champion 1981–83, WBA
cruiserweight champion 1985–86
Record: *50 contests, 39 wins, 1 draw,*
10 defeats

This busy, aggressive fighter, known as "The Camden Buzzsaw", learned his boxing in the toughest school imaginable – Rahway State Penitentiary, New Jersey. He had never boxed as an amateur, but joined the boxing programme to relieve the frustrations of jail life.

He became a professional upon his release in 1978, managed by a former lightweight challenger, Wesley Mouzon, and not surprisingly won only once in his first three starts. But he learned quickly, and a run of 15 straight wins carried him to the WBC light-heavyweight title, which he took from another tough warrior, Matthew Saad Muhammad in December 1981. Curiously, one of his major wins was over a long-term inmate at Rahway, James Scott, and because all of Scott's fights had to be

staged inside the prison, Braxton went back to fight there.

Braxton converted to Islam in 1982, following his second victory over Matthew Saad Muhammad. Boxing as Qawi, he lost to Mike Spinks in a unification match in 1983, but won the WBA cruiserweight title two years later and retained it against Mike's brother Leon before being knocked out by IBF champion Evander Holyfield. Robert Daniels beat him in a WBA title bid in 1989, and he had the last of his 50 fights in October 1992.

Ike Quartey

Real name: *Issifu Quartey*
Born: *Accra, Ghana,*
November 27, 1969
Titles: *WBC International welter-*
weight champion 1992, WBA
welterweight champion 1994–
Record: *31 contests, 31 wins*

The welterweight division boasted amongst its champions in 1995 two of the game's hardest punchers, pound for pound, in IBF champion Felix Trinidad and WBA title-holder Ike Quartey, who by the end of the year had knocked out or stopped 27 of the 31 men he had faced in his so-far unbeaten career.

One of Quartey's brothers, also called Ike, had won the Empire Games gold medal in 1962, and the younger Ike tried without success to emulate him in the world junior championships and in the 1988 Seoul Olympics, where he boxed at light-welterweight. He turned professional on his return from the Games, winning the Ghanaian light-welterweight title in his sixth fight and the All-African championship in his ninth, and came to serious notice when he floored and stopped the American Olympic representative Kelcie Banks in seven rounds.

He won the WBC International title in his next fight, defending it twice before stepping up to welterweight. Quartey then moved to France, where he took the WBA title from the accomplished Venezuelan Crisanto Espana in 11 rounds in June 1994. His first three defences all ended inside the distance.

Frankie Randall

Born: *Birmingham, Alabama, September 25, 1961*
Titles: *WBC light-welterweight champion 1994, WBA light-welterweight champion 1994–95*
Record: *56 contests, 52 wins, 1 draw, 3 defeats*

Few champions have had such a roller-coaster life as Frankie "The Surgeon" Randall, who overcame drugs and alcohol addiction, endured a jail sentence, and beat odds of 15–1 to inflict the first defeat on WBC light-welterweight king Julio Cesar Chavez. Randall started boxing aged nine after moving to Morristown, Tennessee and one of his rare defeats in 236 fights was to future IBF champion Joe Louis Manley in trials for the 1980 Olympics.

He turned pro in 1983, winning 23 straight before ex-champ Edwin Rosario outscored him in London in 1985. He came back strongly with a stoppage of Sammy Fuentes and a draw with Freddie Pendleton, both future world champions, but then, on the verge of a title shot, he was jailed for dealing in drugs in 1990.

By 1993, he was a top contender again with a revenge win over Rosario and in January 1994 he floored Chavez and took a deserved points win. Chavez won a controversial technical decision in the rematch, but Randall rebounded to beat WBA champion Juan Martin Coggi in September 1994 for his second world title, which he defended once in 1995.

Sugar Ray Robinson

see Legends of the Ring (pp 82–83)

Lionel Rose

Born: *Drouin, Australia, June 21, 1948*
Titles: *World banamweight champion 1968–69, Commonwealth champion 1969*
Record: *53 contests, 42 wins, 11 defeats*

The eldest of nine children, Rose was taught to box by his father, an Aboriginal booth fighter. He captured the Australian amateur flyweight title at 15, and turned professional a year later to support the family after his father died of a heart attack. He won and retained the Australian bantamweight title, and victories over respected international opposition in 1966–67 earned him a crack at Fighting Harada's world title in Tokyo in February 1968.

Harada was heavily favoured, but the Australian – whose frequently photographed pipe smoking was no gimmick, but a regular indulgence – floored the champion and boxed brilliantly to take his title. He retained it with split decisions over dangerous contenders in Takao Sakuri, Chuchu Castillo and Alan Rudkin, but then had the misfortune to face Ruben Olivares when the Mexican, who had knocked out 49 of his 52 opponents, was at his peak. Olivares knocked him out in five rounds, in Los Angeles, in August 1969.

Rose boxed on, losing to Yoshiaki Numata for the WBC super-featherweight title in 1971, but the spark was gone and he quit in 1976 after losing four of his last five fights.

Maxie Rosenbloom

Born: *New York, New York, September 6, 1904*
Titles: *World light-heavyweight champion 1930–34*
Record: *299 contests, 210 wins, 26 draws, 23 No Decisions, 2 No Contests, 38 defeats*

Rosenbloom's nickname of "Slapsie Maxie" derived from his tendency to hit with the open glove, which resulted in him winning only 19 of his fights inside schedule. But he was a cagey

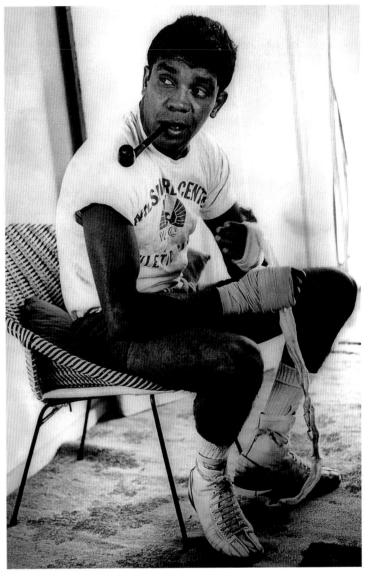

BOXING'S *most successful pipe-smoker, bantamweight king Lionel Rose*

boxer who knew how to avoid trouble, and was himself only stopped twice.

He was a clown in the ring, and because he was an entertainer, Rosenbloom never lacked work. For nearly five years he averaged a fight every fortnight, having 30 in 1932. When Tommy Loughran retired as light-heavyweight champion in September 1929, Jimmy Slattery, an old rival of Rosenbloom's, won New York recognition but lost that to Rosenbloom in June 1930, the NBA subsequently also recognizing Maxie as champion.

The NBA stripped him in June 1931 for failing to defend on time, and their title eventually passed to Bob Godwin on March 1, 1933. Three weeks later Rosenbloom knocked him out to become undisputed king

again, a distinction he held until a disputed points loss to Bob Olin in November 1934. He became a well-known character actor after his retirement in 1939, and died in Los Angeles on March 6, 1976.

Gianfranco Rosi

Born: *Perugia, Italy, August 5, 1957*
Titles: *European welterweight champion 1984–85, WBC light-middleweight champion 1987–88, IBF champion 1989–94, WBO champion 1995*
Record: *63 contests, 57 wins, 1 draw, 1 No Contest, 4 defeats*

The awkward Italian spoiler was a significant figure in light-middleweight affairs between 1987, when he won the

WBC title, and 1995, when after a long spell as IBF title-holder he won the WBO championship, only to be stripped for failing a post-fight drug test.

Rosi won national titles at light-welter and welter as an amateur, turning pro in 1979. He lost only one of his first 33, lifting the Italian and European welterweight titles, but moved up to light-middleweight soon after losing the European belt to Lloyd Honeyghan on a third-round knock-out. After taking his second European title from Chris Pyatt, he outpointed Lupe Aquino for the WBC title, which he held for only nine months until Don Curry knocked him out.

He took the IBF version from Darrin Van Horn in February 1989, retaining it 11 times before Vincent Pettway beat him easily in four rounds in September 1994. Surprisingly, the WBO gave him yet another chance, which he seemed to have taken in style by outpointing Verno Phillips in his hometown of Perugia. A few days later, though, he was a disgraced ex-champion.

Barney Ross

Real name: *Beryl David Rosofsky*
Born: *New York, New York, December 23, 1909*
Titles: *World lightweight and light-welterweight champion 1933–35, world welterweight champion 1934, 1935–38*
Record: *81 contests, 73 wins, 3 draws, 1 No Decision, 4 defeats*

The stylish Ross was a three-weight world champion in the days when that feat was infinitely harder to accomplish than it is today. He was raised in Chicago, turning professional in 1929 after robbers murdered his father, a grocer. His quickly became popular and Al Capone was a regular ringsider, although there was no suggestion that he "helped" Ross.

A points win over Tony Canzoneri in 1933 made him champion at lightweight and light-welterweight, but he relinquished the former after beating Canzoneri in a rematch. He held on to the heavier title, defending that nine times until giving it up in June 1935. He had become a double champion once again in May 1934 when he took the welterweight title from Jimmy McLarnin in the first of three famous meetings, losing to him four months later and then regaining it in May 1935. He finally lost the championship to Henry Armstrong, and immediately retired.

Ross was a much-decorated war hero, and won a long battle against drug addiction caused by medical treatment for his wounds. He died in Chicago on January 17, 1967.

Tommy Ryan

Real name: *Joseph Youngs*
Born: *Redwood, New York, March 31, 1870*
Titles: *World welterweight champion 1891–95, world middleweight champion 1898–1902*
Record: *105 contests, 86 wins, 6 draws, 4 No Decisions, 6 No Contests, 3 defeats*

Ryan reflected the fashion of the time by choosing an Irish ring name, although his father was French and his mother English. He started boxing in 1887, and claimed the welterweight title after the untimely death of champion Paddy Duffy in July 1890. His claim was disputed by Mysterious Billy Smith, but Ryan settled the argument by outpointing Smith. He defended twice, including a stoppage of "Nonpareil" Jack Dempsey, but was subsequently unable to make the championship limit (then 142 lb) even though he continued to style himself as champion until 1898.

Kid McCoy knocked him out in March 1896 to become recognized as middleweight champion following Bob Fitzsimmons's retirement, but when McCoy relinquished the title Ryan took it over and held it for four years until his retirement in 1904. He stayed inactive for two years, and made a brief comeback in 1907.

He lost only three fights, two to McCoy and one on a foul to George Green, which he avenged in his next fight. He died in Van Nuys, California on August 3, 1948.

Joseph "Sandy" Saddler

Born: *Boston, Massachusetts, June 23, 1926*
Titles: *World featherweight champion 1948–49, 1950–57; limited recognition as world junior-lightweight champion 1949–51*
Record: *162 contests, 144 wins, 2 draws, 16 defeats*

A lanky beanpole at 5ft 8½in, Saddler's unusual punching power brought him 103 inside-schedule wins. Of West Indian parentage, Saddler was reared in New York and had only a few amateur fights, turning pro in March 1944.

He worked hard: 22 fights in 1944 and 24

VICENTE SALDIVAR *an outstanding southpaw from the 1960s*

unbeaten in 1945, including 14 consecutive knockouts. But it took him 94 fights to be given a title shot, although he had been rated for three years. Champion Willie Pep performed pathetically when they met in October 1948, losing in four rounds, but the rematch set a new indoor attendance record of 19,097 and this time Pep won comfortably.

Saddler collected a version of the super-featherweight title while he waited for a third fight with Pep, which he won on an eight-round retirement in September 1950. Their fourth meeting a year later earned Saddler (a famously dirty fighter) a 30-day suspension for fouling Pep, who lost in nine rounds. He was still champion when, in 1957, he was forced to retire after being injured in a car crash, later becoming a respected trainer.

Vicente Saldivar

Real name: *Vicente Saldivar Garcia*
Born: *Mexico City, Mexico, May 3, 1943*
Titles: *World featherweight champion 1964–67, WBC champion 1970*
Record: *41 contests, 38 wins, 3 defeats*

Saldivar boasted an abnormally slow heart and pulse rate, which he claimed was the secret of the phenomenal pace he was able to maintain. One of a poor family of nine, he turned professional at 17 in 1961. His hard punching from a southpaw stance and relentless work-rate earned him the Mexican featherweight title in his 24th fight (23 wins).

A points defeat of future lightweight champion Ismael Laguna brought him a chance at the world title held by Mexican-based Cuban Sugar Ramos, and Saldivar won a bloody battle in 12 rounds in September 1964. Eight defences followed in three years, three of them against brilliant Welshman Howard Winstone. Saldivar won the first two on razor-thin verdicts, but stopped Winstone in the 12th round of their third meeting in Mexico City and immediately announced his retirement. He was only 24 and had made eight successful defences.

He stayed out for almost two years, then beat Jose Legra to earn a title match with Johnny Famechon, whom he outpointed in Rome in May 1970 to win the WBC version of his former crown. Kuniaki Shibata dethroned him in December 1970, and he retired after failing to regain the title from Eder Jofre in 1973. He died on July 18, 1985.

Salvador Sanchez

Born: *Santiago, Mexico, February 3, 1958*
Titles: *WBC featherweight champion 1980–82*
Record: *46 contests, 44 wins, 1 draw, 1 defeat*

Salvador Sanchez's tragic death in a car accident robbed the boxing world of an extraordinary performer who may well have gone on to establish himself as the greatest featherweight in history. Three of the men against whom he defended the WBC title went on to win it after his death: Juan LaPorte, Wilfredo Gomez and Azumah Nelson.

The curly-haired Mexican won 17 of his first 18 fights inside the distance before suffering the only loss of his career when Antonio Becerra outpointed him in September 1977 for the vacant national title. He broke into the world ratings with a run of impressive results in 1979, and then battered Danny Lopez to 13th round defeat in February 1980 to become WBC champion.

His challengers, without exception, were all top-drawer, five of them taking him the full 15 rounds. He stopped Nelson in the last round of a bruising fight in Madison Square Garden in July 1982, and a few weeks later, on August 12, was killed at Queretaro in a high-speed, head-on crash in his Porsche.

Dave Sands

Real name: *Ritchie Sands*
Born: *Burnt Ridge, Australia, February 4, 1926*
Titles: *Empire middleweight champion 1949–52*
Record: *104 contests, 93 wins, 1 draw, 2 No Contests, 8 defeats*

By far the most successful of five fighting brothers, Sands owed his striking looks to his Puerto Rican father and Aboriginal mother. Within three years of his debut in 1943, Sands was Australian middleweight and light-heavyweight champion, and without any viable opposition at home he left for England, where under Jack Solomons's promotion he became a major attraction.

Solomons slipped up when classy American light-heavyweight Tommy Yarosz outpointed the youngster. But at middleweight, Sands was unbeatable. A win over highly-ranked Frenchman Robert Villemain was followed by a spectacular knockout of Dick Turpin for the Empire title, Sands disposing of the British champion in two minutes 35 seconds.

He went back to Australia and won the country's heavyweight title, then went to America to pursue a world title chance. Beating Carl "Bobo" Olson made him a leading contender for Ray Robinson's title, and there was every chance that the Australian could emulate Randolph Turpin's success. But on August 11, 1952, his truck overturned, and he died of his injuries.

Johnny Saxton

Born: *Newark, New Jersey, July 4, 1930*
Titles: *World welterweight champion 1954–55, 1956–57*
Record: *66 contests, 55 wins, 2 draws, 9 defeats*

Saxton may have been good enough to become world welterweight champion under his own steam, but given that his manager was Blinky Palermo, the notorious Mob figure who was the most significant of the underworld's links with boxing at the time, he simply couldn't miss.

He was an accomplished Golden Gloves and AAU champion before starting his paid career in 1949. More boxer than puncher, most of his victories at top level were on points. Saxton moved up the ratings in 1952–53, winning the title from Kid Gavilan in October 1954. The verdict was extremely controversial, but as the fight took place in Palermo's power-base, Philadelphia, that was hardly surprising.

He lost it on a 14th round stoppage to Tony deMarco five months later, but regained it from Carmen Basilio in March 1956 on a verdict which was even worse than in the Gavilan fight. Public opinion forced a rematch, which Basilio won in nine rounds, and Basilio then removed all doubts by knocking him out in two rounds in February 1957. Saxton retired in December 1958.

Max Schmeling

Born: *Klein Luckaw, Germany, September 28, 1905*
Titles: *European light-heavyweight champion 1927–28, world heavyweight champion 1930–32, European champion 1939*
Record: *70 contests, 56 wins, 4 draws, 10 defeats*

The heavy-browed German will always be remembered for his two fights with Joe Louis, one a glorious victory and the other an ignominious rout. Yet he was a major figure in the championship scene in the 1930s.

His early career, which began in 1924, was spent in the light-heavyweight division, where he won the European championship in 1927. A first-round knockout by veteran

MAX SCHMELING *won the world heavyweight championship on a foul*

Welshman Gypsy Daniels in February 1928 persuaded him to move up, and he became German heavyweight champion two months later before leaving for America.

When Gene Tunney retired, Schmeling was crowned champion in June 1930 while sitting on the canvas, having been fouled by Jack Sharkey. In the return, Sharkey was lucky to get the verdict. Losses to Max Baer and Steve Hamas pushed Schmeling down the list, and he seemed a safe match for the unbeaten Joe Louis in 1936 – but scored a shock 12th-round knockout. The rematch, for Louis's title two years later, saw the German take a fearful one-round beating. Schmeling staged a brief comeback after the war, and then made a fortune as a senior executive with Coca Cola.

Jack Sharkey

Real name: *Josef Paul Cukoschay*
Born: *Binghampton, New York, October 26, 1902*
Titles: *World heavyweight champion 1932–33*
Record: *55 contests, 38 wins, 3 draws, 1 No Decision, 13 defeats*

Doubts persist about the validity of Sharkey's defeat by Primo Carnera which cost him the heavyweight title in June 1933. The temperamental champion, a former sailor of Lithuanian extraction, had previously outpointed Carnera, yet made a feeble showing in the rematch and was knocked out in six rounds. Sharkey always refused to be drawn on the subject, but the rumours followed him to his grave.

At his best, though, Sharkey was a fine boxer who beat George Godfrey and Harry Wills to qualify for a championship eliminator with Jack Dempsey in 1927. He was clearly outboxing the former champion when, in the seventh round, he turned to complain to the referee and was knocked cold.

He was paired with Max Schmeling for the vacant title in 1930, losing on a foul. He easily beat Carnera to earn another chance to fight for Schmeling's title, and this time was given a dubious verdict over the German. He enjoyed his title for a

DODGING HIS OWN REFLECTION *Battling Siki limbers up for the fray*

year, then lost it to Carnera and his career ended in a third-round humiliation by Joe Louis. After retirement he became a champion angler, and died in August 1994.

Battling Siki

Born: *St Louis, Senegal, September 16, 1897*
Titles: *World light-heavyweight champion 1922–23*
Record: *93 contests, 63 wins, 5 draws, 5 No Decisions, 20 defeats*

His real name will never be known, but when Siki was brought to France as a "toy boy" by a wealthy French woman she called him "Louis Phal" in joking tribute to his chief attribute, and that is what historians have solemnly recorded ever since. He had a few fights before the Great War, in which

he earned the Croix De Guerre, and returned to the ring as Battling Siki in 1919.

He compiled an impressive record, losing only one of 45 fights, but was not considered a threat to Georges Carpentier when the French idol defended his light-heavyweight title in Paris in September 1922. Carpentier had sold the film rights, and to avoid an early finish he spurned repeated chances to win in the first round. But Siki floored him in the second and gave Carpentier a merciless beating, knocking him out in the sixth.

Siki lost the title to Mike McTigue in Dublin on St Patrick's Day, 1923, and moved to America later that year. His wild publicity stunts (he had a lion cub as a pet) kept him in the public eye, but wins were scarce. He was found shot dead in a New York street on December 15, 1925.

Leon Spinks

Born: *St Louis, Missouri, July 11, 1953*
Titles: *World heavyweight champion 1978*
Record: *43 contests, 25 wins, 3 draws, 15 defeats*

It still seems unbelievable, but it happened: Leon Spinks outpointed Muhammad Ali for the world heavyweight title, after only seven professional fights. There was nothing lucky about the verdict, either – Spinks won deservedly, but his tragedy was that the biggest triumph of his life would ultimately destroy him. The gap-toothed, almost illiterate Spinks was singularly ill-equipped to handle the money and the attention which that memorable victory brought him, and his life has been in downward spiral ever since that day in Las Vegas in February 1978.

He had the pedigree to be champion, having won the light-heavyweight gold medal in the 1976 Olympics, but lacked the discipline and sophistication to go with it. Ali easily outpointed him in the rematch in September 1978, and then Gerrie Coetzee destroyed him in a round in a WBA eliminator.

Larry Holmes gave him a title shot in 1981, stopping him in three rounds, and Spinks dropped to cruiserweight to challenge Dwight Muhammad Qawi unsuccessfully for the WBA title in 1986. His money and his talent long gone, Spinks fights on. In 1995, he lost to a youngster making his pro debut.

Mike Spinks

Born: *St Louis, Missouri, July 13, 1956*
Titles: *WBA light-heavyweight champion 1981–83, world light-heavyweight champion 1983–85, IBF heavyweight champion 1985–87*
Record: *32 contests, 31 wins, 1 defeat*

It would be hard to find two brothers less alike in nature than the Spinks. Mike had the qualities Leon lacked, and was able to retire as a wealthy and respected two-weight world champion while his brother, to whom he remained devoted, unfortunately became a joke figure.

They both struck gold in the 1976 Olympic Games, Mike at middleweight, and when Leon found success so quickly, Mike selflessly put his own career on hold to help him. He resumed in 1980, and had won 16 in a row when he outpointed Eddie Mustafa Muhamamd for the WBA light-heavyweight title in November 1981. He retained that five times, then beat WBC champ Dwight Muhammad Qawi for the undisputed title in March 1983.

After a further four defences he relinquished the title on becoming IBF heavyweight champion with a disputed points win over Larry Holmes in September 1985. He won an equally controversial verdict in the rematch, and defended the title only

once before being stripped for fighting Gerry Cooney instead of Tony Tucker. Knocking out Cooney brought a match with Mike Tyson, but Spinks was annihilated inside a round and never boxed again.

Young Stribling

Real name: *William Lawrence Stribling*
Born: *Bainbridge, Georgia, December 26, 1904.*
Titles: *none*
Record: *286 contests, 222 wins, 14 draws, 36 No Decisions, 2 No Contests, 12 defeats*

Known as "The Georgia Peach", Stribling is remembered for his colourful background and lifestyle as much as for his accomplishments in the ring, although they were considerable too. He won 222 out of 286 fights in a remarkably busy 12-year career, which would have easily topped 300 fights had he not been killed in a motorbike accident on October 2, 1933 on his way back from a fight in Houston where he had just beaten the light-heavyweight champion Maxie Rosenbloom in a

non-title match.

His parents were circus acrobats, and Stribling and his brother worked as "midget boxers" in their boyhood. His formidable mother took over his management when he turned professional in January 1921, and worked him hard: he often had more than 30 fights a year.

Paul Berlenbach outpointed him in a light-heavyweight title bid in 1925, but Stribling took on heavyweights with such success that, after a triumphant tour of Europe under Jeff Dickson's promotion, he was given a crack at Max Schmeling's world title in 1931. But he fought an uncharacteristically negative battle, and was knocked out in the 15th.

John L. Sullivan

see Legends of the Ring (pp 84–85)

Ernie Terrell

Born: *Chicago, Illinois, April 4, 1939*
Titles: *WBA heavyweight champion 1965–67*
Record: *55 contests, 46 wins, 9 defeats*

His spoiling style meant that the 6ft 6in Terrell was never a crowd-pleaser, but he frustrated a lot of good fighters. He did not attract much attention until 1963, nearly six years into his career, when he scored back-to-back wins over dangerous puncher Cleveland Williams and long-time contender Zora Folley.

By late 1964 heavyweight champion Muhammad Ali was deeply unpopular with the American establishment because of his alignment with the so-called Black Muslims, so when he signed for a rematch with Sonny Liston the WBA used that as an

excuse to strip him of their title, although return fights were commonplace. Terrell beat Eddie Machen for the vacant title in March 1965, and made some money defending it against George Chuvalo and Doug Jones.

A reunification match with Ali in Houston in February 1967, proved an unedifying spectacle. Terrell insisted on calling Ali by his "slave name", Cassius Clay, so Ali tormented him for 15 rounds, following every punch with the question "What's my name?" The beating finished Terrell as a fighter, and a comeback was a failure. He later became a manager and promoter in Chicago.

Marcel Thil

Born: *Saint-Dizier, France, May 25, 1904*
Titles: *European middleweight champion 1929–30, 1934–38, and light-heavyweight champion 1934–35, IBU middleweight champion 1932–37*
Record: *148 contests, 113 wins, 13 draws, 22 defeats*

Unlike France's other boxing heroes Carpentier and Cerdan, Marcel Thil was not the stuff of which young girls' dreams are made. He was prematurely bald, with a chest hairy enough to pass as a doormat. But he was a competent fighter who won 113 of his 148 fights, and for nearly five years the European-based IBU recognized him as world middleweight champion.

Thil won only 12 of his first 25 fights, but he hit form in 1928 and an unbeaten run of 15 carried him to the French and European titles, losing the latter to Mario Bosisio in November 1930. But his messy, brawling style brought him another 21 consecutive wins, including the 11th-round disqualification victory over the American NBA champion Gorilla Jones which earned Thil IBU recognition.

He retained the title nine times, including surprising points defeats of Len Harvey and Kid Tunero and a pair of disqualification wins over Lou Brouillard. In 1937 he went to New York in the hope of resolving the muddled championship position, but was

MICHAEL SPINKS in his days as undisputed light-heavyweight champion

stopped in 10 rounds by Fred Apostoli and promptly retired. He died in Cannes on August 14, 1968.

Dick Tiger

Real name: *Richard Ihetu*
Born: *Amaigbo, Orlu, Nigeria, August 14, 1929*
Titles: *Empire middleweight champion 1958–60, 1960–62, WBA middleweight champion 1962, world champion 1962–63, 1965–66, world light-heavyweight champion 1966–68*
Record: *81 contests, 61 wins, 3 draws, 17 defeats*

The muscular Tiger lost only one of his 16 bouts in Nigeria, but found it a tougher game when he came to England in 1953 and lost his first four. But he was tough and determined. The breakthrough came when he stopped London favourite Terry Downes in five rounds. Downes earned £125, Tiger £75!

Tiger took the Empire title from Pat McAteer, then settled in New York, scoring a string of wins over the cream of a particularly tough division. The only real setback was the temporary loss of his Empire title to Wilf Greaves in June 1960: he regained it in November.

He outpointed Gene Fullmer for the WBA title, drew with him in a rematch, and then stopped him in seven to earn universal recognition. He lost and won in title fights with Joey Giardello, then lost the title again to Emile Griffith and moved up to become light-heavyweight champion by outpointing Jose Torres. He was beaten in his third defence by Bob Foster, retiring in July 1971. The Nigerian Civil War bankrupted him, and he died of liver cancer on December 14, 1971.

James Toney

Born: *Grand Rapids, Michigan, August 24, 1968*
Titles: *IBF middleweight champion 1991–93, IBF super-middleweight champion 1993–94*
Record: *53 contests, 49 wins, 2 draws, 2 defeats*

LIGHTS OUT *James Toney in the ring before losing his title to Roy Jones Jr*

A truly intimidating fighter, Toney was undefeated in his first 42 fights before Roy Jones dazzled him to a points defeat in November 1994 to take his IBF super-middleweight title. It was an impressive record, considering that Toney (whose hard punching earned him the nickname "Lights Out") had won no titles in his 24-fight amateur career.

But under the guidance of the glamorous Jackie Kallen, one of the few top-flight female managers, he made rapid progress after turning pro in October 1988, winning the Michigan State title and the IBC Americas championship. A victory over dangerous contender Merqui Sosa moved him to the top of the queue to face the unbeaten IBF middleweight champion Michael Nunn, and he stunned the boxing world by knocking out the classy, hitherto elusive Nunn with one punch in the 11th round in May 1991.

He proved less impressive as champion, struggling to retain the title against Reggie Johnson, Mike McCallum (twice) and Dave Tiberi, but he looked much more at home in the 168-lb division when he took the IBF title from Iran Barkley in 1993 and retained it three times before losing to Jones.

Felix Trinidad

Born: *Cupoy Alto, Puerto Rico, January 10, 1973*
Title: *IBF welterweight champion 1993–*
Record: *27 contests, 27 wins*

The tall, rangy Trinidad resembles Thomas Hearns not just in physique but in the speed and impact of his punches. Coached by his father, also Felix Trinidad, he had over 50 amateur fights before turning pro at 17 in March 1990. (Felix Sr had also boxed professionally as a featherweight, his opponents including future world champion Salvador Sanchez, who stopped him in five rounds in 1979.)

The young Trinidad soon earned a world rating, stopping 11 of his first 14 opponents and then coming off the floor in the first round to stop world-ranked Alberto Cortes in the third in Paris in October 1992. That performance brought him a crack at the veteran IBF champion Maurice Blocker, easily the best man Trinidad had faced, but the youngster wrecked him in two rounds in San Diego in June 1993.

Between then and the end of 1995, Trinidad defended his championship six times, and only Hector Camacho went the distance. The highlight was his fourth-round stoppage of Mexican challenger Yori Campos in Las Vegas in 1994, a wildly exciting affair which even drew comparison with the Hagler vs Hearns classic.

Konstantin Tszyu

Born: *Serov, Russia, September 19, 1969*
Titles: *IBF light-welterweight champion 1995–*
Record: *15 contests, 15 wins*

When Tszyu won the IBF light-welterweight title from Jake Rodriguez with a dazzling display in Las Vegas in January 1995, it seemed like a new megastar had appeared. Instead, promotional disputes limited the Russian to just one defence in 1995, and for a while it even looked as though the IBF would strip him for failing to meet their requirements.

Tszyu's amateur achievements

were staggering: 269 wins in 272 contests, a world championship, five Russian titles and two European championships. That kind of potential commands big money in the professional world, and Tszyu recognized that when he defected to Australia to turn pro with promoter Bill Mordey. His amateur pedigree was so impressive that, after only four fights, Mordey felt confident enough to match him with former WBC featherweight champion Juan LaPorte, whom he comfortably outpointed.

Sammy Fuentes, later to win the WBO title, was destroyed in a round and the veteran Livingston Bramble, once the WBA lightweight champion, was floored and outclassed over 10 rounds. Tszyu, who split from Mordey after becoming champion, looked unstoppable – but in his first title defence old pro Roger Mayweather took him the full distance.

Gene Tunney

Real name: *James Joseph Tunney*
Born: *New York, NY, May 25, 1897*
Titles: *American light-heavyweight champion 1922, 1923, world heavyweight champion 1926–28*
Record: *83 contests, 62 wins, 19 No Decisions, 1 No Contest, 1 defeat*

From the time Jack Dempsey became heavyweight champion in 1919, he was in Gene Tunney's sights. The former Marine, son of a comfortably off family from Greenwich Village, always aspired to the championship and turned professional with that in mind in 1915.

He was primarily a scientific boxer, but scored 42 inside-schedule wins in 77 fights. His career began in earnest on his return from service in France in 1919, and an unbeaten run of 22 qualified him to challenge Battling Levinsky for the American title. Tunney won comfortably, but then lost it to Harry Greb and took a fearful beating.

It was the only defeat of his career, and he subsequently trounced Greb twice in title fights and in two No Decision matches. But Dempsey was always the target, and when they met on a rainy afternoon in Philadelphia

TUNNEY *Thinking man's champion*

in September 1926, Tunney had his measure. He outpointed him again in the famous "Battle Of the Long Count", and defended the title only once more. He became a wealthy businessman and father of a US Senator. Tunney died at Greenwich, Connecticut on November 7, 1978.

Randolph Turpin

Born: *Leamington Spa, England, June 7, 1928*
Titles: *British middleweight champion 1950–54, European champion 1951–54, world champion 1951, Empire champion 1952–54, British light-heavyweight champion 1952, 1955, Empire champion 1952–55*
Record: *73 contests, 64 wins, 1 draw, 8 defeats*

For 64 glorious days in 1951, Randolph Turpin was a god. That was the duration of his reign as world middleweight champion, and he was never able to recapture that fleeting glory. He started boxing while working as a Navy cook, and won ABA titles in 1945 and 1946, following his two brothers into the professional ranks later that year.

His unorthodox style and powerful punches had brought him 40 wins in 43 fights (one draw) when, as British and European champion, he challenged the fabulous Sugar Ray Robinson before an 18,000 crowd in London on July 10, 1951. Robinson's

preparations had been casual, and he was soundly outpointed.

The rematch in New York drew 61,370 to watch Robinson, badly cut, stop Turpin in the 10th with a desperation attack. Turpin won the British and Empire light-heavyweight titles in 1953, and was outpointed in a dull fight by Carl "Bobo" Olson for the vacant middleweight title after Robinson's retirement. He lost his European title in a round to Tibero Mitri, but won a Lonsdale Belt outright before his retirement in 1958. His money long gone, he shot himself in Leamington on May 17, 1966.

Mike Tyson

see Legends of the Ring (pp 86–87)

Rodrigo Valdez

Born: *Bolivar, Colombia, December 22, 1946*
Titles: *WBC middleweight champion 1974–76, world champion 1977–78*
Record: *73 contests, 63 wins, 2 draws, 8 defeats*

Valdez would have made a fine world champion, had he not had the misfortune to be a contemporary of the superb Carlos Monzon. Instead, he was obliged to be content with a spell as WBC champion after Monzon was stripped for failing to defend against him, and a five-month reign as undisputed title-holder following the Argentinean's retirement.

Valdez won 23 of 27 fights in Colombia (two draws) before moving to America in 1969. He had some early setbacks, but entered the title picture in 1973 by outpointing the shaven-skulled Philadelphian Bennie Briscoe for the NABF title.

They met again for the vacant WBC title in May 1974, Valdez winning in seven rounds, and the Colombian retained the title four times. Monzon outscored him in a unification match in June 1976 and repeated the result a year later in his last fight, but Valdez snapped up the vacant title by beating Briscoe again. But he had little left, and Hugo Corro outpointed him in his first defence and then beat him again in a rematch. Valdez retired in 1980.

Pancho Villa

Real name: *Francisco Guilledo*
Born: *Illoilo, Philippines, August 1, 1901*
Titles: *American flyweight champion 1922–23, world champion 1923–25*
Record: *105 contests, 73 wins, 4 draws, 23 No Decisions, 5 defeats*

The busy little Filipino, who was taught to box by US military personnel, crammed 105 fights into a six-year career which began in 1919. He lost only twice in 56 fights before leaving for America in the spring of 1922, and promoter Tex Rickard developed the youngster into a major attraction even though he lost to Frankie Genaro in August 1922.

Villa won the American title by knocking out Johnny Buff and

PANCHO VILLA *was a busy battler*

retained it twice before Genaro beat him again. But Rickard kept faith, and persuaded world champion Jimmy Wilde – by then virtually retired – to face his protégé. Wilde was paid $65,000, a flyweight record, but took a pounding and was knocked out in seven rounds.

Villa made four successful defences, the one which gave him most pleasure being his defeat of Jose Sencio in Manila. Sadly, it was his last victory: in July 1925, two months after beating Sencio, Villa was outpointed over 10 rounds by Jimmy McLarnin. He had had a wisdom tooth extracted the previous afternoon, and an abscess developed. Blood poisoning ensued, and Vlila died in San Francisco on July 14, 1925

Joe Walcott

Born: *Barbados, March 13, 1873*
Titles: *World welterweight champion 1897–98, 1901–06*
Record: *134 contests, 69 wins, 18 draws, 21 No Decisions, 3 No Contests, 23 defeats*

One of the better early welterweight champions, Walcott stood only 5ft 1¹/₂in but routinely gave weight away to middleweights and even heavyweights during his 21 years in the ring. Known as the "Barbados Demon", he settled in Boston in 1887, where he boxed and wrestled as an amateur until his professional boxing debut in February 1890.

Boxing as a lightweight, he worked his way up to a match with champion George Lavigne, but lost their fight (which was made at two pounds over the championship limit) on a 12th-round retirement. He stepped up to welterweight, but was held to a draw and then outscored by

Mysterious Billy Smith, their second clash involving Smith's title. They met six times, and their fights were so dirty that Smith had to lodge a "good behaviour" bond of $250 before one of them.

Walcott finally became champion in 1901 when he stopped Rube Ferns, and he retained the title four times before Honey Mellody stopped him in 12 rounds in September 1906. He retired in 1911 and died in a car crash near Massillon, Ohio, on October 1935.

Jersey Joe Walcott

Real name: *Arnold Raymond Cream*
Born: *Merchantville, New Jersey, January 31, 1914*
Titles: *World heavyweight champion 1951–52*
Record: *(approx.) 69 contests, 50 wins, 1 draw, 18 defeats*

Walcott made his name in a spirited challenge for Joe Louis's heavyweight title in December 1947, but the fight almost did not happen. The New York Commission were so unimpressed by Walcott's record, which showed at least 10 defeats in a career stretching back to 1930, that they demanded the fight be billed merely as an exhibition, and only relented under pressure from the champion.

The Commission's attitude was unfair to the challenger, whose form on a comeback from a three-year lay-off between 1941 and 1944 included solid wins over some well-respected names. In fact, Walcott floored Louis twice in the contest, but lost an unpopular split decision.

That showing earned him three more title chances, one against Louis and two against Ezzard Charles. He was given yet another shot, in July 1951, and this time knocked Charles out in seven rounds to become, at 37, the oldest heavyweight champion. He retained the title against Charles, but then was knocked out by Rocky Marciano in the 13th after outboxing the challenger. When Marciano flattened him in a round in the return, Walcott retired. He later became New Jersey Commissioner, and died on February 26, 1994.

ROLE MODEL *Jersey Joe Walcott became world champion at the fifth attempt*

Mickey Walker

Real name: *Edward Patrick Walker*
Born: *Elizabeth, New Jersey, July 13, 1901*
Titles: *World welterweight champion 1922–26, world middleweight champion 1926–31*

Record: *163 contests, 94 wins, 4 draws, 45 No Decisions, 1 No Contest, 19 defeats*

Walker's ring style is conveyed by his nickname, "The Toy Bulldog". He was a relentless battler who loved to fight almost as much he enjoyed drinking and womanizing. He won world titles at welterweight and middleweight, fought twice for the light-heavyweight title, and drew with future heavyweight champion Jack Sharkey. He faced 15 world champions in a 163-fight career and married four women, three of them twice.

Walker took the welterweight title from veteran Jack Britton in November 1922, and made three defences before Pete Latzo outpointed him in May 1926. Joe Dundee knocked him out in eight rounds a few weeks later, prompting a move up to middleweight. He had already challenged Harry Greb in a famous 15-rounder for the middleweight title in July 1925, and he succeeded at the second attempt, outpointing Greb's conqueror Tiger Flowers.

He retained it three times, in between challenging for the light-heavyweight title, then relinquished the championship to box at heavyweight. His busy career ended in 1935, and he subsequently became an internationally known painter. He died at Freehold, New Jersey, on April 28, 1981.

Mike Weaver

Born: *Gatesville, Texas, June 14, 1952*
Titles: *WBA heavyweight champion 1980–82*
Record: *57 contests, 40 wins, 1 draw, 16 defeats*

Body-beautiful Weaver looked the part, but lacked the skill to go with his physique. However, the fights in which he won and lost the WBA heavyweight title were, for different reasons, unforgettable.

He started his career in California in 1972, losing three of his first four, but worked his way up and fought impressively before being stopped in the 12th by Larry Holmes in a 1979 bid for the WBC title. Challenging John Tate for the WBA version the following year, Weaver was trailing on points when, with less

than a minute left in the 15th and final round, he found one perfect punch to drop Tate face-first. He needed the same resilience to hang on to the title in a gruelling fight with Gerrie Coetzee but his other defence, against James Tillis, was less demanding.

He lost the title on perhaps the most controversial stoppage in heavyweight history, when the referee intervened after only 63 seconds, with Weaver in no great trouble, and gave the title to Mike Dokes. A rematch produced an equally unsatisfactory draw, but although Weaver boxed until 1995 he was never given another title chance.

Freddie Welsh

Real name: *Frederick Hall Thomas*
Born: *Pontypridd, Wales, March 5, 1886*
Titles: *European lightweight champion 1909–14, British lightweight champion 1909–11, 1912, Empire champion 1912, world champion 1914–17*
Record: *163 contests, 71 wins, 5 draws, 82 No Decisions, 5 defeats*

A sloppy MC was responsible for Freddie Thomas acquiring his ring name: he neglected to check the boy's name on his pro debut in Philadelphia and, hearing his accent, announced him as "Freddie Welsh". It stuck, and the clever-boxing Welsh soon became a star.

He won the British title from Johnny Summers in September 1909, a month after beating Henri Piet for the European title, and added the Empire championship by outpointing the Australian Hughie Mehegan in 1912. He also won a Lonsdale Belt outright by outpointing

Matt Wells, having put his second notch on it in a bitter clash with his great Welsh contemporary Jim Driscoll.

Wins over top contenders Leach Cross and Joe Rivers earned him a world title chance against Willie Ritchie, although by the time Ritchie had been paid there was virtually nothing left for the challenger. But Welsh won on points and then toured America, boxing mostly No Decision matches. He made only one official defence, and Benny Leonard claimed the title after knocking Welsh out in an overweight fight in May 1917. He died in New York, penniless, on July 29, 1927.

Pernell Whitaker

Born: *Norfolk, Virginia, January 2, 1964*
Titles: *IBF lightweight champion 1989–92, WBC champion 1989– 92, WBA champion 1990–92, IBF light-welterweight champion 1992–93, WBC welterweight champion 1993–, WBA light-middle-weight champion 1995*
Record: *39 contests, 37 wins, 1 draw, 1 defeat*

World titles at every weight from light-weight to light-middleweight mark Whitaker as one of the era's foremost stars. By the end of 1995 he had won 35 of his 37 fights, and the two decisions he failed to win – a points loss to Jose Luis Ramirez for the WBC light-weight title and a draw with Julio Cesar Chavez in defence of the WBC welterweight title – were considered to be gross injustices.

He was America's top amateur, turning professional after taking a gold medal in the 1984 Olympics. The Ramirez "loss" in March 1988 snapped his winning run at 15, but he soon got back on course by taking the IBF title from Greg Haugen, the WBC belt in a rematch with Ramirez, and then the WBA title, which he won on a first-round knockout of Juan Nazario.

He stepped up to win the IBF light-welter title from Rafael Pineda in July 1992, then took the WBC welterweight championship from Buddy

CLOWN PRINCE *Mickey Walker*

PERNELL WHITAKER *is not only multi-talented, but multi-titled*

McGirt. Whitaker completed the four-timer in March 1995 by outscoring Julio Cesar Vasquez for the WBA light-middleweight title – and immediately relinquished it to concentrate in the welterweight championship.

Jimmy Wilde

see Legends of the Ring (pp 88–89)

Jess Willard

Born: *Pottawatomie, Kansas, December 29, 1881*
Titles: *World heavyweight champion 1915–19*
Record: *35 contests, 23 wins, 1 draw, 5 No Decisions, 6 defeats*

Even by today's standards Willard would be considered a big heavyweight, standing 6ft 6½in tall and weighing around 230lb. By the standards of his time he was a giant. He was an exceptionally late starter, not having a fight until he was 29, but his sheer bulk was enough to intimidate most early opponents.

Significantly, though, he was unable to stop any of the higher-grade men he faced, like Gunboat Smith (who outpointed him). Perhaps because of his limitations, Jack Johnson selected him as his opponent in Havana in April 1915 in a fight scheduled for 45 rounds, the longest agreed distance under modern rules. In 103-degree heat, Willard lasted the pace better and Johnson was counted out in the 26th round. Johnson later claimed he had taken a dive, but this was never proven.

Willard was a poor champion: he boxed only once, a No Decision affair with Frank Moran, between winning the title and losing it to Jack Dempsey on July 4,

GALLANT *Jess Willard*

1919. Dempsey gave him a bad beating, but Willard's bravery was memorable. He died in Los Angeles on December 15, 1968.

Ike Williams

Real name: *Isiah Williams*
Born: *Brunswick, Georgia, August 2, 1923*
Titles: *NBA lightweight champion 1945–47, world champion 1947–51*
Record: *153 contests, 123 wins, 5 draws, 25 defeats*

Williams's family moved north when Ike was a boy, and he started boxing professionally at 16 under the co-management of the notorious Blinky Palermo. Fights were plentiful but progress was slow, and a shocking beating by Bob Montgomery, who pounded him for round after round before knocking him out in the 12th, was a real setback.

He rallied with a pair of wins over former champion Sammy Angott, and in April 1945 won the NBA lightweight title by knocking out the Mexican veteran Juan Zurita, who was having the last of his 130 fights. Williams defended it twice, against Enrique Bolanos in Los Angeles and Ronnie James in Cardiff. He then reunified the lightweight championship by beating his former conqueror Montgomery in six rounds.

Williams was a good champion, turning back five challengers before, drained by the effort of shedding 21 lb, he was stopped in the 14th by Jimmy Carter in May 1951. He moved up to welterweight, and retired in 1955 after knocking out another ex-champion, Beau Jack. He died in Los Angeles on September 5, 1994.

Howard Winstone

Born: *Merthyr Tydfil, Wales, April 15, 1939*
Titles: *British featherweight champion 1961–69, European champion 1963–66, WBC champion 1968*
Record: *67 contests, 61 wins, 6 defeats*

If Winstone had carried a worthwhile punch, it is doubtful if any featherweight in history could have beaten him. He had sublime skill, defensive artistry, a left jab of unerring accuracy and withering speed, but the loss of the tops of three fingers in an industrial accident meant that he could not punch his full weight. Despite the handicap, though, he stopped 27 of his 67 opponents.

A former Commonwealth Games and ABA champion, he raced to 34 consecutive wins, including three for the British title, before an obscure American, Leroy Jeffrey, shocked him in two rounds. Winstone put that behind him by winning a second Lonsdale Belt in record time in 1963, and added the European title in July that year.

The first of three wonderful world title challenges came in September 1965, when Vicente Saldivar scraped home on points in London, and Saldivar edged another epic in Cardiff two years later before stopping Winstone in 12 rounds of their third fight. The Mexican immediately retired, and Winstone stopped Mitsunori Seki for the vacant WBC title, which he lost in his first defence – and last fight – to Jose Legra.

Tim Witherspoon

Born: *Pontiac, Michigan, December 27, 1957*
Titles: *WBC heavyweight champion 1984, WBA champion 1986*
Record: *47 contests, 43 wins, 4 defeats*

Lack of dedication prevented this talented heavyweight from achieving his full potential, but he still captured both the WBC and WBA titles. His family settled in Philadelphia, where Witherspoon learned his boxing. He had his first pro fight in 1979, after only seven amateur contests of which he had won six. Before long he was beating good opponents like local rival Marvin Stinson, Alfonzo Ratliff (who later won the WBC cruiserweight title) and Renaldo Snipes.

Larry Holmes inflicted his first defeat in a desperately tough battle to retain the WBC title in May 1983, and when Holmes relinquished the title Witherspoon beat Greg Page for the vacant championship. It should have been the start of a worthwhile reign, but Witherspoon was unsettled by managerial problems and lost to Pinklon Thomas in his first defence.

He worked his way back to the WBA championship, outpointing Tony Tubbs in January 1986 and retaining it in a thriller against Frank Bruno, but then flopped again as Bonecrusher Smith stopped him in the first round. He was still campaigning as 1995 ended, hoping for another title chance after settling a protracted legal battle with Don King.

Ad Wolgast

Real name: *Adolphus Wolgust*
Born: *Cadillac, Michigan,
February 8, 1888*
Titles: *World lightweight champi-
on 1910–12*
Record: *133 contests, 59 wins,
13 draws, 50 No Decisions,
11 defeats*

A lightwieght of legendary ferocity and endurance, Wolgast paid a dreadful price for his hit-or-be-hit style: he became punch-drunk, and was confined to a sanatorium for many years before his death in 1955. Of German extraction, Wolgast had lost only once in 69 fights when he challenged Battling Nelson, the Durable Dane, for the world title in February 1910. They were due to go 45 rounds, but at the end of the 40th Nelson was in such bad shape that the referee stopped the fight.

Wolgast figured in another extraordinary championship fight, against Mexican Joe Rivers at Vernon, California on July 4, 1912. In the 13th round of a gruelling battle they landed simultaneous rights, and both went down. The referee, Jack Welch, started counting, then when it became obvious that neither could rise in time he tucked the champion under his arm and supported him while he counted Rivers out, justifying his action on the grounds that Wolgast's punch had landed first.

Wolgast lost the title on disqualification to Willie Ritchie in 1912, and retired in 1920. He died at Camarillo, California on April 14, 1955.

Tony Zale

Real name: *Anthony Florian
Zaleski*
Born: *Gary, Indiana, May 29, 1913*
Titles: *NBA middleweight
champion 1940–41, world
champion 1941–47, 1948*
Record: *87 contests, 67 wins,
2 draws, 18 defeats*

Zale lost the best four years of his career after joining the US Army in 1942, shortly after becoming middleweight champion, yet the fights which earned him boxing immortality all occurred after his return to the ring. He turned pro in 1934 to supplement his pay at a steel mill, but lost nine times in 29 fights and took a long break, returning in 1937.

This time, he made better progress. A non-title win over NBA champion Al Hostak in January 1940 earned him a rematch for the title in July, and Zale won in 13 rounds. He defended it twice, then outpointed Georgie Abrams to become undisputed champion in 1941 and after one more fight, a points loss to Billy Conn, he joined the Forces.

He faced Graziano for the first time in September 1946, winning a wild battle in six rounds, but was knocked out by the New Yorker in the rematch, also in six rounds, before Zale settled the series with a third-round win. He lost the title in his next fight to Marcel Cerdan, and immediately retired.

Hilario Zapata

Born: *Panama City, Panama,
August 19, 1958*
Titles: *WBC light-flyweight
champion 1980–82, 1982–83,
WBA flyweight champion
1985–87*
Record: *54 contests, 43 wins, 1 draw,
10 defeats*

The fast and stylish Panamanian compiled an impressive championship record: he won 17 and drew one of the 23 world title fights he contested.

He was beaten by Alfonso Lopez, challenging for the Latin American title in his seventh professional fight, but a win over former champion Freddie Castle in June 1979 brought him a trip to Tokyo where he dethroned WBC champion Shigeo Nakajima. He risked his title four times in 1980 and four more in 1981, boxing in Japan, Korea, Venezuela, Panama and America, but then lost it two rounds to the Mexican Amado Ursua in February 1982. But he was champion again before the end of the year, outpointing Tadashi Tomori in Japan.

Zapata won and lost in defences against Jung Koo-Chang, an outstanding champion, and moved up to flyweight. Santos Laciar foiled his first attempt on the WBA title, but he won the vacant championship when the Argentinean retired and retained it five times, eventually losing it to Fidel Bassa, with whom he drew in a rematch. Sung-Kil Moon knocked him out in a round in his final fight, a bid for the WBC super-flyweight crown in 1993.

Carlos Zarate

Born: *Tepito, Mexico, May 23, 1951*
Titles: *WBC bantamweight
champion 1976–79*
Record: *65 contests, 61 wins,
4 defeats*

It would have been a brave man who would have picked a winner between Carlos Zarate and Ruben Olivares, the two hardest-punching bantamweights in history, if they had met in their respective primes. Zarate's phenomenal record showed four losses in 65 fights, with three of the defeats coming in bids for the super-bantamweight championship and the other a split decision which cost him his bantamweight title against Lupe Pintor. And of Zarate's 61 career victories, 58 of them came inside the distance.

When Zarate knocked out his fellow-countryman Rodolfo Martinez in five rounds in May 1976 to win the WBC title, it was his 39th inside the distance win in 40 fights. Only Victor Martinez had heard the final bell in his first 24 fights, and he stopped his next 28 opponents. Zarate defended his title nine times against challengers from four continents – truly a world champion.

He stepped out of his division to challenge the brilliant Wilfredo Gomez for the WBC super-bantamweight title in 1978, but was stopped in five rounds. Subsequent challenges against Jeff Fenech and Daniel Zaragoza, who beat him for the vacant title, also failed and he retired after the Zaragoza fight.

Fritzie Zivic

Born: *Pittsburgh, Pennsylvania,
May 8, 1913*
Titles: *World welterweight
champion 1940–41*
Record: *232 contests, 157 wins,
10 draws, 65 defeats*

In any poll to find the dirtiest fighter in history, Zivic would come near the top. "Kids today think the laces are for tying up the gloves", he remarked once when asked his views on the current, more gentlemanly breed. Despite his reputation he was never disqualified in his 18-year, 232-fight career, but perhaps he always took his own advice: "Always work the ref's blind side."

One of five boxing brothers, Zivic averaged 18 fights a year between 1933 and 1946. He was already a grizzled veteran when he finally got a title chance, against Henry Armstrong in October 1940. It was Armstrong's eighth defence that year, and Zivic gave him a bad beating, closing both his eyes and flooring him for the first time in 26 title bouts with the last punch of the fight. The rematch drew 23,306 New York fans to watch Armstrong take another brutal pounding before being stopped in the 12th round.

Zivic lost the title in his next defence to Freddie Cochrane, an 8–1 outsider with 30 defeats on his record, but he did not retire until 1949, by which time he had faced 12 world champions.

THE LEGENDS OF THE RING

Fine champions like Wilfred Benitez, Carmen Basilio and Iran Barkley can win titles at more than one weight, but they still fail to attain that elusive and indefinable status of "legend". Others, such as Julio Cesar Chavez and Larry Holmes, can build long winning runs or, like Riddick Bowe and Evander Holyfield, earn prodigious amounts of money yet lack the mystique which separates the truly great from the very good. Any list of boxing legends must be arbitrary and personal, but the men featured here are surely very close to automatic selections. They bridge the decades and exemplify vastly different styles of boxing, but they are each landmark figures in the development and history of professional boxing.

MUHAMMAD ALI

The most graceful, original and entertaining heavyweight champion of them all, Ali revolutionized boxing in the 1960s and rewrote the history books by winning the title three times between 1964 and 1978. The impossible was his speciality and the standards he set will probably never be surpassed.

HENRY ARMSTRONG

Armstrong's claim to fame is unique: he was the only man in history to hold championships simultaneously at three different weights, a feat which modern regulations would not permit. His battles with Barney Ross, Lou Ambers and Fritzie Zivic are classics of the ring.

JACK DEMPSEY

The Manassa Mauler became a byword for ferocity, his ring style rooted in his hard and hungry teenage days when he battled in saloons and mining camps for a dollar. He went on to personify the Roaring Twenties, become the game's first million-dollar attraction and remain its most enduring symbol.

ROBERTO DURAN

Arguably the greatest lightweight the sport has seen, Duran moved on to win world titles at welterweight, light-middleweight and middleweight in a fabulous career which began in 1967 and was still going in 1996. He is the ultimate warrior, who fights for money but relishes the thrill of combat almost as much.

JOE LOUIS

Louis was one of that rare breed of athletes who transcend their sport to become figures of true international significance. He held the heavyweight title longer than anyone else, made a record number of defences, and became an icon and an inspiration for American blacks.

JOHN L. SULLIVAN

The last of the bare-knuckle champions, Sullivan gloried in the public image of him as a hard-drinking brawler, the toughest man in the saloon. It was an accurate portrayal of a hero from the gaslight and hansom cab age, a pivotal figure in boxing's development as a major sport.

JACK JOHNSON

In his time he was the most hated man in sport, perhaps even in the whole of American society, but by the sheer weight of his talent Johnson forced his way to the top despite every obstacle. He was the first black heavyweight champion, the forerunner of Muhammad Ali in style as well as spirit.

ROCKY MARCIANO

He was crude, stocky and unskilled – yet nobody beat Rocky Marciano in 49 fights. He had two natural assets: unlimited courage and a thunderous right, and they carried him to the heavyweight championship. He retired in his prime, the only heavyweight champion with a perfect record.

MIKE TYSON

In the second half of the 1980s, Mike Tyson was unbeatable. The youngest heavyweight champion in history, he swept contenders aside with an arrogant ease not seen since the prime of Joe Louis. But then it all went horribly wrong, inside and outside the ring, in an unparalleled fall from grace.

SUGAR RAY LEONARD

Leonard had a huge ego, but ability to match. He was world champion at five weights, from welter to light-heavy inclusive, and he beat magnificent champions like Marvin Hagler, Roberto Duran and Thomas Hearns. There have been few tougher ways to earn that "legend" status.

SUGAR RAY ROBINSON

Robinson was the real Sugar Ray, the original and best. His era spanned 25 years and 202 fights. He was welterweight champion for six years, and held the middleweight title five times. The Sugarman had style, glamour, charisma and class, and 14 of his victims were world champions.

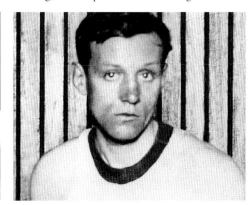

JIMMY WILDE

Wilde was the man who proved, once and for all, that size doesn't matter. He never scaled more than 102 lb in his fighting prime, yet 101 of his 151 opponents failed to last the distance with this fierce-punching little Welshman, whose championship career stretched from 1914 to 1923.

ALI

> **" I'm so fast I can hit the light switch and be in bed before it's dark."**
>
> *Ali, in his glorious prime.*

"GET UP, YOU BUM" – *Muhammad Ali taunts Sonny Liston after his first round "phantom punch" ended their world title rematch*

FLOATED LIKE A BUTTERFLY … STUNG LIKE A BEE

Muhammad Ali transcended sport. In purely boxing terms he was the most original and creative performer of his time, perhaps of all time, but his impact on the wider world was immense. He became a symbol of black pride, just as Joe Louis had been in the 1930s, and through his opposition to the Vietnam War, and the principled (and expensive) stand he took against it, he pricked America's conscience and contributed significantly towards the war's end.

In his own country he has been loved and hated in equal measure, depending on the observer's colour and political leanings. But in Europe, and particularly in Britain, he has been a hero since he first exploded into our consciousness at the 1960 Rome Olympics, and the affection he has inspired is closer to real love than any other sportsman has known.

Boxing was in trouble when Ali – then known by his "slave name" Cassius Clay – came along. The small fight clubs which were the game's breeding ground had virtually gone out of business across America, and the major TV networks were not interested in promoting a sport which, only a few years previously, the Kefauver Commission inquiry into organized crime had shown to be riddled with corruption. Ali changed all that, taking the sport by the scruff of the neck and slapping it back into life with his outrageous mixture of bombast, comedy, innovation and, most of all, sublime and God-given talent. It took nerve to make the kind of boasts in which he specialized but it took genius to make them come true, time after time.

At first, he played by white society's rules, even if privately he seethed, to the point where he threw his Olympic medal into a river in disgust after being refused service in a Southern diner a couple of weeks after his return from Rome. He signed with a consortium of white Kentucky businessmen, who engaged the respected trainer Angelo Dundee to work with him and select the opponents. Dundee, shrewdly, did not seek to impose conventional wisdom on such a free spirit. Instead he took Ali's strengths and polished them to perfection, producing a superbly conditioned athlete whose grace and speed brought a whole new dimension to the sport.

Clay/Ali rewrote the textbooks with his hands-dangling, dancing style, and as he began to trounce men of significant reputation, the feeling grew that he was something special. He came off the floor to beat Henry Cooper, then took on the most feared heavyweight champion for years: the brooding, bullying Sonny Liston. Few gave Clay a chance, but Liston was bamboozled by the youngster's quicksilver attacks and retired, claiming a damaged shoulder, after six rounds. In the rematch, Liston went down and out in the first round from an unconvincing punch. The unsatisfactory nature of both fights helped turn American opinion against the new champion, especially when he announced that he had become a Muslim and changed his name.

He proved to be a truly international champion, defending the title three times in Europe, once in Canada and five times in the US as he battled conscription on the memorable grounds that "I ain't got no quarrel with them Viet Cong." It was a fight he could not win, given the climate of the times, and when he was convicted the sport's governing bodies quickly

READY TO RUMBLE … *Ali prepares to face Henry Cooper in 1966*

disowned him. It took him three years to get his boxing licence back, during which time the majority of his compatriots came to share his opposition to the war.

Joe Frazier foiled his first attempt to regain the title, flooring and outpointing him in a 1971 classic, but Ali kept going and, in 1974, stunned the world when he knocked out the supposedly invincible George Foreman in Zaire. He reigned for three years and 10 defences, then took Leon Spinks too lightly and was outpointed in February 1978. He put that right seven months later, and promptly retired. Financial pressures forced him back in October 1980 to challenge Larry Holmes, who pleaded with him to quit until Angelo Dundee signalled the finish after 10 rounds.

There was one last, pathetic defeat by Trevor Berbick a year later, and then began the long, slow descent into illness and infirmity. How cruel that the game to which he gave so much should, in the end, have demanded so high a price from him.

MUHAMMAD ALI

BORN: January 17, 1942
Louisville, Kentucky

WORLD TITLE FIGHTS:

Feb 25, 1964, w ret 7
Sonny Liston, Miami Beach, FL

May 25, 1965, w ko 1
Sonny Liston, Lewiston, ME

Nov 22, 1965, w rsf 12
Floyd Patterson, Las Vegas, NV

Mar 29, 1966, w pts 15
George Chuvalo, Toronto (Can)

May 21, 1966, w rsf 6
Henry Cooper, London (Eng)

Aug 6, 1966, w ko 3
Brian London, London (Eng)

Sep 10, 1966, w rsf 12
Karl Mildenberger, Frankfurt (Ger)

Nov 14, 1966, w rsf 3
Cleveland Williams, Houston, TX

Feb 6, 1967, w pts 15
Ernie Terrell, Houston, TX
(undisputed)

Mar 22, 1967, w ko 7
Zora Folley, New York, NY

Mar 8, 1971, l pts 15
Joe Frazier, New York, NY

Oct 30, 1974, w ko 8
George Foreman, Kinshasa (Zai)

Mar 24, 1975, w rsf 15
Chuck Wepner, Cleveland, OH

May 16, 1975, w rsf 11
Ron Lyle, Las Vegas, NV

Jul 1, w pts 15
Joe Bugner, Kuala Lumpur (Mal)

Oct 1, 1975, w ret 14
Joe Frazier, Manila (Phi)

Feb 20, 1976, w ko 5
Jean Pierre Coopman, San Juan (PR)

Apr 30, 1976, w pts 15
Jimmy Young, Landover, MD

May 24, 1976, w rsf 5
Richard Dunn, Munich (Ger)

Sep 28, 1976, w pts 15
Ken Norton, New York, NY

May 16, 1977, w pts 15
Alfredo Evangelista, Landover, MD

Sep 29, 1977, w pts 15
Earnie Shavers, New York, NY

Feb 15, 1978, l pts 15
Leon Spinks, Las Vegas, NV

Sep 15, 1978, w pts 15
Leon Spinks, New Orleans, LA (WBA)

Oct 2, 1980, l ret 11
Larry Holmes, Las Vegas, NV (WBC)

OVERALL RECORD:

61 contests
56 wins
5 defeats

ARMSTRONG

TRIPLE HITTER *Henry Armstrong's record is unmatched*

THE HURRICANE THAT STRUCK THRICE

Can you imagine Naseem Hamed, weighing 126 lb, defeating light-weight champion Oscar De La Hoya and welterweight king Pernell Whitaker – and then fighting a draw with Quincy Taylor for the middle-weight championship? Hamed may consider the feat well within his scope, but the rest of us would laugh at the absurdity of the notion. Yet that was what Henry Armstrong achieved in 1937–40, when he won world titles at featherweight, light-weight and welterweight and fought a draw with Ceferino Garcia for a ver-sion of the middleweight title. Even more remarkably, he won his three titles within a span of ten months, and for four glorious months in 1938 he held them simultaneously, some-thing which can no longer happen under modern regulations.

Armstrong's real name was Henry Jackson, and like so many great cham-pions he was born (on December 12, 1912) into appalling poverty, the youngest of 11 children. When he was four, the family moved north to St Louis after the local cotton crop failed, and his obsession with boxing began when he surprised himself with his perfor-mance in a playground fight at school.

After the briefest of amateur careers he turned professional under

ON THE BUTTON *B. Ross takes a right*

the name "Mellody Jackson", in trib-ute to the old welterweight champion Honey Mellody, but made a dismal start as he lost three of his first four fights. He rode the rails west to California, basing himself in Los Angeles where he re-entered the ama-teur ranks under the name he would make immortal – Henry Armstrong. The prodigious work-rate which was a feature of his later career was already in evidence: he travelled the length of California, sometimes boxing three or four times a week. In 1931, he was undefeated in 85 contests, 66 of them won inside the distance. His heart-rate was unusually slow, which allowed him to maintain a pace which would have been beyond normal fighters.

When he relaunched his pro career, his non-stop style brought him the nickname "Hurricane Hank", and he quickly built a large following. In August 1935 he was matched with Baby Arizmendi for the Californian version of the world featherweight title, but the cagey Mexican was too experienced for him and won on

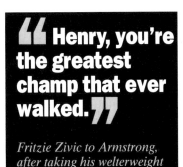
" **Henry, you're the greatest champ that ever walked.** "

Fritzie Zivic to Armstrong, after taking his welterweight title in January 1941.

points. Armstrong reversed the result the following year, but his claim was not taken seriously outside California – although knockouts of champions Mike Belloise and Benny Bass showed that he belonged in championship class. In October 1937, he won the "real" featherweight title in six rounds from Petey Sarron, but never defended it.

Weight was becoming a problem, but instead of making the obvious move, from featherweight to light-weight, he skipped to welterweight and pounded champion Barney Ross into retirement, giving him a bad points beating. Three months later he was a triple champion, outpointing Lou Ambers in a fierce battle to take the lightweight crown. Ambers regained the lightweight title in

August 1939, and Armstrong con-centrated on defending his welter-weight championship, which he did with amazing frequency. The inde-fatigable Armstrong found time to fit in a middleweight title challenge in March 1940, battling to a 10-rounds draw with Ceferino Garcia, whom he had already beaten in a welterweight defence. But the fighting machine was slowly winding down, and he finally lost the welterweight title in his sev-enth defence of the year in 1940, when Fritzie Zivic battered him for 15 rounds and then stopped him in 12 in a rematch.

He had the last of his 181 fights in February 1945 and, in retirement, successfully battled alcoholism and became a Baptist minister. He died in Los Angeles in October 1988.

HENRY ARMSTRONG

BORN: December 12, 1912
Columbus, Mississippi

WORLD TITLE FIGHTS:
Oct 29, 1937, w ko 6
Petey Sarron, New York, NY
(featherweight)

May 31, 1938, w pts 15
Barney Ross, Long Island, NY
(welterweight)

Aug 17, 1938, w pts 15
Lou Ambers, New York, NY (lightweight)

Nov 25, 1938, w pts 15
Ceferino Garcia, New York, NY
(welterweight)

Dec 5, 1938, w rsf 3
Al Manfredo, Cleveland, OH
(welterweight)

Jan 10, 1939, w pts 10
Baby Arizmendi, Los Angeles, LA
(welterweight)

Mar 4, 1939, w rsf 4
Bobby Pacho, Havana (Cub)
(welterweight)

Mar 16, 1939, w ko 1
Lew Feldman, St Louis, MO
(welterweight)

Mar 31, 1939, w ko 12
Davey Day, New York, NY (welterweight)

May 25, 1939, w pts 15
Ernie Roderick, London (Eng)
(welterweight)

Aug 22, 1939, l pts 15
Lou Ambers, New York, NY (lightweight)

Oct 9, 1939, w rsf 4
Al Manfredo, Des Moines, IA
(welterweight)

Oct 13, 1939, w ko 2
Howard Scott, Minneapolis, MN
(welterweight)

Oct 20, 1939, w ko 3
Ritchie Fontaine, Seattle, WA
(welterweight)

Oct 24, 1939, w pts 10
Jimmy Garrison, Los Angeles, CA
(welterweight)

Oct 30, 1939, w rsf 4
Bobby Pacho, Denver, CO
(welterweight)

Dec 11, 1939, w ko 7
Jimmy Garrison, Cleveland, OH
(welterweight)

Jan 4, 1940, w ko 5
Joe Ghnouly, St Louis, MO (welterweight)

Jan 24, 1940, w rsf 9
Pedro Montanez, New York, NY
(welterweight)

Mar 1, 1940, drew 10
Ceferino Garcia, Los Angeles, CA
(middleweight)

(remainder all for welterweight title)
Apr 26, 1940, w rsf 7
Paul Junior, Boston, MA

May 24, 1940, w rsf 5
Ralph Zanelli, Boston, MA

Jun 21, 1940, w rsf 3
Paul Junior, Portland, ME

Sep 23, 1940, w ko 4
Phil Furr, Washington, DC

Oct 4, 1940, l pts 15
Fritzie Zivic, New York, NY

Jan 17, 1941, l rsf 12
Fritzie Zivic, New York, NY

OVERALL RECORD:
181 contests
152 wins
8 draws
21 defeats

DEMPSEY

JACK DEMPSEY *(behind) gave Jess Willard a fierce beating and took his title when Willard quit after three rounds*

THE MAULER WITH A KNOCKOUT PUNCH

Nobody remembers William Harrison Dempsey, but the whole world knows Jack Dempsey. He became part of the fabric of the twentieth century, an original All-American hero whose progress from the hobo camps to the heavyweight championship inspired generations to rise above their background and environment. He won the title with a brand of ferocity and aggression which had rarely been seen before, and his colourful personality – and fondness for pretty women – perfectly captured the spirit of the Roaring Twenties.

He was one of nine children, born in Manassa, Colorado on 24 June, 1895, to parents of exotically mixed ancestry: Irish, Scots, and Native American genes all went into the make-up of this formidable fighting man. His brother Bernie was a part-time professional boxer, taking the name "Jack Dempsey" after the famous middleweight champion, "Nonpareil" Jack. When William was old enough he started boxing as "Young Dempsey" until Bernie retired and he could take over the "Jack Dempsey" name.

Ring earnings were minimal, as he was fighting mainly in bare-knuckle matches in saloons for a share of the gambling winnings. Like thousands of his poor or dispossessed compatriots, he rode the rails across America seeking employment, sleeping in rough-

> ## " When I started I was really bad, and I never got any better. "
>
> *Dempsey, tongue in cheek.*

and-ready "hobo camps" alongside railway tracks and, when he could, working in mining and timber camps.

He had virtually abandoned hope of making a living in the ring, and was working in a Seattle shipyard when news came that one of his brothers had died. Jack accepted another fight to pay for the funeral expenses, and this time he took it seriously. His formal career began in 1914, when he earned $3.50 for his first fight, but he did not break into the big-time until 1918, under the management of the shrewd Jack "Doc" Kearns. He boxed 21 times that year with only one defeat, to "Fat Willie" Meehan, whom Dempsey managed to beat just once in five meetings.

Doc Kearns eventually manoeuvred him into a world title fight with the giant Jess Willard at Toledo on July 4, 1919, confident that his man's ferocious punching would be too much for a champion who had not boxed competitively for over three years. Of Dempsey's previous 26 contests, all but three had ended inside six rounds, and an astonishing 17 had finished in the first. Kearns bet the challenger's entire purse on a first-round win, and Dempsey did his best to oblige. He floored Willard – who outweighed him by 56 lb – seven times in the first round, but the champion's courage kept him going until the third.

Dempsey's reign began well, with three defences in 10 months including boxing's first million-dollar gate, his epic encounter with

Georges Carpentier. But then his pace slowed appreciably, and he did not box again until 1923. The small town of Shelby, Montana, venue for his points win over Tommy Gibbons, was virtually bankrupted when its leading citizens bankrolled the flop, but nobody asked for their money back after his thrilling second-round defeat of Luis Firpo. Dempsey battered the challenger unmercifully, flooring him seven times in the first round before being knocked clean out of the ring in the second. He climbed back, aided by ringside reporters, and promptly flattened Firpo.

That fight was in September 1923, and he was not in serious action again until he

JACK DEMPSEY

BORN: June 24, 1895
Manassa, Colorado

WORLD TITLE FIGHTS:
Jul 4, 1919, w ret 3
Jess Willard, Toledo, OH

Sep 6, 1920, w ko 3
Billy Miske, Benton Harbor, MI

Dec 14, 1920, w ko 12
Bill Brennan, New York, NY

Jul 2, 1921, w ko 4
Georges Carpentier, Jersey City, NJ

Jul 4, 1923, w pts 15
Tommy Gibbons, Shelby, MT

Sep 14, 1923, w ko 2
Luis Angel Firpo, New York, NY

Sep 23, 1926, l pts 10
Gene Tunney, Philadelphia, PA

Sep 22, 1927, l pts 10
Gene Tunney, Chicago, IL

OVERALL RECORD:
79 contests
59 wins
8 draws
6 no decisions
6 defeats

faced Gene Tunney three years later. They fought in driving rain in Philadelphia, and Tunney comfortably outboxed him over 10 rounds. The return, over the same distance in Chicago 364 days later, was the famous "Battle Of The Long Count", in which Dempsey floored Tunney but the referee, Dave Barry, refused to take up the count until he had gone to a neutral corner. Tunney got up within Barry's count of 10, and won a deserved decision.

It was Dempsey's last fight, and the fifth time he had drawn a million-dollar gate. He had brought boxing from the backwoods into mainstream American life, and taken the sport onto a financial plane which would have been unimaginable only a decade earlier.

Dempsey opened a landmark bar/restaurant in New York after his retirement, but had to close it in the 1970s when the owner of the site, who wanted to redevelop it, took out a compulsory purchase order. The owner, it transpired, was Queen Elizabeth, who can thus claim to be the only woman to have knocked out Jack Dempsey. The old champion died on May 31, 1983.

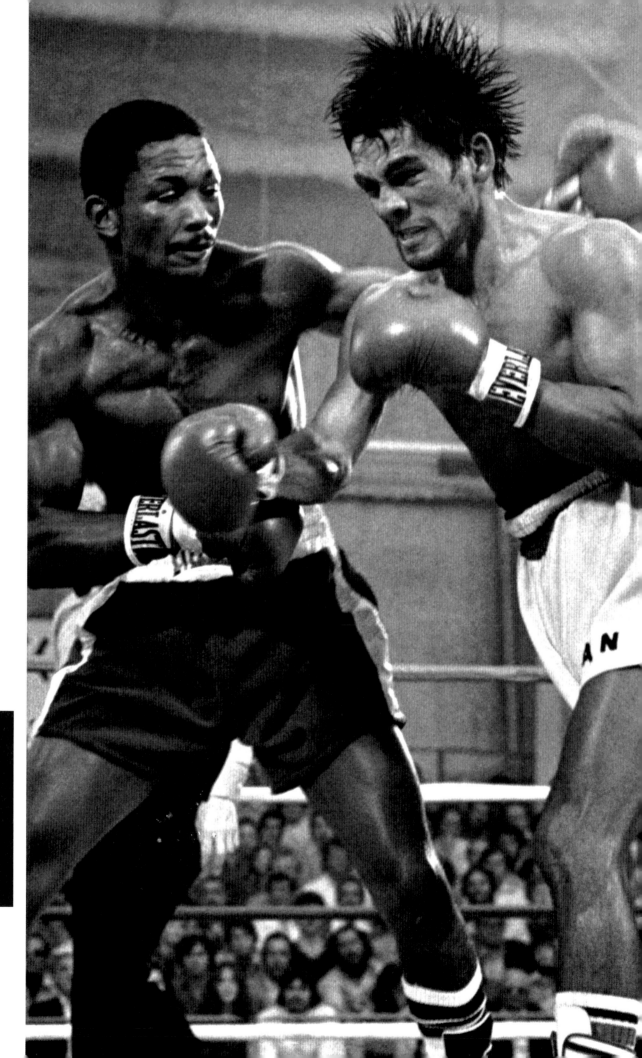

DURAN

> **❝ There's no boxer in the world that doesn't fight for money. ❞**
>
> *Roberto Duran, on his motivation.*

SWEET REVENGE *Roberto Duran (right), ko's Esteban DeJesus, the first man to beat him*

FEROCIOUS SCRAPPER FROM PANAMA

A week before Christmas 1995, Roberto Duran – *Manos de Piedra*, "Hands of Stone" – scored the 97th win of a fabulous career which began 28 years previously. The swashbuckling Panamanian, at 44, is still the pure fighting animal, who loves the thrill of combat the way other men love sex, or drugs. His contemporaries, the men he was destroying in lightweight title fights more than 20 years earlier, have long since retired: some, like the ill-fated Esteban DeJesus, are dead. But Duran fights on, still driven by his demons, and by his dream that, against all logic and evidence, the good times will come back and he will be a champion again.

And they were good times. By any standards, Duran rates with the all-time best, at any weight: four world titles, each of them won from an outstanding champion, prove his worth.

He personified the hungry fighter, clawing his way up from grinding poverty to financial security in the only way that was open to a *cholo*, a youngster of mixed Indian and Spanish blood. He was born in Guarare on 16 June 1951 and grew up in Chorillo, a disease-ridden slum on the east side of the Panama Canal. His father had long since absconded, leaving his wife to raise their nine children alone. By the time he was 13, Duran's schooling, such as it was, had ended and he was hustling money any way he could to support his family,

He even stole fruit from an orchard owned by Carlos Eleta, who ironically was later to become his manager. At 14, Roberto dabbled in amateur boxing, but after winning 13 of his 16 fights, he decided that he might as well be paid for doing what he enjoyed so much. His sheer ferocity in the professional ring was enough to intimidate his early opponents, and he breezed through 21 wins (16 by knockout) before Eleta became involved. The wealthy landowner bought his contract for a derisory $300,

ROBERTO DURAN

BORN: June 16, 1951
Guarare, Panama

WORLD TITLE FIGHTS:
Jun 26, 1972, w rsf 13
Ken Buchanan, New York, NY (WBA lightweight)

Jan 20, 1973, w ko 5
Jimmy Robertson, Panama City (Pan)

Jun 2, 1973, w rsf 8
Hector Thompson, Panama City (Pan)

Sep 8, 1973, w rsf 10
Ishimatsu Susuki, Panama City (Pan)

Mar 16, 1974, w ko 11
Esteban DeJesus, Panama City (Pan)

Dec 21, 1974, w rsf 1
Masataka Takayama, San Jose, CA

Mar 2, 1975, w ko 14
Ray Lampkin, Panama City (Pan)

Dec 14, 1975, w ko 15
Leoncio Ortiz, San Juan (PR)

May 22, 1976, w ko 14
Lou Bizzaro, Erie, PA

Oct 15, 1976, w ko 1
Alvaro Rojas, Hollywood, FL

Jan 29, 1977, w ko 13
Vilomar Fernandez, Miami Beach, FL

Sep 17, 1977, w pts 15
Edwin Viruet, Philadelphia, PA

Jan 21, 1978, w ko 12
Esteban DeJesus, Las Vegas, NV (undisputed lightweight)

Jun 20, 1980, w pts 15
Sugar Ray Leonard, Montreal (Can) (WBC welterweight)

Nov 25, 1980, l ret 8
Sugar Ray Leonard, New Orleans, NV (WBC welterweight)

Jan 30, 1982, l pts 15
Wilfred Benitez, Las Vegas, NV (WBC light-middleweight)

Jun 16, 1983, w rsf 8
Davey Moore, New York, NY (WBA light-middleweight)

Nov 10, 1983, l pts 15
Marvin Hagler, Las Vegas, NV (undisputed middleweight)

Jun 15, 1984, l ko 2
Thomas Hearns, Las Vegas, NV (WBC light-middleweight)

Feb 24, 1989, w pts 15
Iran Barkley, Atlantic City, NJ (WBC middleweight)

Dec 7, 1989, L pts 12
Sugar Ray Leonard, Las Vegas, NV (WBC super-middleweight)

OVERALL RECORD:
108 contests
97 wins
11 defeats

HANDS OF STONE *Duran prepares for his 1986 encounter with Robbie Sims*

and then made the smartest move of all when he hired Ray Arcel and Freddie Brown, two of the game's legendary trainers, and between them they honed and polished Duran's raw talent.

In his 29th fight, 10 days after his 21st birthday, he faced WBA champion Ken Buchanan in Madison Square Garden, and won the title in a fight which illustrated his strengths as well as his dark side. He went on to equal the record for lightweight title defences, earning undisputed recognition in the 12th and last by knocking out Esteban DeJesus, the only man to have beaten him in 64 fights.

Increasing weight forced him to step up to welterweight, and he dethroned champion Ray Leonard in a memorable 15-rounder in June 1980. It was perhaps Duran's finest performance, yet in the rematch three months later he abruptly quit. His fighting reputation was in tatters, but he redeemed it on his 32nd birthday by stopping Davey Moore for the WBA light-middleweight title and then going the full 15 with Marvin Hagler in a middleweight title bid.

Ever unpredictable, Duran was flattened in two rounds by Thomas Hearns next time out, and when he lost again to the modestly talented Robbie Sims (Hagler's half-brother) there seemed no way back. But this astonishing old warhorse had one great victory left. In February 1989, he took on the fearsome Iran Barkley, and outsmarted him in a spell-binding fight for the WBC middleweight title.

His career since then has slipped into a pattern, a string of inconsequential wins building up to a match against a top-grade opponent, who outpoints him. He still draws the crowds, even if they know that they are seeing only the shadow of what he once was. But the old boy always gives value, even in defeat. He is a warrior, neither knowing nor wanting any other trade.

JOHNSON

JACK JOHNSON *(right) went to his grave insisting he threw this 1915 fight against Jess Willard*

CRUSHER OF "GREAT WHITE HOPES"

With the possible exception of Primo Carnera, whose ascent to the title was shamelessly stage-managed, nobody has found it easy to become heavyweight champion of the world. Yet for Jack Johnson, the road was hardest of all.

He was a supremely gifted boxer, one of the handful from that era whose talent still shines through those flickering black-and-white images, yet because of his colour it took him 11 long years to be given the chance to prove himself. To become champion he had to chase the title-holder halfway around the world, finally catching up with him in Australia, and was then obliged to endure a campaign of hatred and vilification which defies the imagination of those born into more liberal times. In the end, he claimed, he was tricked into surrendering his title to a white man in exchange for the dropping of a prosecution which should never have been brought in the first place.

His long journey began in Galveston, Texas, where he was born on March 31, 1878 and where he started fighting for fun at 13 while working as a docker. He had his first professional fight in 1897, and over the next few years built a local reputation despite a third-round loss to the veteran Joe Choynski in 1901. Black vs white matches were not encouraged, unless the outcome was pre-

arranged, so the top black boxers tended to fight each other, over and over again.

Johnson joined that circuit, becoming recognized as the "Negro heavyweight champion" after beating Denver Ed Martin in 1903. He took them all on: Sam Langford, Black Bill, Joe Jeanette, Sam McVey, Frank Childs and a host of other, long-forgotten men who deserved a better deal. Yet despite his own difficulties, Johnson never tried to make life easier for other black fighters after he had become champion. "I won't box any of those coloured boys now", he was quoted as saying to an interviewer in 1913. "I have had a hard time to get a chance. I gave Langford, Jeanette and those boys a chance before I was champ. I'll retire still the only coloured heavyweight champion."

It was a hopeless ambition for him to entertain in those early years, when the "colour bar" raised by John L. Sullivan stayed firmly up. But gradually, as he began to beat white contenders like Jack Monroe, Bill Lang, Bob Fitzsimmons and Fireman Jim Flynn, the boxing world was forced to face up to the unpalatable fact that he would have to be accommodated, sooner or later.

He was kept waiting for as long as possible. Champions came and went; James J. Jeffries, Marvin Hart (who outscored Johnson in 1905) and Tommy Burns all had their day, and in the end it was Burns, the smallest

heavyweight champion in history, who agreed to take him on after Johnson had pursued him across America, on to England and finally to Australia. They met at Rushcutter's Bay, Sydney on December 26, 1908, and Johnson made Burns pay for every moment of frustration and discrimination he had endured over the years, taunting and tormenting the outclassed Canadian until the police intervened in the 14th round.

The search for a white challenger began immediately. Middleweight king Stanley Ketchel floored Johnson in the 12th round, but he got

up to kayo Ketchel with the very next punch. The old champion Jeffries was next, tempted out of retirement to, as novelist Jack London exhorted him, "Wipe the smile off the nigger's face." Johnson was still smiling when it was over, having stopped Jeffries in the 15th round.

He boxed only once more as champion in America, stopping Jim Flynn in a rematch in Las Vegas, New Mexico, and then defended twice in Paris. His penchant for white wives and girlfriends had finally got him into trouble as the Establishment seized on any excuse to bring him down. He was prosecuted under the Mann Act, prohibiting the transportation of women across state lines for immoral purposes, and was given a jail term. He fled to Europe, and, according to his story, worked out a deal to take a dive against Jess Willard if the case would be quashed. He was duly knocked out in Havana in 26 rounds on April 5, 1915, but if a deal had been done it was reneged upon.

He served his time and never got another chance, although he boxed sporadically until 1928. He died in a car crash in Raleigh, North Carolina on June 10, 1946.

> **" No greater defensive fighter than Jack Johnson ever lived. "**
>
> *Damon Runyon.*

PAPA JACK *a gifted boxer who would have thrived in any era*

JACK JOHNSON

BORN: March 31, 1878
Galveston, Texas

WORLD TITLE FIGHTS:
Dec 26, 1908, w rsf 14
Tommy Burns, Sydney (Aus)

Oct 16, 1909, w ko 12
Stanley Ketchel, Colma, CA

Jul 4, 1910, w ko 15
James J. Jeffries, Reno, NV

Jul 4, 1912, w disq 9
Jim Flynn, Las Vegas NM

Dec 19, 1913, drew 10
Jim Johnson, Paris (Fra)

Jun 27, 1914, w pts 20
Frank Moran, Paris (Fra)

Apr 5, 1915, l ko 26
Jess Willard, Havana (Cub)

OVERALL RECORD:
105 contests
68 wins
10 draws
16 no decisions
1 no contest
10 defeats

LEONARD

LOVE HIM or hate him, there was no denying Sugar Ray Leonard's class in the ring

MR COOL WITH A WILL TO WIN

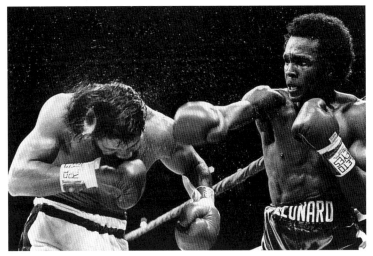

RAY LEONARD'S *sweetest win, over Roberto Duran (left) in November 1980*

It was easy to dislike Ray Leonard for his arrogance, his manipulation of the public and the media, his cynical disregard for the rights of hard-working fellow-professionals whom he would routinely elbow aside from the queue for a title fight or browbeat into signing unfavourable contracts. But it was impossible not to admire Sugar Ray Leonard the fighter, a champion of sublime talent, invention and above all, fighting heart. He never commanded the affections of the public in the way that the original Sugar Ray did, but he is one of the handful who merit mention in the same breath as Robinson. His ego matched his genius ... but, then, perhaps without the ego, the genius could never have flourished.

The natural, instinctive talent was there from the start, as he won 145 of 150 amateur fights in a career which peaked with a gold medal at the 1976 Olympic Games. Even then, Leonard knew how to market himself, enchanting middle America by boxing with a photo of Ray, his young son, tucked in his boot. When he came home from the Games, he approached the decision to turn professional with the icy calculation which marked everything he did. He engaged a lawyer, Mike Trainer, to handle the business deals, set up a company called Sugar Ray Leonard Inc. to ease the tax burdens, and hired Angelo Dundee, the world's best-known trainer, to fine-tune his preparations and select the opponents.

Too many boxers have been exploited, and Leonard was determined that he would never join the list. He negotiated lucrative deals with promoters and advertisers, even

> **" Ray Leonard is the kind of guy who's always looking at the edge of the cliff, to see how close to the edge he can get. "**
>
> *Mike Trainer, Leonard's adviser.*

recruiting his son, Ray Jr, to appear with him in a TV commercial for the soft drink Seven-Up. He had banked $2m before he ever fought for a title, although there was a good reason for the near-three year gap between his pro debut in February 1977 and his WBC welterweight title win over Wilfred Benitez in November 1979: ever the egotist, he wanted to be the first non-heavyweight to command a $1m fee as challenger for a world title.

He stopped Benitez in the final seconds of the 15th round, and fitted in a quick defence against England's Dave Green before taking on the man with whom his name will always be linked: Roberto Duran. The swaggering, uncouth Panamanian was the antithesis of Leonard, in ring style as much as personality, and he used the difference as a weapon. He taunted Leonard endlessly, questioning his masculinity and even insulting his wife – anything to goad Leonard into abandoning his boxing skills and brawling on Duran's terms. The strategy worked, as Duran won deservedly in an unforgettable fight.

Yet Leonard grew in defeat. He had lost for the first time in 28 fights, but he proved that he possessed a champion's heart. In the rematch, he used a similar strategy in reverse, confusing, bewildering and ultimately humiliating Duran.

After that, it was almost an anticlimax when Leonard won his second title, the WBA light-middleweight championship, which he immediately relinquished to concentrate on a welterweight unification match with WBA champion Thomas Hearns. They met in a marvellous contest in Las Vegas in September 1981, Leonard coming from behind to stop Hearns in the 14th. He defended the title once, then was forced into premature retirement because of a detached retina. He made an undistinguished, one-fight comeback two years later, and promptly retired again. But the lure of a fight with middleweight legend Marvin Hagler proved irresistible, and he won a bitterly disputed verdict in April 1987.

Nineteen months later, he was back in the Caesars Palace ring chasing two titles in one fight. WBC light-heavyweight champion Donny Lalonde was

SUGAR RAY LEONARD

BORN: MAY 17, 1956
Wilmington, South Carolina

WORLD TITLE FIGHTS:
Nov 30, 1979, w rsf 15
Wilfred Benitez, Las Vegas, NV (WBC welterweigh)

Mar 31, 1980, w ko 4
Dave Green, Landover, MD (WBC)

Jun 20, 1980, l pts 15
Roberto Duran, Montreal (Can) (WBC)

Nov 25, 1980, w ret 8
Roberto Duran, New Orleans, LA (WBC)

Mar 28, 1981, w rsf 10
Larry Bonds, Syracuse, NY (WBC)

Jun 25, 1981, w ko 9
Ayub Kalule, Houston, TX (WBA light-middleweight)

Sep 16, 1981, w rsf 14
Thomas Hearns, Las Vegas, NV (undisputed welterweight)

Feb 15, 1982, w ko 3
Bruce Finch, Reno, NV (undisputed welterweight)

Apr 6, 1987, w pts 12
Marvin Hagler, Las Vegas, NV (WBC middleweight)

Nov 7, 1988 w rsf 9
Donny Lalonde, Las Vegas, NV (WBC super-middleweight & light-heavyweight)

Jun 12, 1989, drew 12
Thomas Hearns, Las Vegas, NV (WBC super-middleweight title)

Dec 7, 1989, w pts 12
Roberto Duran, Las Vegas, NV (WBC super-middleweight)

Feb 9, 1991, l pts 12
Terry Norris, New York, NY (WBC light-middleweight)

OVERALL RECORD:
39 contest
36 wins
1 draw
2 defeats

persuaded to come in under the super-middleweight limit so that Leonard would be able to claim both titles, which he duly did by stopping the Canadian in nine rounds. He relinquished the 175-lb title but defended the super-middleweight crown twice, getting a lucky draw in a rematch with Hearns and outpointing Duran in a dull 12-rounder. His career ended on a downbeat, when Terry Norris floored and outpointed him to retain the WBC light-middleweight belt in 1991.

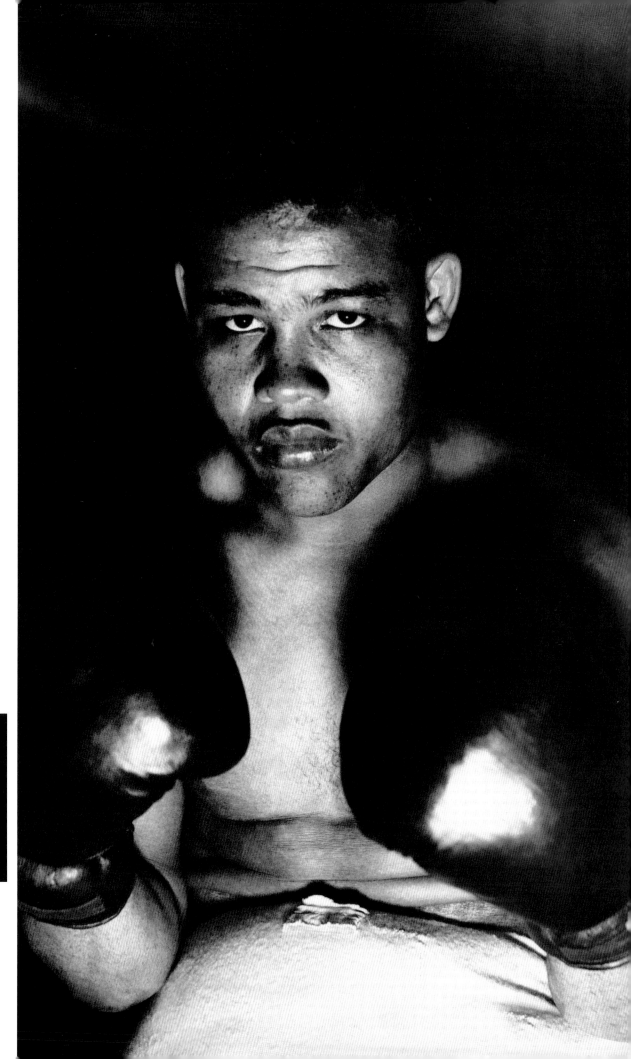

LOUIS

> **"He can run, but he can't hide."**
>
> *Louis's famous – and accurate – preview of his fight with Billy Conn.*

EXPRESSIONLESS *and menacing, Joe Louis could demoralize opponents before the first bell*

BROWN BOMBER WHO BROKE THE COLOUR BAR

When Joe Louis served in the US Army during the Second World War, the authorities ordered him to perform to segregated crowds of American servicemen. He refused. When he died in 1981, the Government had him buried in Arlington National Cemetery, which is reserved for American heroes. There can be few more striking illustrations of the changes in his country's society during his life, or of the importance of the role he played in bringing them about.

Louis led the quiet revolution, which helped erase the divisive memories of Jack Johnson and create a climate in which the talents of other great black performers like Ray Robinson, Archie Moore, and later Muhammad Ali could flourish. Judged by today's radical standards, Louis can sometimes seem obsequious, even servile, but that is a grossly unfair interpretation of who he was and what he did. Much of it is due to the way he was reported at the time, when all black men were quoted in American newspapers as if speaking in some sub-human "Nigger talk", full of "honeychiles", "Massas" and the like. The only roles open to black actors were either eye-rolling comic relief or mindless housemaids, while their music was ignored or else exploited and bastardized by white commercial interests.

Chris Mead, in his definitive biography *Champion – Joe Louis*, wrote: "Not only did (Louis) have to establish himself as a dominant athlete to get a shot at the heavyweight title; he also had to prove that blacks could compete on equal terms with dignity and without exacerbating racial antagonism. Louis

accepted that responsibility and performed so well that he became a challenge to segregation, the challenge that began to crack the system."

Louis knew all about segregation. He was born Joe Louis Barrow in the Alabama cotton belt on May 13, 1914, and lived there until he was 12, when his step-father moved the family north to Detroit. His mother paid for him to have violin lessons, but young Louis used the money to pay for boxing classes instead. In 1933, he reached the finals of the American championships at light-heavyweight, and the following year he won it.

Unusually, he opted to turn professional under a black manager, a gambler called John Roxborough, who recruited an old-time fighter, Jack Blackburn, as trainer. The trio hit it off from the start, and within three years the sensational youngster had beaten just about every heavyweight

ON TARGET *Walcott is ko'd in 1948*

worth considering. The exception was Max Schmeling, who stunned the world – and particularly the world of black America – when he shattered Louis's unbeaten run with a 12th round knockout in June 1934. But Louis put it down to experience, and two months later proved he was unaffected by beating ex-champion Jack Sharkey in three rounds.

Jim Braddock held the title, and he drove a hard bargain for a Louis defence, settling for a huge guarantee of $300,000 and a percentage of Louis's future earnings for the next ten years. It was a fabulous deal, but Braddock earned it by flooring the challenger in the opening round and fighting heroically until he was knocked out in the eighth.

As champion, Louis set new targets in excellence. He retained the title 25 times, and even if some of the opponents were what he cheerfully acknowledged to be "Bums of the Month", there was not a single worth-

while contender of his generation who was not accommodated as well.

On the night he touched perfection, Louis beat Schmeling in 124 seconds, to take revenge for his solitary defeat. Louis gave the champion such a beating that the Nazis ordered the commentary to be cut off because Schmeling's cries of pain were audible after Louis's right to the back had broken two vertebrae.

Louis retired in 1949 as undefeated champion, but tax problems forced him back into the ring. He lost to NBA champion Ezzard Charles, and retired for good after Rocky Marciano knocked him out in 1951. His money gone and debts spiralling, he went downhill fast until President Kennedy wrote off his tax bills as a gesture from the country he had served so well. Caesars Palace in Las Vegas gave him a well-paid sinecure as a greeter in their casino, and he worked there until illness and mental infirmity forced him to stop. He died in Las Vegas on April 12, 1981.

JOE LOUIS

BORN: May 13, 1914
Lafayette, Alabama

WORLD TITLE FIGHTS:

Jun 22, 1937, w ko 8
James J. Braddock, Chicago, IL

Aug 30, 1937, w pts 15
Tommy Farr, New York, NY

Feb 23, 1938, w ko 3
Nathan Mann, New York, NY

Apr 1, 1938, w ko 5
Harry Thomas, Chicago, IL

Jun 22, 1938, w ko 1
Max Schmeling, New York, NY

Jan 25, 1939, w ko 1
John Henry Lewis, New York, NY

Apr 17, 1939, w ko 1
Jack Roper, Los Angeles, CA

Jun 28, 1939, w rsf 4
Tony Galento, New York, NY

Sep 20, 1939, w ko 11
Bob Pastor, Detroit, MI

Feb 9, 1940, w pts 15
Arturo Godoy, New York, NY

Mar 29, 1940, w ko 2
Johnny Paychek, New York, NY

Jun 20, 1940, w rsf 8
Arturo Godoy, New York, NY

Dec 16, 1940, w rsf 6
Al McCoy, Boston, MA

Jan 31, 1941, w ko 5
Red Burman, New York, NY

Feb 17, 1941, w ko 2
Gus Dorazio, Philadelphia, PA

Mar 21, 1941, w rsf 13
Abe Simon, Detroit, MI

Apr 8, 1941, w rsf 9
Tony Musto, St Louis, MO

May 23, 1941, w disq 7
Buddy Baer, Washington, DC

Jun 18, 1941, w ko 13
Billy Conn, New York, NY

Sep 29, 1941, w rsf 6
Lou Nova, New York, NY

Jan 9, 1942, w ko 1
Buddy Baer, New York, NY

Mar 27, 1942, w ko 6
Abe Simon, New York, NY

Jun 19, 1946, w ko 8
Billy Conn, New York, NY

Sep 18, 1946, w ko 1
Tami Mauriello, New York, NY

Dec 5, 1947, w pts 15
Jersey Joe Walcott, New York, NY

Jun 25, 1948, w ko 11
Jersey Joe Walcott, New York, NY

Sep 27, 1950, l pts 15
Ezzard Charles, New York, NY

OVERALL RECORD:
66 contests
63 wins
3 defeats

MARCIANO

ROCKY MARCIANO *(right) trailing on points, and with his left eye closing, knocks out Jersey Joe Walcott to win the world title*

WHIRLWIND PUNCHER WHO NEVER SAID DIE

ROCKY MARCIANO

BORN: September 1, 1923
Brockton, Massachusetts

WORLD TITLE FIGHTS:
Sep 23, 1952, w ko 13
Jersey Joe Walcott, Philadelphia, PA

May 15, 1953, w ko 1
Jersey Joe Walcott, Chicago, IL

Sep 24, 1953, w rsf 11
Roland LaStarza, New York, NY

Jun 17, 1954, w pts 15
Ezzard Charles, New York, NY

Sep 17, 1954, w ko 8
Ezzard Charles, New York, NY

May 16, 1955, w rsf 9
Don Cockell, San Francisco, CA

Sep 21, 1955, w ko 9
Archie Moore, New York, NY

OVERALL RECORD:
49 contests
49 wins

By every known standard, Rocky Marciano lacked the equipment to be a successful fighter. He didn't take up the sport until he was 23, when most aspiring champions are well into their careers; he was short, a little over 5ft 10in; he was not a natural athlete, lacking co-ordination and balance; and he did not even particularly want to box, since his main ambition had been to make the grade in baseball. But he had two assets which, taken together, outweighed all the drawbacks: he was a concussive puncher, especially with the right, and he had unlimited courage and determination – what boxing writers called "bottom".

He was born Rocco Marchegiano, on September 1, 1923, the son of poor Italians who had settled in the Massachusetts town of Brockton where his father, Pasquale, worked in a shoe factory. Rocco did a little boxing in the Army, spending most of his service time in Britain, and only took it up seriously after failing in tryouts for a baseball club. His friend Allie Colombo, who stayed part of the team throughout Marciano's career, persuaded New York manager Al Weill to take him on, which Weill did after seeking advice from veteran trainer Charley Goldman. The 60-year-old Goldman, who had around 300 pro fights himself as a bantamweight, knew championship potential when he saw

it. He worked hard with the raw heavyweight and, under Goldman's patient tuition, Marciano learned to channel his extraordinary punching power into short, destructive blows. In his first pro year, 1948, he flattened all 11 opponents, eight in the first round. In 1949 he was 13–0, with 11 knockouts, and the days of obscure venues and small purses were over.

His breakthrough fight was against Roland LaStarza, a handsome New York-Italian who was unbeaten in 37 fights. They clashed at Madison Square Garden on March 24, 1950, and Marciano won a split decision in a desperately close fight which drew 13,658 fans. Marciano was big business, but Weill was in no rush. He kept him ticking over until he was ready, and then in July 1951 the drive for the title began in earnest. Rex Layne was beaten in six rounds, Freddie Beshore in four, and on October 26, Marciano ended the career of Joe Louis when he clubbed the ex-champion to defeat in nine rounds. Wins over contenders Lee Savold and Harry Matthews maintained the momentum, and Marciano finally fought for the title in Philadelphia on September 23, 1952. Champion Jersey Joe Walcott had been the oldest man to win the heavyweight title, and he did not relinquish it easily. Marciano was floored in the first minute and outboxed for round after round, until by the 13th Walcott had only to stand up to win. But then Marciano landed a single, devastating right, and Walcott crumpled to the floor. That punch took everything out of Walcott as a fighter. In the rematch he went out like a lamb in the first round, and never boxed

again. Marciano removed the lingering doubts about the first LaStarza fight by hammering him to 11th-round defeat in September 1953. He boxed only twice in 1954, but his two wins over former champion Ezzard Charles were classics. In the first, on June 17, Charles defied him for the full 15 rounds, thrilling the crowd of almost 48,000 in Yankee Stadium with his spirited resistance. In the rematch, on September 17, Marciano's left nostril was cut clean in half, and his corner had to plead with the ringside doctor not to stop the fight. As ever, Marciano found the way out of the crisis: a stream of rights floored Charles in the eighth, and the follow-up attack knocked him cold.

There were only two fights after that, a foul-filled victory over England's Don Cockell and a ninth-round knockout of light-heavyweight champion Archie Moore. Rocky's retirement, announced on April 27, 1956, stunned the sporting world. He had a perfect record of 49–0, 43 inside the distance, and there were still large cheques to be earned. But he stuck to his decision, resisting all offers for a comeback. He was killed on August 31, 1969, when the Cessna light aircraft in which he was a passenger crashed near Des Moines. Sonny Liston, the least articulate of men, spoke an eloquent tribute. "This man was one of the greatest champions ever" he said. "He refused to accept defeat. And nobody beat him."

> **" I was a strong guy who trained hard, but I didn't have the talent of Sugar Ray Robinson. "**
>
> *Rocky Marciano.*

ROCKY MARCIANO:
a hard hitter, with a hero's heart

ROBINSON

SUGAR RAY ROBINSON (right) took 10 rounds to defeat Randolph Turpin in their 1951 rematch

MASTER OF THE RING WITH A SENSE OF STYLE

There are not enough superlatives in a thesaurus to do justice to Sugar Ray Robinson, the ego-driven genius who was the greatest middleweight in history and, very probably, the greatest welterweight as well. He held the welterweight crown for four years, and won the middleweight championship an unmatched five times. In a fabulous 25-year career he boxed 202 times, losing only 19, the majority of them in his declining years. He faced 18 men who held world titles, at every weight from lightweight to light-heavyweight, and beat 14 of them, three in his first year as a pro. Some record: some fighter.

The only phony thing about Ray Robinson in the ring was his name. He was born Walker Smith in Detroit on May 3, 1921, and acquired the ring name when he turned up for his first amateur fight without having registered with the authorities and borrowed the card of another boxer. He won, of course – he was beaten only a few times in 85 amateur fights, 69 of which were knockouts, 40 in the first round – and won the

RAY ROBINSON: *Glamour and glory*

featherweight Golden Gloves before turning pro in October 1940. The sheer statistics of what followed still defy belief. He reeled off 40 victories in a row, lost to Jake LaMotta for the only time in their six meetings, and then went unbeaten in his next 91 fights, a streak which brought him the welterweight title in December 1946 and the middleweight championship in February 1951.

But the figures alone do not convey his full impact. He was not just a boxer, but a megastar who, even when TV was in its early years, became known in every corner of the world for his dazzling talent and his astonishing life-style which included pink Cadillacs, a staff barber, masseurs, a shoe-shiner and even a court jester dwarf. In the lean post-war years of his prime, such extravagance was startling. It also took some financing, which was why he maintained a busy programme of defences, non-title matches and exhibition tours.

By 1950 he had run out of opposition, and at 29 was finding it a strain to

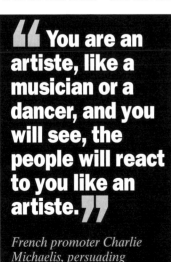

> ❝ **You are an artiste, like a musician or a dancer, and you will see, the people will react to you like an artiste.** ❞

French promoter Charlie Michaelis, persuading Robinson to come to Paris in 1951.

keep down to 147 lb. He went after the middleweight title and, in a blistering 12 fight-spell between June and December, trounced a string of contenders and won three contests which the Pennsylvania Commission recognized as being for the championship. The real champion was his old foe LaMotta, and Robinson hammered him to defeat in the 13th round in Chicago on St Valentine's Day 1951.

Ambitiously, he lined up a seven-fight European tour between May 21 and July 10, culminating in a £30,000 defence against British champion Randolph Turpin. The Continental leg of the trip went smoothly enough, but the awkward Englishman was a different proposition. Robinson had spent as much time partying as training in Europe, and it showed as Turpin out-boxed him in round after round.

The rematch, just 64 days later, drew 61,370 to the Polo Grounds, New York, and again Robinson had problems with Turpin's style. There was nothing much in the first nine rounds, but then Robinson's left eyebrow, which had been cut in the first fight, split open again in the 10th. Referee Ruby Goldstein was poised to intervene when Robinson, wiping the blood away, set up a blistering attack which brought the referee's intervention in his favour with eight seconds left in the round.

Robinson made two quick defences in 1952, outpointing Carl "Bobo" Olson and knocking out Rocky Graziano, and then tried for Joey Maxim's light-heavyweight title. They fought in New York, in 104-degree heat so intense that the referee collapsed and had to be replaced. Robinson was ahead after 13 rounds, but was so drained by the heat that he could not come out for the 14th. He retired, but financial imperatives drove him back to the ring to regain the middleweight title from Olson in December 1955. He lost and regained the title twice more, in famous battles with Gene Fullmer and Carmen Basilio, and then lost it for the final time to Paul Pender in January 1960. He failed three times to regain it, and – the high-spending days now a memory – fought on until December 1965. He suffered Alzheimer's in later life, and died on April 12, 1989.

SUGAR RAY ROBINSON

BORN: May 3, 1921
Detroit, Michigan

WORLD TITLE FIGHTS:
Dec 20, 1946, w pts 15
Tommy Bell, New York, NY
(welterweight)

Jun 24, 1947, w rsf 8
Jimmy Doyle, Cleveland, OH

Dec 19, 1947, w rsf 6
Chuck Taylor, Detroit, MI

Jun 28, 1948, w pts 15
Bernard Docusen, Chicago, IL

Jul 11, 1949, w pts 15
Kid Gavilan, Philadelphia, PA

Aug 9, 1950, w pts 15
Charlie Fusari, Jersey City, NJ

Feb 14, 1951, w rsf 13
Jake LaMotta, Chicago, IL
(middleweight)

Jul 10, 1951, l pts 15
Randolph Turpin, London (Eng)

Sep 12, 1951, w rsf 10
Randolph Turpin, New York, NY

Mar 13, 1952, w pts 15
Carl "Bobo" Olson, San Francisco, CA

Apr 16, 1952, w ko 3
Rocky Graziano, Chicago, IL

Jun 25, 1952, l ret 14
Joey Maxim, New York, NY (light-heavyweight)

Dec 9, 1955, w ko 2
Carl "Bobo" Olson, Chicago, IL
(middleweight)

May 18, 1956, w ko 4
Carl "Bobo" Olson, Los Angeles, CA

Jan 2, 1957, l pts 15
Gene Fullmer, New York, NY

May 1, 1957, w ko 5
Gene Fullmer, Chicago, IL

Sep 23, 1957, l pts 15
Carmen Basilio, New York, NY

Mar 25, 1958, w pts 15
Carmen Basilio, Chicago, IL

Jan 22, 1960, l pts 15
Paul Pender, Boston, MA

Jun 10, 1960, l pts 15
Paul Pender, Boston, MA

Dec 3, 1960, drew 15
Gene Fullmer, Los Angeles, CA
(NBA middleweight)

Mar 4, 1961, l pts 15
Gene Fullmer, Las Vegas, NV
(NBA middleweight)

OVERALL RECORD:
202 contests
175 wins
6 draws
2 no contests
19 defeats

SULLIVAN

CHARLIE MITCHELL *(left) was one of Sullivan's toughest and most persistent opponents*

TOUGH GUY WHO COULD BACK UP HIS BOASTS

Under the avuncular editorship of its founder Nat Fleischer, *Ring* magazine was always concerned about whether a champion was a suitable role model for the growing American boy. It was as well for the roistering, hard-drinking, womanizing braggart John L. Sullivan that he did not depend upon Nat's endorsement, since the old rascal was four years in his grave before *Ring* first appeared in 1922. He may not have been Fleischer's idea of a model citizen, but he was and remains everyone's idea of a prize fighter, a raucous hard man who could cheerfully back up his boast that he could "lick any son-of-a-bitch in the house." Sullivan personified his era, the rough-and-ready years of expansion in America, of the Gold Rush and the rowdy saloons. He earned over a million dollars, which in modern terms is Mike Tyson money, and he got through it all. When he died on February 2, 1918, his estate was tucked under his pillow: a ten-dollar bill, and a five.

He is a pivotal figure in boxing history, as the man who bridged the gap between the worlds of bare-knuckling and boxing as it would be recognized

> ## " I can lick any son-of-a-bitch in the house. "
>
> *Sullivan's legendary, and oft-proven, boast.*

today. His last fight, when he lost the championship to James J. Corbett in 1892, was the first title fight to be staged under an approximation of modern rules and conditions. Corbett's fast and stylish jabbing, contrasting tellingly with Sullivan's lumbering swipes, marked the birth of a new concept of boxing as opposed to brawling. In Sullivan's prime it was enough to be tough: from now on, technique would be needed as well.

He was born in Boston on October 15, 1858, son of a Kerryman from Tralee and a Westmeath woman from Athlone. His mother wanted him to become a priest, but he lacked both the inclination and the academic qualifications and took a series of manual jobs instead, which usually ended in his dismissal for fighting with his boss. He drifted into professional fighting almost by accident, when he accepted a challenge from a touring brawler at the Dudley Street Opera House in Boston and knocked him into the orchestra pit.

A succession of prize-fights followed, and as the colourful youngster acquired a large backing amongst the Irish-Americans of East Coast America, so the clamour grew for him to face Tipperary-born Paddy Ryan for the bare-knuckle championship of the world. Ryan was contemptuous of the youngster – much as Sullivan himself would later be of Corbett – and told him to "go and get a reputation first", but eventually agreed to face him in Mississippi City on February 7, 1882.

The old champion lasted just 11 minutes, much of which time he spent on the ground as Sullivan, 10

pounds lighter and five years younger, battered him into submission. Ryan's corner threw in the sponge when he could not come out for the ninth round, and Sullivan's riotous reign had begun. Most of his so-called fights over the next few years were no more than exhibitions, where he would offer $100 to anyone who could stay three rounds with him, but there was at least one serious opponent: the Englishman Charlie Mitchell, who floored him in the first round before the police stopped it in the third with Mitchell taking a pounding.

There were other good heavyweights around then, like Peter Jackson and George Godfrey, but they never even made it into the exhibition ring with Sullivan. In a newspaper challenge to his contenders, he wrote "In this challenge I include all fighters – first come, first served – who are white. I will not fight a Negro. I never have and never shall." It remains the black mark, so to speak, against his record and achievements.

He defended the title only twice, in a 39-rounds draw with Mitchell in a rematch staged at Chantilly in France in 1888, and a 75th-round knockout of Jake Kilrain in July 1889. A four-rounds exhibition with Corbett in June 1891 should have given him a taste of what was to come, but the purse offer was irresistible

JOHN L. SULLIVAN

BORN: October 15, 1858
Roxbury, Massachusetts.

WORLD TITLE FIGHT:
Sep 7, 1892, l ko 21
James J. Corbett, New Orleans, LA

OVERALL RECORD:
45 contests
41 wins
3 draws
1 defeat

and they met for the title, with gloves, in New Orleans on September 7, 1892. Sullivan barely hit Corbett in 21 rounds, and was counted out, exhausted, in the 21st round.

He retired to drink the rest of his fortune away, but in later life became a temperance lecturer. He died in Abingdon, Massachusetts, of cirrhosis of the liver.

JOHN L. SULLIVAN *drew boxing's colour line*

TYSON

MIKE TYSON *(right) was not very impressive, but still too good for Donovan Ruddock in 1991*

TROUBLE MAN WITH IRON IN HIS SOUL

POWERHOUSE
The young Mike Tyson

History will not be kind to Mike Tyson, who wasted the potential and the opportunity to be the greatest heavyweight of them all. Despite regaining the WBC version of the title from Frank Bruno in March 1996, the chances are that he will never again be the irresistible force he was in the years from 1985 to 1988.

But then Tyson always had the air of a man whose built-in self-destruct was ticking away, and considering the background he came from, that is scarcely surprising. He was born in Brooklyn, New York on June 30, 1966, and grew up wild on the toughest streets of the Brownsville ghetto. His father had left even before he was born, and his mother, a drinker, struggled to cope with her four children on welfare. By the time he was 10, the boy was an accomplished mugger, a sociopath who beat up other children, and occasionally adults, for the sheer pleasure of doing so. He was incorrigible, in and out of a succession of juvenile detention centres and medium-security facilities until, at 13, he was sent to the Tryon School for Boys, a last-resort establishment where he could be detained until the age of 16.

An instructor there, Bobby Stewart, saw possibilities in the boy, who even at that age was 200 lb of solid muscle. He taught him the basics, and referred him to Cus D'Amato, a 72-year-old manager and trainer who had steered Floyd Patterson and Jose Torres to

world titles. On his 14th birthday, Tyson was released into D'Amato's care and his life began afresh. D'Amato had rich backers, Jim Jacobs and Bill Cayton, who owned the world's largest collection of fight films. Jacobs, in particular, struck up a close relationship with the youngster, and they spent endless hours studying the great fighters on film until Tyson's encyclopaedic knowledge matched his mentor's.

He turned professional in May 1985, boxing mainly on small shows bankrolled by Jacobs and Cayton. The policy was deliberate, to keep him off national TV until public curiosity about the sensational heavyweight with the knockout record mounted to the right pitch of hysteria. Of his 15 fights in 1985, 11 finished in the first round. The pace continued in 1986, when 13 straight wins culminated in a second-round destruction of Trevor Berbick to win the WBC title. At 20 years and 145 days, he had broken Patterson's record as the youngest-ever heavyweight champion.

Within 10 months, he had unified the championship, and in 1988 he reached his peak. Larry Holmes, a fine champion in his time, was taken apart in four rounds; Tony Tubbs in two; and, most impressive of all, he took out the undefeated Mike Spinks in the first round with a performance of such terrifying precision that it recalled Joe Louis' annihilation of Max Schmeling.

But Tyson's life was falling apart. D'Amato and Jacobs had died, and the ubiquitous Don King had ousted Cayton from the driving seat. There was a catastrophic marriage to actress Robin Givens, which ended in predictable but painful divorce, and a bitter split from trainer Kevin Rooney, who as D'Amato's protégé and professional heir had played such a significant part in the fighter's development. The champion looked vulnerable in stopping Frank Bruno,

> **" I'm just a normal guy with heart. "**
>
> *Mike Tyson, in 1990.*

MIKE TYSON

BORN: June 30, 1966
Brooklyn, New York

WORLD TITLE FIGHTS:
Non 22, 1986, w rsf 2
Trevor Berbick, Las Vegas, NV (WBC)

Mar 7, 1987, w pts 12
James "Bonecrusher" Smith, Las Vegas, NV (WBC and WBA)

Aug 1, 1987, w pts 12
Tony Tucker, Las Vegas, NV (undisputed)

Oct 16, 1987, w rsf 7
Tyrell Biggs, Atlantic City, NJ

Jan 22, 1988, w rsf 4
Larry Holmes, Atlantic City, NJ

Mar 21, 1988, w rsf 2
Tony Tubbs, Tokyo (Jap)

Jun 27, 1988, w ko 1
Mike Spinks, Atlantic City, NJ

Feb 25, 1989, w rsf 5
Frank Bruno, Las Vegas, NV

Jun 21, 1989, w rsf 1
Carl Williams, Atlantic City, NJ (WBC, WBA, IBF)

Feb 11, 1990, l ko 10
James "Buster" Douglas, Tokyo (Jap)

Mar 16, 1996, w rsf 3
Frank Bruno, Las Vegas, NV (WBC)

OVERALL RECORD:
45 contests
44 wins
1 defeat

but more like the old Tyson in flattening Carl Williams in the first round. But it ended, shockingly, in Tokyo on February 11, 1990 when James "Buster" Douglas climbed off the floor to knock out an ill-prepared and unfocused Tyson in the 10th.

He came back with four wins of varying quality, struggling twice to beat Razor Ruddock, and then was jailed for six years for raping a beauty pageant contestant. The conviction looked shaky, but appeals failed and he spent more than three years in prison before being released in 1995. The fortune he had earned, estimated at more than $100m, had allegedly dwindled to $15m, but he quickly topped that up with a farcical comeback win over Peter McNeeley, whose cornerman jumped into the ring in the first round to earn his man automatic disqualification. His second test, against Buster Mathis in December, left the questions unanswered. but at least he looked like a hungry fighter again in beating Bruno.

WILDE

JIMMY WILDE *(right) suffers a rare defeat by former bantam-weight champion Pete Herman*

THE GHOST WITH A HAMMER IN HIS HAND

Jimmy Wilde never scaled more than 102 lb in his prime, yet he knocked out or stopped 101 of the 151 men he faced in his 12-year career, and lost to just four of them. Wilde claimed to have had 854 fights, but he was including hundreds in the booths and in the semi-professional fighting which was popular in Wales in the early part of the century. If those are included, then his figure may not be far short of the truth.

He was born into a mining family in Tylerstown on May 15, 1892, and as soon as he was old enough he, too, went down the pit. But he soon discovered he could fight, and with disproportionate punching power. When he was 18 his landlord, an old bare-knuckler called Dai Davies, encouraged him to join Jack Scarrott's travelling booth to gain experience. He was backed by Davies's daughter Elizabeth, whom he later married and who became, effectively, his manager and even, when necessary, his sparring partner.

His formal professional career began on December 26, 1910, and he set a hot pace. In 1911 he had 28 fights, winning 27 and drawing once. However, all but two of them were staged in Pontypridd. Even though he had won 22 by knockout, he couldn't seem to get noticed outside his home area. Eventually, he travelled to London and pestered Dick Burge, promoter at the Blackfriars Ring, for a booking. Burge matched him with a protégé of lightweight champion Matt Wells, and Wilde won in 45 seconds. But a second booking was not forthcoming, and after a trial at the National Sporting Club proved equally unproductive, he went back to Wales.

There, he compiled a further 54 straight wins, 33 inside the distance, to bring his tally to 81 wins (55 inside schedule), one draw and no defeats. Even yet, London did not want to

THE CHAMP'S *last fighting portrait, in June 1923*

know. Peggy Bettinson, matchmaker at the NSC, explained that Wilde was simply too small, and would provoke complaints from his members about bad match-making. Eventually, though, they found a Frenchman who was actually lighter than Wilde, Eugene Husson. He scaled under 100 lb for his fight with Wilde at the NSC on March 30, 1914, and while Wilde probably could have knocked him out

quickly he chose instead to put on an exhibition of the full range of his boxing skills before disposing of Husson in the sixth.

Having convinced the game's most powerful promoters of his worth, Wilde was quickly moved ahead and, in January 1915, was matched with Tancy Lee for the British and European titles. Wilde went through with the fight despite a strength-sapping dose of flu, and took a shocking beating before his corner threw in the towel in the 17th round. Five months later the little Welshman was back in action, and by early 1916 had earned a match with Joe Symonds for the world and British titles at the NSC on February 14, Wilde winning on a 12th-round retirement after a gruelling battle which was settled in the end by a blow to the Englishman's Adam's Apple.

Symonds's world title claims were disputed by two Americans, Johnny Rosner and Giuseppe di Mefi, who took his ring name of Young Zulu Kid from the golliwog mascot he carried. Wilde stopped Rosner in 11 rounds, and while he waited for the match with the Zulu Kid to be finalized he stopped his old rival Tancy Lee, also in the 11th. The championship fight took place in London on December 18, 1916, Wilde yet again winning in 11 rounds to become the undisputed title-holder.

War service severely restricted his activity after that, and he spent 1920 on a well-paid tour of America and Canada. He came home to fight former bantamweight champion Pete Herman, but found the American much too big and strong for him and was rescued by the referee in the 17th round. After two years' inactivity he accepted a £13,000 offer to defend against Pancho Villa in New York, and took such a terrible beating that

he later admitted that, for four months after the fight, he could not recognize anyone.

He never boxed again, but made a useful second career as a newspaper columnist. When he was 72 he was beaten up by a gang of thugs at Cardiff railway station, and lived out the last four years of his life unaware of who he was or what he had achieved. He died on March 10, 1969.

JIMMY WILDE

BORN: May 15, 1892
Tylorstown, Wales

WORLD TITLE FIGHTS:
Nov 16, 1914, w pts 15
Joe Symonds, London (Eng)

Dec 3, 1914, w ko 9
Sid Smith, Liverpool (Eng)

Jan 25, 1915, l rsf 17
Tancy Lee, London (Eng)

Feb 14, 1916, w rsf 12
Joe Symonds, London (Eng)

Apr 24, 1916, w rsf 11
Johnny Rosner, Liverpool (Eng)

Jun 26, 1916, w rsf 11
Tancy Lee, London (Eng)

Jul 31, 1916, w ko 10
Johnny Hughes, London (Eng)

Dec 18, 1916, w ko 11
Young Zulu Kid, London (Eng)

Mar 12, 1917, w rsf 4
George Clark, London (Eng)

Apr 29, 1918, w rsf 2
Dick Heasman, London (Eng)

Jun 18, 1923, l ko 7
Pancho Villa, New York, NY

OVERALL RECORD:
145 contests
136 wins
1 draw
5 no decisions
3 defeats

> ## " Give me a chance, Mr Burge – you won't regret it. "

Wilde, pleading with promoter Dick Burge for his first London booking.

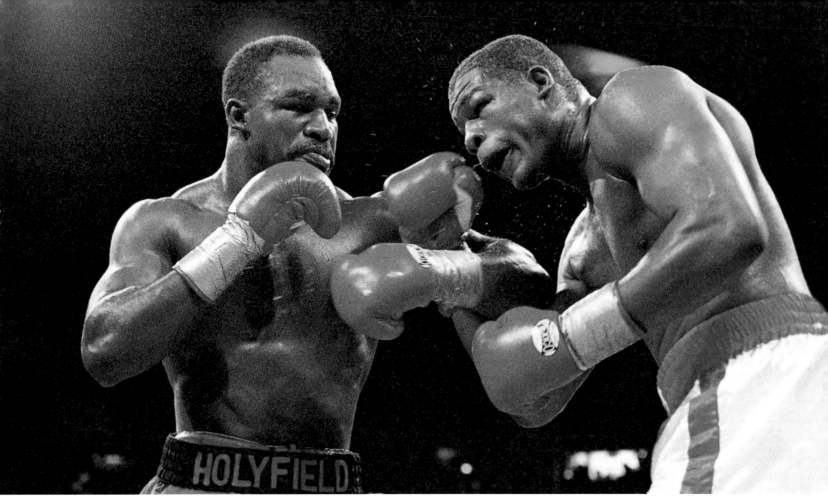

EVANDER HOLYFIELD *loses the heavyweight title to Riddick Bowe in the first of their three classic encounters, at Caesars Palace in 1992*

THE GREAT FIGHTS

There have been many better fights than the 15 chronicled here. Some were obscure six-rounders in tiny halls, or minor epics where area titles or just local pride were at stake. Others were multi-million-dollar encounters between the greatest fighters of their time: who can forget Julio Cesar Chavez stopping Meldrick Taylor with just two seconds to go in their classic clash at Caesars Palace in 1990?

It is impossible to condense 100 years of boxing history into 15 fights, so inevitably your favourite fight may not be on our list. Chavez vs. Taylor didn't make it, but Jake LaMotta vs. Laurent Dauthuille did. That was also a last-gasp victory, but in its way it was even more impressive than Chavez's success because LaMotta had been so comprehensively outboxed for fourteen and a half rounds. His win defined him as a fighter, a true triumph for heart, courage and simple refusal to acknowledge defeat. There was always a chance that Chavez could stop Taylor, but until it happened, there wasn't a hope that LaMotta could stop Dauthuille.

Other fights are included because of their social significance, such as Jack Johnson's defeat of James J. Jeffries in the most hate-laden fight in boxing history. Marvin Hagler's win over Thomas Hearns is there, since it was one of those special nights when two great talents collided at the peak of their powers. Muhammad Ali's win over George Foreman is included because it was the supreme moment of an unmatched career, while his triumph over Joe Frazier in Manila was simply one of the greatest fights of all time. It was not an easy shortlist to compile, but then that is yet another illustration of boxing's eternal appeal.

THE END OF AN ERA

JAMES J. CORBETT vs. JOHN L. SULLIVAN

It is one of the many ironies of boxing that the man who wins like a bullying lout will often lose with the chivalry and generosity of a Corinthian sportsman. So it was with John L. Sullivan, the Boston Strong Boy, terror of a thousand bar-rooms, when the time came for him to acknowledge that after 42 "official" fights and countless other short-lived brawls, he had met a better man than himself. Sullivan's grace in the moments after James J. Corbett had knocked him out in the 21st round of an embarrassingly one-sided fight served to cement his legend, and won him admirers who would have shunned him in the days when he was the old high-living, hard-drinking, rough-talking John L.

The result shocked the world as much as it stunned Sullivan. For a decade, ever since he knocked out Paddy Ryan to win the bare-knuckle championship of the world, Sullivan was the epitome of the fighting man, a brawler who battled for pleasure as much as for cash, and who had never even come close to defeat. Oddly, it was Sullivan who insisted that this fight be the first championship to be contested with gloves (five-ouncers), although Corbett, a skilled technician who relied on speed and skill rather than brawn, raised no objections – especially as his hands were known to be brittle.

Their clash was a landmark in boxing history. Louisiana had recently legalised decision fights under the Queensberry Rules, and the Sullivan–Corbett match, apart from being the first gloved heavyweight title fight of the modern era, would also be the climax of a boxing carnival at the New Orleans Olympic Club at 636 Royal Street. Boxing had become respectable, and the club celebrated the fact by organizing a series of championship fights. On the Monday, George Dixon and Jack Skelly met for the featherweight title; on Tuesday, Jack McAuliffe retained the lightweight crown against Billy Meyers, and on Wednesday John L. faced Corbett. McAuliffe, a close friend of Sullivan's who also acted as his chief second, bet his entire purse of $18,500 on Sullivan at 1–4.

The first few rows were occupied by the Club members, all of them dinner-suited and wearing a white gardenia in their buttonholes, but the rest of the 10,000 crowd were more the traditional fight fans. Unusually, the champion was the first to enter the ring, and looked to be carrying more weight than was good for him at 212 lb to Corbett's 180 lb.

From the first bell, the outcome was painfully apparent. Corbett danced around the lumbering champion, seven years his senior at 33, and stabbed away with left jabs. Sullivan ploughed forward for round after round, swiping punches at a more elusive target than he had ever faced, and often missing so badly that he swung himself in a full circle. Even when he finally connected in the fourth round, Corbett shrugged it off and laughed as he broke away. The sustained punishment took its toll on the veteran: as early as the third round his nose was broken, his lips split, and all the while those relentless jabs were eroding his resistance.

By the 21st round, he was spent. Corbett floored him early in the round, and John L. only just beat the count. Corbett showed no mercy: another flurry of punches, and Sullivan crashed face first. Halfway through the count he rolled on to his right side, but he was finished. Afterwards, he raised his arm to silence the crowd who were applauding Corbett's victory. "All I have to say is that I came to the ring once too often," he said, before adding the sentence which confirmed him as an American folk hero: "If I had to get licked, I'm glad it was by an American."

The Ex-Champion

ROUND 21 SULLIVAN'S VAIN ATTEMPT TO RISE.

Gentleman Jim whips the Boston Strong Boy at New Orleans on September 7, 1892.

JAMES J. CORBETT *(right) controlled every moment of their historic fight*

ᏥᏥ Fighting under the new rules before gentlemen is a pleasure. 🔊🔊

John L. Sullivan, describing the difference between the sport he had dominated and boxing under the Marquess of Queensbury Rules.

BLACK POWER UNSETTLES WHITE AMERICA

FIGHT FACTS

DATE: July 4, 1910
VENUE: Reno, NV
TITLE: World heavyweight
RESULT: Jack Johnson won (stoppage, round 15)

JACK JOHNSON vs. JAMES J. JEFFRIES

Squinting at the world through a white pointed hood must give a peculiar perspective on life, which may explain how otherwise sane people argued in 1910 that James J. Jeffries, who had not thrown a punch for money since 1904, was the rightful heavyweight champion of the world. Jeffries had retired as unde-

"HOW DO YOU LIKE THIS, MR JEFF?" *Johnson taunts his challenger*

feated champion, and his title passed to Marvin Hart, then to Tommy Burns and finally to Jack Johnson – the first black champion, and the object of an unprecedented outpouring of hatred.

The cry went up for Jeffries to return to the ring and reclaim the title for the "white race". His advocates – led by the famous novelist Jack London – claimed that since Jeffries had never been beaten in the ring he remained the rightful champion.

Johnson, more amused than insulted by the suggestion that a man who was now a fat and comfortable farmer had more right than he to regard himself as the world's best fighting man,

encouraged speculation about the match, with one eye on the potential receipts.

Jeffries proved initially unreceptive to the idea, at first claiming the right to draw the infamous "colour line" as laid down by his predecessor John L. Sullivan, who proclaimed that he had "never fought a Negro, and never will". Jeffries criticized Burns for defending the title against Johnson, and accused him of betraying his pride and the Caucasian race by doing so. Jeffries's father, a minister, threatened to disown his son if he fought Johnson, conveniently ignoring the fact that his other son, Jack, had fought and lost to Johnson eight years earlier.

Finally, the pressure on Jeffries to challenge Johnson became intolerable, and he agreed to the match. It was a troublesome affair from the start. Tex Rickard won an auction for the right to promote it, offering the then-staggering sum of $120,000 to be shared between the pair.

He initially planned to stage the fight in Salt Lake City, but then switched to San Francisco and built an arena there specially for the fight. But after $300,000 worth of tickets had been sold, the State Governor suddenly withdrew permission, costing Rickard $50,000.

He had offers from Goldfield, Reno and Ely, all in Nevada, to host the fight and made a theatrical tour of all three venues, being greeted each time by a brass band, before announcing that the fight – the first to be billed as "The Battle of the Century" – would take place in Reno on July 4, 1910.

It was scheduled for 45 rounds, and 15,710 paid to watch Jeffries attempt to reclaim the championship. The ex-champion, never beaten in 20 fights, had shed 70 lb in training and looked drawn and haggard as he entered the ring under the blazing summer sun.

Johnson had split acrimoniously

with his manager George Little in the weeks before the fight (in a dispute over a poker hand) and the disgruntled Little bet heavily on Jeffries and spread the rumour that the fight was fixed, which caused the odds to plummet and left the challenger a 5–2 favourite by fight time.

But when the action began, it was immediately apparent that the 35-year-old veteran had no business in the ring with a champion at the peak of his powers. Johnson taunted and tormented him unmercifully, just as he had done against Burns, landing at will with jabs and hooks and evading Jeffries's crude swings.

It was all so easy for Johnson that he later claimed he deliberately held off on Jeffries because he didn't want to cause him permanent damage, and certainly from the sixth round onwards the crowd were calling for Rickard (who doubled as referee) to stop the fight.

Jeffries was game and had his pride, though, and he kept trying his limited best, all the while walking into a bewildering barrage of punches from the quicksilver Johnson, who punctuated bursts of punches with sneers like "How do you like this jab then, Mr Jeff?"

It went on like that for 14 rounds, until the end came in the 15th. A succession of short punches to the head dropped Jeffries for the first time in his life, and when he rose he was immediately floored again by two hooks to the jaw. As he crawled across the ring on his hands and knees the crowd again called on Rickard to intervene, but when Jeffries got to his feet, Rickard waved him back into action.

Jeffries was defenceless, and sagged to the ground for the third time as Johnson rained punches on him. The challenger finished with one arm draped over the middle rope, and this time Rickard signalled the end without completing the count.

DAZED AND HURT *Tunney tries to haul himself upright in the seventh round*

THE BATTLE OF THE LONG COUNT

GENE TUNNEY vs. JACK DEMPSEY

There was deep and lasting respect between Jack Dempsey and Gene Tunney. Dempsey, the glamorous and charismatic heavyweight champion, was always the man in Tunney's sights from the day the former Marine, still only a light-heavyweight, decided to make boxing his career. He worked his way up to challenge for Dempsey's title, beat him then and in the rematch, and earned the old champ's undying esteem.

And yet Dempsey might have been excused a degree of bitterness towards his old rival, since half the world was convinced that he had been robbed of victory when they met for the second time in what history came to know as "The Battle of the Long Count". Dempsey never shared that view, acknowledging that he had been in breach of the rules by not immediately going to a neutral corner when Tunney was floored in the seventh round. Referee Dave Barry, quite properly, did not commence his count until Dempsey had obeyed the letter of the law, and Tunney took full advantage by remaining on one knee until Barry had reached "nine", by which point he had been on the floor for considerably longer than the traditional ten seconds.

The incident offered a telling insight into both men and their backgrounds …Dempsey, the hard nut who brawled his way out of the mining camps and hobo camps, the fighting animal who ignored the rules in his eagerness to get at his opponent; and Tunney, the cold and calculating professional who, even in his moment of supreme crisis, remained cool enough to exploit every angle to his maximum advantage.

Dempsey had grown complacent and soft during long spells of inactivity before facing Tunney for the first time in Philadelphia on September 23, 1926, and was easily outboxed by his fast-punching and clever challenger. But when they met again, a year all but a day later, Dempsey was a different man. The shock of defeat had concentrated his mind on his business. Tunney, too, was different. He wanted to knock Dempsey out this time and, uncharacteristically, missed with a whole stream of rights as Dempsey, boxing much more cagily than in their first encounter, slipped and ducked most of his efforts.

Tunney got through in the fourth and rocked the ex-champ to his heels, but Dempsey, ignoring blood from cuts over both eyes, came back strongly in the fifth. He had a tendency to rabbit punch, and time and again he crashed blows off the back of Tunney's neck until finally the champion's bodyguard, Sergeant Bill Smith of the Chicago Police, got onto the ring apron during the interval between the fifth and sixth rounds and yelled to Barry that if he didn't stop the rabbit punches he'd "be carried out of here dead".

A minute into the seventh, Dempsey crossed a right over Tunney's jab and shook him, following up with a barrage of six unanswered hooks which sent the champion into a crouch, almost sitting on the bottom rope before crumpling to the canvas for the first knockdown of his long career. His fighting instinct hauled him into a sitting position, and there he waited until Barry at last persuaded Dempsey to move to a neutral corner. Fourteen seconds had elapsed before Barry's count reached nine, time enough for Tunney's head to clear.

When he got up, Tunney met Dempsey's charge with a right to the heart so severe that Dempsey later described it as "the hardest blow I have ever received. It was not a question in my mind of being knocked out – I thought I was going to die." That punch turned the fight back Tunney's way, and he never lost control of it again. Dempsey was floored in the eighth, and when the final bell sounded at the end of the 10th round, he immediately acknowledged Tunney's superiority. The game's toughest competitor could also lose with style.

FIGHT FACTS

DATE:	September 22, 1927
VENUE:	Soldier Field, Chicago, IL
TITLE:	World heavyweight
RESULT:	Gene Tunney won (points decision, 10 rounds)

BILLY CONN *full of confidence, has Joe Louis under severe pressure*

NO HIDING PLACE

JOE LOUIS vs. BILLY CONN

So many great fighters have had in-built flaws which prevented them from achieving their maximum potential. Billy Conn was one such, though in his case the flaw was in his temperament more than his technique. He was a brilliant boxer, but he was also of "fighting Irish" stock and, on the biggest night of his life, he allowed his Irish love of a punch-up to deny him the heavyweight championship of the world.

Conn was in his prime when he challenged Joe Louis for the title at the Polo Grounds, New York on June 18, 1941. A huge crowd of 54,487 came out that Wednesday evening to watch Louis make his 18th title defence, and despite the weight disparity (174 lb against Louis's 199½ lb) there was plenty of support for the handsome Irish-American, the former light-heavyweight champion. The betting odds opened at 18–5, making him the shortest-priced challenger for three years, and by fight time they had come right down to 11–5.

Conn, at 23, was a veteran of 67 fights of which he had won 58 and drawn one. His skill was unquestioned, but it was not complemented by punching power: his 58 wins included only 12 inside the distance, although a run of four consecutive knockouts on the lead-in to the Louis fight was a major confidence-booster. It was widely accepted that if Conn were to win, it would have to be by exploiting his speed to outmanoeuvre the slow-footed champion. Louis, though, was unconcerned. "He can run, but he can't hide," he said, coining a phrase which passed into the language.

And running was all Conn did for the first two rounds, skipping around the ring as Louis plodded after him. The challenger took a more positive approach in the third, but did not have any real success until a left jab and two following rights to the jaw stopped Louis in his tracks early in the fourth. Conn switched on to the attack, driving Louis back with quick and well-placed jabs and hooks, but the champion took over again in the fifth when he staggered Conn with a left hook to the jaw and split open a cut over the right eye and another on the nose. At the bell, Conn was so dazed that he went to the wrong corner, and had to be revived with smelling salts between rounds.

But the fast pace was telling on Louis, and from the seventh onwards he was in pain from a damaged right wrist, which he'd jarred on the top of Conn's head. As Louis faded, Conn grew in self-belief, finding the confidence to step in with quick combinations and constantly stabbing left jabs into Louis's bewildered face.

The 12th was Conn's best round. Time and again he rocked Louis with left hooks and rights, which he seemed able to land at will. In the corner, Louis's trainer Jack Blackburn spelt it out to him between rounds. "You're losing on points", he told Louis. "You've got to knock him out." A knockout was on Conn's mind, too – his success in the 12th encouraged him to believe he could finish the exhausted champion in the 13th, and he came out looking for it.

Louis soaked up the first flurry, then suddenly caught Conn with a perfect right to the chin. Three more rights sent him into the ropes, but Conn rallied fiercely. But now he was fighting on Louis's terms, and that was what Joe had been waiting for all night. A right uppercut stunned Conn, and a burst of hooks, culminating in a right to the head which spun him in a half-circle, sent the challenger down and out. He was almost on his feet when referee Eddie Joseph reached "out" after 2:58 of the round. He'd been just six minutes away from the heavyweight championship of the world.

> **❝ Of all the times to be a wise guy, I had to pick it against him. ❞**
>
> *A rueful Billy Conn, years later.*

FIGHT FACTS

DATE:	June 18, 1941
VENUE:	Polo Grounds, New York, NY
TITLE:	World heavyweight
RESULT:	Joe Louis won (knockout in 2:58, round 13)

RAGING BULL SEES RED ...

JAKE LaMOTTA vs. LAURENT DAUTHUILLE

Laurent Dauthuille had every reason to feel confident when he ducked through the ropes in front of 11,424 fans at the Detroit Olympia on September 13, 1950 to challenge Jake LaMotta for the middleweight championship of the world. He had faced the champion before, on 21 February 1949 in Montreal, and stood head-to-head with the toughest man in the division for 10 gory rounds. LaMotta finished the fight in a mess, his face smeared in his own blood, and Dauthuille got the unanimous verdict.

It was considered a huge upset. The Frenchman was regarded as, at best, a "fringe" contender, with a solid reputation in Europe but virtually unknown on the other side of the Atlantic. LaMotta, though, was the leading contender for the title, the Raging Bull who was the only man to beat Sugar Ray Robinson in Robinson's first 132 fights. He should have had a title chance years before, but it suited the shadowy figures who unofficially ran the business in those days to keep him waiting. LaMotta even threw a fight with the light-heavyweight Billy Fox, a Mob-controlled fighter, on the understanding that he would be rewarded with a crack at the middleweight title, but instead it was Marcel Cerdan who was matched with Tony Zale.

Eventually, four months after losing to Dauthuille, LaMotta was paired with Cerdan and took the title when the Algerian retired with a damaged shoulder after nine punishing rounds. Success had come late in LaMotta's career, and when he lost his next fight, a non-title 10-rounder with yet another Frenchman, Robert Villemain, it looked as though his competitive fires were burning low. There was another problem; he was finding it increasingly hard to get down to the middleweight limit of 160 lb, and had to lose more than 20 lb in training. He did it the hard way, by starving himself and "drying out", denying himself liquid until his body was weakened and dehydrated.

The peak LaMotta might have been able to bulldoze his way through the Frenchman's defences, but instead the weight-drained champion tried to hang back and jab. Dauthuille, who had soaked up some severe punishment last time they met, couldn't believe his luck. He was able to back LaMotta up, scoring easily on the slow-moving and floundering target. Fighters hate having to box out of their usual style, rarely doing so with ease or grace, and LaMotta was no exception.

For round after round Dauthuille piled up points, landing with such ease that the suspicion grew – even in LaMotta's own corner – that there might be something "peculiar" about the fight. At times LaMotta was reduced to charging at the challenger with his left arm extended like a lance, but invariably Dauthuille avoided him easily and banged in counters.

Referee Lou Handler cautioned LaMotta in the sixth and seventh rounds that he had better start working, and for a while he did manage to string a few worthwhile attacks together. By the ninth, though, the quick-fisted challenger was once again scoring at will with bursts of combinations.

LaMotta had a habit of lying back on the ropes as if he was exhausted or badly hurt, then switching onto the attack when his opponent came in to finish him off. He tried it in the 12th round, and Dauthuille obligingly fell for the well-worn ploy, but LaMotta was too arm-weary to sustain the counter-attack for long enough to do any damage. By the end of the 14th round, he was hopelessly behind on points.

As he sat on his stool before the 15th round, his left eye bleeding and almost closed, the champion was told, "You've got to knock him out."

LaMotta came out for the final round throwing everything he had, but Dauthuille knew that he needed only to survive the last three minutes to be crowned champion. He covered up and clinched, and as the round wore on LaMotta's attacks became ever more desperate. And then, in the middle of a maul, the champion spotted an opening and fired the best left hook he'd ever thrown.

The blow landed perfectly on Dauthuille's jaw, and as the Frenchman sagged back into the ropes LaMotta stormed after him, clubbing blows to the head until the challenger finally slumped to the floor. Dauthuille was brave: he struggled to haul himself up by the ropes, and as the referee completed the count he was already on one knee. There were just 13 seconds left in the fight.

THE INDOMITABLE *Jake LaMotta completes the unlikeliest of comebacks*

A DAMN CLOSE RUN THING

FIGHT FACTS

DATE: September 23, 1952
VENUE: Municipal Stadium, Philadelphia, PA
TITLE: World heavyweight
RESULT: Rocky Marciano won
(knockout in 43 seconds, round 13)

ROCKY MARCIANO vs. JOE WALCOTT

It was the night Rocky Marciano won the heavyweight championship of the world and lost his trousers, stolen from his dressing room at the Municipal Stadium, Philadelphia by a souvenir hunter with an eye for the off-beat. The list of suspects would have been lengthy, for it seemed that the entire population of Brockton, Mass. had crammed into the room to celebrate their hometown boy's success.

It had been a painfully won victory, achieved with perhaps the hardest single punch ever thrown in a heavyweight title fight. For the 29-year-old winner, the fight marked the launch of a fabulous championship reign, while the loser, Jersey Joe Walcott, earned more respect in defeat that he had ever done in victory.

Marciano, a rugged Italian-American, was a late starter, not making his pro debut until he was 23. He made it to a title fight in five years, but it had taken Walcott at least 17 – the champion's official record went back to 1930, but he was probably boxing even before then. Marciano had never been beaten in 42 fights, all but five of which he had won inside the distance. He was a 9–5 favourite, but the bookies' hearts (if that is not a contradiction in terms) must have been in their mouths in the opening round when the veteran landed a perfect left hook to drop Marciano for a count of four. He ignored his corner's calls to take an eight count, and charged at the champion. But Walcott's punches were infinitely more accurate and crisp, and by the end of a tumultuous round Marciano was bleeding from the lip and had a swelling over the left eye.

Walcott was 10 lb heavier, two inches taller and had a seven-inch reach advantage, and he used all those assets brilliantly in the first five

rounds. But however hard he landed, he could not reproduce that first-round success as Marciano ploughed forward, walking through the champion's punches in a futile bid to land his own clubbing blows. In the sixth, as the stocky challenger came up out of his customary crouch with the fighters at close range, their heads cracked together and blood spewed from a deep cut on Marciano's forehead and from a gash on Walcott's left eye-lid. The champion's injury looked the worse, but in the succeeding rounds it was Marciano who suffered. A combination of blood from his own cut and some form of medication used on Walcott's wound found its way into Marciano's eyes, leaving him virtually blind and defenceless as Walcott ripped in hooks and uppercuts. Between rounds his corner team of Freddie Brown, Charlie Goldman and Allie Colombo worked frantically, rinsing their man's inflamed eyes with small sponges soaked in cold water.

By the ninth, the eyes had started to clear but Walcott, boxing as one observer put it "with the legs of a 20-year-old", continued to outmanoeuvre and outpunch the increasingly ragged challenger. In the 11th, he landed a ferocious right to the heart which would have dropped a lesser man, and then opened a cut over Marciano's right eye. But Marciano's spirit was unbreakable, and he kept pressuring, pressuring, pressuring.

Finally, in the 13th round, it paid off. He hooked a left to the body, and as Walcott retreated to the ropes Marciano fired a short, six-inch right which exploded on Walcott's jaw with dramatic and instantaneous effect. The champion looked as though he had been filleted; he seemed to fold towards the floor in stages, ending up with his head and one knee on the canvas and his left arm hooked behind the middle rope. He had been ahead on all three cards (8–4, 7–4–1 and 7–5 in rounds), but that was academic now. After 43 seconds of the 13th round, the Marciano Era had begun.

ROCKY MARCIANO *doesn't need the left hook which followed that spectacular right – Walcott is already down and out*

YVON DURELLE *goes down for the final time in the 11th round*

THE STREET OF DREAMS

ARCHIE MOORE vs. YVON DURELLE

Durelle, the rugged and unpolished French-Canadian from Baie Ste Anne, who seemed the champion-elect. Their fight is part of boxing legend, and has become Moore's passport to immortality.

Moore was three days short of his 45th birthday, although his precise age was a matter of intense speculation. Much of that was mischievously fuelled by the man himself, who knew a good selling point when he saw one. He was a supreme salesman, principally of himself. He had talked, written and self-publicised his way into two cracks at the world heavyweight title, losing to Rocky Marciano in 1955 and Floyd Patterson a year later, and he still dreamt of a third chance.

Durelle, 29, had 11 years as a pro behind him when his big chance arrived. It hardly compared to Moore's 23 years in the business, but after 96 fights he was a seasoned, battle-hardened performer whose brawling style had carried him to the Canadian and British Empire titles. Moore, with an eye on the gate receipts, emphasized Durelle's ability. "Many regard him as just a rough club-fighter with no style or class", he said. "I fought another fellow who fitted this description – Rocky Marciano."

Moore should have heeded his own caution, because less than a minute into the fight Durelle electrified the 8,484 fans when he came up from a crouch with a booming right to the chin. Moore stood frozen by the impact, then pitched to the floor.

Somehow, he got up as referee Jack Sharkey (the former heavyweight champion) reached "nine", but Durelle was on him at once and half-punched, half-pushed him down again. This time Moore rose without a count and, adopting his familiar cross-arm defence, tried to ride out the storm. But Durelle kept firing, and another right put Moore down for the third time for a "nine" count.

Curiously, Durelle did not go all out for the knockout: he explained afterwards that he'd "forgotten this was a championship fight and that three knockdowns didn't halt the fight". Moore jabbed his way back into the fight in the second and third, though Durelle shook him in the third with a left-right to the head that made the veteran hold on briefly. After a brisk fourth round, in which the exchanges continued after the bell, Durelle found the range once more in the fifth and sent Moore sprawling with a sweeping right hook. He was up at six, and hung on frantically as Durelle went for the finish.

But in the closing moments of the round Moore hurt Durelle for the first time, and the momentum of the fight swung his way. The champion outboxed him in the sixth, and floored him for two in the seventh. The eighth and ninth were big rounds for Moore, whose left jab bloodied Durelle's nose and kept him off-balance. By the 10th, the challenger was spent: Moore battered him throughout the round, which finished with the Canadian on his knees with the count at seven.

The end came swiftly in the 11th. Durelle was floored for nine almost immediately, and Moore, who scored more knockouts than any man in history, completed the job with clinical efficiency. Another right stretched Durelle on the canvas, and he was still struggling to rise when, after 49 seconds of the round, Sharkey completed the count.

> **❝ I felt as if the top of my head was blown off. I walked the street of dreams. ❞**
>
> *Archie Moore, describing his first-round knockdown.*

Take a world champion who is generally accepted as one of the best pound-for-pound fighters of his era, maybe even the best-ever in his weight division, and match him with a contender who's been beaten 20 times, six of them by knockout or stoppage, and what do you expect to happen? A one-sided mismatch? Well, that's what it looked like in the first round when Archie Moore faced Yvon Durelle in the Montreal Forum on 10 December 1958 – except that it was Moore, the veteran light-heavyweight champion, who fought like the sacrificial offering and

FIGHT FACTS

DATE:	December 10, 1958
VENUE:	The Forum, Montreal (Canada)
TITLE:	World light-heavyweight
RESULT:	Archie Moore won (knockout in 49 seconds of round 11)

SLACKER TURNS UP THE HEAT

INGEMAR JOHANSSON vs. FLOYD PATTERSON

FIGHT FACTS

DATE: June 26, 1959
VENUE: Yankee Stadium, New York, NY
TITLE: World heavyweight
RESULT: Ingemar Johansson won
(stoppage in 2:03, round 3)

Ingemar Johansson broke all the rules. That is not to say that the handsome, dimple-chinned Swede was a dirty fighter – his behaviour inside the ring was always impeccable. What outraged the purists and the traditionalists – and in those strait-laced pre-Ali days everybody was a traditionalist – was his attitude to training.

Roadwork was something best done on the dance floor, and as for abstinence, he showed what he thought of that by installing his gorgeous girl-friend Brigit in the training camp where he was ostensibly preparing to challenge Floyd Patterson for the heavyweight championship of the world at the Yankee Stadium, New York on June 25, 1959. (Rain caused a 24-hour postponement until the 26th.) No wonder the American writers gave him no chance of dethroning even such a brittle-chinned champion as Patterson, who had been floored in one of his previous defences by Pete Rademacher, having his first professional fight.

Their opinions were largely based on the pair's respective performances in the 1952 Olympic Games in Helsinki. Patterson, a dazzlingly fast 17-year-old middleweight, won the gold medal but Johansson suffered the ultimate indignity of being disqualified in the heavyweight final for "not trying" against the giant American, Ed Sanders.

He tried to live down that disgrace by building an impressive unbeaten 21-fight run, winning the European title which he retained against British challengers Henry Cooper and Joe Erskine. But the result of which the Americans should have taken note was dismissed as a fluke: his one-round, one-punch knockout of the top-ranked Eddie Machen in the fight before he faced Patterson. The bookies reckoned him a 4–1 shot, and the public showed their apathy by staying away – only 18,215 turned up. Curiously, though, the closed-circuit takings of over $1 million were the highest so far recorded for that relatively new medium.

For two rounds, there was little to cheer about. Johansson moved back behind a light, flicking left jab, never landing hard enough to inconvenience Patterson, who won both rounds on all three judges' cards.

But there was a subtle strategy at work, as Patterson later acknowledged. "Three times he shoved out the left hand, and three times I found myself moving straight towards the right hand", he wrote in his autobiography *Victory Over Myself*. "I was directly in line with it, but three times he didn't do anything about throwing the right and I said to myself 'He's not going to throw that right at all.'"

That proved a monumental miscalculation. Early in the third, Johansson showed him another jab and Patterson once more disregarded the right. This time, though, Johansson threw it hard and straight at the champion's jaw, and Patterson went down. He was so dazed when he rose at nine that he walked towards a neutral corner, having assumed that it was he who had knocked Johansson down.

Johansson moved after him and landed a left to the back of Patterson's head and a right to the jaw, sending him down again for nine. Referee Ruby Goldstein, a former top-class lightweight, could have stopped the fight at that point but instead allowed the rout to continue. Johansson was merciless, firing right after right until Patterson dropped again. He was up at seven, down again for six, then for seven and finally for another count of nine. He tried gamely to fight back when he rose, but there was nothing left and Goldstein intervened as Johansson rocked the bewildered champion yet again with a left-right-left.

It had taken Johansson just eight minutes and three seconds of action to erase for ever the stigma of his Olympic disgrace.

FLOYD PATTERSON *cannot believe what is happening to him as "Ingo's Bingo" floors him in the third round*

TOP OF THE WORLD *Muhammad Ali is champion again*

THE RUMBLE IN THE JUNGLE

MUHAMMAD ALI vs. GEORGE FOREMAN

If you still don't understand why Muhammad Ali's knockout of George Foreman in the Stade du Mai, Kinshasa on October 30, 1974 had such world-wide impact, look again at the famous photograph of Foreman as he waits for the first bell, tree-trunk arms thrust aloft into the African night. He looks carved from stone, omnipotent, unbeatable, and that's how he seemed to all but the most loyal Ali fans at the time. There was serious concern for the ex-champion's well-being, faced with this monster whose bearing in the ring made Sonny Liston seem benevolent. This, after all, was the man who had butchered Joe Frazier and Ken Norton in two rounds apiece – and Frazier and Norton had both beaten Ali.

FIGHT FACTS

DATE:	October 30, 1974
VENUE:	Kinshasa (Zaire)
TITLE:	World Heavyweight
RESULT:	Muhammad Ali won (knockout, round 8)

Muhammad was 32, still clawing his way back from that shock, jaw-breaking defeat by Norton in March 1973. But, against all logic and visual evidence, Ali was convinced that he knew how to beat Foreman. Hugh McIlvanney, then writing for the London *Observer*, also knew how to beat Foreman. "First you shell him for three days, and then you send in the infantry", he wrote after watching George pulverize Norton in Caracas.

A confident Ali seemed unfazed by all the concern for his health. "I'm not scared of George," he said. "George ain't all that tough.'

The match was originally scheduled for September 24, but had to be postponed when, a week before the fight, sparring partner Bill McMurray caught Foreman with his elbow and split open a cut over the champion's eye. The postponement seemed more likely to damage the challenger's chances than Foreman's: older fighters find it harder to reach peak condition twice in quick succession.

Instead, it was Ali who put the delay to better use. While the moody Foreman – who had wanted to go home to America while the cut healed – brooded in his quarters, Ali played the Zaire public like a politician running for office. By fight time, he was the most popular man in the country, and George didn't have a friend in the place.

Ali's arrival in the ring at 4 a.m. local time (to facilitate live TV coverage to America) was greeted with chants of "Ali, bomba-ya" ("Ali, kill him!"), and the uproar continued in the first two rounds as Ali, shooting out quick left jabs, frustrated Foreman and tied him up at close range. Foreman swung those mighty arms like a man chopping a tree, but hardly any got through. The challenger's corner, led by Angelo Dundee, were screaming at him to stay off the ropes and use his superior mobility, but Ali – alone in the stadium – knew what he was about.

In the third, Foreman drove a powerful right to Ali's heart. It was the hardest punch he had landed, but Ali merely retreated again to the ropes and covered up, allowing Foreman to pound away at his forearms and sides. Slowly, the champion was being revealed as a one-paced fighter with only one-strategy stratetgy in his head and not even the technical wizardry of former light-heavyweight champion Archie Moore in his corner could devise a way to prise open Ali's defences.

It was a whole new experience for Foreman, the archetypal ring bully, who was not accustomed to facing opponents who did not crumble when they sampled the big man's power.

By the sixth, Foreman looked sluggish and arm-weary, but Ali's sharp little jabs were as stingingly accurate as ever. Foreman's rare successes were received in silence, while every punch Ali landed was greeted ecstatically. It all served to erode Foreman's fighting spirit. He had minimal experience of long contests, as all but six of his 40 fights had finished inside four rounds, and had no concept of pacing himself. The power had left Foreman's blows in the seventh, and Ali taunted him with "Come on, George, show me something. Is that all you got?" Foreman tried to rush Ali in the eighth, knocking him backwards into a corner where he moved sideways along the ropes.

Foreman lunged after him, off-balance, and moved straight into a left and a long right to the head which sent him stumbling to the floor. He was fully conscious, but too exhausted and demoralized to beat referee Zack Clayton's count. The Greatest had pulled off his most improbable win: after seven years, Ali was king again.

EARLY ACTION *Joe Frazier's left hand forces Muhammad Ali back in the opening round*

THE THRILLA IN MANILA

MUHAMMAD ALI vs. JOE FRAZIER

Great fights do not always involve boxers at their peak: sometimes they happen between men on the way down, like one last burst of bright sunlight before the dusk. That was the case when Muhammad Ali and Joe Frazier concluded their epic rivalry in Manila on October 1, 1975, in a clash so unrelentingly savage that neither was quite the same again.

Theirs was one of the ring's great feuds, and each time they met a classic ensued. Partly that was because of the happy blend of styles – the snarling, snorting aggression of Frazier against the inventive genius of Ali – but it was rooted too in their natures

and their personalities. Frazier was born into poverty in the Deep South, and battled his way out of it when the family transplanted to Philadelphia. Ali had a comfortable upbringing in a family which, if never wealthy, at least had no experience of real deprivation.

Frazier's upbringing left its scar on his personality: he was abrasive and monosyllabic, at least in public, and Ali's fluency and wit often made Frazier seem dull and unintelligent, which did him less than justice. Frazier bitterly resented the way Ali used his glib tongue as a weapon to diminish and humiliate him in the build-up to their first fight in 1971, when Frazier defended the title Ali had never lost in the ring. With Ali, as always, it was just promotional hype, but Frazier took it all seriously and the hurt was real.

Even when he floored and outpointed Ali, the resentment still burned, and when Ali outscored him in the rematch in 1974 the scene was set for the dream fight, the one to settle the issue between them once and for all. The fight drew a crowd of 25,000, causing a three-hour traffic jam, and world-wide television revenue set new records

This time, there was no dancing from Ali. He set himself solidly in mid-ring and lashed hard punches at Frazier, who soaked them up impassively and kept firing those short, dazzling left hooks. Ali taunted and teased Frazier in the third, talking to him in the few clinches permitted by Filipino referee Carlos Padilla, but in the fourth the tide began to flow the challenger's way. Ali spent more time

on the ropes in the fifth and sixth rounds, blocking a fair few of Frazier's hooks but being jarred to his boots by others. At the end of the sixth Ali, significantly, sat down for the first time between rounds. It was the clearest possible indication that he knew he was engaged in the fight of his life.

The seventh saw him on his toes, slamming jabs into Frazier's face, but Frazier, coming in close, buried his head on the champion's shoulder and drove home strength-draining body hooks. That was the pattern until the 12th round: a test of iron will and endurance as much as skill. Ali's title was in the balance, and he produced a champion's effort in the 12th. Frazier was driven back under a sustained barrage which left his face swollen and his left eye closing, and with restricted vision he was suddenly a vulnerable target for the revitalised Ali's sharp right hands.

In the 13th, it seemed that Frazier was on the brink of collapse. Ali's rights wobbled him, and once Joe did a crazy backwards dance, his legs out of control. But Ali too was in what he graphically called "the near room", the ante-room to death itself. It took a massive effort of will to haul himself off the stool for the 14th round, three minutes of hell as the two drained and barely conscious battlers flailed punches at each other. Frazier was in worse shape, though, and Ali scored with nine successive rights to his battered head.

At the bell, Padilla had to lead him to his corner. Trainer Eddie Futch had seen enough. "Sit down, son, it's all over", he told Joe. "But nobody will ever forget what you did here today."

Ali, ever gracious in victory, summed up his bitter-sweet relationship with Frazier when he said. "Without him I couldn't be who I am, and without me he couldn't be who he is. We've been a pretty good team."

FIGHT FACTS

DATE:	October 1, 1975
VENUE:	Manila (Philippines)
TITLE:	World heavyweight
RESULT:	Muhammad Ali won (retirement, after 14 rounds)

BRIEF, BLOODY AND BRUTAL GRUDGE MATCH

MARVIN HAGLER vs. THOMAS HEARNS

When a great fighter produces his peak performance, those lucky enough to have been there count themselves blessed. But when two great fighters hit their peak against each other, something magical is in the air and their fight lives on in the memory, growing to epic proportions with each re-telling. When middleweight champion Marvin Hagler went up against his most dangerous challenger, Thomas "Hit Man" Hearns, at Caesars Palace on April 15, 1985, it was a match made in heaven, pitting the cold professionalism of Hagler against the explosive punching of Hearns, the former WBA welterweight and WBC light-middleweight champion.

The fight had been three years in the making, partly because of the genuine animosity existing between these two proud champions, each of whom accused the other of ducking out of the match. It had taken Hagler seven years to prove what the trade had known for at least three years before then: that he was the best middleweight in the world. This was his 11th defence of the championship, and he looked absolutely invulnerable. Virtually all his challengers had been top-flight contenders, and only slippery old Roberto Duran had taken

him the full 15-rounds championship course. But Duran, who won the WBA light-middleweight title in 1984 and relinquished it to challenge for Hearns' WBC version, was flattened by the Hit Man in two rounds; on that form-line, Hearns had a real chance of upsetting the shaven-skulled, muscular champion.

The Detroit puncher had lost just once in 41 fights, a welterweight unification match with Ray Leonard, and only six of his fights had gone the full distance. Hagler's record was equally impressive: 64 fights, two draws and two defeats, and all four men who blemished his record had been beaten inside the distance in rematches.

When they came together under the evening sky at Caesars' outdoor arena, there was no feeling-out period, no jabbing for distance or range. Instead they tore from their corners like greyhounds released from their traps, smashing hooks at each other with terminal intent. Every blow was designed to produce a knockout, and against other opponents they may well have succeeded.

It was, surely, only the adrenaline of the moment which kept them upright as they rocked each other with terrifying punches. Hearns was finally forced to concede the centre of the ring and retreated to the ropes, where he traded punches with the snarling Hagler for at least 30 seconds.

MARVIN HAGLER, *a relentless fighting, machine sets Hearns up for the finish*

And then, with less than a minute to go in the round, blood suddenly spouted from a long vertical cut on the champion's forehead. He brushed the blood away with the irritated gesture of a man swatting at a fly, but he knew how serious the injury was. It was now a case of stopping Hearns quickly, or losing his title.

He tried hard for the finish in the second, but Hearns sensed victory and he punched with him, splitting open a second, horrible cut under Hagler's right eye. With nothing to gain from caution, Hagler threw everything at his man in a blistering, sustained attack, but the deceptively spindly challenger soaked it up and punched back.

Referee Richard Steele, a former professional boxer himself, stopped the action to enquire of Hagler "Can you see him?" Hagler's response was unforgettable. "I'm hitting him, aren't I?"

It ended, abruptly, in the third as Hagler proved his right to be ranked alongside Robinson, Greb and Monzon with the middleweight greats. A right hook caught Hearns flush on the chin, and his legs went into spasm as he staggered back, turning almost a full circle.

Hagler literally ran after him, landing three clubbing rights which spread-eagled him. Hearns somehow beat the count, but was defenceless and Steele took the compassionate course, throwing his arms around the beaten fighter to signal the end of an epic encounter.

FIGHT FACTS

DATE:	April 15, 1985
VENUE:	Caesars Palace, Las Vegas, NV
TITLE:	World middleweight
RESULT:	Marvin Hagler won (stoppage, round 3)

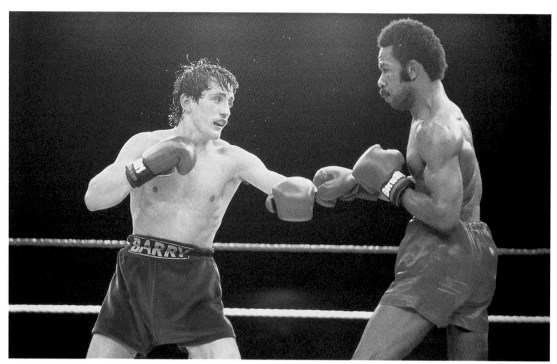

EUSEBIO PEDROZA *used all the craft acquired in 19 title defences, but could not keep McGuigan at bay*

BRILLIANT BARRY GETS THE PARTY GOING

BARRY McGUIGAN vs. EUSEBIO PEDROZA

Barry McGuigan's grip on the affections of the British sporting public in the mid-1980s was a unique product of the times and the circumstances. He was a Catholic from south of the Irish Border, married to a Northern Protestant, and his Belfast manager Barney Eastwood marketed him brilliantly as a symbol of peace and unity at a time when the only images of Ireland being presented to the British was of soldiers sprawled dead in the streets, or bombed-out buildings, or hooded corpses in ditches. The concept of McGuigan as peacemaker was nonsense, but appealing none the less: the partisans came together in the King's Hall in Belfast to roar him up the world rankings, but when the fight was over they resumed business as usual.

It helped, of course, that McGuigan could fight better than any European of his era. He was a superb pressure fighter, whose hooks to the short ribs drew anguished gasps from ringsiders as often as opponents. He built his reputation and his rating on a series of victories over world-class opposition, including the former WBC featherweight champion Juan LaPorte.

The Puerto Rican came nearer than anyone else to spoiling the Irish script when he bounced two thunderous rights off McGuigan's chin at the King's Hall, but when his protégé took them unflinchingly and roared back to win on points, Eastwood knew that McGuigan was ready to go for glory.

The title was in dispute then as now, but there was little doubt that the real champion was Eusebio Pedroza. The lanky Panamanian veteran had been champion for seven years, making 19 defences around the world, including places like Papua New Guinea, where championship boxing had never been seen. He was, in the truest sense of the words, the world champion, and Eastwood paid him almost £1 million to risk his crown against McGuigan at Loftus Road football ground on a warm summer's evening on June 8, 1985.

English soccer grounds in the 1980s tended to be forbidding, threatening places, where violence always hung in the air, but the vast Irish contingent amongst the 26,000 crowd were concerned only with celebrations. Afterwards. the police would record only two arrests, a tribute to the crowd's participation in a sporting event which is still recalled with a warm glow.

Pedroza had a well-deserved reputation as a rough handful who knew all the tricks in the book, while McGuigan's body punching had often brought him perilously close to disqualification. But for this night, they behaved with impeccable sportsmanship, as if sensing they were part of history in the making. Pedroza, tall and spindly, concentrated on his boxing in the early rounds, mixing sharp jabs with whipping right uppercuts. McGuigan was invariably slow to build an attacking rhythm, and it took him three or four rounds to force his way into contention against a masterly boxer who was having one of the best nights of an illustrious career.

But in the seventh, the Irishman surged ahead when he fired a perfect right through the gap as Pedroza's left hand dropped momentarily. The champion fell on his left side, rising at three and nodding reassurance to his corner as South African referee Stanley Christodolou completed the mandatory eight count. He somehow got through the remainder of the round, mainly by holding and frustrating McGuigan, and raised his arms aloft in mock triumph at the bell.

The Panamanian rallied splendidly to win the eighth round, but another booming right knocked the defiance from him in the ninth. From then on it became a grim battle for survival, with the proud old champion using every ounce of experience to hold his boxing together as McGuigan launched attack after attack. Whatever doubts lingered about the outcome were vanquished in the 13th, when Pedroza tottered on the brink of defeat but kept going on pride alone.

At the final bell, the verdict was announced – unanimously in favour of McGuigan – and the biggest sporting party London had seen for years got under way.

FIGHT FACTS

DATE: June 8, 1985
VENUE: Loftus Road, London (England)
TITLE: WBA featherweight
RESULT: Barry McGuigan won (unanimous decision, 15 rounds)

TOO CLOSE TO CALL

SUGAR RAY LEONARD vs. MARVIN HAGLER

There is a hoary old tradition in boxing that great champions shouldn't lose their titles on razor-thin calls, but somebody forgot to tell that to the judges when Marvin Hagler risked his WBC middleweight title against Sugar Ray Leonard at Caesars Palace on April 6, 1987. It was the fight the whole world wanted to see, even if it should have happened five years earlier before Leonard was driven into temporary retirement by an eye injury. He didn't deserve to leapfrog over the other contenders when he decided to return to action to challenge Hagler, but such considerations never worried the insufferably self-centred Sugarman. His ego was enormous, but then that was probably a large part of what made him such an outstanding performer.

Even those who were repelled by Leonard's cloyingly sweet public persona had to acknowledge that he was a rock-hard fighting man, while Hagler's worth had been proven in the furnace of more championship defences than any middleweight since Carlos Monzon, whose record he would equal were he to beat Leonard. The betting odds said he would, but the crowd's sympathies were with Leonard rather than the bleak, single-minded Hagler, who had never been able to capture the public's affection despite a magnificent seven-year reign.

Between them they secured a fabulous deal that guaranteed them a split of $23 million. Caesars Palace sold all 15,000 seats within weeks and an estimated 300 million watched worldwide on television. Leonard looked edgy and nervous when he ducked through the ropes in his short jacket-type gown, and he kept giving Hagler furtive glances during the preliminaries. He knew Hagler's strengths as well as he knew his own, and he spelt out his battle-plan from the opening bell, moving back and smothering Hagler's attacks. The champion, as ever, switched between orthodox and southpaw stances, but did not land effectively until a left hook in the second round made Leonard's eyes widen in apprehension.

Hagler's pressure took the third round, but there was an edge of frustration creeping into his work as the elusive challenger denied him a clean shot. Leonard's confidence was growing, to the point where he felt able to wind up a theatrical right and land it cleanly on Hagler's shaven skull. When Hagler tried to counter-attack, Leonard simply walked away with the unconcerned air of a man strolling in the park. It was sound psychological warfare and it was working: Hagler shouted in irritation at Leonard as they turned away at the end of the round.

But Hagler at last got on top in the fifth, hurting Leonard with a big left hook which drove the challenger to the ropes and forced him to duck and roll for survival. Leonard rallied well in the sixth with sharp counter-punching and clever defensive work on the ropes, but Hagler had him in trouble briefly again in the seventh.

Leonard's left eye looked swollen in the eighth, but he found the heart to stand, open-mouthed and weary, trading punches with Hagler in a wildly exciting ninth round. By the 10th the challenger was so tired that he stood flat-footed and missed crudely, something totally out of character for such a consummate stylist, but his heart hauled him back into the fight as he danced his way through the 11th.

There was nothing between them in a hard-fought final round, although Hagler had the last word with a left hook which sent Leonard spinning towards his own corner in the closing moments. And then there was the long wait for the verdict and the look of stunned disbelief on Hagler's face when it was announced. Dave Moretti scored 115–113 Leonard, Lou Filippo 115–113 Hagler, and Mexican Judge Jo Jo Guerra a ludicrous 118–110 for Leonard. Somehow, he had given Hagler just two rounds, rough justice indeed for a man who had proved himself one of the division's finest champions.

> **❝ If I were a betting man, I'd bet on Hagler. If I were a smart man, I'd bet on me. ❞**
>
> *Leonard's fight prediction.*

TWO WEARY BATTLERS *trade punches in a wildly exciting ninth round*

FIGHT FACTS

DATE:	April 6, 1987
VENUE:	Caesars Palace, Las Vegas, NV
TITLE:	WBC middleweight
RESULT:	Sugar Ray Leonard won (split points decision, 12 rounds)

TURN UP FOR THE BOOKS

JAMES DOUGLAS vs. MIKE TYSON

FIGHT FACTS

DATE: February 11, 1990
VENUE: Tokyo (Japan)
TITLE: World heavyweight
RESULT: Buster Douglas won
(knockout in 1:23, round 10)

Journeymen professionals like James "Buster" Douglas are not supposed to topple ring legends like Mike Tyson, but occasionally they do: that is part of boxing's mystique, part of the unpredictability which is at the core of the sport's appeal. With hindsight, of course, it was not such a surprise when Douglas knocked out Tyson in the 10th round in the massive, domed Korakuen Stadium in Tokyo. The champion was self-destructing at an alarming rate. His life was in chaos, and the team which brought him to the title had been replaced by men whose lack of professional expertise was glaringly obvious.

The problem was that no one, least of all the bookies who installed Douglas as a 42–1 outsider, had understood the speed at which Tyson was unravelling. Great fighters do not become mediocre overnight, they reasoned, nor do mediocre fighters like Douglas become great. They were wrong, on both counts. On this one night, alone among the many mundane evenings of Douglas's undistinguished career, he touched the peaks and shattered the myth which had grown up around Iron Mike, the unbeatable monster who terrified a generation of heavyweight pretenders.

Douglas, though, was an improbable dragon-slayer, who seemed to have settled for life as a middle-ranking contender. There had been one previous title chance, when he fought Tony Tucker for the vacant IBF championship and quit in the 10th round. He had lost four of his 35 fights, and was considered such a sacrificial offering that promoter Don King refused him even a single complimentary ticket for the fight.

But he was a man with motivation, beset by so many griefs and upsets that he focused totally on the fight as a bolt-hole from his problems. Just 23 days before the fight his mother died of a stroke. His wife had left him, and the mother of his 11-year-old son was dying of cancer. Douglas sought distraction and comfort in the fight, and found it. He drove himself hard in training, and for the first time came to the ring as a superbly conditioned heavyweight rather than the blubbery slob who had gone through the motions for most of his career.

Tyson, by contrast, looked soft and ill-prepared: unlike Douglas, he had not been able to turn his problems into a plus. Douglas, trim and sharp at 231 lb, outboxed Tyson easily with jabs in the opener and, in the second, introduced right uppercuts which were the perfect counter to the champion's crouching attacks. By the fourth Tyson's left eye had started to swell, and the injury progressively worsened until he was peering through a slit.

Douglas, virtually alone amongst the men Tyson had so far faced, was not intimidated by the champion's air of brooding menace. He stood toe-to-toe with him when he had to, but preferred to keep him on the end of those long jabs and whipping uppercuts. There was confusion, approaching panic, in the champion's inexperienced corner as the rounds went past and their man dropped further behind, but there was no one there with the tactical nous to devise a fight-winning strategy.

Thrown back on his own resources, Tyson almost rose to the challenge. A perfect right uppercut dropped Douglas on his back in the eighth round. Referee Octavio Meyran was slow to pick up the count, and Douglas – who had recovered by the count of "two", took full advantage of Meyran's indecision to stay on one knee until he had reached "nine", by which time Douglas had actually been down for 13 seconds.

It was Tyson's last chance, and the world watched in open-mouthed amazement as the once-formidable champion absorbed a merciless pounding throughout the ninth. The end, in the 10th, was almost a relief: a right uppercut and a four-punch combination sent Tyson to his knees, and he was counted out as he fumbled with his gumshield, cramming it lopsidedly into his mouth as Meyran signalled the end of his reign.

MIKE TYSON *takes a pounding from Buster Douglas as the unthinkable becomes reality*

DESERT SHOOT-OUT FOR OLD RIVALS

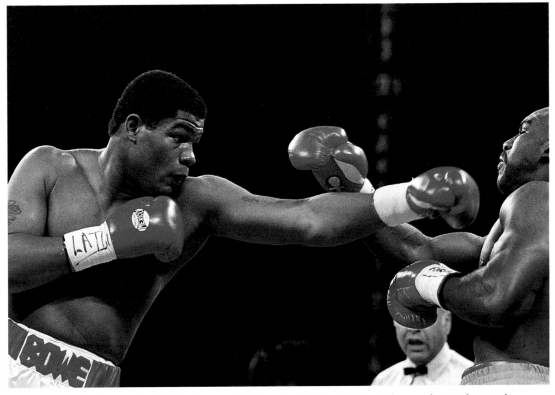

RIDDICK BOWE *lands a perfect left jab, but usually it was the lighter Holyfied who was first to the punch*

EVANDER HOLYFIELD vs. RIDDICK BOWE

Riddick Bowe and Evander Holyfield: the names are inextricably linked in the history of heavyweight boxing, like Dempsey and Tunney, Louis and Conn, or Frazier and Ali. The pair provided one of the ring's epic rivalries, clashing three times in the 1990s in fights which set new standards in courage and endurance. Bowe won the first, Holyfield the second and Bowe the decider, but they were so perfectly matched that even in their third fight, the only one to end inside the distance, Bowe had to survive a crushing knockdown to win.

They were cut from the same cloth, both scandal-free, religious men who shunned the kind of company and pastimes favoured by Mike Tyson. They were each fiercely loyal to the managers they had joined from the amateurs: Holyfield to the Duva family, and Bowe to Rock Newman. Both had competed in the Olympic Games and, by their own standards, failed. Holyfield had won a light-heavyweight bronze in 1984, while Bowe had been stopped by Lennox Lewis in the 1988 super-heavyweight final.

Holyfield won and quickly unified the cruiserweight title, but when he ran out of competition in that division he embarked on an extraordinary training programme designed to bulk his weight up into the more lucrative heavyweight class. It worked, and he duly knocked out Tyson's conqueror Buster Douglas to win the title, losing it eventually to Bowe in their first meeting at Caesars Palace in November 1992.

The rematch was set for the same venue, and the undefeated Bowe – who had outweighed Holyfield by 30 lb last time – was widely expected to repeat the result. Holyfield was 31, and was attempting what only three men had ever achieved – to regain the heavyweight title.

The first surprise was Bowe's

condition. He had allowed his weight to balloon to gross proportions and, anticipating an easy night's work, had only bothered to train down to a career-heaviest 246 lb. Holyfield, trained for this fight by Emanuel Steward, was a sculpted 217 lb. Last time, Holyfield neglected his boxing to stand head-to-head with Bowe, but Steward had devised new tactics for the rematch and Holyfield implemented them brilliantly. He darted in and out with quick bursts of punches, making Bowe seem flat-footed and ponderous, only rarely able to land his heavier blows.

By the fourth, it was clear to Bowe that he faced a tough task. Holyfield had taken the hardest punches he could land, and was still as fresh as ever. Bowe was bleeding from a cut by the right eye, and there was an uncharacteristically nasty brawl after the bell to end the round. Holyfield dominated the fifth, switching attacks effectively between head and body, and opened another cut between Bowe's eyes in the sixth.

The seventh round was a minute old when boxing's most bizarre incident occurred: a paraglider swooped down out of the night sky and landed on the ring apron, his parachute entangled in the ring canopy. There was a moment of frozen disbelief, and then Bowe's entourage grabbed the man and beat him unconscious before hotel security staff could get to him. Bowe's pregnant wife Judy, who was sitting six feet away, fainted and was taken to hospital. The fighters paced the ring trying to keep warm in the chill desert air during the 22-minute delay while the canopy was cleared and order restored.

Holyfield's accurate punches soon had blood flowing again from Bowe's cuts when the action resumed, but the champion almost turned the fight around with a fierce ninth-round onslaught which had Holyfield reeling. A full-blooded left hook, thrown after the bell, hurt the challenger badly, and he was in trouble again after taking a low left in the 10th. But he clawed his way back on top in the 11th, and soaked up Bowe's pressure in the final round to take the closest of verdicts on scores of 115–113, 115–114 and 114–114.

FIGHT FACTS

DATE: November 6, 1993
VENUE: Caesars Palace, Las Vegas, NV
TITLE: WBA and IBF heavyweight titles
RESULT: Evander Holyfield won
(points decision, 12 rounds)

TRAINERS AND MANAGERS

Boxing is, at first sight, the most individual of sports, where a man stands or falls on his own merits. It is the classic one-on-one confrontation, and if things go wrong there is nowhere the man in trouble can look to for help except inside himself. That, at least, is the theory: in practice, a boxer depends as much on his back-up team of trainer, manager, cuts man and corner help as he does on his own resources. He may be good enough to win the fight, but if his training has been inadequate or the corner work is sloppy, or self-doubt is allowed to creep into his mind, then all the talent in the world may not be enough to see him through.

If that sounds an extravagant claim to make for men who may never have taken a punch in their lives, consider the number of times an important fight has been won because of what was done in the corner. Muhammad Ali (Cassius Clay, as he then was) gained vital extra seconds' recovery time after being floored by Henry Cooper at the end of the fourth round in 1963 because of the quick-wittedness of trainer Angelo Dundee, who stuck his finger into a slight tear in one of Ali's gloves, pulled it apart, and then called the referee's attention to the damage. By the time it was established that a replacement glove could not be found, Dundee's dazed fighter had regained control of himself and went on to stop Cooper in the next round.

Then there was Teddy Atlas, whose inspired pep-talk to Michael Moorer at the end of the eighth round of his world heavyweight title challenge against Evander Holyfield in April 1994 helped make Moorer world champion. The notoriously belligerent Atlas, a fireball who once held a gun to Mike Tyson's head during a row in the days when he trained the teenager, was becoming increasingly exasperated by the way the lethargic Moorer was allowing the fight to drift away from him against a man whom Atlas could see was not the fighter he had once been. (Holyfield was later diagnosed as having a heart condition which forced him to announce his retirement, later rescinded.)

When Moorer trudged back to his stool, Atlas leapt into the ring and, planting himself in front of the fighter with his face couple of inches from Moorer's, gave a speech which has become, in its way, as famous as the "Coulda been a

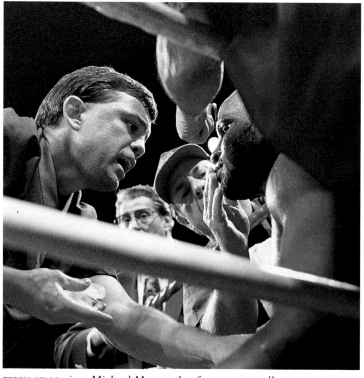

TEDDY ATLAS *gives Michael Moorer that famous pep-talk*

106

contender" monologue from *On The Waterfront*. "Do you want me to fight, huh, do you?", he yelled at Moorer. "Do you want me to change places with you – do you? Listen, this guy is finished. There comes a time in a man's life when he makes a decision – makes a decision – to just live, survive. Or he wants to win. You're doing just enough to keep him off you and hope he leaves you alone.

"You're lying to yourself, but you're gonna cry tomorrow! You're lying to yourself and I'd lie to you if I let you get away with that! You're gonna cry tomorrow because of this. Do you want to cry tomorrow, huh? Then don't lie to yourself. There's something wrong with this guy. Back him up and fight a full round." Moorer took heed, and won on points.

Ironically, Holyfield himself contributed to his own defeat by making two false economies in training. He split with trainer Emanuel Steward (Moorer's former mentor) in an argument over $100,000 – a minuscule percentage of what he earned from the fight, and what the title was worth to him; and he was badly hampered by a cut left eye, after refusing to pay top cuts man Ace Marotta $25,000 to work in his corner.

HARD DAYS AT THE OFFICE

Famous gymnasia

For 40 years Stillman's was the most famous gymnasium in boxing – home to revered trainers like Ray Arcel, Charley Goldman, Whitey Bimstein and Chickie Ferrera, and the boxing academy to which Angelo Dundee came to listen, watch and learn. New York was the world capital of boxing then, in the decades before the Las Vegas casinos discovered the sport, and at one time or another all the fighters of any consequence would train either at Stillman's or at the nearby Gleason's.

Lou Stillman opened his gym, situated at 54th and Eighth, in 1920 and ran it with an autocratic hand until its closure in 1959.

EVANDER HOLYFIELD *in his state-of-the-art gym; not all gymnasia are so well-equipped*

It was a large, long room up one flight of stairs, with a main floor 125 feet long and 50 feet wide, accommodating two rings. Up a spiral staircase, on the next level, was an area set aside for skipping and ground work. There was seating on the main floor for 200 spectators, and Stillman himself, seated on a high chair, would act as master of ceremonies, introducing the boxers who were sparring to the punters who paid their 50 cents to climb the stairs and watch the champions and contenders at work.

The closest modern equivalent to Stillman's is Johnny Tocco's, on Charleston Boulevard in downtown Las Vegas. It is small, dark, smelly and the air conditioning consists of an open back door, but the fighters love it. It has the feel and atmosphere of an old-time gym, and it is no coincidence that the boxers who felt most at home here, and who opted to train at Tocco's rather than in the casino facilities a mile up the Strip, were the blue-collar, hard-working champions like Marvin Hagler, Cornelius Boza-Edwards and Mike Tyson – when he was younger. But gyms like this are hard to find. The modern gym is much more likely to be a state-of-the-art fitness centre, where computers play a bigger role than spit buckets and skipping ropes.

Evander Holyfield is the best-known product of such an establishment. He bulked up from cruiserweight (190 lb) to heavyweight under the guidance of Tim Hallmark, a pioneer in the field who described himself as Holyfield's "Director Of Physical Build-up". Hallmark devised for him a programme combining diet control with cardiovascular exercise and resistance weight training, constantly monitoring his heart and pulse rates. Where old-time fighters strengthened their upper body by swinging an axe at a tree or hoisting barbells, Holyfield used something called a pec-deck machine, a weights-and-pulley arrangement which concentrated on the pectoral muscles.

Hallmark had Holyfield punch through water, and devised a 12-minute routine in which the boxer, feet together, jumped on and off a 2½ feet high block. He even had Holyfield taking ballet lessons, to improve his balance and movement. Somehow, one suspects Jack Dempsey or John L. Sullivan might have drawn the line there. But Hallmark's ideas worked, since Holyfield became a superbly muscled heavyweight good enough to beat George Foreman, Larry Holmes and Riddick Bowe.

His success has inspired many others to follow his example, but however much new technology and medical knowledge impacts on boxing, some things will never change. Boxers will still have to leave their beds for long runs in the early morning air, to strengthen their legs and improve their lung capacity; they will still have to do back-breaking, muscle-aching floor exercises, and they will still skip rope just as their predecessors were doing a century ago. (Sullivan, never an enthusiastic trainer, used a variation on road-work: rather than run, he used to walk a brisk eight miles every morning, doubling the distance on Saturdays.)

TRAINERS

Trainers traditionally get 10 per cent of the purse, although in these days of seven or eight-figure purses, it is commonplace for a fee to be negotiated which is much less than that. But whatever he earns, a good trainer is worth the money. He fills any number of roles: conditioner, confidante, psychologist, motivator, and strategist. Brendan Ingle, the Sheffield-based Dubliner who developed talent like Naseem Hamed, Herol Graham and Johnny Nelson, defines himself as "a

professor of boxing, a professor of psychology and a professor of kidology all rolled into one. You have to be."

Ingle has a better grasp than many of the importance of the psychological aspect of boxing. His fighters are trained to confuse and bewilder their opponents – in Ingle's phrase, to "Do their head in" rather than damage them physically. Herol Graham was the prime exponent of this kind of boxing, an artful dodger in the ring who could

reduce opponents to tears of frustration by his evasive moves. Mark Kaylor, a brave and hard-hitting middleweight, retired on his stool after eight rounds of a European title fight with Graham, telling his corner "How can I beat a man I can't even hit?"

Because Ingle likes to start them young (Hamed was seven when he first came to the Sheffield gym) he gets to know his boxers inside out, and that is essential to a successful trainer–boxer relationship. The trainer must know his man so intimately that he can sense every change of mood, every nuance of expression. That way, he can be sure of getting the best out of his man,

whereas the manager, whose role is primarily to negotiate the fee and hire the trainer, is a much more distant figure who, if he knows what is best for the boxer, will leave the corner work to the experts.

It is a two-way relationship, of course: the boxer must have absolute faith in the trainer, since he will entrust his future career to the trainer's judgement by implementing the strategies devised for him. Sometimes the trainer's art will be in kidding the fighter that a particular move or punch is the boxer's own creation, and then flattering him into constant repetition of the move until it has been mastered. Angelo Dundee, who used the

THE SIXTY-SECOND SURGEONS

The cuts man

The cuts man is an often unsung but vitally important member of the team, particularly with boxers who are cut-prone. By the time a bleeding fighter has made his way back to the corner, sat down, and the cuts man has climbed through the ropes to go to work on the injury, maybe 15 seconds of the allotted 60 have elapsed. That does not leave much time for treatment, and it is in those crucial moments that an expert cuts man comes into his own. First he will clean the cut with a cotton wool swab, taking care to change swabs between rounds to avoid the danger of dust or dirt gathering on a used swab. Hollywood films like to depict the cuts man working with a swab-stick in his mouth, but a good operator will be more hygiene-conscious than that.

Next he will soak a swab in the adrenaline solution and hold in on the wound, pressing down with his other hand. What he will never do – and here again Hollywood too often gets it wrong – is douse the man with water, since water serves to accelerate the blood flow. If there is a swelling developing, he will either use the Endswell – a small flat iron – to smooth down the lump, or else apply an ice-pack.

It is a specialized field, and the few top men working in it are always in demand. They tend to operate as freelances, rather than commit themselves to one particular camp. In Britain Paddy Byrne is much in demand, and his services are also used by anxious managers in South Africa and Denmark. In America, experts like Ace Marotta and Ralph Citro are highly paid, while some, like the late Freddie Brown (who treated Rocky Marciano's often horrible cuts) become the most valuable member of the fighter's entourage.

While the fight is underway, the trainer and his corner team will be watching closely, comparing notes and devising strategic changes, if such are needed. During the interval between rounds, in a well-run corner, only one man will be talking: too many voices distract a boxer, who has little enough time in which to absorb what may be complicated instructions. Usually, too, the trainer will not welcome comments from his boxer, who needs the recovery time and should not waste his breath and energy in talking.

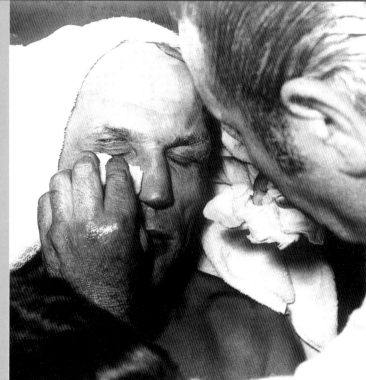

CUTS MAN *Danny Holland at work on Henry Cooper*

The final service a good trainer will do for his man is to pull him out of the fight once it becomes unwinnable, as Eddie Futch memorably did for Joe Frazier in the "Thrilla in Manila" against Muhammad Ali in 1975 with the words "Sit down, son, it's all over. But nobody will forget what you did here today." Dundee had to fight off his own corner helper, Bundini Brown, when he retired Ali against Larry Holmes in 1980. Brown grabbed Dundee's shirt, shouting for "One more round", but Dundee furiously shoved him away and yelled "Take your hands off me. He can't take any more. Get the hell away from me. I'm the boss here. It's over."

ploy to great effect with Muhammad Ali, explained: "What you have to do is make the fighter feel he's the innovator. I'd say to Ali 'You're really putting your left hand into that jab. You're really snapping it', or I'd say 'I've never seen such a great left uppercut'. Then he'd throw it again, and again."

In the long build-up to a title fight, the trainer will be responsible for supervising his man's workouts, monitoring his weight and diet, shielding him from distractions, and devising tactics, often done nowadays by studying videotapes of the opponent to analyse his style and spot his flaws. He will hire sparring partners capable of imitating the opponent's style, and will study his own man's sparring to see how he copes. Either the trainer or his assistant will "work the pads", donning large pads like a baseball catcher's mitt and moving around the ring, hands up in a boxing stance, while the boxer throws punches in combinations at the pads. The routine is intended to develop timing and accuracy.

On fight night, the trainer will wrap his man's hands in the dressing room, under the supervision of a Board of Control official and a representative of the opponent's camp.

Bandaging sounds a straight-forward procedure, but is a skill in itself. Badly wrapped hands are prone to damage, and carelessness at this stage could have catastrophic consequences for a boxer's career. The human hand is a delicate piece of engineering, with a vast number of small bones which can be broken, splintered, or jarred by the impact of a punch. Good bandaging holds the bones firmly in place, and minimizes the risk of injury. When the procedure is complete, the Board official will rubber-stamp the bandages to certify that only the permitted 18 feet length of wrapping and 11 feet of zinc oxide sticky tape has been used, and that there has been no "skulduggery". (Jess Willard claimed that Jack Dempsey's bandages had been sprinkled with a powder which, when mixed with the sweat of his hands, hardened into a type of plaster of Paris, but that allegation was never substantiated and was always vehemently denied by Dempsey.)

He may then rub Vaseline over the boxer's face and body, the theory being that the opponent's punches will slide over the grease. So long as only a reasonable amount of Vaseline is used, the referee will permit it. But if he feels there is excessive grease on the man's face, he will call for a towel to wipe away the excess before allowing the action to commence. Before leaving the dressing room, the cuts man will have checked his tool box to ensure that nothing has been overlooked. The kit contains swab-sticks, scissors, sticking tape (used to secure the glove laces), cotton wool, and a solution of 1:1000 adrenaline and water solution, which in Britain is the only coagu-lant permitted by the Board of Control. Regulations vary in America, where some Commissions allow very much stronger solutions and other States have no Athletic Commission, so anything goes. The discrepancy between Britain and America in this area has often led to unseemly scenes in corners, with Board officials attempting to confiscate solutions which they suspect to be stronger than their permitted limits.

NASEEM HAMED
and trainer Brendan Ingle (second left) celebrate victory over Freddy Cruz in 1994

MANAGERS

The importance of good management is also one of the game's constants. The roles of promoter and manager are often blurred in the modern game, where old-style independent managers, negotiating fiercely with rival promoters to secure the best deal for their fighter, are the exception rather than the rule. In the era before TV cash attracted entrepreneurs like Don King and Bob Arum into the business, managers acted like theatrical agents, hustling their clients' talent around the industry and bargaining for their services. There were "front" managers then as now, the difference being that in America they would be fronting for the Mob while in the modern era they front for big-name promoters, who have gained the exclusive services of the boxers by signing them to long-term, multi-fight contracts.

Some manage to avoid this form of commitment, but it takes enormous nerve and a lot of talent to maintain independence. Ray Leonard looked outside boxing for guidance, and placed his future in the hands of a lawyer, Mike Trainer, who was not hamstrung by the sport's customs or conventions and approached the idea of managing a fighter as he would have done any other business proposition. The pair were brilliantly successful, making Leonard enormously wealthy yet allowing him to dictate to the big promoters and TV networks rather than the other way round. Rock Newman did a similar service for Riddick Bowe, remaining stubbornly a free agent yet still managing to steer Bowe to the heavyweight championship. Roy Jones, the current (1996) IBF super-middleweight champion, has also consistently refused to grant any promoter options on his future fights, but his talent is so immense that, with the aid of two lawyers who serve as advisors, he has won world titles at two weights and become the hottest property in boxing.

Most managers, though, either double as promoters or else have close – often exclusive – links with a major promoter. Thus, for example, Lou Duva manages fighters but his family group, Main Events, do the promoting. Carl King has been "manager of record" for a host of world champions, but the chances of any of them appearing on a show promoted by one of Don King's rivals are laughably slight.

In Britain, the main promoters – Frank Warren, Mickey Duff, Frank Maloney and Barry Hearn – also manage their own extensive stables of boxers, who appear on their shows or those of their provincial associates. It is rare indeed for boxers from one camp to appear on another's promotions, unless a championship is involved. The small-time managers tend to serve as "feeders" to the major operators, with their boxers generally used as "fodder" to fatten the record of the promoter's rising stars.

In the old days, the business was very different. Managers like Doc Kearns, who looked after a host of champions like Jack Dempsey, Mickey Walker and Archie Moore, became major personalities in their own right, even if many of the business deals they struck either on their own behalf or for their clients would be considered wildly unethical today. Kearns was a larger-than-life character who worked his way through several fortunes, at least one of them his own. Jack Dempsey, his most successful fighter, recalled him in this way in his autobiography: "Jack Kearns was not the type of guy to sit still and watch the world go by. He tackled just about anything, whether it was acceptable or not. He was a crafty alligator, a real slicker, as expert at

ROCK NEWMAN *has made a fortune for his client, heavyweight champion Riddick Bowe, while preserving his fighter's independence*

making a fortune as losing one. He was a man who connived for success, and any method was good enough just so long as it worked."

Kearns and Dempsey were at loggerheads as often as they were bosom pals, but overall Kearns did a good job for his man. So, too, did Billy Gibson, who steered Gene Tunney to the championship he acquired at Dempsey's expense. Tunney was an exceptionally bright and shrewd individual, and Gibson probably would not have been able to cheat him even had he wanted to.

Kearns took over Archie Moore's management at a time when Moore's career was apparently drifting towards its conclusion. Moore had been a top contender for years, first at middleweight and then at light-heavyweight, but was just too good for his own

good: successive champions in both divisions gave him the cold shoulder. Kearns managed Joey Maxim, a competent but colourless performer who held the light-heavyweight title, and he saw Moore as a much more marketable commodity. He moved in on the fighter's then-manager, Charley Johnson, and bought his contract on exceptionally favourable terms, and then promptly matched him with Maxim. Whatever the outcome, Kearns would be a winner.

Not all managers were so mercenary. Cus D'Amato was never motivated primarily by money when he was developing the skills of Floyd Patterson, Jose Torres or the teenage Mike Tyson: he was searching for the perfect fighting machine, and it was his tragedy that, having discovered him in Tyson, he died before his protégé's talent

MICKEY DUFF *and Lloyd Honeyghan had a volatile but very successful partnership, peaking with the world welterweight championship*

had flowered. D'Amato cherished his independence above everything else, even at a time when the International Boxing Club under Jim Norris enjoyed a virtual monopoly on world championship fights. D'Amato refused to do business with the IBC, since he knew that there were more shadowy and sinister figures than Norris involved, and he performed an astonishing feat of managerial skill to bring Patterson through the ranks to the heavyweight championship.

Having got him there, he kept him champion by matching him with a selection of no-hopers in well-paid defences, which after all is a manager's first responsibility to his charge. When Sonny Liston emerged as leading contender, D'Amato opposed the match so strongly that Patterson, his professional pride stung, broke with his mentor and insisted on taking the fight anyway, with disastrous consequences.

In Britain, as in America, the contrast between caring and callous managers was striking. Ted Broadribb's daughter Chrissie married Freddie Mills, yet Broadribb matched Mills in one brutal fight after another until the fighter was spent. Perhaps the consequences of absorbing repeated poundings was not as widely understood then as it is now, but it remains hard to believe that Broadribb could watch his man take a merciless beating from Gus Lesnevich in a world light-heavyweight title challenge on May 14, 1946 and then put him in with British heavyweight champion Bruce Woodcock in a tough 12-rounder on June 4.

The other side of the coin was Jim "The Bishop" Wicks, who guided Henry Cooper throughout his long career. Wicks involved Cooper in every stage of the deals he made on his behalf, usually insisting that Cooper attend his meetings with the rival promoters who were bidding for his services. Wicks' concern was always to get the best deal going for "My 'Enery", as he always called him, and he did his job so well that Cooper retired a wealthy man and remained friends with his old manager until Wicks' death.

Such a close relationship between manager and boxer is unusual. Mickey Duff, himself a hugely successful manager and promoter, summed up his role perfectly when he was being quizzed by a reporter about yet another dispute with his world welterweight champion, Lloyd Honeyghan. "There's nothing in our contract that says we have to like each other", Duff said, and the shades of generations of harassed managers raised ghostly glasses in agreement.

THE FAMOUS PROMOTERS

Promotion is a multi-million pound business of companies usually headed by single promoters. Barry Hearn is promoter for Matchroom, Frank Warren for Sports Network and Mickey Duff for National Promotions. In the USA, the business is dominated by three groups: Don King, Bob Arum (Top Rank) and the Duva family's Main Events.

In bare-knuckle days bouts were promoted by agreement between the backers of the respective pugilists. Terms would usually be thrashed out in a tavern or "sporting house" when the fight was set up. Each side would then go away to train, the prize money having already been lodged with a trusted independent. Pugilism had its own society and largely looked after itself, with varying fortunes according to the social mood of the time.

Only towards the end of the nineteenth century did bouts become promoted by either a single entrepreneur or an organization. The most powerful organization in early British boxing was the National Sporting Club, which established what amounted to an autocratic grip on the championship scene. They allocated the Lonsdale Belts, which were the "badges" of the British champions, and they matched men accordingly.

Before the National Sporting Club was formed in 1891 boxing was illegal, except for sparring sessions and small-time competitions in amateur clubs. Anyone caught boxing, with gloves or bare-knuckle, in a discernible competition, was arrested as a common criminal. The Pelican Club existed from 1887 to 1892 more or less as a house for gambling on bare-knuckle fights, providing for the upper classes, and the National Sporting Club was formed with similar aims, for those who considered themselves respectable gentlemen but were not of sufficient social standing to gain admittance to the Pelican Club.

However, because of the dedication of two principal members, John Fleming and A.F. "Peggy" Bettinson, the club grew in stature and drew members from the City of London and the West End. Men went to the club's Covent Garden headquarters straight from work, ate a steak or chops in the grill room, downed it with a pint of beer or three, and then settled down to watch the boxing. It increased from a gambling alternative to the Pelican to a genuine "organizer" of all things appertaining to boxing. It gave British boxing a firm base, although gradually Fleming and Bettinson chased the favours of a wealthier clientele to add greater financial stability and so took it further away from its original supporters.

When the Pelican Club closed, the NSC moved "up-market". This, of course, took boxing away from the common man, but it did afford it a more powerful social standing. And this in turn enabled it to survive the death of Walter Croot of Leytonstone following a fight with Jimmy Barry of Chicago at the club in 1897. Calls for the club to be closed down were resisted, but the crisis deepened as four boxers died there in the space of four years. The arguments then were pretty much the same as they are now. Bettinson took the "accidents will happen" line, while the critics said such accidents could not happen if boxers didn't box. But the club was so well established that in a test case at the Old Bailey in 1901 boxing received the tacit backing of the law. The jury took only two minutes to decide that the death of a boxer named Billy Smith was an accident and the result of a legitimate boxing contest, not a prize-fight. By the time the National Sporting Club closed its doors in 1929, boxing was established as a national sport.

As boxing grew in popularity in the early years of the century, so its business expanded beyond the doors of the NSC. And try as they might, they could not control either the earning power of the boxers or the matches that were made.

By 1910 the old champion Dick Burge was promoting at the Blackfriars Ring, a former chapel in south London. He regularly drew packed houses and in 1914 was established enough to promote a huge fight between Georges Carpentier and Gunboat Smith at Olympia. Burge died of pneumonia in 1918 and his widow Bella continued promoting shows at The Ring until the Second World War broke out. In October 1940 the Ring was blown to rubble by a German bomb.

Solomons wisdom

Premierland and Manor Hall were popular venues in the 20s and in 1931 a fishmonger named Jack Solomons began promoting at an old church in Devonshire Street, Hackney, in north London. He called it the Devonshire Club. Solomons lost £275 – a small fortune in those days – on an over-ambitious first promotion at the Clapton Stadium when he staged a British bantamweight title fight between Johnny King and Dick Corbett.

Solomons went on to be one of the greatest boxing promoters in history, taking over from men like Jeff Dickson and Sydney Hulls, primarily because of his success with one of the greatest crowd pleasers of the day, the Chatteris lightweight Eric "Boy" Boon, who was so good he won a Lonsdale Belt outright before his twentieth birthday.

Solomons fell out with the Board of Control at one point and handed back his licence, continuing to promote without one. The Board, as a self-appointed body, could do nothing to stop him. Solomons and Hulls worked together on major shows, and eventually he grew to be the dominant force in British, indeed European boxing, staging all the great outdoor shows in the post-war boom. His first major success was the Jack London-Bruce Woodcock British heavyweight title fight at White Hart Lane football ground in front of an official crowd of 26,479 in 1945.

"I made £400 profit," Solomons recalled in his autobiography. "Far, far more important to me was the fact that at long last I had laid the foundations of Solomons Promotions. I was in, and I meant to stay in."

Solomons saw off all rivals for the next decade and a half, putting on classics involving Woodcock, Freddie Mills and the greatest night in all those post-War years, the 1951 world middleweight title bout between Sugar Ray Robinson and Randy Turpin at Earls Court in west London.

Eventually Solomons was challenged by Harry Levene in the 1960s and was superseded, retreating to the World Sporting Club, a dinner and boxing establishment at a Mayfair hotel, and branching out

only occasionally with men like the British heavyweight champion Danny McAlinden.

Levene and his partners Mike Barrett, Mickey Duff and Jarvis Astaire were in control by the late 1960s and established themselves as one of the major forces in world boxing in the 1970s. They promoted a string of world champions, including John Conteh, Alan Minter, Jim Watt, Maurice Hope, John H. Stracey and, in the 1980s, Charlie Magri and Cornelius Boza-Edwards.

Frank Warren and ITV

Their dominance was such that they virtually monopolised boxing shows on BBC television. And because of that, they were able to hold all challengers to their supremacy at bay. That stranglehold was broken only by the interest shown by ITV in the early 1980s when they supported the brash young north London promoter Frank Warren, who had previously operated outside the British Board of Control.

Warren shook the boxing establishment to its core, challenging its rulings repeatedly and eventually forcing the Board to take out membership of the World Boxing Association. Since the formation of the World Boxing Council in 1962, the British Board had allied itself to the WBC and ignored the rival body, the WBA. No British boxer of the time was allowed to fight for a WBA belt.

Warren, however, challenged even that status quo – and, as always, with no legal standing, the Board were forced to accept not only him,

JACK SOLOMONS *was the leading British promoter in 1940s and '50s*

but the WBA and any other world bodies that chose to introduce themselves. Eventually, this led to "world" title fights approved by the International Boxing Federation, the World Boxing Organization and

even the virtually meaningless World Boxing Federation being staged in Britain.

Warren and ITV opened up British boxing in the 1980s until by the end of the decade it was more or

THE FAMOUS BOXING ARENAS

White City

Boxing was big business in Britain in the years after the Second World War, and promoter Jack Solomons regularly drew crowds like this to his open-air shows at White City Stadium in west London. The stadium was home to the athletics events in the 1908 Olympic Games, and was used primarily for athletic meetings (many world records were broken there) and greyhound racing, although it also hosted some of the games in the 1966 soccer World Cup. It was demolished in the late 1980s.

THE FAMOUS BOXING ARENAS

Royal Albert Hall

Virtually every British world champion from the 1960s onwards boxed at the the Royal Albert Hall. It has always been a popular venue – Jack "Kid" Berg won his world light-welterweight title there in 1930. For nearly 20 years, from the mid-1960s to the mid-1980s, Mickey Duff and Mike Barrett had exclusive promotional rights, and ran shows there at least once a month.

less a free market. His first world champion was the IBF light-welterweight champion Terry Marsh and he went on to promote some of the biggest names in boxing: Nigel Benn, Frank Bruno, Steve Collins, Colin McMillan, Steve Robinson and Naseem Hamed were all world champions in the 1990s.

Meanwhile, snooker impresario Barry Hearn brought his Matchroom organization into boxing in the late 1980s, beginning with a stake in the lucrative 1987 fight between Bruno and veteran Joe Bugner. Hearn forged links with ITV and also branched out into the new satellite market, working with the ill-fated Screensport channel as well as Eurosport through his own series, Pro-Box.

Hearn's major success was in the shape of the eccentric but talented Chris Eubank, who was WBO middleweight and super-middleweight champion through more than 20 title fights, a record for a British boxer. Hearn and Eubank negotiated a 12-month deal worth a reported £10 million with the major satellite channel Sky Sports. Eubank's demise in 1995 sparked a split with Hearn, but the promoter continued to flourish, guiding WBO welterweight champion Eamonn Loughran and the former WBO

heavyweight title holder Herbie Hide.

Sky Sports became a major player as television's hold on boxing increased in the 1990s. They snatched the services of Lennox Lewis through Lewis's promoter Frank Maloney, after ITV had built him up, and it was Sky who covered all of Lewis's winning WBC heavyweight title fights in 1993 and 1994. The following year they sealed a multi-million pound deal with Frank Warren to lure him away from ITV.

Warren, by now, was also a partner of the controversial American promoter Don King. Consequently,

in spite of his years working with Mickey Duff and first manager Terry Lawless, and becoming a household name on the BBC, Bruno won the WBC heavyweight crown (at the fourth attempt) on a Sky Sports show.

The proliferation of television channels had made boxing more open market by the middle 1990s, preventing the kind of monopoly held in the 1970s by the BBC and the promotional partnership of Duff, Barrett, Levene and Astaire from happening again.

So much for British boxing.

Tex Rickard

In the USA, where power transferred from Britain towards the end of the bare-knuckle era, promoters have often seemed larger than life figures. "Sunny Jim" Coffroth was the best of the promoters in the early years of the century. He was a Californian entrepreneur who staged the Jack Johnson-Stanley Ketchel world heavyweight title fight in Colma, just outside San Francisco, in 1909.

Coffroth was an opportunist, not above guiding a boxer to act in both of their interests. For example, he is said to have told Johnson to hold Ketchel up because he was having the fight filmed and didn't want it killed at the box office by a quick ending. Johnson was knocked down in the 12th round, and got up to flatten the middleweight Ketchel with his next attack. The film sold rapidly, giving Coffroth a lucrative bonus.

Coffroth and his arch rival "Tuxedo" Eddie Graney, the man

BARRY HEARNS *celebrates Chris Eubank's victory over Henry Wharton in Manchester in 1994*

who refereed the last three of Jim Jeffries's title defences in San Francisco, thought they had only each other to worry about when the Johnson–Jeffries bout was up for grabs in 1910. In those days negotiations were different to those of today. Jeffries and Johnson agreed to fight each other and then threw it open to offers from promoters, which were opened in a hotel in Hoboken, New Jersey.

Other promoters present apart from Coffroth and Graney were Tom McCarey, who had worked with Johnson in the past out of the Pacific Club in Los Angeles, Hugh McIntosh, the Australian who had staged the incredible Johnson-Tommy Burns fight in Rushcutter's Bay near Sydney, and a newcomer George Lewis (also known as Tex) Rickard. To general amazement when the bids were opened the winning bid was made by Rickard, who guaranteed the boxers $101,000 and two-thirds of the movie rights. Each fighter would also get a $10,000 bonus for just signing for the contest.

Rickard was backed by a Minnesota millionaire named Thomas Cole, who owned silver and gold mines in the USA and Alaska. Rickard had previously promoted a lightweight title tight between the great Joe Gans and Battling Nelson, which lasted 42 rounds in Goldfield, Nevada, where Tex had a gambling saloon at the time.

He was a gambler by nature and had already won and lost fortunes in gaming houses and business deals when he struck it rich with the Johnson–Jeffries fight (which he refereed

TEX RICKARD *He and Jack Dempsey became the world's best-known promoters*

himself) which became known as the Fight of the Century, even though the century was but a decade old. But it was Jack Dempsey and the Roaring Twenties which made Tex Rickard into one of the greatest, perhaps the greatest, boxing promoter in history.

Paul Gallico, who made his name as a sports writer before moving into "serious" literature, said Rickard understood how to make money work. "He knew how to exhibit it, use it, spend it … " Rickard knew that by paying out big money, he attracted big attention. If his fighters looked as if they were wealthy, then they drew the attention of the wealthy … and Rickard himself could feed off that and increase his business, and that of his fighters, by association alone.

Through Tex Rickard as much as through his own fists; Jack Dempsey became a "somebody". Other men before him had held the heavyweight championship of the world, but nobody had made it work for him the way Dempsey did. In his autobiography *Massacre In The Sun*, the world champ said: "We never had a contract. You didn't need one with Tex Rickard. He was the great man of my life. They don't make them like Rickard any more … I hadn't met a promoter before who gave a damn whether I lived or croaked."

Rickard promoted Dempsey's major fights from the day in the blazing sun of Toledo, Ohio, when he destroyed Jess Willard in three rounds to the night in the pouring rain of Philadelphia when 120,757 packed themselves into the Sesquicentennial Stadium to see Dempsey lose the title to Gene Tunney. Rickard promoted the first fight to gross $1 million, Dempsey's defence against Georges Carpentier at Boyle's Thirty Acres in Jersey City, New Jersey. Around 91,000

fans showed up and shelled out an official $1,626,580.

The only one of Dempsey's title defences not promoted by Rickard was the 15-rounder with Tommy Gibbons in Shelby, Montana, which was financed by a haphazard conglomerate of local businessmen. The town was more or less ruined and the challenger, Gibbons, went 15 rounds for nothing because hardly anyone turned up and most of those who did somehow omitted to pay at the gate. Rickard died of peritonitis in Miami in January 1929, leaving a huge hole in boxing's finances.

The 1930s were a poor time for everybody. The Wall Street Crash ruined investment plans the world over. Money was scarce. Jimmy Johnston promoted men like Jack Sharkey and then became matchmaker at Madison Square Garden in 1931. But it fell to Mike Jacobs, a former ticket hustler and wheeler-dealer who used to work Rickard's fights to take boxing into a new era. Johnston was one of many who believed black fighters couldn't sell tickets. The bad publicity generated by Jack Johnson's seven-year reign had also prejudiced boxing promoters, Rickard included, against using black heavyweights in particular.

Consequently, when Joe Louis came along, Johnston didn't want to know. But Jacobs, already tipped off about his remarkable ability by the editor of *Ring* magazine, Nat Fleischer, showed no such bias. As Louis himself was to recall: "Mike had no prejudice about a man's colour so long as he could make a

THE FAMOUS BOXING ARENAS

Madison Square Garden

The funeral cortege of Joe Humphreys, the best-known boxing MC of his time, pauses outside Madison Square Garden, New York in July 1936. This was the second Garden: the original, built in 1882 and rebuilt only eight years later, occupied a site in Madison Square. It was pulled down in 1925, and Tex Rickard erected the building shown here on 8th Avenue. In 1968, the latest Garden opened at 7th and 31st, opposite Penn Station.

green buck for him." Louis's managers Julian Black and John Roxborough signed the young man over to Jacobs's Twentieth Century Sporting Club and the partnership lasted for the next decade and a half.

Jacobs staged all of Louis's title fights, eventually also working out of Madison Square Garden and establishing himself as the most powerful boxing figure in the world from the late 1930s all the way through to the end of the next decade. "Uncle Mike" was old and ill when Joe Louis switched his attention to the newly formed International Boxing Club owned by millionaires Jim Norris and Arthur Wirtz in 1949. They bought Louis's attention, and persuaded him to retire in return for an annual salary of $20,000. They also bought Jacobs out as Madison Square Garden matchmaker, then helped Louis launch his comeback and bought out all the major contenders.

Eventually they persuaded Louis to take one last fight against Rocky Marciano, whom they were also pushing, and just as Rickard and Jacobs prospered because of Dempsey and Louis the IBC blossomed because of its control of Marciano, who reigned as world heavyweight champion from 1952 to 1956. However, when the US Government won an anti-trust law case against the IBC it was forced to disband. Norris fought on to the end of the decade, but by then the IBC had faded as a viable promotional force.

New Governing Bodies

In 1962 the World Boxing Association was formed, quickly followed by its rival, the World Boxing Council, in what was at least partially an attempt to prevent any single promoter obtaining absolute power again. And for a while at least, it looked as if it would work. The governing bodies controlled the championship bouts and ensured different promoters got a fair crack ... or so it seemed.

However, the governing bodies fell some way short of the ideal. The weakness of the theory is simple – it relies on integrity and on a completely unbiased sense of fair play for it to work. If deep working relationships were formed between boxing promoters and the governing bodies, then the system becomes open to favouritism and prejudice. Some promoters, inevitably, become more powerful than others – and not simply because of their ability to conduct their businesses successfully. There was, of course, nothing to stop anybody setting up a world boxing authority, but it took until the early 1980s for a third organization to come into being.

The major promoters of the late 1970s were Bob Arum, a New York lawyer, and Don King, who had risen from the streets of Cleveland, Ohio, where he had once worked as a numbers man, and who had served time for killing a man. (He was later pardoned.) King formed a working relationship with WBC president Jose Sulaiman, who assumed a level of control within the organization that many perceived to be beyond the duties expected from a man in his position. But as undemocratic as the system appeared, it worked.

The WBA was accused of corruption by Arum in 1982 when in an interview with *Ring* magazine he admitted paying a bagman, a Puerto Rican named Pepe Cordero, to "get things done" in the WBA. The flaws in the governing body system became exposed, and the increased influence of television enabled a new authority, the International Boxing Federation, to grow out of foundations laid by a disenchanted number of WBA members who walked out of an annual convention in frustration at being unable to make changes they felt were necessary. Bobby Lee of New Jersey ran the IBF, with the help of his son Bobby Jnr. The hunger of television companies for world championships enabled first the IBF to obtain TV revenue and then, in 1988, for the WBO to do the same. The WBO was formed by none other than Pepe Cordero, who had himself become fed up with the WBA.

The proliferation of world title bouts in this time was quite staggering. In 1963 there were 20. In 1973 there were 40. In 1993 there were 140! By then the dominant world promoters were King and Arum and the South African Cedric Kushner, who worked predominantly with the IBF. In 1993, Kushner promoted 21 world title fights either solely or in association with minor promoters. King and Arum promoted 20 and 17 respectively. Barry Hearn's Matchroom organization was a party to 14 championship bouts, while the Duvas' Main Events team had 12. This was a bad year for the Duvas. In the four-year period from 1990 to 1993, Kushner promoted 71, Dan Duva 69, Bob Arum 61, and Don King 47. King had business problems in this period following the controversial defeat of Mike Tyson by Buster Douglas in Tokyo in February 1990, and his figure was low because he was in a rebuilding period at the time.

Cedric Kushner is a South African who made his first significant money as a promoter of rock concerts. But by 1985 he was firmly established as one of the rising stars in boxing and today, based in New York State, he is one of the most powerful men in the boxing business.

Main Events is a family affair. The patriarch, Lou, acts as a trainer and manager with the organization's fighters, who include Evander Holyfield and Pernell Whitaker. They cemented their position at the head of the business when they signed up virtually all of the American medallists in the brilliant 1984 Olympic team. Lou's son Dan wore the promoter's hat until his untimely death, aged only 44, in January 1996, but this is very much a team effort with no distinct leader.

Don King roadshow

Don King continues to carve his own path. "Jail was my school," he said of the four years he spent in prison from 1967 to 1971 for the manslaughter of a man named Sam Garrett, whom he had suspected of cheating him on a numbers

THE FAMOUS BOXING ARENAS

Caesars Palace

Caesars Palace (the missing apostrophe is deliberate), in Las Vegas, has hosted some of the greatest fights of the last 20 years in its famous outdoor arena. Marvin Hagler battled Thomas Hearns, John Mugabi and Sugar Ray Leonard there, and Leonard won his epic welterweight title clash with Hearns at Caesars. Larry Holmes won his WBC title in the indoor arena behind the major stadium, and retained it against Muhammad Ali on an emotional night there. Caesars Palace also hosted all three of the Riddick Bowe vs Evander Holyfield classics.

DON KING *(left) rose to power on the back of Muhammad Ali, but has stayed there on merit.*

deal. King managed heavyweight Earnie Shavers and in 1974 worked as a consultant on the videoing of the George Foreman-Ken Norton fight. But he really launched himself because of his association with Muhammad Ali, which superseded that of Ali and Bob Arum, and he came to dominate the heavyweight division through Larry Holmes in the first half of the 1980s. He also bought up most of the top ten heavyweights and so controlled who fought for the championship. The WBC rarely, if ever, chose to work with another promoter as long as King wanted to be in on the fight. The relationship was perceived as unhealthy, but that was the way it was.

The arrival of Mike Tyson under co-managers Jim Jacobs and Bill Cayton threatened King's heavyweight supremacy, but Jacobs's untimely death altered the situation. Tyson and Cayton were never close and by 1988 the young champion had switched allegiance to King. His empire continued to prosper until Tyson's defeat by Buster Douglas in Tokyo. Douglas successfully

bought himself out of his promotional contract with King in the courts, and promptly lost the title to the Main Events fighter, Evander Holyfield.

King was thus in the heavyweight wilderness for the first half of the 1990s and therefore was forced to concentrate his attentions on the lighter divisions, focusing in particular on the Mexican superstar Julio Cesar Chavez. Tyson in turn spent three years in jail after being convicted of rape. King, however, climbed back after a suitable period of taking stock and by the close of 1995 was once more in a commanding position.

Tyson was out of jail and King had under contract three of the four heavyweight champions recognized by the governing bodies. Through his association with British promoter Frank Warren, King controlled the immediate destiny of Frank Bruno, the WBC champion. He also had the WBA champion Bruce Seldon and the IBF champion, the South African Frans Botha. Only WBO champion Riddick Bowe, whose manager Rock Newman stayed steadfastly

independent remained outside King's heavyweight net. King survived wire fraud charges heard late in 1995 and remains one of the hardest working, certainly one of the noisiest promoters in history.

Arum, the son of a New York accountant, graduated from Harvard Law School in 1956. He has been involved with boxing since 1962 when he was working for the United States Attorney's Office in New York and was involved when the Internal Revenue Service

impounded the revenue from the closed circuit rights to the first Floyd Patterson–Sonny Liston fight. Arum liked what he saw and got involved, promoting several of Muhammad Ali's world championship bouts before Ali was stripped of the title in 1967 for refusing to fight in Vietnam. Arum also promoted Ali's comeback fights from 1970 and today promotes the extremely marketable lightweight champion Oscar De La Hoya.

THE IRREPRESSIBLE DON KING *with two of his round-card girls*

THE ADMINISTRATION OF BOXING

Boxing is one of the few major international sports that is not run by a simple, regulatory body – it has at least four, each of whom install their own "world champions". Anarchy rules, but then there's nothing new about that ...

In the days before any so-called world governing bodies existed there were usually just eight world champions, acknowledged by their peers and by the fans as the best at their weight. Today, there are four widely accepted ruling bodies and a myriad of minor organizations each with their own champion in 17 weight divisions. At least half the names in any listing of the top ten in each division can claim to be "world champion" in their category, while the champions of some of the lunatic fringe organizations would struggle to command a place among an impartially assessed top 50 in their division, let alone the top 10. A state of near-anarchy prevails, and since it is profitable for all concerned, that is how it will remain.

Only the purists, those with a feel for the game's history, are offended by the proliferation of titles. As far as the average television viewer or casual fan is concerned, one

world title is as good as another. Thus, the Danes happily pay to watch contests for the obscure International Boxing Organization (IBO) titles, which command zero respect in America and are not welcomed in any other European country; thus, the British have turned the World Boxing Organization (WBO)

CHAMPIONS *were appointed by popular acclaim in the bare-knuckle era*

into a major force, despite its low profile in America. Many US publications do not even mention the WBO when publishing lists of the rival world title claimants, so lightly is it regarded there, yet British boxers like Chris Eubank, Herbie Hide, Steve Robinson, Duke McKenzie and Naseem Hamed have earned well in WBO title fights. Steve Collins failed twice to win World Boxing Association (WBA) titles and was carefully avoided by the champions of the rival bodies, yet became an instant millionaire by taking Eubank's WBO super-middleweight championship. The customer is always right: market forces prevail.

Television, a mixed blessing for boxing, bears much of the responsibility for the multiplicity of titles. The label "World Championship Boxing" attracts viewers and sells commercial slots, and there will always be a promoter prepared to stage a title fight and a TV company willing to screen it regardless of the organization's status or the degree of public acceptance it commands.

CHAOS DESCENDS *as cameramen, photographers and assorted nonentities pile in to the ring after Mike Tyson's defeat of Razor Ruddock in 1991*

Bob Arum, one of the world's top promoters, puts on championships under the aegis of the World Boxing Union, the most recent addition to the throng, which is run from a village in Norfolk, England by its founder, Jon Robinson. The WBU is not even recognized by the British Boxing Board of Control, which is affiliated to the four major bodies, but that has not prevented it acquiring the services of a few big-name champions including George Foreman, Thomas Hearns and James Toney.

For the fighters, as well as the promoters and TV companies, it seems that one championship belt is as good as another. Managers, unsurprisingly, take a more pragmatic view than their clients. "With that plastic championship belt and a dime I can ride the city buses", Curtis Ramsey's manager told him as the fighter was proudly displaying his newly won World Athletic Association welterweight title belt. The manager had been so underwhelmed by the occasion that he stayed at home watching TV rather than attend the fight.

The Power of the Press

There is nothing new about the media influencing boxing, or the appointment of its champions. In the days before television, Commissions or Boards of Control, it was the print press who formed public opinion as to the merits of rival claimants. In bare-knuckle Britain Pierce Egan's *Boxiana* and, later, Henry Downes Miles's *Pugilistica* recorded their deeds and traced the course of the championships, while in America, in the last quarter of the nineteenth century, as prize-fighting grew in popularity there, Richard

Kyle Fox's *Police Gazette* fulfilled the same function. Fox was a Dubliner who emigrated to America in 1871 when he was 29. Like so many of his countrymen he brought nothing with him but an eagerness to work and a hunger for advancement, and within two years he had saved half of the $400 needed to buy a discredited and failing scandal sheet called the *National Police Gazette*.

Fox proved a publishing genius, and quickly turned the paper's fortunes around. He had a flair for imaginative sales gimmicks, designed to boost public awareness of his 10-cent product. In addition to giving away more than $250,000 in cash prizes, he awarded a whole range of belts, trophies and cups commemorating the most bizarre and obscure achievements of the type which today are chronicled

in the *Guinness Book of Records*. But the real key to his success was that he was the first newspaper publisher to identify and service the public's craving for sports news. He introduced a full sports section, and the leap in circulation which followed convinced rival publishers to do likewise.

Fox appreciated that prize-fighting was among the most popular sports with his readership, even though it was still illegal in all the (then) 38 states of America. He concentrated his coverage on fights and races, and soon the *Gazette* had attained a position of influence and power in the sport unmatched by any other publication until *Ring* magazine was founded in 1922. It was so successful that there was even a British edition, which was launched in 1896. In the same year he published the first of his annual record books, which continued until a fire in 1918 unfortunately destroyed the paper's offices and all its records.

Changing public tastes, coupled with the competition from *Ring,* finally killed the *Police Gazette* off in 1932. But it had served a worthwhile purpose, and in the years before boxing was legalized and the various states set up Athletic Commissions to regulate it, the Gazette effectively controlled the sport in America and had a large say in who the public regarded as champions.

Ring, under the editorship of its founder Nat Fleischer, became recognized as the sport's most authoritative voice, for two reasons. Fleischer made it his policy to record the result of every fight, however obscure, in tiny type at the back of the magazine, thus making it compulsory reading for the serious fan; and more importantly, he introduced the first monthly ratings of the top ten in each division, which rapidly acquired quasi-official status and were enormously influential in determining a boxer's progress towards a title fight. It is no exaggeration to say that, in the years before any of the present controlling bodies emerged, the *Ring* ratings effectively governed world championships. It was unheard-of for a man to get a title fight if he was not in the magazine's top ten, and fans around the world would eagerly chart their favourite's progress up the lists month by month.

The early ratings were compiled by Tex Rickard, the leading promoter of the time. He was an odd choice by Fleischer, rather like the World Boxing Council entrusting their ratings to Don King, and Rickard would have needed to be a saint not to be swayed in his judgements by promotional considerations. Given a choice between advancing a fighter from, say, Nebraska who was not under his control and a contender from New York who drew large crowds to his promotions, the New Yorker would get the vote every time. Fleischer eventually took over the ratings himself, and they retained a high level of accuracy and impartiality until his death in 1972.

HOW THE *POLICE GAZETTE,* *the most influential sports paper of its time, saw the Sullivan–Kilrain fight in 1889*

New York vs. The NBA

New York was ideally placed to dictate the course of world boxing. At the turn of the century it was the business and sporting capital of America, with a number of purpose-built arenas which were suitable to stage boxing. The original Madison Square Garden, whose name was to become synonymous with the sport, hosted its first prize-fight in 1882. It was rebuilt in 1890, and staged its last show (with Sid Terris beating Johnny Dundee over 12 rounds) on 5 May 1925. Tex Rickard built the new Garden, and opened it on 11 December 1925 with a world light-heavyweight title fight between Paul Berlanbach and Jack Delaney. In the following decades, notably under the promotional reign of Mike Jacobs, the Garden was boxing's headquarters, and an appearance there was the summit of a fighter's career. The outdoor stadia like the Polo Grounds and Yankee Stadium would also become as well-known for boxing shows as for the sport which they were built to house.

There were other factors which helped make New York pre-eminent. The country's leading newspapers (and, later, its radio stations) were based there, as were most of the prominent promoters and managers. As the century progressed, the city's importance in boxing terms grew. Since it was the first point of entry to the United States, most of the prominent European boxers appeared there and some, like the Englishman Jack "Kid" Berg, became major attractions.

Boxing was legalized in the state in 1900 when the Horton Law, permitting shows in members-only clubs, was passed. Predictably, the law proved unworkable, since membership would be granted to anyone purchasing a ticket for the fight. In 1911 it was replaced by the Frawley Law, permitting boxing to take place freely provided no points decision was awarded and the fights did not exceed 10 rounds in duration. The New York State Athletic Commission also came into being in 1911, but did not take over the administration of boxing until 1920 when the Walker Law ended the No Decision era in the state (although various other states continued to enforce their own version of the Frawley Law until later in the decade.)

The New York Commission was the first of its kind in America, and soon established itself as a firm ruling body by stripping Johnny Kilbane of his featherweight title because of his failure to defend it, and by regularizing the weight limits for all the divisions to bring them into line with the rest of the world. They also approved a new weight class, the junior lightweight class (130 lb) although this did not gain acceptance outside America. Other local controlling bodies around the world began to follow New York's leads,

and whoever the NYSAC recognized as world champion was usually also regarded as such in Britain and, after the collapse of the International Boxing Union, in Europe generally.

But New York's domination was viewed with suspicion and envy in other states where the sport flourished, and in 1920 representatives of 13 states came together to establish the rival National Boxing Association. The choice of venue for the meeting was ironic, in several senses: they gathered at the Flatiron Building in

New York. The meeting was called by an Englishman, William A. Gavin. He had his own agenda – he wanted to set up an International Sporting Club in the city to be run on the same lines as London's National Sporting Club, which was effectively the controlling body in British boxing at the time. Gavin's project never got off the ground, but the NBA did and over the next 40 years it grew in both strength and influence.

The NBA frequently opposed the New York

MIKE JACOBS, *boxing's top promoter in the 1930s and 1940s*

choice as world champion, and (particularly in the 1930s) split titles were commonplace as the two organizations vied for supremacy. New York usually won, and when the European Boxing Union was formed in 1948 and allied itself with New York and Britain, the NBA struggled to keep pace. But the coming of the television age weakened New York's unique position. Now, fights could be staged anywhere, and when the Las Vegas casinos discovered boxing, or vice versa, the city's glory days were over. Suddenly, Las Vegas was the new hub of the sport, and New York, almost overnight, was reduced to the status of a fringe player.

Apart from a spurt of activity in the early 1970s (when, continuing Jack "Kid" Berg's tradition, Ken Buchanan of Scotland was the house favourite) the Garden ceased to host regular big-time boxing, and with the decline of the small fight clubs in the city, which in the 1940s and 1950s staged four or five shows a week, boxing became a side show. The Felt Forum, a small arena in the basement of the latest Madison Square Garden, continued to stage regular minor shows, but the balance of power in American boxing had shifted, permanently, westwards to Nevada.

The Rise of the Alphabet Boys

In August 1962, at its annual convention in Tacoma, Washington the NBA renamed itself the World Boxing Association, although its officers remained American or Canadian for the next 12 years. The new body boasted affiliations from 51 state commissions and other organizations. This was the second attempt to establish a world controlling body: in 1957 a World Championship Committee was established consisting of a representative from the NBA, the NYSAC, the European Boxing Union, and the British Boxing Board Of Control, but it was unsuccessful in its well-meaning attempt to end split titles. In 1959, the NBA broke ranks when it stripped Sugar Ray Robinson of the middleweight championship for his failure to defend it against Carmen Basilio, and matched Basilio with Gene Fullmer for its version of the vacant title.

The WBA started issuing its own monthly ratings and set up a Championship Committee, and by the late 1960s had succeeded in splitting almost all the world titles. In 1974 two Panamanians, Rodrigo Sanchez and Elias Cordova, engineered a voting coup which turned the WBA into a Latin-dominated organization and removed it from American control entirely. It was a well-planned operation. The WBA constitution offered voting rights at the annual convention to delegates who represented any body which controlled boxing at any level, be it national or regional. Cordova and Sanchez imported delegates by the busload for the 1974 convention, including three from the Virgin Islands (where no boxing commission existed), six from Venezuela, four from Panama and four from El Salvador. Cordova became the new President, and Sanchez took over from his successor in 1979.

Since then the WBA has remained predominately a Latin organization, although American promoters, notably Bob Arum, worked with it extensively. Arum revealed the extent of WBA corruption in memorable interviews with *Sports Illustrated* and *Ring* magazine, in which he detailed how he had to pay large amounts in bribes to a Puerto Rican, Pepe Cordero, who held no official position whatever in the organization. To get Ray Mancini a crack at the WBA lightweight title, Arum paid Cordero $10,000 and $25,000 from each of Mancini's first three defences, and had to agree to give Cordero's fighter Ernesto Espana a title fight for a purse of $250,000, of which Cordero took a third.

The status of the WBA improved somewhat when South Africans like Mike Mortimer and Judge Klopper were elected to office. South Africa at that time was an international sporting leper because of its apartheid policy, and the WBA was the only boxing organization which would grant it

membership. There was plenty of South African money to inject into the WBA coffers, particularly when the Sun City gambling resort opened, but Mortimer and Klopper were men of high integrity who did their best to combat the financial excesses.

In 1983 an American group, headed by Robert Lee of the New Jersey State Athletic Commission, attempted to regain control of the WBA. When the coup failed, Lee and his associates walked out of the convention and announced the formation of their own organization, the International Boxing Federation. They succeeded in attracting strong support from American promoters who, like Arum, resented having to pay costly sanctioning fees to the WBA as well as the additional under-the-table demands which had become routine. The IBF also drew support from the Orient, particularly from the rapidly expanding Korean market and from the Philippines.

The British Boxing Board of Control remained aloof from both the WBA and IBF, as they had been founder-members of the World Boxing Council in 1963. Sixteen countries took part in the WBC's inaugural meeting in Mexico City on 14 February 1963, and the new body sub-divided itself into seven federations representing North America, South America, Central America /Caribbean, Europe, Africa, Britain and the Orient. Unlike the WBA, it was Latin-dominated from the start. The United States shared North America's voting rights with Mexico and Canada, and so would always be outvoted by any combination of the South and Central American votes.

The driving force behind the rapid expansion of the WBC was Jose Sulaiman, a Mexican businessman who has been its president since 1975 and who enjoys a mutually rewarding friendship with the sport's most powerful promoter, Don King. Under Sulaiman's energetic presidency the WBC has grown to embrace more than 100 countries, making it easily the most significant of the rival organizations. Despite the

JOSE SULAIMAN, *WBC president since 1975*

often-justified complaints about his dictatorial methods and his constant readiness to oblige King, Sulaiman cares passionately about the sport and has worked hard to improve it, particularly in the safety area. He was responsible for the reduction in the number of championship rounds from 15 to 12, which the other bodies eventually adopted, and he has also set up insurance schemes for boxers and initiated medical research programmes.

The British Board held out against the WBA for many years, even refusing permission in 1969 for the country's best-loved champion, Henry Cooper, to challenge for the WBA version of the heavyweight title held by Jimmy Ellis. Cooper was outraged by the lack of support from his own country, and gave up his British title in protest. The Board finally relented in the early 1980s, when they were under pressure from a new organization called the National Boxing Council, whose star promoter and standard-bearer was the young and hard-pushing Londoner, Frank Warren.

Warren aimed to steer the NBC into membership of the WBA, which would then put it on the same legal footing as the BBBC and force its acceptance as a properly constituted rival body. The WBA wanted the BBBC in their fold, but were being manoeuvred into a position where they would have to grant the NBC's application – and, since the WBA constitution

barred membership by two bodies from the same country, that would have put the WBA and the British Board on a collision course. Through an intermediary, Mike Mortimer approached the Board and spelt out their predicament, which finally convinced the BBBC to take membership. Shrewdly, they invited Warren to apply for a Board licence at the same time and, deprived of its leading promoter and without the prospect of international recognition, the NBC faded from the British scene.

Warren, in turn, battled successfully for the right to stage IBF title fights in Britain, and because of his persistence the Board eventually affiliated to the IBF as well. The Warren-promoted Terry Marsh won the IBF light-welterweight title, and he also promoted the super featherweight champion Barry Michael, but when they departed Warren turned his attention elsewhere and an IBF title fight in Britain is now a rarity. In contrast, the World Boxing Organization has made giant strides in Britain, which is now its strongest power base outside its native Puerto Rico.

The WBO was another breakaway from the WBA, and was set up by the former WBA "bag man" Pepe Cordero, although its president was an American lawyer, Ed Levine. The organization was banned from France and Denmark after initial acceptance, but has flourished in Germany and Britain where first Barry Hearn and then Warren promoted WBO title fights. Cordero died in 1995, but the headquarters remained in Puerto Rico under the control of his son. The WBO, despite its shaky start, has greatly enhanced its status over the last few years by the efforts of outstanding champions like Marco Antonio Barrera, Oscar De La Hoya, Riddick Bowe, Chris Eubank and Naseem Hamed.

Britain and Europe
The International Boxing Union, a loose alliance of interested parties from those European countries in which boxing took place, was formed in 1911 with a view to admin-

istering European championships but immediately set about creating its own world champions as well. Those were chaotic times, with any number of boxers claiming world titles at whatever weight best suited them, there being in those days few universally recognized limits for any category. In those circumstances, the IBU had as much right to nominate its own champions as anybody else, and it continued to do so until the outbreak of the First World War in 1914.

The IBU reappeared between the wars, principally as a means of protecting the interests of European contenders like Marcel Thil, Valentin Angelmann, Maurice Holtzer and Gustav Roth. At a convention in Rome in May 1938 the delegates agreed to withdraw recognition from their own champions, to facilitate the reunification of the titles. The IBU was then overtaken by the Second World War in 1939, and its successor, the European Boxing Union, was not formed until 1948.

Claiming the affiliation of every European country in which boxing is staged, it is one of the strongest federations in the world and, in recent years, has increased its efficiency and impartiality after long years of Italian domination. The EBU now issues its own monthly ratings, which are compiled by consultation among the member countries, and titles can only be contested by rated boxers.

In Britain, the Pelican Club was the principal venue for boxing in the late nineteenth century, but it was eventually supplanted by the National Sporting Club, a much more up-market venture founded by John Fleming and A.F. "Peggy" Bettinson at 43 King Street, Covent Garden in 1891. The NSC drew a titled clientele, and quickly became recognized as the sport's quasi-official governing body. It drew up its own set of boxing rules, and reinforced its position as boxing's administrator by introducing the Lonsdale Belts for British title fights. Since the belts could only be awarded for contests which took place at the Club, the NSC

established a monopoly on British championships which endured until the 1920s, by which time the sport in Britain had outgrown the Club's 1,300-seat headquarters to become a major crowd-puller.

The NSC lacked the resources to run what was rapidly becoming a very big and lucrative business, and disputes mounted between the commercial promoters and the autocratic, self-appointed Club committee. A Board of Control was set up in 1921, but was largely under the direction of the NSC

and did little to alleviate the tensions. Finally, in 1929, the Board was reconstituted, and this time it worked. The NSC was originally granted a permanent seat on the new Board, but had to relinquish that in 1936 when the Club set up as a commercial promoter in its own right.

The Board, composed almost entirely of men with no direct financial interest in the business, took on the

MARCO ANTONIO BARRERA, *an outstanding WBO champion, celebrates another victory*

responsibility for running every aspect of boxing including licensing all participants, supervising tournaments, controlling championships and adjudicating on disputes between licence-holders. The Board is sub-divided into eight area councils, most of which contain representatives from local licence-holders in various capacities. It is funded by licence fees and by taxes on promotions and TV revenue, and has long been recognized as one of the world's most efficient boxing organizations. The Board was a founder member of the EBU, the WBC and the Commonwealth Championships Council, which controls the sport in British Commonwealth countries, and has been a powerful influence in them all.

BOXING RULES, CONVENTIONS AND SCORING

To the uniniated, there is nothing very complicated about the scoring of boxing; if boxer A hits boxer B more frequently and harder than boxer B hits him, he wins the fight. But the reality is different, with wide variations in scoring methods, rules and conventions.

JACK BROUGHTON
drew up the first prize ring rules in 1743

Fritzie Zivic, by popular consensus the dirtiest fighter ever to hold a world title, had a simple justification for his tactics in the ring. "I'd give 'em the head, choke 'em, hit 'em in the balls," he said. "You're fighting, not playing the piano, you know". Curiously, Zivic was never disqualified in 232 fights, which is either an indictment of the laxity of the referees who handled his fights, or a compliment to their common sense in adhering rigidly to the first rule of the ring, that a boxer must protect himself at all times.

Zivic would have been at home in the old days, before rules and referees got in the way of a straightforward fight to the finish. Just about anything was permissible, short of actually taking a weapon into the ring. Blows to the Adam's Apple (a target unreachable with a gloved fist) were a favourite, since they almost always incapacitated an opponent. Even grabbing a man by the hair or by the moustache was allowed, which was why fighters kept their heads shaven and forfeited their moustaches before a contest. A round ended when a man was floored, so in theory its duration could be ten minutes or ten seconds. Unscrupulous boxers would drop without taking a punch, to gain additional recovery time, and fights would often drag on interminably without many actual punches being landed.

It was not until Jack Broughton, the champion of England, drew up his own set of rules in 1743 that order began to be imposed on the chaotic world of the prize ring. Broughton did so in reaction to the death of an opponent, George Stevenson, and the rules he devised became the basis of boxing as we know it today. They were short and uncomplicated. Complete with eccentric punctuation and capitals, they read:

1 – That a square of a Yard be chalked in the middle of the Stage, and in each fresh set-to after a fall, or being from the rails, each second is to bring his Man to the side of the Square and place him opposite to the other, and until they are fairly set-to at the Lines, it shall not be lawful for one to strike at the other.

2 – That, in order to prevent any Disputes, the time a man lies after a fall if the Second does not bring his Man to the side of the square within the space of half a minute, he shall be deemed a beaten Man.

3 – That in every Main Battle no person whatever shall be upon the Stage, except the Principals and their Seconds, the same rule to be observed in Bye-battles, except that in the latter Mr. Broughton is allowed to be upon the Stage to keep decorum and to assist Gentlemen in getting to their places, provided always he does not interfere in the Battle; and whoever pretends to infringe these Rules to be turned immediately out of the house. Everybody is to quit the Stage as soon as the Champions are stripped, before the set-to.

4 – That no Champion be deemed beaten, unless he fails coming up to the line in the limited time or that his own Second declares him beaten. No Second is to be allowed to ask his Man's adversary any questions or advise him to give out.

5 – That in Bye-battles the winning man have two-thirds of the Money given, which shall be publicly divided upon the Stage, notwithstanding private agreements to the contrary.

6 – That, to prevent Disputes, in every Main Battle the Principals shall, upon coming to the Stage, choose from among the Gentlemen present two Umpires, who shall absolutely decide all Disputes that may arise about the Battle; and if the two Umpires cannot agree, the said Umpires to choose a third, who is to determine it.

7 – That no person is to hit his Adversary when he is down or seize him by the ham, the breeches, or any part below the waist; a man on his knees to be reckoned down.

One of Broughton's successors, Gentleman John Jackson, founded an organization called the Pugilistic Society in 1814 in an attempt to regularize the sport, and Broughton's Rules were superseded in 1838 by the London Prize Rules (which were revised in 1853 and again in 1866). These provided for a 24-ft square ring, bounded with ropes. When a man was floored or thrown (wrestling was still an integral part of the developing sport) the round ended and the fighter was helped to his corner, being allowed

GENTLEMAN JOHN JACKSON *founded the Pugilistic Society in 1814, the sport's first regulatory body*

a full 30 seconds to recover and a further eight seconds to "come up to scratch", which was a line scratched in the turf of the ring floor. Kicking, butting, biting and low blows were declared fouls, as was the previously common practice of going down without being hit, automatically finishing the round.

The London Rules did service until 1867, when John Graham Chambers of the London Amateur Athletic Club drew up another set of 12 rules which differed in four main aspects: contestants must wear padded gloves, rounds would be of three-minute duration with a minute's interval, wrestling throws

would not be permitted, and a floored boxer had to rise within ten seconds or be declared the loser. Chambers devised the rules to cover amateur boxing, and persuaded the Marquess of Queensberry, John Sholto Douglas, to sponsor them and lend them his name. For a while the two sets of rules co-existed, but as boxing techniques developed the Queensberry Rules became the more popular. They suited fast boxers rather than slow brawlers, since without a minute's rest between rounds the style would be exhausting.

The introduction of the Queensberry Rules brought about

another basic change: the classic "squaring up" posture adopted by bare-knucklers gave way to one more closely resembling the modern stance. In bare-knuckle fighting, the elbows and forearms were used to ward off punches, hence the peculiar stance the "knucklers" adopted. Under Queensberry Rules, the gloves could be used for the same purpose, and so the modern stance evolved.

Jem Mace won the championship under London Rules in 1861, but his technique (and particularly his defensive skills, not hitherto considered an important element of a fighter's art) was more at home under Queensberry Rules. Mace fought under both codes, but favoured Queensberry's and encouraged their adoption on his extensive travels around the world. In America, rapidly overtaking England as the home of prize-fighting, the Queensberry Rules took a long time to gain acceptance.

John L. Sullivan won and defended his title under London Prize Rules, but it was he who was responsible for the adoption of the Queensberry Rules. Because prize-fighting was illegal, the fighters and organizers constantly ran the risk of arrest and imprisonment, and Sullivan had frequent experience of both. The final straw was his arrest in 1889 for defending his title against Jake Kilrain, in the last bare-knuckle championship fight. Sullivan was fined $500, and Kilrain was given two months on an assault-and-battery charge. Sullivan had had enough. "In all the fights I have been in under the London Prize Ring Rules I have not only lost money but have also had the care and worriment incidental to arrests, trials and penalties," he announced. "It has always cost me more money to get out of my fights under those rules than I have ever gained by them. Again, I have never seen a fight under the London Prize Ring Rules but what those present were of a rougher character than I have ever seen under Marquess of Queensberry Rules, and wherever the rowdy element predominates there is always sure to be trouble."

When he issued his famous challenge to Frank Slavin, Charlie Mitchell and James J. Corbett, he stipulated that "The Marquess of Queensberry Rules must govern this contest, as I want fighting, not foot racing." With that announcement, the Prize Ring era died and boxing entered the modern world.

The No-Decision Era

By the early 1900s America had replaced England as the world's leading boxing nation, but the sport was not universally welcomed by all the states. Fights under the old Prize Ring Rules were banned, and the unruly element which boxing attracted caused many authorities to outlaw gloved contests as well. In New York, the Horton Law was passed in 1900, which permitted only those fights which took place in a members-only club, but this proved near-impossible to enforce since the "membership requirements" were usually extremely elastic. In 1911, the state replaced it with the Frawley Law, which enabled boxing to take place openly but restricted contests to ten rounds and prohibited points decisions.

This practice became commonplace across America, which is why the records of champions from that period contain so many "No Decision" entries. The only way a title could change hands was by a knockout or stoppage, provided both men were inside the weight limit for their division. The limits had evolved over the years, often with wildly differing standards on either side of the Atlantic, but by the century's second decade they had stabilized at their present limits: flyweight 112 lb, bantam 118 lb, featherweight 126 lb, lightweight 135 lb, welterweight 147 lb, middleweight 160 lb, light-heavyweight 175 lb, and heavyweight over 175 lb. There were only the eight categories, although two more (junior lightweight, 130 lb and junior welter-

JIMMY WALKER *(right, with President Roosevelt) was responsible for ending the "No Decision" era in New York*

weight, 140 lb) were introduced with limited success in the 1920s.

The No Decision law was designed also to curb betting on fights, but the ever-inventive punters found a way round that. The parties would agree to accept the opinion of a nominated newspaper reporter as to who had proved the better man. It was a system with obvious scope for corruption, but at least the so-called "Newspaper decisions" – assuming they were honest – gave the public some means of assessing a man's progress. This prevailed until the Walker Law (sponsored by New York's famous Mayor Jimmy Walker) legalized boxing completely in 1920. The rest of America took its lead from New York, whose State Athletic Commission became the sport's governing body there and, because most big fights now took place in that city, the Athletic Commission quickly established itself as one of the most influential controlling bodies in the world.

British Rules and Conventions

Boxing in Britain continued to be governed by the Marquess of Queensberry Rules until the emergence of the Pelican Club as the sport's quasi-official governing body in the late nineteenth century. In about 1890 the Club produced their own set of rules, modelled largely on Queensberry's. These restricted the maximum number of rounds to 20, and set the minimum weight for gloves at six ounces. When the Pelican faded from the scene to be replaced by the National Sporting Club as the sport's self-appointed administrator, the rules were revised in 1909 and again in 1923. The British Boxing Board Of Control used the NSC's rules when it took over the sport, and updated them in 1947. There have been occasional changes and variations since then, notably in the scoring system and, in 1948, the abolition of the obnoxious "colour bar" which restricted British championships to white boxers.

The colour bar, which prevented fine craftsmen like the Manchester welterweight Len Johnson from

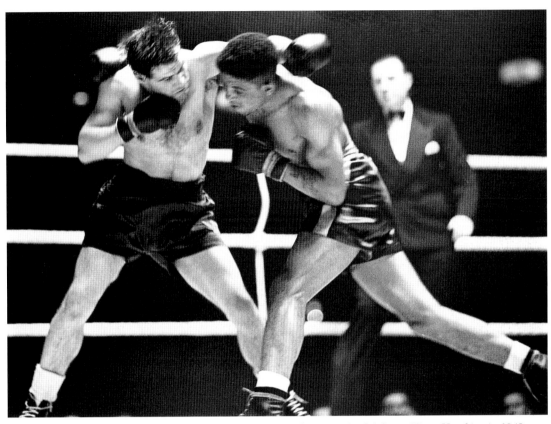

THE END *of the odious "colour bar" in British boxing as Dick Turpin (right) beats Vince Hawkins in 1948*

achieving their potential, was the legacy of what the NSC perceived to have been a slight inflicted on them by Jack Johnson, and at this distance it seems unbelievable that it took so long to get rid of it. Dick Turpin, whose brother Randolph went on to become world middleweight champion, was the first to benefit: he outpointed Vince Hawkins in 1948 to win the British middleweight title. Turpin's success led the way for black boxers to make their mark in the sport – although, curiously, one weight division, the bantamweight, has yet to produce a black champion.

With the wave of immigration from former colonies in the 1950s and 1960s, the Board relaxed the rules to permit immigrants to contest British titles after living in the country for 10 years, and later reduced the qualifying period to six years. Bunny Sterling was the first immigrant to win a title, taking the middleweight championship from Mark Rowe in 1970, and three years later Des Morrison from Jamaica outpointed Joe Tetteh of Ghana for the light-welterweight title in the first

championship match between immigrants.

Britain remains one of the few countries to leave the scoring of fights in the referee's sole hands. Most others employ three judges and a non-scoring referee, or two judges and a scoring referee but the British Board have always resisted the change. Fights used to be scored on a fraction system with the winner of a round being awarded five points and the loser 4¾ or, if he clearly lost the round, 4½. This led to unnecessarily complicated arithmetic, not always easily done in the pressure of the moment, and finally Britain opted to fall in line with most other countries and adopt the 10-point must system, with the winner of the round getting 10 points and the loser nine or less.

But because the rules also called for the referee to record, in the event of a knockout, 10 points for the winner and none for the loser, a truly farcical situation developed in a British lightweight title fight in Derry in 1978 between champion Charlie Nash and London challenger Johnny Claydon. Nash was winning

the fight clearly, but all the rounds were hard-fought and Claydon, who had not been hurt at any stage, was still firmly in contention. At the end of the 12th round the referee caused consternation by announcing that the fight was over: it transpired that Claydon was so far behind on points, having been edged out of most rounds by a 10–9 margin, that even if he scored a knockout and was awarded 10 points against none for Nash, he would still have lost the fight on points! The rule was amended to avoid this happening again, with fights now being scored on a half-point basis.

There are other areas in which Britain remains stubbornly isolated. Foreign boxers are frequently confused by the absence of a mandatory eight count, which is in almost universal use elsewhere. Two-minute rounds, originally designed for novice professionals, are now commonplace in British rings but rare elsewhere. There is minimal co-operation between the amateur and professional governing bodies, although in many European countries relations between the two codes

LLOYD HONEYGHAN *disposes of challenger Johnny Bumphus in one of his many controversial title fights*

are so good that often they are administered by the same organization and amateurs are routinely featured on professional shows. France even has a special "in between" category called "independents", which allows boxers to compete professionally for a maximum of two seasons and then, if they so choose, to be reinstated as amateurs. There are encouraging signs of a thaw between the amateur authorities and the British Board, and the fact that only two British boxers qualified to take part in the 1996 Olympic Games has underlined the urgent need for change if the amateur sport is to survive.

Rules Disputes

Bob Arum, who shares the caustic wit of most fight promoters, once announced at a press conference before a championship fight which was taking place under the joint jurisdiction of the WBA and the New York State Athletic Commission:

"The rules meeting for this fight as usual will be conducted in Spanish in order that nobody understands a word that is said." He was no doubt speaking from long experience of such terminally boring events, but the pre-fight rules meeting is now an inflexible part of the procedure. Given the variations in rules and practice between the many governing bodies, they are a necessary evil.

They are usually held on the evening before the fight, in the presence of the boxers, their representatives and the host Commission, under the chairmanship of the supervisor from the championship organization whose title is being contested.

The meeting affords an opportunity to clarify issues like whether there is a mandatory eight count; a standing count; a three-knock-down rule (under which three knockdowns in the same round automatically ends the fight); who is

empowered to stop the fight (a doctor as well as the referee); what will happen in the event of an accidental cut which forces a stoppage (in some jurisdictions a technical points decision will be rendered, in others a No Contest will be ruled); whether the "no foul" rule is in operation (meaning that a man cannot be disqualified.) These are all important issues, and it is preferable to settle any disputes at this stage rather than have arguments and confusion in the ring.

The No Foul rule is not applied in Britain, where it seems directly to contradict all the old-fashioned notions of sportsmanship and fair play, but it is in operation in most American states. Its most striking use in recent times was on an extraordinary afternoon in Atlantic City in July 1988, when Britain's Lloyd Honeyghan defended the WBC welterweight title against Yung-kil Chang of Korea and Marlon

Starling risked the WBA version of the title against Tomas Molinares of Colombia. Chang was hit low, and finally refused to continue in the fifth round after being given time to recover from the latest low punch. Honeyghan was credited with a fifth-round retirement victory – and then Starling lost his title when he was knocked out by a punch thrown after the bell, but Molinares was nonetheless credited with a knockout win.

Honeyghan figured in some riotous and controversial title fights. He raced across the ring at Wembley to flatten Johnny Bumphus before the American challenger had got off the stool to answer the bell for the second round. He was perfectly within his rights to do so, since the bell had sounded and Bumphus, like all fighters, was obliged to protect himself at all times. "The bell went 'ding' and I went 'dong'", was Lloyd's laconic explanation.

He lost his title on a curious technical decision to Jorge Vaca in 1987, when after an accidental cut Vaca was unable to continue in the eighth round. A points total was called for, which included the eighth round even though it had not been completed, and Honeyghan was declared a narrow loser. That fight, incidentally, involved both the WBC and IBF titles, but Vaca was immediately stripped by the IBF as the fight had been scheduled for the WBC distance of 12 rounds, rather than the 15 which the IBF still regarded as the championship distance. (Since then the IBF, and all other governing bodies, have agreed to accept the 12 rounds limit, on safety grounds.)

How to Score

Boxing is probably the only one-on-one competitive sport in existence where the spectators don't know at any stage who is winning – where, in fact, that knowledge is restricted to, at most, four people in the arena (the three officials and the supervisor) or, in Britain, just to the referee. The spectators may think they know who's in front, but even if one boxer has floored the other a couple of times there is no guarantee that the judges have not taken other factors into account: maybe the man who has scored the knockdowns has tended to slap with the open glove rather than punch correctly with the knuckle part, or maybe the floored boxer has, with the exception of the knockdown blows, avoided most of his opponents punches and steadily outboxed him throughout the fight.

So much depends upon personal interpretation, on which kind of boxing style you like. If Tony Zale or Gene Fullmer is your prototype fighting man, then you'll give points for aggression even if the aggression is not particularly effective. If you marvelled at the defensive artistry of Herol Graham, then you will reward the man who makes his opponent miss and counters him smartly. Quite a few referees and judges have been fighters themselves in their youth, but it does not automatically follow that they will lean towards the man whose style reminds them of their own. They may go the other way, and vote for the man whose style is the one they

would have loved to have had in their days in the ring. After all, inside every Chris Eubank there may be a Nigel Benn bursting to get out.

In theory, scoring fights is a simple process. Points are awarded for punches landed on the target area (above the waist, on the front and sides of the body or head) with the front or the knuckle part of the closed glove. Open handed cuffs do not score, and back-handed blows are illegal. In world title fights, the principal governing bodies advise their judges to award a 10-8 score in a round in which a knockdown has occurred, but this not always a fair or accurate reading of the round. For example, boxer A may have built up a big lead in the round, outscoring his opponent by a 3:1 ratio, and then boxer B scores a flash knockdown from which his opponent gets up almost at once, to carry on where he left off. Who then should win the round?

Where possible, good judges/ referees try to avoid giving even rounds. It is barely conceiv-

able that, in three minutes of sustained action, one man did not land at least a few more punches than the other, or show a wider range of skill. European judges are particularly prone to fence sit. When Britain's Dave Needham drew with Daniel Trioulaire of France in a European bantamweight title fight in 1975, one judge marked 11 of the 15 rounds even and another was unable to split them in 10 of the rounds. Such scores suggest a worrying lack of confidence in their own ability to find a winner, and do an injustice to the boxers.

Even rounds often seem like a "cop-out", a case of the judge taking an easy way out. The late Chuck Minker, a forward-looking chairman of the Nevada State Athletic Commision, used to make his officials review with him the film of fights they had worked and explain to him precisely how and why they had scored each individual round as they did. While this was a commendable practice, it did little to dispel the notion that Las Vegas judges apply their own peculiar standards and often come up with verdicts which are, to put it mildly, controversial.

Marvin Hagler, who lost to Ray Leonard on such a verdict, gave a prophetic interview a month before the fight in which he said "I'm not sure you can get a fair shake in Las Vegas. I mean, they've got very bad judges there, and it's a town where they'll bet on which cockroach will get across the sidewalk first."

Larry Holmes was twice outscored by Mike Spinks in heavyweight title fights in Las Vegas, and after the second one expressed his opinion of the judges in succinct terms which later cost him a fine. "The referees and judges can kiss me where the sun don't shine – my big black behind."

Chris Eubank figured in many close calls during his reign as WBO super-middleweight champion. He had mastered an art of which oldtimers like Archie Moore were prime exponents: fine-judging the time remaining in the round so that judges will be swayed by a fast finishing burst and forget what had gone on before. Muhammad Ali, too, tended to fight in well-judged spurts rather than sustained action.

There is an argument that the referee is the only man well-enough placed to score a fight, since he can move around with the boxers and see virtually all punches while judges, seated in a fixed position at ringside, only see the action which is within their eye-line. By the same token, it is often possible to watch a fight on television, with the benefit of multi-angled camera shots which show you all the action, and find a different winner than you did at ringside. For once, arguably, the armchair experts can get it right.

OUT FOR THE COUNT *the referee signals the end of a fight*

CULTURE AND CONTROVERSY

Boxing's appeal crosses all barriers of class, race, religion and sex. Gangsters and cabinet ministers sit elbow-by-elbow at ringside; Popes and princes are equally fascinated by its indefinable, sometimes seedy glamour. It has a culture all its own, and a history littered with scandals and controversy.

Let's face it, boxing never has been politically correct. It is a macho world, where violence is venerated and rewarded, and where (with a few exceptions) women are little more than attractive set-dressings. Men who are hard inside the ring draw the admiration of men who are hard outside it: the biggest gangster in London will defer to the lowliest six-rounder, because the boxer has asserted his masculinity in a way that a gunman never could. The underworld has always flirted with the fight game, and the sometimes sleazy, slightly raffish glamour of the ring is part of its attraction.

That was certainly true in the old days, when bare-knuckle fights were illegal and attending them offered otherwise law-abiding citizens a little *frisson* of naughtiness. Prize-fights and public executions drew much the same range of spectators. Contemporary accounts such as in Pierce Egan's *Boxiana* or William Hazlitt's famous essay *The Fight* paint a vivid picture of a sport patronized by obscenely wealthy and worthless aristocrats who gambled fortunes on the outcome, and who travelled to the fights accompanied by ladies of spectacularly less than the highest moral standards. Prize fights were no place for a "proper" lady to be seen, but they afforded a busy market-place for whores and camp-followers. Pickpockets, too, thrived among the vast throngs who were drawn to the spectacle - 30,000 watched Tom Spring beat Bill Neat in 1823, and gatherings of 20,000 or more were not unusual. "Fences" were always on hand to buy the stolen items, which would then be sold on again in the same afternoon.

Fixed fights were commonplace especially in the later part of the eighteenth century when the sport was in decline and the rewards for "straight" fights had diminished. Given the amounts which were staked, it was always worth a fighter's while to oblige a gambler in return for a slice of his winnings.

CHRISTY MARTIN *(right) battles Ireland's Deidre Gogarty in Las Vegas in March 1996*

Maybe, in a variation on the scene so beloved of Hollywood film makers of the 1930s and 1940s, a sinister-looking character would open the door of the carriage in which the fighter was changing and hiss: "The boss says you go in the 117th."

Bill Stevens, a notorious "fixer", won the championship in dubious circumstances from Jack Slack in 1760 and lost it to George Meggs a year later in a blatantly prearranged affair. Stevens justified himself to an outraged friend by saying: "I got 50 guineas more than I should otherwise have done by letting George beat me, and damme, ain't I the same man still?" Peter Corcoran and Jem Ward, who presumably shared Stevens's cheerful pragmatism, also figured in their share of fixed fights.

Many prize-fighters turned to the pub business when they retired, a tradition which endures. Nineteenth-century gin palaces were a far cry from the discreet and orderly modern pub, and it helped to have a respected fighting man behind the bar. Since the upper levels of society did not patronize such places, the links between boxing and the underworld were strengthened. Pubs were gathering places for criminals and their associates, and even Tom Cribb, a figure of legendary propriety while a fighter, set up his pub in Panton Street just off the Haymarket in London, right in the heart of what was then the city's red-light district.

There were close links too between boxing and the theatre, or more specifically the music hall. Champions like John L. Sullivan, James J. Corbett and Bob Fitzsimmons earned more on the boards than they did in the ring, either in touring melodramas or by giving sparring and training exhibitions. Sullivan took that a stage further: he would offer $50 to any man in the audience who thought he could beat the champion, and never had to pay out. According to Sullivan's biographer Donald Barr Chidsey his 11 theatrical tours earned a total of $83,000, a staggering total for the time. By comparison, his fight purses were meagre - $11,000 for the

JACK DEMPSEY *(with wife Estelle Taylor in 1927) was one of the many champions who flirted with the movies*

first Charlie Mitchell fight, $8,500 for the rematch with Dominick McCaffrey, and $10,000 for his last bare-knuckle championship defence against Jake Kilrain.

When moving pictures came in, the champions of the day found themselves in demand. Jack Dempsey – who married several actresses – and Max Baer both starred in a number of decidedly lightweight films. (Baer's nephew, Buddy Baer Jr., became well

known in the 1960s playing Jed Clampett's affable but slow-thinking son in the long-running TV series *The Beverly Hillbillies.*) It became fashionable for film stars to be seen with fighters, even to manage them: George Raft and Al Jolson, for example, were both involved in Henry Armstrong's management, with the Mob-connected Eddie Mead actually doing the business deals for the triple champion.

In Europe, too, boxing and

show-business shared the same clientele and often the same bed. The long-running affair between Marcel Cerdan and Edith Piaf entranced the French public for years (with the possible exception of Madame Cerdan), while in Britain the heavyweight sensation Jack Doyle earned well on the music halls and eventually married the film actress Movita, who subsequently divorced him and married Marlon Brando instead. Brando, to complete the circle, used boxing as

his vehicle to stardom with his unforgettable portrayal of the broken-down ex-fighter Terry Malloy in *On The Waterfront*.

Paul Newman and Robert DeNiro had huge successes playing former middleweight champions Rocky Graziano and Jake LaMotta in, respectively, *Somebody Up There Likes Me* and *Raging Bull*. The Graziano role was Newman's first big break, and – as did DeNiro – he prepared for it by immersing himself in the world of boxing and learning enough of the basic moves to look convincing in the ring. Other stars, notably Jon Voight in *The Champ* and, oddly, Elvis Presley in *Kid Galahad*, did this so well that they might even have won a couple of fights in the professional ring. Mickey Rourke, who cherishes his screen "tough guy" image, believed his own publicity to the extent of actually taking out a professional licence and winning a handful of four-rounders, although sceptical observers noted that the opponents may have been better actors than he was.

Boxing is such a colourful world that film makers have always been fascinated by it. Apart from tear-jerkers like *The Champ* or ludicrous yarns like the *Rocky* series there have been cinema classics made about the game. *The Harder They Fall* is a bleak and moving retelling of the Primo Carnera story with Humphrey Bogart - an inveterate fight fan - outstanding as the world-weary press hack who knows what is going on but lacks the moral courage to do anything about it. John Huston's *Fat City* has never been bettered for its accurate depiction of the other side of the boxing coin, the life of a down-the-bill "opponent" who is always just a Greyhound Bus ride away from another defeat.

A few such fighters manage a twist in the story by turning to movies themselves and becoming stars. Bob Hope was a woefully inept boxer who later worked his ring experiences into his stage act. ("I was called Rembrandt Hope because I was on the canvas so much. My last fight, a guy hit me so hard I bounced right into dancing school.") Jack Palance and Dean Martin were competent performers in the

(ABOVE) ROBERT DeNIRO *played Jake LaMotta in "Raging Bull"*
(OPPOSITE) FRANK SINATRA *a lifetime boxing fan, claimed to have had 10 fights and looks the part in a 1947 publicity picture*

ring, as was Martin's former drinking partner Frank Sinatra. The son of a fighter, Sinatra had 10 fights himself and has enjoyed a life-long affinity with the sport and its stars. He has even claimed his own little corner of boxing immortality. One of the most famous fight photographs ever taken shows Muhammad Ali snarling over the prostrate Sonny Liston in their rematch in Lewiston, Maine in 1965. Note the picture credit: Frank Sinatra.

Fixes, Scandals and the Mob

The popular perception of boxing as a crooked business dominated by sinister men in camel-hair overcoats who talk out of the sides of their mouths

owes everything to Hollywood and little to reality, or at least to reality in the modern game. Fifty or 60 years ago, of course, it was very different: then, the Mob virtually ran big-time boxing in America, and since America dominated the world championship scene, it followed that titles were at their disposal and in their gift. It took a US Senate investigation, the Kefauver Commission, to expose the extent of organized crime involvement and eradicate it.

Britain has always run a cleaner operation, partly because the sport has been rigorously controlled first by the National Sporting Club and, since 1929, by the British Boxing Board of Control. Many American states

lack an effective Commission to regulate the business, and the absence of a national controlling body has resulted in conditions of near-anarchy which made it easy for the criminal element to infiltrate and take over boxing there. British criminals would no doubt have relished those kind of opportunities, but simple geography worked against them. The country is too small to allow, for instance, a phoney record like Primo Carnera's to be compiled in out-of-the-way places where opponents could swan-dive without attracting unwelcome attention from either Commission Inspectors or national newspapermen.

British gangsters have always loved to be seen around fighters and at ringside, but the strict licensing procedures operated by the Board of Control make it difficult for them to pursue any active involvement in the sport. Applications for managerial or promotional licences are carefully vetted, and any hint of criminality is usually enough to guarantee rejection. Similarly, a boxer who breaks the law risks forfeiture of his licence, however prominent he may be. Chic Calderwood was British light-heavyweight champion and a world-ranked contender when his licence was suspended following his conviction on an assault charge in the 1960s, and there have been many similar cases.

The Kray brothers, acknowledged bosses of London gangland in the early 1960s, were all former pros who were also genuine *aficionados,* as were their arch-rivals the Richardsons. Any world champion or ex-champion visiting London in the early 1960s would sooner or later find a Kray arm around his shoulders and a photographer on hand to record the moment, and the twins relished these encounters like wide-eyed fans. London villains like Frankie Fraser, Joey Pyle and Freddie Foreman were all regular big-fight patrons (Her Majesty's Pleasure permitting), and their provincial counterparts shared their enthusiasm for the sport.

Many former boxers, even some ex-champions, turned to crime when their ring careers ended. It is easy to understand why they would do so: generally they were

THE KRAY TWINS *Ronnie and Reggie at Klein's Gym in London in 1952*

ill-educated men whose only trade was boxing, and who had grown accustomed to the life-style their ring earnings brought them. When the income ceased abruptly on retirement, they had to look elsewhere for sources of revenue - and crime offered a quick and easy way of maintaining their living standards. Happily, that does not happen so often today. Educational standards are higher, and television has helped make people more aware and sophisticated than their parents' generation were. The modern British boxer knows that he needs top-class lawyers and accountants just as much as he needs a good cuts man, and the emergence of the Professional Boxers Association has served to make fighters more aware of their rights and of the need to safeguard their financial future.

Despite the tight control exercised by the Board of Control, there have been occasional scandals in British boxing. One such was Bruce Woodcock's fourth-round knockout of the American, Lee Oma, in London in September 1948. Woodcock was European and British heavyweight champion, and his promoter Jack Solomons was trying to bring him back from a catastrophic defeat by another American, Joe Baksi. Oma had beaten Baksi, as well as top men like Lou Nova, Tami Mauriello and light-heavyweight champion Gus Lesnevich. He looked a tough proposition for Woodcock and the fight generated so much interest that all 10,600 seats at Harringay Arena were sold out nearly a fortnight before the show.

The rumours began when Oma was seen to be lackadaisical in training and soon they hardened to a specific allegation: that he had been paid £5,000 to take a dive. When the fight got under way, the American was strangely lethargic, scarcely throwing a punch for three rounds. At the end of the third, boos came from all around the arena as the fans showed their displeasure with his lack of effort. Oma made a slight show of aggression early in the fourth, but then crashed for the full count when Woodcock landed a right to the jaw. The press were scathing, and the result produced one of the great headlines in British sports journalism: "Oma Coma Aroma".

Woodcock vigorously denied that anything improper had occurred. In his autobiography, he wrote: "So far as I am concerned, I can honestly say that I have never taken part in a fixed fight in my life." And then he added, perhaps significantly, "It would, I suppose, be possible for one man to have agreed to lose without the other knowing about it, but such is the bush-telegraph system of the training camps of boxing that even that possibility is remote."

The truth of the Oma affair will never be ascertained. If the fight was fixed, then only Oma and Solomons need have known about it. Woodcock was a fighter of blazing honesty and exemplary courage, who would never knowingly have allowed himself to be a part of such a shoddy deal, but it would be naive to pretend that such arrangements did not occasionally happen. British libel laws are so strict that they prohibit discussion of other possible fixes involving boxers who are still living, but the number of questionable results in the last 40 years is reassuringly low.

There have been instances where perhaps a man may not have tried as hard as he should have done, or where he neglected his training to such an extent that he left himself with little chance of victory. But outright prearrangements are rare and almost impossible to prove, since they require only two men to know in advance - the fixer and the diver, and as they have each committed a criminal act, they are unlikely to admit it. Only the man on the receiving end of a punch knows for certain whether the punch is of knockout quality or not. What looks an innocuous blow from the safe side of the ropes can have a dramatic effect on the recipient, with the second Muhammad Ali vs. Sonny Liston "phantom punch" knockdown being the best-known case in point.

As television became ever more involved in boxing, the incentive to fix fights lessened. This was partly because, with TV revenue underwriting the show, more money could be made legitimately from purses and receipts than from gambling, which had always been the prime reason for fixing results. Another factor was that TV companies, ever eager for spectacular knockouts, were perfectly happy to settle for blatantly one-sided matches in which the fighter they were projecting, the audience-puller, had at least an 80 per cent chance of success. In the absence of any kind of quality control on tele-

BRUCE WOODCOCK *(right) and Lee Oma weigh-in for their 1948 fight*

vised matches, promoters were able to build long winning records for their protégés against imported losers, while the Board of Control – who had the power to veto unsuitable opponents – too often turned a blind eye to mismatches.

The explosion in purse levels in recent years makes it simply uneconomic for a boxer to "throw" a title fight. The heavyweight championship, conservatively, is worth at least $50 million to the holder: how much, then, would Michael Moorer have needed to be paid to give the title away to George Foreman, or how large a bribe would Lennox Lewis have required to lose to Oliver McCall? Fixing a title fight is just too expensive to contemplate and, given the hundreds of millions of people watching the fight around the world, too public a spectacle to get away with a pre-arranged result.

No such inhibitions applied in the wild, anything-goes days of boxing's early development. Barry Hugman's outstanding research on world title history for his *British Boxing Yearbook* has unearthed some gems, such as the match in San Francisco in April 1904 between Joe Walcott, defending his claim to the welterweight title, and Dixie Kid. Walcott was winning easily when, for no apparent reason, he was disqualified in the 20th round. It later transpired that the referee had backed the Kid, and disqualified Walcott to protect his investment. (Traditionally, a disqualification meant that all bets were off.) Walcott continued to be regarded as champion.

Dixie Kid was involved in another scandalous decision seven years later to the very day, though this time he was the injured party. France was effectively the capital of world boxing in those pre-war years, and matches between American stars were big attractions. Kid (whose real name was Aaron Brown) boxed Willie Lewis in a 20-rounder and, in what was suspected to be a betting coup, was adjudged to have lost when in fact he had outboxed Lewis convincingly. The verdict caused such uproar that a jury

of leading Parisian sportsmen was convened to reconsider it, and they duly reversed the decision in the Kid's favour.

Lewis was appointed to referee Dixie Kid's defence of his International Boxing Union version of the championship against George Bernard of France in Paris in April 1912, and disqualified his old opponent when Bernard fell to the canvas in the 11th round, writhing in apparent pain and claiming a foul. Three doctors examined the Frenchman and found no trace of injury, and the decision was overturned with the Kid being declared the winner by retirement.

This tradition of French fair play was maintained when Battling Siki took the light-heavyweight title from Georges Carpentier in 1922. Carpentier had agreed to a fixed fight, in which he would hold up the challenger for at least four rounds to give the fight film some sale value, and then knock him out in the fifth. But Siki double-crossed him, and gave the out-of-condition Frenchman a bad beating before Carpentier's corner threw in the towel in the sixth round. The referee, however, disregarded their action and instead disqualified Siki for tripping the champion, which caused such an uproar that the French Boxing Federation went into a hurried conference and, an hour later, declared Siki the new champion.

Only eight months after the Lewis debacle, Bernard figured in the most blatant case of "nobbling" a fighter on record when, challenging Billy Papke for the middleweight title, he fell sound asleep in his corner between the sixth and seventh rounds and could not be roused in time to answer the bell. There was an echo of that affair 43 years on when Harold Johnson, working his way back from a light-heavyweight title loss to Archie Moore, was surprisingly knocked out in two rounds by Julio Mederos, whom he had previously outpointed. Johnson claimed afterwards that he had been given a drugged orange to eat before the fight, which had the effect of slowing his reflexes drastically. The episode seriously damaged Johnson's

career: he did not get another fight for 19 months, and had to wait until 1961 for a second championship chance.

Benny Leonard is rightly remembered as one of the greatest lightweight champions of all time, but he took part in a contest which, if not actually fixed, he at least contrived deliberately to lose. Challenging Jack Britton for the welterweight title in New York in June 1922, Leonard was comfortably outboxing the veteran until, having floored Britton in the 13th round, he struck the champion while he was down, incurring instant disqualification. In this case, at least, it seems that betting was not involved. Leonard

YOUNG STRIBLING, *who figured in a riotous affair against Mike McTigue in 1923*

was really only a lightweight, and did not particularly want the burden of winning the welterweight title and having to concede weight every time he defended it, so he opted for a disqualification as a means of losing the fight without forfeiting any of his status or prestige.

It was normal practice in those days for champions to insist that their favourite referees handle their fights, to give them every possible edge. It was often a wise precaution. Mike McTigue, who took the light-heavyweight title from Battling Siki, needed a little help from the referee when he faced Young Stribling, the "Georgia Peach", in 1923. It was, even by the standards of the time, a chaotic affair. McTigue broke his hand and wanted to retire, but was "persuaded" at gun-point to complete the 10

THE TRUTH *about his knockout by Primo Carnera (above) died with Jack Sharkey in 1994*

rounds, of which Stribling had won eight. The referee saved the Irishman's title by declaring a draw, but then hastily changed that to a win for Stribling when the crowd, which included Ku Klux Klansmen in full regalia, threatened to string him up. Once he was safely out of the state, the official announced that his original drawn decision stood.

Controversy endures about the heavyweight title fight in which Jack Johnson lost to Jess Willard in 1915. Johnson insisted that a deal had been done for him to surrender the title in exchange for the dropping of outstanding criminal charges against him, and pointed as evidence to a famous photograph of him on his back in the 26th round, his forearm apparently shielding his eyes from the glare of the Havana sun. Yet the fight film showed that as the count was completed both of Johnson's arms were lying on the scorching canvas. Willard offered the most convincing refutation of Johnson's story when he remarked that: "If he was going to throw the fight, I sure wish he hadn't waited until the 26th

round to do it - it was hotter 'n' Hell out there."

Jack Sharkey's sixth-round knockout by Primo Carnera in 1933, which cost the American the heavyweight title, is still viewed with suspicion, given the fact that so many of the challenger's previous fights had been blatant fixes and that Sharkey had been much too smart for Carnera when they first boxed, in 1931. Accounts vary of how the fight finished. Some described the finishing blow as "a phantom punch", while the *New York Times* wrote of "a tremendous right uppercut." Sharkey claimed that as the sixth round began he had seen a vision of Ernie Schaaf, a protégé of his who had recently died in the ring, which threw his mind into such turmoil that he could not concentrate on the fight. But, as he conceded to author Peter Heller in a 1971 interview, "Even my wife has her doubts", and the truth died with Sharkey in 1994.

Charley Phil Rosenberg, a bantamweight contemporary of Sharkey's, was dogged by scandal throughout his championship

career. He was suspended indefinitely by the New York Commission, and his opponent Eddie Shea banned for life, after Shea went down for the count in the fourth round in July 1925. Shea had reportedly been threatened with death unless he threw the fight, and armed gangsters were said to be at ringside to ensure that he obliged. The story may be true: Rosenberg was friendly with Al Capone, whom he described to Heller in *In This Corner* as: "A fine man. I don't know what he done on the outside. He may have had hundreds of people killed. I don't know. I'm not interested. To me, he was a fine person."

Rosenberg's suspension was lifted to allow him to defend against Bushy Graham, whom he outpointed, but he was then suspended again when a secret agreement was unearthed concerning the purse split. He was finally stripped of the title after failing to make the championship weight, which upset him greatly as he had done a deal to go to Philadelphia and lose the title there for $50,000.

Battling Battalino lost his featherweight title in 1931 following a fixed fight with Freddie Miller, whose contract Battalino and his manager Pete Reilly had bought for $3,500. Battalino came in three pounds overweight, but the fight went ahead as a non-title match. Battalino made no effort, and laid down in the third round. "I stretched out", he recalled years later. "The referee says for me to get up. I told him to count. He says 'No Contest'". The title was immediately declared vacant, and was eventually won by Miller two years later.

One of the best-known fixes involved Jake LaMotta, who took a dive against the Mob-controlled Blackjack Billy Fox in 1947 in return for the promise of a crack at the middleweight title. Fox was an undefeated light-heavyweight, and LaMotta reasoned that losing to him would not affect his status as a middleweight contender. But he had his pride: he refused to be counted out, and stood against the ropes in the fourth round allowing Fox to land at will until the referee stopped it. Even then, he had to wait almost two years for his chance, and pay a "fee" of $20,000 for the privilege.

LaMotta told the story to the Kefauver Commission, a US Senate body investigating organized crime in 1960, and his evidence was instrumental in breaking the stranglehold which gangsters like Frankie Carbo and Blinky Palermo had on the business. They were actual or undercover managers of a host of champions. They decided who won and who lost, and through their manipulation of James Norris's International Boxing Club, which enjoyed an effective monopoly on world championship shows, they controlled the promotional side of the business as well. The power of the IBC was eventually broken by an anti-trust (monopoly) action brought against it at the instigation of Cus D'Amato, the manager of the heavyweight champion Floyd Patterson.

Through an organization called the Boxing Guild, the Mob kept recalcitrant fighters in line. The Guild was a kind of managers' union, and any boxer who tried to leave his manager was blackballed by the Guild and denied work. Not even Ike Williams, NBA lightweight champion at the time, could beat the Guild. He was blackballed, until he agreed to sign contracts with Palermo, who promptly got him a match with Bob Montgomery, which he won, for the undisputed title.

Carbo and his like, once omnipotent, would struggle to survive in the modern game. Today, contracts are hammered out by corporate lawyers in boardrooms rather than haggled over in smoky bars or sweaty changing rooms, and a length of lead pipe won't get you as far in the negotiating process as a degree in business administration or law. The game is unquestionably cleaner than it was in the bad old days, but to the uninvolved and uncommitted outside observer, it's also a lot duller.

Death in the Ring

Tragedy is never far from the ring. This is a violent sport, and only the ignorant or incurably naive would argue that it leaves its participants unscathed. Every punch to the head inflicts a degree of irreversible brain damage, since it kills off cells which do not regenerate. Some men are lucky, and can walk away from a long career with their faculties intact, but most will be affected to some extent. Boxers understand the risks they take, and weigh them against the potential rewards. As Barry McGuigan, a perceptive and articulate former featherweight champion, said: "This is the price we pay, and we budget for it."

But for some, mercifully few, the price is too high. Every year, a handful of men die in the ring. Some are killed in obscure corners of the world, fighting for small purses in primitive arenas in Latin America or the Philippines. Others die or suffer lasting injury fighting for world titles with millions watching around the world. When that happens, as it did when Gerald McClellan was dreadfully injured against Nigel Benn in London in 1995, the calls to outlaw boxing are heard loud and clear

and the sport is forced on to the defensive.

For the present, at least, the law is on boxing's side. Two prosecutions at the turn of the century, each arising from ring deaths at the National Sporting Club in London, established the principle that deaths resulting from a properly organized and controlled boxing contest, as opposed to an unregulated prize fight, were accidental. The first was in 1897 when Walter Croot of Leytonstone died after being knocked out by Jimmy Barry of Chicago in a world bantamweight title fight. In that instance, the magistrate found there was no case to answer, and that position was reinforced in 1901 when Jack Roberts was acquitted on a charge of "feloniously killing and slaying Murray Livingstone" (boxing as Billy Smith), who died in a fight with Roberts at the Club. Smith's death was the fourth in as many years at the NSC, following Croot (1897), Tom Turner (1898) and Mike Riley (1900).

The first to die in a championship ring this century was welterweight Jimmy Doyle, who never regained

consciousness after Ray Robinson knocked him out in the eighth round at Cleveland in 1947. Robinson had dreamt the precise circumstances of Doyle's death the night before the fight, and had to be persuaded to go through with it by Doyle's parish priest.

Benny Paret died following his 12th round stoppage by Emile Griffith in a welterweight title defence in New York in 1962: he had been unable to extricate himself from the ropes and was defenceless as Griffith pounded him, a tragedy which led to the introduction of the four-roped ring. Just under a year later, featherweight champion Davey Moore lost his life against Sugar Ramos in Los Angeles, which was also the scene of a bizarre, tragic coincidence. Welsh bantamweight Johnny Owen was fatally injured when challenging Lupe Pintor for the WBC title there in September 1980, dying 46 days later, and in 1983 Kiko Bejines died of a blood clot on the brain three days after losing to Albert Davila in the same ring, for the same title. Both fights ended in the same round, the 12th.

Four sometime-world heavyweight champions have been involved in ring fatalities: Jess Willard against Bull Young (1913), Max Baer against Frankie Campbell (1930), Primo Carnera against Ernie Schaaf (1933) and Ezzard Charles against Sam Baroudi (1948.) Other world champions who went through that trauma included Barry McGuigan, Alan Minter, Ray Mancini, Brian Mitchell and Lou Ambers, who echoed the experiences of many fighters in those circumstances when he described how, after Tony Scarpati died when Ambers knocked him out in 1936: "Every once in a while I'd look in that corner and I'd see like a picture of Tony, God rest his soul." McGuigan, too, spoke movingly of the death of his opponent, Young Ali of Nigeria. "It was as though the world had stopped for me. I never thought something like this could happen. I had always thought boxing was just a sport, just a game."

But it isn't, and as long as men compete in a ring, the casualty list will grow. That is the real price of boxing's transient glory.

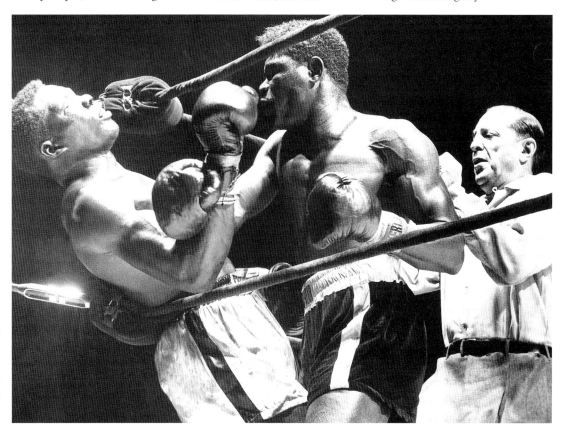

MOMENT OF TRAGEDY: *Benny Paret, trapped on the ropes, is battered into a coma by Emile Griffith in 1962*

THE WORLD CHAMPIONSHIPS

The history of each weight division from heavyweight down to strawweight, tracing how the world championship has passed from boxer to boxer from the start of each division to the present day.

VICTORY AT LAST *for one of boxing's most persistent challengers as Frank Bruno wins the WBC title from Oliver McCall – it was the British boxer's fourth challenge for a version of the title*

For reasons of sanity as much as space, this list of world championship fights has been restricted to those involving the four major organizations: the World Boxing Council (WBC), World Boxing Association (WBA), International Boxing Federation (IBF) and World Boxing Organization (WBO). There are any number of other would-be governing bodies, including the World Boxing Union, the Intercontinental Boxing Council, the International Boxing Organization and so on *ad nauseam*, but they lack even the limited credibility of their more established rivals.

The chaos which reigns today in world boxing is deplorable but inevitable, given the close association which the various organizations enjoy with individual promoters and power groups within the sport. The bulk of their income derives from fees for sanctioning championships: the more title fights, the greater the cash flow. The simple days of eight weight divisions and eight champions have gone forever, and it is startling to realize just how far back in history they are.

The last time an undisputed world championship was contested in each of the 17 weight categories was:

Heavyweight: February 25, 1989: Mike Tyson vs. Frank Bruno
Cruiserweight: April 9, 1988: Evander Holyfield vs. Carlos DeLeon
Light-heavyweight: June 6, 1985: Mike Spinks vs. Jim MacDonald
Super-middleweight: July 26, 1987 Chang-Pal Park vs. Emmanuel Otti
Middleweight: March 10, 1986: Marvin Hagler vs. John Mugabi
Light-middle: January 21, 1975: Koichi Wajima vs. Oscar Albarado
Welterweight: September 27, 1986: Lloyd Honeyghan vs. Don Curry
Light-welterweight: November 16, 1967: Paul Fuji vs. Willi Quator
Lightweight: January 21, 1978: Roberto Duran vs. Esteban DeJesus

Super-featherweight: October 6, 1968: Hiroshi Kobayashi vs. Jaime Valladeres
Featherweight: October 14, 1967: Vicente Saldivar vs. Howard Winstone
Super-bantamweight: July 11, 1977: Wilfredo Gomez vs. Raul Tirado
Bantamweight: July 30, 1972: Enrique Pinder vs. Rafael Herrera
Super-flyweight: July 29, 1981: Chul-Ho Kim vs. Willie Jensen
Flyweight: April 23, 1965: Salvatore Burruni vs. Pone Kingpetch
Light-flyweight: April 4, 1975: Franco Udella vs. Valentin Martinez
Strawweight: June 14, 1987: Kyung-Yun Lee vs. Masaharu Kawakami

In several of those cases, the championship was "undisputed" only in so far as the other organizations had not yet followed the lead of the body which inaugurated the division. To be strictly accurate, none of the men who have styled themselves world champions since the dates shown above was anything more than the champion of the particular organization he represented – and that includes magnificent fighters like Julio Cesar Chavez, Azumah Nelson or Sot Chitalada, who would have won titles in any era.

For ease of reference, the various strands of each title have been disentangled rather than merely listing them all in indiscriminate chronological order. The history of the championships in the early days is cloudy, and there were often several versions of a title in circulation: nothing changes. The situation is further complicated by the sketchy records of the period, and the fact that many American states permitted boxing matches only on condition that no decision was given.

Barry Hugman, compiler of the estimable *British Boxing Yearbook*, has scoured newspaper files on both sides of the Atlantic in an effort to clarify the story, and future historians will be in his debt.

Heavyweight

Some historians' researches lead him to take the controversial view that the distinction of being the first world heavyweight champion in the modern sense belongs to the Australian Frank Slavin rather than to John L. Sullivan, who was the last of the bare-knuckle champions. Slavin stopped Jake Kilrain in nine rounds in June 1891 in a match made with four-ounce gloves, and was then knocked out by his compatriot

Peter Jackson in the National Sporting Club, London a year later.

But Jackson was black, and Sullivan, to his lasting discredit, put up the so-called "colour bar" which would remain in place until Jack Johnson's victory over Tommy Burns in 1908. When Sullivan finally came out of semi-retirement to fight James J. Corbett in September 1892, the gloved era had truly begun.

World Heavyweight Championship Bouts

Feb 7,	1882*	**John L. Sullivan** (US) w ko 9 Paddy Ryan (US)	Mississippi City, MS
Mar 10,	1888*	John L. Sullivan drew 39 Charlie Mitchell (Eng)	Chantilly (Fra)
Aug 8,	1889*	John L. Sullivan w rsf 75 Jake Kilrain (US)	Richburg, MS
		* Under London Prize Ring rules (bare-knuckle)	
Sep 7,	1892	**James J. Corbett** (US) w ko 21 John L. Sullivan	New Orleans, LA
Jan 25,	1894	James J. Corbett w ko 3 Charlie Mitchell	Jacksonville, FL
Mar 17,	1897	**Bob Fitzsimmons** (Eng) w ko 14 James J. Corbett	Carson City, NV
Jun 9,	1899	**James J. Jeffries** (US) w ko 11 Bob Fitzsimmons	Coney Island, NY
Nov 3,	1899	James J. Jeffries w pts 25 Tom Sharkey (Ire)	Coney Island, NY
Apr 6,	1900	James J. Jeffries w ko 1 Jack Finnegan (US)	Detroit, MI
May 11,	1900	James J. Jeffries w ko 23 James J. Corbett	Coney Island, NY
Nov 15,	1901	James J. Jeffries w ret 5 Gus Ruhlin (US)	San Francisco, CA
Jul 25,	1902	James J. Jeffries w ko 8 Bob Fitzsimmons	San Francisco, CA
Aug 14,	1903	James J. Jeffries w ko 10 James J. Corbett	San Francisco, CA
Aug 26,	1904	James J. Jeffries w ko 2 Jack Munroe (US)	San Francisco, CA
		Jeffries announced retirement	
Jul 3,	1905	**Marvin Hart** (US) w rsf 12 Jack Root (US)	Reno, NV
Feb 23,	1906	**Tommy Burns** (Can) w pts 20 Marvin Hart	Los Angeles, CA
Oct 2,	1906	Tommy Burns w ko 15 Jim Flynn (US)	Los Angeles, CA
Nov 28,	1906	Tommy Burns drew 20 Philadelphia Jack O'Brien (US)	Los Angeles, CA
May 8,	1907	Tommy Burns w pts 20 Philadelphia Jack O'Brien	Los Angeles, CA
Jul 4,	1907	Tommy Burns w ko 1 Bill Squires (Aus)	Colma, CA
Dec 2,	1907	Tommy Burns w ko 10 Gunner Moir (Eng)	London (Eng)
Feb 10,	1908	Tommy Burns w ko 4 Jack Palmer (Eng)	London (Eng)
Mar 17,	1908	Tommy Burns w ko 1 Jem Roche (Ire)	Dublin (Ire)
Apr 18,	1908	Tommy Burns w ko 5 Jewey Smith (Eng)	Paris (Fra)
Jun 13,	1908	Tommy Burns w ko 13 Bill Squires	Paris (Fra)
Aug 24,	1908	Tommy Burns w ko 13 Bill Squires	Sydney (Aus)
Sep 2,	1908	Tommy Burns w ko 6 Bill Lang (Aus)	Melbourne (Aus)
Dec 26,	1908	**Jack Johnson** (US) w rsf 14 Tommy Burns	Sydney (Aus)
Oct 16,	1909	Jack Johnson w ko 12 Stanley Ketchel (US)	Colma, CA
Jul 4,	1910	Jack Johnson w rsf 15 James J. Jeffries	Reno, NV
Jul 4,	1912	Jack Johnson w ko 9 Jim Flynn	Las Vegas, NM
Dec 19,	1913	Jack Johnson drew 10 Jim Johnson (US)	Paris (Fra)
Jun 27,	1914	Jack Johnson w pts 20 Frank Moran (US)	Paris (Fra)
Apr 5,	1915	**Jess Willard** (US) w ko 26 Jack Johnson	Havana (Cub)
Mar 25,	1916	Jess Willard no dec 10 Frank Moran	New York, NY
Jul 4,	1919	**Jack Dempsey** (US) w ret 3 Jess Willard	Toledo, OH
Sep 6,	1920	Jack Dempsey w ko 3 Billy Miske (US)	Benton Harbor, MI
Dec 14,	1920	Jack Dempsey w ko 12 Bill Brennan (US)	New York, NY
Jul 2,	1921	Jack Dempsey w ko 4 Georges Carpentier (Fra)	Jersey City, NJ
Jul 4,	1923	Jack Dempsey w pts 15 Tommy Gibbons (US)	Shelby, MT
Sep 14,	1923	Jack Dempsey w ko 2 Luis Angel Firpo (Arg)	New York, NY
Sep 23,	1926	**Gene Tunney** (US) w pts 10 Jack Dempsey	Philadelphia, PA
Sep 22,	1927	Gene Tunney w pts 10 Jack Dempsey	Chicago, IL
Jul 23,	1928	Gene Tunney w rsf 11 Tom Heeney (NZ)	New York, NY
		Tunney announced retirement	
Jun 12,	1930	**Max Schmeling** (Ger) w dis 4 Jack Sharkey (US)	New York, NY
Jul 3,	1931	Max Schmeling w rsf 15 Young Stribling (US)	Cleveland, OH
Jun 21,	1932	**Jack Sharkey** w pts 15 Max Schmeling	Long Island, NY
Jun 29,	1933	**Primo Carnera** (Ita) w ko 6 Jack Sharkey	Long Island, NY
Oct 22,	1933	Primo Carnera w pts 15 Paulino Uzcudun (Sp)	Rome (Ita)
Mar 1,	1934	Primo Carnera w pts 15 Tommy Loughran (US)	Miami, FL

Jun 14,	1934	**Max Baer** (US) w rsf 11 Primo Carnera	Long Island, NY
Jun 13,	1935	**James J. Braddock** (US) w pts 15 Max Baer	Long Island, NY
Jun 22,	1937	**Joe Louis** (US) w ko 8 James J. Braddock	Chicago, IL
Aug 30,	1937	Joe Louis w pts 15 Tommy Farr (Wal)	New York, NY
Feb 23,	1938	Joe Louis w ko 3 Nathan Mann (US)	New York, NY
Apr 1,	1938	Joe Louis w ko 5 Harry Thomas (US)	Chicago, IL
Jun 22,	1938	Joe Louis w ko 1 Max Schmeling	New York, NY
Jan 25,	1939	Joe Louis w rsf 1 John Henry Lewis (US)	New York, NY
Apr 17,	1939	Joe Louis w ko 1 Jack Roper (US)	Los Angeles, CA
Jun 28,	1939	Joe Louis w rsf 4 Tony Galento (US)	New York, NY
Sep 20,	1939	Joe Louis w ko 11 Bob Pastor (US)	Detroit, MI
Feb 9,	1940	Joe Louis w pts 15 Arturo Godoy (Ch)	New York, NY
Mar 29,	1940	Joe Louis w rsf 2 Johnny Paycheck (US)	New York, NY
Jun 20,	1940	Joe Louis w rsf 8 Arturo Godoy	New York, NY
Dec 16,	1940	Joe Louis w ret 6 Al McCoy (US)	Boston, MA
Jan 31,	1941	Joe Louis w ko 5 Red Burman (US)	New York, NY
Feb 17,	1941	Joe Louis w ko 2 Gus Dorazio (US)	Philadelphia, PA
Mar 21,	1941	Joe Louis w rsf 13 Abe Simon (US)	Detroit, MI
Apr 8,	1941	Joe Louis w rsf 9 Tony Musto (US)	St Louis, MO
May 23,	1941	Joe Louis w dis 7 Buddy Baer (US)	Washington, DC
Jun 18,	1941	Joe Louis w ko 13 Billy Conn (US)	New York, NY
Sep 29,	1941	Joe Louis w rsf 6 Lou Nova (US)	New York, NY
Jan 9,	1942	Joe Louis w ko 1 Buddy Baer	New York, NY
Mar 27,	1942	Joe Louis w ko 6 Abe Simon	New York, NY
Jun 19,	1946	Joe Louis w ko 8 Billy Conn	New York, NY
Sep 18,	1946	Joe Louis w ko 1 Tami Mauriello (US)	New York, NY
Dec 5,	1947	Joe Louis w pts 15 Jersey Joe Walcott (US)	New York, NY
Jun 25,	1948	Joe Louis w ko 11 Jersey Joe Walcott	New York, NY
		Louis announced retirement	
Jun 22,	1949	**Ezzard Charles** (US) w pts 15 Jersey Joe Walcott	Chicago, IL
		For vacant NBA title	
Aug 10,	1949	Ezzard Charles w rsf 7 Gus Lesnevich (US)	New York, NY
Oct 14,	1949	Ezzard Charles w ko 8 Pat Valentino (US)	San Francisco, CA
Aug 15,	1950	Ezzard Charles w rsf 14 Freddy Beshore (US)	Buffalo, NY
Sep 27,	1950	Ezzard Charles w pts 15 Joe Louis	New York, NY
		(Undisputed title)	
Dec 5,	1950	Ezzard Charles w ko 11 Nick Barone (US)	Cincinnati, OH
Jan 12,	1951	Ezzard Charles w rsf 10 Lee Oma (US)	New York, NY
Mar 7,	1951	Ezzard Charles w pts 15 Jersey Joe Walcott	Detroit, MI
May 30,	1951	Ezzard Charles w pts 15 Joey Maxim (US)	Chicago, IL
Jul 18,	1951	**Jersey Joe Walcott** w ko 7 Ezzard Charles	Pittsburgh, PA
Jun 5,	1952	Jersey Joe Walcott w pts 15 Ezzard Charles	Philadelphia, PA
Sep 23,	1952	**Rocky Marciano** (US) w ko 13 Jersey Joe Walcott	Philadelphia, PA
May 15,	1953	Rocky Marciano w ko 1 Jersey Joe Walcott	Chicago, IL
Sep 24,	1953	Rocky Marciano w rsf 11 Roland La Starza (US)	New York, NY
Jun 17,	1954	Rocky Marciano w pts 15 Ezzard Charles	New York, NY
Sep 17,	1954	Rocky Marciano w ko 8 Ezzard Charles	New York, NY

EZZARD CHARLES *(left) gave Rocky Marciano the toughest of his 49 fights*

JOHN L. SULLIVAN *and Jake Kilrain in the last championship fight staged under London Prize Ring rules*

May 16, 1955	Rocky Marciano w rsf 9 Don Cockell (Eng)	San Francisco, CA
Sep 21, 1955	Rocky Marciano w ko 9 Archie Moore (US)	New York, NY
	Marciano announced retirement	
Nov 30, 1956	**Floyd Patterson** (US) w ko 5 Archie Moore	Chicago, IL
Jul 29, 1957	Floyd Patterson w rsf 10 Tommy Jackson (US)	New York, NY
Aug 22, 1957	Floyd Patterson w ko 6 Pete Rademacher (US)	Seattle, WA
Aug 18, 1958	Floyd Patterson w ret 12 Roy Harris (US)	Los Angeles, CA
May 1, 1959	Floyd Patterson w ko 11 Brian London (Eng)	Indianapolis, IN
Jun 26, 1959	**Ingemar Johansson** (Swe) w rsf 3 Floyd Patterson	New York, NY
Jun 20, 1960	**Floyd Patterson** w ko 5 Ingemar Johansson	New York, NY
Mar 13, 1961	Floyd Patterson w ko 6 Ingemar Johansson	Miami, FL
Dec 4, 1961	Floyd Patterson w ko 4 Tom McNeeley (US)	Toronto (Can)
Sep 25, 1962	**Sonny Liston** (US) w ko 1 Floyd Patterson	Chicago, IL
Jul 22, 1963	Sonny Liston w ko 1 Floyd Patterson	Las Vegas, NV
Feb 25, 1964	**Cassius Clay** (US) w ret 6 Sonny Liston	Miami, FL

	Clay announced he would henceforth be known as Muhammad Ali	
Sep 14, 1964	*WBA withdrew recognition of Ali because he signed for return bout with Sonny Liston*	
Mar 5, 1965	**Ernie Terrell** (US) w pts 15 Eddie Machen (US)	Chicago, IL
	For vacant WBA title	
May 25, 1965	Muhammad Ali w ko 1 Sonny Liston	Lewiston, ME
Nov 1, 1965	Ernie Terrell w pts 15 George Chuvalo (Can)	Toronto (Can)
	WBA title	
Nov 22, 1965	Muhammad Ali w rsf 12 Floyd Patterson	Las Vegas, NV
Mar 29, 1966	Muhammad Ali w pts 15 George Chuvalo	Toronto (Can)
May 21, 1966	Muhammad Ali w rsf 6 Henry Cooper (Eng)	London (Eng)
Jun 28, 1966	Ernie Terrell w pts 15 Doug Jones	Houston, TX
	WBA title	
Aug 6, 1966	Muhammad Ali w ko 3 Brian London	London (Eng)
Sep 10, 1966	Muhammad Ali w rsf 12 Karl Mildenberger (Ger)	Frankfurt (Ger)

Nov 14, 1966	Muhammad Ali w rsf 3 Cleveland Williams (US)	....	Houston, TX
Feb 6, 1967	Muhammad Ali w pts 15 Ernie Terrell	....	Houston, TX
	(Undisputed title)		
Mar 22, 1967	Muhammad Ali w ko 7 Zora Folley (US)	....	New York, NY
Apr 28, 1967	*Ali stripped of title by WBA and New York State Athletic Commission for refusing to join US Army*		

New York title

Mar 4, 1968	**Joe Frazier** (US) w rsf 11 Buster Mathis (US)	....	New York, NY
	For vacant title		
Jun 24, 1968	Joe Frazier w ret 2 Manuel Ramos (Mex)	....	New York, NY
Dec 10, 1968	Joe Frazier w pts 15 Oscar Bonavena (Arg)	....	Philadelphia, PA
Apr 22, 1969	Joe Frazier w ko 1 Dave Zyglewicz (US)	....	Houston, TX
Jun 23, 1969	Joe Frazier w rsf 7 Jerry Quarry (US)	....	New York, NY
Feb 16, 1970	Joe Frazier w ret 4 Jimmy Ellis (US)	....	New York, NY
	Undisputed title		

WBA title

Apr 27, 1968	**Jimmy Ellis** w pts 15 Jerry Quarry	....	Oakland, CA
	For vacant title		
Sep 14, 1968	Jimmy Ellis w pts 15 Floyd Patterson	....	Stockholm (Swe)
Feb 16, 1970	**Joe Frazier** w ret 4 Jimmy Ellis	....	New York, NY
	Undisputed title		

Undisputed title

Nov 18, 1970	Joe Frazier w ko 2 Bob Foster (US)	....	Detroit, MI
Mar 8, 1971	Joe Frazier w pts 15 Muhammad Ali	....	New York, NY
Jan 15, 1972	Joe Frazier w rsf 4 Terry Daniels (US)	....	New Orleans, LA
May 25, 1972	Joe Frazier w rsf 4 Ron Stander (US)	....	Omaha, NE
Jan 22, 1973	**George Foreman** (US) w rsf 2 Joe Frazier	....	Kingston (Jam)
Sep 1, 1973	George Foreman w ko 1 Joe Roman (PR)	....	Tokyo (Jap)
Mar 26, 1974	George Foreman w rsf 2 Ken Norton (US)	....	Caracas (Ven)
Oct 30, 1974	**Muhammad Ali** w ko 8 George Foreman	....	Kinshasa (Za)
Mar 24, 1975	Muhammad Ali w rsf 15 Chuck Wepner (US)	....	Cleveland, OH
May 16, 1975	Muhammad Ali w rsf 11 Ron Lyle (US)	....	Las Vegas, NV
Jul 1, 1975	Muhammad Ali w pts 15 Joe Bugner (Eng)	....	Kuala Lumpur (Mal)
Oct 1, 1975	Muhammad Ali w ret 14 Joe Frazier	....	Manila (Phil)
Feb 10, 1976	Muhammad Ali w ko 5 Jean-Pierre Coopman (Bel)	....	San Juan, CA
Apr 30, 1976	Muhammad Ali w pts 15 Jimmy Young (US)	....	Landover, MD
May 25, 1976	Muhammad Ali w rsf 5 Richard Dunn (Eng)	....	Munich (Ger)
Sep 28, 1976	Muhammad Ali w pts 15 Ken Norton	....	New York, NY
May 16, 1977	Muhammad Ali w pts 15 Alfredo Evangelista (Sp)	....	Landover, MD
Sep 29, 1977	Muhammad Ali w pts 15 Earnie Shavers (US)	....	New York, NY
Feb 15, 1978	**Leon Spinks** (US) w pts 15 Muhammad Ali	....	Las Vegas, NV
Mar 18, 1978	*Spinks stripped by the WBC for his failure to defend against Ken Norton. The WBC then proclaimed Norton champion on the basis of his 15-rounds points win over Jimmy Young in their final eliminator in Las Vegas on November 5, 1977*		

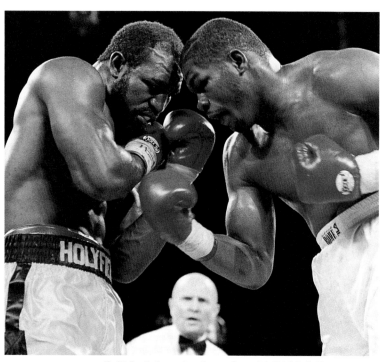

EVANDER HOLYFIELD *(left) had three titanic tussles with Riddick Bowe*

Jul 7, 1980	Larry Holmes w rsf 7 Scott LeDoux (US)	....	Bloomington, MN
Oct 2, 1980	Larry Holmes w ret 10 Muhammad Ali	....	Las Vegas, NV
Apr 11, 1981	Larry Holmes w pts 15 Trevor Berbick	....	Las Vegas, NV
Jun 12, 1981	Larry Holmes w rsf 3 Leon Spinks	....	Detroit, MI
Nov 6, 1981	Larry Holmes w rsf 11 Renaldo Snipes (US)	....	Pittsburgh, PA
Jun 11, 1982	Larry Holmes w dis 13 Gerry Cooney (US)	....	Las Vegas, NV
Nov 26, 1982	Larry Holmes w pts 15 Randy "Tex" Cobb (US)	....	Houston, TX
Mar 27, 1983	Larry Holmes w pts 12 Lucien Rodriguez (Fra)	....	Scranton, PA
May 20, 1983	Larry Holmes w pts 12 Tim Witherspoon (US)	....	Las Vegas, NV
Sep 10, 1983	Larry Holmes w rsf 5 Scott Frank (US)	....	Atlantic City, NJ
Dec 1983	*Holmes relinquished WBC title and accepted recognition from the newly-formed International Boxing Federation*		
Mar 9, 1984	**Tim Witherspoon** w pts 12 Greg Page (US)	....	Las Vegas, NV
	For vacant title		
Aug 31, 1984	**Pinklon Thomas** (US) w pts 12 Tim Witherspoon	....	Las Vegas, NV
Jun 15, 1985	Pinklon Thomas w ko 8 Mike Weaver	....	Las Vegas, NV
Mar 22, 1986	**Trevor Berbick** w pts 12 Pinklon Thomas	....	Las Vegas, NV
Nov 22, 1986	**Mike Tyson** (US) w rsf 2 Trevor Berbick	....	Las Vegas, NV
Mar 7, 1987	Mike Tyson w pts 12 James "Bonecrusher" Smith (US)	...	Las Vegas, NV
	Tyson won Smith's WBA title		
May 30, 1987	Mike Tyson w rsf 6 Pinklon Thomas	....	Las Vegas, NV
Aug 1, 1987	Mike Tyson w pts 12 Tony Tucker (US)	....	Las Vegas, NV
	For unified and undisputed world title		

WBA title

Sep 15, 1978	**Muhammad Ali** w pts 15 Leon Spinks	....	New Orleans, LA
	Muhammad Ali announced his retirement as WBA champion		
Oct 20, 1979	**John Tate** (US) w pts 15 Gerrie Coetzee (SA)	....	Pretoria (SA)
	For vacant title		
Mar 31, 1980	**Mike Weaver** w ko 15 John Tate	....	Knoxville, TN
Oct 25, 1980	Mike Weaver w ko 13 Gerrie Coetzee	....	Sun City (Bop)
Oct 3, 1981	Mike Weaver w pts 15 James Tillis (US)	....	Rosemount, IL
Dec 10, 1982	**Mike Dokes** (US) w rsf 1 Mike Weaver	....	Las Vegas, NV
May 20, 1983	Mike Dokes drew 15 Mike Weaver	....	Las Vegas, NV
Sep 23, 1983	**Gerrie Coetzee** w ko 10 Mike Dokes	....	Richfield, OH
Dec 1, 1984	**Greg Page** w ko 8 Gerrie Coetzee	....	Sun City (Bop)
Apr 29, 1985	**Tony Tubbs** (US) w pts 15 Greg Page	....	Buffalo, NY
Jan 17, 1986	**Tim Witherspoon** w pts 15 Tony Tubbs	....	Atlanta, GA
Jul 19, 1986	Tim Witherspoon w rsf 11 Frank Bruno (Eng)	....	Wembley (Eng)
Dec 12, 1986	**James "Bonecrusher" Smith** w rsf 1 Tim Witherspoon	....	New York, NY
Mar 7, 1987	**Mike Tyson** w pts 12 James Smith	....	Las Vegas, NV
May 30, 1987	Mike Tyson w rsf 6 Pinklon Thomas	....	Las Vegas, NV
Aug 1, 1987	Mike Tyson w pts 12 Tony Tucker	....	Las Vegas, NV
	For unified and undisputed world title		

WBC title

Jun 10, 1978	**Larry Holmes** (US) w pts 15 Ken Norton	....	Las Vegas, NV
Nov 10, 1978	Larry Holmes w ko 7 Alfredo Evangelista	....	Las Vegas, NV
Mar 24, 1979	Larry Holmes w rsf 7 Osvaldo Ocasio (PR)	....	Las Vegas, NV
Jun 22, 1979	Larry Holmes w rsf 12 Mike Weaver (US)	....	New York, NY
Sep 28, 1979	Larry Holmes w rsf 11 Earnie Shavers (US)	....	Las Vegas, NV
Feb 3, 1980	Larry Holmes w ko 6 Lorenzo Zanon (Ita)	....	Las Vegas, NV
Mar 31, 1980	Larry Holmes w pts 15 Trevor Berbick (Jam)	....	Las Vegas, NV

IBF title

Dec 1983	*The IBF proclaimed Holmes champion after he had given up the WBC title*	
Nov 9, 1984	**Larry Holmes** w rsf 12 James "Bonecrusher" Smith	Las Vegas, NV
Mar 15, 1985	Larry Holmes w rsf 10 David Bey (US)	Las Vegas, NV
May 20, 1985	Larry Holmes w pts 15 Carl Williams (US)	Reno, NV
Sep 21, 1985	**Mike Spinks** (US) w pts 15 Larry Holmes	Las Vegas, NV
Apr 19, 1986	Mike Spinks w pts 15 Larry Holmes	Las Vegas, NV
Sep 6, 1986	Mike Spinks w rsf 4 Steffen Tangstad (Nor)	Las Vegas, NV
Feb 1987	*Spinks was stripped for signing to fight Gerry Cooney rather than the IBF No. 1, Tony Tucker*	
May 30, 1987	**Tony Tucker** (US) w rsf 10 James "Buster" Douglas (US)	Las Vegas, NV
	For vacant title	
Aug 1, 1987	**Mike Tyson** w pts 12 Tony Tucker	Las Vegas, NV
	For unified and undisputed world title	

Undisputed title

Oct 16, 1987	**Mike Tyson** w rsf 7 Tyrell Biggs (US)	Atlantic City, NJ
Jan 22, 1988	Mike Tyson w rsf 4 Larry Holmes	Atlantic City, NJ
Mar 21, 1988	Mike Tyson w rsf 2 Tony Tubbs	Tokyo (Jap)
Jun 27, 1988	Mike Tyson w ko 1 Mike Spinks	Atlantic City, NJ
Feb 25, 1989	Mike Tyson w rsf 5 Frank Bruno	Las Vegas, NV

The newly-formed WBO announced that they would recognize the winner between Francesco Damiani and Johnny Du Plooy as champion, rather than Tyson, a decision which set new standards in eccentricity

WBC/WBA/IBF titles

Jul 21, 1989	**Mike Tyson** w rsf 1 Carl Williams	Atlantic City, NJ
Feb 11, 1990	**James "Buster" Douglas** w ko 10 Mike Tyson	Tokyo (Jap)
Oct 25, 1990	**Evander Holyfield** (US) w ko 3 James "Buster" Douglas	Las Vegas, NV
Apr 19, 1991	Evander Holyfield w pts 12 George Foreman	Atlantic City, NJ
Nov 23, 1991	Evander Holyfield w rsf 7 Bert Cooper (US)	Atlanta, GA
Jun 19, 1992	Evander Holyfield w pts 12 Larry Holmes	in Las Vegas, NV
Nov 14, 1992	**Riddick Bowe** (US) w pts 12 Evander Holyfield	Las Vegas, NV
Dec 1992	*Bowe relinquished the WBC title rather than defend against Britain's Lennox Lewis, who was awarded the championship retrospectively on the basis of his second-round stoppage of Razor Ruddock in London on October 31, 1992 in an official WBC final eliminator*	

WBA/IBF titles

Feb 6, 1993	**Riddick Bowe** w rsf 1 Mike Dokes	New York, NY
May 22, 1993	Riddick Bowe w rsf 2 Jesse Ferguson (US)	Washington, DC
Nov 6, 1993	**Evander Holyfield** w pts 12 Riddick Bowe	Las Vegas, NV
Apr 22, 1994	**Michael Moorer** (US) w pts 12 Evander Holyfield	Las Vegas, NV
Nov 5, 1994	**George Foreman** w ko 10 Michael Moorer	Las Vegas, NV
Mar 1995	*Foreman was stripped of the WBA title for failing to defend against a suitable contender*	

WBC title

May 8, 1993	**Lennox Lewis** (Eng) w pts 12 Tony Tucker	Las Vegas, NV
Oct 1, 1993	Lennox Lewis w rsf 7 Frank Bruno	Cardiff (Wal)
May 6, 1994	Lennox Lewis w rsf 8 Phil Jackson (US)	Atlantic City, NJ
Sep 24, 1994	**Oliver McCall** (US) w rsf 2 Lennox Lewis	London (Eng)
Apr 8, 1995	Oliver McCall w pts 12 Larry Holmes	Las Vegas, NV
Sep 2, 1995	**Frank Bruno** w pts 12 Oliver McCall	Wembley (Eng)

WBA title

Apr 8, 1995	**Bruce Seldon** (US) w rtd 7 Tony Tucker (US)	Las Vegas, NV
	For vacant title	
Aug 19, 1995	Bruce Seldon w rsf 10 Joe Hipp (US)	Las Vegas, NV

IBF title

Apr 22, 1995	**George Foreman** w pts 12 Axel Schulz (Ger)	Las Vegas, NV
Jul 1995	*Foreman vacated title rather than face Schulz in a rematch in Germany*	
Dec 9, 1995	**Frans Botha** w pts 12 Axel Schulz	Suttgart, (Ger)
	For vacant title	

WBO title

| May 6, 1989 | **Francesco Damiani** (Ita) w ko 3 Johnny Du Plooy (SA) | Syracuse, NY |
| | *For vacant title* | |

Dec 16, 1989	Francesco Damiani w ret 2 Daniel Netto (Arg)	Cesena (Ita)
Jan 11, 1991	**Ray Mercer** (US) w ko 9 Francesco Damiani	Atlantic City, NJ
Oct 18, 1991	Ray Mercer w rsf 5 Tommy Morrison (US)	Atlantic City, NJ
Jan 1992	*Mercer was stripped for failing to defend against Michael Moorer*	
May 15, 1992	**Michael Moorer** w rsf 5 Bert Cooper	Atlantic City, NJ
Feb 1993	*Moorer relinquished the WBO title because it was "retarding his career"*	
Jun 7, 1993	**Tommy Morrison** w pts 12 George Foreman	Las Vegas, NV
	For vacant title	
Oct 29, 1993	**Michael Bentt** (US) w rsf 1 Tommy Morrison	Tulsa, OK
Mar 19, 1994	**Herbie Hide** (Eng) w ko 7 Michael Bentt	London (Eng)
Mar 11, 1995	**Riddick Bowe** w ko 6 Herbie Hide	Las Vegas, NV
Jun 17, 1995	Riddick Bowe w ko 6 Jorge Luis Gonzalez (Cub)	Las Vegas, NV
Jul 1995	*Bowe vacated title*	
Oct 1995	*Bowe requested reinstatement as champion, although his third fight with Evander Holyfield in Las Vegas on November 4, 1995, which Bowe won on an eighth-round stoppage, was not billed as a title defence*	

RINGSIDE VIEW

Mike Tyson
vs
Frank Bruno

ONE PUNCH FROM GLORY

This was expected to be an easy win for Tyson, and that's how it looked in the opening seconds at the Las Vegas Hilton on February 25, 1989, when Tyson floored the challenger heavily. But Bruno beat the count, and rocked the advancing champion with a thunderous right hook. Tyson was dazed and hurt, but Bruno failed to realise just how close he was to victory and the moment soon passed. One more punch, and the big Englishman may well have changed the course of boxing history.

GEORGE FOREMAN *(right) became the oldest ever champion in 1994*

Cruiserweight

In the near-20 years which separated the reigns of Floyd Patterson and George Foreman, the physical dimensions of the average heavyweight boxer changed dramatically. Patterson was little more than a light-heavyweight, as was his great British contemporary Henry Cooper, and in their era a heavyweight scaling over 210 lb would have been considered exceptional. By the time the massive Foreman was champion, 210-lb heavyweights would have looked undernourished.

Yet there were still a substantial number of good fighters who were too heavy for the 175 lb light-heavyweight division but who would have been hopelessly overmatched against genuine heavyweights. There was an urgent need for an in-between division, and in 1979 the WBC instituted the cruiserweight class with a weight limit of 190 lb. Three years later, they raised the limit to 195 lb, while the WBA and IBF – who set up their own champions in 1982 and 1983 respectively – stayed with the original limit. It was not until Evander Holyfield unified the titles in 1988 that the limit was standardized at 190 lb.

The division, which the WBA call "junior heavyweight", has struggled for acceptance, with Holyfield its sole champion of real quality and the only man to have held the undisputed title.

CARLOS DELEON *(left) beat Sammy Reeson to win his fourth WBC title*

World Cruiserweight Championship Bouts

WBC title

Dec 8,	1979	Marvin Camel (US) drew 15 Mate Parlov (Yug) . . . . Split (Yug)	
		For vacant title	
Mar 31,	1980	**Marvin Camel** w pts 15 Mate Parlov . . . . Las Vegas, NV	
		For vacant title	
Nov 26,	1980	**Carlos DeLeon** (PR) w pts 15 Marvin Camel . . . . New Orleans, LA	
Feb 24,	1982	Carlos DeLeon w rsf 7 Marvin Camel . . . . Atlantic City, NJ	
Jun 27,	1982	**S.T. Gordon** (US) w rsf 2 Carlos De Leon . . . . Cleveland, OH	
Feb 16,	1983	S.T. Gordon w rsf 2 Jesse Burnett (US) . . . . East Rutherford, NJ	
Jul 17,	1983	**Carlos DeLeon** w pts 12 S.T. Gordon . . . . Las Vegas, NV	
Sep 21,	1983	Carlos DeLeon w rsf 4 Alvaro Lopez (US) . . . . San Jose, CA	
Mar 9,	1984	Carlos DeLeon w pts 12 Anthony Davis (US) . . . . Las Vegas, NV	
Jun 2,	1984	Carlos DeLeon w pts 12 Bashiru Ali (Nig) . . . . Oakland, CA	
Jun 6,	1985	**Alfonso Ratliff** (US) w pts 12 Carlos DeLeon . . . . Las Vegas, NV	
Sep 21,	1985	**Bernard Benton** (US) w pts 12 Alfonso Ratliff . . . . Las Vegas, NV	
Mar 22,	1986	**Carlos DeLeon** w pts 12 Bernard Benton . . . . Las Vegas, NV	
Aug 10,	1986	Carlos DeLeon w rsf 8 Michael Greer (US) . . . . Giardini Naxos (Ita)	
Feb 21,	1987	Carlos DeLeon w rsf 5 Angelo Rottoli (Ita) . . . . Bergamo (Ita)	
Jan, 22	1988	Carlos DeLeon w pts 12 Jose Maria Flores Burlon (Ur.) . . . Atlantic City, NJ	
Apr 9,	1988	**Evander Holyfield** w ko 8 Carlos DeLeon . . . . Las Vegas, NV	
		Undisputed title	

WBA title

Feb 9,	1982	**Ossie Ocasio** (PR) w pts 15 Robbie Williams (SA) . . . Johannesburg (SA)	
		For vacant title	
Dec 16,	1982	Ossie Ocasio w pts 15 Young Joe Louis (US) . . . . Chicago, IL	
May 20,	1983	Ossie Ocasio w pts 15 Randy Stephens (US) . . . . Las Vegas, NV	
May 5,	1984	Ossie Ocasio w rsf 15 John Odhiambo (Ken) . . . . San Juan, CA	
Dec 1,	1984	**Piet Crous** (SA) w pts 15 Ossie Ocasio . . . . Sun City (Bop)	

Mar 29,	1985	Piet Crous w pts 15 Ossie Ocasio . . . . Sun City (Bop)	
Jul 27,	1985	**Dwight Muhammad Qawi** (US) w ko 11 Piet Crous . . . . . . Sun City (Bop)	
Mar 23,	1986	Dwight Muhammad Qawi w rsf 6 Leon Spinks (US) . . . . Reno, NV	
Jul 12,	1986	**Evander Holyfield** (US) w pts 15 Dwight Muhammad Qawi . . . Atlanta, GA	
Feb 14,	1987	Evander Holyfield w rsf 7 Henry Tillman (US) . . . . Reno, NV	

IBF title

May 21,	1983	**Marvin Camel** w ko 9 Rick Sekorski (US) . . . . Billings, MT	
Dec 13,	1983	Marvin Camel w ko 5 Roddy McDonald (Can) . . . . Halifax (Can)	
Oct 6,	1984	**Lee Roy Murphy** (US) w rsf 14 Marvin Camel . . . . Billings, MT	
Dec 20,	1984	Lee Roy Murphy w rsf 12 Young Joe Louis (US) . . . . Chicago, IL	
Oct 19,	1985	Lee Roy Murphy w ko 12 Chisanda Mutti (Zam) . . . . . . Monte Carlo (Mon)	
Apr 19,	1986	Lee Roy Murphy w ko 9 Dorcey Gaymon (US) . . . . San Remo (Ita)	
Oct 25,	1986	**Rickey Parkey** (US) w rsf 10 Lee Roy Murphy . . . . Marsala (Ita)	
May 15,	1987	**Evander Holyfield** w rsf 3 Rickey Parkey . . . . Las Vegas, NV	

WBA/IBF titles

Aug 15,	1987	**Evander Holyfield** w rsf 11 Ossie Ocasio . . . . St Tropez (Fra)	
Dec 6,	1987	Evander Holyfield w ko 4 Dwight Muhammad Qawi . . . . . . Atlantic City, NJ	

Undisputed title

Apr 9, 1988   **Evander Holyfield** w ko 8 Carlos DeLeon .... Las Vegas, NV
Nov 88   *Holyfield relinquished the title to box at heavyweight*

WBC title

May 17, 1989   **Carlos DeLeon** w rsf 9 Sammy Reeson (Eng) .... London (Eng)
   For vacant title
Jan 27, 1990   Carlos DeLeon drew 12 Johnny Nelson (Eng) .... Sheffield (Eng)
Jul 27, 1990   **Masimiliano Duran** (Ita) w dis 11 Carlos DeLeon ... Capo D'Orlando (Ita)
Dec 8, 1990   Masimiliano Duran w dis 12 Anaclet Wamba (Fra) ..... Ferrera (Ita)
Jul 20, 1991   **Anaclet Wamba** w rsf 11 Masimiliano Duran .... Palermo (Ita)
Dec 13, 1991   Anaclet Wamba w rsf 11 Masimiliano Duran .... Paris (Fra)
Jun 13, 1992   Anaclet Wamba w rsf 5 Andrei Rudenko (Rus) .... Paris (Fra)
Oct 16, 1992   Anaclet Wamba w pts 12 Andrew Maynard (US) .... Paris (Fra)
Mar 6, 1993   Anaclet Wamba w pts 12 David Vedder (US) .... Paris (Fra)
Oct 16, 1993   Anaclet Wamba w ret 7 Akim Tafer (Fra) .... Paris (Fra)
Jul 14, 1994   Anaclet Wamba drew 12 Adolpho Washington (US) ... Monte Carlo (Mon)
Dec 3, 1994   Anaclet Wamba w pts 12 Marcelo Dominguez (Arg) .... Salta (Arg)

WBA title

Mar 25, 1989   **Taoufik Belbouli** (Fra) w rsf 8 Michael Greer .... Casablanca (Mor)
   For vacant title, which Belbouli then relinquished in August 1989
   because of a knee injury
Nov 28, 1989   **Robert Daniels** (US) w pts 12 Dwight Muhammad Qawi ....
   .... Nogent-Sur-Marne (Fra)
   For vacant title
Jul 19, 1990   Robert Daniels w pts 12 Craig Bodzianowski (US) .... Seattle, WA
Nov 22, 1990   Robert Daniels drew 12 Taoufik Belbouli (Fra) .... Madrid (Sp)
Mar 9, 1991   **Bobby Czyz** (US) w pts 12 Robert Daniels .... Atlantic City, NJ
Aug 9, 1991   Bobby Czyz w pts 12 Bash Ali (Nig) .... Atlantic City, NJ
May 8, 1992   Bobby Czyz w pts 12 Donny Lalonde (Can) .... Las Vegas, NV
Sep 1993   *Czyz stripped for failure to defend*
Nov 6, 1993   **Orlin Norris** (US) w rsf 6 Marcelo Figueroa (Arg) .... Paris (Fra)
   For vacant title
Mar 4, 1994   Orlin Norris w pts 12 Arthur Williams (US) .... Las Vegas, NV

Jul 2, 1994   Orlin Norris w ko 3 Arthur Williams .... Las Vegas, NV
Nov 12, 1994   Orlin Norris w ko 2 James Heath (US) .... Mexico City (Mex)
Mar 17, 1995   Orlin Norris w pts 12 Adolpho Washington .... Worcester, MA
Jul 22, 1995   **Nate Miller** (US) w ko 8 Orlin Norris .... London (Eng)

IBF title

Jun 3, 1989   **Glenn McCrory** (Eng) w pts 12 Patrick Lumumba (Ken) .... Stanley (Eng)
   For vacant title
Oct 21, 1989   Glenn McCrory w ko 11 Siza Makhathini (SA) ...... Middlesbrough (Eng)
Mar 22, 1990   **Jeff Lampkin** (US) w ko 3 Glenn McCrory .... Gateshead (Eng)
Jul 29, 1990   Jeff Lampkin w ko 8 Sika Makhatini .... St Petersburg (Rus)
Jul 1991   *Lampkin relinquished title*
Sep 6, 1991   **James Warring** (US) w ko 1 James Pritchard (US) .... Salemi (Ita)
   For vacant title
Nov 15, 1991   James Warring (US) w ko 5 Donnell Wingfield (US) .... Roanoke, VA
May 16, 1992   James Warring w pts 12 Johnny Nelson (Eng) .... Fredericksburg, VA
Jul 30, 1992   **Al Cole** (US) w pts 12 James Warring .... Stanhope, NJ
Feb 28, 1993   Al Cole w pts 12 Uriah Grant (Jam) .... Atlantic City, NJ
Jul 16, 1993   Al Cole w pts 12 Glenn McCrory .... Moscow (Rus)
Nov 17, 1993   Al Cole w rsf 5 Vince Boulware (US) .... Atlantic City, NJ
Jul 23, 1994   Al Cole w pts 12 Nate Miller (US) .... Bismark, ND
Jun 24, 1995   Al Cole w pts 12 Uriah Grant .... Atlantic City, NJ

WBO title

Dec 3, 1989   **Boone Pultz** (US) w pts 12 Magne Havnaa (Nor) ..... Copenhagen (Den)
   For vacant title
May 17, 1990   **Magne Havnaa** w rsf 5 Boone Pultz .... Aars (Den)
Dec 8, 1990   Magne Havnaa w pts 12 Daniel Netto (Arg) .... Aalborg (Den)
Feb 15, 1991   Magne Havnaa w pts 12 Tyrone Booze (US) .... Randers (Den)
Feb 1992   *Havnaa relinquished the title because of weight problems*
Jul 25, 1992   **Tyrone Booze** (US) w ko 7 Derek Angol (Eng) .... Manchester (Eng)
   For vacant title
Oct 2, 1992   Tyrone Booze w pts 12 Ralf Rocchigiani (Ger) .... Berlin (Ger)
Feb 13, 1993   **Marcus Bott** (Ger) w pts 12 Tyrone Booze .... Hamburg (Ger)
Mar 26, 1993   **Nestor Giovannini** (Arg) w pts 12 Marcus Bott .... Hamburg (Ger)
Nov 20, 1993   Nestor Giovannini w pts 12 Marcus Bott .... Hamburg (Ger)
Oct 1, 1994   Nestor Giovannini w ret 6 Larry Carlisle (US) .... Buenos Aires (Arg)
Dec 17, 1994   **Dariusz Michalczewski** (Ger) w rsf 10 Nestor Giovannini .. Hamburg (Ger)
Mar 1995   *Michalczewski relinquished the cruiserweight title to concentrate on*
   defending his WBO light-heavyweight championship
Jun 10, 1995   **Ralf Rocchigiani** (Ger) w rsf 11 Carl Thompson (Eng) .. Manchester (Eng)
   For vacant title
Sep 30, 1995   Ralf Rocchigiani w pts 12 Mark Randazzo (US) .... Hanover (Ger)
Nov 25, 1995   Ralf Rocchigiani w ko 8 Dan Ward (US) .... Brunswick (Ger)

ANDREW MAYNARD *(right) lost to Anaclet Wamba in a 1992 WBC fight*

Light-Heavyweight

Although it is one of the eight "classic" divisions in boxing, the light-heavyweight category took a long time to become established. It was the brain-child of a Chicago newspaperman, Lou Houseman, who made a few false starts before finally steering his own protégé, Jack Root, to the title in 1903. The weight limit in the early days fluctuated between 165 lb and 170 lb before settling, in the reign of Jack Dillon, at the present 175 lb.

Like all of boxing's weight categories it needed a charismatic champion to earn it popular recognition, and Frenchman Georges Carpentier brought the division to centre stage. Throughout the 1920s and 1930s it saw plenty of title action with quality performers like Tommy Loughran, Maxie Rosenbloom and John Henry Lewis.

Before the introduction of the cruiserweight class it was traditionally seen as a launch-pad into the heavyweight division, but although light-heavyweight champions Carpentier, Loughran, Lewis, Billy Conn, Gus Lesnevich, Joey Maxim, Archie Moore and Bob Foster all tried for the heavy-weight crown, none succeeded until Mike Spinks beat Larry Holmes in 1985.

World Light-Heavyweight Championship Bouts

Apr 22,	1903	**Jack Root** (US) w pts 10 Kid McCoy (US)	....	in Detroit, MI
Jul 4,	1903	**George Gardner** (Ire) w ko 12 Jack Root	....	Fort Erie (Can)
Nov 25,	1903	**Bob Fitzsimmons** (Eng) w pts 20 George Gardner	.....	San Francisco, CA
Dec 20,	1905	**Philadelphia Jack O'Brien** (US) w ko 13 Bob Fitzsimmons	....	
				San Francisco, CA
Nov 28,	1906	Philadelphia Jack O'Brien drew 20 Tommy Burns (Can)	....	
				Los Angeles, CA

There was no further championship activity in the division until Jack Dillon claimed the title after beating Hugo Kelly in 1912

May 28,	1912	**Jack Dillon** (US) w ko 3 Hugo Kelly (US)	....	Indianapolis, IN
Apr 14,	1914	Jack Dillon w pts 12 Battling Levinsky (US)	....	Butte, MT
Apr 28,	1914	Jack Dillon w pts 10 Al Norton (US)	....	Kansas City, KS
Jun 15,	1914	Jack Dillon w pts 12 Bob Moha (US)	....	Butte, MT
Jul 3,	1914	Jack Dillon w pts 10 Sailor Petroskey (US)	....	Kansas City, KS
Apr 25,	1916	Jack Dillon w pts 15 Battling Levinsky	....	Kansas City, KS
Oct 24,	1916	**Battling Levinsky** w pts 12 Jack Dillon	....	Boston, MA
Oct 12,	1920	**Georges Carpentier** (Fra) w ko 4 Battling Levinsky	....	New York, NY
May 11,	1922	Georges Carpentier w ko 1 Ted "Kid" Lewis (Eng)	....	London (Eng)
Sep 24,	1922	**Battling Siki** (Sen) w ko 6 Georges Carpentier	....	Paris (Fra)
Mar 17,	1923	**Mike McTigue** (Ire) w pts 20 Battling Siki	....	Dublin (Ire)
Oct 4,	1923	Mike McTigue drew 10 Young Stribling (US)	....	Columbus, OH
May 30,	1925	**Paul Berlenbach** (US) w pts 15 Mike McTigue	....	New York, NY
Sep 11,	1925	Paul Berlenbach w rsf 11 Jimmy Slattery (US)	....	New York, NY
Dec 11,	1925	Paul Berlenbach w pts 15 Jack Delaney (Can)	....	New York, NY
Jun 10,	1926	Paul Berlenbach w pts 15 Young Stribling	....	New York, NY
Jul 16,	1926	**Jack Delaney** w pts 15 Paul Berlenbach	....	Brooklyn, NY
Dec 10,	1926	Jack Delaney w ko 3 Jamaica Kid (US)	....	Waterbury, CT

RINGSIDE VIEW

Mike McTigue
vs
Battling Siki

EXPLOSIVE ATMOSPHERE

Gunfire and grenade explosions were audible in the street outside the Dublin cinema where Mike McTigue from Co. Clare, boxing on St Patrick's Day 1923 during the height of the Irish Civil War, was challenging Battling Siki for the light-heavyweight title ... but there was little excitement in the ring as McTigue won a dull points decision.

June	1927	*Delaney relinquished title to box at heavyweight*		
Aug 30,	1927	**Jimmy Slattery** w pts 10 Maxie Rosenbloom (US)	....	Hartford, CT
		For vacant NBA title		
Oct 7,	1927	**Tommy Loughran** (US) w pts 15 Mike McTigue	....	New York, NY
		For vacant New York title		
Dec 12,	1927	Tommy Loughran w pts 15 Jimmy Slattery	....	New York, NY
		For undisputed title		
Jan 6,	1928	Tommy Loughran w pts 15 Leo Lomski (US)	....	New York, NY
Jun 1,	1928	Tommy Loughran w pts 15 Pete Latzo (US)	....	New York, NY
Jul 16,	1928	Tommy Loughran w pts 10 Pete Latzo	....	Wilkes-Barre, PA
Mar 28,	1929	Tommy Loughran w pts 10 Mickey Walker (US)	....	Chicago, IL
Jul 18,	1929	Tommy Loughran w pts 15 James J. Braddock (US)	......	New York, NY
Sep	1929	*Loughran relinquished title to box at heavyweight*		
Feb 10,	1930	**Jimmy Slattery** w pts 15 Lou Scozza (US)	....	Buffalo, NY
		For vacant New York title		
Jun 25,	1930	**Maxie Rosenbloom** w pts 15 Jimmy Slattery	....	New York, NY
		For undisputed title		
Oct 22,	1930	Maxie Rosenbloom w rsf 11 Abe Bain (US)	....	New York, NY
Jun 6,	1931	*NBA withdrew recognition from Rosenbloom for failing to defend within a stipulated period*		
Aug 5,	1931	Maxie Rosenbloom w pts 15 Jimmy Slattery	....	New York, NY
Mar 18,	1932	**George Nichols** (US) w pts 10 Dave Maier (US)	....	Chicago, IL
		For vacant NBA title		
Jul 14,	1932	Maxie Rosenbloom w pts 15 Lou Scozza	....	Buffalo, NY
Dec	1932	*NBA vacated Nichols' title*		
Mar 1,	1933	**Bob Godwin** (US) w pts 10 Joe Knight (US)	....	Palm Beach, FL
		For vacant NBA title		
Mar 10,	1933	Maxie Rosenbloom w pts 15 Adolf Heuser (Ger)	....	New York, NY
Mar 24,	1933	Maxie Rosenbloom w ko 4 Bob Godwin	....	New York, NY
		For undisputed title		
Nov 3,	1933	Maxie Rosenbloom w pts 15 Mickey Walker	....	New York, NY
Feb 5,	1934	Maxie Rosenbloom drew 15 Joe Knight	....	Miami, FL
Nov 16,	1934	**Bob Olin** (US) w pts 15 Maxie Rosenbloom	....	New York, NY
Aug	1935	*The European-based IBU withdrew recognition from Olin and matched Hein Lazek with Merlo Preciso for their version of the title, although the British Board continued to recognize Olin*		

IBU title

Sep 17,	1935	**Hein Lazek** (Aut) w dis 13 Merlo Preciso (Ita)	....	Vienna (Aut)
		For vacant title		
Feb 25,	1936	Hein Lazek w ko 6 Reinus de Boer (Hol)	....	Vienna (Aut)
Aug 3,	1936	Hein Lazek w ko 9 Emil Olive (Fra)	....	Vienna (Aut)
Sep 1,	1936	**Gustav Roth** (Bel) w pts 15 Hein Lazek	....	Vienna (Aut)
Oct 29,	1936	Gustav Roth w pts 15 Adolph Witt (Ger)	....	Berlin (Ger)
Jan 12,	1937	Gustav Roth drew 15 Antonio Rodriguez (Br)	....	Rio de Janeiro (Br)
Mar 24,	1937	Gustav Roth w pts 15 Merlo Preciso	....	Brussels (Bel)
May 1,	1937	Gustav Roth w pts 15 John Andersson (Swe)	....	Antwerp (Bel)
Dec 1,	1937	Gustav Roth drew 15 Karel Sys (Bel)	....	Brussels (Bel)
Jan 21,	1938	Gustav Roth w pts 15 Josef Besselmann (Ger)	....	Berlin (Ger)
Mar 25,	1938	**Adolf Heuser** w ko 7 Gustav Roth	....	Berlin (Ger)
May	1938	*The IBU, in an effort to unify the title, withdrew recognition from Heuser*		

New York/NBA titles

Oct 31,	1935	**John Henry Lewis** (US) w pts 15 Bob Olin	....	St Louis, MO
Mar 30,	1936	John Henry Lewis w pts 15 Jock McAvoy (Eng)	....	New York, NY
Nov 9,	1936	John Henry Lewis w pts 15 Len Harvey (Eng)	....	London (Eng)
Jun 3,	1937	John Henry Lewis w rsf 8 Bob Olin	....	St Louis, MO
Apr 25,	1938	John Henry Lewis w ko 4 Emilio Martinez (US)	....	Minneapolis, MN
Jul 27,	1938	*The New York Commission withdrew recognition from Lewis*		
Oct 28,	1938	John Henry Lewis w pts 15 Al Gainer (US)	....	New Haven, CT
Feb 23,	1939	**Melio Bettina** (US) w rsf 9 Tiger Jack Fox (US)	....	New York, NY
		For vacant New York title		
Jun 19,	1939	*Lewis announced his retirement*		
Jul 13,	1939	**Billy Conn** (US) w pts 15 Melio Bettina	....	Pittsburgh, PA
		For New York and NBA titles: the British Board decided instead to recognize Len Harvey's 15-rounds points win over Jock McAvoy in London on July 10, 1939 as being for the vacant world title. No other body supported Harvey's claim		
Sep 25,	1939	Billy Conn w pts 15 Melio Bettina	....	Pittsburgh, PA
Nov 17,	1939	Billy Conn w pts 15 Gus Lesnevich (US)	....	New York, NY

Jun 5,	1940	Billy Conn w pts 15 Gus Lesnevich . . . . Detroit, MI
Dec	1940	*The NBA withdrew recognition from Conn, who had moved into the heavyweight division*
Jan 13,	1941	**Anton Christoforidis** (Gr) w pts 15 Melio Bettina . . . . Cleveland, OH
		For vacant NBA title
Mar	1941	*New York stripped Conn*
May 22,	1941	**Gus Lesnevich** w pts 15 Anton Christoforidis . . . . New York, NY
		For NBA and NY titles
Aug 26,	1941	Gus Lesnevich w pts 15 Tami Mauriello (US) . . . . New York, NY
Nov 14,	1941	Gus Lesnevich w pts 15 Tami Mauriello . . . . New York, NY
Jun 20,	1942	**Freddie Mills** (Eng) w ko 2 Len Harvey . . . . London (Eng)
		For British version of title
May 14,	1946	Gus Lesnevich w rsf 10 Freddie Mills . . . . London (Eng)
		For undisputed title
Feb 8,	19247	Gus Lesnevich w ko 10 Billy Fox (US) . . . . New York, NY
Mar 5,	1948	Gus Lesnevich w ko 1 Billy Fox . . . . New York, NY
Jul 26,	1948	**Freddie Mills** w pts 15 Gus Lesnevich . . . . London (Eng)
Jan 24,	1950	Joey Maxim (US) w ko 10 Freddie Mills . . . . London (Eng)
Aug 22,	1951	Joey Maxim w pts 15 Bob Murphy (US) . . . . New York, NY
Jun 25,	1952	Joey Maxim w ret 14 Sugar Ray Robinson (US) . . . . New York, NY
Dec 17,	1952	**Archie Moore** (US) w pts 15 Joey Maxim . . . . St Louis, MO
Jun 24,	1953	Archie Moore w pts 15 Joey Maxim . . . . Ogden, UT
Jan 27,	1954	Archie Moore w pts 15 Joey Maxim . . . . Miami, FL
Aug 11,	1954	Archie Moore w rsf 14 Harold Johnson (US) . . . . New York, NY
Jun 22,	1955	Archie Moore w ko 3 Carl "Bobo" Olson (US) . . . . New York, NY
Jun 5,	1956	Archie Moore w rsf 10 Yolande Pompey (Tr) . . . . London (Eng)
Sep 20,	1957	Archie Moore w rsf 7 Tony Anthony (US) . . . . Los Angeles, CA
Dec 10,	1958	Archie Moore w ko 11 Yvon Durelle (Can) . . . . Montreal (Can)
Aug 12,	1959	Archie Moore w ko 3 Yvon Durelle . . . . Montreal (Can)
Oct	1960	*The NBA stripped Moore for failing to defend*
Feb 7,	1961	**Harold Johnson** w rsf 9 Jesse Bowdrey (US) . . . . Miami, FL
		For vacant NBA title
Apr 24,	1961	Harold Johnson w rsf 2 Von Clay (US) . . . . Philadelphia, PA
Jun 10,	1961	Archie Moore w pts 15 Guilio Rinaldi (Ita) . . . . New York, NY
Aug 29,	1961	Harold Johnson w pts 15 Eddie Cotton (US) . . . . Seattle, WA
Feb	1962	*The New York Commission and the EBU withdrew recognition from Moore because of his failure to meet Johnson*
May 12,	1962	Harold Johnson w pts 15 Doug Jones (US) . . . . Philadelphia, PA
		For vacant undisputed title
Jun 23,	1962	Harold Johnson w pts 15 Gustav Scholz (Ger) . . . . Berlin (Ger)
Jun 1,	1963	**Willie Pastrano** (US) w pts 15 Harold Johnson . . . . Las Vegas, NV
Apr 10,	1964	Willie Pastrano w rsf 5 Gregorio Peralta (Arg) . . . . New Orleans, LA
Nov 30,	1964	Willie Pastrano w rsf 11 Terry Downes (Eng) . . . . Manchester (Eng)
Mar 30,	1965	**Jose Torres** (PR) w rsf 9 Willie Pastrano . . . . New York, NY
May 21,	1966	Jose Torres w pts 15 Wayne Thornton (US) . . . . New York, NY
Aug 15,	1966	Jose Torres w pts 15 Eddie Cotton . . . . Las Vegas, NV
Oct 15,	1966	Jose Torres w ko 2 Chic Calderwood (Sco) . . . . San Juan, CA
Dec 16,	1966	**Dick Tiger** (Nig) w pts 15 Jose Torres . . . . New York, NY
May 16,	1967	Dick Tiger w pts 15 Jose Torres . . . . New York, NY
Nov 17,	1967	Dick Tiger w rsf 12 Roger Rouse (US) . . . . Las Vegas, NV
May 24,	1968	**Bob Foster** (US) w ko 4 Dick Tiger . . . . New York, NY
Jan 22,	1969	Bob Foster w ko. 1 Frank DePaula (US) . . . . New York, NY
May 24,	1969	Bob Foster w rsf 4 Andy Kendall (US) . . . . Springfield, MA
Apr 4,	1970	Bob Foster w rsf 4 Roger Rouse . . . . Missoula, MT
Jun 27,	1970	Bob Foster w ko 10 Mark Tessman (US) . . . . Baltimore, MD
Dec 9,	1970	*Foster stripped of title by WBA for refusing to meet their deadline for defence against No. 1 WBA challenger, Jimmy Dupree*

WBA title

Feb 27,	1971	**Vicente Rondon** (Ven) w rsf 6 Jimmy Dupree (US) . . . . Caracas (Ven)
		For vacant title
Jun 5,	1971	Vicente Rondon w ko 1 Piero Del Papa (Ita) . . . . Caracas (Ven)
Aug 21,	1971	Vicente Rondon w pts 15 Eddie Jones (US) . . . . Caracas (Ven)
Oct 26,	1971	Vicente Rondon w ko 13 Gomeo Brennan (Bah) . . . . Miami, FL
Dec 15,	1971	Vicente Rondon w ko 8 Doyle Baird (US) . . . . Cleveland, OH
Apr 7,	1972	**Bob Foster** w ko 2 Vicente Rondon . . . . Miami Beach, FL
		Undisputed title

WBC title

Mar 2,	1971	**Bob Foster** w ko 4 Hal Carroll (US) . . . . Scranton, PA
Apr 24,	1971	Bob Foster w pts 15 Ray Anderson (US) . . . . Tampa, FL
Oct 29,	1971	Bob Foster w rsf 8 Tommy Hicks (US) . . . . Scranton, PA
Dec 16,	1971	Bob Foster w rsf 3 Brian Kelly (US) . . . . Oklahoma City, OK
Apr 7,	1972	Bob Foster w ko 2 Vicente Rondon . . . . Miami Beach, FL
		(Undisputed title)

RINGSIDE VIEW

Victor Galindez
vs
Richie Kates

TO THE VICTOR THE SPOILS

Victor Galindez enlivened the history of the light-heavyweight division with some heroic performances, but his finest hour came on May 22, 1976 in Johannesburg when he knocked out American challenger Richie Kates with just one second remaining in the 15th and final round of a blood-soaked epic.

Undisputed title

Jun 27,	1972	**Bob Foster** w ko 4 Mike Quarry (US) . . . . Las Vegas, NV
Sep 26,	1972	Bob Foster w ko 14 Chris Finnegan (Eng) . . . . Wembley (Eng)
Aug 21,	1973	Bob Foster w pts 15 Pierre Fourie (SA) . . . . Albuquerque, NM
Dec 1,	1973	Bob Foster w pts 15 Pierre Fourie . . . . Johannesburg (SA)
Jun 17,	1974	Bob Foster drew 15 Jorge Ahumada (Arg) . . . . Albuquerque, NM
Aug	1974	*World Boxing Council withdrew recognition of Foster as world champion for failure to sign for a title defence against John Conteh or Jorge Ahumada. Foster later announced his retirement*

WBC title

Oct 1,	1974	**John Conteh** (Eng) w pts 15 Jorge Ahumada . . . . Wembley (Eng)
		For vacant title
Mar 11,	1975	John Conteh w rsf 5 Lonnie Bennett (US) . . . . Wembley (Eng)
Oct 9,	1976	John Conteh w pts 15 Alvaro "Yaqui" Lopez (US) . . . . . Copenhagen (Den)
Mar 5,	1977	John Conteh w rsf 3 Len Hutchins (US) . . . . Liverpool (Eng)
May	1977	*Conteh stripped of his title by the WBC for failure to go through with a contracted defence against Miguel Angel Cuello*
May 21,	1977	**Miguel Cuello** (Arg) w ko 9 Jesse Burnett (US) . . . . . . Monte Carlo (Mon)
		For vacant title
Jan 7,	1978	**Mate Parlov** (Yug) w ko 9 Miguel Cuello . . . . Milan (Ita)
Jun 17,	1978	Mate Parlov w pts 15 John Conteh . . . . Belgrade (Yug)
Dec 2,	1978	**Marvin Johnson** (US) w rsf 10 Mate Parlov . . . . Marsala (Ita)
Apr 22,	1979	**Matthew Saad Muhammad** *[formerly known as Matt Franklin]* (US) w rsf 8 Marvin Johnson . . . . Indianapolis, IN
Aug 18,	1979	Matthew Saad Muhammad w pts 15 John Conteh . . . . Atlantic City, NJ
Mar 29,	1980	Matthew Saad Muhammad w rsf 4 John Conteh . . . . Atlantic City, NJ
May 11,	1980	Matthew Saad Muhammad w rsf 5 Louis Pergaud (Fra) . . . . . Halifax (Can)
Jul 13,	1980	Matthew Saad Muhammad w rsf 14 Alvaro Lopez . . . . McAfee, NJ
Nov 28,	1980	Matthew Saad Muhammad w ko 4 Lotte Mwale (Zam) . . . . San Diego, CA
Feb 28,	1981	Matthew Saad Muhammad w rsf 11 Vonzell Johnson (US) . . . . Atlantic City, NJ
Apr 25,	1981	Matthew Saad Muhammad w ko 9 Murray Sutherland (Sco) . . . . Atlantic City, NJ
Sep 26,	1981	Matthew Saad Muhammad w rsf 11 Jerry Martin (US) . . . . Atlantic City, NJ
Dec 19,	1981	**Dwight Braxton** (US) w rsf 10 Matthew Saad Muhammad . Atlantic City, NJ
Mar 21,	1982	Dwight Braxton w rsf 6 Jerry Martin . . . . Las Vegas, NV
Aug 7,	1982	Dwight Braxton w rsf 6 Matthew Saad Muhammad . . . . . Philadelphia, PA
Nov 28,	1982	**Dwight Muhammad Qawi** *[formerly known as Dwight Braxton]* w rsf 11 Eddie Davis (US) . . . . Atlantic City, NJ
Mar 18,	1983	**Michael Spinks** (US) w pts 15 Dwight Muhammad Qawi . Atlantic City, NJ
		Undisputed title

WBA title

Dec 7,	1974	**Victor Galindez** (Arg) w ret 12 Len Hutchins . . . . Buenos Aires (Arg)
		For vacant title
Apr 7,	1975	Victor Galindez w pts 15 Pierre Fourie . . . . Johannesburg (SA)
Jun 30,	1975	Victor Galindez w pts 15 Jorge Ahumada . . . . New York, NY
Sep 13,	1975	Victor Galindez w pts 15 Pierre Fourie . . . . Johannesburg (SA)
Mar 28,	1976	Victor Galindez w ret 3 Harald Skog (Nor) . . . . Oslo (Nor)
May 22,	1976	Victor Galindez w ko 15 Richie Kates (US) . . . . Johannesburg (SA)
Oct 5,	1976	Victor Galindez w pts 15 Kosie Smith (SA) . . . . Johannesburg (SA)
Jun 18,	1977	Victor Galindez w pts 15 Richie Kates . . . . Rome (Ita)
Sep 17,	1977	Victor Galindez w pts 15 Alvaro "Yaqui" Lopez (US) . . . . Rome (Ita)
Nov 20,	1977	Victor Galindez w pts 15 Eddie Mustafa Muhammad *[formerly known as Eddie Gregory]* (US) . . . . Turin (Ita)

May 6, 1978	Victor Galindez w pts 15 Alvaro "Yaqui" Lopez	Reggio (Ita)
Sep 15, 1978	**Mike Rossman** (US) w rsf 13 Victor Galindez	New Orleans, LA
Dec 5, 1978	Mike Rossman w rsf 6 Aldo Traversaro (Ita)	Philadelphia, PA
Apr 14, 1979	**Victor Galindez** w ret 9 Mike Rossman	New Orleans, LA
Nov 30, 1979	**Marvin Johnson** (US) w rsf 11 Victor Galindez	New Orleans, LA
Mar 31, 1980	**Eddie Mustafa Muhammad** w rsf 11 Marvin Johnson	Knoxville, TN
Jul 20, 1980	Eddie Mustafa Muhammad w rsf 10 Jerry Martin (US)	McAfee, NJ
Nov 29, 1980	Eddie Mustafa Muhammad w rsf 3 Rudi Koopman (Hol)	Los Angeles, CA
Jul 18, 1981	**Michael Spinks** (US) w pts 15 Eddie Mustafa Muhammad	Las Vegas, NV
Nov 7, 1981	Michael Spinks w rsf 7 Vonzell Johnson	Atlantic City, NJ
Feb 13, 1982	Michael Spinks w pts 15 Mustapha Wassaja (Ug)	Atlantic City, NJ
Apr 11, 1982	Michael Spinks w rsf 8 Murray Sutherland	Atlantic City, NJ
Jun 12, 1982	Michael Spinks w rsf 8 Jerry Celestine (US)	Atlantic City, NJ
Sep 18, 1982	Michael Spinks w rsf 9 Johnny Davis (US)	Atlantic City, NJ
Mar 18, 1983	Michael Spinks w pts 15 Dwight Muhammad Qawi	Atlantic City, NJ
	For undisputed title	

Undisputed title

Nov 25, 1983	**Michael Spinks** w rsf 11 Oscar Rivadeneyra (Peru)	Vancouver (Can)
Feb 25, 1984	Michael Spinks w pts 12 Eddie Davis	Atlantic City, NJ
Feb 23, 1985	Michael Spinks w rsf 3 David Sears (US)	Atlantic City, NJ
Jun 6, 1985	Michael Spinks w rsf 8 Jim MacDonald (US)	Las Vegas, NV
Sep 1985	*Spinks relinquished the title when he became IBF heavyweight champion, and the light-heavyweight title once more fragmented*	

WBC title

Dec 10, 1985	**J. B. Williamson** (US) w pts 12 Prince Mama Muhammad (Gha)	Los Angeles, CA
Apr 30, 1986	**Dennis Andries** (Eng) w pts 12 J. B. Williamson	London (Eng)
Sep 10, 1986	Dennis Andries w rsf 9 Tony Sibson (Eng)	London (Eng)
Mar 7, 1987	**Thomas Hearns** (US) w rsf 10 Dennis Andries	Detroit, MI
Aug 1987	*Hearns gave up the title to fight for the WBC middleweight championship*	
Nov 27, 1987	**Donny Lalonde** (Can) w rsf 2 Eddie Davis	Port of Spain (Trin)
	For vacant title	
May 29, 1988	Donny Lalonde w rsf 5 Leslie Stewart	Port of Spain (Trin)
Nov 7, 1988	**Sugar Ray Leonard** (US) w rsf 9 Donny Lalonde	Las Vegas, NV
	The fight was also for the vacant WBC super-middleweight title, and Lalonde scaled 167 lb. Leonard immediately relinquished the light-heavyweight title	
Feb 21, 1989	**Dennis Andries** w rsf 5 Tony Willis (US)	Tucson, AZ
	For vacant title	
Jun 24, 1989	**Jeff Harding** (Aus) w rsf 12 Dennis Andries	Atlantic City, NJ
Oct 24, 1989	Jeff Harding w ret 2 Tom Collins (Eng)	Brisbane (Aus)
Mar 18, 1990	Jeff Harding w rsf 11 Nestor Giovannini (Arg)	Atlantic City, NJ
Jul 28, 1990	**Dennis Andries** w ko 7 Jeff Harding	Melbourne (Aus)
Oct 10, 1990	Dennis Andries w ret 4 Sergio Merani (Arg)	London (Eng)
Jan 10, 1991	Dennis Andries w pts 12 Guy Waters (Aus)	Adelaide (Aus)
Sep 11, 1991	**Jeff Harding** w pts 12 Dennis Andries	London (Eng)
Jun 5, 1992	Jeff Harding w rsf 8 Christophe Tiozzo (Fra)	Marseilles (Fra)
Dec 3, 1992	Jeff Harding w pts 12 David Vedder (US)	St-Jean-de-Luz (Fra)
Jul 23, 1994	**Mike McCallum** (Jam) w pts 12 Jeff Harding	Bismark, ND
Feb 25, 1995	Mike McCallum w rsf 7 Carl Jones (US)	London (Eng)
Jun 16, 1995	**Fabrice Tiozzo** (Fra) w pts 12 Mike McCallum	Lyon (Fra)

WBA title

Feb 9, 1986	**Marvin Johnson** (US) w rsf 7 Leslie Stewart (Tr)	Indianapolis, IN
	For vacant title	
Sep 20, 1986	Marvin Johnson w rsf 13 Jean-Marie Emebe (Cam)	Indianapolis, IN
May 23, 1987	**Leslie Stewart** w ret 8 Marvin Johnson	Port of Spain (Trin)
Sep 5, 1987	**Virgil Hill** (US) w rsf 4 Leslie Stewart	Atlantic City, NJ
Nov 21, 1987	Virgil Hill w pts 12 Rufino Angulo(Fr)	Paris (Fra)
Apr 3, 1988	Virgil Hill w rsf 11 Jean-Marie Emebe	Bismark, ND
Jun 6, 1988	Virgil Hill w pts 12 Ramzi Hassan (US)	Las Vegas, NV
Nov 11, 1988	Virgil Hill w rsf 10 Willie Featherstone (Can)	Bismark, ND
Mar 4, 1989	Virgil Hill w pts 12 Bobby Czyz (US)	Bismark, ND
May 27, 1989	Virgil Hill w rsf 7 Joe Lasisi (Nig)	Bismark, ND
Oct 24, 1989	Virgil Hill w pts 12 James Kinchen (US)	Bismark, ND
Feb 25, 1990	Virgil Hill w pts 12 David Vedder	Bismark, ND
Jul 7, 1990	Virgil Hill w pts 12 Tyrone Frazier (US)	Bismark, ND
Jan 6, 1991	Virgil Hill w pts 12 Mike Peak (US)	Bismark, ND
Jun 3, 1991	**Thomas Hearns** w pts 12 Virgil Hill	Las Vegas, NV
Mar 20, 1992	**Iran Barkley** (US) w pts 12 Thomas Hearns	Las Vegas, NV
Apr 1992	*Barkley gave up the light-heavyweight title to concentrate on defending his IBF super-middleweight title*	

Sep 29, 1992	**Virgil Hill** w pts 12 Frank Tate (US)	Bismark, ND
	For vacant title	
Feb 20, 1993	Virgil Hill w ret 11 Adolfo Washington (US)	Fargo, ND
Nov 9, 1993	Virgil Hill w rsf 10 Saul Montana (US)	Bismark, ND
Dec 17, 1993	Virgil Hill w pts 12 Guy Waters	Minot, ND
Jul 23, 1994	Virgil Hill w pts 12 Frank Tate	Bismark, ND
Apr 1, 1995	Virgil Hill w pts 12 Crawford Ashley (Eng)	Stateline, NV
Sep 2, 1995	Virgil Hill w pts 12 Drake Thadzi (Mal)	London (Eng)

IBF title

Dec 12, 1985	**Slobodan Kacar** (Yug) w pts 15 Eddie Mustafa Muhammad	Pesaro (Ita)
	For vacant title	
Sep 6, 1986	**Bobby Czyz** (US) w rsf 5 Slobodan Kacar	Las Vegas, NV
Dec 26, 1986	Bobby Czyz w rsf 1 David Sears (US)	West Orange, NJ
Feb 21, 1987	Bobby Czyz w ko 2 Willie Edwards (US)	Atlantic City, NJ
May 3, 1987	Bobby Czyz w rsf 6 Jim MacDonald	Atlantic City, NJ
Oct 29, 1987	**Prince Charles Williams** (US) w ret 9 Bobby Czyz	Las Vegas, NV
Jun 10, 1988	Prince Charles Williams w ret 11 Richard Caramanolis (Fra)	Annecy (Fra)
Oct 21, 1988	Prince Charles Williams w rsf 3 Rufino Angulo (Fra)	Bordeaux (Fra)
Jun 25, 1989	Prince Charles Williams w ret 10 Bobby Czyz	Atlantic City, NJ
Jan 7, 1990	Prince Charles Williams w rsf 8 Frankie Swindell (US)	Atlantic City, NJ
Jan 12, 1991	Prince Charles Williams w pts 12 Mwehu Beya (Ita)	St Vincent (Ita)
Apr 20, 1991	Prince Charles Williams w rsf 2 James Kinchen	Atlantic City, NJ
Jul 20, 1991	Prince Charles Williams w ko 3 Vince Boulaire (US)	San Remo (Ita)
Oct 19, 1991	Prince Charles Williams w rsf 2 Freddie Delgado (PR)	Williamsburg, VA
Mar 20, 1993	**Henry Maske** (Ger) w pts 12 Prince Charles Williams	Dusseldorf (Ger)
Dec 11, 1993	Henry Maske w pts 12 David Vedder	Dusseldorf (Ger)
Mar 26, 1994	Henry Maske w rsf 9 Ernesto Magdelano (US)	Dortmund (Ger)
Jun 4, 1994	Henry Maske w pts 12 Andrea Magi	Dortmund (Ger)
Oct 8, 1994	Henry Maske w ret 9 Iran Barkley (US)	Halle (Ger)
Feb 11, 1995	Henry Maske w pts 12 Egerton Marcus (Can)	Frankfurt (Ger)
May 27, 1995	Henry Maske w pts 12 Graciano Rocchigiani (Ger)	Dortmund (Ger)
Oct 14, 1995	Henry Maske w pts 12 Graciano Rocchigiani (Ger)	Munich (Ger)

WBO title

Dec 3, 1988	**Michael Moorer** (US) w rsf 5 Ramzi Hassan	Cleveland, OH
Jan 14, 1989	Michael Moorer w rsf 2 Victor Claudio (PR)	Detroit, MI
Feb 19, 1989	Michael Moorer w rsf 6 Frankie Swindell (US)	Monessen, PA
Apr 22, 1989	Michael Moorer w rsf 1 Freddie Delgado (PR)	Detroit, MI
Jun 25, 1989	Michael Moorer w rsf 8 Leslie Stewart	Atlantic City, NJ
Nov 16, 1989	Michael Moorer w rsf 1 Jeff Thompson (US)	Atlantic City, NJ
Dec 22, 1989	Michael Moorer w rsf 6 Mike Sedillo (US)	Detroit, MI
Feb 3, 1990	Michael Moorer w rsf 9 Marcellus Allen (US)	Atlantic City, NJ
Apr 28, 1990	Michael Moorer w ko 1 Mario Melo (Arg)	Atlantic City, NJ
Dec 15, 1990	Michael Moorer w ko 8 Danny Lindstrom (Can)	Pittsburgh, PA
Apr 1991	*Moorer relinquished the title to box at heavyweight*	
May 9, 1991	**Leeonzer Barber** (US) w ret 5 Tom Collins	Leeds (Eng)
	For vacant title	
Jan 7, 1992	Leeonzer Barber w pts 12 Anthony Hembrick (US)	Detroit, MI
Feb 27, 1993	Leeonzer Barber w pts 12 Mike Sedillo	Bejing (Chn)
Sep 29, 1993	Leeonzer Barber w pts 12 Andrea Magi (Ita)	Pesaro (Ita)
Jan 29, 1994	Leeonzer Barber w rsf 9 Nicky Piper (Wal)	Cardiff (Wal)
Sep 10, 1994	**Dariusz Michalczewski** (Ger) w pts 12 Leeonzer Barber	Hamburg (Ger)
Mar 11, 1995	Dariusz Michalczewski w rsf 2 Roberto Dominguez (Sp)	Cologne (Ger)
May 20, 1995	Dariusz Michalczewski w ko 4 Paul Carlo (US)	Hamburg (Ger)
Aug 19, 1995	Dariusz Michalczewski w ko 5 Everardo Armenta (Mex)	Dusseldorf (Ger)
Oct 7, 1995	Dariusz Michalczewski w pts 12 Philippe Michel (Fra)	Frankfurt (Ger)

RINGSIDE VIEW

Leeonzer Barber
vs
Nicky Piper

THE UNKINDEST CUT

After eight rounds, Nicky Piper only had to stand up and the WBO light-heavyweight title would be his. Champion Leeonzer Barber's right eye was horribly swollen and his cornermen were going to pull him out at the end of the ninth. But the American felled Piper for a seven count with a left hook. With another long right the fight ended.

DENNIS ANDRIES *recaptures the WBC title from Jeff Harding in 1990*

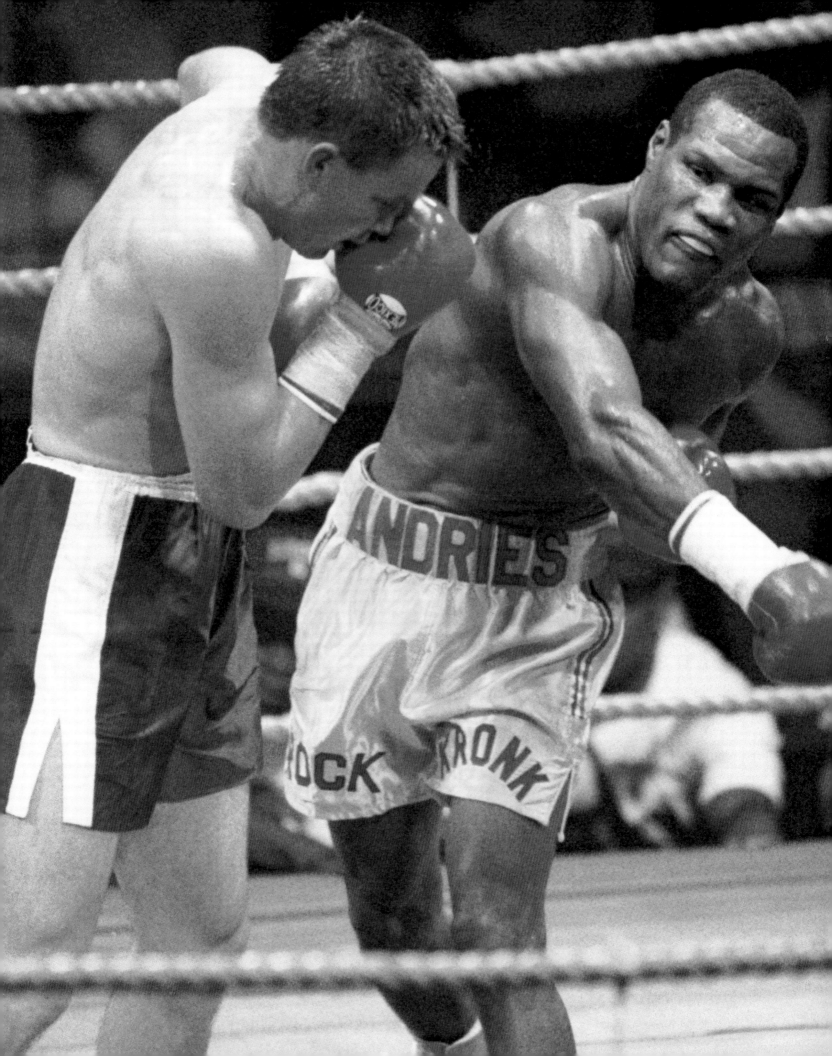

Super-Middleweight

One of Scottish boxing's unsung heroes, Murray Sutherland, holds the distinction of being the first generally accepted champion of the super-middleweight division (weight limit 168 lb). Sutherland was born in Edinburgh, but the family emigrated to Canada. Sutherland made his name in the "Tough Guy" free-for-all contests in America in the late 1970s before he became a well respected professional, operating between the middleweight and light-heavyweight classes.

There had been sporadic attempts to cater for men of his weight: Don Fullmer – brother of former middleweight champion Gene – and Danny Brewer both enjoyed recognition from their home states as world champion, but the category did not become officially recognized until the IBF matched Sutherland with Ernie Singletary for the vacant title. The new category was clearly needed, since the gulf between middleweight (160 lb) and light-heavyweight (175 lb) was the biggest in boxing, and the WBA followed suit in 1987. The WBC, unusually, were slowest off the mark – their first championship was not contested until Ray Leonard stopped Donny Lalonde in 1988.

Since then the class has become one of boxing's busiest and most popular, due in large measure to the efforts of the rival British title-holders Chris Eubank (WBO) and Nigel Benn (WBC).

World Super-Middleweight Championship Bouts

IBF title

Mar 28,	1984	**Murray Sutherland** (Sco) w pts 15 Ernie Singletary (US) . Atlantic City, NJ	
		For inaugural title	
Jul 22,	1984	**Chong-Pal Park** (Kor) w ko 11 Murray Sutherland . . . . Seoul (Kor)	
Jan 2,	1985	Chong-Pal Park w ko 2 Roy Gumbs (Eng) . . . . Seoul (Kor)	
Jun 30,	1985	Chong-Pal Park w pts 15 Vinnie Curto (US) . . . . Seoul (Kor)	
Apr 11,	1986	Chong-Pal Park w ko 15 Vinnie Curto . . . . Los Angeles, CA	
Jul 6,	1986	Chong-Pal Park tech draw 2 Lindell Holmes (US) . . . . Chungju (Kor)	
Sep 14,	1986	Chong-Pal Park w pts 15 Marvin Mack (US) . . . . Pusan (Kor)	
Jan 25,	1987	Chong Pal-Park w rsf 15 Doug Sam (Aus) . . . . Seoul (Kor)	
May 3,	1987	Chong-Pal Park w pts 15 Lindell Holmes . . . . Inchon (Kor)	
Jul 26,	1987	Chong-Pal Park w rsf 4 Emmanuel Otti (Ug) . . . . Kwangju (Kor)	
Dec	1987	*Park relinquished IBF title to box for vacant WBA version*	
Mar 12,	1988	**Graciano Rocchigiani** (Ger) w rsf 8 Vince Boulware (US) Dusseldorf (Ger)	
		For vacant title	
Jun 3,	1988	Graciano Rocchigiani w pts 15 Nicky Walker (US) . . . . Berlin (Ger)	
Oct 7,	1988	Graciano Rocchigiani w rsf 11 Chris Reid (US) . . . . Berlin (Ger)	
Jan 27,	1989	Graciano Rocchigiani w pts 12 Sugar Boy Malinga (SA) . . . . . Berlin (Ger)	
Sep	1989	*Rocchigani relinquished the title because of weight problems*	
Jan 27,	1990	**Lindell Holmes** w pts 12 Frank Tate (US) . . . . New Orleans, LA	
		For vacant title	
Jul 19,	1990	Lindell Holmes w rsf 9 Carl Sullivan (US) . . . . Seattle, WA	
Dec 16,	1990	Lindell Holmes w pts 12 Sugar Boy Malinga . . . . Marino (Ita)	
Mar 7,	1991	Lindell Holmes w pts 12 Antoine Byrd (US) . . . . Madrid (Sp)	
May 18,	1991	**Darrin Van Horn** (US) w ko 11 Lindell Holmes . . . . Verbania (Ita)	
Aug 17,	1991	Darrin Van Horn w ko 3 John Jarvis (US) . . . . Irvine, CA	
Jan 10,	1992	**Iran Barkley** (US) w rsf 2 Darrin Van Horn . . . . New York, NJ	
Feb 13,	1993	**James Toney** (US) w ret 9 Iran Barkley . . . . Las Vegas, NV	
Oct 29,	1993	James Toney w pts 12 Tony Thornton (US) . . . . Tulsa, OK	
Mar 5,	1994	James Toney w rsf 4 Tim Littles (US) . . . . Los Angeles, CA	
Jul 29,	1994	James Toney w ko 12 Prince Charles Williams (US) . . . . . . Las Vegas, NV	
Nov 18,	1994	**Roy Jones** (US) w pts 12 James Toney . . . . Las Vegas, NV	
Mar 18,	1995	Roy Jones w rsf 1 Antoine Byrd (US) . . . . Pensacola, FL	
Jun 24,	1995	Roy Jones w rsf 6 Vinny Pazienza (US) . . . . Atlantic City, NJ	
Sep 30,	1995	Roy Jones w rsf 3 Tony Thornton . . . . Pensacola, FL	

WBA title

Dec 6,	1987	**Chong-Pal Park** w rsf 2 Jesus Gallardo (Mex) . . . . Seoul (Kor)	
		For vacant title	
Mar 1,	1988	Chong Pal-Park w ko 5 Polly Pasieron (Indo) . . . . Chungju (Kor)	
May 23,	1988	**Fulgencio Obelmejias** (Ven) w pts 12 Chong-Pal Park . . . . Chungju (Kor)	
May 27,	1989	**Inchul Baek** (Kor) w rsf 11 Fulgencio Obelmejias . . . . Seoul (Kor)	
Oct 8,	1989	Inchul Baek w rsf 11 Ron Essett (US) . . . . Seoul (Kor)	
Jan 13,	1990	Inchul Baek w ret 7 Yoshiaki Tajima (Jap) . . . . Ulsan (Kor)	
Mar 30,	1990	**Christophe Tiozzo** (Fra) w rsf 6 Inchul Baek . . . . Lyon (Fra)	
Jul 20,	1990	Christophe Tiozzo w rsf 8 Paul Whittaker (US) . . . . Arles (Fra)	
Nov 23,	1990	Christophe Tiozzo w rsf 2 Danny Morgan (US) . . . . . Cergy Pontoise (Fra)	
Apr 9,	1991	**Victor Cordoba** (Pan) w rsf 9 Christophe Tiozzo . . . . Marseilles (Fra)	
Dec 13,	1991	Victor Cordoba w rsf 11 Vincenzo Nardiello (Ita) . . . . Paris (Fra)	
Sep 12,	1992	**Michael Nunn** (US) w pts 12 Victor Cordoba . . . . Las Vegas, NV	
Jan 30,	1993	Michael Nunn w pts 12 Victor Cordoba . . . . Memphis, TN	
Feb 20,	1993	Michael Nunn w ko 1 Danny Morgan (US) . . . . Mexico City (Mex)	
Apr 23,	1993	Michael Nunn w rsf 6 Crawford Ashley (Eng) . . . . Memphis, TN	
Dec 18,	1993	Michael Nunn w pts 12 Merqui Sosa (DR) . . . . Puebla (Mex)	
Feb 26,	1904	**Steve Little** (US) w pts 12 Michael Nunn . . . . London (Eng)	
Aug 12,	1994	**Frank Liles** (US) w pts 12 Steve Little . . . . Tucuman (Arg)	
Dec 16,	1994	Frank Liles w pts 12 Michael Nunn . . . . Quito (Ecu)	
May 27,	1995	Frank Liles w rsf 6 Frederic Seillier (Fra) . . . . Fort Lauderdale, FL	
Dec 9,	1995	Frank Liles w pts 12 Mauricio Amaral (Bra) . . . . Stuttgart (Ger)	

WBC title

Nov 7,	1988	**Sugar Ray Leonard** (US) w rsf 9 Donny Lalonde (Can) . . . . Las Vegas, NV	
		For vacant title: Lalonde's WBC light-heavyweight title was also at stake, even though he scaled only 167 lb	
Jun 12,	1989	Sugar Ray Leonard drew l2 Thomas Hearns . . . . Las Vegas, NV	
Dec 7,	1989	Sugar Ray Leonard w pts 12 Roberto Duran (Pan) . . . . . Las Vegas, NV	
Aug	1990	*Leonard relinquished the title to pursue the light-middleweight championship*	
Dec 15,	1990	**Mauro Galvano** (Ita) w pts 12 Dario Matteoni (Arg) . . . Monte Carlo (Mon)	
		For vacant title	
Jul 27,	1991	Mauro Galvano w pts 12 Ron Essett (US) . . . . Capo D'Orlando (Ita)	
Feb 6,	1992	Mauro Galvano w pts 12 Juan Carlos Giminez (Par) . . . . Marino (Ita)	
Oct 3,	1992	**Nigel Benn** (Eng) w ret 3 Mauro Galvano . . . . Marino (Ita)	
Mar 6,	1993	Nigel Benn w pts 12 Mauro Galvano . . . . Glasgow (Sco)	
Jun 26,	1993	Nigel Benn w rsf 4 Lou Gent (Eng) . . . . London (Eng)	
Oct 9,	1993	Nigel Benn drew 12 Chris Eubank (Eng) . . . . Manchester (Eng)	
		WBC/WBO unification match	
Feb 26,	1994	Nigel Benn w pts 12 Henry Wharton (Eng) . . . . London (Eng)	
Sep 10,	1994	Nigel Benn w pts 12 Juan Carlos Gimenez (Par) . . . . . . Birmingham (Eng)	
Feb 25,	1995	Nigel Benn w ko 10 Gerald McClellan (US) . . . . London (Eng)	
Jul 22,	1995	Nigel Benn w rsf 8 Vincenzo Nardiello (Ita) . . . . London (Eng)	
Sep 2,	1995	Nigel Benn w ko 7 Danny Ray Perez (US) . . . . London (Eng)	

WBO title

Nov 4,	1988	**Thomas Hearns** (US) w pts 12 James Kinchen (US) . . . . . . Las Vegas, NV	
		For vacant title	
Apr 28,	1990	Thomas Hearns w pts 12 Michael Olajide (Can) . . . . Atlantic City, NJ	
Apr	1991	*Hearns relinquished the title to box at light-heavyweight*	
Sep 21,	1991	**Chris Eubank** (Eng) w rsf 12 Michael Watson (Eng) . . . . . . London (Eng)	
		For vacant title	
Feb 1,	1992	Chris Eubank w pts 12 Sugar Boy Malinga . . . . Birmingham (Eng)	
Apr 25,	1992	Chris Eubank w ko 3 John Jarvis . . . . Manchester (Eng)	
Jun 27,	1992	Chris Eubank w pts 12 Ron Essett . . . . Quinto do Lago (Por)	

RINGSIDE VIEW

Chris Eubank
vs
Michael Watson

TRADING BLOWS

When the exhausted Chris Eubank was sent crashing in the final moments of the 11th round against Michael Watson on September 21, 1991, he looked a beaten man. Yet he floored Watson heavily with the very next punch, leaving him an easy target for the 12th round finish from which, tragically, the Londoner never recovered.

Sep 19,	1992	Chris Eubank w pts 12 Tony Thornton	Glasgow (Sco)
Nov 28,	1992	Chris Eubank w pts 12 Juan Carlos Giminez	Manchester (Eng)
Feb 20,	1993	Chris Eubank w pts 12 Lindell Holmes	London (Eng)
May 15,	1993	Chris Eubank drew 12 Ray Close (Ire)	Glasgow (Sco)
Oct 9,	1993	Chris Eubank drew 12 Nigel Benn	Manchester (Eng)
		(WBC/WBO unification match)	
Feb 5,	1994	Chris Eubank w pts 12 Graciano Rocchigiani	Berlin (Ger)
May 21,	1994	Chris Eubank w pts 12 Ray Close	Belfast (N. Ire)
Jul 9,	1994	Chris Eubank w pts 12 Mauricio Amaral (Bra)	London (Eng)
Aug 27,	1994	Chris Eubank w rsf 7 Sam Storey (Ire)	Cardiff (Wal)
Oct 25,	1994	Chris Eubank w pts 12 Dan Schommer (US)	Sun City (Bop)
Dec 10,	1994	Chris Eubank w pts 12 Henry Wharton	Manchester (Eng)
Mar 18,	1995	**Steve Collins** (Ire) w pts 12 Chris Eubank	Millstreet (Ire)
Sep 9,	1995	Steve Collins w pts 12 Chris Eubank	Cork (Ire)
Nov 25,	1995	Steve Collins w pts 12 Cornelius Carr (Eng)	Dublin (Ire)

RINGSIDE VIEW

Chris Eubank
vs
Henry Wharton

EUBANK GIVES A MASTERCLASS

Ironically, Chris Eubank's last world title victory was one of his best: indeed, he boxed so well in beating Henry Wharton in Manchester on December 10, 1994, that it was unthinkable that his reign was about to end. He entered the ring in style, transported over the heads of the crowd on a spotlit crane, and poor Wharton, as brave as they come, was upstaged for the rest of the night as the engimatic Eubank gave him a boxing lesson to win widely on points.

NIGEL BENN *(right) beating Mauro Galvano, has been a popular champ*

RINGSIDE VIEW

Sugar Ray Leonard
vs
Thomas Hearns

LAS VEGAS STALEMATE

Ray Leonard and Thomas Hearns provided one of the greatest contests in boxing history when they met for the welterweight title in Las Vegas in 1981, but their rematch in the same ring eight years later, in which Leonard scraped a draw to retain his WBC super-middleweight title, was a sad echo of past glories.

Leonard, never the most gracious of men, at least had the class to acknowledge that the draw favoured him more than Hearns, although he soon retracted that view and claimed, against all the evidence, that he had deserved to win. When he produced another low-key display to win his next defence, a third meeting with Roberto Duran, the signs were clear to all but him that it was to get out of the game.

But the fighter is always the last to know, and it took a beating by Terry Norris in a bid for the light-middleweight title to convince Leonard that his fabulous career was over.

Middleweight

The Irish-born Jack Dempsey – the original, "Nonpariel" Dempsey – earns his place in boxing history as the man who bridged the eras from bare-knuckles to gloves to become the first world middleweight champion. Dempsey had been accepted as the American champion at the new weight (154 lb), and his win over Billy McCarthy (English-born but Australian based) was the first proper international contest in the division.

Dempsey was dethroned by Bob Fitzsimmons, who, in keeping with the practice of the time, named a new weight limit of 158 lb, since he could no longer make

154 lb. The limit crept up to the modern 160 lb in stages. It was first accepted in Europe, where France hosted a series of famous middleweight matches in the years immediately before the First World War, but America did not adopt the new poundage until 1921.

Middleweight has produced more of boxing's legendary champions than any other: Harry Greb, Sugar Ray Robinson, Carlos Monzon and Marvin Hagler each became international superstars. Perhaps because they combine speed, skill and power so perfectly, the middleweights are properly regarded as the sport's thoroughbreds.

World Middleweight Championship Bouts

Feb 3,	1886	**"Nonpariel" Jack Dempsey** (Ire) w ko 27 Jack Fogarty (US)	New York, NY
Mar 4,	1886	"Nonpariel" Jack Dempsey w ko 13 George LaBlanche (Can)	Larchmont, NY
Dec 13,	1887	"Nonpariel" Jack Dempsey w ko 15 Johnny Reagan (US)	Long Island, NY
Feb 18,	1890	"Nonpariel" Jack Dempsey w rsf 28 Billy McCarthy (Aus)	San Francisco, CA
Jan 14,	1891	**Bob Fitzsimmons** (Eng) w ko 12 "Nonpariel" Jack Dempsey	New Orleans, LA
Sep 26,	1894	Bob Fitzsimmons w ko 2 Dan Creedon (NZ)	New Orleans, LA

Fitzsimmons gave up the title to pursue the heavyweight championship. There was no clear-cut successor, but Kid McCoy (US) established a solid claim to the title by beating welterweight champion Tommy Ryan

Mar 2,	1896	**Kid McCoy** w ko 15 Tommy Ryan (US)	Long Island, NY
May 18,	1896	Kid McCoy w dis 6 Mysterious Billy Smith (US)	Boston, MA
Dec 26,	1896	Kid McCoy w ko 9 Billy Doherty (Aus)	Johannesburg (SA)
Dec 17,	1897	Kid McCoy w ko 15 Dan Creedon	Long Island, NY

Creedon had gained recognition in England as the world champion. McCoy subsequently relinquished the title, which was claimed by Tommy Ryan

Oct 24,	1898	**Tommy Ryan** w pts 20 Jack Bonner (US)	Coney Island, NY
Aug 31,	1899	Tommy Ryan w pts 20 Jack Moffatt (US)	Dubuque, IA
Mar 4,	1901	Tommy Ryan w ret 17 Tommy West (US)	Louisville, KY
Jun 24,	1902	Tommy Ryan w ko 3 Johnny Gorman (US)	London (Eng)
Sep 15,	1902	Tommy Ryan w ko 6 Kid Carter (US)	Fort Erie (Can)

Ryan retired, and once more confusion reigned. Hugo Kelly, Jack "Twin" Sullivan, Stanley Ketchel and Billy Papke all claimed the title. Ketchel's wins over the other three established him as the rightful champion

May 9,	1908	**Stanley Ketchel** (US) w ko 20 Jack "Twin" Sullivan (US)	Colma, CA
Jun 4,	1908	Stanley Ketchel w pts 10 Billy Papke (US)	Milwaukee, WI
Jul 31,	1908	Stanley Ketchel w ko 3 Hugo Kelly (US)	San Francisco, CA
Sep 7,	1908	**Billy Papke** w ko 12 Stanley Ketchel	Los Angeles, CA
Nov 26,	1908	**Stanley Ketchel** w ko 11 Billy Papke	Colma, CA
Jul 5,	1909	Stanley Ketchel w pts 20 Billy Papke	Colma, CA
Jan	1910	*Ketchel announced that he could no longer make the weight (then 158 lb) and Papke and Willie Lewis were matched for the vacant title*	
Mar 19,	1910	**Billy Papke** w ko 3 Willie Lewis (US)	Paris (Fra)
Mar	1910	*Ketchel reclaimed the title*	
May 27,	1910	**Stanley Ketchel** w ko 2 Willie Lewis	New York, NY
Oct 15,	1910	*Ketchel was shot to death, and Papke reclaimed the title Various other claimants emerged during the next couple of years, cluding Frank Mantell, Frank Klaus and Georges Carpentier, but Papke's claim was generally regarded as the strongest*	
Jun 8,	1911	**Billy Papke** w ret 9 Jim Sullivan (Eng)	London (Eng)
Jun 29,	1912	Billy Papke w rsf 6 Marcel Moreau (Fra)	Paris (Fra)
Dec 4,	1912	Billy Papke w ret 7 George Bernard (Fra)	Paris (Fra)
Mar 5,	1913	**Frank Klaus** (US) w dis 15 Billy Papke	Paris (Fra)
Oct 11,	1913	**George Chip** (US) w ko 6 Frank Klaus	Pittsburgh, PA
Dec 23,	1913	George Chip w ko 5 Frank Klaus	Pittsburgh, PA

With these two wins over Klaus, Chip earned recognition in America as

champion, even though he had been over the division limit on each occasion. Meanwhile, the Australians set up their own version of the title

Australian version of world title

Jan 1,	1914	**Eddie McGoorty** (US) w ko 1 Dave Smith (US)	Sydney (Aus)
Feb 7,	1914	Eddie McGoorty w pts 20 Pat Bradley (Aus)	Sydney (Aus)
Mar 14,	1914	**Jeff Smith** (US) w pts 20 Eddie McGoorty	Sydney (Aus)
Apr 13,	1914	Jeff Smith w ko 16 Pat Bradley	Sydney (Aus)
Jun 6,	1914	Jeff Smith w pts 20 Jimmy Clabby (US)	Sydney (Aus)
Nov 28,	1914	**Mick King** (Aus) w pts 20 Jeff Smith	Sydney (Aus)
Dec 26,	1914	**Jeff Smith** w pts 20 Mick King	Sydney (Aus)
Jan 23,	1915	Jeff Smith w dis 5 Les Darcy (Aus)	Sydney (Aus)
Feb 20,	1915	Jeff Smith w pts 20 Mick King	Melbourne (Aus)
May 22,	1915	**Les Darcy** w dis 2 Jeff Smith	Sydney (Aus)
Jun 12,	1915	Les Darcy w ko 10 Mick King	Sydney (Aus)
Jul 31,	1915	Les Darcy w rsf 15 Eddie McGoorty	Sydney (Aus)
Sep 4,	1915	Les Darcy w pts 20 Billy Murray (US)	Sydney (Aus)
Oct 9,	1915	Les Darcy w ret 6 Fred Dyer (Eng)	Sydney (Aus)
Oct 23,	1915	Les Darcy w pts 20 Jimmy Clabby	Sydney (Aus)
Jan 15,	1916	Les Darcy w pts 20 George "KO" Brown (US)	Sydney (Aus)
May 15,	1916	Les Darcy w ko 4 Alex Costica (Rom)	Sydney (Aus)
Sep 9,	1916	Les Darcy w pts 20 Jimmy Clabby	Sydney (Aus)
Sep 30,	1916	Les Darcy w ko 9 George Chip	Sydney (Aus)

Darcy went to America to pursue his claim to the championship, but died in Memphis on May 27, 1917

World title

Apr 6,	1914	**Al McCoy** (US) w ko 1 George Chip	Brooklyn, NY
Nov 14,	1917	**Mike O'Dowd** (US) w ko 6 Al McCoy	Brooklyn, NY
Nov 6,	1919	Mike O'Dowd w ko 2 Billy Kramer (US)	Paterson, NJ
Mar 1,	1920	Mike O'Dowd w ko 2 Jack McCarron (US)	Philadelphia, PA
Mar 31,	1920	Mike O'Dowd w ko 5 Joe Eagan (US)	Boston, MA
May 6,	1920	**Johnny Wilson** (US) w pts 12 Mike O'Dowd	Boston, MA
Mar 17,	1921	Johnny Wilson w pts 15 Mike O'Dowd	New York, NY
		The division limit was now set at 160 lb	
Jul 27,	1921	Johnny Wilson w dis 7 Bryan Downey (US)	Cleveland, OH
		Although this was not a title fight, Wilson scaling 165 lb, the result was so controversial that the New York Commission declared the title vacant	
Aug 14,	1922	**Dave Rosenburg** (US) w pts 15 Phil Krug (US)	New York, NY
		For vacant New York title	

Nov 30,	1922	**Mike O'Dowd** w dis 8 Dave Rosenburg	New York, NY
Mar 16,	1923	*O'Dowd retired after being knocked out in the first round of a non-title fight against Jock Malone in St Paul. Harry Greb was universally recognized as champion after his wins over Johnny Wilson and Bryan Downey in 1923*	
Aug 31,	1923	**Harry Greb** (US) w pts 15 Johnny Wilson	New York, NY
Dec 3,	1923	Harry Greb w pts 10 Bryan Downey (US)	Pittsburgh, PA
Jan 18,	1924	Harry Greb w pts 15 Johnny Wilson	New York, NY
Mar 24,	1924	Harry Greb w ko 12 Fay Kaiser (US)	Baltimore, MD
Jul 2,	1925	Harry Greb w pts 15 Mickey Walker (US)	New York, NY
Jun 26,	1924	Harry Greb w pts 15 Ted Moore (Eng)	New York, NY
Feb 26,	1926	**Tiger Flowers** (US) w pts 15 Harry Greb	New York, NY
Aug 19,	1926	Tiger Flowers w pts 15 Harry Greb	New York, NY
Dec 3,	1926	**Mickey Walker** (US) w pts 10 Tiger Flowers	Chicago, IL

Jun 30,	1927	Mickey Walker w ko 10 Tommy Milligan (Sco) .... London (Eng)
Jun 21,	1928	Mickey Walker w pts 10 Ace Hudkins (US) .... Chicago, IL
Oct 29,	1929	Mickey Walker w pts 10 Ace Hudkins .... Los Angeles, CA
June	1931	*Walker relinquished the title, and the division again became chaotic, with various versions of the championship on offer*

National Boxing Association (NBA) title

Jan 25,	1932	**Gorilla Jones** (US) w ko 6 Oddone Piazza (Ita) .... Milwaukee, WI
		For vacant title
Apr 26,	1932	Gorilla Jones w pts 12 Young Terry (US) .... Trenton, NJ
		The NBA withdrew recognition from Jones after his loss to Marcel Thil
Aug 9,	1933	**Lou Brouillard** (Can) w ko 7 Ben Jeby .... New York, NY
		For NBA and New York versions

International Boxing Union (IBU) title

Jun 11,	1932	**Marcel Thil** (Fra) w dis 11 Gorilla Jones .... Paris (Fra)
		Thil was recognized as champion following this result, even though the NBA did not regard it as a championship defence by Jones
Jul 4,	1932	Marcel Thil w pts 15 Len Harvey (Eng) .... London (Eng)
Oct 2,	1933	Marcel Thil w pts 15 Kid Tunero (Cub) .... Paris (Fra)
Feb 26,	1934	Marcel Thil w pts 15 Ignacio Ara (Sp) .... Paris (Fra)
May 3,	1934	Marcel Thil w pts 15 Gustave Roth (Bel) .... Paris (Fra)
Oct 15,	1934	Marcel Thil drew 15 Carmelo Candel (Fra) .... Paris (Fra)
May 4,	1935	Marcel Thil w ret 14 Vilda "Kid" Jaks (Cze) .... Paris (Fra)
Jun 1,	1935	Marcel Thil w pts 15 Ignacio Ara (Sp) .... Madrid (Sp)
Jan 20,	1936	Marcel Thil w dis 4 Lou Brouillard .... Paris (Fra)
Feb 15,	1937	Marcel Thil w dis 6 Lou Brouillard .... Paris (Fra)
		Thil retired after being stopped in 10 rounds by Fred Apostoli (US) in New York on September 23, 1937. Although they fought under championship conditions, both men had to sign a pre-fight agreement that the world title would not be at stake, so as to protect the position of New York's champion Freddie Steele
Apr 7,	1938	**Edouard Tenet** (Fra) w ret 12 Josef Besselmann (Ger) .... Berlin (Ger)
		For vacant title
May 1938		*The IBU withdrew recognition from Tenet (and their other champions) in an effort to reunite the world titles*

New York title

Jan 13,	1933	**Ben Jeby** (US) w rsf 12 Frank Battaglia (Can) .... New York, NY
		For vacant title
Mar 17,	1933	Ben Jeby drew 15 Vince Dundee (US) .... New York, NY
Jul 10,	1933	Ben Jeby w pts 15 Young Terry .... Newark, NJ
Aug 9,	1933	**Lou Brouillard** w ko 7 Ben Jeby .... New York, NY
		(For NY and NBA recognition)

NY/NBA titles

Oct 30,	1933	**Vince Dundee** (US) w pts 15 Lou Brouillard .... Boston, MA
Dec 8,	1933	Vince Dundee w pts15 Andy Callahan (US) .... Boston, MA
May 1,	1934	Vince Dundee w pts15 Al Diamond (US) .... Paterson, NJ
Sep 11,	1934	**Teddy Yarosz** (US) w pts 15 Vince Dundee .... Pittsburgh, PA
Sep 19,	1935	**Ed "Babe" Risko** (US) w pts 15 Teddy Yarosz .... New York, NY
Feb 10,	1936	Ed "Babe" Risko w pts 15 Tony Fisher (US) .... Newark, NJ
Jul 11,	1936	**Freddie Steele** (US) w pts 15 Ed "Babe" Risko .... New York, NY
Jan 1,	1937	Freddie Steele w pts 10 Gorilla Jones .... Milwaukee, WI
Feb 19,	1937	Freddie Steele w pts 15 Ed "Babe" Risko .... New York, NY
May 11,	1937	Freddie Steele w ko 3 Frank Battaglia (Can) .... Seattle, WA
Sep 11,	1937	Freddie Steele w ko 4 Ken Overlin (US) .... Seattle, WA
Feb 19,	1938	Freddie Steele w ko 7 Carmen Barth (US) .... Cleveland, OH
May	1938	*The NY Commission vacated Steele's title for his failure to defend against Fred Apostoli*

New York title

Nov 18,	1938	**Fred Apostoli** (US) w ko 8 Young Corbett III (US) .... New York, NY
		For vacant title
Oct 2,	1939	**Ceferino Garcia** (Phil) w rsf 7 Fred Apostoli .... New York, NY
Dec 23,	1939	Ceferino Garcia w ko 13 Glen Lee (US) .... Manila (Phil)
Mar 1,	1940	Ceferino Garcia drew 10 Henry Armstrong (US) .... Los Angeles, CA
May 23,	1940	**Ken Overlin** w pts 15 Ceferino Garcia .... New York, NY
Nov 1,	1940	Ken Overlin w pts 15 Steve Belloise (US) .... New York, NY
Dec 13,	1940	Ken Overlin w pts 15 Steve Belloise .... New York, NY
May 9,	1941	**Billy Soose** (US) w pts 15 Ken Overlin .... New York, NY
		Soose was stripped for failing to defend the title

NBA title

Jul 26,	1938	**Al Hostak** (US) w ko 1 Freddie Steele .... Seattle, WA
		For vacant title
Nov 1,	1938	**Solly Kreiger** (US) w pts 15 Al Hostak .... Seattle, WA
Jun 27,	1939	**Al Hostak** w ko 4 Solly Kreiger .... Seattle, WA
Dec 11,	1939	Al Hostak w ko 1 Eric Seelig (Ger) .... Cleveland, OH
Jul 19,	1940	**Tony Zale** (US) w ret 13 Al Hostak .... Chicago, IL
Feb 21,	1941	Tony Zale w ko 14 Steve Mamakos (US) .... Chicago, IL
May 28,	1941	Tony Zale w ko 2 Al Hostak .... in Chicago, IL
Nov 28,	1941	Tony Zale w pts 15 Georgie Abrams (US) .... New York, NY
		For undisputed title

Undisputed title

Sep 27,	1946	**Tony Zale** w ko 6 Rocky Graziano (US) .... New York, NY
Jul 16,	1947	**Rocky Graziano** (US) w rsf 6 Tony Zale .... Chicago, IL
Jun 10,	1948	**Tony Zale** w ko 3 Rocky Graziano .... Newark, NJ
Sep 21,	1948	**Marcel Cerdan** (Fra) w ret 11 Tony Zale .... Jersey City, NJ
Jun 16,	1949	**Jake LaMotta** (US) w ret 10 Marcel Cerdan .... Detroit, MI
Jul 12,	1950	Jake LaMotta w pts 15 Tibero Mitri (Ita) .... New York, NY
Sep 13,	1950	Jake LaMotta w ko 15 Laurent Dauthuille (Fra) .... Detroit, MI
Feb 14,	1951	**Sugar Ray Robinson** (US) w rsf 13 Jake LaMotta .... Chicago, IL
Jul 10,	1951	**Randolph Turpin** (Eng) w pts 15 Sugar Ray Robinson ..... London (Eng)
Sep 12,	1951	**Sugar Ray Robinson** w rsf 10 Randolph Turpin .... New York, NY
Mar 13,	1952	Sugar Ray Robinson w pts 15 Carl "Bobo" Olson (US) . San Francisco, CA
Apr 16,	1952	Sugar Ray Robinson w ko 3 Rocky Graziano .... Chicago, IL
Dec 18,	1952	*Robinson announced his retirement*
Oct 21,	1953	**Carl "Bobo" Olson** (US) w pts 15 Randolph Turpin .... New York, NY
		For vacant title
Apr 2,	1954	Carl "Bobo" Olson w pts 15 Kid Gavilan (Cub) .... Chicago, IL
Aug 20,	1954	Carl "Bobo" Olson w pts 15 Rocky Castellani (US) .... San Francisco, CA
Dec 15,	1954	Carl "Bobo" Olson w rsf 11 Pierre Langlois (Fra) ...... San Francisco, CA
Dec 9,	1955	**Sugar Ray Robinson** w ko 2 Carl "Bobo" Olson .... Chicago, IL
May 18,	1956	Sugar Ray Robinson w ko 4 Carl "Bobo" Olson .... Los Angeles, CA
Jan 2,	1957	**Gene Fullmer** (US) w pts 15 Sugar Ray Robinson .... New York, NY
May 1,	1957	**Sugar Ray Robinson** w ko 5 Gene Fullmer .... Chicago, IL
Sep 23,	1957	**Carmen Basilio** (US) w pts 15 Sugar Ray Robinson .... New York, NY
Mar 25,	1958	**Sugar Ray Robinson** w pts 15 Carmen Basilio .... Chicago, IL
May	1959	*The NBA stripped Robinson for his failure to defend against Basilio*

NBA title

Aug 28,	1959	**Gene Fullmer** w rsf 14 Carmen Basilio .... San Francisco, CA
		For vacant title
Dec 4,	1959	Gene Fullmer w pts 15 Spider Webb (US) .... Logan (Can)
Apr 20,	1960	Gene Fullmer drew 15 Joey Giardello (US) .... Bozeman, MT
Jun 29,	1960	Gene Fullmer w rsf 12 Carmen Basilio .... Salt Lake City, UT
Dec 3,	1960	Gene Fullmer drew 15 Sugar Ray Robinson .... Los Angeles, CA
Mar 4,	1961	Gene Fullmer w pts 15 Sugar Ray Robinson .... Las Vegas, NV
Aug 5,	1961	Gene Fullmer w pts 15 Florentino Fernandez (Cub) .... Ogden, UT
Oct 9,	1961	Gene Fullmer w ko 10 Benny "Kid" Paret (Cub) .... Las Vegas, NV
Oct 23,	1962	**Dick Tiger** (Nig) w pts 15 Gene Fullmer .... San Francisco, CA
Feb 23,	1963	Dick Tiger drew 15 Gene Fullmer .... Las Vegas, NV
Aug 10,	1963	Dick Tiger w ret 7 Gene Fullmer .... Ibadan (Nig)
		For undisputed title

New York and European versions

Jan 22,	1960	**Paul Pender** (US) w pts 15 Sugar Ray Robinson .... Boston, MA
Jun 10,	1960	Paul Pender w pts 15 Sugar Ray Robinson .... Boston, MA
Jan 14,	1961	Paul Pender w rsf 7 Terry Downes (Eng) .... Boston, MA
Apr 22,	1961	Paul Pender w pts 15 Carmen Basilio .... Boston, MA
Jul 11,	1961	**Terry Downes** w ret 9 Paul Pender .... London (Eng)
Apr 7,	1962	**Paul Pender** w pts 15 Terry Downes .... Boston, MA
Nov 9,	1962	*Pender forfeited the title for failing to defend it within a stipulated period*

Undisputed title

Dec 7,	1963	**Joey Giardello** (US) w pts 15 Dick Tiger .... Atlantic City, NJ
Dec 14,	1964	Joey Giardello w pts 15 Rubin Carter (US) .... Philadelphia, PA
Oct 21,	1965	**Dick Tiger** w pts 15 Joey Giardello .... New York, NY
Apr 25,	1966	**Emile Griffith** (VI) w pts 15 Dick Tiger .... New York, NY
Jul 13,	1966	Emile Griffith w pts 15 Joey Archer (US) .... New York, NY
Jan 23,	1967	Emile Griffith w pts 15 Joey Archer .... New York, NY
Apr 17,	1967	**Nino Benvenuti** (Ita) w pts 15 Emile Griffith .... New York, NY
Sep 29,	1967	**Emile Griffith** w pts 15 Nino Benvenuti .... New York, NY

CARLOS MONZON *(left) embraces Rodrigo Valdes after their 1976 battle*

Mar 4,	1968	**Nino Benvenuti** w pts 15 Emile Griffith	New York, NY
Dec 14,	1968	Nino Benvenuti w pts 15 Don Fullmer (US)	San Remo (Ita)
Oct 4,	1969	Nino Benvenuti w dis 7 Fraser Scott (US)	Naples (Ita)
Nov 22,	1969	Nino Benvenuti w ko 11 Luis Rodriguez (Cub)	Rome (Ita)
May 23,	1970	Nino Benvenuti w ko 8 Tom Bethea (US)	Umag (Yug)
Nov 7,	1970	**Carlos Monzon** (Arg) w ko 12 Nino Benvenuti	Rome (Ita)
May 8,	1971	Carlos Monzon w rsf 3 Nino Benvenuti	Monte Carlo (Mon)
Sep 25,	1971	Carlos Monzon w rsf 14 Emile Griffith	Buenos Aires (Arg)
Mar 4,	1972	Carlos Monzon w rsf 5 Denny Moyer (US)	Rome (Ita)
Jun 17,	1972	Carlos Monzon w ret 12 Jean-Claude Bouttier (Fra)	Paris (Fra)
Aug 19,	1972	Carlos Monzon w rsf 5 Tom Bogs (Den)	Copenhagen (Den)
Nov 11,	1972	Carlos Monzon w pts 15 Bennie Briscoe (US)	Buenos Aires (Arg)
Jun 2,	1973	Carlos Monzon w pts 15 Emile Griffith	Monte Carlo (Mon)
Sep 29,	1973	Carlos Monzon w pts 15 Jean-Claude Bouttier	Paris (Fra)
Feb 9,	1974	Carlos Monzon w ret 6 Jose Napoles (Cub)	Paris (Fra)
Apr	1974	*The World Boxing Council withdrew recognition of Monzon as champion for his failure to defend against their official contender, Rodrigo Valdes*	

WBC title

May 25,	1974	**Rodrigo Valdes** (Col) w ko 7 Bennie Briscoe (US)	Monte Carlo (Mon)
		For vacant title	
Nov 13,	1974	Rodrigo Valdes w ko 11 Gratien Tonna (Fra)	Paris (Fra)
May 31,	1975	Rodrigo Valdes w rsf 8 Ramon Mendez (Arg)	Cali (Col)
Aug 16,	1975	Rodrigo Vales w pts 15 Rudy Robles (Mex)	Cartagena (Col)
Mar 28,	1976	Rodrigo Valdes w ret 4 Max Cohen (Fra)	Paris (Fra)
Jun 26,	1976	**Carlos Monzon** w pts 15 Rodrigo Valdes	Monte Carlo (Mon)
		For undisputed title	

WBA title

Oct 5,	1974	**Carlos Monzon** w ko 7 Tony Mundine (Aus)	Buenos Aires (Arg)
Jun 30,	1975	Carlos Monzon w ko 10 Tony Licata (US)	New York, NY
Dec 13,	1975	Carlos Monzon w ko 5 Gratien Tonna	Paris (Fra)
Jun 26,	1976	Carlos Monzon w pts 15 Rodrigo Valdes	Monte Carlo (Mon)
		For undisputed title	

Undisputed title

Jul 30,	1977	**Carlos Monzon** w pts 15 Rodrigo Valdes	Monte Carlo (Mon)
Aug	1977	*Monzon retired*	
Nov 5,	1977	**Rodrigo Valdes** w pts 15 Bennie Briscoe	Campione d'Italia (Ita)
		For vacant undisputed title	
Apr 22,	1978	**Hugo Corro** (Arg) w pts 15 Rodrigo Valdes	Buenos Aires (Arg)
Aug 5,	1978	Hugo Corro w pts 15 Ronnie Harris (US)	Buenos Aires (Arg)
Nov 11,	1978	Hugo Corro w pts 15 Rodrigo Valdes	Buenos Aires (Arg)
Jun 30,	1979	**Vito Antuofermo** (Ita) w pts 15 Hugo Corro	Monte Carlo (Mon)
Nov 30,	1979	Vito Antuofermo drew 15 Marvin Hagler (US)	Las Vegas, NV
Mar 16,	1980	**Alan Minter** (Eng) w pts 15 Vito Antuofermo	Las Vegas, NV
Jun 28,	1980	Alan Minter w ret 8 Vito Antuofermo	Wembley (Eng)
Sep 27,	1980	**Marvin Hagler** (US) w rsf 3 Alan Minter	Wembley (Eng)
Jan 17,	1981	Marvin Hagler w rsf 8 Fulgencio Obelmejias (Ven)	Boston, MA
Jun 13,	1981	Marvin Hagler w ret 4 Vito Antuofermo	Boston, MA
Oct 3,	1981	Marvin Hagler w rsf 11 Mustafa Hamsho (Syr)	Rosemount, IL
Mar 7,	1982	Marvin Hagler w rsf 1 William "Caveman" Lee (US)	Atlantic City, NJ
Oct 31,	1982	Marvin Hagler w rsf 5 Fulgencio Obelmejias	San Remo (Ita)
Feb 11,	1983	Marvin Hagler w rsf 6 Tony Sibson (Eng)	Worcester, MA
May 27,	1983	Marvin Hagler w ko 4 Wilford Scypion (US)	Providence, RI
Nov 10,	1983	Marvin Hagler w pts 15 Roberto Duran (Pan)	Las Vegas, NV
Mar 30,	1984	Marvin Hagler w rsf 10 Juan Domingo Roldan (Arg)	Las Vegas, NV
Oct 19,	1984	Marvin Hagler w rsf 3 Mustafa Hamsho	New York, NY
Apr 15,	1985	Marvin Hagler w rsf 3 Thomas Hearns (US)	Las Vegas, NV
Mar 10,	1986	Marvin Hagler w ko 11 John Mugabi (Ug)	Las Vegas, NV
Feb	1987	*WBA stripped Hagler for his failure to defend against Herol Graham*	

WBC/IBF titles

Apr 6,	1987	**Sugar Ray Leonard** (US) w pts 12 Marvin Hagler	Las Vegas, NV
Apr	1987	*The IBF vacated the title because they felt unable to recognise Leonard as champion*	
June	1987	*Leonard relinquished the WBC title, leaving all versions of the title vacant*	

IBF title

Oct 10,	1987	**Frank Tate** (US) w pts 15 Michael Olajide (Can)	Las Vegas, NV
		For vacant title	
Feb 7,	1988	Frank Tate w ko 10 Tony Sibson	Stafford (Eng)
Jul 28,	1988	**Michael Nunn** (US) w rsf 9 Frank Tate	Las Vegas, NV
Nov 4,	1988	Michael Nunn w ko 8 Juan Domingo Roldan	Las Vegas, NV
Mar 25,	1989	Michael Nunn w ko 1 Sumbu Kalambay (Zai)	Las Vegas, NV
Aug 14,	1989	Michael Nunn w pts 12 Iran Barkley (US)	Reno, NV
Apr 14,	1990	Michael Nunn w pts 12 Marlon Starling (US)	Las Vegas, NV
Oct 18,	1990	Michael Nunn w rsf 10 Don Curry (US)	Paris (Fra)
May 10,	1991	**James Toney** (US) w rsf 11 Michael Nunn	Davenport, IA
Jun 29,	1991	James Toney w pts 12 Reggie Johnson (US)	Las Vegas, NV
Oct 12,	1991	James Toney w rsf 4 Francisco Dell'Aquila (Ita)	Monte Carlo (Mon)
Dec 13,	1991	James Toney drew 12 Mike McCallum (Jam)	Atlantic City, NJ
Feb 8,	1992	James Toney w pts 12 Dave Tiberi (US)	Atlantic City, NJ
Apr 11,	1992	James Toney w pts 12 Glenn Wolfe (US)	Las Vegas, NV
Aug 29,	1992	James Toney w pts 12 Mike McCallum	Reno, NV
Feb	1993	*Toney relinquished the title on becoming IBF super-middleweight champion*	
May 22,	1993	**Roy Jones** (US) w pts 12 Bernard Hopkins (US)	Washington, DC
		For vacant title	
May 27,	1994	Roy Jones w rsf 2 Thomas Tate (US)	Las Vegas, NV
		Jones relinquished the title to box at super-middleweight	
Dec 16,	1994	**Bernard Hopkins** drew 12 Segundo Mercado (Ecu)	Quito (Ecu)
		For vacant title	
Apr 29,	1995	Bernard Hopkins w rsf 7 Segundo Mercado	Landover, MD
		For vacant title	

WBA title

Oct 23,	1987	**Sumbu Kalambay** (Zai) w pts 15 Iran Barkley	Livorno (Ita)
		For vacant title	
Mar 5,	1988	Sumbu Kalambay w pts 12 Mike McCallum	Pesaro (Ita)
Jun 12,	1988	Sumbu Kalambay w pts 12 Robbie Sims (US)	Ravenna (Ita)
Nov 8,	1988	Sumbu Kalambay w ko 7 Doug De Witt (US)	Monte Carlo (Mon)
Mar	1989	*Kalambay was stripped for failing to defend against Herol Graham*	
May 10,	1989	**Mike McCallum** w pts 12 Herol Graham (Eng)	London (Eng)
		For vacant title	
Feb 3,	1990	Mike McCallum w pts 12 Steve Collins (Ire)	Boston, MA
Apr 14,	1990	Mike McCallum w ko 11 Michael Watson (Eng)	London (Eng)
Apr 1,	1991	Mike McCallum w pts 12 Sumbu Kalambay	Monte Carlo (Mon)

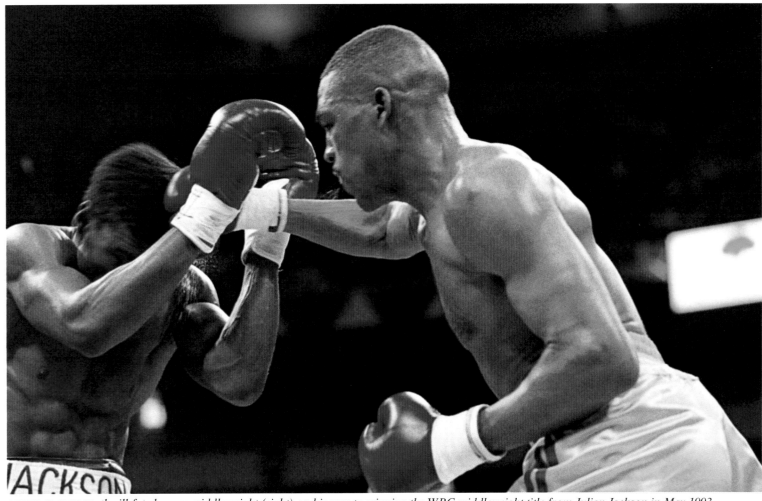

GERALD McCLELLAN *the ill-fated super-middleweight (right) on his way to winning the WBC middleweight title from Julian Jackson in May 1993*

Dec	1991	*The WBA stripped McCallum for agreeing to box for James Toney's IBF title*
Apr 22,	1992	**Reggie Johnson** w pts 12 Steve Collins . . . . East Rutherford, NJ
		For vacant title
Oct 27,	1992	Reggie Johnson w pts 12 Lamar Parks (US) . . . . Houston, TX
Jan 19,	1993	Reggie Johnson w rsf 8 Ki-Yun Song (Kor) . . . . Boise, ID
May 4,	1993	Reggie Johnson w pts 12 Wayne Harris (US) . . . . Denver, CO
Oct 1,	1993	**John David Jackson** (US) w pts 12 Reggie Johnson . . Buenos Aires (Arg)
May	1994	*Jackson was stripped by the WBA for taking a non-title fight without having first sought their permission*
Aug 12,	1994	**Jorge Castro** (Arg) w pts 12 Reggie Johnson . . . . Tucuman (Arg)
		For vacant title
Nov 5,	1994	Jorge Castro w ko 2 Alex Ramos (US) . . . . Caleta Olivia (Arg)
Dec 10,	1994	Jorge Castro w rsf 9 John David Jackson . . . . Monterrey (Mex)
May 27,	1995	Jorge Castro w rsf 12 Anthony Andrews (Guy) . . . . . . Fort Lauderdale, FL
Oct 14,	1995	Jorge Castro w pts 12 Reggie Johnson . . . . . . Comodoro Rivadavoa (Arg)
Dec 19,	1995	**Shinji Takehara** (Jap) w pts 12 Jorge Castro . . . . Tokyo (Jap)

WBC title

Oct 29,	1987	**Thomas Hearns** w ko 4 Juan Domingo Roldan . . . . Las Vegas, NV
		For vacant title
Jun 6,	1988	**Iran Barkley** w rsf 3 Thomas Hearns . . . . Las Vegas, NV
Feb 24,	1989	**Roberto Duran** w pts 12 Iran Barkley . . . . Atlantic City, NJ
Jan	1990	*Duran was stripped for failing to give a written undertaking to defend the title*
Nov 24,	1990	**Julian Jackson** (VI) w ko 4 Herol Graham . . . . Benalmadena (Sp)
		For vacant title
Sep 14,	1991	Julian Jackson w ko 1 Dennis Milton (US) . . . . Las Vegas, NV
Feb 15,	1992	Julian Jackson w ko 1 Ismael Negron (US) . . . . Las Vegas, NV
Apr 10,	1992	Julian Jackson w rsf 5 Ron Collins (US) . . . . Mexico City (Mex)
Aug 1,	1992	Julian Jackson w pts 12 Thomas Tate . . . . Las Vegas, NV
May 8,	1993	**Gerald McClellan** (US) w rsf 5 Julian Jackson . . . . Las Vegas, NV
Aug 6,	1993	Gerald McClellan w ko 1 Jay Bell (US) . . . . Bayamon (PR)
Mar 4,	1994	Gerald McClellan w rsf 1 Gilbert Baptist (US) . . . . Las Vegas, NV

May 7,	1994	Gerald McClellan w ko 1 Julian Jackson . . . . Las Vegas, NV
		McClellan relinquished the title to box at super-middleweight
Mar 7,	1995	**Julian Jackson** w rsf 2 Agostino Cardamone (Ita) . . . . Worcester, MA
		For vacant title
Aug 19,	1995	**Quincy Taylor** (US) w rsf 6 Julian Jackson . . . . Las Vegas, NV

WBO title

Apr 18,	1989	**Doug DeWitt** w pts 12 Robbie Sims . . . . Atlantic City, NJ
		For vacant title
Jan 15,	1990	Doug DeWitt w ret 11 Matthew Hilton (Can) . . . . Atlantic City, NJ
Apr 29,	1990	**Nigel Benn** (Eng) w rsf 8 Doug DeWitt . . . . Atlantic City, NJ
Aug 18,	1990	Nigel Benn w rsf 1 Iran Barkley . . . . Las Vegas, NV
Nov 18,	1990	**Chris Eubank** (Eng) w rsf 9 Nigel Benn . . . . Birmingham (Eng)
Feb 23,	1991	Chris Eubank w tech dec 10 Dan Sherry (Can) . . . . Brighton (Eng)
Apr 18,	1991	Chris Eubank w rsf 6 Gary Stretch (Eng) . . . . London (Eng)
Jun 22,	1991	Chris Eubank w pts 12 Michael Watson . . . . London (Eng)
Jul	1991	*Eubank vacated the title to box for the WBO super-middleweight title*
Nov 20,	1991	**Gerald McClellan** w rsf 1 John Mugabi . . . . London (Eng)
		For vacant title
Mar	1993	*McClellan relinquished the WBO title to box for the WBC version*
May 19,	1993	**Chris Pyatt** (Eng) w pts 12 Sumbu Kalambay . . . . Leicester (Eng)
		For vacant title
Sep 18,	1993	Chris Pyatt w ko 6 Hugo Corti (Arg) . . . . Leicester (Eng)
Feb 9,	1994	Chris Pyatt w ko 1 Mark Cameron (SA) . . . . Brentwood (Eng)
May 11,	1994	**Steve Collins** (Ire) w rsf 5 Chris Pyatt . . . . Sheffield (Eng)
Mar	1995	*Collins relinquished the title on becoming WBO super-middleweight champion*
May 19,	1995	**Lonnie Bradley** (US) w rsf 12 David Mendez (Mex) . . . . Jean (Sp)
		For vacant title
Jul 15,	1995	Lonnie Bradley w rsf 1 Dario Galindez (Arg) . . . . Inglewood, CA

Light-Middleweight

Sugar Ray Robinson would have been unbeatable in the 154 lb division had it been around in his day, but instead Robinson had to move up from 147 to 160 lb to become a double champion. Emile Griffith, who made the same leap in the 1960s, at least managed to get a finger-hold on the first light-middleweight world championship. The Austrian Board of Control, which existed at that time mainly to facilitate the career of the great Hungarian Laszlo Papp, who boxed out of Vienna, approved a match in 1962 between Griffith and Teddy Wright, a middleweight who was just short of top ten quality.

They billed it as a world title fight, but the fact that three days later the WBA staged the first "real" world championship at the new weight ensured that the Austrian initiative would soon peter out. Griffith beat Wright on points and defended his paper title only once, against the Dane Chris Christensen in Copenhagen, before quietly forgetting about it and concentrating instead on his welterweight title. He made one brave attempt to win the WBC light-middleweight title, 13 years later, but was outpointed by Eckhard Dagge.

The division, which the Americans prefer to call "junior middleweight" took a long time to become accepted. The WBC did not create its own championship until 1975, with the first IBF champion being crowned nine years later.

World Light-Middleweight Championship Bouts

WBA title

Oct 20,	1962	**Denny Moyer** (US) w pts 15 Joey Giambra (US)	Portland, OR
		For vacant title	
Feb 19,	1963	Denny Moyer w pts 15 Stan Harrington (US)	Honolulu, HI
Apr 29,	1963	**Ralph Dupas** (US) w pts 15 Denny Moyer	New Orleans, LA
Jun 17,	1963	Ralph Dupas w pts 15 Denny Moyer	Baltimore, MD
Sep 7,	1963	**Sandro Mazzinghi** (Ita) w ko 9 Ralph Dupas	Milan (Ita)
Dec 2,	1963	Sandro Mazzinghi w rsf 13 Ralph Dupas	Sydney (Aus)
Dec 11,	1964	Sandro Mazzinghi w pts 15 Fortunato Manca (Ita)	Rome (Ita)
Jun 18,	1965	**Nino Benvenuti** (Ita) w ko 6 Sandro Mazzinghi	Milan (Ita)
Dec 17,	1965	Nino Benvenuti w pts 15 Sandro Mazzinghi	Rome (Ita)
Jun 25,	1966	**Kim Ki-Soo** (Kor) w pts 15 Nino Benvenuti	Seoul (Kor)
Dec 17,	1966	Kim Ki-Soo w pts 15 Stan Harrington	Seoul (Kor)
Oct 3,	1967	Kim Ki-Soo w pts 15 Freddie Little (US)	Seoul (Kor)
May 26,	1968	**Sandro Mazzinghi** w pts 15 Kim Ki-Soo	Milan (Ita)
Oct 25,	1968	Sandro Mazzinghi no contest 9 Freddie Little	Rome (Ita)
		Mazzinghi was unable to come out for the ninth round because he was badly cut. The referee ruled a no contest, claiming that EBU rules applied. However, the rule in question only applied if a contest ended on injury before the second half of the eighth round. Mazzinghi refused to give Little a rematch, and the WBA declared his title vacant in January 1969	
Mar 17,	1969	**Freddie Little** w pts 15 Stan Hayward (US)	Las Vegas, NV
		For vacant title	

Sep 9,	1969	Freddie Little w ko 2 Hisao Minami (Jap)	Osaka (Jap)
Mar 20,	1970	Freddie Little w pts 15 Gerhard Piaskowy (Ger)	Berlin (Ger)
Jul 9,	1970	**Carmelo Bossi** (Ita) w pts 15 Freddie Little	Monza (Ita)
Apr 29,	1971	Carmelo Bossi drew 15 Jose Hernandez (Sp)	Madrid (Sp)
Oct 31,	1971	**Koichi Wajima** (Jap) w pts 15 Carmelo Bossi	Tokyo (Jap)
May 7,	1972	Koichi Wajima w ko 1 Domenico Tiberia (Ita)	Tokyo (Jap)
Oct 3,	1972	Koichi Wajima w ko 3 Matt Donovan (Tr)	Tokyo (Jap)
Jan 9,	1973	Koichi Wajima drew 15 Miguel DeOliveira (Bra)	Tokyo (Jap)
Apr 19,	1973	Koichi Wajima w pts 15 Ryu Sorimachi (Jap)	Osaka (Jap)
Aug 14,	1973	Koichi Wajima w rsf 13 Silvani Bertini (1ta)	Sapporo (Jap)
Feb 5,	1974	Koichi Wajima w pts 15 Miguel DeOliveira (Bra)	Tokyo (Jap)
Jun 4,	1974	**Oscar Albarado** (US) w ko 15 Koichi Wajima	Tokyo (Jap)
Oct 8,	1974	Oscar Albarado w rsf 7 Ryu Sorimachi (Jap)	Tokyo (Jap)
Jan 21,	1975	**Koichi Wajima** w pts 15 Oscar Albarado	Tokyo (Jap)
		The WBC, hitherto prepared to accepted the imcumbent as world champion, withdrew recognition from Wajima for failing to agree to a defence against their top contender, Miguel DeOliveira and set up their own title	

WBC title

May 7,	1975	**Miguel DeOliveira** w pts 15 Jose Duran (Sp)	Monte Carlo (Mon)
		For vacant title	
Nov 13,	1975	**Elisha Obed** (Bah) w ret 10 Miguel DeOliveira	Paris (Fra)
Feb 28,	1976	Elisha Obed w ko 2 Tony Gardner (US)	Nassau (Bah)
Apr 25,	1976	Elisha Obed w pts 15 Sea Robinson (IC)	Abidjan (IC)
Jun 18,	1976	**Eckhard Dagge** (Ger) w ret 10 Elisha Obed	Berlin (Ger)
Sep 18,	1976	Eckhard Dagge w pts 15 Emile Griffith (VI)	Berlin (Ger)
Mar 15,	1977	Eckhard Dagge drew 15 Maurice Hope (Eng)	Berlin (Ger)
Aug 6,	1977	**Rocky Mattioli** (Ita) w ko 5 Eckhard Dagge	Berlin (Ger)
Mar 11,	1978	Rocky Mattioli w ko 7 Elisha Obed	Melbourne (Aus)
May 14,	1978	Rocky Mattioli w rsf 5 Jose Duran	Pescara (Ita)
Mar 4,	1979	**Maurice Hope** w ret 8 Rocky Mattioli	San Remo (Ita)
Sep 25,	1979	Maurice Hope w rsf 7 Mike Baker (US)	Wembley (Eng)
Jul 12,	1980	Maurice Hope w rsf 11 Rocky Mattioli	Wembley (Eng)
Nov 26,	1980	Maurice Hope w pts 15 Carlos Herrera (Arg)	Wembley (Eng)
May 24,	1981	**Wilfred Benitez** (PR) w ko 12 Maurice Hope	Las Vegas, NV
Nov 14,	1981	Wilfred Benitez w pts 15 Carlos Santos (PR)	Las Vegas, NV
Jan 30,	1982	Wilfred Benitez w pts 15 Roberto Duran (Pan)	Las Vegas, NV
Dec 3,	1982	**Thomas Hearns** (US) w pts 15 Wilfred Benitez	New Orleans, LA
Feb 11,	1984	Thomas Hearns w pts 12 Luigi Minchillo (Ita)	Detroit, MI
Jun 15,	1984	Thomas Hearns w ko 2 Roberto Duran	Las Vegas, NV
Sep 15,	1984	Thomas Hearns w rsf 3 Fred Hutchings (US)	Saginaw, MI
Jun 23,	1986	Thomas Hearns w rsf 8 Mark Medal (US)	Las Vegas, NV
Sep	1986	*Hearns relinquished the title because of weight problems*	
Dec 5,	1986	**Duane Thomas** (US) w rsf 3 John Mugabi (Ug)	Las Vegas, NV
		For vacant title	
Jul 12,	1987	**Lupe Aquino** (Mex) w pts 12 Duane Thomas	Bordeaux (Fra)
Oct 2,	1987	**Gianfranco Rosi** (Ita) w pts 12 Lupe Aquino	Perugia (Ita)
Jan 3,	1988	Gianfranco Rosi w ko 7 Duane Thomas	Genoa (Ita)
Jul 8,	1988	**Don Curry** (US) w ret 9 Gianfranco Rosi	San Remo (Ita)
Feb 11,	1989	**Rene Jacquot** (Fra) w pts 12 Don Curry	Grenoble (Fra)
Jul 9,	1989	**John Mugabi** w rsf 1 Rene Jacquot	Paris (Fra)
Mar 31,	1990	**Terry Norris** (US) w ko 1 John Mugabi	Tampa, FL
Jul 13,	1990	Terry Norris w pts 12 Rene Jacquot	Annecy (Fra)
Feb 9,	1991	Terry Norris w pts 12 Sugar Ray Leonard (US)	New York, NY
Jun 1,	1991	Terry Norris w ko 8 Don Curry	Palm Springs, CA
Aug 16,	1991	Terry Norris w rsf 1 Brett Lally (US)	San Diego, CA
Dec 13,	1991	Terry Norris w pts 12 Jorge Castro (Arg)	Paris (Fra)
Feb 22,	1992	Terry Norris w rsf 9 Carl Daniels (US)	San Diego, CA
May 9,	1992	Terry Norris w rsf 4 Meldrick Taylor (US)	Las Vegas, NV
Feb 20,	1993	Terry Norris w rsf 2 Maurice Blocker (US)	Mexico City (Mex)
Jun 19,	1993	Terry Norris w ret 3 Troy Waters (Aus)	San Diego, CA
Sep 10,	1993	Terry Norris w rsf 1 Joe Gatti (US)	San Antonio, TX
Dec 18,	1993	**Simon Brown** (Jam) w ko 4 Terry Norris	Puebla (Mex)
Jan 29,	1994	Simon Brown w pts 12 Troy Waters	Las Vegas, NV
May 7,	1994	**Terry Norris** w pts 12 Simon Brown	Las Vegas, NV
Nov 12,	1994	**Luis Santana** (DR) w dis 5 Terry Norris	Mexico City (Mex)
Apr 8,	1995	Luis Santana w dis 3 Terry Norris	Las Vegas, NV
Aug 19,	1995	**Terry Norris** w rsf 2 Luis Santana	Las Vegas, NV
Sep 16,	1995	Terry Norris w rsf 9 David Gonzales (US)	Las Vegas, NV
Dec 16,	1995	Terry Norris w pts 12 Paul Vaden (US)	Philadelphia, PA
		Norris retained WBC title and won Vaden's IBF Championship	

RINGSIDE VIEW

Nino Benvenuti
vs
Sandro Mazzinghi

AN ITALIAN AFFAIR

Italian pride was at stake as well as the light-middleweight championship when Sandro Mazzinghi (left) faced former Olympic gold medallist Nino Benvenuti in Milan on June 18, 1965. Benvenuti, later to win the middleweight title as well, kayoed Mazzinghi in six rounds and outpointed him in a rematch six months later.

MAURICE HOPE *(right) retained his title by outpointing Carlos Herrera*

WBA title

Jun 7,	1975	**Jae Do Yuh** (Kor) w ko 7 Koichi Wajima	. . . .	Kitakyushu (Jap)
Nov 11,	1975	Jae-Do Yuh w rsf 6 Masahiro Masaki (Jap)	. . . .	Shizuoka (Jap)
Feb 17,	1976	**Koichi Wajima** w ko 15 Jae Do Yuh	. . . .	Tokyo (Jap)
May 18,	1976	**Jose Duran** (Sp) w ko 14 Koichi Wajima	. . . .	Tokyo (Jap)
Oct 8,	1976	**Miguel Angel Castellini** (Arg) w pts 15 Jose Duran	. . . .	Madrid (Sp)
Mar 5,	1977	**Eddie Gazo** (Nic) w pts 15 Miguel Angel Castellini	. . . .	Managua (Nic)
Jun 7,	1977	Eddie Gazo w rsf 11 Koichi Wajima	. . . .	Tokyo (Jap)
Sep 13,	1977	Eddie Gazo w pts15 Kenji Shibata (Jap)	. . . .	Tokyo (Jap)
Dec 18,	1977	Eddie Gazo w pts 15 Chae-Keun Lim (Kor)	. . . .	Inchon (Kor)
Aug 9,	1978	**Masashi Kudo** (Jap) w pts 15 Eddie Gazo	. . . .	Akita (Jap)
Dec 13,	1978	Masashi Kudo w pts 15 Ho-In Joo (Kor)	. . . .	Osaka (Jap)
Mar 14,	1979	Masashi Kudo w pts 15 Manuel Ricardo Gonzalez (Arg)	. . . . .	Tokyo (Jap)
Jun 20,	1979	Masashi Kudo w rsf 12 Manuel Ricardo Gonzalez	. . . .	Yokkaichi (Jap)
Oct 24,	1979	**Ayub Kalule** (Ug) w pts 15 Masashi Kudo	. . . .	Akita (Jap)
Dec 6,	1979	Ayub Kalule w pts 15 Steve Gregory (US)	. . . .	Copenhagen (Den)
Apr 17,	1980	Ayub Kalule w ret 11 Emiliano Villa (Col)	. . . .	Copenhagen (Den)
Jun 12,	1980	Ayub Kalule w pts 15 Marijan Benes (Yug)	. . . .	Randers (Den)
Sep 6,	1980	Ayub Kalule w pts 15 Bushy Bester (SA)	. . . .	Aarhus (Den)
Jun 25,	1981	**Sugar Ray Leonard** w rsf 9 Ayub Kalule	. . . .	Houston, TX
Jul	1981	*Leonard vacated WBA title to concentrate on welterweight division*		
Nov 7,	1981	**Tadashi Mihara** (Jap) w pts 15 Rocky Fratto (US)	. . . .	Rochester, NY
		For vacant title		
Feb 2,	1982	**Davey Moore** (US) w rsf 6 Tadashi Mihara	. . . .	Tokyo (Jap)
Apr 26,	1982	Davey Moore w ko 5 Charlie Weir (SA)	. . . .	Johannesburg (SA)
Jul 17,	1982	Davey Moore w rsf 10 Ayub Kalule	. . . .	Atlantic City, NJ
Jan 29,	1983	Davey Moore w ko 4 Gary Guiden (US)	. . . .	Atlantic City, NJ
Jun 16,	1983	**Roberto Duran** w rsf 8 Davey Moore	. . . .	New York, NY
Jun	1984	*Duran relinquished the title to challenge Thomas Hearns for the WBC version*		
Oct 19,	1984	**Mike McCallum** (Jam) w pts 15 Sean Mannion (Ire)	. . . . . .	New York, NY
		For vacant title		
Dec 1,	1984	Mike McCallum w rsf 14 Luigi Minchillo (Ita)	. . . .	Milan (Ita)
Jul 28,	1985	Mike McCallum w rsf 8 David Braxton (US)	. . . .	Miami, FL
Aug 23,	1986	Mike McCallum w rsf 2 Julian Jackson (VI)	. . . .	Miami, FL
Oct 25,	1986	Mike McCallum w rsf 9 Said Skouma (Alg)	. . . .	Paris (Fra)
Apr 19,	1987	Mike McCallum w rsf 10 Milton McCrory (US)	. . . .	Phoenix, AZ
Jul 18,	1987	Mike McCallum w ko 5 Don Curry (US)	. . . .	Las Vegas, NV
Sep	1987	*McCallum relinquished the title to box at middleweight*		
Nov 21,	1987	**Julian Jackson** w rsf 3 In-Chul Baek (Kor)	. . . .	Las Vegas, NV
		For vacant title		
Jul 30,	1988	Julian Jackson w rsf 3 Buster Drayton (US)	. . . .	Atlantic City, NJ
Feb 25,	1989	Julian Jackson w ko 8 Francisco DeJesus (Bra)	. . . .	Las Vegas, NV
Jul 30,	1989	Julian Jackson w rsf 2 Terry Norris (US)	. . . .	Atlantic City, NJ

RINGSIDE VIEW

Thomas Hearns
vs
Roberto Duran

SLEDGEHAMMER BLOW

One single, chilling right hand was all Thomas Hearns needed to demolish Roberto Duran in the second round of their Las Vegas showdown on June 15, 1984. The Panamanian, who had given up his WBA title to try for Hearns's WBC title, was sent sprawling face-first for his only knockout loss.

Sep	1990	*Jackson gave up the WBA title to fight for the WBC middleweight title*		
Feb 23,	1991	**Gilbert Dele** (Fra) w rsf 7 Carlos Elliott (US)	. . . .	Point-à-Pitre (Guad)
		For vacant title		
May 5,	1991	Gilbert Dele w pts 12 Jun-Suk Hwang (Kor)	. . . .	Paris (Fra)
Oct 3,	1991	**Vinny Pazienza** (US) w rsf 12 Gilbert Dele	. . . .	Providence, RI
Oct	1992	*Pazienza gave up the title because of injuries he sustained in a car crash*		
Dec 21,	1992	**Julio Cesar Vasquez** (Arg) w rsf 1 Hitoshi Kamiyama (Jap)	. .	Buenos Aires
		For vacant title		
Apr 24,	1993	Julio Cesar Vasquez w pts 12 Javier Castillejos (Sp)	. . . .	Madrid (Sp)
Jul 10,	1993	Julio Cesar Vasquez w pts 12 Alejandro Ugueto (Ven)	. . . .	Tucuman (Arg)
Aug 21,	1993	Julio Cesar Vasquez w pts 12 Aaron Davis (US)	. . . . . .	Monte Carlo (Mon)
Jan 22,	1994	Julio Cesar Vasquez w pts 12 Juan Medina Padilla (Sp)	. . .	Alma Ata (Kaz)
Mar 4,	1994	Julio Cesar Vasquez w rsf 2 Armand Picar (Phil)	. . . . .	Las Vegas, NV
Apr 8,	1994	Julio Cesar Vasquez w pts 12 Ricardo Nunez (Arg)	. . . . . .	Tucuman (Arg)
May 21,	1994	Julio Cesar Vasquez w rsf 10 Ahmet Dottuev (Rus)	. . . . .	Belfast (N. Ire)
Aug 21,	1994	Julio Cesar Vasquez w pts 12 Ronald Wright (US)	. . .	St-Jean-de-Luz (Fra)
Nov 11,	1994	Julio Cesar Vasquez w pts 12 Tony Marshall (US)	. . . . . .	Tucuman (Arg)
Mar 4,	1995	**Pernell Whitaker** (US) w pts 12 Julio Cesar Vasquez	. . . .	Atlantic City, NJ
Mar	1995	*Whitaker relinquished the title to defend his welterweight championship*		
Jun 16,	1995	**Carl Daniels** (US) w pts 12 Julio Cesar Green (US)	. . . .	Lyon (Fra)
		For vacant title		
Dec 16,	1995	**Julio Cesar Vasquez** w rsf 11 Carl Daniels	. . . .	Philadelphia, PA

IBF title

Mar 11,	1984	**Mark Medal** (US) w rsf 5 Earl Hargrove (US)	. . . .	Atlantic City, NJ
		For vacant title		
Nov 2,	1984	**Carlos Santos** w pts 15 Mark Medal	. . . .	New York, NY
Jun 1,	1985	Carlos Santos w pts 15 Louis Acaries (Fra)	. . . .	Paris (Fra)
Feb	1986	*The IBF withdrew recognition from Santos for his failure to defend against Davey Moore*		
Jun 4,	1986	**Buster Drayton** w pts 15 Carlos Santos	. . . .	East Rutherford, NJ
		For vacant title		
Aug 24,	1986	Buster Drayton w rsf 10 Davey Moore	. . . .	Juan-les-Pins (Fra)
Mar 27,	1987	Buster Drayton w ret 10 Said Skouma (Alg)	. . . .	Cannes (Fra)
Jun 27,	1987	**Matthew Hilton** (Can) w pts 15 Buster Drayton	. . . .	Montreal (Can)
Oct 16,	1987	Matthew Hilton w rsf 2 Jack Callahan (US)	. . . .	Atlantic City, NJ
Nov 4,	1988	**Robert Hines** (US) w rsf 12 Matthew Hilton	. . . .	Las Vegas, NV
Feb 5,	1989	**Darrin van Horn** (US) w pts 12 Robert Hines	. . . .	Atlantic City, NJ
Jul 15,	1989	**Gianfranco Rosi** w pts 12 Darrin van Horn	. . . .	Atlantic City, NJ
Oct 27,	1989	Gianfranco Rosi w pts 12 Troy Waters (Aus)	. . . .	St Vincent (Ita)
Apr 14,	1990	Gianfranco Rosi w rsf 7 Kevin Daigle	. . . .	Monte Carlo (Mon)
Jul 21,	1990	Gianfranco Rosi w pts 12 Darrin Van Horn	. . . .	Marino (Ita)
Nov 30,	1990	Gianfranco Rosi w pts 12 Rene Jacquot	. . . .	Marsala (Ita)
Mar 16,	1991	Gianfranco Rosi w pts 12 Ron Amundsen (US)	. . . .	St Vincent (Ita)
Jul 13,	1991	Gianfranco Rosi w pts 12 Glenn Wolfe (US)	. . . .	Avezzano (Ita)
Nov 21,	1991	Gianfranco Rosi w pts 12 Gilbert Baptist (US)	. . . .	Perugia (Ita)
Apr 9,	1992	Gianfranco Rosi w rsf 6 Angel Hernandez (Sp)	. . . .	Celano (Ita)
Jul 11,	1992	Gianfranco Rosi w pts 12 Gilbert Dele	. . . .	Monte Carlo (Mon)
Jan 20,	1993	Gianfranco Rosi w pts 12 Gilbert Dele	. . . .	Avoriaz (Ita)
Mar 4,	1994	Gianfranco Rosi tech draw 6 Vincent Pettway (US)	. . . .	Las Vegas, NV
Sep 17,	1994	**Vincent Pettway** w ko 4 Gianfranco Rosi	. . . .	Las Vegas, NV
Apr 29,	1995	Vincent Pettway w ko 6 Simon Brown	. . . .	Landover, MD
Aug 12,	1995	**Paul Vaden** w rsf 12 Vincent Pettway	. . . .	Las Vegas, NV
Dec 16,	1995	**Terry Norris** w pts 12 Paul Vaden	. . . .	Philadelphia, PA

WBO title

Dec 8,	1988	**John David Jackson** (US) w ret 7 Lupe Aquino	. . . .	Detroit, MI
		For vacant title		
Apr 22,	1989	John David Jackson w rsf 8 Steve Little (US)	. . . .	Detroit, MI
Feb 17,	1990	John David Jackson no contest 11 Martin Camara (Fra)	. . .	Deauville (Fra)
		This decision caused such a scandal that the French Federation prohibited any further WBO championships from taking place under their jurisdiction		
Nov 23,	1990	John David Jackson w pts 12 Chris Pyatt (Eng)	. . . .	Leicester (Eng)
Jul 20,	1991	John David Jackson w pts 12 Tyrone Trice (US)	. . . .	McKee, NJ
Jun 9,	1992	John David Jackson w ret 9 Pat Lawlor (US)	. . . .	San Francisco, CA
Dec 19,	1992	John David Jackson w ret 10 Michele Mastrodonato (Ita)	.	San Severo (Ita)
Jul	1993	*Jackson gave up the title to box at middleweight*		
Oct 30,	1993	**Verno Phillips** (US) w rsf 7 Lupe Aquino	. . . .	Phoenix, AZ
		For vacant title		
Jul 25,	1994	Verno Phillips w rsf 7 Jaime Llanes (Mex)	. . . .	Inglewood, CA
Nov 9,	1994	Verno Phillips w pts 12 Santos Cardona (PR)	. . . .	New Orleans, LA
Feb 3,	1995	Verno Phillips w pts 12 Santos Cardona	. . . .	Bushkill
May 17,	1995	**Gianfranco Rosi** (Ita) w pts 12 Verno Phillips	. . . .	Perugia (Ita)
		Rosi failed a post-fight drugs test and Phillips was reinstated as champion		
Nov 22,	1995	**Paul Jones** (Eng) w pts 12 Verno Phillips	. . . .	Sheffield (Eng)

Welterweight

Paddy Duffy, an Irish-American from Boston, was the first crossover champion of the welterweight division; he won the 142 lb championship (as the limit then was) under London Prize Ring rules and then knocked out Billy McMillan under Queensberry Rules in the first gloved championship match, even if the gloves were only skin-tight. His disqualification win over the Australian-based Englishman Tom Meadows is generally accepted as the inaugural international match of the gloved era in the welterweight class, which Duffy had helped to popularize in the Prize Ring.

Sadly, it was his last fight: he died of tuberculosis a year later, and set off one of the periodic scrambles for recognition to which the division was particularly prone in its first 30 years. His successors included colourful characters like Joe Walcott, the Barbados Demon, and the gloriously named Mysterious Billy Smith. (A disgruntled ex-opponent of his explained that Smith was so called because "He was always doing something mysterious in the ring.") That larger-than-life tradition has been maintained by great champions like Ted "Kid" Lewis, Mickey Walker, Henry Armstrong, Jose Napoles and Emile Griffith.

The championship limit fluctuated between 142 and 145 lb for the first two decades of the century, until the present poundage was universally accepted in 1920 during Jack Britton's second spell as champion.

World Welterweight Championship Bouts

Oct 30,	1888	**Paddy Duffy** (US) w ko 17 Billy McMillan (US)	Fort Foote, VA
Mar 29,	1889	Paddy Duffy w dis 45 Tom Meadows (Eng)	San Francisco, CA
Jul 19,	1890	*Duffy died, and the title was claimed by Tommy Ryan and Mysterious Billy Smith*	
Aug 9,	1891	**Tommy Ryan** (US) w ko 3 Billy McMillan	Richardson (Can)
Dec 13,	1891	Tommy Ryan w ko 14 Frank Howson (Eng)	Chicago, IL
Dec 14,	1892	**Mysterious Billy Smith** (US) w ko 14 Danny Needham (US) .San Francisco, CA	
Apr 17,	1893	Mysterious Billy Smith w ko 2 Tom Williams (Aus)	Brooklyn, NY
Jul 26,	1894	**Tommy Ryan** w pts 20 Mysterious Billy Smith	Minneapolis, MN
Jan 18,	1895	Tommy Ryan w rsf 3 "Nonpareil" Jack Dempsey (Ire)	New York, NY
May 27,	1895	Tommy Ryan no contest 18 Mysterious Billy Smith	New York, NY
		Ryan was subsequently unable to make the championship weight, then 142 lb, although he continued to style himself champion until 1898	
Mar 17,	1897	**George Green** (US) w ko 12 Mysterious Billy Smith	Carson City, NV
Aug 26,	1897	**Joe Walcott** (Bar) w ko 18 George Green	San Francisco, CA
Aug 27,	1898	**Mysterious Billy Smith** w pts 25 Matty Matthews (US)	New York, NY
		With this victory Smith, who had outpointed Green in an overweight match a month earlier, was generally accepted as champion	
Oct 7,	1898	Mysterious Billy Smith w pts 25 Charley McKeever (US) . . .	New York, NY
Dec 6,	1898	Mysterious Billy Smith w pts 20 Joe Walcott	New York, NY
		Although the match was made at 145 lb, Smith's victory helped consolidate his claim to the title	
Mar 10,	1899	Mysterious Billy Smith w rsf 14 George Lavigne (US) . .	San Francisco, CA
Apr 17,	1900	**Matty Matthews** w ko 19 Mysterious Billy Smith	New York, NY
Jun 5,	1900	**Eddie Connolly** (Can) w pts 25 Matty Matthews	Brooklyn, NY
Aug 13,	1900	**Jim "Rube" Ferns** (US) w ret 15 Eddie Connolly	Buffalo, NY
Oct 16,	1900	**Matty Matthews** w pts 15 Jim "Rube" Ferns	Detroit, MI
Apr 20,	1901	Matty Matthews w pts 20 Tom Couhig (US)	Louisville, KY
May 24,	1901	**Jim "Rube" Ferns** w ko 10 Matty Matthews	Toronto (Can)
Sep 23,	1901	Jim "Rube" Ferns w ko 9 Frank Erne (US)	Fort Erie (Can)
Dec 18,	1901	**Joe Walcott** w rsf 5 Jim "Rube" Ferns	Fort Erie (Can)
Sep 5,	1904	Joe Walcott drew 15 Sam Langford (US)	Manchester, NH
Sep 30,	1904	Joe Walcott drew 20 Joe Gans (US)	San Francisco, CA
Jul 10,	1906	Joe Walcott w ko 8 Jack Dougherty (US)	Chelsea, MA
Sep 29,	1906	Joe Walcott drew 20 Billy Rhodes (US)	Kansas City, KS
Nov 29,	1906	**Honey Mellody** (US) w rsf 12 Joe Walcott	Chelsea, MA
Apr 23,	1907	**Mike "Twin" Sullivan** w pts 20 Honey Mellody	Los Angeles, CA
		The title was in dispute during this period with Sullivan, Frank Mantell and Harry Lewis calling themselves champion, with varying degrees of authenticity. Sullivan relinquished his claim in April 1908 because of	

weight problems, and Lewis, who had beaten Mellody and Mantell, became accepted as champion at the division's new limit of 147 lb

Feb 19,	1910	**Harry Lewis** (US) drew 25 Willie Lewis (US)	Paris (Fra)
Apr 23,	1910	Harry Lewis drew 25 Willie Lewis	Paris (Fra)
May 4,	1910	Harry Lewis w ko 3 Peter Brown (Eng)	Paris (Fra)
Jun 27,	1910	Harry Lewis w ret 7 Harry "Young" Joseph (Eng)	London (Eng)
Feb	1911	*Lewis gave up the title to box at middleweight*	
Nov 9,	1911	**Dixie Kid** (US) w ko 2 Johnny Summers (Eng)	Liverpool (Eng)
Apr 24,	1912	Dixie Kid w ret 11 George Bernard (Fra)	Paris (Fra)
Oct 4,	1912	**Marcel Thomas** (Fra) w pts 15 Dixie Kid	Paris (Fra)
		For IBU version of title	
Jul 22,	1913	**Mike Glover** (US) w rsf 4 Marcel Thomas	Boston, MA
		Glover was widely accepted in America and Europe as champion, but a separate version of the title was contested in Australia	

Australian version

Jan 1,	1914	**Waldemar Holberg** (Den) w pts 20 Ray Bronson (US) . .	Melbourne (Aus)
Jan 24,	1914	**Tom McCormick** (Eng) w dis 6 Waldemar Holberg	Melbourne (Aus)
Mar 21,	1914	**Matt Wells** (Eng) w pts 20 Tom McCormick	Sydney (Aus)

World title

Jun 1,	1915	**Mike Glover** w pts 12 Matt Wells	Boston, MA
		Glover lost his claim to the title when he was outpointed over 12 rounds by Jack Britton (US) in Boston on June 26, 1915, although the fight was not billed as for the championship and no weights were announced. The title was variously claimed by Britton, Ted "Kid" Lewis and Eddie Moha (US), with Britton finally gaining acceptance by beating Lewis	
Apr 24,	1916	**Jack Britton** w pts 20 Ted "Kid" Lewis (Eng)	New Orleans, LA
Oct 17,	1916	Jack Britton w pts 12 Ted "Kid" Lewis	Boston, MA
Nov 21,	1916	Jack Britton w pts 12 Charlie White (US)	Boston, MA
Jun 25,	1917	**Ted "Kid" Lewis** w pts 20 Jack Britton	Dayton, OH
May 17,	1918	Ted "Kid" Lewis w pts 20 Johnny Tillman (US)	Denver, CO
Mar 17,	1919	**Jack Britton** w ko 9 Ted "Kid" Lewis	Canton, OH
Aug 23,	1920	Jack Briton drew 12 Lou Bogash (US)	Bridgeport, CT
Feb 7,	1921	Jack Britton w pts 15 Ted "Kid" Lewis	New York, NY
Feb 17,	1922	Jack Britton drew 15 Dave Shade (US)	New York, NY
Jun 26,	1922	Jack Britton w dis 13 Benny Leonard (US)	New York, NY
Oct 10,	1922	Jack Britton w pts 12 Jimmy Kelly (US)	Havana (Cub)
Nov 1,	1922	**Mickey Walker** (US) w pts 15 Jack Britton	New York, NY
Jun 6,	1923	*The New York Commission stripped Walker for his failure to defend against Dave Shade, whom they proclaimed champion*	
Jul 27,	1923	**Jimmy Jones** (US) w pts 10 Dave Shade	Boston, MA
		For New York title	
Oct 11,	1923	*The NY Commission withdrew recognition from Jones, after he and Mickey Walker had both been disqualified for "not trying" in their overweight match in Newark three days earlier*	
Jun 2,	1924	**Mickey Walker** w pts 10 Lew Tendler (US)	Philadelphia, PA
Oct 1,	1924	Mickey Walker w ko 6 Bobby Barrett (US)	Philadelphia, PA
Sep 21,	1925	Mickey Walker w pts 15 Dave Shade	New York, NY
May 20,	1926	**Pete Latzo** (US) w pts 10 Mickey Walker	Scranton, PA
Jul 9,	1926	Pete Latzo w dis 4 George Levine (US)	New York, NY
Jun 3,	1927	**Joe Dundee** (US) w pts 15 Pete Latzo	New York, NY
Jul 13,	1927	Joe Dundee w pts 10 Billy Drako (US)	Cincinnati, OH
Sep	1928	*Dundee was stripped by the NBA for failing to defend against Young Jack Thompson (who had stopped him in two rounds in an overweight match on August 30, 1928) or Jackie Fields*	
Mar 25,	1929	**Jackie Fields** (US) w pts 10 Young Jack Thompson (US)	Chicago, IL
		For vacant NBA title	
Jul 25,	1929	Jackie Fields w dis 2 Joe Dundee	Detroit, MI
		For undisputed title	
May 9,	1930	**Young Jack Thompson** w pts 15 Jackie Fields	Detroit, MI

CARMEN BASILIO *(left) twice stopped Tony DeMarco in the 12th round*

Sep 5, 1930	**Tommy Freeman** (US) w pts 15 Young Jack Thompson . . . . Cleveland, OH
Apr 14, 1931	**Young Jack Thompson** w ret 12 Tommy Freeman . . . . Cleveland, OH
Oct 23, 1931	**Lou Brouillard** (Can) w pts 15 Young Jack Thompson . . . . . . Boston, MA
Jan 28, 1932	**Jackie Fields** w pts 10 Lou Brouillard . . . . Chicago, IL
Feb 22, 1933	**Young Corbett III** (US) w pts10 Jackie Fields . . . . San Francisco, CA
May 29, 1933	**Jimmy McLarnin** (Ire) w ko 1 Young Corbett III . . . . Los Angeles, CA
May 28, 1934	**Barney Ross** (US) w pts 15 Jimmy McLarnin . . . . New York, NY
Sep 17, 1934	**Jimmy McLarnin** w pts 15 Barney Ross . . . . New York, NY
May 28, 1935	**Barney Ross** w pts 15 Jimmy McLarnin . . . . New York, NY
Nov 27, 1936	Barney Ross w pts 15 Izzy Jannazzo (US) . . . . New York, NY
Sep 23, 1937	Barney Ross w pts 15 Ceferino Garcia (Phil) . . . . New York, NY
Jan 1938	*The IBU withdrew recognition from Ross in favour of Felix Wouters (Bel), who outpointed Gustav Eder (Ger) over 15 rounds in Brussels on February 16, 1938. In May that year the IBU agreed to recognize Ross again, in the interests of unity*
May 31, 1938	**Henry Armstrong** (US) w pts 15 Barney Ross . . . . New York, NY
Nov 25, 1938	Henry Armstrong w pts 15 Ceferino Garcia . . . . New York, NY
Dec 5, 1938	Henry Armstrong w rsf 3 Al Manfredo (US) . . . . Cleveland, OH
Jan 10, 1939	Henry Armstrong w pts 10 Baby Arizmendi (Mex) . . . . . . Los Angeles, CA
Mar 4, 1939	Henry Armstrong w rsf 4 Bobby Pacho (US) . . . . Havana (Cub)
Mar 16, 1939	Henry Armstrong w ko 1 Lew Feldman (US) . . . . St Louis, MO
	Armstrong's lightweight title was also at stake
Mar 31, 1939	Henry Armstrong w ko 12 Davey Day (US) . . . . New York, NY
May 25, 1939	Henry Armstrong w pts 15 Ernie Roderick (Eng) . . . . London (Eng)
Oct 9, 1939	Henry Armstrong w rsf 4 Al Manfredo . . . . Des Moines, IA
Oct 13, 1939	Henry Armstrong w ko 2 Howard Scott (US) . . . . Minneapolis, MN
Oct 20, 1939	Henry Armstrong w ko 3 Richie Fontaine (US) . . . . Seattle, WA
Oct 24, 1939	Henry Armstrong w pts 10 Jimmy Garrison (US) . . . . New York, NY
Oct 30, 1939	Henry Armstrong w rsf 4 Bobby Pacho . . . . Denver, CO
Dec 11, 1939	Henry Armstrong w ko 7 Jimmy Garrison . . . . Cleveland, OH
Jan 4, 1940	Henry Armstrong w ko 5 Joe Ghnouly (US) . . . . St Louis, MO
Jan 24, 1940	Henry Armstrong w rsf 9 Pedro Montanez (PR) . . . . New York, NY
Apr 26, 1940	Henry Armstrong w rsf 7 Paul Junior (Can) . . . . Boston, MA
May 24, 1940	Henry Armstrong w rsf 5 Ralph Zanelli (US) . . . . Boston, MA
Jun 21, 1940	Henry Armstrong w rsf 3 Paul Junior . . . . Portland, ME
Sep 23, 1940	Henry Armstrong w ko 4 Phil Furr (US) . . . . Washington, DC
Oct 4, 1940	**Fritzie Zivic (US)** w pts 15 Henry Armstrong . . . . New York, NY
Jan 17, 1941	Fritzie Zivic w rsf 12 Henry Armstrong . . . . New York, NY
Jul 21, 1941	**Freddie (Red) Cochrane** (US) w pts 15 Fritzie Zivic . . . . Newark, NJ
Feb 1, 1946	**Marty Servo** w ko 4 Freddie (Red) Cochrane . . . . New York, NY
Sep 25, 1946	*Servo retired*
Dec 20, 1946	**Sugar Ray Robinson** (US) w pts 15 Tommy Bell (US) . . . . . New York, NY
	For vacant title
Jun 24, 1947	Sugar Ray Robinson w rsf 8 Jimmy Doyle (US) . . . . Cleveland, OH
Dec 19, 1947	Sugar Ray Robinson w rsf 6 Chuck Taylor (US) . . . . Detroit, MI
Jun 28, 1948	Sugar Ray Robinson w pts 15 Bernard Docusen (US) . . . . . . Chicago, IL
Jul 11, 1949	Sugar Ray Robinson w pts 15 Kid Gavilan (Cub) . . . . Philadelphia, PA
Aug 9, 1950	Sugar Ray Robinson w pts 15 Charlie Fusari (US) . . . . . . Jersey City, NJ
Feb 15, 1951	*Robinson gave up welterweight title on becoming middleweight champion*
Mar 14, 1951	**Johnny Bratton** (US) w pts 15 Charlie Fusari . . . . Chicago, IL
	For vacant NBA title

May 18, 1951	**Kid Gavilan** w pts 15 Johnny Bratton . . . . New York, NY
	For undisputed title
Aug 29, 1951	Kid Gavilan w pts 15 Billy Graham (US) . . . . New York, NY
Feb 4, 1952	Kid Gavilan w pts 15 Bobby Dykes (US) . . . . Miami, FL
Jul 7, 1952	Kid Gavilan w rsf 11 Gil Turner (US) . . . . Philadelphia, PA
Oct 5, 1952	Kid Gavilan w pts 15 Billy Graham . . . . Havana (Cub)
Feb 11, 1953	Kid Gavilan w ret 9 Chuck Davey (US) . . . . Chicago, IL
Sep 18, 1953	Kid Gavilan w pts 15 Carmen Basilio (US) . . . . Syracuse, NY
Nov 13, 1953	Kid Gavilan w pts 15 Johnny Bratton . . . . Chicago, IL
Oct 20, 1954	**Johnny Saxton** (US) w pts 15 Kid Gavilan . . . . Philadelphia, PA
Apr 1, 1955	**Tony DeMarco** (US) w rsf 14 Johnny Saxton . . . . Boston, MA
Jun 10, 1955	**Carmen Basilio** w rsf 12 Tony DeMarco . . . . Syracuse, NY
Nov 30, 1955	Carmen Basilio w rsf 12 Tony DeMarco . . . . Boston, MA
Mar 14, 1956	**Johnny Saxton** w pts 15 Carmen Basilio . . . . Chicago, IL
Sep 12, 1956	**Carmen Basilio** w rsf 9 Johnny Saxton . . . . Syracuse, NY
Feb 22, 1957	Carmen Basilio w ko 2 Johnny Saxton . . . . Cleveland, OH
Sep 1957	*Basilio relinquished the title on winning the middleweight championship*
Jun 6, 1958	**Virgil Akins** (US) w rsf 4 Vince Martinez (US) . . . . St Louis, MO
	For vacant title
Dec 5, 1958	**Don Jordan** (US) w pts 15 Virgil Akins . . . . Los Angeles, CA
Apr 24, 1959	Don Jordan w pts 15 Virgil Akins . . . . St Louis, MO
Jul 10, 1959	Don Jordan w pts 15 Denny Moyer (US) . . . . Portland, ME
May 27, 1960	**Benny (Kid) Paret** (Cub) w pts 15 Don Jordan . . . . Las Vegas, NV
Dec 10, 1960	Benny (Kid) Paret w pts 15 Federico Thompson (Pan) . . . . New York, NY
Apr 1, 1961	**Emile Griffith** (VI) w ko 13 Benny (Kid) Paret . . . . Miami, FL
Jun 3, 1961	Emile Griffith w rsf 12 Gaspar Ortega (Mex) . . . . Los Angeles, CA
Sep 30, 1961	**Benny (Kid) Paret** w pts 15 Emile Griffith . . . . New York, NY
Mar 24, 1962	**Emile Griffith** w rsf 12 Benny (Kid) Paret . . . . New York, NY
Jul 13, 1962	Emile Griffith w pts 15 Ralph Dupas (US) . . . . Las Vegas, NV
Dec 8, 1962	Emile Griffith w ret 9 Jorge Fernandez (Arg) . . . . Las Vegas, NV
Mar 21, 1963	**Luis Rodriguez** (Cub) w pts 15 Emile Griffith . . . . Los Angeles, CA
Jun 8, 1963	**Emile Griffith** w pts 15 Luis Rodriguez . . . . New York, NY
Jun 12, 1964	Emile Griffith w pts 15 Luis Rodriguez . . . . Las Vegas, NV
Sep 22, 1964	Emile Griffith w pts 15 Brian Curvis (Wal) . . . . London (Eng)
Mar 30, 1965	Emile Griffith w pts 15 Jose Stable (Cub) . . . . New York, NY
Dec 10, 1965	Emile Griffith w pts 15 Manny Gonzalez (US) . . . . New York, NY
Apr 1966	*Griffith relinquished the title on winning the middleweight championship*
Aug 24, 1966	**Curtis Cokes** (US) w pts 15 Manny Gonzalez . . . . New Orleans, LA
	For vacant WBA title
Nov 28, 1966	Curtis Cokes w pts 15 Jean Josselin (Fra) . . . . Dallas, TX
	For undisputed title
May 19, 1967	Curtis Cokes w rsf 10 Francois Pavilla (Fra) . . . . Dallas, TX
Oct 2, 1967	Curtis Cokes w rsf 8 Charlie Shipes (US) . . . . Oakland, CA
Apr 16, 1968	Curtis Cokes w rsf 5 Willie Ludick (SA) . . . . Dallas, TX
Oct 21, 1968	Curtis Cokes w pts 15 Ramon La Cruz (Arg) . . . . New Orleans, LA
Apr 18, 1969	**Jose Napoles** (Cub) w rsf 13 Curtis Cokes . . . . Inglewood, CA
Jun 29, 1969	Jose Napoles w ret 10 Curtis Cokes . . . . Mexico City (Mex)
Oct 17, 1969	Jose Napoles w pts 15 Emile Griffith . . . . Inglewood, CA
Feb 15, 1970	Jose Napoles w rsf 15 Ernie Lopez (US) . . . . Los Angeles, CA
Dec 3, 1970	**Billy Backus** (US) w rsf 4 Jose Napoles . . . . Syracuse, NY
Jun 4, 1971	**Jose Napoles** w rsf 8 Billy Backus . . . . Inglewood, CA
Dec 14, 1971	Jose Napoles w pts 15 Hedgemon Lewis (US) . . . . Inglewood, CA
Mar 28, 1972	Jose Napoles w ko 7 Ralph Charles (Eng) . . . . Wembley (Eng)
Jun 10, 1972	Jose Napoles w rsf 2 Adolph Pruitt (US) . . . . Monterrey (Mex)
May 1972	*The NY Commission stripped Napoles for refusing to meet Backus again*
Jun 16, 1972	**Hedgemon Lewis** w pts 15 Billy Backus . . . . Syracuse, NY
	For vacant NY version of title
Dec 8, 1972	Hedgemon Lewis w pts 15 Billy Backus . . . . Syracuse, NY
Feb 28, 1973	Jose Napoles w ko 7 Ernie Lopez . . . . Inglewood, CA
Jun 23, 1973	Jose Napoles w pts 15 Roger Menetrey (Fra) . . . . Grenoble (Fra)
Sep 22, 1973	Jose Napoles w pts 15 Clyde Gray (Can) . . . . Toronto (Can)
Aug 3, 1974	Jose Napoles w rsf 9 Hedgemon Lewis . . . . Mexico City (Mex)
	For undisputed title
Dec 14, 1974	Jose Napoles w ko 3 Horacio Saldano (Arg) . . . . Mexico City (Mex)
Mar 30, 1975	Jose Napoles w tech dec 12 Armando Muniz (US) . . . . . . Acapulco (Mex)
May 14, 1975	*Napoles announced he would relinquish WBA title to concentrate on defending the WBC version*

WBC title

Jul 12, 1975	**Jose Napoles** w pts 15 Armando Muniz . . . . Mexico City (Mex)
Dec 6, 1975	**John H. Stracey** (Eng) w rsf 6 Jose Napoles . . . . Mexico City (Mex)
Mar 20, 1976	John H. Stracey w rsf 10 Hedgemon Lewis . . . . Wembley (Eng)
Jun 22, 1976	**Carlos Palomino** (US) w rsf 12 John H. Stracey . . . . Wembley (Eng)
Jan 22, 1977	Carlos Palomino w rsf 15 Armando Muniz . . . . Los Angeles, CA
Jun 14, 1977	Carlos Palomino w ko 11 Dave Green (Eng) . . . . Wembley (Eng)
Sep 13, 1977	Carlos Palomino w pts 15 Everaldo Costa Azevedo (Bra) . Los Angeles, CA

Dec 10,	1977	Carlos Palomino w ko 13 Jose Palacios (Mex)	Los Angeles, CA
Feb 11,	1978	Carlos Palomino w ko 7 Ryu Sorimachi (Jap)	Las Vegas, NV
Mar 18,	1978	Carlos Palomino w rsf 9 Mimoun Mohatar (Mor)	Las Vegas, NV
May 27,	1978	Carlos Palomino w pts 15 Armando Muniz	Los Angeles, CA
Jan 14,	1979	**Wilfred Benitez** (PR) w pts 15 Carlos Palomino	San Juan, CA
Mar 25,	1979	Wilfred Benitez w pts 15 Harold Weston (US)	San Juan, CA
Nov 30,	1979	**Sugar Ray Leonard** (US) w rsf 15 Wilfred Benitez	Las Vegas, NV
Mar 31,	1980	Sugar Ray Leonard w ko 4 Dave Green	Landover, MD
Jun 20,	1980	**Roberto Duran** (Pan) w pts 15 Sugar Ray Leonard	Montreal (Can)
Nov 25,	1980	**Sugar Ray Leonard** w ret 8 Roberto Duran	New Orleans, LA
Mar 28,	1981	Sugar Ray Leonard w rsf 10 Larry Bonds (US)	Syracuse, NY
Sep 16,	1981	Sugar Ray Leonard w rsf 14 Thomas Hearns (US)	Las Vegas, NV
		For undisputed title	

WBA title

Jun 28,	1975	**Angel Espada** (PR) w pts 15 Clyde Gray	San Juan, CA
		For vacant title	
Oct 11,	1975	Angel Espada w pts 15 Johnny Gant (US)	San Juan, CA
Jul 17,	1976	**Jose Pipino Cuevas** (Mex) w rsf 2 Angel Espada	Mexicali (Mex)
Oct 27,	1976	Jose Pipino Cuevas w ko 2 Shoji Tsujimoto (Jap)	Kanazawa (Jap)
Mar 12,	1977	Jose Pipino Cuevas w ko 2 Miguel Campanino (Arg)	Mexico City (Mex)
Aug 6,	1977	Jose Pipino Cuevas w ko 2 Clyde Gray	Los Angeles, CA
Nov 19,	1977	Jose Pipino Cuevas w rsf 11 Angel Espada	San Juan, CA
Mar 4,	1978	Jose Pipino Cuevas w rsf 9 Harold Weston (US)	Los Angeles, CA
May 20,	1978	Jose Pipino Cuevas w rsf 1 Billy Backus	Los Angeles, CA
Sep 9,	1978	Jose Pipino Cuevas w rsf 2 Pete Ranzany (US)	Sacramento, CA
Jan 29,	1979	Jose Pipino Cuevas w rsf 2 Scott Clark (US)	Los Angeles, CA
Jul 30,	1979	Jose Pipino Cuevas w pts 15 Randy Shields (US)	Chicago, IL
Dec 8,	1979	Jose Pipino Cuevas w rsf 10 Angel Espada	Los Angeles, CA
Apr 6,	1980	Jose Pipino Cuevas w ko 5 Harold Volbrecht (SA)	Houston, TX
Aug 2,	1980	**Thomas Hearns** w rsf 2 Jose Pipino Cuevas	Detroit, MI

Dec 6,	1980	Thomas Hearns w ko 6 Luis Primera (Ven)	Detroit, MI
Apr 25,	1981	Thomas Hearns w rsf 12 Randy Shields	Phoenix, AZ
Jun 25,	1981	Thomas Hearns w rsf 4 Pablo Baez (US)	Houston, TX
Sep 16,	1981	**Sugar Ray Leonard** w rsf 14 Thomas Hearns	Las Vegas, NV
		For undisputed title	

Undisputed title

Feb 5,	1982	**Sugar Ray Leonard** w rsf 3 Bruce Finch (US)	Reno, NV
Nov	1982	*Leonard retired as undisputed champion*	

WBA title

Feb 13,	1983	**Don Curry** (US) w pts 15 Junsok Hwang (Kor)	Fort Worth, TX
		For vacant title	
Sep 3,	1983	Don Curry w rsf 1 Roger Stafford (US)	Marsala (Ita)
Feb 4,	1984	Don Curry w pts 15 Marlon Starling (US)	Atlantic City, NJ
Apr 21,	1984	Don Curry w ret 7 Elio Diaz (Ven)	Fort Worth, TX
Sep 22,	1984	Don Curry w rsf 6 Nino LaRocca (Ita)	Monte Carlo (Mon)
Jan 19,	1985	Don Curry w rsf 4 Colin Jones (Wal)	Birmingham (Eng)
Dec 6,	1985	Don Curry w ko 2 Milton McCrory (US)	Las Vegas, NV
		For undisputed title	

WBC title

Mar 19,	1983	**Milton McCrory** drew 12 Colin Jones	Reno, NV
		For vacant title	
Aug 13,	1983	Milton McCrory w pts 12 Colin Jones	Las Vegas, NV
Jan 14,	1984	Milton McCrory w rsf 6 Milton Guest (US)	Detroit, MI
Apr 15,	1984	Milton McCrory w rsf 6 Gilles Ebilia (Fra)	Detroit, MI
Mar 9,	1985	Milton McCrory w pts 12 Pedro Villela (PR)	Paris (Fra)
Jul 14,	1985	Milton McCrory w rsf 3 Carlos Trujillo (Pan)	Monte Carlo (Mon)

PERNELL WHITAKER *(left) was the victim of a rank injustice when Julio Cesar Chavez was given a draw in their 1993 WBC title clash*

RINGSIDE VIEW

Lloyd Honeyghan
vs
Don Curry

SWEET AS HONEY

Curry was widely accepted as the world's best pound-for-pound champion until Sepember 1986 when he defended his undisputed welterweight title against Lloyd Honeyghan, who backed himself to win $25,000, and gave a stunning performance which left Curry a battered ex-champion.

Dec 6, 1985 **Don Curry** w ko 2 Milton McCrory . . . . Las Vegas, NV
For undisputed title

Undisputed title
Mar 9, 1986 **Don Curry** w ko 2 Eduardo Rodriguez (Pan) . . . . Fort Worth, TX
Sep 27, 1986 **Lloyd Honeyghan** (Eng) w ret 6 Don Curry . . . . Atlantic City, NJ
Dec 1986 *Honeyghan relinquished the WBA title rather than defend against the official challenger, Harold Volbrecht of South Africa. He continued to be recognized by the WBC and the IBF*

WBC/IBF titles
Feb 22, 1987 **Lloyd Honeyghan** w rsf 2 Johnny Bumphus (US) . . . . Wembley (Eng)
Apr 18, 1987 Lloyd Honeyghan w pts 12 Maurice Blocker (US) . . . . London (Eng)
Aug 30, 1987 Lloyd Honeyghan w rsf 1 Gene Hatcher (US) . . . . Marbella (Sp)
Oct 28, 1987 **Jorge Vaca** (Mex) w tech dec 8 Lloyd Honeyghan . . . . Wembley (Eng)
The IBF withdrew recognition from Vaca as the bout had been scheduled for 12 rounds rather than their championship distance, which was still 15 rounds

WBA title
Feb 6, 1987 **Mark Breland** (US) w ko 7 Harold Volbrecht . . . . Atlantic City, NJ
For vacant title
Aug 22, 1987 **Marlon Starling** (US) w ko 11 Mark Breland . . . . Columbia, SC
Feb 5, 1988 Marlon Starling w pts 12 Fujio Ozaki (Jap) . . . . Atlantic City, NJ
Apr 16, 1988 Marlon Starling drew 12 Mark Breland . . . . Las Vegas, NV
Jul 29, 1988 **Thomas Molinares** (Col) w ko 6 Marlon Starling . . . . Atlantic City, NJ
Jan 1989 *Molinares was stripped of the title because of his inability to make the weight*
Feb 5, 1989 **Mark Breland** w rsf 1 Seung-Soon Lee (Kor) . . . . Las Vegas, NV
For vacant title
Apr 22, 1989 Mark Breland w rsf 5 Rafael Pineda (Col) . . . . Atlantic City, NJ
Oct 13, 1989 Mark Breland w rsf 2 Mauro Martelli (Swi) . . . . Geneva (Swi)
Dec 10, 1989 Mark Breland w rsf 4 Fujio Ozaki . . . . Tokyo (Jap)
Mar 3, 1990 Mark Breland w rsf 3 Lloyd Honeyghan . . . . Wembley (Eng)
Jul 8, 1990 **Aaron Davis** w ko 9 Mark Breland . . . . Reno, NV
Jan 19, 1991 **Meldrick Taylor** (US) w pts 12 Aaron Davis . . . . Atlantic City, NJ
Jun 1, 1991 Meldrick Taylor w pts 12 Luis Garcia (Ven) . . . . Palm Springs, CA
Jan 18, 1992 Meldrick Taylor w pts 12 Glenwood Brown (US) . . . . Atlantic City, NJ
Oct 31, 1992 **Crisanto Espana** (Ven) w rsf 8 Meldrick Taylor . . . . London (Eng)
May 5, 1993 Crisanto Espana w pts 12 Rodolfo Aguilar (Pan) . . . . Belfast (N. Ire)
Oct 9, 1993 Crisanto Espana w rsf 10 Donovan Boucher (Can) . . . . . Manchester (Eng)
Jun 4, 1994 **Ike Quartey** (Gha) w rsf 11 Crisanto Espana . . Levallois Perret, Paris (Fra)
Oct 1, 1994 Ike Quartey w ko 5 Alberto Cortes (Arg) . . . . Carpentras (Fra)
Mar 4, 1995 Ike Quartey w rsf 4 Jung-Oh Park (Kor) . . . . Atlantic City, NJ
Aug 23, 1995 Ike Quartey w rsf 4 Andrew Murray (Guy) . . . . Le Cannet (Fra)

WBC title
Mar 29, 1988 **Lloyd Honeyghan** w ko 3 Jorge Vaca . . . . Wembley (Eng)
Jul 29, 1988 Lloyd Honeyghan w ret 5 Yung-Kil Chang (Kor) . . . . Atlantic City, NJ
Feb 5, 1989 **Marlon Starling** w rsf 9 Lloyd Honeyghan . . . . Las Vegas, NV
Aug 15, 1989 Marlon Starling w pts 12 Yung-Kil Chung (Kor) . . . . Hartford, CT
Aug 19, 1990 **Maurice Blocker** w pts 12 Marlon Starling . . . . Reno, NV
Mar 18, 1991 Simon Brown (Jam) w rsf 10 Maurice Blocker . . . . Las Vegas, NV
Nov 29, 1991 **James "Buddy" McGirt** (US) w pts 12 Simon Brown . . . . . Las Vegas, NV

Jun 25, 1992 James "Buddy" McGirt w pts 12 Patrizio Oliva (Ita) . . . . Naples (Ita)
Jan 12, 1993 James "Buddy" McGirt w pts 12 Genaro Leon (Mex) . . . . . . New York, NY
Mar 6, 1993 **Pernell Whitaker** (US) w pts 12 James "Buddy" McGirt . . . New York, NY
Sep 10, 1993 Pernell Whitaker drew 12 Julio Cesar Chavez (Mex) . . . . . San Antonio, TX
Apr 9, 1994 Pernell Whitaker w pts 12 Santos Cardona (PR) . . . . Norfolk, VA
Oct 1, 1994 Pernell Whitaker w pts 12 James "Buddy" McGirt . . . . Norfolk, VA
Aug 26, 1995 Pernell Whitaker w pts 12 Gary Jacobs (Sco) . . . . Atlantic City, NJ
Nov 17, 1995 Pernell Whitaker w ko 6 Jake Rodriguez (US) . . . . Atlantic City, NJ

IBF title
Apr 23, 1988 **Simon Brown** (Jam) w rsf 14 Tyrone Trice (US) . . . . . Berck-sur-Mer (Fra)
For vacant title
Jul 16, 1988 Simon Brown w rsf 3 Jorge Vaca . . . . Kingston (Jam)
Oct 14, 1988 Simon Brown w pts 12 Mauro Martelli . . . . Lausanne (Swi)
Feb 18, 1989 Simon Brown w rsf 3 Jorge Maysonet (PR) . . . . Budapest (Hun)
Apr 27, 1989 Simon Brown w ko 7 Al Long (US) . . . . Washington, DC
Sep 20, 1989 Simon Brown w rsf 2 Bobby Joe Young (US) . . . . Rochester, NY
Nov 9, 1989 Simon Brown w pts 12 Luis Santana (DR) . . . . Springfield, MA
Apr 1, 1990 Simon Brown w rsf 10 Tyrone Trice . . . . Washington, DC
Mar 1991 *Brown relinquished the IBF title to challenge for the WBC version*
Oct 4, 1991 **Maurice Blocker** w pts 12 Glenwood Brown (US) . . . . Atlantic City, NJ
For vacant title
Aug 28, 1992 Maurice Blocker w pts 12 Luis Garcia (Ven) . . . . Atlantic City, NJ
Jun 19, 1993 **Felix Trinidad** (PR) w ko 2 Maurice Blocker . . . . San Diego, CA
Aug 6, 1993 Felix Trinidad w rsf 1 Luis Garcia . . . . Bayamon (PR)
Oct 23, 1993 Felix Trinidad w ko 10 Anthony Stephens (US) . . . . Fort Lauderdale, FL
Jan 20, 1994 Felix Trinidad w pts 12 Hector Camacho (PR) . . . . Las Vegas, NV
Sep 17, 1994 Felix Trinidad w rsf 4 Yori Boy Campas (Mex) . . . . Las Vegas, NV
Dec 10, 1994 Felix Trinidad w rsf 8 Oba Carr (US) . . . . Monterrey (Mex)
Apr 8, 1995 Felix Trinidad w rsf 2 Roger Turner (US) . . . . Las Vegas, NV
Nov 17, 1995 Felix Trinidad w ko 4 Larry Barnes (US) . . . . Atlantic City, NJ

WBO title
May 8, 1989 **Genaro Leon** (Mex) w ko 1 Danny Garcia (PR) . . . . Santa Ana
For vacant title
Oct 1989 *Leon gave up the WBO title*
Dec 15, 1989 **Manning Galloway** (US) w pts 12 Al Hamza (US) . . . . Yabucoa
For vacant title
Aug 25, 1990 Manning Galloway w pts 12 Nike Khumalo (SA) . . . . Lewiston, MT
Feb 15, 1991 Manning Galloway w ret 8 Gert Bo Jacobsen (Den) . . . . . . Randers (Den)
May 17, 1991 Manning Galloway w ret 7 Racheed Lawal (Den) . . . . . . Copenhagen (Den)
Sep 15, 1991 Manning Galloway w pts 12 Jeff Malcolm (Aus) . . . . Broadbeach
Dec 14, 1991 Manning Galloway w pts 12 Nike Khumalo . . . . Cape Town (SA)
Jul 25, 1992 Manning Galloway w pts 12 Pat Barrett (Eng) . . . . Manchester (Eng)
Nov 27, 1992 Manning Galloway no contest 1 Gert Bo Jacobsen . . . . . . Randers (Den)
Feb 12, 1993 **Gert Bo Jacobsen** w pts 12 Manning Galloway . . . . Randers (Den)
Oct 1993 *Jacobsen relinquished the title*
Oct 16, 1993 **Eamonn Loughran** (Ire) w pts 12 Lorenzo Smith (US) . . . . . . Belfast (Ire)
For vacant title
Jan 22, 1994 Eamonn Loughran w pts 12 Alessandro Duran (Ita) . . . . Belfast (Ire)
Dec 10, 1994 Eamonn Loughran w tech dec 5 Manning Galloway . . . . Manchester (Eng)
May 27, 1995 Eamonn Loughran no contest 3 Angel Beltre (DR) . . . . Belfast (Ire)
Aug 26, 1995 Eamonn Loughran w rsf 6 Tony Ganarelli (US) . . . . Belfast (Ire)
Oct 7, 1995 Eamonn Loughran w pts 12 Angel Beltre . . . . Belfast (Ire)

RINGSIDE VIEW

Crisanto Espana
vs
Meldrick Taylor

ONE FIGHT TOO MANY

Meldrick Taylor had been a fine champion at light-welterweight and welterweight, but the tank was almost empty by the time he defended his WBA title against Crisanto Espana in London on October 31, 1992. The long-armed Venezuelan, based in Belfast, was far too young and fresh for the American, who was coming off a stoppage loss to Terry Norris for the light-middleweight title, and it was a relief when the referee rescued Taylor in the eighth round.

Light-Welterweight

The light-welterweight or "junior welterweight" class had an uncertain beginning when its first champion, Pinkey Mitchell, was elected to the title by the readers of a weekly boxing magazine called the *Boxing Blade*, which was published in Minneapolis. Since the owner of *Boxing Blade*, Mike Collins, was also Mitchell's manager the outcome of the poll astonished nobody. Mitchell lost his title at the first defence and subsequently won only three of his remaining 35 fights.

Controversy dogged the new division, weight limit 140 lb. The New York Commission withdrew recognition in 1930, and the British Board would not even accept their own Jack "Kid" Berg as world champion when he beat Mushy Callahan at the Albert Hall in 1930. The category fell out of favour in 1935 when champion Barney Ross opted to defend his welter-weight title instead, and there were sporadic unsuccessful efforts to revive it before Carlos Ortiz, a fine boxer from Puerto Rico, at last got it up and running in 1959. At first the weight was accepted only by the NBA and their successors, the WBA, but the WBC set up their own champion in 1968.

World Light-Welterweight Championship Bouts

Sep 21, 1926	**Mushy Callahan** (US) w pts 10 Pinkey Mitchell (US)	. . .Vernon, California
	For NBA title	
Jan 22, 1926	Mushy Callahan w ko 2 Charlie Pitts (Aus)	Los Angeles, CA
Mar 14, 1927	Mushy Callahan w ko 2 Andy Divodi	New York, NY
	For NBA and New York recognition	
May 31, 1927	Mushy Callahan w pts 10 Spug Myers (US)	Chicago, IL
May 28, 1929	Mushy Callahan w ko 3 Fred Mahan (US)	Los Angeles, CA
Jan 1, 1930	*The New York Commission decided not to recognize the so-called "junior" weight classes*	
Jan 30, 1930	*The NBA withdrew recognition from Callahan after he had signed to defend the title in London*	
Feb 18, 1930	**Jack "Kid" Berg** (Eng) w ret 10 Mushy Callahan	London (Eng)
Apr 4, 1930	Jack "Kid" Berg w pts 10 Joe Glick (US)	New York, NY
May 29, 1930	Jack "Kid" Berg w rsf 4 Al Delmont (US)	Newark, NJ
Jun 12, 1930	Jack "Kid" Berg w pts 10 Herman Perlick (US)	New York, NY
Aug 7, 1930	Jack "Kid" Berg w pts 10 Kid Chocolate (Cub)	New York, NY
Sep 3, 1930	Jack "Kid" Berg w pts 10 Buster Brown (US)	Newark, NJ
Sep 18, 1930	Jack "Kid" Berg w pts 10 Joe Glick	Long Island, NY
Oct 10, 1930	Jack "Kid" Berg w pts 10 Billy Petrolle (US)	New York, NY
Jan 23, 1931	Jack "Kid" Berg w pts 10 Goldie Hess (US)	Chicago, IL
	(Berg won NBA recognition as champion)	
Jan 30, 1931	Jack "Kid" Berg w pts 10 Herman Perlick	New York, NY
Apr 10, 1931	Jack "Kid" Berg w pts 10 Billy Wallace (US)	Detroit, MI
Apr 24, 1931	**Tony Canzoneri** w ko 3 Jack "Kid" Berg	Chicago, IL
	Billed as a lightweight title defence by Canzoneri, but as both were within the light-welterweight limit that title was automatically at stake. Berg refused to accept this, and continued to bill himself as world champion even though only Ring magazine supported his claim	
Jun 25, 1931	Tony Canzoneri w pts 10 Herman Perlick	New Haven, CT
Jul 13, 1931	Tony Canzoneri w pts 10 Cecil Payne (US)	Los Angeles, CA
Sep 10, 1931	Tony Canzoneri w pts 15 Jack "Kid" Berg	New York, NY
	Billed as lightweight title defence	
Oct 29, 1931	Tony Canzoneri w pts 10 Phillie Griffin (US)	Newark, NJ
Nov 20, 1931	Tony Canzoneri w pts 15 Kid Chocolate (Cub)	New York, NY
	Billed as lightweight title defence	
Jan 18, 1932	**Johnny Jadick** (US) w pts 10 Tony Canzoneri	Philadelphia, PA
Jul 18, 1932	Johnny Jadick (US) w pts 10 Tony Canzoneri	Philadelphia, PA
Sep 20, 1932	*The NBA withdrew recognition from the division*	
Feb 20, 1933	**Battling Shaw** (Mex) w pts 10 Johnny Jadick	New Orleans, LA
May 21, 1933	**Tony Canzoneri** w pts 10 Battling Shaw	New Orleans, LA
Jun 23, 1933	**Barney Ross** (US) w pts 10 Tony Canzoneri	Chicago, IL
	Canzoneri's lightweight title was also at stake	
Jul 26, 1933	Barney Ross w rsf 6 Johnny Farr (US)	Kansas City, KS
Sep 12, 1933	Barney Ross w pts 15 Tony Canzoneri	New York, NY
	Billed as lightweight title defence	
Nov 17, 1933	Barney Ross w pts 10 Sammy Fuller	Chicago, IL
Feb 7, 1934	Barney Ross w pts 12 Pete Nebo (US)	Kansas City, KS
Mar 5, 1934	Barney Ross drew 10 Frankie Klick	San Francisco, CA
Mar 27, 1934	Barney Ross w pts 10 Bobby Pacho (US)	Los Angeles, CA
Dec 10, 1934	Barney Ross w pts 12 Bobby Pacho	Cleveland, OH
Jan 28, 1935	Barney Ross w pts Frankie Klick	Miami, FL
Apr 9, 1935	Barney Ross w pts 12 Harry Woods (US)	Seattle, WA
Jun 1935	*Ross relinquished the title on regaining the welterweight championship*	
Jul 5, 1939	**Maxie Berger** (Can) w pts 10 Wes Ramey (US)	Montreal (Can)
	Recognized in Canada as being for the vacant title, which Berger never defended	
Oct 28, 1940	**Harry Weekly** (US) w pts 15 Jerome Conforto (US)	New Orleans, LA
	Recognized by the Louisiana Commission as a title fight	
Jun 27, 1941	Harry Weekly w pts 10 Carmelo Fenoy (US)	Birmingham, AL
Jul 28, 1941	Harry Weekly w pts 15 Baby Breese (US)	New Orleans, LA
Oct 20, 1941	Harry Weekly w ko 5 Ervin Berlier (US)	New Orleans, LA
	The title fell into disuse when Weekly joined the Army, and was not contested again until the Massachusetts Commission approved the first Tippy Larkin v Willie Joyce fight. The New York Commission agreed to recognize their second fight as involving the world title	
Apr 29, 1946	**Tippy Larkin** w pts 12 Willie Joyce	Boston, MA
Sep 13, 1946	Tippy Larkin w pts 12 Willie Joyce	New York, NY
Jun 1947	*The New York and Massachusetts Commissions withdrew recognition from Larkin after his fourth-round knockout by lightweight champion Ike Williams, and the title was not revived again until 1959*	
Jun 12, 1959	**Carlos Ortiz** (PR) w ret 2 Kenny Lane (US)	New York, NY

RINGSIDE VIEW

Jack "Kid" Berg vs Mushy Callahan

LONDON PRIDE

The busy championship career of London's Jack "Kid" Berg, began at the Albert Hall, London, on February 18, 1930, with this 10th round win over Mushy Callahan of America. He went on to defend the title 12 times in 14 months, and his buzzsaw fighting style made him a big favourite in American rings.

Feb 4, 1960	Carlos Ortiz w ko 10 Battling Torres (Mex) . . . . Los Angeles, CA
Jun 15, 1960	Carlos Ortiz w pts 15 Duilio Loi (Ita) . . . . San Francisco, CA
Sep 1, 1960	**Duilio Loi** w pts 15 Carlos Ortiz . . . . Milan (Ita)
May 10, 1961	Duilio Loi w pts 15 Carlos Ortiz . . . . Milan (Ita)
Oct 21, 1961	Duilio Loi drew 15 Eddie Perkins (US) . . . . Milan (Ita)
Sep 14, 1962	**Eddie Perkins** w pts 15 Duilio Loi . . . . Milan (Ita)
Dec 15, 1962	**Duilio Loi** w pts 15 Eddie Perkins . . . . Milan (Ita)
	Loi announced retirement in January, 1963
Mar 21, 1963	**Roberto Cruz** (Phil) w ko 1 Battling Torres . . . . Los Angeles, CA
	For vacant title
Jun 15, 1963	**Eddie Perkins** w pts 15 Roberto Cruz . . . . Manila (Phil)
Jan 4, 1964	Eddie Perkins w rsf 13 Yoshinori Takahashi (Jap) . . . . Tokyo (Jap)
Apr 18, 1964	Eddie Perkins w pts 15 Bunny Grant (Jam) . . . . Kingston (Jam)
Jan 18, 1965	**Carlos Hernandez** (Ven) w pts 15 Eddie Perkins . . . . Caracas (Ven)
May 15, 1965	Carlos Hernandez w rsf 4 Mario Rossito (Col) . . . . Maracaibo (Ven)
Jul 10, 1965	Carlos Hernandez w ko 3 Percy Hayles (Jam) . . . . Kingston (Jam)
Apr 29, 1966	**Sandro Lopopolo** (Ita) w pts 15 Carlos Hernandez . . . . Rome (Ita)
Oct 21, 1966	Sandro Lopopolo w rsf 7 Vicente Rivas (Ven) . . . . Rome (Ita)
Apr 30, 1967	**Paul Fuji** (US) w ret 2 Sandro Lopopolo . . . . Tokyo (Jap)
Nov 16, 1967	Paul Fuji w ko 4 Willi Quator (Ger) . . . . Tokyo (Jap)
	The WBC stripped Fuji of title for failure to defend against the No. 1 challenger Pedro Adigue, and set up their own version of the title. The WBA continued to recognize Fuji as the champion

WBA title

Dec 12, 1968	**Nicolino Loche** (Arg) w ret 9 Paul Fuji . . . . Tokyo (Jap)
May 3, 1969	Nicolino Loche w pts 15 Carlos Hernandez . . . . Buenos Aires (Arg)
Oct 11, 1969	Nicolino Loche w pts 15 Joao Henrique (Bra) . . . . Buenos Aires (Arg)
May 16, 1970	Nicolino Loche w pts 15 Adolph Pruitt (US) . . . . Buenos Aires (Arg)
Apr 3, 1971	Nicolino Loche w pts 15 Domingo Barrera (Sp) . . . . . . Buenos Aires (Arg)
Dec 11, 1971	Nicolino Loche w pts 15 Antonio Cervantes (Col) . . . . . Buenos Aires (Arg)
Mar 10, 1972	**Alfonso Frazer** (Pan) w pts 15 Nicolino Loche . . . . Panama City (Pan)
Jun 17, 1972	Alfonso Frazer w ret 4 Al Ford (Can) . . . . Panama City (Pan)
Oct 28, 1972	**Antonio Cervantes** w ko 10 Alfonso Frazer . . . . Panama City (Pan)
Feb 16, 1973	Antonio Cervantes w pts 15 Josua Marquez (PR) . . . . San Juan, CA
Mar 17, 1973	Antonio Cervantes w ret 9 Nicolino Loche . . . . Maracay (Ven)
May 19, 1973	Antonio Cervantes w rsf 5 Alfonso Frazer . . . . Panama City (Pan)
Sep 8, 1973	Antonio Cervantes w rsf 5 Carlos Giminez (Arg) . . . . Bogota (Col)
Dec 4, 1973	Antonio Cervantes w pts 15 Lion Furuyama (Jap) . . . . . Panama City (Pan)
Mar 2, 1974	Antonio Cervantes w ko 6 Chang-Kil Lee (Kor) . . . . Cartagena (Col)
Jul 27, 1974	Antonio Cervantes w ko 2 Victor Ortiz (PR) . . . . Cartagena (Col)
Oct 26, 1974	Antonio Cervantes w ko 8 Shinchi Kadota (Jap) . . . . Tokyo (Jap)
May 17, 1975	Antonio Cervantes w pts 15 Esteban De Jesus (PR) . . . Panama City (Pan)
Nov 15, 1975	Antonio Cervantes w ret 7 Hector Thompson (Aus) . . . . Panama City (Pan)
Mar 6, 1976	**Wilfredo Benitez** (PR) w pts 15 Antonio Cervantes . . . . San Juan, CA
May 31, 1976	Wilfredo Benitez w pts 15 Emiliano Villa (Col) . . . . San Juan, CA
Oct 16, 1976	Wilfredo Benitez w rsf 3 Tony Petronelli (US) . . . . San Juan, CA
Dec 1976	*WBA stripped Benitez for failing to defend against Antonio Cervantes*
Jun 25, 1977	**Antonio Cervantes** w rsf 5 Carlos Gimenez . . . . Maracaibo (Ven)
	For vacant title
Nov 5, 1977	Antonio Cervantes w pts 15 Adriano Marrero (DR) . . . . Maracay (Ven)
Apr 28, 1978	Antonio Cervantes w ko 6 Tonga Kiatvayupakdi (Thai) . . . . Udon (Thai)
Aug 26, 1978	Antonio Cervantes w rsf 9 Norman Sekgapane (SA) . . . . . Mabatho (Bots)
Jan 18, 1979	Antonio Cervantes w pts 15 Miguel Montilla (DR) . . . . New York, NY
Aug 25, 1979	Antonio Cervantes w pts 15 Kwang-Min Kim (Kor) . . . . Seoul (Kor)
Mar 29, 1980	Antonio Cervantes w rsf 7 Miguel Montilla . . . . Cartagena (Col)
Aug 2, 1980	**Aaron Pryor** (US) w ko 4 Antonio Cervantes . . . . Cincinnati, OH
Nov 22, 1980	Aaron Pryor w rsf 6 Gaetan Hart (Can) . . . . Cincinnati, OH
Jun 27, 1981	Aaron Pryor w rsf 2 Lennox Blackmoore (Guy) . . . . Las Vegas, NV
Nov 14, 1981	Aaron Pryor w rsf 7 Dujuan Johnson (US) . . . . Cleveland, OH
Mar 21, 1982	Aaron Pryor w rsf 12 Miguel Montilla . . . . Atlantic City, NJ
Jul 4, 1982	Aaron Pryor w rsf 6 Akio Kameda (Jap) . . . . Cincinnati, OH
Nov 12, 1982	Aaron Pryor w rsf 14 Alexis Arguello (Nic) . . . . Miami, FL
Apr 2, 1983	Aaron Pryor w rsf 3 Kim Sang Hyun (Kor) . . . . Atlantic City, NJ
Sep 9, 1983	Aaron Pryor w ko 10 Alexis Arguello . . . . Las Vegas, NV
	Pryor gave up the WBA title and was proclaimed champion by the IBF
Jan 22, 1984	**Johnny Bumphus** (US) w pts.15 Lorenzo Garcia (Arg . . . . .Atlantic City, NJ
	For vacant title
Jun 1, 1984	**Gene Hatcher** (US) w rsf 11 Johnny Bumphus . . . . Buffalo, NY
Dec 15, 1984	Gene Hatcher w pts 15 Ubaldo Sacco (Arg) . . . . Fort Worth, TX
Jul 21, 1985	**Ubaldo Sacco** w rsf 9 Gene Hatcher . . . . Campione (Ita)
Mar 15, 1986	**Patrizio Oliva** (Ita) w pts 15 Ubaldo Sacco . . . . Monte Carlo (Mon)
Sep 6, 1986	Patrizio Oliva w rsf 3 Brian Brunette (US) . . . . Naples (Ita)
Jan 10, 1987	Patrizio Oliva w pts 15 Rodolfo Gonzalez (Mex) . . . . Agrigento (Ita)
Jul 4, 1987	**Juan Martin Coggi** (Arg) w ko 3 Patrizio Oliva . . . . Ribera (Sp)
May 7, 1988	Juan Martin Coggi w ko 2 Sang-Ho Lee (Kor) . . . . Roseto (Ita)
Jan 21, 1989	Juan Martin Coggi w pts 12 Harold Brazier (US) . . . . Vasto (Ita)
Apr 29, 1989	Juan Martin Coggi w pts 12 Akinobu Hiranaka (Jap) . . . . Vasto (Ita)
Mar 24, 1990	Juan Martin Coggi w pts 12 Jose Luis Ramirez (Mex) . . . . . Arjaccio (Arg)
Aug 17, 1990	**Loreto Garza** (US) w pts 12 Juan Martin Coggi . . . . Nice (Fra)
Dec 1, 1990	Loreto Garza w dis 11 Vinny Pazienza (US) . . . . Sacramento, CA
Jun 14, 1991	**Edwin Rosario** (PR) w rsf 3 Loreto Garza . . . . Sacramento, CA
Apr 10, 1992	**Akinobu Hiranaka** (Jap) w rsf 1 Edwin Rosario . . . . Mexico City (Mex)
Sep 9, 1992	**Morris East** (Phil) w rsf 11 Akinobu Hiranaka . . . . Tokyo (Jap)
Jan 13, 1993	**Juan M. Coggi** w rsf 8 Morris East . . . . Mar del Plata (Arg)
Apr 10, 1993	Juan Martin Coggi w rsf 7 Jose Rivera (PR) . . . . Mar del Plata (Arg)
Jun 23, 1993	Juan Martin Coggi w ko 5 Hiroyuki Yoshino (Jap) . . . . Tokyo (Jap)
Aug 13, 1993	Juan Martin Coggi w pts 12 Jose Barboza (Ven) . . . . . Buenos Aires (Arg)
Sep 24, 1993	Juan Martin Coggi w rsf 10 Guillermo Cruz (Mex) . . . . Tucuman (Arg)
Dec 17, 1993	Juan Martin Coggi w rsf 7 Eder Gonzalez (Col) . . . . Tucuman (Arg)
Mar 18, 1994	Juan Martin Coggi w rsf 3 Eder Gonzalez . . . . Las Vegas, NV
Sep 17, 1994	**Frankie Randall** w pts 12 Juan Martin Coggi . . . . Las Vegas, NV
Dec 10, 1994	Frankie Randall w rsf 7 Rodney Moore (US) . . . . Monterrey (Mex)
Jun 16, 1995	Frankie Randall w pts 12 Jose Barboza . . . . Lyon (Fra)

New York title

The New York Commission continued to regard Benitez as champion until he announced in August 1977 that he could no longer make the weight

Aug 3, 1977	**Wilfredo Benitez** w rsf 15 Guerrero Chavez (Can) . . . . New York, NY

WBC title

Dec 14, 1968	**Pedro Adigue** (Phil) w pts 15 Adolph Pruitt . . . . Manila (Phil)
	For vacant title
Jan 31, 1970	**Bruno Arcari** (Ita) w pts 15 Pedro Adigue . . . . Rome (Ita)
Jul 10, 1970	Bruno Arcari w dis 6 Rene Roque (Fra) . . . . Lignano (Ita)
Oct 30, 1970	Bruno Arcari w ko 3 Raimundo Dias (Bra) . . . . Genoa (Ita)
Mar 6, 1971	Bruno Arcari w pts 15 Joao Henrique . . . . Rome (Ita)
Jun 26, 1971	Bruno Arcari w rsf 9 Enrique Jana (Arg) . . . . Palermo (Ita)
Oct 10, 1971	Bruno Arcari w ko 10 Domingo Barrera . . . . Genoa (Ita)
Jun 10, 1972	Bruno Arcari w ko 12 Joao Henrique . . . . Genoa (Ita)
Dec 2, 1972	Bruno Arcari w pts 15 Everaldo Costa Azevedo (Bra) . . . . Turin (Ita)
Feb 16, 1974	Bruno Arcari w dis 8 Tony Ortiz (Sp) . . . . Turin (Ita)
Aug 1974	*Arcari relinquished the title because of weight problems*
Sep 21, 1974	**Perico Fernandez** (Sp) w pts 15 Lion Furuyama . . . . Rome (Ita)
	For vacant title
Apr 19, 1975	Perico Fernandez w ko 9 Joao Henrique . . . . Barcelona (Sp)
Jul 15, 1975	**Saensak Muangsurin** (Thai) w ret 8 Perico Fernandez . . . . Bangkok (Thai)
Jan 25, 1976	Saensak Muangsurin w pts 15 Lion Furuyama . . . . Tokyo (Jap)
Jun 30, 1976	**Miguel Velasquez** (Sp) w dis 4 Saensak Muangsurin . . . . Madrid (Sp)
Oct 29, 1976	**Saensak Muangsurin** w rsf 2 Miguel Velasquez . . . . Segovia (Sp)
Jan 5, 1977	Saensak Muangsurin w rsf 15 Monroe Brooks (US) . . . . Chiang (Thai)
Apr 2, 1977	Saensak Muangsurin w ko 6 Guts Ishimatsu (Jap) . . . . Tokyo (Jap)
Jun 17, 1977	Saensak Muangsurin w pts 15 Perico Fernandez . . . . Madrid (Sp)
Aug 20, 1977	Saensak Muangsurin w rsf 6 Mike Everett (US) . . . . Roi-Et (Thai)
Oct 22, 1977	Saensak Muangsurin w pts 15 Saoul Mamby (US) . . . . Korat (Thai)
Dec 29, 1977	Saensak Muangsurin w ret 13 Jo Kimpuani (Zai) . . . . . Chanthabun (Thai)
Apr 8, 1977	Saensak Muangsurin w ko 13 Francisco Moreno (Ven) . . . . . Hat Yai (Thai)
Dec 30, 1978	**Kim Sang Hyun** w rsf 13 Saensak Muangsurin . . . . Seoul (Kor)
Jun 3, 1979	Kim Sang Hyun w pts 15 Fitzroy Guiseppe (Tr) . . . . Seoul (Kor)
Oct 4, 1979	Kim Sang Hyun w ko 11 Masahiro Yokai (Jap) . . . . Tokyo (Jap)
Feb 23, 1980	**Saoul Mamby** w ko 14 Kim Sang Hyun . . . . Seoul (Kor)
Jul 7, 1980	Saoul Mamby w rsf 13 Esteban De Jesus . . . . Bloomington, MN
Oct 2, 1980	Saoul Mamby w pts 15 Maurice "Termite" Watkins (US) . . . Las Vegas, NV
Jun 12, 1981	Saoul Mamby w pts 15 Jo Kimpuani . . . . Detroit, MI
Aug 29, 1981	Saoul Mamby w pts 15 Thomas Americo (Indo) . . . . Jakarta (Indo)
Dec 20, 1981	Saoul Mamby w pts 15 Obisia Nwankpa (Nig) . . . . Lagos (Nig)
Jun 26, 1982	**Leroy Haley** (US) w pts 15 Saoul Mamby . . . . Cleveland, OH
Oct 20, 1982	Leroy Haley w pts 15 Juan Jose Giminez (Arg) . . . . Cleveland, OH
Feb 13, 1983	Leroy Haley w pts 15 Saoul Mamby . . . . Cleveland, OH
May 18, 1983	**Bruce Curry** (US) w pts 12 Leroy Haley . . . . Las Vegas, NV
Jul 7, 1983	Bruce Curry w rsf 7 Hidekazu Akai (Jap) . . . . Osaka (Jap)
Oct 19, 1983	Bruce Curry w pts 12 Leroy Haley . . . . Las Vegas, NV
Jan 29, 1984	**Bill Costello** (US) w rsf 10 Bruce Curry . . . . Beaumont, TX
Jul 15, 1984	Bill Costello w pts 12 Ronnie Shields (US) . . . . Kingston, NY
Nov 3, 1984	Bill Costello w pts 12 Saoul Mamby . . . . Kingston, NY
Feb 16, 1985	Bill Costello w pts 12 Leroy Haley . . . . Kingston, NY
Aug 21, 1985	**Lonnie Smith** (US) w rsf 8 Bill Costello . . . . New York, NY
May 5, 1986	**Rene Arredondo** (Mex) w rsf 5 Lonnie Smith . . . . Los Angeles, CA
Jul 24, 1986	**Tsuyoshi Hamada** (Jap) w ko 1 Rene Arredondo . . . . Tokyo (Jap)
Dec 2, 1986	Tsuyoshi Hamada w pts 12 Ronnie Shields . . . . Tokyo (Jap)
Jul 22, 1987	**Rene Arredondo** w rsf 6 Tsuyoshi Hamada . . . . Tokyo (Jap)

Nov 12, 1987	**Roger Mayweather** (US) w rsf 6 Rene Arredondo	Los Angeles, CA
Mar 24, 1988	Roger Mayweather w ko 3 Maurico Aceves (Mex)	Los Angeles, CA
Jun 6, 1988	Roger Mayweather w pts 12 Harold Brazier	Las Vegas, NV
Sep 22, 1988	Roger Mayweather w rsf 12 Rodolfo Gonzalez (Mex)	Los Angeles, CA
Nov 7, 1988	Roger Mayweather w pts 12 Vinny Pazienza	Las Vegas, NV
May 13, 1989	**Julio Cesar Chavez** (Mex) w ret 10 Roger Mayweather	Los Angeles, CA
Nov 18, 1989	Julio Cesar Chavez w rsf 10 Sammy Fuentes (PR)	Las Vegas, NV
Dec 16, 1989	Julio Cesar Chavez w ko 3 Alberto Cortes (Arg)	Mexico City (Mex)
Mar 17, 1990	Julio Cesar Chavez w rsf 12 Meldrick Taylor (US)	Las Vegas, NV
	For WBC and IBF titles	

IBF title

Jun 22, 1984	**Aaron Pryor** w pts 15 Nicky Furlano (Can)	Toronto (Can)
Mar 2, 1985	Aaron Pryor w pts 15 Gary Hinton (US)	Atlantic City, NJ
Dec 1985	*The IBF stripped Pryor for inactivity*	
Apr 26, 1986	**Gary Hinton** w pts 15 Antonio Reyes Cruz (DR)	Lucca (Ita)
	For vacant title	
Oct 30, 1986	**Joe Manley** (US) w ko 10 Gary Hinton	Hartford, CT
Mar 4, 1987	**Terry Marsh** (Eng) w rsf 10 Joe Manley	Basildon (Eng)
Jul 1, 1987	Terry Marsh w ret 6 Akio Kameda	London (Eng)
Sep 1987	*Marsh retired*	
Feb 14, 1988	**James "Buddy" McGirt** (US) w rsf 12 Frankie Warren (US)	Corpus Christi, TX
	For vacant title	
Jul 31, 1988	James "Buddy" McGirt w ko 1 Howard Davis (US)	New York, NY
Sep 3, 1988	**Meldrick Taylor** w rsf 12 James "Buddy" McGirt	Atlantic City, NJ
Jan 21, 1989	Meldrick Taylor w rsf 7 John Meekins (US)	Atlantic City, NJ
Sep 11, 1989	Meldrick Taylor w pts 12 Courtney Hooper (US)	Atlantic City, NJ
Mar 17, 1990	**Julio Cesar Chavez** w rsf 12 Meldrick Taylor	Las Vegas, NV
	For WBC and IBF titles	

WBC/IBF titles

Dec 8, 1990	**Julio Cesar Chavez** w rsf 3 Kyung-Duk Ahn (Kor)	Atlantic City, NJ
Mar 18, 1991	Julio Cesar Chavez w rsf 4 John Duplessis (US)	Las Vegas, NV
Apr 1991	*Chavez relinquished the IBF title*	

WBC title

Sep 14, 1991	**Julio Cesar Chavez** w pts 12 Lonnie Smith	Las Vegas, NV
Apr 10, 1992	Julio Cesar Chavez w ko 5 Angel Hernandez (PR)	Mexico City (Mex)
Aug 1, 1992	Julio Cesar Chavez w rsf 4 Frankie Mitchell (US)	Las Vegas, NV
Sep 12, 1992	Julio Cesar Chavez w pts 12 Hector Camacho (PR)	Las Vegas, NV
Feb 20, 1993	Julio Cesar Chavez w rsf 5 Greg Haugen (US)	Mexico City (Mex)
May 8, 1993	Julio Cesar Chavez w rsf 6 Terrence Alli (Guy)	Las Vegas, NV
Dec 18, 1993	Julio Cesar Chavez w ret 5 Andy Holligan (Eng)	Mexico City (Mex)
Jan 29, 1994	**Frankie Randall** (US) w pts 12 Julio Cesar Chavez	Las Vegas, NV

May 7, 1994	**Julio Cesar Chavez** w tech dec 8 Frankie Randall	Las Vegas, NV
Sep 17, 1994	Julio Cesar Chavez w rsf 8 Meldrick Taylor	Las Vegas, NV
Dec 10, 1994	Julio Cesar Chavez w rsf 10 Tony Lopez (US)	Monterrey (Mex)
Apr 8, 1995	Julio Cesar Chavez w pts 12 Giovanni Parisi (Ita)	Las Vegas, NV
Sep 16, 1995	Julio Cesar Chavez w pts 12 David Kamau (Ken)	Las Vegas, NV

IBF title

Dec 7, 1991	**Rafael Pineda** (Col) w rsf 9 Roger Mayweather	Reno, NV
	For vacant title	
May 22, 1992	Rafael Pineda w rsf 7 Clarence Coleman (US)	Mexico City (Mex)
Jul 18, 1992	**Pernell Whitaker** (US) w pts 12 Rafael Pineda	Las Vegas, NV
Mar 1993	*Whitaker relinquished the title on becoming WBC welterweight champion*	
May 15, 1993	**Charles Murray** (US) w pts 12 Rodney Moore	Atlantic City, NJ
	For vacant title	
Jul 24, 1993	Charles Murray w pts 12 Juan LaPorte (PR)	Atlantic City, NJ
Nov 19, 1993	Charles Murray w ret 5 Courtney Hooper	Atlantic City, NJ
Feb 13, 1994	**Jake Rodriguez** (US) w pts 12 Charles Murray	Atlantic City, NJ
Apr 21, 1994	Jake Rodriguez w pts 12 Ray Oliveira (US)	Ledyard, CT
Aug 27, 1994	Jake Rodriguez w rsf 9 George Scott (Swe)	Bushkill
Jan 28, 1995	**Konstantin Tszyu** (Rus) w rsf 6 Jake Rodriguez	Las Vegas, NV
Jun 25, 1995	Konstantin Tszyu w pts 12 Roger Mayweather	Newcastle (Aus)

WBO title

Mar 6, 1989	**Hector Camacho** w pts 12 Ray Mancini (US)	Reno, NV
	For vacant title	
Feb 3, 1990	Hector Camacho w pts 12 Vinny Pazienza	Atlantic City, NJ
Aug 11, 1990	Hector Camacho w pts 12 Tony Baltazar (US)	Stateline, NV
Feb 23, 1991	**Greg Haugen** w pts 12 Hector Camacho	Las Vegas, NV
Mar 1991	*Haugen was stripped of the title for failing a post-fight drugs test*	
May 18, 1991	**Hector Camacho** w pts 12 Greg Haugen	Reno, NV
Mar 1992	*Camacho was stripped of the title for failure to defend it*	
Jun 30, 1992	**Carlos Gonzalez** (Mex) w rsf 2 Jimmy Paul (US)	Los Angeles, CA
	For vacant title	
Nov 9, 1992	Carlos Gonzalez w ret 6 Lorenzo Smith (US)	Los Angeles, CA
Dec 14, 1992	Carlos Gonzalez w rsf 1 Rafael Ortiz (DR)	Mexico City (Mex)
Mar 22, 1993	Carlos Gonzalez w rsf 1 Tony Baltazar	Los Angeles, CA
Jun 7, 1993	**Zack Padilla** (US) w pts 12 Carlos Gonzalez	Las Vegas, NV
Nov 19, 1993	Zack Padilla w ret 7 Efrem Calamati (Ita)	Arezzo (Ita)
Dec 16, 1993	Zack Padilla w pts 12 Ray Oliveira	Ledyard, CT
Apr 18, 1994	Zack Padilla w ret 6 Harold Miller (US)	Rotterdam (Hol)
Jul 24, 1994	Zack Padilla w ret 11 Juan LaPorte	Los Angeles, CA
	Padilla was forced to retire on medical grounds	
Feb 20, 1995	**Sammy Fuentes** w rsf 2 Fidel Avendano (Mex)	Inglewood, CA
	For vacant title	
Jun 10, 1995	Sammy Fuentes w pts 12 Hector Lopez (US)	Las Vegas, NV

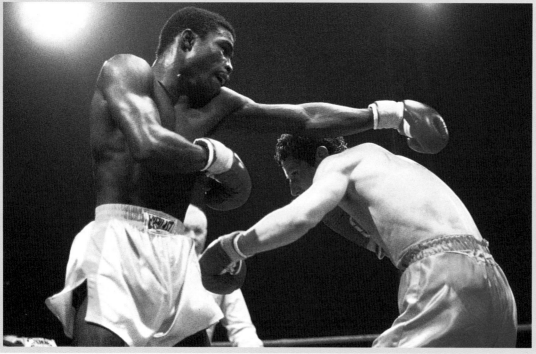

Terry Marsh
vs
Joe Manley

CALL THE FIRE BRIGADE
Promoter Frank Warren came up with an original setting for the IBF light-welterweight title fight between Terry Marsh, whom he managed, and Joe Manley of America: a marquee erected on the outskirts of Marsh's hometown, Basildon. Marsh, a full-time fireman, who went on to become the only British world champion to retire undefeated, stopped Manley in the 10th round.

Lightweight

The lightweight division had a long and colourful history under Prize Ring rules, but the scandal which surrounded the outcome of an international match between Jack McAuliffe and the English champion Jem Carney in 1887 was so great that it was nine years before the first gloved championship could be staged between American champion George Lavigne and his British counterpart Dick Burge.

The weight limit then was 133 lb in America and 134 lb in Britain, although Freddie Welsh had it increased to 135 lb in 1912 and Willie Ritchie, who was also claiming the title at the time, raised the American limit by a pound. A year later Ritchie again increased the limit to bring it into line with the British mark, at which it has remained ever since.

Racism was rampant in the division's early years, to the extent that because the black Joe Gans dominated the weight so thoroughly his rivals had to set up a "white lightweight championship", which was contested frequently during the eight years of Gans' pre-eminence. Gans was the first major figure the category produced, but his successors have included Benny Leonard, Tony Canzoneri, Barney Ross, Henry Armstrong, Joe Brown and Roberto Duran.

World Lightweight Championship Bouts

Jun 1,	1896	**George "Kid" Lavigne** (US) w ko 17 Dick Burge (Eng)	NSC, London (Eng)
Feb 8,	1897	George "Kid" Lavigne w pts 25 Kid McPartland (US)	New York, NY
Apr 30,	1897	George "Kid" Lavigne w rsf 11 Eddie Connolly (Can)	New York, NY
Sep 28,	1898	George "Kid" Lavigne drew 25 Frank Erne (US)	Coney Island, NY
Jul 3,	1899	**Frank Erne** w pts 20 George "Kid" Lavigne	Buffalo, NY
Dec 4,	1899	Frank Erne drew 25 Jack O'Brien (US)	Coney Island, NY
Mar 23,	1900	Frank Erne w ret 12 Joe Gans (US)	New York, NY
May 12,	1902	**Joe Gans** w ko 1 Frank Erne	Fort Erie (Can)
Sep 17,	1902	Joe Gans w ko 5 Gus Gardner (US)	Baltimore, MD
Oct 31,	1904	Joe Gans w dis 5 Jimmy Britt (US)	San Francisco, CA
Sep 3,	1906	Joe Gans w dis 42 Battling Nelson (Den)	Goldfield, NV
Jan 1,	1907	Joe Gans w ko 8 Kid Herman (US)	Tonopah, NV
Sep 27,	1907	Joe Gans w pts 20 George Memsic (US)	Los Angeles, CA
May 14,	1908	Joe Gans w rsf 11 Rudy Unholz (US)	San Francisco, CA
Jul 4,	1908	**Battling Nelson** w ko 17 Joe Gans	San Francisco, CA
Sep 9,	1908	Battling Nelson w ko 21 Joe Gans	San Francisco, CA
May 29,	1909	Battling Nelson w ko 23 Dick Hyland (US)	San Francisco, CA
Feb 22,	1910	**Ad Wolgast** (US) w rsf 40 Battling Nelson	Port Richmond, CA
Mar 17,	1911	Ad Wolgast w rsf 9 George Memsic (US)	Los Angeles, CA
Mar 31,	1911	Ad Wolgast w ret 5 Antonio la Grave (US)	San Francisco, CA
May 27,	1911	Ad Wolgast w ret 16 Frankie Burns (US)	San Francisco, CA
Jul 4,	1911	Ad Wolgast w ko 13 Owen Moran (Eng)	San Francisco, CA
Jul 4,	1912	Ad Wolgast w ko 13 Joe Rivers (Mex)	Los Angeles, CA
Nov 28,	1912	**Willie Ritchie** (US) w dis 16 Ad Wolgast	Daly City, CA
Jul 4,	1913	Willie Ritchie w ko 11 Joe Rivers	San Francisco, CA
Apr 17,	1914	Willie Ritchie w pts 20 Tommy Murphy (US)	San Francisco, CA
Jul 7,	1914	**Freddie Welsh** (Wal) w pts 20 Willie Ritchie	London (Eng)
Sep 4,	1916	Freddie Welsh w pts 20 Charlie White (US)	Colorado Springs, CO
May 28,	1917	**Benny Leonard** (US) w rsf 9 Freddie Welsh	New York, NY
		Leonard was recognized as champion on the basis of this result, even though Welsh was overweight and the fight, like most of Leonard's subsequent contests, was a "no decision" affair	
Nov 26,	1920	Benny Leonard w rsf 14 Joe Welling (US)	New York, NY
Oct 14,	1921	Benny Leonard w rsf 6 Richie Mitchell (US)	New York, NY
Feb 10,	1922	Benny Leonard w pts 15 Rocky Kansas (US)	New York, NY
Jan	1925	*Leonard relinquished title*	
Jul 3,	1925	**Jimmy Goodrich** (US) w rsf 2 Stanislaus Loayza (Cze)	Long Island, NY
		For vacant title	
Dec 7,	1925	**Rocky Kansas** w pts 15 Jimmy Goodrich	Buffalo, NY
Jul 3,	1926	**Sammy Mandell** (US) w pts 10 Rocky Kansas	Chicago, IL
May 21,	1928	Sammy Mandell w pts 15 Jimmy McLarnin (Ire)	New York, NY
Aug 2,	1929	Sammy Mandell w pts 10 Tony Canzoneri (US)	Chicago, IL
Jul 17,	1930	**Al Singer** (US) w ko 1 Sammy Mandell	New York, NY
Nov 14,	1930	**Tony Canzoneri** w ko 1 Al Singer	New York, NY
Apr 24,	1931	Tony Canzoneri w ko 3 Jack "Kid" Berg (Eng)	Chicago, IL
Sep 10,	1931	Tony Canzoneri w pts 15 Jack "Kid" Berg	New York, NY
Nov 20,	1931	Tony Canzoneri w pts 15 Kid Chocolate (Cub)	New York, NY
Nov 4,	1932	Tony Canzoneri w pts 15 Billy Petrolle	New York, NY
Jun 23,	1933	**Barney Ross** (US) w pts 10 Tony Canzoneri	Chicago, IL
Sep 12,	1933	Barney Ross w pts 15 Tony Canzoneri	New York, NY
Apr	1935	*Ross relinquished title*	
May 10,	1935	**Tony Canzoneri** w pts 15 Lou Ambers (US)	New York, NY
		For vacant title	
Oct 4,	1935	Tony Canzoneri w pts 15 Al Roth (US)	New York, NY
Sep 3,	1936	**Lou Ambers** w pts 15 Tony Canzoneri	New York, NY
May 7,	1937	Lou Ambers w pts 15 Tony Canzoneri	New York, NY
Sep 23,	1937	Lou Ambers w pts 15 Pedro Montanez (PR)	New York, NY
Aug 17,	1938	**Henry Armstrong** (US) w pts 15 Lou Ambers	New York, NY
Mar 16,	1939	Henry Armstrong w ko 1 Lew Feldman (US)	St Louis, MO
		Billed as a welterweight title defence by Armstrong, but both were inside the lightweight limit	
Aug 22,	1939	**Lou Ambers** w pts 15 Henry Armstrong	New York, NY
April	1940	*The NBA withdrew recognition from Ambers for his failure to defend against Davey Day*	
May 3,	1940	**Sammy Angott** (US) w pts 15 Davey Day (US)	Louisville, KY
		For vacant NBA title	
May 10,	1940	**Lew Jenkins** (US) w rsf 3 Lou Ambers	New York, NY
Nov 22,	1940	Lew Jenkins w rsf 2 Pete Lello (US)	New York, NY
Dec 19,	1941	Sammy Angott w pts 15 Lew Jenkins	New York, NY
		For undisputed title	
May 15,	1942	Sammy Angott w pts 15 Allie Stolz (US)	New York, NY
Nov	1942	*Angott retired and relinquished the title, although he changed his mind in 1943 and was installed as a challenger for the vacant NBA version of the championship*	

New York title

Dec 18,	1942	**Beau Jack** (US) w ko 3 Tippy Larkin (US)	New York, NY
		For vacant title	
May 21,	1943	**Bob Montgomery** (US) w pts 15 Beau Jack (US)	New York, NY
Nov 19,	1943	**Beau Jack** w pts 15 Bob Montgomery	New York, NY
Mar 3,	1944	**Bob Montgomery** w pts 15 Beau Jack	New York, NY
Jun 28,	1946	Bob Montgomery w ko 13 Allie Stolz	New York, NY
Nov 26,	1946	Bob Montgomery w ko 8 Wesley Mouzon (US)	Philadelphia, PA
Aug 4,	1947	**Ike Williams** (US) w ko 6 Bob Montgomery	Philadelphia, PA
		For undisputed title	

NBA title

Oct 27,	1943	**Sammy Angott** w pts 15 Slugger White (US)	Los Angeles, CA
		For vacant title	
Mar 8,	1944	**Juan Zurita** (Mex) w pts 15 Sammy Angott	Hollywood, CA
Apr 18,	1945	**Ike Williams** w ko 2 Juan Zurita	Mexico City (Mex)
Apr 30,	1946	Ike Williams w rsf 8 Enrique Bolanos (US)	Los Angeles, CA
Sep 4,	1946	Ike Williams w ko 9 Ronnie James (Wal)	Cardiff (Wal)
Aug 4,	1947	Ike Williams w ko 6 Bob Montgomery	Philadelphia, PA
		For undisputed title	

Undisputed title

May 25,	1948	**Ike Williams** w pts 15 Enrique Bolanos	Los Angeles, CA
Jul 12,	1948	Ike Williams w rsf 6 Beau Jack	Philadelphia, PA
Sep 23,	1948	Ike Williams w ko 10 Jesse Flores (US)	New York, NY
Jul 21,	1949	Ike Williams w rsf 4 Enrique Bolanos	Los Angeles, CA
Dec 5,	1949	Ike Williams w pts 15 Freddie Dawson (US)	Philadelphia, PA
May 25,	1951	**Jimmy Carter** (US) w rsf 14 Ike Williams	New York, NY
Nov 14,	1951	Jimmy Carter w pts 15 Art Aragon (US)	Los Angeles, CA
Apr 1,	1952	Jimmy Carter w pts 15 Lauro Salas (Mex)	Los Angeles, CA

RINGSIDE VIEW

Benny Leonard
vs
Freddie Welsh

DOUBLE WHAMMY

Insult was added to injury when Freddie Welsh lost his lightweight title to the stylish American Benny Leonard in New York on May 28, 1917: his manager had bet the entire purse, $4,000, on a Welsh victory, so poor Freddie returned to Cardiff without either championship or cash.

ROBERTO DURAN *(left) and Ken Buchanan, two of the great modern lightweights, battle it out for the world title in Madison Square Garden in 1972*

May 14, 1952	**Lauro Salas** w pts 15 Jimmy Carter	Los Angeles, CA
Oct 15, 1952	**Jimmy Carter** w pts 15 Lauro Salas	Chicago, IL
Apr 24, 1953	Jimmy Carter w rsf 4 Tommy Collins (US)	Boston, MA
Jun 12, 1953	Jimmy Carter w rsf 13 George Araujo (US)	New York, NY
Nov 11, 1953	Jimmy Carter w ko 5 Armand Savoie (Can)	Montreal (Can)
Mar 5, 1954	**Paddy DeMarco** (US) w pts 15 Jimmy Carter	New York, NY
Nov 17, 1954	**Jimmy Carter** w rsf 15 Paddy DeMarco	San Francisco, CA
Jun 29, 1955	**Wallace (Bud) Smith** (US) w pts 15 Jimmy Carter	Boston, MA
Oct 19, 1955	Wallace (Bud) Smith (US) w pts 15 Jimmy Carter	Cincinnati, OH
Aug 24, 1956	**Joe Brown** (US) w pts 15 Wallace (Bud) Smith	New Orleans, LA
Feb 13, 1957	Joe Brown w rsf 10 Wallace (Bud) Smith	Miami, FL
Jun 19, 1957	Joe Brown w rsf 15 Orlando Zulueta (Cub)	Denver, CO
Dec 4, 1957	Joe Brown w rsf 11 Joey Lopes (US)	Chicago, IL
May 7, 1958	Joe Brown w rsf 8 Ralph Dupas (US)	Houston, TX
Jul 23, 1958	Joe Brown w pts 15 Ralph Dupas	Houston, TX
Feb 11, 1959	Joe Brown w pts 15 Johnny Busso (US)	Houston, TX
Jun 3, 1959	Joe Brown w ret 8 Paolo Rosi (Ita)	Washington, DC
Dec 2, 1959	Joe Brown w ret 5 Dave Charnley (Eng)	Houston, TX

Oct 28, 1960	Joe Brown w pts 15 Cisco Andrade (US)	Los Angeles, CA
Apr 18, 1961	Joe Brown w pts 15 Dave Charnley	London (Eng)
Oct 28, 1961	Joe Brown w pts 15 Bert Somodio (Phil)	Quezon City (Phil)
Apr 21, 1962	**Carlos Ortiz** (PR) w pts 15 Joe Brown	Las Vegas, NV
Dec 3, 1962	Carlos Ortiz w ko 5 Teruo Kosaka (Jap)	Tokyo (Jap)
Apr 7, 1963	Carlos Ortiz w rsf 13 Doug Vaillant (Cub)	San Juan, CA
Feb 15, 1964	Carlos Ortiz w rsf 14 Flash Elorde(Phil)	Manila (Phil)
Apr 11, 1964	Carlos Ortiz w pts 15 Kenny Lane (US)	San Juan, CA
Apr 10, 1965	**Ismael Laguna** (Pan) w pts 15 Carlos Ortiz	Panama City (Pan)
Nov 13, 1965	**Carlos Ortiz** w pts 15 Ismael Laguna	San Juan, CA
Jun 20, 1966	Carlos Ortiz w rsf 12 Johnny Bizzaro (US)	Pittsburgh, PA
Oct 22, 1966	Carlos Ortiz w rsf 5 Sugar Ramos (Cub)	Mexico City (Mex)

A riot ensued when Ramos was stopped because of a cut eye. The WBC supervisor ordered Ortiz to return to the ring and resume the fight, and he refused. Two days later, the WBC vacated his title

Nov 28, 1966	Carlos Ortiz w ko 14 Flash Elorde	New York, NY

For WBA title

Jul 1, 1967	Carlos Ortiz w rsf 4 Sugar Ramos	San Juan, CA

For undisputed title

Aug 16, 1967	Carlos Ortiz w pts 15 Ismael Laguna	New York, NY
Jun 29, 1968	**Carlos Teo Cruz** (DR) w pts 15 Carlos Ortiz	Santo Domingo (DR)
Sep 28, 1968	Carlos Teo Cruz w pts 15 Mando Ramos (US)	Los Angeles, CA
Feb 18, 1969	**Mando Ramos** w rsf 11 Carlos Teo Cruz	Los Angeles, CA
Oct 4, 1969	Mando Ramos w rsf 6 Yoshiaki Numata (Jap)	Los Angeles, CA
Mar 3, 1970	**Ismael Laguna** w ret 9 Mando Ramos	Los Angeles, CA
May 1970	*WBC stripped Laguna of title for allegedly breaking a contract to make his first defence in Los Angeles for promoter Aileen Eaton. The following two fights involved only the WBA title*	
Jun 7, 1970	Ismael Laguna w rsf 13 Guts Ishimatsu (Jap)	Panama City (Pan)
Sep 26, 1970	**Ken Buchanan** (Sco) w pts 15 Ismael Laguna	San Juan, CA
Feb 12, 1971	Ken Buchanan w pts 15 Ruben Navarro (US)	Los Angeles, CA

For undisputed title

Jun 1971	*WBC stripped Buchanan for signing to meet Laguna instead of their No. 1 challenger, Pedro Carrasco. The British Boxing Board, although affiliated to the WBC, upheld Buchanan as world champion*	

RINGSIDE VIEW

Mando Ramos
vs
Pedro Carrasco

SURPRISE VERDICT
Pedro Carrasco had been floored four times in 11 rounds before being declared WBC lightweight champion in Madrid on November 5, 1971 when the Nigerian referee Samuel Ahubota disqualified his American opponent Mando Ramos for "hitting on top of the head and below the belt". The WBC declared the verdict null and void.

WBA title

Sep 13,	1971	**Ken Buchanan** w pts 15 Ismael Laguna		New York, NY
Jun 26,	1972	**Roberto Duran** (Pan) w rsf 13 Ken Buchanan		New York, NY
		For WBA, New York and British recognition		
Jan 20,	1973	Roberto Duran w ko 5 Jimmy Robertson (US)		Panama City (Pan)
Jun 2,	1973	Roberto Duran w rsf 8 Hector Thompson (Aus)		Panama City (Pan)
Sep	1973	*Britain and New York withdrew recognition of Duran for failing to honour a contract with Madison Square Garden to defend against Ken Buchanan*		
Sep 8,	1973	Roberto Duran w rsf 10 Guts Ishimatsu		Panama City (Pan)
Mar 16,	1974	Roberto Duran w rsf 11 Esteban De Jesus (PR)		Panama City (Pan)
Dec 21,	1974	Roberto Duran w rsf 1 Masataka Takayama (Jap)		San Jose, CA
Mar 2,	1975	Roberto Duran w ko 14 Ray Lampkin (US)		Panama City (Pan)
Dec 14,	1975	Roberto Duran w ko 15 Leoncio Ortiz (Mex)		San Juan, CA
May 22,	1976	Roberto Duran w ko 14 Lou Bizzaro (US)		Fort Erie (Can)
Oct 15,	1976	Roberto Duran w ko 1 Alvaro Rojas (CR)		Los Angeles, CA
Jan 29,	1977	Roberto Duran w ko 13 Vilomar Fernandez (DR)		Miami, FL
Sep 17,	1977	Roberto Duran w pts 15 Edwin Viruet (PR)		Philadelphia, PA
Jan 21,	1978	Roberto Duran w ko 12 Esteban De Jesus		Las Vegas, NV
		For undisputed title		
Jan 1979		*Duran relinquished the title because of difficulty in making the weight*		
Jun 16,	1979	**Ernesto Espana** (Ven) w ko 13 Claude Noel (Tr)		San Juan, CA
		For vacant WBA title		
Aug 4,	1979	Ernesto Espana w rsf 9 Johnny Lira (US)		Chicago, IL
Mar 2,	1980	**Hilmer Kenty** (US) w rsf 9 Ernesto Espana		Detroit, MI
Aug 2,	1980	Hilmer Kenty w rsf 9 Yong-Ho Oh (Kor)		Detroit, MI
Sep 20,	1980	Hilmer Kenty w rsf 4 Ernesto Espana		San Juan, CA
Nov 8,	1980	Hilmer Kenty w pts 15 Vilomar Fernandez		Detroit, MI
Apr 12,	1981	**Sean O'Grady** (US) w pts 15 Hilmer Kenty		Atlantic City, NJ
Aug	1981	*The WBA vacated O'Grady's title because of a contractual dispute*		
Sep 12,	1981	**Claude Noel** w pts 15 Rodolfo Gonzalez (Mex)		Atlantic City, NJ
		For vacant title		
Dec 5,	1981	**Arturo Frias** (US) w ko 8 Claude Noel		Las Vegas, NV
Jan 30,	1982	Arturo Frias w tech dec 9 Ernesto Espana		Atlantic City, NJ
May 8,	1982	**Ray Mancini** (US) w rsf 1 Arturo Frias		Las Vegas, NV
Jul 24,	1982	Ray Mancini w rsf 6 Ernesto Espana		Warren, OH
Nov 13,	1982	Ray Mancini w rsf 14 Deuk-Koo Kim (Kor)		Las Vegas, NV
Sep 15,	1983	Ray Mancini w ko 9 Orlando Romero (Peru)		Atlantic City, NJ
Jan 14,	1984	Ray Mancini w rsf 3 Bobby Chacon (US)		Reno, NV
Jun 1,	1984	**Livingstone Bramble** (VI) w rsf 14 Ray Mancini		Buffalo, NY
Feb 16,	1985	Livingstone Bramble w pts 15 Ray Mancini		Reno, NV
Feb 16,	1986	Livingstone Bramble w rsf 13 Tyrone Crawley (US)		Reno, NV
Sep 26,	1986	**Edwin Rosario** (PR) w ko 2 Livingstone Bramble		Miami, FL
Aug 11,	1987	Edwin Rosario w ko 8 Juan Nazario (PR)		Chicago, IL
Nov 21,	1987	**Julio Cesar Chavez** (Mex) w rsf 11 Edwin Rosario		Las Vegas, NV
Apr 16,	1988	Julio Cesar Chavez w rsf 6 Rodolfo Aguilar (Pan)		Las Vegas, NV
Oct 29,	1988	Julio Cesar Chavez w tech dec 11 Jose Luis Ramirez (Mex)		Las Vegas, NV
		For WBA and WBC titles, both of which Chavez relinquished in May 1989 when he won the WBC light-welterweight title		
Jul 9,	1989	**Edwin Rosario** w rsf 6 Anthony Jones (US)		Atlantic City, NJ
		For vacant WBA title		
Apr 4,	1990	**Juan Nazario** w rsf 8 Edwin Rosario		New York, NY
Aug 11,	1990	**Pernell Whitaker** w ko 1 Juan Nazario		Stateline, NV
		For WBC, IBF and WBA titles		

WBC title

Nov 5,	1971	**Pedro Carrasco** (Sp) w dis 11 Mando Ramos		Madrid (Sp)
		For vacant title. Because of the controversy surrounding Ramos's disqualification the verdict was declared "null and void" at a WBC meeting in Mexico City on November 20, and a rematch was ordered		
Feb 18,	1972	**Mando Ramos** w pts 15 Pedro Carrasco		Los Angeles, CA
		For vacant title: the WBC later withdrew recognition of the fight as a world championship because the decision was "locally influenced"		
Jun 28,	1972	Mando Ramos w pts 15 Pedro Carrasco		Madrid (Sp)
		For vacant title		
Sep 15,	1972	**Chango Carmona** (Mex) w rsf 8 Mando Ramos		Los Angeles, CA
Nov 10,	1972	**Rodolfo Gonzalez** (Mex) w ret 12 Chango Carmona		Los Angeles, CA
Mar 17,	1973	Rodolfo Gonzalez w rsf 9 Ruben Navarro		Los Angeles, CA
Oct 27,	1973	Rodolfo Gonzalez w ret 10 Antonio Puddu (Ita)		Los Angeles, CA
Apr 11,	1974	**Guts Ishimatsu** w ko 8 Rodolfo Gonzalez		Tokyo (Jap)
Sep 13,	1974	Guts Ishimatsu drew 15 Turi Pineda (Mex)		Nagoya (Jap)
Nov 28,	1974	Guts Ishimatsu w ko 12 Rodolfo Gonzalez		Osaka (Jap)
Feb 21,	1975	Guts Ishimatsu w pts 15 Ken Buchanan		Tokyo (Jap)
Jun 5,	1975	Guts Ishimatsu w pts 15 Turi Pineda		Osaka (Jap)
Dec 4,	1975	Guts Ishimatsu w ko 14 Alvaro Rojas		Tokyo (Jap)
May 8,	1976	**Esteban De Jesus** w pts 15 Guts Ishimatsu		San Juan, CA
Sep 10,	1976	Esteban De Jesus w ko 7 Hector Medina (DR)		Bayamon (PR)
Feb 12,	1977	Esteban De Jesus w rsf 6 Buzzsaw Yamabe (Jap)		Bayamon (PR)
Jun 25,	1977	Esteban De Jesus w ko 11 Vicente Mijares (Mex)		Bayamon (PR)
Jan 21,	1978	**Roberto Duran** w ko 12 Esteban De Jesus		Las Vegas, NV
		For undisputed title		
Jan	1979	*Duran relinquished the title because of difficulty making the weight*		
Apr 17,	1979	**Jim Watt** (Sco) w rsf 12 Alfredo Pitalua (Col)		Glasgow (Sco)
		For vacant WBC title		
Nov 3,	1979	Jim Watt w rsf 9 Roberto Vasquez (US)		Glasgow (Sco)
Mar 14,	1980	Jim Watt w rsf 4 Charlie Nash (Ire)		Glasgow (Sco)
Jun 7,	1980	Jim Watt w pts 15 Howard Davis (US)		Glasgow (Sco)
Nov 1,	1980	Jim Watt w rsf 12 Sean O'Grady		Glasgow (Sco)
Jun 20,	1981	**Alexis Arguello** (Nic) w pts 15 Jim Watt		Wembley (Eng)
Oct 3,	1981	Alexis Arguello w rsf 14 Ray Mancini		Atlantic City, NJ
Nov 21,	1981	Alexis Arguello w ko 7 Roberto Elizondo (US)		Las Vegas, NV
Feb 13,	1982	Alexis Arguello w rsf 6 James "Bubba" Busceme (US)		Beaumont, TX
May 22,	1982	Alexis Arguello w ko 5 Andy Ganigan (US)		Las Vegas, NV
Feb	1983	*Arguello relinquished WBC title*		
May 1,	1983	**Edwin Rosario** (PR) w pts 12 Jose Luis Ramirez		San Juan, CA
		For vacant title		
Mar 17,	1984	Edwin Rosario w rsf 1 Roberto Elizondo		San Juan, CA
Jun 23,	1984	Edwin Rosario w pts 12 Howard Davis		San Juan, CA
Nov 3,	1984	**Jose Luis Ramirez** w rsf 4 Edwin Rosario		San Juan, CA
Aug 10,	1985	**Hector Camacho** (PR) w pts 12 Jose Luis Ramirez		New York, NY
Jun 13,	1986	Hector Camacho w pts 12 Edwin Rosario		New York, NY
Sep 26,	1986	Hector Camacho w pts 12 Cornelius Boza-Edwards (Eng)		Miami, FL
May	1987	*Camacho relinquished the title because of weight problems*		
Jul 19,	1987	**Jose Luis Ramirez** w pts 12 Terrence Alli (Guy)		St Tropez (Fra)
		For vacant title		
Oct 10,	1987	Jose Luis Ramirez w ko 5 Cornelius Boza-Edwards		Paris (Fra)
Mar 12,	1988	Jose Luis Ramirez w pts 12 Pernell Whitaker (US)		Paris (Fra)
Oct 29,	1988	**Julio Cesar Chavez** w tech dec 11 Jose Luis Ramirez		Las Vegas, NV
		For WBA and WBC titles, both of which Chavez relinquished in May 1989 when he won the WBC light-welterweight title		
Aug 20,	1989	**Pernell Whitaker** (US) w pts 12 Jose Luis Ramirez		Norfolk, VA
		For IBF and vacant WBC titles		

IBF title

Jan 30,	1984	**Charlie "Choo Choo" Brown** (US) w pts 15 Melvin Paul (US)		Atlantic City, NJ
		For vacant title		
Apr 15,	1984	**Harry Arroyo** (US) w rsf 14 Charlie "Choo Choo" Brown		Atlantic City, NJ
Sep 1,	1984	Harry Arroyo w rsf 8 Charlie "White Lightning" Brown (US)		Youngstown, OH
Jan 12,	1985	Harry Arroyo w rsf 11 Terrence Alli		Atlantic City, NJ
Apr 6,	1985	**Jimmy Paul** (US) w pts 15 Harry Arroyo		Atlantic City, NJ
Jun 30,	1985	Jimmy Paul w rsf 14 Robin Blake (US)		Las Vegas, NV
Jun 4,	1986	Jimmy Paul w pts 15 Irleis Perez (Cub)		East Rutherford, NJ
Aug 15,	1986	Jimmy Paul w pts 15 Darryl Tyson (US)		Detroit, MI
Dec 5,	1986	**Greg Haugen** (US) w pts 15 Jimmy Paul		Las Vegas, NV
Jun 7,	1987	**Vinny Pazienza** (US) w pts 15 Greg Haugen		Providence, RI
Feb 6,	1988	**Greg Haugen** w pts 15 Vinny Pazienza		Atlantic City, NJ
Apr 11,	1988	Greg Haugen w tech dec 11 Miguel Santana (PR)		Tacoma, WA
Oct 28,	1988	Greg Haugen w ret 10 Gert Bo Jacobsen (Den)		Copenhagen (Den)
Feb 18,	1989	**Pernell Whitaker** w pts 12 Greg Haugen		Hampton, VA
Apr 30,	1989	Pernell Whitaker w rsf 3 Louie Lomeli (US)		Norfolk, VA
Aug 20,	1989	Pernell Whitaker (US) w pts 12 Jose Luis Ramirez		Norfolk, VA
		For IBF and vacant WBC titles		

WBC/IBF titles

Feb 3,	1990	**Pernell Whitaker** w pts 12 Fred Pendleton (US)		Atlantic City, NJ
May 19,	1990	Pernell Whitaker w pts 12 Azumah Nelson (Gha)		Las Vegas, NV
Aug 11,	1990	Pernell Whitaker w ko 1 Juan Nazario		Stateline, NV
		For WBC, IBF and WBA titles		

WBC/WBA/IBF titles

Feb 23,	1991	**Pernell Whitaker** w pts 12 Anthony Jones		Las Vegas, NV
Jul 27,	1991	Pernell Whitaker w pts 12 Poli Diaz (Sp)		Norfolk, VA
Oct 5,	1991	Pernell Whitaker w pts 12 Jorge Paez (Mex)		Reno, NV
Feb	1992	*Whitaker relinquished the lightweight titles to box at light-welterweight*		

WBA title

Jun 12,	1992	**Joey Gamache** (US) w ret 8 Chil-Sung Chun (Kor) . . . . Portland, ME
		For vacant title
Oct 24,	1992	**Tony Lopez** (US) w rsf 11 Joey Gamache . . . . Portland, ME
Feb 12,	1993	Tony Lopez w pts 12 Dingaan Thobela (SA) . . . . Sacramento, CA
Jun 26,	1993	**Dingaan Thobela** w pts 12 Tony Lopez . . . . Sun City (Bop)
Oct 30,	1993	**Orzoubek Nazarov** (Rus) w pts 12 Dingaan Thobela . . Johannesburg (SA)
Mar 19,	1994	Orzoubek Nazarov w pts 12 Dingaan Thobela . . . . Hammanskraal
Dec 10,	1994	Orzoubek Nazarov w ko 2 Joey Gamache . . . . Portland, ME
May 15,	1995	Orzoubek Nazarov w ko 2 Won Park (Kor) . . . . Tokyo (Jap)
Nov 15,	1995	Orzoubek Nazarov w pts 12 Dindo Canoy (Phi) . . . . Iwaki (Jap)

WBC title

Aug 24,	1992	**Miguel Angel Gonzalez** (Mex) w ret 9 Wilfredo Rocha (Col) . . . .
		. . . . Mexico City (Mex)
		For vacant title
Dec 5,	1992	Miguel Angel Gonzalez w pts 12 Darryl Tyson . . . . Mexico City (Mex)
Apr 26,	1993	Miguel Angel Gonzalez w pts 12 Hector Lopez (Mex) Aguascalientes (Mex)
Aug 13,	1993	Miguel Angel Gonzalez w pts 12 David Sample (US) . . . Guadalajara (Mex)
Nov 27,	1993	Miguel Angel Gonzalez w rsf 10 Wilfredo Rocha . . . . . . Mexico City (Mex)
Mar 29,	1994	Miguel Angel Gonzalez w rsf 5 Jean Baptiste Mendy (Fra) . . . . . Paris (Fra)
Aug 6,	1994	Miguel Angel Gonzalez w rsf 8 Leavander Johnson (US) . Ciudad Juarez (Mex)
Dec 13,	1994	Miguel Angel Gonzalez w ret 5 Calvin Grove (US) . . . . . . Albuquerque, NM
Apr 25,	1995	Miguel Angel Gonzalez w pts 12 Ricardo Silva (Arg) . . South Padre Island, TX
Jun 2,	1995	Miguel Angel Gonzalez w pts 12 Marty Jakubowski (US) . . . . . Ledyard, CT
Aug 19,	1995	Miguel Angel Gonzalez w pts 12 Lamar Murphy (US) . . . . . Las Vegas, NV

IBF title

Aug 29,	1992	**Fred Pendleton** tech draw 2 Tracy Spann (US) . . . . Reno, NV
		For vacant title
Jan 10,	1993	Fred Pendleton w pts 12 Tracy Spann . . . . Atlantic City, NJ
Jul 17,	1993	Fred Pendleton w pts 12 Jorge Paez . . . . Las Vegas, NV

Feb 19,	1994	**Rafael Ruelas** (US) w pts 12 Fred Pendleton . . . . Inglewood, CA
May 27,	1994	Rafael Ruelas w rsf 3 Mike Evgen (US) . . . . Las Vegas, NV
Jan 28,	1995	Rafael Ruelas w rsf 8 Billy Schwer (Eng) . . . . Las Vegas, NV
May 6,	1995	**Oscar De La Hoya** (US) w rsf 2 Rafael Ruelas . . . . Las Vegas, NV
		For WBO and IBF titles
Jul	1995	*De La Hoya vacated IBF title*
Aug 19,	1995	**Phillip Holiday** (SA) w ret 11 Miguel Julio (Col) . . . . Sun City (Bop)
		For vacant title
Sep 9,	1995	Phillip Holiday w pts 12 Ray Martinez (US) . . . . Sun City (Bop)

WBO title

Jan 21,	1989	**Mauricio Aceves** (Mex) drew 12 Amancio Castro (Col) . . . . Monteria (Col)
		For vacant title
May 8,	1989	Mauricio Aceves w pts 12 Amancio Castro . . . . Santa Ana, CA
Aug 30,	1989	Mauricio Aceves w rsf 10 Oscar Bejines (Mex) . . . . Los Angeles, CA
Sep 22,	1990	**Dingaan Thobela** w pts 12 Mauricio Aceves . . . . Brownsville, TX
Feb 2,	1991	Dingaan Thobela w pts 12 Mario Martinez (Mex) . . . . San Jose, CA
Sep 14,	1991	Dingaan Thobela w pts 12 Antonio Rivera (PR) . . . . . . Johannesburg (SA)
Jul	1992	*Thobela relinquished the WBO title to box for the WBA version*
Sep 25,	1992	**Giovanni Parisi** (Ita) w rsf 10 Javier Altamirano (Mex) . . . . . Voghera (Ita)
		For vacant title
Apr 16,	1993	Giovanni Parisi w pts 12 Michael Ayers (Eng) . . . . Rome (Ita)
Sep 24,	1993	Giovanni Parisi w pts 12 Antonio Rivera (PR) . . . . Rome (Ita)
Apr	1994	*Parisi relinquished the title to box at light-welterweight*
Jul 29,	1994	**Oscar De La Hoya** w ko 2 Jorge Paez . . . . Las Vegas, NV
		For vacant title
Nov 18,	1994	Oscar De La Hoya w rsf 3 Carl Griffith (US) . . . . Las Vegas, NV
Dec 10,	1994	Oscar De La Hoya w rsf 9 Johnny Avila (US) . . . . Los Angeles, CA
Feb 18,	1995	Oscar De La Hoya w pts 12 Juan "John-John" Molina (PR) . Las Vegas, NV
May 6,	1995	Oscar De La Hoya w rsf 2 Rafael Ruelas . . . . Las Vegas, NV
		For WBO and IBF titles
Jul	1995	*De La Hoya vacated IBF title*
Sep 9,	1995	Oscar De La Hoya w ret 6 Genaro Hernandez (US) . . . . Las Vegas, NV
Dec 15,	1995	Oscar De La Hoya w rsf 2 Jesse James Leija (US) . . . . New York, NY

OSCAR DE LA HOYA *(right), the dazzling Californian destroys defending IBF champion Rafael Ruelas inside two rounds in May 1995*

Super-Featherweight

The super-featherweight or junior lightweight class was popularized by the promoter Tex Rickard, who put up a $2,500 championship belt in 1921 which prompted the New York Commission to approve the new division, which can be considered to have been launched by Johnny Dundee and George Chaney's fight in New York in November 1921.

The NBA added their blessing in 1923, and when Tod Morgan became champion between 1925 and 1929, the category's future looked assured. But Morgan's reign ended in scandal, when both he and Benny Bass had their purses suspended on suspicion of a betting coup after Bass knocked him out in two rounds. The evidence was inconclusive, but in January 1930 New York withdrew recognition from the division. The NBA did likewise two years later, and although the 130 lb class stumbled on for a few more years it effectively went out of business from 1933 until 1949, when Sandy Saddler briefly revived it.

There was an eight-year beak between 1951, when Saddler ceased to claim the title, and 1959, when the NBA brought it back. This time, due mainly to the outstanding Filipino champion Flash Elorde, the category flourished. The inevitable split came in 1968, when the WBC stripped Hiroshi Kobayashi, and not even outstanding performers like Julio Cesar Chavez, Alexis Arguello or Brian Mitchell were able to reunite the championship.

World Super-Featherweight Championship Bouts

Nov 18, 1921	**Johnny Dundee** (US) w dis 5 George "KO" Chaney (US) . . . New York, NY
	For vacant title
Jul 6, 1922	Johnny Dundee w pts 15 Jackie Sharkey (US) . . . . New York, NY
Aug 28, 1922	Johnny Dundee w pts 15 Vincent "Pepper" Martin (US) . . . . New York, NY
Feb 2, 1923	Johnny Dundee w pts 15 Elino Flores (Phil) . . . . New York, NY
May 30, 1923	**Jack Bernstein** (US) w pts 15 Johnny Dundee . . . . New York, NY
Dec 17, 1923	**Johnny Dundee** w pts 15 Jack Bernstein . . . . New York, NY
Jun 20, 1924	**Steve "Kid" Sullivan** (US) w pts 10 Johnny Dundee . . . . . . Brooklyn, NY
Aug 18, 1924	Steve "Kid" Sullivan w pts 15 Pepper Martin . . . . New York, NY
Oct 15, 1924	Steve "Kid" Sullivan w ko 5 Mike Ballerino (US) . . . . New York, NY
Apr 1, 1925	**Mike Ballerino** w pts 10 Steve "Kid" Sullivan . . . . Philadelphia, PA
Jul 6, 1925	Mike Ballerino w pts 15 Vincent "Pepper" Martin . . . . Long Island, NY
Dec 2, 1925	**Tod Morgan** (US) w ret 10 Mike Ballerino . . . . Los Angeles, CA
Jun 3, 1926	Tod Morgan w ret 6 Steve "Kid" Sullivan . . . . Brooklyn, NY
Sep 30, 1926	Tod Morgan w pts 15 Joe Glick (US) . . . . New York, NY
Oct 19, 1926	Tod Morgan w pts 10 Johnny Dundee . . . . San Francisco, CA
Nov 19, 1926	Tod Morgan w pts 15 Carl Duane (US) . . . . New York, NY
May 28, 1927	Tod Morgan w pts 12 Vic Foley (US) . . . . Vancouver (Can)
Dec 16, 1927	Tod Morgan w dis 14 Joe Glick . . . . New York, NY
May 24, 1928	Tod Morgan w pts 15 Eddie Martin (US) . . . . New York, NY
Jul 18, 1928	Tod Morgan w pts 15 Eddie Martin . . . . Brooklyn, NY
Dec 3, 1928	Tod Morgan drew 10 Santiago Zorilla (Pan) . . . . San Francisco, CA
Apr 5, 1929	Tod Morgan w pts 10 Santiago Zorilla . . . . Los Angeles, CA
May 20, 1929	Tod Morgan w pts 10 Sal Sorio (US) . . . . Los Angeles, CA
Dec 19, 1929	**Benny Bass** (Rus) w ko 2 Tod Morgan . . . . New York, NY
Jan 1930	*NY Commission withdrew recognition of the weight class, leaving Bass recognized only by the NBA*

Jan 5, 1931	Benny Bass w pts 10 Lew Massey (US) . . . . Philadelphia, PA
Jul 15, 1931	**Kid Chocolate** (Cub) w rsf 7 Benny Bass . . . . Philadelphia, PA
Apr 10, 1932	Kid Chocolate w pts 15 Davey Abad (Pan) . . . . Havana (Cub)
Aug 4, 1932	Kid Chocolate w pts 10 Eddie Shea (US) . . . . Chicago, IL
Sep 20, 1932	*The NBA also withdrew recognition from the division, although individual Commissions were free to authorize title fights in their jurisdiction*
Oct 13, 1932	Kid Chocolate w rsf 12 Lew Feldman (US) . . . . New York, NY
Dec 9, 1932	Kid Chocolate w pts 15 Fidel la Barba (US) . . . . New York, NY
	Both the above contests were billed as featherweight title defences by Chocolate, but as the boxers were inside the 130 lb limit that title was automatically at stake also
May 1, 1933	Kid Chocolate w pts 10 Johnny Farr (US) . . . . Philadelphia, PA
May 19, 1933	Kid Chocolate w pts 15 Seaman Tommy Watson (Eng) . . . . . New York, NY
	Billed as a featherweight title defence
Dec 4, 1933	Kid Chocolate w pts 10 Frankie Wallace (US) . . . . Cleveland, OH
Dec 26, 1933	**Frankie Klick** (US) w rsf 7 Kid Chocolate . . . . Philadelphia, PA
	Klick never defended the title, which fell into disuse until Sandy Saddler revived it briefly, with the backing of the Ohio Commission, in 1949
Dec 6, 1949	**Sandy Saddler** (US) w pts 10 Orlando Zulueta (Cub) . . . . . . Cleveland, OH
Apr 18, 1950	Sandy Saddler w rsf 9 Lauro Salas (Mex) . . . . Cleveland, OH
Feb 28, 1951	Sandy Saddler w ko 2 Diego Sosa (Cub) . . . . Havana (Cub)
	Saddler thereafter concentrated on the featherweight title, and the division did not become active again until 1959
Jul 20, 1959	**Harold Gomes** (US) w pts 15 Paul Jorgensen (US) . . . . . . Providence, RI
Mar 16, 1960	**Gabriel "Flash" Elorde** (Phil) w ko 7 Harold Gomes . . . Quezon City (Phil)
Aug 17, 1960	Gabriel "Flash" Elorde w ko 1 Harold Gomes . . . . San Francisco, CA
Mar 19, 1961	Gabriel "Flash" Elorde w pts 15 Joey Lopes (US) . . . . Manila (Phil)
Dec 16, 1961	Gabriel "Flash" Elorde w rsf 1 Sergio Caprari (Ita) . . . . Manila (Phil)

Jun 23, 1962	Gabriel "Flash" Elorde w pts 15 Auburn Copeland (US) . . . . . Manila (Phil)
Feb 16, 1963	Gabriel "Flash" Elorde w pts 15 Johnny Bizzaro (US) . . . . . . Manila (Phil)
Nov 16, 1963	Gabriel "Flash" Elorde w dis 11 Love Allotey (Gha) . . . . Quezon City (Phil)
Jul 27, 1964	Gabriel "Flash" Elorde w rsf 12 Teruo Kosaka (Jap) . . . . Tokyo (Jap)
Jun 5, 1965	Gabriel "Flash" Elorde w ko 15 Teruo Kosaka . . . . Quezon City (Phil)
Dec 4, 1965	Gabriel "Flash" Elorde w pts 15 Kang-Il Suh (Kor) . . . . . Quezon City (Phil)
Oct 22, 1966	Gabriel "Flash" Elorde w pts 15 Vicente Derado (Arg) . . Quezon City (Phil)
Jun 15, 1967	**Yoshiaki Numata** (Jap) w pts 15 Gabriel "Flash" Elorde . . . . . Tokyo (Jap)
Dec 14, 1967	**Hiroshi Kobayashi** (Jap) w ko 12 Yoshiaki Numata . . . . Tokyo (Jap)
Mar 30, 1968	Hiroshi Kobayashi drew 15 Rene Barrientos (Phil) . . . . Tokyo (Jap)
Oct 6, 1968	Hiroshi Kobayashi w pts 15 Jaime Valladeres (Ecu) . . . . Tokyo (Jap)
	The WBC vacated Kobayashi's title for his failure to defend against Rene Barrientos

WBA title

Apr 6, 1969	**Hiroshi Kobayashi** w pts 15 Antonio Amaya (Pan) . . . . Tokyo (Jap)
Nov 9, 1969	Hiroshi Kobayashi w pts 15 Carlos Canete (Arg) . . . . Tokyo (Jap)
Aug 23, 1970	Hiroshi Kobayashi w pts 15 Antonio Amaya . . . . Tokyo (Jap)
Mar 3, 1971	Hiroshi Kobayashi w pts 15 Ricardo Arredondo (Mex) . . . . Tokyo (Jap)
Jul 29, 1971	**Alfredo Marcano** (Ven) w ret 10 Hiroshi Kobayashi . . . . Aomari (Jap)
Nov 7, 1971	Alfredo Marcano w rsf 4 Kenji Iwata (Jap) . . . . Caracas (Ven)
Apr 25, 1972	**Ben Villaflor** (Phil) w pts 15 Alfredo Marcano . . . . Honolulu, HI

Sep 5,	1972	Ben Villaflor drew 15 Victor Echegaray (Arg)	Honolulu, HI
Mar 12,	1973	**Kuniaki Shibata** (Jap) w pts 15 Ben Villaflor	Honolulu, HI
Jun 19,	1973	Kuniaki Shibata w pts 15 Victor Echegaray	Tokyo (Jap)
Oct 17,	1973	**Ben Villaflor** w ko 1 Kuniaki Shibata	Honolulu, HI
Mar 14,	1974	Ben Villaflor drew 15 Apollo Yoshio (Jap)	Toyama (Jap)
Aug 24,	1974	Ben Villaflor w rsf 2 Yasutsune Uehara (Jap)	Honolulu, HI
Mar 13,	1975	Ben Villaflor w pts 15 Hyun-Chi Kim (Kor)	Quezon City (Phil)
Jan 12,	1976	Ben Villaflor w rsf 13 Morito Kashiwaba (Jap)	Tokyo (Jap)
Apr 13,	1976	Ben Villaflor drew 15 Sam Serrano (PR)	Honolulu, HI
Oct 16,	1976	**Sam Serrano** w pts 15 Ben Villaflor	San Juan, CA
Jan 15,	1977	Sam Serrano w rsf 11 Alberto Herrera (Ecu)	Guayaquil (Ecu)
Jun 26,	1977	Sam Serrano w pts 15 Leonel Hernandez (Ven)	Puerta La Cruz (Ven)
Aug 27,	1977	Sam Serrano w pts 15 Apollo Yoshio	San Juan, CA
Nov 19,	1977	Sam Serrano w rsf 10 Tae-Ho Kim (Kor)	San Juan, CA
Feb 18,	1978	Sam Serrano w pts 15 Mario Martinez (Nic)	San Juan, CA
Jul 8,	1978	Sam Serrano w rsf 9 Yong-Ho Oh (Kor)	San Juan, CA
Nov 29,	1978	Sam Serrano w pts 15 Takas Maruki (Jap)	Nagoya (Jap)
Feb 18,	1979	Sam Serrano w pts 15 Julio Valdez (DR)	San Juan, CA
Apr 14,	1979	Sam Serrano w rsf 8 Nkosana Mgxaji (SA)	Cape Town (SA)
Apr 3,	1980	Sam Serrano w rsf 13 Kiyoshi Kazama (Jap)	Nara (Jap)
Aug 2,	1980	**Yasutsune Uehara** (Jap) w ko 6 Sam Serrano	Detroit, MI
Nov 20,	1980	Yasutsune Uehara w pts 15 Leonel Hernandez	San Juan, CA
Apr 9,	1981	**Sam Serrano** w pts 15 Yasutsune Uehara	Wakayama (Jap)
Jun 29,	1981	Sam Serrano w pts 15 Leonel Hernandez	Caracas (Ven)
Dec 10,	1981	Sam Serrano w rsf 12 Hikaru Tomonari (Jap)	San Juan, CA
Jun 5,	1982	Sam Serrano no contest 11 Benedicto Villablanca (Ch)	Santiago (Ch)
Jan 19,	1983	**Roger Mayweather** (US) w ko 8 Sam Serrano	San Juan, CA
Apr 20,	1983	Roger Mayweather w rsf 8 Jorge Alvarado (PR)	San Jose, CA
Aug 17,	1983	Roger Mayweather w ko 1 Benedicto Villablanca	Las Vegas, NV
Feb 26,	1984	**Rocky Lockridge** (US) w ko 1 Roger Mayweather	Beaumont, TX
Jun 12,	1984	Rocky Lockridge w rsf 11 Taej-In Moon (Kor)	Anchorage, AK
Jan 27,	1985	Rocky Lockridge w rsf 6 Kamel Bou-Ali (Tun)	Riva del Garda (Ita)
May 19,	1985	**Wilfredo Gomez** (PR) w pts 12 Rocky Lockridge	San Juan, CA
May 24,	1986	**Alfredo Layne** (Pan) w rsf 9 Wilfredo Gomez	San Juan, CA
Sep 27,	1986	**Brian Mitchell** (SA) w rsf 10 Alfredo Layne	Sun City (Bop)
Mar 27,	1987	Brian Mitchell drew 15 Jose Rivera (PR)	San Juan, CA
Jul 31,	1987	Brian Mitchell w rsf 14 Francisco Fernandez (Pan)	Panama City (Pan)
Oct 3,	1987	Brian Mitchell w pts 15 Daniel Londas (Fra)	Gravelines (Fra)
Dec 19,	1987	Brian Mitchell w rsf 8 Salvatore Curcetti (Ita)	Capo D'Orlando (Ita)
Apr 26,	1988	Brian Mitchell w pts 12 Jose Rivera	Madrid (Sp)
Nov 2,	1988	Brian Mitchell w pts 12 Jim McDonnell (Eng)	London (Eng)
Feb 10,	1989	Brian Mitchell w rsf 8 Salvatore Bottiglieri (Ita)	Capo D'Orlando (Ita)
Jul 1,	1989	Brian Mitchell w tech dec 9 Jackie Beard (US)	Crotone (Ita)
Sep 28,	1989	Brian Mitchell w rsf 7 Irving Mitchell (US)	Lewiston, ME
Mar 14,	1990	Brian Mitchell w pts 12 Jackie Beard	Grossetto (Ita)
Sep 29,	1990	Brian Mitchell w pts 12 Frankie Mitchell (US)	Aosta (Ita)
Mar 15,	1991	Brian Mitchell drew 12 Tony Lopez (US)	Sacramento, CA
		For WBA and IBF titles	
April 1991		*Mitchell relinquished the WBA title to challenge again for the IBF version*	
Jun 28,	1991	**Joey Gamache** (US) w rsf 10 Jerry N'Gobeni (SA)	Lewiston, ME
		For vacant title	
Oct	1991	*Gamache relinquished the title because of weight problems*	
Nov 22,	1991	**Genaro Hernandez** (US) w ret 9 Daniel Londas	Epernay (Fra)
		For vacant title	
Feb 24,	1992	Genaro Hernandez w pts 12 Omar Catari (Ven)	Los Angeles, CA
Jul 15,	1992	Genaro Hernandez w pts 12 Masuaki Takeda (Jap)	Fukuoka (Jap)
Nov 20,	1992	Genaro Hernandez w rsf 6 Yuji Watanabe (Jap)	Tokyo (Jap)
Apr 26,	1993	Genaro Hernandez tech draw 1 Raul Perez (Mex)	Los Angeles, CA
Jun 28,	1993	Genaro Hernandez w ko 8 Raul Perez	Los Angeles, CA
Oct 11,	1993	Genaro Hernandez w pts 12 Harold Warren (US)	Inglewood, CA
Jan 31,	1994	Genaro Hernandez w rsf 8 Jorge Ramirez (Mex)	Inglewood, CA
Nov 12,	1994	Genaro Hernandez w pts 12 Jimmy Garcia (Col)	Mexico City (Mex)
Aug	1995	*Hernandez relinquished the title*	
Oct 21,	1995	**Yong Soo Choi** (Kor) w rsf 10 Victor Hugo Paz (Arg)	Salta (Arg)
		For vacant title	

WBC title

Feb 15,	1969	**Rene Barrientos** w pts 15 Ruben Navarro (US)	Manila (Phil)
		For vacant WBC title	
Apr 5,	1970	**Yoshiaki Numata** (Jap) w pts 15 Rene Barrientos	Tokyo (Jap)
Sep 27,	1970	Yoshiaki Numata w ko 5 Raul Rojas (US)	Tokyo (Jap)
Jan 3,	1971	Yoshiaki Numata w pts 15 Rene Barrientos	Shizuoka (Jap)
May 3,	1971	Yoshiaki Numata w pts 15 Lionel Rose (Aus)	Hiroshima (Jap)
Oct 10,	1971	**Ricardo Arredondo** w ko 10 Yoshiaki Numata	Sendai (Jap)
Jan 29,	1972	Ricardo Arredondo w pts 15 Jose Marin (CR)	San Jose, CA
Apr 22,	1972	Ricardo Arredondo w ko 5 William Martinez (Nic)	Mexico City (Mex)

Sep 15,	1972	Ricardo Arredondo w ko 12 Susumu Okabe (Jap)	Tokyo (Jap)
Mar 6,	1973	Ricardo Arredondo w pts 15 Apollo Yoshio (Jap)	Fukuoka (Jap)
Sep 1,	1973	Ricardo Arredondo w rsf 6 Morito Kashiwaba (Jap)	Tokyo (Jap)
Feb 28,	1974	**Kuniaki Shibata** w pts 15 Ricardo Arredondo	Tokyo (Jap)
Jun 27,	1974	Kuniaki Shibata w pts 15 Antonio Amaya	Tokyo (Jap)
Aug 3,	1974	Kuniaki Shibata w rsf 15 Ramiro Clay Bolanos (Ecu)	Tokyo (Jap)
Mar 27,	1975	Kuniaki Shibata w pts 15 Ould Makloufi (Alg)	Fukuoka (Jap)
Jul 5,	1975	**Alfredo Escalera** (PR) w ko 2 Kuniaki Shibata	Mito (Jap)
Sep 20,	1975	Alfredo Escalera drew 15 Leonel Hernandez (Ven)	Caracas (Ven)
Dec 12,	1975	Alfredo Escalera w rsf 9 Sven-Erik Paulsen (Nor)	Oslo (Nor)
Feb 20,	1976	Alfredo Escalera w rsf 13 Jose Fernandez (DR)	San Juan, CA
Apr 1,	1976	Alfredo Escalera w ko 6 Buzzsaw Yamabe (Jap)	Nara (Jap)
Jul 1,	1976	Alfredo Escalera w pts 15 Buzzsaw Yamabe	Nara (Jap)
Sep 18,	1976	Alfredo Escalera w ret 12 Ray Lunny (US)	San Juan, CA
Nov 30,	1976	Alfredo Escalera w pts 15 Tyrone Everett (US)	Philadelphia, PA
Mar 17,	1977	Alfredo Escalera w rsf 6 Ronnie McGarvey (US)	San Juan, CA
May 16,	1977	Alfredo Escalera w ko 8 Carlos Becerril (Mex)	Landover, MD
Sep 10,	1977	Alfredo Escalera w pts 15 Sigfredo Rodriguez (Mex)	San Juan, CA
Jan 28,	1978	**Alexis Arguello** (Nic) w rsf 13 Alfredo Escalera	San Juan, CA
Apr 29,	1978	Alexis Arguello w rsf 5 Rey Tam (Phil)	Los Angeles, CA
Jun 3,	1978	Alexis Arguello w ko 1 Diego Alcala (Pan)	San Juan, CA
Nov 10,	1978	Alexis Arguello w pts 15 Arturo Leon (Mex)	Las Vegas, NV
Feb 4,	1979	Alexis Arguello w ko 13 Alfredo Escalera	Rimini (Ita)
Jul 8,	1979	Alexis Arguello w rsf 1 Rafael Limon (Mex)	New York, NY
Nov 16,	1979	Alexis Arguello w ret 7 Bobby Chacon (US)	Los Angeles, CA
Jan 20,	1980	Alexis Arguello w rsf 11 Ruben Castillo (US)	Tucson, AZ
Apr 27,	1980	Alexis Arguello w rsf 4 Rolando Navarette (Phil)	San Juan, CA
Oct	1980	*Arguello relinquished WBC title to campaign as a lightweight*	
Dec 11,	1980	**Rafael Limon** w rsf 15 Idelfonso Bethelmi (Ven)	Los Angeles, CA
		For vacant title	
Mar 8,	1981	**Cornelius Boza-Edwards** (Eng) w pts 15 Rafael Limon	Stockton, CA
May 30,	1981	Cornelius Boza-Edwards w ret 13 Bobby Chacon (US)	Las Vegas, NV
Aug 29,	1981	**Rolando Navarette** w ko 5 Cornelius Boza-Edwards	Via Reggio (Ita)
Jan 16,	1982	Rolando Navarette w ko 11 Chung-Il Choi (Kor)	Manila (Phil)
May 29,	1982	**Rafael Limon** w ko 12 Rolando Navarette	Las Vegas, NV
Sep 18,	1982	Rafael Limon w rsf 7 Chung-Il Choi	Los Angeles, CA
Dec 11,	1982	**Bobby Chacon** w pts 15 Rafael Limon	Sacramento, CA
May 15,	1983	Bobby Chacon w pts 12 Cornelius Boza-Edwards	Las Vegas, NV
June	1983	*The WBC stripped Chacon of the title because of a contractual dispute*	
Aug 7,	1983	**Hector Camacho** (PR) w rsf 5 Rafael Limon	San Juan, CA
		For vacant title	
Nov 18,	1983	Hector Camacho w ko 5 Rafael Solis (PR)	San Juan, CA
June	1984	*Camacho relinquished WBC title to box as a lightweight*	
Sep 13,	1984	**Julio Cesar Chavez** (Mex) w rsf 8 Mario Martinez (Mex)	Los Angeles, CA
		For vacant title	
Apr 19,	1985	Julio Cesar Chavez w rsf 6 Ruben Castillo	Los Angeles, CA
Jul 7,	1985	Julio Cesar Chavez w rsf 2 Roger Mayweather	Las Vegas, NV
Sep 22,	1985	Julio Cesar Chavez w pts 12 Dwight Pratchett (US)	Las Vegas, NV
May 15,	1986	Julio Cesar Chavez w rsf 5 Faustino Barrios (Arg)	Paris (Fra)
Jun 13,	1986	Julio Cesar Chavez w rsf 7 Refugio Rojas (US)	New York, NY
Aug 3,	1986	Julio Cesar Chavez w pts 12 Rocky Lockridge	Monte Carlo (Mon)
Dec 12,	1986	Julio Cesar Chavez w pts 12 Juan LaPorte (PR)	New York, NY
Apr 18,	1987	Julio Cesar Chavez w rsf 3 Francisco Tomas Da Cruz (Bra)	Nimes (Fra)
Aug 21,	1987	Julio Cesar Chavez w pts 12 Danilo Cabrera (DR)	Tijuana Mex)
Nov 21,	1987	*Chavez relinquished the title on becoming WBA lightweight champion*	
Feb 29,	1988	**Azumah Nelson** (Gha) w pts 12 Mario Martinez (Mex)	Los Angeles, CA
		For vacant title	
Jun 25,	1988	Azumah Nelson w rsf 9 Lupe Suarez (US)	Atlantic City, NJ
Dec 10,	1988	Azumah Nelson w ko 3 Sydnei dal Rovere (Bra)	Accra (Gha)
Feb 25,	1989	Azumah Nelson w rsf 12 Mario Martinez (Mex)	Las Vegas, NV
Nov 5,	1989	Azumah Nelson w ko 12 Jim McDonnell	London (Eng)
Oct 13,	1990	Azumah Nelson w pts 12 Juan LaPorte	Sydney (Aus)
Jun 28,	1991	Azumah Nelson drew 12 Jeff Fenech (Aus)	Las Vegas, NV
Mar 1,	1992	Azumah Nelson w rsf 8 Jeff Fenech	Melbourne (Aus)
Nov 7,	1992	Azumah Nelson w pts 12 Calvin Grove (US)	Lake Tahoe, CA
Feb 20,	1993	Azumah Nelson w pts 12 Gabriel Ruelas (Mex)	Mexico City (Mex)
Sep 10,	1993	Azumah Nelson drew 12 Jesse James Leija (US)	San Antonio, TX
May 7,	1994	**Jesse James Leija** w pts 12 Azumah Nelson	Las Vegas, NV
Sep 17,	1994	**Gabriel Ruelas** w pts 12 Jesse James Leija	Las Vegas, NV
Jan 28,	1995	Gabriel Ruelas w ret 2 Freddie Liberatore (US)	Las Vegas, NV
May 6,	1995	Gabriel Ruelas w rsf 11 Jimmy Garcia	Las Vegas, NV
May 6,	1995	**Azumah Nelson** w rsf 5 Gabriel Ruelas	Indio Springs, CA

IBF title

Apr 22,	1984	**Hwan-Kil Yuh** (Kor) w pts 15 Rod Sequenan (Phil)	Seoul (Kor)
		For vacant title	

Sep 16, 1984	Hwan-Kil Yuh w ko 6 Sak Galexi (Thai)	Pohang (Kor)
Feb 15, 1985	**Lester Ellis** (Aus) w pts 15 Hwan-Kil Yuh	Melbourne (Aus)
Apr 26, 1985	Lester Ellis w ko 13 Rod Sequenan	Melbourne (Aus)
Jul 12, 1985	**Barry Michael** (Aus) w pts 15 Lester Ellis	Melbourne (Aus)
Oct 18, 1985	Barry Michael w rsf 4 Jin-Shik Choi (Kor)	Darwin (Aus)
May 23, 1986	Barry Michael w rsf 4 Mark Fernandez (US)	Melbourne (Aus)
Aug 23, 1986	Barry Michael w pts 12 Najib Daho (Eng)	Manchester (Eng)
Aug 9, 1987	**Rocky Lockridge** w ret 8 Barry Michael	Windsor (Eng)
Oct 25, 1987	Rocky Lockridge w rsf 10 Johnny De La Rosa (DR)	Tucson, AZ
Apr 2, 1988	Rocky Lockridge w pts 15 Harold Knight (US)	Atlantic City, NJ
Jul 27, 1988	**Tony Lopez** (US) w pts 12 Rocky Lockridge	Sacramento, CA
Oct 27, 1988	Tony Lopez w pts 12 Juan "John-John" Molina (PR)	Sacramento, CA
Mar 5, 1989	Tony Lopez w pts 12 Rocky Lockridge	Sacramento, CA
Jun 18, 1989	Tony Lopez w rsf 8 Tyrone Jackson (US)	Stateline, NV
Oct 7, 1989	**Juan "John-John" Molina** w rsf 10 Tony Lopez	Sacramento, CA
Jan 28, 1990	Juan "John-John" Molina w rsf 6 Lupe Suarez	Atlantic City, NJ
May 20, 1990	**Tony Lopez** w pts 12 Juan "John-John" Molina	Reno, NV
Sep 22, 1990	Tony Lopez w pts 12 Jorge Paez (Mex)	Sacramento, CA
Mar 15, 1991	Tony Lopez drew 15 Brian Mitchell	Sacramento, CA
	For IBF and WBA titles	
Jul 12, 1991	Tony Lopez w rsf 6 Lupe Guttierez (US)	Lake Tahoe, CA
Sep 13, 1991	**Brian Mitchell** w pts 12 Tony Lopez	Sacramento, CA
Jan 1992	*Mitchell announced his retirement*	
Feb 22, 1992	**Juan "John-John" Molina** w rsf 4 Jackie Gunguluza (SA)	Sun City (Bop)
	For vacant title	
Aug 22, 1992	Juan "John-John" Molina w rsf 4 Fernando Caicedo (Col)	Bayamon (PR)
Feb 13, 1993	Juan "John-John" Molina w rsf 8 Francisco Segura (Mex)	Bayamon (PR)
Jun 26, 1993	Juan "John-John" Molina w pts 12 Manuel Medina (Mex)	Atlantic City, NJ
Oct 9, 1993	Juan "John-John" Molina w ko 8 Bernard Taylor (US)	San Juan, CA
Jan 22, 1994	Juan "John-John" Molina w ret 6 Floyd Havard (Wal)	Cardiff (Wal)
Apr 22, 1994	Juan "John-John" Molina w pts 12 Gregorio Vargas (Mex)	Las Vegas, NV
Nov 26, 1994	Juan "John-John" Molina w ko 10 Wilson Rodriguez (DR)	Bayamon (PR)
Jan 1995	*Molina vacated the title to move up to lightweight*	
Apr 22, 1995	**Eddie Hopson** (US) w ko 7 Moises Pedroza (Col)	Atlantic City, NJ
	For vacant title	
Jul 9, 1995	**Tracy Harris Patterson** (US) w rsf 2 Eddie Hopson	Reno, NV
Dec 15, 1995	**Arturo Gatti** (US) w rsf 2 Tracy Harris Patterson	Reno, NV

WBO title

Apr 29, 1989	**Juan "John-John" Molina** (PR) w pts 12 Juan LaPorte (PR)	San Juan, CA
	For vacant title	
Sep 1989	*Molina relinquished the title to challenge for the IBF version*	
Dec 9, 1989	**Kamel Bou-Ali** (Tun) w ko 8 Antonio Rivera (PR)	Terano
	For vacant title	
Oct 20, 1990	Kamel Bou-Ali no contest 2 Pedro Villegas (Arg)	Cesena (Ita)
Jun 1, 1991	Kamel Bou-Ali w ko 3 Joey Jacobs (Eng)	Ragusa (Ita)
Mar 21, 1992	**Daniel Londas** w pts 12 Kamel Bou-Ali	San Rufo
Sep 4, 1992	**Jimmi Bredahl** (Den) w pts 12 Daniel Londas	Copenhagen (Den)
Sep 17, 1993	Jimmi Bredahl w pts 12 Renato Cornett (Aus)	Copenhagen (Den)
Mar 5, 1994	**Oscar De La Hoya** (US) w ret 10 Jimmi Bredahl	Los Angeles, CA
May 27, 1994	Oscar De La Hoya w rsf 3 Giorgio Campanella (Ita)	Las Vegas, NV
June 1994	*De La Hoya vacated title to box at lightweight*	
Sep 24, 1994	**Regilio Tuur** (Hol) w pts 12 Eugene Speed (US)	Rotterdam (Hol)
	For vacant title	
Mar 9, 1995	Regilio Tuur w pts 12 Tony Pep (Can)	Groningen (Hol)
Jun 17, 1995	Regilio Tuur w rsf 5 Pete Taliefero (US)	New Orleans, LA
Sep 17, 1995	Regilio Tuur w ret 10 Luis Mendoza (Col)	Arnhem (Hol)
Dec 23, 1995	Regilio Tuur w rsf 12 Giorgio Campanella	Amsterdam (Hol)

JEFF FENECH *(right) held Azumah Nelso to a controversial draw in this 1991 title fight, but was easily beaten in the rematch in March 1992*

Featherweight

The featherweight class first became active in the Prize Ring around 1860, but did not gain widespread acceptance until the Irishman with the English name, Ike Weir, fought the Englishman with the Irish name, Frank Murphy, to a draw in 1889. Weir was generally considered to be getting on top when the police intervened, but when he got a second chance at the title he was knocked out by "Torpedo" Billy Murphy of New Zealand. There was at this time a wide gap between the division limits in Britain and America. The British regarded it as being anywhere from 122 to 126 lb, while the Americans favoured 112 to 114 lb.

The pick of the early champions was George Dixon, a black Canadian who was known as "Little Chocolate". He was responsible for moving the American limit first to 117, then 120, and finally 122 lb. It was not until 1920 that the Americans accepted the British figure of 126 lb at which it has remained.

As the list below shows, the story of the featherweight class is complicated, with the title frequently in dispute. That is still the case: the last time there was just one champion was almost 30 years ago, in 1967. But the featherweights have always had a place in the public's affections, and champions of the quality of Willie Pep, Eusbeio Pedroza, Sandy Saddler and Salvador Sanchez stand pound-for-pound comparison with the best in the game.

World Featherweight Championship Bouts

Mar 31,	1889	**Ike Weir** (Ire) drew 80 Frank Murphy (Eng) . . . . Kouts, IN
Jan 13,	1890	**Billy Murphy** (NZ) w ko 14 Ike Weir . . . . San Francisco, CA
Sep 2,	1890	**Young Griffo** (Aus) w rsf 15 Billy Murphy . . . . Sydney (Aus)
		Griffo outgrew the division
Jun 27,	1892	**George Dixon** (Can) w ko 14 Fred Johnson (Eng) . . . . . . Coney Island, NY
Sep 6,	1892	George Dixon w ko 8 Jack Skelly (US) . . . . New Orleans, LA
Aug 7,	1893	George Dixon w ko 3 Eddie Pierce (US) . . . . Coney Island, NY
Sep 25,	1893	George Dixon w ko 7 Solly Smith (US) . . . . Coney Island, NY
Jun 29,	1894	George Dixon drew 20 Young Griffo . . . . Boston, MA
Nov 27,	1896	**Frank Erne** (US) w pts 20 George Dixon . . . . New York, NY
Mar 24,	1897	**George Dixon** w pts 25 Frank Erne . . . . New York, NY
Oct 4,	1897	**Solly Smith** (US) w pts 20 George Dixon . . . . San Francisco, CA
		Dixon argued that as Smith was two pounds over the agreed weight of 118 lb, the title was not at stake. Smith was widely regarded as the new champion, but Dixon continued to style himself as such and to defend his "title". In Britain, a rival version of the championship (limit 122 lb) was claimed by Ben Jordan of Bermondsey, London, who outpointed Dixon over 25 rounds in New York on July 1, 1898
Aug 1,	1898	Solly Smith drew 25 Tommy White (US) . . . . Coney Island, NY
Sep 26,	1898	**Dave Sullivan** (US) w ret 5 Solly Smith . . . . Coney Island, NY
Nov 11,	1898	**George Dixon** w dis 10 Dave Sullivan . . . . New York, NY
Nov 29,	1898	George Dixon w pts 25 Oscar Gardner (US) . . . . New York, NY
Jan 17,	1899	George Dixon w ko 10 Young Pluto (Aus) . . . . New York, NY
May 29,	1899	**Ben Jordan** (Eng) w ko 9 Harry Greenfield . . . . London (Eng)
Oct 10,	1899	**Eddie Santry** w ko 15 Ben Jordan . . . . New York, NY
		Above two were for British version of title
Nov 2,	1899	George Dixon w pts 25 Will Curley (Eng) . . . . New York, NY
Nov 21,	1899	George Dixon w pts 25 Eddie Lenny (US) . . . . New York, NY
Jan 9,	1900	**Terry McGovern** (US) w rsf 8 George Dixon . . . . New York, NY
Feb 1,	1900	Terry McGovern w ko 5 Eddie Santry (US) . . . . Chicago, IL
		For undisputed title
Mar 9,	1900	Terry McGovern w ko 3 Oscar Gardner . . . . New York, NY
Nov 2,	1900	Terry McGovern w ko 7 Joe Bernstein (US) . . . . Louisville, KY
Nov 28,	1901	**Young Corbett** II (US) w ko 2 Terry McGovern . . . . Hartford, CT
		Corbett could no longer make the championship limit and Abe Attell, who had drawn with and beaten George Dixon in 1901, was regarded as the best man at the weight
Sep 3,	1903	**Abe Attell** (US) w pts 25 Johnny Reagan (US) . . . . St Louis, MO
Feb 1,	1904	Abe Attell w ko 5 Harry Forbes (US) . . . . St Louis, MO
Feb 22,	1906	Abe Attell w pts 15 Jimmy Walsh (US) . . . . Chelsea, MA
May 11,	1906	Abe Attell drew 20 Kid Herman (US) . . . . Los Angeles, CA
Jul 4,	1906	Abe Attell w pts 20 Frankie Neil (US) . . . . Los Angeles, CA

Oct 30,	1906	Abe Attell w pts 20 Harry Baker (US) . . . . Los Angeles, CA
Nov 16,	1906	Abe Attell w pts 15 Billy de Coursey (US) . . . . San Diego, CA
Dec 7,	1906	Abe Attell w ko 8 Jimmy Walsh . . . . Los Angeles, CA
Jan 18,	1907	Abe Attell w ko 8 Harry Baker . . . . Los Angeles, CA
May 24,	1907	Abe Attell w pts 20 Kid Solomon (US) . . . . Los Angeles, CA
Oct 29,	1907	Abe Attell w ko 4 Freddie Weeks (US) . . . . Los Angeles, CA
Jan 1,	1908	Abe Attell drew 25 Owen Moran (Eng) . . . . San Francisco, CA
Jan 31,	1908	Abe Attell w ret 13 Frankie Neil . . . . San Francisco, CA
Feb 28,	1908	Abe Attell w rsf 7 Eddie Kelly (US) . . . . San Francisco, CA
Sep 7,	1908	Abe Attell drew 23 Owen Moran . . . . San Francisco, CA
Dec 29,	1908	Abe Attell w ko 8 Biz Mackey (US) . . . . New Orleans, LA
Jan 14,	1909	Abe Attell w ko 10 Freddie Weeks . . . . Goldfield, NV
Feb 4,	1909	Abe Attell w ret 7 Eddie Kelly . . . . New Orleans, LA
Feb 19,	1909	**Jim Driscoll** (Wal) no decision 10 Abe Attell . . . . New York, NY
		Driscoll was clearly the better man, but Attell refused to give him a rematch for the championship. However, on the basis of this performance Driscoll was recognized as world champion by Britain and the IBU
Oct 24,	1910	Abe Attell w pts 10 Johnny Kilbane (US) . . . . Kansas City, KS
Feb 22,	1912	**Johnny Kilbane** w pts 20 Abe Attell . . . . Vernon, CA
Jun 3,	1912	Jim Driscoll w ko 12 Jean Poesy (Fra) . . . . London (Eng)
Jan 27,	1913	Jim Driscoll drew 20 Owen Moran . . . . NSC, London (Eng)
Feb	1913	*Driscoll retired*
Apr 29,	1913	Johnny Kilbane drew 20 Johnny Dundee (US) . . . . Los Angeles, CA
Sep 6,	1913	Johnny Kilbane w pts 12 Jimmy Walsh . . . . Boston, MA
Sep 4,	1916	Johnny Kilbane w ko 3 Kid Chaney (US) . . . . Cedar Point, OH
Sep 17,	1921	Johnny Kilbane w ko 7 Danny Frush (Eng) . . . . Cleveland, OH
		New York Commission stripped Kilbane of the title for failing to defend against Johnny Dundee, and matched Dundee and Danny Frush for the vacant title
Aug 15,	1922	**Johnny Dundee** w ko 9 Danny Frush . . . . Brooklyn, NY
Jun 2,	1923	**Eugene Criqui** (Fra) w ko 6 Johnny Kilbane . . . . New York, NY
Jul 26,	1923	**Johnny Dundee** w ko 6 Eugene Criqui . . . . New York, NY
		For undisputed title
Aug 10,	1924	*Dundee relinquished title because of weight problems*
Jan 2,	1925	**Louis "Kid" Kaplan** (US) w ret 9 Danny Kramer (US) . . . . . New York, NY
Aug 27,	1925	Louis "Kid" Kaplan drew 15 Babe Herman (US) . . . . Waterbury, CT
Dec 18,	1925	Louis "Kid" Kaplan w pts 15 Babe Herman . . . . New York, NY
July	1927	*Kaplan relinquished the title because of weight problems*
Sep 19,	1927	**Benny Bass** (Rus) w pts 10 Red Chapman (US) . . . . Philadelphia, PA
		For vacant NBA title
Oct 24,	1927	**Tony Canzoneri** (US) w pts 15 Johnny Dundee . . . . New York, NY
		NY version of vacant title
Feb 10,	1928	Tony Canzoneri w pts 15 Benny Bass . . . . New York, NY
		For undisputed title
Sep 28,	1928	**Andre Routis** (Fra) w pts 15 Tony Canzoneri . . . . New York, NY
May 27,	1929	Andre Routis w rsf 3 Buster Brown (US) . . . . Baltimore, MD
Sep 23,	1929	**Battling Battalino** (US) w pts 15 Andre Routis . . . . Hartford, CT
Jul 15,	1930	Battling Battalino w ko 5 Ignacio Fernandez (Phil) . . . . Hartford, CT
Dec 12,	1930	Battling Battalino w pts 15 Kid Chocolate (Cub) . . . . New York, NY
May 22,	1931	Battling Battalino w pts 15 Fidel LaBarba (US) . . . . New York, NY
Jul 23,	1931	Battling Battalino w pts 10 Freddie Miller (US) . . . . Cincinnati, OH
Nov 4,	1931	Battling Battalino w pts 10 Earl Mastro (US) . . . . Chicago, IL
Jan	1932	*The NBA and NY Commission declared the title vacant after Battalino had been three pounds overweight for a scheduled defence against Freddie Miller*

NBA title

May 26,	1932	**Tommy Paul** (US) w pts 15 Johnny Pena (PR) . . . . Detroit, MI
		For vacant title
Jan13,	1933	**Freddie Miller** w pts 10 Tommy Paul . . . . Chicago, IL
Feb 28,	1933	Freddie Miller w pts 10 Baby Arizmendi (Mex) . . . . Los Angeles, CA
Mar 21,	1933	Freddie Miller w pts 10 Speedy Dado (Phil) . . . . Los Angeles, CA
Jul 11,	1933	Freddie Miller w ko 4 Abie Israel (US) . . . . Seattle, WA
Jan 1,	1934	Freddie Miller w pts 10 Jackie Sharkey (US) . . . . Cincinnati, OH
Jul 13,	1934	Freddie Miller w ko 8 Gene Espinosa (US) . . . . Watsonville, CA
Sep 21,	1934	Freddie Miller w pts 15 Nel Tarleton (Eng) . . . . Liverpool (Eng)
Feb 17,	1935	Freddie Miller w ko 1 Jose Girones (Sp) . . . . Barcelona (Sp)
Jun 12,	1935	Freddie Miller w pts 15 Nel Tarleton . . . . Liverpool (Eng)
Oct 22,	1935	Freddie Miller w pts 15 Vernon Cormier (US) . . . . Boston, MA
Feb 18,	1936	Freddie Miller w pts 15 Johnny Pena . . . . Seattle, WA
Mar 2,	1936	Freddie Miller w pts 15 Petey Sarron (US) . . . . Miami, FL
May 11,	1936	**Petey Sarron** w pts 15 Freddie Miller . . . . Washington, DC
Jul 22,	1936	Petey Sarron w pts 15 Baby Manuel (US) . . . . Dallas, TX
Sep 4,	1937	Petey Sarron w pts 12 Freddie Miller . . . . Johannesburg (SA)
Oct 29,	1937	**Henry Armstrong** (US) w ko 6 Petey Sarron . . . . New York, NY
		For NBA and vacant NY titles, which Armstrong relinquished on becoming lightweight champion in August 1938

Dec 29, 1938   **Leo Rodak** (US) w pts 10 Leone Efrati (US) . . . . Chicago, IL
Although this was an overweight match, the NBA agreed to recognize Rodak as their new champion

Apr 18, 1939   **Joey Archibald** (US) w pts 15 Leo Rodak . . . . Providence, RI
For undisputed title

New York title

13Oct, 1932   **Kid Chocolate** w rsf 12 Lew Feldman (US) . . . . New York, NY
For vacant title

Dec 9, 1932   Kid Chocolate w pts 15 Fidel LaBarba . . . . New York, NY

May 19, 1933   Kid Chocolate w pts 15 Tommy Watson (Eng) . . . . New York, NY

Mar 1934   *NY Commission stripped Chocolate for failing to defend against Frankie Klick*

May 1936   *NY Commission recognized Mike Belloise as champion*

Sep 3, 1936   **Mike Belloise (US)** w ko 9 Dave Crowley (Eng) . . . . New York, NY

Oct 27, 1936   **Henry Armstrong** w pts 10 Mike Belloise . . . . Los Angeles, CA
This was a defence by Armstrong of the California version of the title, which he had won by outpointing Baby Arizmendi over 10 rounds in Los Angeles on August 4, 1936. The NY Commission did not regard it as involving Belloise's title, and continued to recognize him as champion until Belloise was forced to give up the title because of injury

Aug 10, 1937   *Belloise relinquished title*

Oct 29, 1937   Henry Armstrong w ko 6 Petey Sarron . . . . New York, NY
For NBA and vacant NY titles, which Armstrong relinquished on becoming lightweight champion in August 1938

Oct 17, 1938   **Joey Archibald** (US) w pts 15 Mike Belloise . . . . New York, NY
For vacant title

Apr 18, 1939   Joey Archibald w pts 15 Leo Rodak . . . . Providence, RI
For undisputed title

IBU title

Oct 5, 1937   **Maurice Holtzer** (Fra) w pts 15 Phil Dolhem (Bel) . . . . Algiers (Alg)
For vacant title

Feb 19, 1938   Maurice Holtzer drew 15 Maurice Dubois (Swi) . . . . Geneva (Swi)

May 1938   *The IBU agreed to recognize Armstrong, in an effort to promote unity*

Undisputed title

Sep 28, 1939   **Joey Archibald** w pts 15 Harry Jeffra (US) . . . . Washington, DC

May 1, 1940   *The NBA withdrew recognition from Archibald for his failure to defend against Petey Scalzo, who had knocked him out in a non-title fight in December 1938. They declared Scalzo champion*

New York title

May 20, 1940   **Harry Jeffra** w pts 15 Joey Archibald . . . . Baltimore, MD

Jul 29, 1940   Harry Jeffra w pts 15 Spider Armstrong (Can) . . . . Baltimore, MD

May 12, 1941   **Joey Archibald** w pts 15 Harry Jeffra . . . . Washington, DC

Sep 11, 1941   **Chalky Wright** (Mex) w ko 11 Joey Archibald . . . . Washington, DC

Jun 19, 1942   Chalky Wright w rsf 10 Harry Jeffra . . . . Baltimore, MD

Sep 25, 1942   Chalky Wright w pts 15 Lulu Constantino (US) . . . . New York, NY

Nov 20, 1942   **Willie Pep** (US) w pts 15 Chalky Wright . . . . New York, NY

Jun 8, 1943   Willie Pep w pts 15 Sal Bartolo (US) . . . . Boston, MA

Sep 29, 1944   Willie Pep w pts 15 Chalky Wright . . . . New York, NY

Feb 19, 1945   Willie Pep w pts 15 Phil Terranova (US) . . . . New York, NY

Jun 7, 1946   Willie Pep w ko 12 Sal Bartolo . . . . New York, NY
For undisputed title

NBA title

Jul 10, 1940   **Petey Scalzo** (US) w rsf 15 Bobby "Poison" Ivy (US) . . . . Hartford, CT

May 19, 1941   Petey Scalzo w pts 15 Phil Zwick (US) . . . . Milwaukee, WI

Jul 1, 1941   **Richie Lemos** (US) w ko 5 Petey Scalzo . . . . Los Angeles, CA

Nov 18, 1941   **Jackie Wilson** (US) w pts 12 Richie Lemos . . . . Los Angeles, CA

Dec 16, 1941   Jackie Wilson w pts 12 Richie Lemos . . . . Los Angeles, CA

Jan 18, 1943   **Jackie Callura** (Can) w pts 15 Jackie Wilson . . . . Providence, RI

Mar 18, 1943   Jackie Callura w pts 15 Jackie Wilson . . . . Boston, MA

Aug 16, 1943   **Phil Terranova** (US) w ko 8 Jackie Callura . . . . New Orleans, LA

Dec 27, 1943   Phil Terranova w rsf 6 Jackie Callura . . . . New Orleans, LA

Mar 10, 1944   **Sal Bartolo** w pts 15 Phil Terranova . . . . Boston, MA

May 5, 1944   Sal Bartolo w pts 15 Phil Terranova . . . . Boston, MA

Dec 15, 1944   Sal Bartolo w pts 15 Willie Roache (US) . . . . Boston, MA

May 3, 1946   Sal Bartolo w ko 6 Spider Armstrong (Can) . . . . Boston, MA

Jun 7, 1946   **Willie Pep** w ko 12 Sal Bartolo . . . . New York, NY
For undisputed title

Undisputed title

Aug 22, 1947   **Willie Pep** w ko 12 Jock Leslie (US) . . . . Flint, MI

Feb 24, 1948   Willie Pep w rsf 10 Humberto Sierra (Cub) . . . . Miami, FL

Oct 29, 1948   **Sandy Saddler** (US) w ko 4 Willie Pep . . . . New York, NY

Feb 11, 1949   **Willie Pep** w pts 15 Sandy Saddler . . . . New York, NY

Sep 20, 1949   Willie Pep w rsf 7 Eddie Compo (US) . . . . Waterbury, CT

Jan 16, 1950   Willie Pep w ko 5 Charlie Riley (US) . . . . St Louis, MO

Mar 17, 1950   Willie Pep w pts 15 Ray Famechon (Fra) . . . . New York, NY

Sep 8, 1950   **Sandy Saddler** w ret 7 Willie Pep . . . . New York, NY

Sep 26, 1951   Sandy Saddler w ret 9 Willie Pep . . . . New York, NY

Feb 25, 1955   Sandy Saddler w pts 15 Teddy Davis (US) . . . . New York, NY

Jan 18, 1956   Sandy Saddler w rsf 13 Gabriel "Flash" Elorde (Phil) . . . San Francisco, CA

Jan 1957   *Saddler retired because of injuries sustained in a car crash*

Jun 24, 1957   **Hogan Bassey** (Nig) w rsf 10 Cherif Hamia (Fra) . . . . Paris (Fra)
For vacant title

Apr 1, 1958   Hogan Bassey w ko 3 Ricardo Moreno (Mex) . . . . Los Angeles, CA

Mar 18, 1959   **Davey Moore** (US) w ret 13 Hogan Bassey . . . . Los Angeles, CA

Aug 19, 1959   Davey Moore w ret 10 Hogan Bassey . . . . Los Angeles, CA

Aug 29, 1960   Davey Moore w pts 15 Kazuo Takayama (Jap) . . . . Tokyo (Jap)

Apr 8, 1961   Davey Moore w ko 1 Danny Valdez (US) . . . . Los Angeles, CA

Nov 13, 1961   Davey Moore w pts 15 Kazuo Takayama . . . . Tokyo (Jap)

Aug 17, 1962   Davey Moore w rsf 2 Olli Maki (Fin) . . . . Helsinki (Fin)

Mar 21, 1963   **Sugar Ramos** (Cub) w ret 10 Davey Moore . . . . Los Angeles, CA

Jul 13, 1963   Sugar Ramos w pts 15 Rafiu King (Nig) . . . . Mexico City (Mex)

Feb 28, 1964   Sugar Ramos w ret 6 Mitsunori Seki (Jap) . . . . Tokyo (Jap)

May 9, 1964   Sugar Ramos w pts 15 Floyd Robertson (Gha) . . . . Accra (Gha)

Sep 26, 1964   **Vicente Saldivar** (Mex) w ret 11 Sugar Ramos . . . . Mexico City (Mex)

Dec 6, 1964   Vicente Saldivar w rsf 11 Delfino Rosales (Mex) . . . . . . Guanajuato (Mex)

May 7, 1965   Vicente Saldivar w rsf 15 Raul Rojas (US) . . . . Los Angeles, CA

Sep 7, 1965   Vicente Saldivar w pts 15 Howard Winstone (Wal) . . . . London (Eng)

Feb 12, 1966   Vicente Saldivar w ko 2 Floyd Robertson . . . . Mexico City (Mex)

Aug 7, 1966   Vicente Saldivar w pts 15 Mitsunori Seki . . . . Mexico City (Mex)

Jan 29, 1967   Vicente Saldivar w rsf 7 Mitsunori Seki . . . . Mexico City (Mex)

Jun 15, 1967   Vicente Saldivar w pts 15 Howard Winstone . . . . Cardiff (Wal)

Oct 14, 1967   Vicente Saldivar w ret 12 Howard Winstone . . . . Mexico City (Mex)
Saldivar announced his retirement in the ring immediately after the fight

WBC title

Jan 23, 1968   **Howard Winstone** w rsf 9 Mitsunori Seki . . . . London (Eng)
For vacant title

Jul 24, 1968   **Jose Legra** (Cub) w rsf 5 Howard Winstone . . . . Porthcawl (Wal)

Jan 21, 1969   **Johnny Famechon** (Aus) w pts 15 Jose Legra . . . . London (Eng)

Jul 28, 1969   Johnny Famechon w pts 15 Fighting Harada (Jap) . . . . Sydney (Aus)

Jan 6, 1970   Johnny Famechon w ko 14 Fighting Harada . . . . Tokyo (Jap)

May 9, 1970   **Vicente Saldivar** w pts 15 Johnny Famechon . . . . Rome (Ita)

Dec 11, 1970   **Kuniaki Shibata** (Jap) w rsf 12 Vicente Saldivar . . . . Tijuana (Mex)

Jun,3 1971   Kuniaki Shibata w ko 1 Raul Cruz (Mex) . . . . Tokyo (Jap)

Nov 11, 1971   Kuniaki Shibata drew 15 Ernesto Marcel (Pan) . . . . Matsuyama (Jap)

May 19, 1972   **Clemente Sanchez** (Mex) w ko 3 Kuniaki Shibata . . . . Tokyo (Jap)

Dec 16, 1972   **Jose Legra** w rsf 10 Clemente Sanchez . . . . Monterrey (Mex)
(Sanchez was overweight, but Legra was recognized as champion by the WBC)

May 5, 1973   **Eder Jofre** (Bra) w pts 15 Jose Legra . . . . Brasilia (Bra)

Oct 21, 1973   Eder Jofre w ko 4 Vicente Saldivar . . . . Salvador (Bra)

Jun 1974   *WBC withdrew recognition of Jofre for failing to defend against their official challenger, Alfredo Marcano*

RINGSIDE VIEW

Willie Pep
vs
Sandy Saddler

PEPPING IT UP

Sandy Saddler had swept Willie Pep aside with astonishing ease when they met for the featherweight title in October 1948, and was expected to do likewise in the return on February 11, 1949. Instead, Pep gave a consummate display of classic boxing skills to regain his championship in a match which broke attendance and receipt records for the division.

RINGSIDE VIEW

Danny "Little Red" Lopez
vs
David Kotey

"LITTLE RED" CHECKS IN

The largest attendance in featherweight history, 100,000, watched Ghana's first world champion David Kotey lose to the explosive-punching Californian Danny "Little Red" Lopez in Accra on November 5, 1976. It was the only time in 11 title fights, nine of which he won, that Lopez went the full 15 rounds.

Date		Result	Location
Sep 7,	1974	**Bobby Chacon** (US) w rsf 9 Alfredo Marcano (Ven)	Los Angeles, CA
		For vacant title	
Mar 1,	1975	Bobby Chacon w ko 2 Jesus Estrada (Mex)	Los Angeles, CA
Jun 20,	1975	**Ruben Olivares** (Mex) w rsf 2 Bobby Chacon	Inglewood, CA
Sep 20,	1975	**David Kotey** (Gha) w pts 15 Ruben Olivares	Inglewood, CA
Mar 6,	1976	David Kotey w rsf 12 Flipper Uehara (Jap)	Accra (Gha)
Jul 16,	1976	David Kotey w rsf 3 Shigeo Fukuyama (Jap)	Tokyo (Jap)
Nov 5,	1976	**Danny Lopez** (US) w pts 15 David Kotey	Accra (Gha)
Sep 13,	1977	Danny Lopez w rsf 7 Jose Torres (Mex)	Los Angeles, CA
Feb 15,	1978	Danny Lopez w rsf 6 David Kotey	Las Vegas, NV
Apr 23,	1978	Danny Lopez w rsf 6 Jose de Paula (Bra)	Los Angeles, CA
Sep 15,	1978	Danny Lopez w ko 2 Juan Malvarez (Arg)	New Orleans, LA
Oct 21,	1978	Danny Lopez w dis 4 Fel Clemente (Phil)	Pesaro (Ita)
Mar 10,	1979	Danny Lopez w ko 2 Roberto Castanon (Sp)	Salt Lake City, UT
Jun 17,	1979	Danny Lopez w ko 15 Mike Ayala (US)	San Antonio, TX
Sep 25,	1979	Danny Lopez w rsf 3 Jose Caba (DR)	Los Angeles, CA
Feb 2,	1980	**Salvador Sanchez** (Mex) w rsf 13 Danny Lopez	Phoenix, AZ
Apr 12,	1980	Salvador Sanchez w pts 15 Ruben Castillo (US)	Tucson, AZ
Jun 21,	1980	Salvador Sanchez w rsf 14 Danny Lopez	Las Vegas, NV
Sep 13,	1980	Salvador Sanchez w pts 15 Pat Ford (Guy)	San Antonio, TX
Dec 13,	1980	Salvador Sanchez w pts 15 Juan LaPorte (PR)	El Paso, NM
Mar 22,	1981	Salvador Sanchez w rsf 10 Roberto Castanon (Sp)	Las Vegas, NV
Aug 21,	1981	Salvador Sanchez w rsf 8 Wilfredo Gomez (PR)	Las Vegas, NV
Dec 12,	1981	Salvador Sanchez w pts 15 Pat Cowdell (Eng)	Houston, TX
May 8,	1982	Salvador Sanchez w pts 15 Rocky Garcia (US)	Dallas, TX
Jul 21,	1982	Salvador Sanchez w rsf 15 Azumah Nelson (Gha)	New York, NY
Aug	1982	*Sanchez was killed in a car crash*	
Sep 15,	1982	**Juan LaPorte** w ret 10 Mario Miranda (Col)	New York, NY
		For vacant title	
Feb 20,	1983	Juan LaPorte w pts 12 Ruben Castillo	San Juan, CA
Jun 25,	1983	Juan LaPorte w pts 12 Johnny De La Rosa (DR)	San Juan, CA
Mar 31,	1984	**Wilfredo Gomez** w pts 12 Juan LaPorte	San Juan, CA
Dec 8,	1984	**Azumah Nelson** w rsf 11 Wilfredo Gomez	San Juan, CA
Sep 6,	1985	Azumah Nelson w ko 5 Juvenal Ordenes (Ch)	Miami, FL
Oct 12,	1985	Azumah Nelson w ko 1 Pat Cowdell	Birmingham (Eng)
Feb 25,	1986	Azumah Nelson w pts 12 Marcos Villasana (Mex)	Los Angeles, CA
Jun 22,	1986	Azumah Nelson w rsf 10 Danilo Cabrera (DR)	San Juan, CA
Mar 7,	1987	Azumah Nelson w ko 6 Mauro Gutierrez (Mex)	Las Vegas, NV
Aug 29,	1987	Azumah Nelson w pts 12 Marcos Villasana	Los Angeles, CA
Jan	1988	*Nelson relinquished the title to box at super-featherweight*	
Mar 7,	1988	**Jeff Fenech** (Aus) w rsf 10 Victor Callejas (PR)	Sydney (Aus)
		For vacant title	
Aug 12,	1988	Jeff Fenech w rsf 5 Tyrone Downes (Bar)	Melbourne (Aus)
Nov 30,	1988	Jeff Fenech w rsf 5 George Navarro (US)	Melbourne (Aus)
Apr 8,	1989	Jeff Fenech w pts 12 Marcos Villasana	Melbourne (Aus)
		Fenech relinquished the title immediately because of weight problems	
Jun 2,	1990	**Marcos Villasana** w rsf 8 Paul Hodkinson (Eng)	Manchester (Eng)
		For vacant title	
Sep 30,	1990	Marcos Villasana w rsf 8 Javier Marquez (Mex)	Mexico City (Mex)
Apr 11,	1991	Marcos Villasana w rsf 6 Rafael Zuniga (Col)	Mexico City (Mex)
Aug 16,	1991	Marcos Villasana w pts 12 Ricardo Cepeda (PR)	Marbella (Sp)
Nov 13,	1991	**Paul Hodkinson** w pts 12 Marcos Villasana	Belfast (N. Ire)
Apr 25,	1992	Paul Hodkinson w rsf 3 Steve Cruz (US)	Belfast (N. Ire)
Sep 12,	1992	Paul Hodkinson w rsf 10 Fabrice Benichou (Fra)	Blagnac (Fra)
Feb 3,	1993	Paul Hodkinson w ret 4 Ricardo Cepeda	London (Eng)
Apr 28,	1993	**Gregorio Vargas** (Mex) w ret 7 Paul Hodkinson	Dublin (Ire)
Dec 4,	1993	**Kevin Kelley** (US) w pts 12 Gregorio Vargas	Reno, NV
May 6,	1994	Kevin Kelley w pts 12 Jesse Benavides (USA)	Atlantic City, NJ
Jan 7,	1995	**Alejandro Gonzalez** (Mex) w ret 11 Kevin Kelley	San Antonio, TX
Mar 31,	1995	Alejandro Gonzalez w pts 12 Louie Espinosa (US)	Anaheim, CA
Jun 2,	1995	Alejandro Gonzalez w rsf 9 Tony Green (USA)	Ledyard, CT
Sep 23,	1995	**Manuel Medina** w pts 12 Alejandro Gonzalez	Sacramento, CA
Dec 11,	1995	**Luisito Espinosa** (Phil) w pts 12 Manuel Medina	Tokyo (Jap)

WBA title

Date		Result	Location
Mar 28,	1968	**Raul Rojas** w pts 15 Enrique Higgins (Col)	Los Angeles, CA
		For vacant title	
Sep 27,	1968	**Shozo Saijo** (Jap) w pts 15 Raul Rojas	Los Angeles, CA
Feb 9,	1969	Shozo Saijo w pts 15 Pedro Gomez (Ven)	Tokyo (Jap)
Sep 7,	1969	Shozo Saijo w ko 2 Jose Luis Pimental (Mex)	Sapporo (Jap)
Feb 8,	1970	Shozo Saijo w pts 15 Godfrey Stevens (Ch)	Tokyo (Jap)
Jul 5,	1970	Shozo Saijo w pts 15 Frankie Crawford (US)	Sendai (Jap)
Feb 28,	1971	Shozo Saijo w pts 15 Frankie Crawford	Utsonomija (Jap)
Sep 2,	1971	**Antonio Gomez** (Ven) w rsf 5 Shozo Saijo	Tokyo (Jap)
Feb 6,	1972	Antonio Gomez w ko 7 Raul Martinez (Mex)	Maracay (Ven)
Aug 19,	1972	**Ernesto Marcel** w pts 15 Antonio Gomez	Maracay (Ven)
Dec 3,	1972	Ernesto Marcel w rsf 6 Enrique Garcia (Mex)	Panama City (Pan)
Jul 14,	1973	Ernesto Marcel w ret 11 Antonio Gomez	Panama City (Pan)
Sep 8,	1973	Ernesto Marcel w ko 9 Spider Nemoto (Jap)	Panama City (Pan)
Feb 16,	1974	Ernesto Marcel w pts 15 Alexis Arguello (Nic)	Panama City (Pan)
May	1974	*Marcel retired*	
Jul 9,	1974	**Ruben Olivares** w ko 7 Zensuke Utagawa (Jap)	Inglewood, CA
		For vacant title	
Nov 23,	1974	**Alexis Arguello** w ko 13 Ruben Olivares	Inglewood, CA
Mar 15,	1975	Alexis Arguello w rsf 8 Leonel Hernandez (Ven)	Caracas (Ven)
May 31,	1975	Alexis Arguello w rsf 2 Rigoberto Riasco (Pan)	Managua (Nic)
Oct 12,	1975	Alexis Arguello w ko 5 Royal Kobayashi (Jap)	Tokyo (Jap)
Jun 19,	1976	Alexis Arguello w ko 3 Salvatore Torres (Mex)	Los Angeles, CA
Jun	1976	*Arguello gave up WBA title due to weight-making difficulties*	
Jan 15,	1977	**Rafael Ortega** (Pan) w pts 15 Francisco Coronado (Nic)	Panama City (Pan)
		For vacant title	
May 29,	1977	Rafael Ortega w pts 15 Flipper Uehara	Okinawa (Jap)
Dec 17,	1977	**Cecilio Lastra** (Sp) w pts 15 Rafael Ortega	Torrelavega (Sp)
Apr 15,	1978	**Eusebio Pedroza** (Pan) w ko 13 Cecilio Lastra	Panama City (Pan)
Jul 2,	1978	Eusebio Pedroza w rsf 12 Ernesto Herrera (Mex)	Panama City (Pan)
Nov 27,	1978	Eusebio Pedroza w pts 15 Enrique Solis (PR)	San Juan, CA
Jan 9,	1979	Eusebio Pedroza w ret 13 Royal Kobayashi	Tokyo (Jap)
Apr 8,	1979	Eusebio Pedroza w rsf 11 Hector Carrasquilla (Pan)	Panama City (Pan)
Jul 21,	1979	Eusebio Pedroza w rsf 12 Ruben Olivares	Houston, TX
Nov 17,	1979	Eusebio Pedroza w rsf 11 Johnny Aba (PNG)	Port Moresby (PNG)
Jan 22,	1980	Eusebio Pedroza w pts 15 Spider Nemoto (Jap)	Tokyo (Jap)
Mar 29,	1980	Eusebio Pedroza w ko 9 Juan Malvarez (Arg)	Panama City (Pan)
Jul 20,	1980	Eusebio Pedroza w ko 9 Sa-Wang Kim (Kor)	Seoul (Kor)
Oct 4,	1980	Eusebio Pedroza w pts 15 Rocky Lockridge (US)	McAfee, NJ
Feb 14,	1981	Eusebio Pedroza w ko 13 Pat Ford (Guy)	Panama City (Pan)
Aug 1,	1981	Eusebio Pedroza w ko 7 Carlos Pinango (Ven)	Caracas (Ven)
Dec 5,	1981	Eusebio Pedroza w ko 5 Bashew Sibaca (SA)	Panama City (Pan)
Jan 24,	1982	Eusebio Pedroza w pts 15 Juan LaPorte	Atlantic City, NJ
Oct 16,	1982	Eusebio Pedroza drew 15 Bernard Taylor (US)	Charlotte, NC
Apr 24,	1983	Eusebio Pedroza w pts 15 Rocky Lockridge	San Remo (Ita)
Oct 22,	1983	Eusebio Pedroza w pts 15 Jose Caba	St Vincent (Ita)
May 27,	1984	Eusebio Pedroza w pts 15 Angel Mayor (Ven)	Maracaibo (Ven)
Feb 2,	1985	Eusebio Pedroza w pts 15 Jorge Lujan (Pan)	Panama City (Pan)
Jun 8,	1985	**Barry McGuigan** (Ire) w pts 15 Eusebio Pedroza	London (Eng)
Sep 28,	1985	Barry McGuigan w ret 8 Bernard Taylor	Belfast (Ire)
Feb 15,	1986	Barry McGuigan w rsf 14 Danilo Cabrera	Dublin (Ire)
Jun 23,	1986	**Steve Cruz** w pts 15 Barry McGuigan	Las Vegas, NV
Mar 6,	1987	**Antonio Esparragoza** (Ven) w rsf 12 Steve Cruz	Fort Worth, TX
Jul 26,	1987	Antonio Esparragoza w ko 10 Pascual Aranda (Mex)	Houston, TX
Jun 23,	1988	Antonio Esparragoza drew 12 Marcos Villasana	Los Angeles, CA
Nov 5,	1988	Antonio Esparragoza w ko 8 Jose Marmolejo (Pan)	Marsala (Ita)
Mar 25,	1989	Antonio Esparragoza w ko 10 Mitsuri Sugiya (Jap)	Kawasaki Jap)
Jun 2,	1989	Antonio Esparragoza w ko 6 Jean Marc Renard (Bel)	Namur (Bel)
Sep 22,	1989	Antonio Esparragoza w ko 5 Eduardo Montoya (Mex)	Mexicali (Mex)
May 12,	1990	Antonio Esparragoza w pts 12 Chan-Mok Park (Kor)	Seoul (Kor)
Mar 30,	1991	**Kyun-Yung Park** (Kor) w pts 12 Antonio Esparragoza	Kwangju (Kor)
Jun 15,	1991	Kyun-Yung Park w rsf 6 Masuaki Takeda (Jap)	Seoul (Kor)
Sep 14,	1991	Kyun-Yung Park w pts 12 Eloy Rojas (Ven)	Mokpo (Kor)
Jan 25,	1992	Kyun-Yung Park w ko 9 Seiji Asakawa (Jap)	Seoul (Kor)
Apr 25,	1992	Kyun-Yung Park w rsf 11 Koji Matsumoto (Jap)	Ansan (Kor)
Aug 29,	1992	Kyun-Yung Park w pts 12 Giovanni Neves (Ven)	Taeju (Kor)
Dec 19,	1992	Kyun-Yung Park w pts 12 Ever Beleno (Col)	Changwon (Kor)
Mar 20,	1993	Kyun-Yung Park w rsf 4 Thanomchit Kiatkriengkrai (Thai)	Cheju Do (Kor)
Sep 3,	1993	Kyun-Yung Park w pts 12 Tae-Shik Chun (Kor)	Damyang (Kor)
Dec 4,	1993	**Eloy Rojas** w pts 12 Kyun-Yung Park	Kwangmong
Mar 19,	1994	Eloy Rojas w ko 5 Seiji Asakawa (Jap)	Kobe (Jap)
Sep 11,	1994	Eloy Rojas w rsf 8 Samart Payakaroon (Thai)	Trang (Thai)
Dec 3,	1994	Eloy Rojas w pts 12 Luis Mendoza (Col)	Bogota (Col)
May 27,	1995	Eloy Rojas w pts 12 Kyun-Yung Park	Soeul (Kor)
Aug 13,	1995	Eloy Rojas w pts 12 Nobutoshi Hiranaka (Jap)	Tagawa

IBF title

Mar 4,	1984	**Min-Keun Oh** (Kor) w ko 2 Joko Arter (Phil)	. . . .	Seoul (Kor)

For vacant title

Jun 10,	1984	Min-Keun Oh w pts 15 Kelvin Lampkin (US)	. . . .	Seoul (Kor)
Apr 7,	1985	Min-Keun Oh w pts 15 Irving Mitchell (US)	. . . .	Pusan (Kor)
Nov 29,	1985	**Ki-Yung Chung** (Kor) w rsf 15 Min-Keun Oh	. . . .	Chonju (Kor)
Feb 16,	1986	Ki-Yung Chung w ret 6 Tyrone Jackson (US)	. . . .	Ulsan (Kor)
May 18,	1986	Ki-Yung Chung w pts 15 Richard Savage (US)	. . . .	Taegu (Kor)
Aug 30,	1986	**Antonio Rivera** (PR) w ret 10 Ki-Yung Chung	. . . .	Osan (Kor)
Jan 23,	1988	**Calvin Grove** (US) w rsf 4 Antonio Rivera	. . . .	Gamaches (Fra)
May 17,	1988	Calvin Grove w pts 15 Myron Taylor (US)	. . . .	Atlantic City, NJ
Sep 4,	1988	**Jorge Paez** (Mex) w pts 15 Calvin Grove	. . . .	Mexicali (Mex)
Mar 30,	1989	Jorge Paez w ko 11 Calvin Grove	. . . .	Mexicali (Mex)
May 21,	1989	Jorge Paez drew 12 Louie Espinosa	. . . .	Phoenix, AZ
Aug 6,	1989	Jorge Paez w pts 12 Steve Cruz	. . . .	El Paso, NM
Sep 16,	1989	Jorge Paez w rsf 2 Jose Mario Lopez (Arg)	. . . .	Mexico City (Mex)
Dec 9,	1989	Jorge Paez w rsf 6 Lupe Guttierez (US)	. . . .	Reno, NV
Feb 4,	1990	Jorge Paez w pts 12 Troy Dorsey (US)	. . . .	Las Vegas, NV
Apr 7,	1990	Jorge Paez w pts 12 Louie Espinosa	. . . .	Las Vegas, NV

For IBF and WBO titles

WBO title

Jan 28,	1989	**Maurizio Stecca** (Ita) w rsf 6 Pedro Nolasco (DR)	. . . .	Milan (Ita)

For vacant title

Jun 16,	1989	Maurizio Stecca w rsf 9 Angel Mayor	. . . .	Milan (Ita)
Nov 11,	1989	**Louie Espinosa** (US) w rsf 7 Maurizio Stecca	. . . .	Rimini (Ita)
Apr 7,	1990	**Jorge Paez** w pts 12 Louie Espinosa	. . . .	Las Vegas, NV

For IBF and WBO titles

IBF/WBO titles

Jul 8,	1990	**Jorge Paez** drew 12 Troy Dorsey	. . . .	Las Vegas, NV
April	1991	*Paez relinquished both titles to box at lightweight*		

IBF title

Jun 3,	1991	**Troy Dorsey** w ko 1 Alfred Rangel (US)	. . . .	Las Vegas, NV

For vacant title

Aug 12,	1991	**Manuel Medina** (Mex) w pts 12 Troy Dorsey	. . . .	Los Angeles, CA

Nov 18,	1991	Manuel Medina w tech dec 9 Tom Johnson (US)	. . . .	Los Angeles, CA
Mar 14,	1992	Manuel Medina w pts 12 Fabrice Benichou	. . . .	Antibes (Fra)
Jul 22,	1992	Manuel Medina w ret 10 Fabrizio Cappai (Ita)	. . . . . .	Capo D'Orlando (Ita)
Oct 23,	1992	Manuel Medina w pts 12 Moussa Sangare (Fra)	. . . .	Gravelines (Fra)
Feb 26,	1993	**Tom Johnson** w pts 12 Manuel Medina	. . . .	Melun (Fra)
Sep 11,	1993	Tom Johnson w pts 12 Sugar Baby Rojas (Col)	. . . .	Miami, FL
Nov 30,	1993	Tom Johnson w rsf 9 Stephane Haccoun (Fra)	. . . .	Marseilles (Fra)
Feb 12,	1994	Tom Johnson w pts 12 Orlando Soto (Pan)	. . . .	St Louis, MO
Jun 11,	1994	Tom Johnson w rsf 12 Benny Amparo (DR)	. . . .	Atlantic City, NJ
Oct 22,	1994	Tom Johnson w pts 12 Francisco Segura (US)	. . . .	Atlantic City, NJ
Jan 28,	1995	Tom Johnson w pts 12 Manuel Medina	. . . .	Atlantic City, NJ
May 28,	1995	Tom Johnson w pts 12 Eddie Croft (US)	. . . .	South Padre Island, TX
Dec 9,	1995	Tom Johnson w pts 12 Jose Badillo (PR)	. . . .	Stuttgart (Ger)

WBO title

Jan 26,	1991	**Maurizio Stecca** w rsf 5 Armando Reyes (DR)	. . . .	Sassari (Ita)

For vacant title

Jun 15,	1991	Maurizio Stecca w pts 12 Fernando Ramos (Mex)	. . . .	Mantichiari (Ita)
Nov 9,	1991	Maurizio Stecca w ret 9 Tim Driscoll (Eng)	. . . . . .	Campione d'Italia (Ita)
May 16,	1992	**Colin McMillan** (Eng) w pts 12 Maurizio Stecca	. . . .	London (Eng)
Sep 26,	1992	**Ruben Palacio** (Col) w ret 8 Colin McMillan	. . . .	London (Eng)
Apr	1993	*Palacio forfeited the title on medical grounds*		
Apr 17,	1993	**Steve Robinson** (Wal) w pts 12 John Davison (Eng)	. . .	Washington (Eng)

For vacant title

Jul 10,	1993	Steve Robinson w rsf 9 Sean Murphy (Eng)	. . . .	Cardiff (Wal)
Oct 23,	1993	Steve Robinson w pts 12 Colin McMillan	. . . .	Cardiff (Wal)
Mar 12,	1994	Steve Robinson w ko 12 Paul Hodkinson (Eng)	. . . .	Cardiff (Wal)
Jun 4,	1994	Steve Robinson w pts 12 Freddy Cruz (DR)	. . . .	Cardiff (Wal)
Oct 1,	1994	Steve Robinson w ko 9 Duke McKenzie (Eng)	. . . .	Cardiff (Wal)
Feb 4,	1995	Steve Robinson w pts 12 Domingo Damigella (Arg)	. . . .	Cardiff (Wal)
Jul 7,	1995	Steve Robinson w rsf 7 Pedro Ferradas (Sp)	. . . .	Cardiff (Wal)
Sep 30,	1995	**Naseem Hamed** (Eng) w rsf 8 Steve Robinson	. . . .	Cardiff (Wal)

NASEEM HAMED *(left) colourful and extravagantly talented, ends Steve Robinson's reign as WBO featherweight champion*

Super-Bantamweight

There was sporadic championship activity in the 122 lb class in the early 1920s, but the promoters who were trying to establish the new division could not get any organization to give it official sanction and, without that status, the super-bantams slipped back into obscurity. A long-forgotten body called the American Federation of Boxing failed to revive the category in the early 1940s, but the WBC were more successful in 1976. The phenomenal Wilfredo Gomez defended the WBC title 17 times before relinquishing it, became a major star and thus established the division with the fans. The WBA set up their own title in 1977, but have yet to produce a champion of Gomez's stature.

World Super-Bantamweight Championship Bouts

WBC title

Apr 3,	1976	**Rigoberto Riasco** (Pan) w ret 8 Waruinge Nakayama (Ken) .... Panama City (Pan)
Jun 12,	1976	Rigoberto Riasco w ko 10 Livio Nolasco (DR) ...... Panama City (Pan)
Aug 1,	1976	Rigoberto Riasco w pts 15 Dong-Kyun Yum (Kor) .... Pusan (Kor)
Oct 10,	1976	**Royal Kobayashi** (Jap) w rsf 8 Rigoberto Riasco .... Tokyo (Jap)
Nov 24,	1976	**Dong Kyun Yum** w pts 15 Royal Kobayashi .... Seoul (Kor)
Feb 13,	1977	Dong Kyun Yum w pts 15 Jose Cervantes (Col) .... Seoul (Kor)
May 21,	1977	**Wilfredo Gomez** (PR) w ko 12 Dong Kyun Yum .... San Juan, CA
Jul 11,	1977	Wilfredo Gomez w ko 5 Raul Tirado (Mex) .... San Juan, CA
Jan 19,	1978	Wilfredo Gomez w ko 3 Royal Kobayashi .... Kitakyushu (Jap)
Apr 8,	1978	Wilfredo Gomez w rsf 7 Juan Antonio Lopez (Mex) .... Bayamon (PR)
Jun 2,	1978	Wilfredo Gomez w rsf 3 Sakad Petchyindee (Thai) .... Korat (Thai)
Sep 9,	1978	Wilfredo Gomez w rsf 13 Leonardo Cruz (DR) .... San Juan, CA
Oct 28,	1978	Wilfredo Gomez w rsf 5 Carlos Zarate (Mex) .... San Juan, CA
Mar 9,	1979	Wilfredo Gomez w rsf 5 Nestor Jiminez (Col) .... New York, NY
Jun 16,	1979	Wilfredo Gomez w rsf 5 Jesus Hernandcz (Nic) .... San Juan, CA
Sep 28,	1979	Wilfredo Gomez w rsf 10 Carlos Mendoza (Pan) .... Las Vegas, NV
Oct 26,	1979	Wilfredo Gomez w rsf 5 Nicky Perez (US) .... New York, NY
Feb 3,	1980	Wilfredo Gomez w ret 6 Ruben Valdez (Col) .... Las Vegas, NV
Aug 22,	1980	Wilfredo Gomez w rsf 5 Derrick Holmes (US) .... Las Vegas, NV
Dec 13,	1980	Wilfredo Gomez w ko 3 Jose Cervantes .... Miami, FL
Mar 27,	1982	Wilfredo Gomez w rsf 6 Juan Meza (Mex) .... Atlantic City, NJ
Jun 11,	1982	Wilfredo Gomez w ko 10 Juan Antonio Lopez .... Las Vegas, NV
Aug 18,	1982	Wilfredo Gomez w ret 7 Roberto Rubaldino (Mex) .... San Juan, CA
Dec 3,	1982	Wilfredo Gomez w rsf 14 Lupe Pintor (Mex) .... New Orleans, LA
April	1983	*Gomez relinquished the title because of weight problems*
Jun 15,	1983	**Jaime Garza** (US) w rsf 2 Bobby Berna (Phil) .... Los Angeles, CA
		For vacant title
May 26,	1984	Jaime Garza w ko 3 Felipe Orozco (Col) .... Miami, FL
Nov 3,	1984	**Juan Meza** (Mex) w ko 1 Jaime Garza .... Kingston, NY
Apr 19,	1985	Juan Meza w rsf 6 Mike Ayala (US) .... Los Angeles, CA
Aug 18,	1985	**Lupe Pintor** (Mex) w pts 12 Juan Meza .... Mexico City (Mex)
Jan 18,	1986	**Samart Payakarun** (Thai) w ko 5 Lupe Pintor .... Bangkok (Thai)
		Pintor forfeited the title by being three pounds overweight, but the WBC agreed to recognize Payakarun as the new champion if he won
Dec 10,	1986	**Samart Payakarun** w ko 12 Juan Meza .... Bangkok (Thai)

May 8,	1987	**Jeff Fenech** (Aus) w rsf 4 Samart Parakarun .... Sydney (Aus)
Jul 10,	1987	Jeff Fenech w rsf 5 Greg Richardson (US) .... Sydney (Aus)
Oct 16,	1987	Jeff Fenech w tech dec 4 Carlos Zarate .... Sydney (Aus)
Jan	1988	*Fenech relinquished the title to challenge for the WBC featherweight title*
Feb 29,	1988	**Daniel Zaragoza** (Mex) w rsf 10 Carlos Zarate .... Los Angeles, CA
		For vacant title
May 29,	1988	Daniel Zaragoza drew 12 Seung-Hoon Lee (Kor) .... Youchan (Kor)
Nov 21,	1988	Daniel Zaragoza w ko 5 Valerio Nati (Ita) .... Forli (Ita)
Jun 22,	1989	Daniel Zaragoza w pts 12 Paul Banke (US) .... Los Angeles, CA
Sep 1,	1989	Daniel Zaragoza w rsf 10 Frankie Duarte (US) .... Los Angeles, CA
Dec 3,	1989	Daniel Zaragoza w pts 12 Chan-Young Park (Kor) .... Seoul (Kor)
Apr 23,	1990	**Paul Banke** w rsf 9 Daniel Zaragoza .... Los Angeles, CA
Aug 12,	1990	Paul Banke w rsf 12 Ki-Jun Lee (Kor) .... Seoul (Kor)
Nov 5,	1990	**Pedro Decima** (Arg) w rsf 4 Paul Banke .... Los Angeles, CA
Feb 3,	1991	**Kiyoshi Hatanaka** (Jap) w rsf 8 Pedro Decima .... Nagoya (Jap)
Jun 14,	1991	**Daniel Zaragoza** w pts 12 Kiyoshi Hatanaka .... Tokyo (Jap)
Aug 24,	1991	Daniel Zaragoza w pts 12 Huh Chin (Kor) .... Seoul (Kor)
Dec 9,	1991	Daniel Zaragoza w pts 12 Paul Banke .... Los Angeles, CA
Mar 20,	1992	**Thierry Jacob** (Fra) w pts 12 Daniel Zaragoza .... Calais (Fra)
Jun 23,	1992	**Tracy Harris Patterson** (US) w rsf 2 Thierry Jacob .... Albany, NY
Dec 5,	1992	Tracy Harris Patterson drew 12 Daniel Zaragoza .... Berck-sur-Mer (Fra)
Mar 13,	1993	Tracy Harris Patterson w pts 12 Jesse Benavides (US) . Poughkeepsie, NY
Apr 9,	1994	Tracy Harris Patterson w pts 12 Richard Duran (US) .... Reno, NV
Aug 26,	1994	**Hector Acero Sanchez** (DR) w pts 12 Tracy Harris Patterson .... Atlantic City, NJ
Mar 11,	1995	Hector Acero-Sanchez w pts 12 Julio Gervacio (PR) ..... Atlantic City, NJ
Jun 2,	1995	Hector Acero-Sanchez drew 12 Daniel Zaragoza .... Ledyard, CT
Nov 6,	1995	**Daniel Zaragoza** w pts 12 Hector Acero-Sanchez .... Inglewood, CA

WBA title

Nov 26,	1977	**Soo Hwan Hong** (Kor) w ko 3 Hector Carasquilla (Pan) Panama City (Pan)
		For vacant title
Feb 1,	1978	Soo Hwan Hong w pts 15 Yu Kasahara (Jap) .... Tokyo (Jap)
May 6,	1978	**Ricardo Cardona** (Col) w rsf 12 Soo Hwan Hong .... Seoul (Kor)
Sep 2,	1978	Ricardo Cardona w pts 15 Ruben Valdez (Col) .... Cartagena (Col)
Nov 12,	1978	Ricardo Cardona w pts 15 Soon-Hyun Chung (Kor) .... Seoul (Kor)
Jun 23,	1979	Ricardo Cardona w pts 15 Soon-Hyun Chung .... Seoul (Kor)
Sep 6,	1979	Ricardo Cardona w pts 15 Yukio Segawa (Jap) .... Hachinhoe (Jap)
Dec 15,	1979	Ricardo Cardona w pts 15 Sergio Palma (Arg) .... Barranquilla (Col)
May 4,	1980	**Leo Randolph** (US) w rsf 15 Ricardo Cardona .... Seattle, WA
Aug 9,	1980	**Sergio Palma** w ko 6 Leo Randolph .... Spokane, WA
Nov 8,	1980	Sergio Palma w rsf 9 Ulisses Morales (Pan) .... Buenos Aires (Arg)
Apr 4,	1981	Sergio Palma w pts 15 Leonardo Cruz (DR) .... Buenos Aires (Arg)
Aug 15,	1981	Sergio Palma w rsf 12 Ricardo Cardona .... Buenos Aires (Arg)
Oct 3,	1981	Sergio Palma w pts 15 Vichit Muangroi-et (Thai) ..... Buenos Aires (Arg)
Jan 15,	1982	Sergio Palma w pts 15 Jorge Lujan (Pan) .... Cordoba (Sp)
Jun 12,	1982	**Leonardo Cruz** w pts 15 Sergio Palma .... Miami Beach, FL
Nov 13,	1982	Leonardo Cruz w ko 8 Benito Badilla (Ch) .... San Juan, CA
Mar 16,	1983	Leonardo Cruz w pts 15 Soon-Hyun Chung .... San Juan, CA
Aug 26,	1983	Leonardo Cruz w pts 15 Cleo Garcia (Nic) .... Santa Domingo (Bah)
Feb 22,	1984	**Loris Stecca** (Ita) w rsf 12 Leonardo Cruz .... Milan (Ita)
May 26,	1984	**Victor Callejas** (PR) w rsf 8 Loris Stecca .... Guaynabo (PR)
Feb 2,	1985	Victor Callejas w pts 15 Seung-Hoon Lee .... San Juan, CA
Nov 8,	1985	Victor Callejas w ret 6 Loris Stecca .... Rimini (Ita)
Dec	1986	*The WBA stripped Callejas for failing to defend against Louie Espinosa*
Jan 16,	1987	**Louie Espinosa** (US) w rsf 4 Tommy Valoy (DR) .... Phoenix, AZ
		For vacant title
Jul 15,	1987	Louie Espinosa w rsf 15 Manuel Vilchez (Ven) .... Phoenix, AZ
Aug 15,	1987	Louie Espinosa w ko 9 Mike Ayala (US) .... San Antonio, TX
Nov 28,	1987	**Julio Gervacio** (DR) w pts 12 Louie Espinosa .... San Juan, CA
Feb 27,	1988	**Bernardo Pinango** (Ven) w pts 12 Julio Gervacio .... San Juan, CA
May 28,	1988	**Juan Jose Estrada** (Mex) w pts 12 Bernardo Pinango ..... Tijuana (Mex)
Oct 15,	1988	Juan Jose Estrada w rsf I1 Takuya Muguruma (Jap) .... Osaka (Jap)
Apr 4,	1989	Juan Jose Estrada w rsf 10 Jesus Poll (Ven) .... Los Angeles, CA
Jul 10,	1989	Juan Jose Estrada w pts 12 Luis Mendoza (Col) .... Tijuana (Mex)
Dec 11,	1989	**Jesus Salud** (US) w dis 9 Juan Jose Estrada .... Los Angeles, CA
April	1990	*The WBA stripped Salud for failing to defend against Luis Mendoza*
May 25,	1990	**Luis Mendoza** drew 12 Ruben Palacio (Col) .... Cartagena (Col)
		For vacant title
Sep 11,	1990	Luis Mendoza w rsf 3 Ruben Palacio .... Miami, FL

RINGSIDE VIEW

Wilfredo Gomez
vs
Dong-Kyun Yum

START OF SOMETHING BIG
When Wilfredo Gomez took the WBC title from Dong-Kyun Yum in San Juan on May 21,1977, he embarked on a championship career which remains unmatched in the division's history. He won all 18 title fights inside the distance, and then stepped up to featherweight and super-feather to become a triple champion.

Jeff Fenech
vs
Samart Payakarun

MONASTIC RETREAT

Samart Payakarun of Thailand, who became champion in controversial circumstances when Lupe Pintor came in three pounds overweight for a defence against him, made a drastic career change after losing his WBC super-bantamweight title to Jeff Fenech in Sydney on May 8, 1987 – he retired to become a Buddhist monk!

Oct 18,	1990	Luis Mendoza w pts 12 Fabrice Benichou	Paris (Fra)
Jan 19,	1991	Luis Mendoza w rsf 8 Noree Jockygym (Thai)	Bangkok (Thai)
Apr 21,	1991	Luis Mendoza w pts 12 Carlos Uribe (Ch)	Cartagena (Col)
May 30,	1991	Luis Mendoza w ko 7 Jose Cardosa de Oliveira (Bra)	Madrid (Sp)
Oct 7,	1991	**Raul Perez** (Mex) w pts 12 Luis Mendoza	Los Angeles, CA
Mar 27,	1992	**Wilfredo Vasquez** (PR) w rsf 3 Raul Perez	Mexico City (Mex)
Jun 27,	1992	Wilfredo Vasquez w pts 12 Freddy Cruz (DR)	Gorle (Ita)
Dec 5,	1992	Wilfredo Vasquez w rsf 8 Thierry Jacob (Fra)	Berck- sur-Mer (Fra)
Mar 6,	1993	Wilfredo Vasquez w pts 12 Luis Mendoza	Paris (Fra)
Jun 24,	1993	Wilfredo Vasquez w ko 10 Thierry Jacob	Bordeaux (Fra)
Nov 18,	1993	Wilfredo Vasquez w pts 12 Horoaki Yokota (Jap)	Tokyo (Jap)
Mar 2,	1994	Wilfredo Vasquez w rsf 1 Yuichi Kasai (Jap)	Tokyo (Jap)
Jul 2,	1994	Wilfredo Vasquez w rsf 2 Jae-Won Choi (Kor)	Las Vegas, NV
Oct 13,	1994	Wilfredo Vasquez w pts 12 Juan Polo-Perez (Col)	Paris (Fra)
Jan 7,	1995	Wilfredo Vasquez w pts 12 Orlando Canizales (US)	San Antonio, TX
May 13,	1995	**Antonio Cermeno** (Ven) w pts 12 Wilfredo Vasquez	Bayamon (PR)
Nov 26,	1995	Antonio Cermeno w pts 12 Jesus Salud	Caracas (Ven)

IBF title

Dec 14,	1983	**Bobby Berna** (Phil) w ret 11 Seung-In Suh (Kor)	Seoul (Kor)
		For vacant title	
Apr 15,	1984	**Seung-In Suh** w ko 10 Bobby Berna	Seoul (Kor)
Jul 8,	1984	Seung-In Suh w ko 4 Cleo Garcia	Seoul (Kor)
Jan 3,	1985	**Ji-Won Kim** (Kor) w ko 10 Seung-In Sun	Seoul (Kor)
Mar 30,	1985	Ji-Won Kim w pts 15 Dario Palacio (Col)	Suwon (Kor)

Jun 28,	1985	Ji-Won Kim w ko 4 Bobby Berna	Pusan (Kor)
Oct 9,	1985	Ji-Won Kim w ko 1 Seung-In Suh	Chungju (Kor)
Jun 1,	1986	Ji-Won Kim w ko 2 Rudy Casicas (Phil)	Inchon (Kor)
Nov	1986	*Kim retired*	
Jan 18,	1987	**Seung-Hoon Lee** w ko 9 Prayoonsak Muangsurin (Thai)	Pohang (Kor)
		For vacant title	
Apr 5,	1987	Seung-Hoon Lee w ko 10 Jorge Urbina Diaz (Mex)	Seoul (Kor)
Jul 19,	1987	Seung-Hoon Lee w ko 5 Lion Collins (Phil)	Seoul (Kor)
Dec 27,	1987	Seung-Hoon Lee w pts 15 Jose Sanabria (Ven)	Pohang (Kor)
Mar	1988	*Lee relinquished the title to challenge for the WBC version*	
May 21,	1988	**Jose Sanabria** w ko 5 Moises Fuentes (Col)	Bucaramanga (Col)
		For vacant title	
Aug 21,	1988	Jose Sanabria w pts 12 Vincenzo Belcastro (Ita)	Capo D'Orlando (Ita)
Sep 26,	1988	Jose Sanabria w rsf 10 Fabrice Benichou	Paris (Fra)
Nov 11,	1988	Jose Sanabria w rsf 6 Thierry Jacob	Gravelines (Fra)
Mar 10,	1989	**Fabrice Benichou** w pts 12 Jose Sanabria	Limoges (Fra)
Jun 10,	1989	Fabrice Benichou w ko 5 Franie Badenhorst (SA)	Frasnone (Ita)
Oct 7,	1989	Fabrice Benichou w pts 12 Ramon Cruz (PR)	Bordeaux (Fra)
Mar 10,	1990	**Welcome Ncita** (SA) w pts 12 Fabrice Benichou	Tel Aviv (Is)
Jun 2,	1990	Welcome Ncita w rsf 7 Ramon Cruz (DR)	Rome (Ita)
Sep 29,	1990	Welcome Ncita w rsf 8 Gerardo Lopez (Pan)	Aosta (Ita)
Feb 27,	1991	Welcome Ncita w pts 12 Jesus Rojas (Col)	St Vincent (Ita)
Jun 15,	1991	Welcome Ncita w pts 12 Hurley Snead (US)	San Antonio, TX
Sep 28,	1991	Welcome Ncita w pts 12 Jesus Rojas	Sun City (Bop)
Apr 18,	1992	Welcome Ncita w pts 12 Jesus Salud	Treviola
Dec 2,	1992	**Kennedy McKinney** (US) w ko 11 Welcome Ncita	Tortoli
Apr 17,	1993	Kennedy McKinney w pts 12 Richard Duran (US)	Sacramento, CA
Oct 17,	1993	Kennedy McKinney w pts 12 Jesus Salud	Lake Tahoe, CA
Apr 16,	1994	Kennedy McKinney w pts 12 Welcome Ncita	South Padre Island, TX
Aug 20,	1994	**Vuyani Bungu** (SA) w pts 12 Kennedy McKinney	Hammanskraal (SA)
Nov 19,	1994	Vuyani Bungu w pts 12 Felix Camacho (PR)	Hammanskraal (SA)
Mar 4,	1995	Vuyani Bungu w pts 12 Mohammed Al Haji Nurhuda (Indo)	Hammanskraal (SA)
Apr 29,	1995	Vuyani Bungu w pts 12 Victor Llerena (Col)	Johannesburg (SA)
Sep 26,	1995	Vuyani Bungu w pts 12 Laureano Ramirez (DR)	Hammanskraal (SA)

WBO title

Apr 29,	1989	**Kenny Mitchell** (US) w pts 12 Julio Gervacio	San Juan, CA
		For vacant title	
Sep 9,	1989	Kenny Mitchell w pts 12 Simon Skosana (SA)	San Juan, CA
Dec 9,	1989	**Valerio Nati** w dis 4 Kenny Mitchell	Teramo (Ita)
May 12,	1990	**Orlando Fernandez** (PR) w rsf 10 Valerio Nati	Sassari (Ita)
May 24,	1991	**Jesse Benavides** w pts 12 Orlando Fernandez	Corpus Christi, TX
Aug 31,	1991	Jesse Benavides w rsf 5 Fernando Ramos (Mex)	Corpus Christi, TX
Oct 15,	1992	**Duke McKenzie** (Eng) w pts 12 Jesse Benavides	London (Eng)
Jun 9,	1993	**Daniel Jiminez** (PR) w pts 12 Duke McKenzie	London (Eng)
Oct 29,	1993	Daniel Jiminez w rsf 5 Felix Garcia Losada (Sp)	Zaragoza (Sp)
Jan 7,	1994	Daniel Jiminez w pts 12 Felix Garcia Losada	Palma, Majorca (Sp)
Jun 25,	1994	Daniel Jiminez w pts 12 Cristobal Pascual (Sp)	Utrera, Seville (Sp)
Sep 3,	1994	Daniel Jiminez w ko 1 Harald Geier (Aut)	Wiener Neustadt (Aut)
Mar 31,	1995	**Marco Antonio Barrera** (Mex) w pts 12 Daniel Jiminez	Anaheim, CA
Jun 2,	1995	Marco Antonio Barrera w rsf 2 Frankie Toledo (US)	Ledyard, CT
Jul 15,	1995	Marco Antonio Barrera w rsf 1 Mauri Diaz (US)	Inglewood, CA
Aug 22,	1995	Marco Antonio Barrera w pts 12 Agapito Sanchez (DR)	South Padre Island, TX
Nov 4,	1995	Marco Antonio Barrera w rsf 7 Eddie Croft (US)	Las Vegas, NV

Jesse Benavides
vs
Duke McKenzie

DUKE BECOMES A KING

Bob Fitzsimmons had become an American citizen by the time he won his third world title at the turn of the century, so Duke McKenzie could reasonably claim to be the first Englishman to complete the three-timer. He had already been the IBF flyweight and WBO bantamweight champion, and achieved the historic treble by outboxing tough American Jesse Benavides to wake the WBO super-bantamweight crown in London on October 15, 1992.

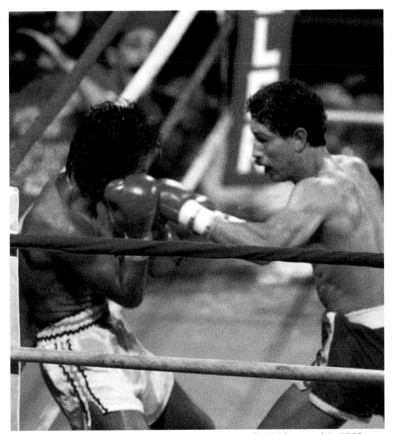

WILFREDO GOMEZ *(right) stopped Lupe Pintor in the 14th round in 1982*

Bantamweight

The bantamweight gloved era began when Chappie Moran from Manchester beat Tommy Kelly in 1889. The weight limit in America at that time was 110 lb, but it crept up pound by pound from 112 to 114, 115, and 116 lb until finally settling in 1915 at the present 118 lb, which the British had introduced in 1910.

The early history of the division is even more confused than most, with the championship almost continuously in dispute until the 1920s, sometimes with parallel versions on offer on either side of the Atlantic. Since the record-breaking eight-year

reign of the Mexican-American Manuel Ortiz, who made 19 successful defences, the bantamweight class has been dominated by Mexicans like Joe Becerra, Ruben Olivares, Carlos Zarate, Lupe Pintor and Alfonso Zamora, while Eder Jofre (Brazil) and Jorge Lujan (Panama) both made their mark.

Champions Jeff Chandler, Richard Sandoval and Orlando Canizales from America revived interest there in the division, with Canizales – whose brother Gaby held the WBO title at the same time – enjoying a remarkable run as IBF champion.

World Bantamweight Championship Bouts

Jun 5,	1889	**Chappie Moran** (Eng) w pts 10 Tommy Kelly (US)	Brooklyn, NY
Jan 31,	1890	**Tommy Kelly** w ko 10 Chappie Moran	New York, NY
May 9,	1892	**Billy Plimmer** (Eng) w pts 10 Tommy Kelly	Coney Island, NY
Dec 28,	1892	Billy Plimmer w rsf 8 Joe McGrath (US)	Coney Island, NY
May 28,	1895	Billy Plimmer w ko 7 George Corfield (Eng)	London (Eng)
Nov 25,	1895	**Pedlar Palmer** (Eng) w dis 14 Billy Plimmer	London (Eng)
Oct 12,	1896	Pedlar Palmer w pts 20 Johnny Murphy (US)	London (Eng)
Jan 25,	1897	Pedlar Palmer w rsf 14 Ernie Stanton (US)	London (Eng)
Dec 12,	1898	Pedlar Palmer w rsf 17 Billy Plimmer	London (Eng)
Apr 17,	1899	Pedlar Palmer w rsf 3 Billy Rotchford (US)	London (Eng)
Sep 12,	1899	**Terry McGovern** (US) w ko 1 Pedlar Palmer	Tuckahoe
Dec 31,	1899	*McGovern relinquished the title because of weight trouble*	
Sep 6,	1900	Harry Forbes (US) drew 20 Caspar Leon (US)	St Joseph
		For vacant title	
Mar 18,	1901	**Harry Harris** w pts 20 Pedlar Palmer	London (Eng)
		Harris claimed the vacant title, but soon relinquished it to box at featherweight	
Apr 2,	1901	**Harry Forbes** w pts 15 Casper Leon	Memphis, TN
Nov 11,	1901	Harry Forbes w ko 2 Dan Dougherty (US)	St Louis, MO
Jan 23,	1902	Harry Forbes w ko 4 Dan Dougherty	St Louis, MO
Feb 27,	1902	Harry Forbes w pts 15 Tommy Feltz (US)	St Louis, MO
May 1,	1902	Harry Forbes drew 20 Johnny Reagan (US)	St Louis, MO
Dec 23,	1902	Harry Forbes w rsf 7 Frankie Neil (US)	Oakland, CA
Feb 27,	1903	Harry Forbes w pts 10 Andy Tokell (Eng)	Detroit, MI
Aug 13,	1903	**Frankie Neil** w ko 2 Harry Forbes	San Francisco, CA
Sep 4,	1903	Frankie Neil w ko 15 Billy de Coursey (US)	Los Angeles, CA
Oct 16,	1903	Frankie Neil drew 20 Johnny Reagan	Los Angeles, CA
Oct 17,	1904	**Joe Bowker** (Eng) w pts 20 Frankie Neil	London (Eng)
May 29,	1905	Joe Bowker w pts 20 Pinky Evans (US)	London (Eng)
		Bowker relinquished the title, which was claimed for America by Jimmy Walsh and for Britain by Digger Stanley	
Oct 20,	1905	**Jimmy Walsh** (US) w pts 15 Digger Stanley (Eng)	in Chelsea, MA
		Walsh relinquished the title due to weight problems. There followed a most confused period, with several claimants including Johnny Coulon, Digger Stanley, Monte Attell, Frankie Conley, and Walsh (on his comeback)	

British/IBU version of title

Jan 20,	1906	**Digger Stanley** w pts 20 Ike Bradley (Eng)	Newcastle (Eng)
Dec 13,	1906	Digger Stanley w pts 20 Ike Bradley	Liverpool (Eng)
May 24,	1909	Digger Stanley drew 15 Jimmy Walsh	London (Eng)
Oct 17,	1910	Digger Stanley w ko 8 Joe Bowker	London (Eng)
Dec 5,	1910	Digger Stanley w pts 20 Johnny Condon (Eng)	London (Eng)
Sep 14,	1911	Digger Stanley w pts 20 Ike Bradley	Liverpool (Eng)
Apr 22,	1912	Digger Stanley w pts 20 Charles Ledoux (Fra)	London (Eng)
		The IBU recognized this as a title fight	
Jun 23,	1912	**Charles Ledoux** w ko 7 Digger Stanley	Dieppe (Fra)
Jun 24,	1913	**Eddie Campi** (US) w pts 20 Charles Ledoux	Vernon, CA
Oct 10,	1913	Eddie Campi drew 15 Frankie Burns (US)	Denver, CO
Jan 31,	1914	**Kid Williams** (US) w ko 12 Eddie Campi	Los Angeles, CA
Jun 9,	1914	Kid Williams w ko 3 Johnny Coulon (Can)	Los Angeles, CA
		For undisputed title	

American versions

Jun 26,	1908	**Jimmy Walsh** w ko 11 Jimmy Carroll	San Francisco, CA
Oct 9,	1908	Jimmy Walsh w pts 15 Young Britt (US)	Baltimore, MD
Dec 21,	1908	Jimmy Walsh drew 15 Monte Attell (US)	San Francisco, CA
May 24,	1909	Jimmy Walsh drew 15 Digger Stanley	London (Eng)
		Walsh moved back to featherweight again	
Jun 19,	1909	**Monte Attell** w rsf 18 Frankie Neil	San Francisco, CA
Dec 17,	1909	Monte Attell drew 20 Danny Webster (US)	San Francisco, CA
Feb 22,	1910	**Frankie Conley** (US) w ret 42 Monte Attell	Vernon, CA
Mar 6,	1910	**Johnny Coulon** w ko 19 Jim Kendrick (Eng)	New Orleans, LA
Feb 26,	1911	Johnny Coulon w pts 20 Frankie Conley	New Orleans, LA
Feb 3,	1912	Johnny Coulon w pts 20 Frankie Conley	Los Angeles, CA
Feb 18,	1912	Johnny Coulon w pts 20 Frankie Burns	New Orleans, LA
Jun 9,	1914	**Kid Williams** w ko 3 Johnny Coulon	Los Angeles, CA
		For undisputed title	

Undisputed title

Dec 6,	1915	**Kid Williams** drew 20 Frankie Burns	New Orleans, LA
Feb 7,	1916	Kid Williams drew 20 Pete Herman (US)	New Orleans, LA
Jan 9,	1917	**Pete Herman** w pts 20 Kid Williams	New Orleans, LA
Nov 5,	1917	Pete Herman w pts 20 Frankie Burns	New Orleans, LA
Dec 22,	1920	**Joe Lynch** (US) w pts 15 Pete Herman	New York, NY
Jul 25,	1921	**Pete Herman** w pts 15 Joe Lynch	New York, NY
Sep 23,	1921	**Johnny Buff** (US) w pts 15 Pete Herman	New York, NY
Nov 10,	1921	Johnny Buff w pts 15 Jackie Sharkey (US)	New York, NY
Jul 10,	1922	**Joe Lynch** w ret 14 Johnny Buff	New York, NY
Dec 22,	1922	Joe Lynch w pts 15 Midget Smith (US)	New York, NY
Mar 21,	1924	**Abe Goldstein** (US) w pts 15 Joe Lynch	New York, NY
Jul 17,	1924	Abe Goldstein w pts 15 Charles Ledoux	New York, NY
Sep 9,	1924	Abe Goldstein w pts 15 Tommy Ryan (US)	Long Island, NY
Dec 19,	1924	**Eddie Martin** (US) w pts 15 Abe Goldstein	New York, NY
Mar 20,	1925	**Charlie Rosenberg** (US) w pts 15 Eddie Martin	New York, NY
Jul 23,	1925	Charlie Rosenberg w ko 4 Eddie Shea (US)	New York, NY
		Rosenberg was suspended indefinitely by the NY Commission because of suspicion that the fight was fixed	
Feb	1927	*Rosenberg's suspension was lifted to allow him to defend against Bushy Graham in New York on February 4, 1927. Rosenberg lost his title on the scales when he came in at 122½ lb, although he won a 15-rounds decision. He was then suspended again for making a secret agreement with Graham concerning the percentage split of the purse money*	
Feb 24,	1927	**Bud Taylor** (US) w pts 10 Eddie Shea	Chicago, IL
		Taylor won recognition in four States as champion	
Mar 26,	1927	Bud Taylor drew 10 Tony Canzoneri (US)	Chicago, IL
		For vacant NBA title	
May 5,	1927	**Teddy Baldock** (Eng) w pts 15 Archie Bell (US)	London (Eng)
		British version of vacant title	
Jun 24,	1927	Bud Taylor w pts 10 Tony Canzoneri	Chicago, IL
		For vacant NBA title	
Oct 6,	1927	**Willie Smith** (SA) w pts 15 Teddy Baldock	London (Eng)
		For British version of title. Smith never defended it, and moved up to featherweight	
May 23,	1928	**Bushy Graham** (US) w pts 15 Cpl Izzy Schwarz (US)	New York, NY
		For vacant New York title	
Aug	1928	*Taylor relinquished the NBA title to box at featherweight*	
Jan	1929	*Graham gave up the NY title because of weight problems*	

Pete Herman
vs
Frankie Burns

WORTH POSTPONING THE HONEYMOON

Bantamweight champion Pete Herman celebrated a unique double event on November 5, 1917: he was married in the afternoon and made a successful first defence of his title in the evening, outpointing Frankie Burns in New Orleans, LA. The fact that Burns had been the only man to beat him inside the distance was the icing on the cake.

Bantamweight

Jun 18, 1929 **Al Brown** (Pan) w pts 15 Vidal Gregorio (Sp) . . . . New York, NY
For vacant title
Feb 8, 1930 Al Brown w dis 4 Johnny Erickson (US) . . . . New York, NY
Oct 4, 1930 Al Brown w pts 15 Eugene Huat (Fra) . . . . Paris (Fra)
May 20, 1931 **Pete Sanstol** (Nor) w pts 10 Archie Bell . . . . Montreal (Can)
Recognized in Canada as being for the title
Jun 17, 1931 Pete Sanstol w pts 15 Art Giroux (Can) . . . . Montreal (Can)
Aug 25, 1931 Al Brown w pts 15 Pete Sanstol . . . . Montreal (Can)
For undisputed title
Oct 27, 1931 Al Brown w pts 15 Eugene Huat . . . . Montreal (Can)
Jul 10, 1932 Al Brown w pts 15 Kid Francis (Ita) . . . . Marseilles (Fra)
Sep 19, 1932 Al Brown w ko 1 Emile Pladner (Fra) . . . . Toronto (Can)
Mar 18, 1933 Al Brown w pts 12 Dom Bernasconi (Ita) . . . . Milan (Ita)
Jul 3, 1933 Al Brown w pts 15 Johnny King (Eng) . . . . Manchester (Eng)
Feb 19, 1934 Al Brown w pts 15 Young Perez (Tun) . . . . Paris (Fra)
May 1934 *The NBA stripped Brown for his failure to defend against Baby Casanova*

NBA title

Jun 26, 1934 **Sixto Escobar** (PR) w ko 9 Baby Casanova (Mex) . . . . Montreal (Can)
For vacant title
Aug 8, 1934 Sixto Escobar w pts 15 Eugene Huat . . . . Montreal (Can)

New York/IBU titles

Nov 1, 1934 **Al Brown** w ko 10 Young Perez . . . . Tunis (Tun)
Jun 1, 1935 **Baltazar Sangchilli** (Sp) w pts 15 Al Brown . . . . Valencia (Sp)
The NY Commission and the NBA decided to recognize the winner between Lou Salica and Sixto Escobar as champion

NY/NBA titles

Aug 26, 1935 **Lou Salica** (US) w pts 15 Sixto Escobar . . . . New York, NY
Nov 15, 1935 **Sixto Escobar** w pts 15 Lou Salica . . . . New York, NY

IBU title

Jun 29, 1936 **Tony Marino** (US) w ko 14 Baltazar Sangchilli . . . . New York, NY

Aug 31, 1936 **Sixto Escobar** w rsf 13 Tony Marino . . . . New York, NY
For undisputed title

Undisputed title

Oct 13, 1936 **Sixto Escobar** w ko 1 Carlos Quintana (Pan) . . . . New York, NY
Feb 21, 1937 Sixto Escobar w pts 15 Lou Salica . . . . New York, NY
Sep 23, 1937 **Harry Jeffra** (US) w pts 15 Sixto Escobar . . . . New York, NY
Feb 20, 1938 **Sixto Escobar** w pts 15 Harry Jeffra . . . . San Juan, CA
The IBU withdrew recognition from Escobar

IBU title

Mar 4, 1938 **Al Brown** w pts 15 Baltazar Sangchilli . . . . Paris (Fra)
May 1938 *The IBU, in the interests of unity, withdrew recognition from Brown*

Undisputed title

Apr 2, 1939 **Sixto Escobar** w pts 15 Kayo Morgan (US) . . . . San Juan, CA
Oct 1939 *Escobar relinquished the title because of difficulty in making the weight. The NBA nominated Georgie Pace as champion*

NBA title

Mar 4, 1940 **Georgie Pace** (US) drew 15 Lou Salica . . . . Toronto (Can)
Sep 24, 1940 **Lou Salica** w pts 15 Georgie Pace . . . . New York, NY
Dec 2, 1940 Lou Salica w rsf 3 Small Montana (Phil) . . . . Toronto (Can)
Jan 13, 1941 Lou Salica w pts 15 Tommy Forte (US) . . . . Philadelphia, PA
Apr 25, 1941 Lou Salica w pts 15 Lou Transparenti (US) . . . . Baltimore, MD
For undisputed title

Undisputed title

Jun 16, 1941 **Lou Salica** w pts 15 Tommy Forte . . . . Philadelphia, PA
Aug 7, 1942 **Manuel Ortiz** (Mex) w pts 12 Lou Salica . . . . Hollywood, CA
The NY Commission refused to accept this as a title fight because it had been contested over 12 rounds rather than their 15, and they continued to regard Salica as champion

JIMMY CARRUTHERS *(right) the Australian challenger rips the bantamweight title away from Vic Toweel, whom he knocked out in the first round*

NBA title

Jan 1,	1943	**Manuel Ortiz** w pts 10 Kenny Lindsay (Can)	. . . .	Portland, OR
Jan 27,	1943	Manuel Ortiz w rsf 10 George Freitas (US)	. . . .	Oakland, CA
Mar 10,	1943	Manuel Ortiz w rsf 11 Lou Salica	. . . .	Oakland, CA
		For undisputed title		

Undisputed title

Apr 28,	1943	**Manuel Ortiz** w ko 6 Lupe Cordoza (US)	. . . .	Fort Worth, TX
May 26,	1943	Manuel Ortiz w pts 15 Joe Robelto (US)	. . . .	Los Angeles, CA
Jul 12,	1943	Manuel Ortiz w ko 7 Joe Robelto	. . . .	Seattle, WA
Oct 1,	1943	Manuel Ortiz w ko 4 Leonardo Lopez (US)	. . . .	Los Angeles, CA
Nov 23,	1943	Manuel Ortiz w pts 15 Benny Goldberg (US)	. . . .	Los Angeles, CA
Mar 14,	1944	Manuel Ortiz w pts 15 Ernesto Aguilar (Mex)	. . . .	Los Angeles, CA
Apr 4,	1944	Manuel Ortiz w pts 15 Tony Olivera (US)	. . . .	Los Angeles, CA
Sep 12,	1944	Manuel Ortiz w ko 4 Luis Castillo (Mex)	. . . .	Los Angeles, CA
Nov 14,	1944	Manuel Ortiz w rsf 9 Luis Castillo	. . . .	Los Angeles, CA
Feb 25,	1946	Manuel Ortiz w ko 13 Luis Castillo	. . . .	San Francisco, CA
May 26,	1946	Manuel Ortiz w ko 5 Kenny Lindsay (Can)	. . . .	Los Angeles, CA
Jun 10,	1946	Manuel Ortiz w ko 11 Jackie Jurich (US)	. . . .	San Francisco, CA
Jan 6,	1947	**Harold Dade** (US) w pts 15 Manuel Ortiz	. . . .	San Francisco, CA
Mar 11,	1947	**Manuel Ortiz** w pts 15 Harold Dade	. . . .	Los Angeles, CA
May 30,	1947	Manuel Ortiz w pts 15 Kui Kong Young (Haw)	. . . .	Honolulu, HI
Dec 20,	1947	Manuel Ortiz w pts 15 Tirso del Rosario (Phil)	. . . .	Manila (Phil)
Jul 4,	1948	Manuel Ortiz w rsf 8 Memo Valero (Mex)	. . . .	Mexicali (Mex)
Mar 1,	1949	Manuel Ortiz w pts 15 Dado Marino (Haw)	. . . .	Honolulu, HI
May 31,	1950	**Vic Toweel** (SA) w pts 15 Manuel Ortiz	. . . .	Johannesburg (SA)
Dec 2,	1950	Vic Toweel w ret 10 Danny O'Sullivan (Eng)	. . . .	Johannesburg (SA)
Nov 17,	1951	Vic Toweel w pts 15 Luis Romero (Sp)	. . . .	Johannesburg (SA)
Jan 26,	1952	Vic Toweel w pts 15 Peter Keenan (Sco)	. . . .	Johannesburg (SA)
Nov 15,	1952	**Jimmy Carruthers** (Aus) w ko 1 Vic Toweel	. . . .	Johannesburg (SA)
Mar 21,	1953	Jimmy Carruthers w ko 10 Vic Toweel	. . . .	Johannesburg (SA)
Nov 13,	1953	Jimmy Carruthers w pts 15 Henry "Pappy" Gault (US)	. . . . .	Sydney (Aus)
May 2,	1954	Jimmy Carruthers w pts 15 Chamrern Songkitrat (Thai)	. . .	Bangkok (Thai)
May 16,	1954	*Carruthers retired as undefeated champion*		
Sep 18,	1954	**Robert Cohen** (Alg) w pts 15 Chamrern Songkitrat	. . . . . .	Bangkok (Thai)
		For vacant title		
Jan	1955	*The NBA stripped Cohen because of his failure to defend against Raton Macias*		

NY/EBU title

Sep 3,	1955	**Robert Cohen** drew 15 Willie Toweel (SA)	. . . .	Johannesburg (SA)
Jun 29,	1956	**Mario D'Agata** (Ita) w ret 6 Robert Cohen	. . . .	Rome (Ita)
Apr 1,	1957	**Alphonse Halimi** (Fra) w pts 15 Mario D'Agata	. . . .	Paris (Fra)
Nov 6,	1957	Alphonse Halimi w pts 15 Raton Macias (Mex)	. . . .	Los Angeles, CA
		For undisputed title		

NBA title

Mar 9,	1955	**Raton Macias** w ko 11 Chamrern Songkitrat	. . . .	San Francisco, CA
		For vacant title		
Mar 25,	1956	Raton Macias w ko 10 Leo Espinosa (Phil)	. . . .	Mexico City (Mex)
Jun 15,	1957	Raton Macias w rsf 11 Dommy Ursua (Phil)	. . . .	San Francisco, CA

Nov 6,	1957	**Alphonse Halimi** w pts 15 Raton Macias	. . . .	Los Angeles, CA
		For undisputed title		

Undisputed title

Jul 8,	1959	**Joe Becerra** (Mex) w ko 8 Alphonse Halimi	. . . .	Los Angeles, CA
Feb 4,	1960	Joe Becerra w ko 9 Alphonse Halimi	. . . .	Los Angeles, CA
May 23,	1960	Joe Becerra w pts 15 Kenji Yonekura (Jap)	. . . .	Tokyo (Jap)
Aug 30,	1960	*Becerra retired as undefeated champion*		

European version of title

Oct 25,	1960	**Alphonse Halimi** w pts 15 Freddie Gilroy (Ire)	. . . .	Wembley (Eng)
		For vacant title		
May 30,	1961	**John Caldwell** (Ire) w pts 15 Alphonse Halimi	. . . .	Wembley (Eng)
Oct 31,	1961	John Caldwell w pts 15 Alphonse Halimi	. . . .	Wembley (Eng)
Jan 18,	1962	**Eder Jofre** (Bra) w ret 10 John Caldwell	. . . .	Sao Paulo (Bra)
		For undisputed title		

NBA title

Nov 18,	1960	**Eder Jofre** (Bra) w ko 6 Eloy Sanchez (Mex)	. . . .	Los Angeles, CA
		For vacant title		
Mar 25,	1961	Eder Jofre w ret 9 Piero Rollo (Ita)	. . . .	Rio de Janiro (Bra)
Aug 19,	1961	Eder Jofre w rsf 7 Ramon Arias (Ven)	. . . .	Caracas (Ven)
Jan 18,	1962	Eder Jofre w ret 10 John Caldwell	. . . .	Sao Paulo (Bra)
		For undisputed title		

Undisputed title

May 4,	1962	**Eder Jofre** w rsf 10 Herman Marquez (US)	. . . .	San Francisco, CA
Sep 11,	1962	Eder Jofre w ko 6 Joe Medel (Mex)	. . . .	Sao Paulo (Bra)
Apr 4,	1963	Eder Jofre w ko 3 Katsutoshi Aoki (Jap)	. . . .	Tokyo (Jap)
May 18,	1963	Eder Jofre w ret 11 Johnny Jamito (Phil)	. . . .	Quezon City (Phil)
Nov 27,	1964	Eder Jofre w ko 7 Bernardo Caraballo (Col)	. . . .	Bogota (Col)
May 18,	1965	**Masahiko "Fighting" Harada** (Jap) w pts 15 Eder Jofre	. . . .	Nagoya (Jap)
Nov 30,	1965	Masahiko "Fighting" Harada w pts 15 Alan Rudkin (Eng)	. . . . .	Tokyo (Jap)
Jun 1,	1966	Masahiko "Fighting" Harada w pts 15 Eder Jofre	. . . .	Tokyo (Jap)
Jan 3,	1967	Masahiko "Fighting" Harada w pts 15 Joe Medel	. . . .	Nagoya (Jap)
Jul 4,	1967	Masahiko "Fighting" Harada w pts 15 Bernardo Caraballo	. . . .	Tokyo (Jap)
Feb 27,	1968	**Lionel Rose** (Aus) w pts 15 Masahiko "Fighting" Harada	. . . .	Tokyo (Jap)
Jul 2,	1968	Lionel Rose w pts 15 Takao Sakuri (Jap)	. . . .	Tokyo (Jap)
Dec 6,	1968	Lionel Rose w pts 15 Jesus "Chuchu" Castillo (Mex)	. . . .	Los Angeles, CA
Mar 8,	1969	Lionel Rose w pts 15 Alan Rudkin	. . . .	Melbourne (Aus)
Aug 22,	1969	**Ruben Olivares** (Mex) w ko 5 Lionel Rose	. . . .	Inglewood, CA
Dec 12,	1969	Ruben Olivares w rsf 2 Alan Rudkin	. . . .	Inglewood, CA
Apr 18,	1970	Ruben Olivares w pts 15 Jesus "Chuchu" Castillo	. . . . . .	Los Angeles, CA
Oct 16,	1970	**Jesus "Chuchu" Castillo** w rsf 14 Ruben Olivares	. . . .	Mexico City (Mex)
Apr 3,	1971	**Ruben Olivares** w pts 15 Jesus "Chuchu" Castillo	. . . .	Inglewood, CA
Oct 25,	1971	Ruben Olivares w rsf 14 Katsutoshi Kanazawa (Jap)	. . . .	Nagoya (Jap)
Dec 14,	1971	Ruben Olivares w rsf 11 Jesus Pimentel (Mex)	. . . .	Los Angeles, CA
Mar 19,	1972	**Rafael Herrera** (Mex) w ko 8 Ruben Olivares	. . . .	Mexico City (Mex)
Jul 30,	1972	**Enrique Pinder** (Pan) w pts 15 Rafael Herrera	. . . .	Panama City (Pan)
Dec 1972		*The WBC stripped Pinder when he signed to defend against Romeo Anaya, whom they did not consider a suitable challenger*		

RINGSIDE VIEW

Ruben Olivares
vs
Lionel Rose

THE LIGHTS TURNED OUT
Nobody hit harder than Ruben Olivares, the Mexican bantamweight who won the world title by knocking out Lionel Rose in California on August 22, 1969. It was his 49th knockout in a 52-fight unbeaten career, and there were many more to come – including one over Bobby Chacon for the featherweight championship in 1975.

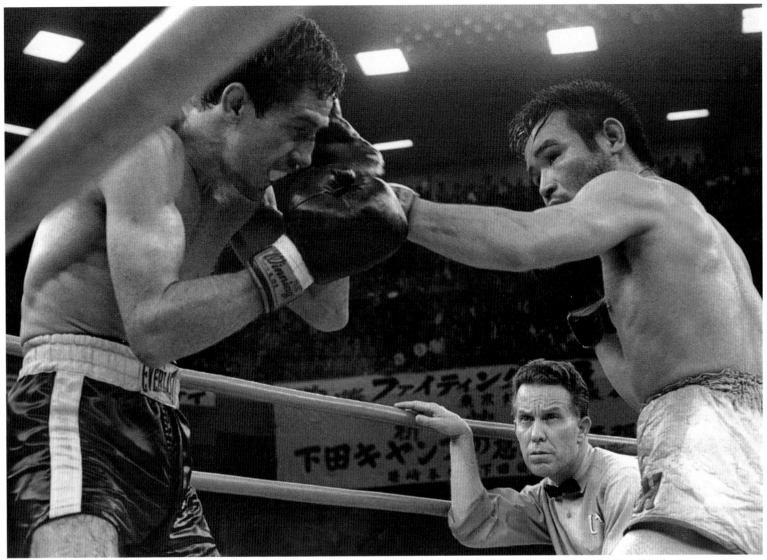

EDER JOFRE *(left) has his fabulous unbeaten run brought to an end by Japan's Masahiko "Fighting" Harada at Nagoya, the Brazilian losing on points*

WBA title

Jan 20, 1973	**Romeo Anaya** (Mex) w ko 3 Enrique Pinder	....	Panama City (Pan)
Apr 28, 1973	Romeo Anaya w pts 15 Rogelio Lara (Mex)	....	Los Angeles, CA
Aug 18, 1973	Romeo Anaya w ko 3 Enrique Pinder	....	Los Angeles, CA
Nov 3, 1973	**Arnold Taylor** (SA) w ko 14 Romeo Anaya	....	Johannesburg (SA)
Jul 3, 1974	**Soo Hwan-Hong** (Kor) w pts 15 Arnold Taylor	....	Durban (SA)
Dec 28, 1974	Soo Hwan-Hong w pts 15 Fernando Canabela (Phil)	....	Seoul (Kor)
Mar 14, 1975	**Alfonso Zamora** (Mex) w ko 4 Soo Hwan Hong	....	Inglewood, CA
Aug 30, 1975	Alfonso Zamora w ko 4 Thanomjit Sukhothai (Thai)	.....	Los Angeles, CA
Dec 6, 1975	Alfonso Zamora w ko 1 Socrates Batoto (Phil)	....	Mexico City (Mex)
Apr 3, 1976	Alfonso Zamora w ko 2 Eusebio Pedroza (Col)	....	Mexicali (Mex)
Jul 10, 1976	Alfonso Zamora w ko 3 Gilberto Illueca (Pan)	....	Juarez (Mex)
Oct 16, 1976	Alfonso Zamora w rsf 12 Soo-Hwan Hong	....	Inchon (Kor)
Nov 19, 1977	**Jorge Lujan** (Pan) w ko 10 Alfonso Zamora	....	Los Angeles, CA
Mar 18, 1978	Jorge Lujan w ret 11 Roberto Rubaldino (Mex)	....	San Antonio, TX
Sep 15, 1978	Jorge Lujan w pts 15 Albert Davila	....	New Orleans, LA
Apr 8, 1979	Jorge Lujan w rsf 15 Cleo Garcia	....	Las Vegas, NV
Oct 6, 1979	Jorge Lujan w ko 15 Roberto Rubaldino	....	McAllen, TX
Apr 2, 1980	Jorge Lujan w rsf 9 Shuichi Isogami (Jap)	....	Tokyo (Jap)
Aug 29, 1980	**Julian Solis** (PR) w pts 15 Jorge Lujan	....	Miami, FL
Nov 14, 1980	**Jeff Chandler** (US) w rsf 14 Julian Solis	....	Miami Beach, FL
Jan 31, 1981	Jeff Chandler w pts 15 Jorge Lujan	....	Philadelphia, PA
Apr 5, 1981	Jeff Chandler drew 15 Eijiro Murata (Jap)	....	Tokyo (Jap)
Jul 25, 1981	Jeff Chandler w ko 7 Julian Solis	....	Atlantic City, NJ
Dec 10, 1981	Jeff Chandler w rsf 13 Eijiro Murata	....	Atlantic City, NJ
Mar 27, 1982	Jeff Chandler w rsf 6 Johnny Carter (US)	....	Philadelphia, PA
Oct 27, 1982	Jeff Chandler w rsf 9 Miguel Iriale (Pan)	....	Atlantic City, NJ
Mar 13, 1983	Jeff Chandler w pts 15 Gaby Canizales (US)	....	Atlantic City, NJ
Sep 11, 1983	Jeff Chandler w rsf 10 Eijiro Murata	....	Tokyo (Jap)
Dec 17, 1983	Jeff Chandler w rsf 7 Oscar Muniz (US)	....	Atlantic City, NJ
Apr 7, 1984	**Richard Sandoval** (US) w rsf 15 Jeff Chandler	....	Atlantic City, NJ
Sep 22, 1984	Richard Sandoval w pts 15 Edgar Roman (Ven)	.....	Monte Carlo (Mon)
Dec 15, 1984	Richard Sandoval w rsf 8 Cardenio Ulloa (Ch)	....	Miami, FL
Mar 10, 1986	**Gaby Canizales** w rsf 7 Richard Sandoval	....	Las Vegas, NV
Jun 4, 1986	**Bernardo Pinango** (Ven) w pts 15 Gaby Canizales	...	East Rutherford, NJ
Oct 4, 1986	Bernardo Pinango w rsf 10 Ciro De Leva (Ita)	....	Turin (Ita)
Nov 22, 1986	Bernardo Pinango w rsf 15 Simon Skosana (SA)	.....	Johannesburg (SA)
Feb 3, 1987	Bernardo Pinango w pts 15 Frankie Duarte (US)	....	Los Angeles, CA
	Pinango immediately relinquished the title because of weight problems		
Mar 29, 1987	**Takuya Muguruma** (Jap) w ko 5 Azael Moran (Pan)	.....	Moriguchi (Jap)
	For vacant title		
May 24, 1987	**Chan-Yong Park** (Kor) w rsf 11 Takuya Muguruma	.....	Moriguchi (Jap)
Oct 4, 1987	**Wilfredo Vasquez** (PR) w rsf 10 Chan-Yong Park	......	Seoul (Kor)
Jan 17, 1988	Wilfredo Vasquez drew 12 Takuya Muguruma	....	Osaka (Jap)
May 9, 1988	**Kaokor Galaxy** (Thai) w pts 12 Wilfredo Vasquez	....	Bangkok (Thai)
Aug 14, 1988	**Sung-Il Moon** (Kor) w tech dec 6 Kaokor Galaxy	....	Pusan (Kor)
Nov 27, 1988	Sung-Il Moon w ko 7 Edgar Monserrat (Pan)	....	Seoul (Kor)
Feb 19, 1989	Sung-Il Moon w rsf 5 Chaiki Kobayashi (Jap)	....	Taejon (Kor)
Jul 8, 1989	**Kaokor Galaxy** w pts 12 Sung-Il Moon	....	Bangkok (Thai)
Oct 18, 1989	**Luisito Espinosa** (Phil) w rsf 1 Kaokor Galaxy	....	Bangkok (Thai)
May 30, 1990	Luisito Espinosa w ret 8 Hurley Snead (US)	....	Bangkok (Thai)
Oct 12, 1990	Luisito Espinosa w ko 1 Yong-Man Chung (Kor)	....	Manila (Phil)
Nov 29, 1990	Luisito Espinosa w pts 12 Thalerngsak Sitbobay (Thai)	...	Bangkok (Thai)
Oct 19, 1991	**Israel Contrerras** (Ven) w ko 5 Luisito Espinosa	....	Manila (Phil)
Mar 15, 1992	**Eddie Cook** (US) w ko 5 Israel Contrerras	....	Las Vegas, NV
Oct 9, 1992	**Jorge Elicier Julio** (Col) w pts 12 Eddie Cook	....	Cartagena (Col)
Jul 8, 1992	Jorge Elicier Julio w pts 12 Ricardo Vargas (Mex)	....	Tijuana (Mex)

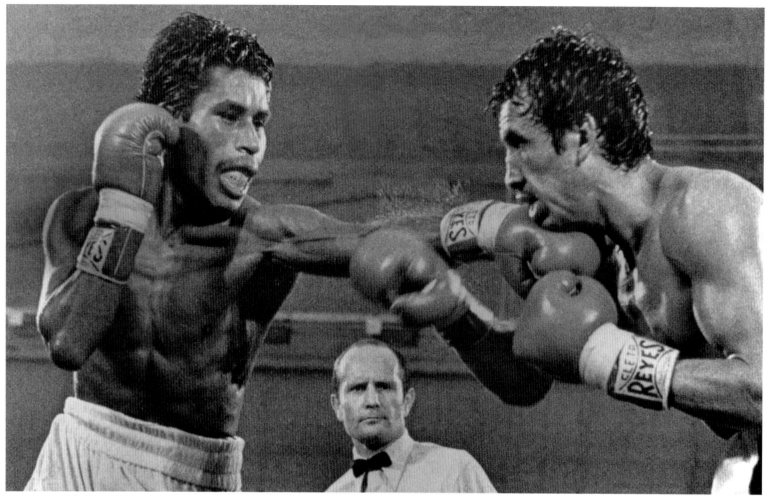

LUPE PINTOR *(left) was the controversial points winner of the clash with defending champion, Mexican compatriot Carlos Zarate*

Oct 23, 1993	**Junior Jones** (US) w pts 12 Jorge Elicier Julio .... Atlantic City, NJ	
Jan 8, 1994	Junior Jones w pts 12 Elvis Alvarez (Col) .... Catskill, NY	
Apr 22, 1994	**John Michael Johnson** (USA) w rsf 11 Junior Jones ..... Las Vegas, NV	
Jul 16, 1994	**Daorung Chuvatana** [*aka MP Petroleum*] (Thai) w rsf 1	
	John Michael Johnson .... Bangkok (Thai)	
Nov 20, 1994	Daorung MP Petroleum w rsf 5 Koh In Sik (Kor) ...... Bangkok (Thai)	
May 27, 1995	Daorung MP Petroleum drew 12 Lakhin CP Gym (Thai) ... Bangkok (Thai)	
Sep 17, 1995	**Veeraphol Sahaprom** (Thai) w pts 12 Daorung MP Petroleum	
	.... Nongtha Buri (Thai)	

WBC title

Apr 14, 1973	**Rafael Herrera** w rsf 12 Rodolfo Martinez (Mex) ...... Monterrey (Mex)	
	For vacant title	
Oct 13, 1973	Rafael Herrera w pts 15 Venice Borkorsor (Thai) .... Los Angeles, CA	
May 25, 1974	Rafael Herrera w ko 6 Romeo Anaya .... Mexico City (Mex)	
Dec 7, 1974	**Rodolfo Martinez** w rsf 4 Rafael Herrera .... Merida (Mex)	
May 31, 1975	Rodolfo Martinez w rsf 7 Nestor Jiminez (Col) .... Bogota (Col)	
Oct 8, 1975	Rodolfo Martinez w pts 15 Hisami Numata (Jap) .... Sendai (Jap)	
Jan 30, 1976	Rodolfo Martinez w pts 15 Venice Borkorsor .... Bangkok (Thai)	
May 8, 1976	**Carlos Zarate** (Mex) w ko 9 Rodolfo Martinez .... Inglewood, CA	
Aug 28, 1976	Carlos Zarate w rsf 12 Paul Ferreri (Aus) .... Los Angeles, CA	
Nov 13, 1976	Carlos Zarate w ko 4 Waruinge Nakayama (Ken) .... Culiacan (Mex)	
Feb 5, 1977	Carlos Zarate w rsf 3 Fernando Cabanela .... Mexico City (Mex)	
Oct 29, 1977	Carlos Zarate w rsf 6 Danilo Batista (Bra) .... Los Angeles, CA	
Dec 2, 1977	Carlos Zarate w rsf 5 Juan Francisco Rodriguez (Sp) ...... Madrid (Sp)	
Feb 25, 1978	Carlos Zarate w rsf 8 Albert Davila (US) .... Los Angeles, CA	
Apr 22, 1978	Carlos Zarate w rsf 13 Andres Hernandez (PR) .... San Juan, CA	
Jun 9, 1978	Carlos Zarate w ko 4 Emilio Hernandez (Ven) .... Las Vegas, NV	
Mar 10, 1979	Carlos Zarate w ko 3 Mensah Kpalongo (Togo) .... Los Angeles, CA	
Jun 2, 1979	**Lupe Pintor** (Mex) w pts 15 Carlos Zarate .... Las Vegas, NV	
Feb 9, 1980	Lupe Pintor w rsf 12 Alberto Sandoval (US) .... Los Angeles, CA	
Jun 11, 1980	Lupe Pintor drew 15 Ejiro Murata (Jap) .... Tokyo (Jap)	
Sep 19, 1980	Lupe Pintor w ko 12 Johnny Owen (Wal) .... Los Angeles, CA	

Dec 19, 1980	Lupe Pintor w pts 15 Albert Davila .... Las Vegas, NV	
Feb 22, 1981	Lupe Pintor w pts 15 Jose Uziga (Arg) .... Houston, TX	
Jul 26, 1981	Lupe Pintor w rsf 8 Jovio Rengifo (Ven) .... Las Vegas, NV	
Sep 22, 1981	Lupe Pintor w ko 15 Hurricane Teru (Jap) .... Nagoya (Jap)	
Jun 3, 1982	Lupe Pintor w rsf 11 Seung-Hoon Lee (Kor) .... Los Angeles, CA	
Jul 1983	*Pintor relinquished the title because of injuries sustained in a motor bike accident*	
Sep 1, 1983	**Albert Davila** w ko 12 Francisco "Kiko" Bejines (Mex) ... Los Angeles, CA	
	For vacant title	
May 26, 1984	Albert Davila w rsf 11 Enrique Sanchez (DR) .... Miami, FL	
Feb 1985	*The WBC stripped Davila for his failure to defend*	
May 4, 1985	**Daniel Zaragoza** (Mex) w dis 7 Freddie Jackson (US) ... Aruba (Neth Ant)	
	For vacant title	
Aug 9, 1985	**Miguel Lora** (Col) w pts 12 Daniel Zaragoza .... Miami, FL	
Feb 8, 1986	Miguel Lora w pts 12 Wilfredo Vasquez (PR) .... Miami, FL	
Aug 23, 1986	Miguel Lora w rsf 6 Enrique Sanchez (DR) .... Miami, FL	
Nov 15, 1986	Miguel Lora w pts 12 Albert Davila .... Barranquilla (Col)	
Jul 25, 1987	Miguel Lora w rsf 4 Antonio Avelar (Mex) .... Miami, FL	
Nov 27, 1987	Miguel Lora w pts 12 Ray Minus (Bah) .... Miami, FL	
Apr 30, 1988	Miguel Lora w pts 12 Lucio Lopez (Arg) .... Cartagena (Col)	
Aug 1, 1988	Miguel Lora w pts 12 Albert Davila .... Los Angeles, CA	
Oct 29, 1988	**Raul Perez** (Mex) w pts 12 Miguel Lora .... Las Vegas, NV	
Mar 9, 1989	Raul Perez w pts 12 Lucio Lopez .... Los Angeles, CA	
Aug 26, 1989	Raul Perez w ret 7 Cardenio Ulloa .... Santiago (Ch)	
Oct 23, 1989	Raul Perez w pts 12 Diego Avila (Mex) .... Los Angeles, CA	
Jan 22, 1990	Raul Perez w pts 12 Gaby Canizales .... Los Angeles, CA	
May 7, 1990	Raul Perez w rsf 9 Gerardo Martinez (US) .... Los Angeles, CA	
Dec 17, 1990	Raul Perez w ko 8 Chanquito Carmona (Mex) .... Tijuana (Mex)	
Feb 25, 1991	**Greg Richardson** (US) w pts 12 Raul Perez .... Los Angeles, CA	
May 20, 1991	Greg Richardson w pts 12 Victor Rabanales (Mex) ...... Los Angeles, CA	
Sep 19, 1991	**Joichiro Tatsuyushi** (Jap) w ret 10 Greg Richardson .... Tokyo (Jap)	
March 1992	*Tatsuyushi relinquished the title because of injury*	
Mar 30, 1992	**Victor Rabanales** w tech dec 9 Yong-Hoon Lee (Kor) ... Los Angeles, CA	
	For vacant title	

May 16, 1992	Victor Rabanales w rsf 4 Luis Ocampo (Arg)	Tuxtla Gutierrez Mex
Jul 27, 1992	Victor Rabanales w pts 12 Chang-Kyun Oh (Kor)	Los Angeles, CA
Sep 17, 1992	Victor Rabanales w rsf 9 Joichiro Tatsuyoshi	Osaka (Jap)
Jan 25, 1993	Victor Rabanales w pts 12 Dio Andujar (Phil)	Los Angeles, CA
Mar 28, 1993	**Jung-Il Byun** (Kor) w pts 12 Victor Rabanales	Kyungju
May 28, 1993	Jung-Il Byun w pts 12 Josefino Suarez (Mex)	Seoul (Kor)
Dec 23, 1993	**Yasuei Yakushiji** (Jap) w pts 12 Jung-Il Byun	Nagoya (Jap)
Apr 16, 1994	Yasuei Yakushiji (Jap) w ko 10 Josefino Suarez	Nagoya (Jap)
Aug 1, 1994	Yasuei Yakushiji w rsf 11 Jung-Il Byun (Kor)	Nagoya (Jap)
Dec 4, 1994	Yasuei Yakushiji w pts 12 Joichiro Tatsuyoshi	Nagoya (Jap)
Apr 2, 1995	Yasuei Yakushiji w pts 12 Cuauhtemoc Gomez (Mex)	Nagoya (Jap)
Jul 30, 1995	**Wayne McCullough** (Ire) w pts 12 Yasuei Yakushiji	Nagoya (Jap)
Dec 4, 1995	Wayne McCullough w rsf 8 Johnny Bredhal (Den)	Belfast (Ire)

IBF title

Apr 16, 1984	**Satoshi Shingaki** (Jap) w rsf 8 Elmer Magallano (Phil)	Kashiwa (Jap)
	For vacant title	
Aug 4, 1984	Satoshi Shingaki w pts 15 Joves de la Puz (Phil)	Kashiwa (Jap)
Apr 26, 1985	**Jeff Fenech** (Aus) w rsf 9 Satoshi Shingaki	Sydney (Aus)
Aug 23, 1985	Jeff Fenech w ko 3 Satoshi Shingaki	Sydney (Aus)
Dec 2, 1985	Jeff Fenech w pts 15 Jerome Coffee (US)	Sydney (Aus)
Jul 18, 1986	Jeff Fenech w rsf 14 Steve McCrory (US)	Sydney (Aus)
Feb 1987	*Fenech relinquished the title to challenge for the WBC super-bantamweight championship*	
May 15, 1987	**Kelvin Seabrooks** (US) w ko 5 Miguel Maturana (Col)	Cartagena (Col)
	For vacant title	
Jul 4, 1987	Kelvin Seabrooks No Contest 9 Thierry Jacob (Fra)	Calais (Fra)
Nov 18, 1987	Kelvin Seabrooks w rsf 4 Ernie Cataluna (Phil)	San Cataldo Ita
Feb 6, 1988	Kelvin Seabrooks w rsf 2 Fernando Beltran (Mex)	Paris (Fra)
Jul 9, 1988	**Orlando Canizales** (US) w rsf 15 Kelvin Seabrooks	Atlantic City, NJ
Nov 29, 1988	Orlando Canizales w ko 1 Jimmy Navarro (US)	San Antonio, TX
Jun 24, 1989	Orlando Canizales w rsf 11 Kelvin Seabrooks	Atlantic City, NJ
Jan 24, 1990	Orlando Canizales w pts 12 Billy Hardy (Eng)	Sunderland (Eng)
Jun 10, 1990	Orlando Canizales w rsf 2 Paul Gonzalez (US)	El Paso, NM
Aug 14, 1990	Orlando Canizales w rsf 5 Eddie Rangel (US)	Saratoga Springs, NY
May 4, 1991	Orlando Canizales w rsf 8 Billy Hardy	Laredo, TX

Sep 22, 1991	Orlando Canizales w pts 12 Fernie Morales (US)	Indio, CA
Dec 21, 1991	Orlando Canizales w rsf 11 Ray Minus	Laredo, TX
Apr 23, 1992	Orlando Canizales w pts 12 Francisco Alvarez (Col)	Paris (Fra)
Sep 18, 1992	Orlando Canizales w pts 12 Samuel Duran (Phil)	Bozeman, MT
Mar 27, 1993	Orlando Canizales w ret 11 Clarence Adams (US)	Evian les Bains (Fra)
Jun 19, 1993	Orlando Canizales No Contest 3 Derrick Whiteboy (SA)	Houston, TX
Nov 20, 1993	Orlando Canizales w pts 12 Juvenal Berrio (Col)	Hammanskraal
Feb 26, 1994	Orlando Canizales w rsf 4 Gerardo Martinez (USA)	San Jose, CA
Jun 7, 1994	Orlando Canizales w ko 5 Rolando Bohol (Phil)	South Padre Island, TX
Oct 15, 1994	Orlando Canizales w pts 12 Sergio Reyes (USA)	Laredo, TX
Dec 1994	*Canizales relinquished the title*	
Jan 21, 1995	**Harold Mestre** (Col) w rsf 8 Juvenal Berrio (Col)	Cartagena (Col)
	For vacant title	
Apr 29, 1995	**Mbulelo Botile** (SA) w ko 2 Harold Mestre	Johannesburg (SA)
Jul 4, 1995	Mbulelo Botile w pts 12 Sam Stewart (Lib)	Hammanskraal (SA)
Jul 4, 1995	Mbulelo Botile w ko 2 Reynaldo Hurtado (Col)	East London (SA)

WBO title

Feb 3, 1989	**Israel Contrerras** (Ven) w ko 1 Maurizio Lupino (Ita)	Caracas (Ven)
	For vacant title	
Sep 2, 1990	Israel Contrerras w rsf 9 Ray Minus	Nassau (Bah)
Jan 1991	*Contrerras relinquished the WBO title to challenge for the WBA version*	
Mar 12, 1991	**Gaby Canizales** w ko 2 Miguel Lora	Detroit, MI
	For vacant title	
Jun 30, 1991	**Duke McKenzie** (Eng) w pts 12 Gaby Canizales	London (Eng)
Sep 12, 1991	Duke McKenzie w pts 12 Cesar Soto (Mex)	London (Eng)
Mar 25, 1992	Duke McKenzie w rsf 8 Wilfredo Vargas (PR)	London (Eng)
May 13, 1992	**Rafael Del Valle** (PR) w ko 1 Duke McKenzie	London (Eng)
Mar 24, 1993	Rafael Del Valle w rsf 5 Wilfredo Vargas	Conado (PR)
Jun 19, 1993	Rafael Del Valle w pts 12 Miguel Lora	Hato Rey (PR)
Jul 30, 1994	**Alfred Kotey** (Gha) w pts 12 Rafael Del Valle	London (Eng)
Oct 25, 1994	Alfred Kotey w pts 12 Armando Castro (Mex)	Middlesbrough (Eng)
Feb 17, 1995	Alfred Kotey w rsf 4 Drew Docherty (Sco)	Cumbernauld (Sco)
Oct 21, 1995	**Daniel Jimenez** (PR) w pts 12 Alfred Kotey	London (Eng)

BILLY HARDY *(left) the Sunderland based bantamweight made a heroic bid to take the IBF title away from Orlando Canizales*

Super-Flyweight

The super-flyweight division, weight limit 115 lb, was introduced by the World Boxing Council in 1979, in response particularly to pressure from their Latin and Oriental members who felt that the gap from flyweight (112 lb) to bantamweight (118 lb) was too great. The first champion, Rafael Orono, had been a professional for less than a year when he won a split decision over Seung-Hoon Lee in 1980, but he soon established himself as a worthwhile performer. In fact, the division has been blessed with a high proportion of outstanding champions, including Jiro Watanabe, Gilberto Roman and Kaosai Galaxy.

The WBA were slow to recognize the potential of what quickly became one of boxing's brighter innovations: they did not establish their own championship until 1981, with the IBF following in 1983.

World Super-Flyweight Championship Bouts

WBC title

Feb 2,	1980	**Rafael Orono** (Ven) w pts 15 Seung-Hoon Lee (Kor)	Caracas (Ven)
		For vacant title	
Apr 14,	1980	Rafael Orono w pts 15 Ramon Soria (Arg)	Caracas (Ven)
Jul 28,	1980	Rafael Orono drew 15 Willie Jensen (US)	Caracas (Ven)
Sep 15,	1980	Rafael Orono w rsf 3 Jovito Rengifo (Ven)	Barquisimeto (Ven)
Jan 24,	1981	**Chul-Ho Kim** (Kor) w ko 9 Rafael Orono	San Cristobal (Ven)
Apr 22,	1981	Chul-Ho Kim w pts 15 Jiro Watanabe (Jap)	Seoul (Kor)
Jul 29,	1981	Chul-Ho Kim w ko 12 Willie Jensen	Pusan (Kor)
Nov 18,	1981	Chul-Ho Kim w rsf 9 Jackal Maruyama (Jap)	Pusan (Kor)
Feb 10,	1982	Chul-Ho Kim w ko 8 Koki Ishii (Jap)	Taegu (Kor)
Jul 4,	1982	Chul-Ho Kim drew 15 Raul Valdez (Mex)	Daejon (Kor)
Nov 28,	1982	**Rafael Orono** w ko 6 Chul-Ho Kim	Seoul (Kor)
Jan 30,	1983	Rafael Orono w ko 4 Pedro Romero (Pan)	Caracas (Ven)
May 9,	1983	Rafael Orono w pts 15 Raul Valdez	Caracas (Ven)
Oct 29,	1983	Rafael Orono w rsf 5 Orlando Maldonado (PR)	Caracas (Ven)
Nov 27,	1983	**Payao Poontarat** (Thai) w pts 12 Rafael Orono	Pattaya (Thai)
Mar 28,	1984	Payao Poontarat w rsf 10 Guty Espadas (Mex)	Bangkok (Thai)
Jul 5,	1984	**Jiro Watanabe** w pts 12 Payao Poontarat	Osaka (Jap)
		The fight was for the WBC title, Watanabe was immediately stripped by the WBA for failing to defend against their leading contender, Kaosai Galaxy	
Nov 29,	1984	**Jiro Watanabe** w rsf 11 Payao Poontarat	Kumamoto (Jap)
May 9,	1985	Jiro Watanabe w pts 12 Julio Solano (DR)	Tokyo (Jap)
Sep 17,	1985	Jiro Watanabe w rsf 7 Katsuo Katsuma (Jap)	Osaka (Jap)
Dec 13,	1985	Jiro Watanabe w ko 5 Yun-Sok Hwang (Kor)	Taegu (Kor)
Mar 30,	1986	**Gilberto Roman** (Mex) w pts 12 Jiro Watanabe	Osaka (Jap)
May 15,	1986	Gilberto Roman w pts 12 Edgar Monserrat (Pan)	Paris (Fra)
Jul 18,	1986	Gilberto Roman w pts 12 Ruben Condori (Mex)	Salta (Arg)
Aug 30,	1986	Gilberto Roman drew 12 Santos Laciar (Arg)	Cordoba (Arg)
Dec 15,	1986	Gilberto Roman w pts 12 Kongtoranee Payakarun (Thai) ..	Bangkok (Thai)
Jan 31,	1987	Gilberto Roman w rsf 9 Antoine Montero (Fra)	Montpelier (Fra)
Mar 19,	1987	Gilberto Roman w pts 12 Frank Cedeno (Phil)	Mexicali (Mex)
May 16,	1987	**Santos Laciar** w rsf 11 Gilberto Roman	Reims (Fra)
Aug 8,	1987	**Sugar Baby Rojas** (Col) w pts 12 Santos Laciar ...	Miami, FL
Oct 24,	1987	Sugar Baby Rojas w rsf 4 Gustavo Ballas (Arg)	Miami, FL
Apr 8,	1988	**Gilberto Roman** w pts 12 Sugar Baby Rojas	Miami, FL
Jul 9,	1988	Gilberto Roman w rsf 5 Yoshiyuki Uchida (Jap)	Kawagoe (Jap)
Sep 3,	1988	Gilberto Roman w pts 12 Kiyoshi Hatanaka (Jap)	Nagoya (Jap)

JIRO WATANABE *(right) launches a fine championship career by outpointing over 15 rounds Rafael Pedroza at Osaka in April 1982*

Nov 7,	1988	Gilberto Roman w pts 12 Sugar Baby Rojas	Las Vegas, NV
Jun 5,	1989	Gilberto Roman w pts 12 Juan Carazo (PR)	Los Angeles, CA
Sep 12,	1989	Gilberto Roman w pts 12 Santos Laciar	Los Angeles, CA
Nov 7,	1989	**Nana Yaw Konadu** (Gha) w pts 12 Gilberto Roman	Mexico City (Mex)
Jan 20,	1990	**Sung-Il Moon** (Kor) w pts 12 Nana Yaw Konadu	Seoul (Kor)
Jun 9,	1990	Sung-Il Moon w ret 8 Gilberto Roman	Seoul (Kor)
Oct 20,	1990	Sung-Il Moon w tech dec 5 Kenji Matsumara (Jap)	Seoul (Kor)
Mar 16,	1991	Sung-Il Moon w rsf 4 Nana Yaw Konadu	Zaragoza (Sp)
Jul 20,	1991	Sung-Il Moon w ko 5 Ernesto Ford (Pan)	Seoul (Kor)
Dec 22,	1991	Sung-Il Moon w rsf 6 Torsak Pongsupa (Thai)	Inchon (Kor)
Jul 4,	1992	Sung-Il Moon w rsf 8 Armando Salazar (Mex)	Inchon (Kor)
Oct 31,	1992	Sung-Il Moon w pts 12 Greg Richardson (US)	Seoul (Kor)
Feb 27,	1993	Sung-Il Moon w rsf 1 Hilario Zapata (Pan)	Seoul (Kor)
Jul 3,	1993	Sung-Il Moon w pts 12 Carlos Salazar (Arg)	Seoul (Kor)
Nov 13,	1993	**Jose Luis Bueno** (Mex) w pts 12 Sung-Il Moon	Seoul (Kor)
May 4,	1994	**Hiroshi Kawashima** (Jap) w pts 12 Jose Luis Bueno	Yokohama (Jap)
Aug 7,	1994	Hiroshi Kawashima w pts 12 Carlos Salazar	Tokyo (Jap)
Jan 18,	1995	Hiroshi Kawashima w pts 12 Jose Luis Bueno	Yokohama (Jap)
May 24,	1995	Hiroshi Kawashima w pts 12 Seung Koo Lee (Kor)	Yokohama (Jap)
Nov 8,	1995	Hiroshi Kawashima w rsf 3 Boy Aruan (Indo)	Tokyo (Jap)

WBA title

Sep 12,	1981	**Gustavo Ballas** w rsf 8 Sok-Chul Baek (Kor)	Buenos Aires (Arg)
		For vacant WBA title	
Dec 5,	1981	**Rafael Pedroza** (Pan) w pts 15 Gustavo Ballas	Panama City (Pan)
Apr 8,	1982	**Jiro Watanabe** (Jap) w pts 15 Rafael Pedroza	Osaka (Jap)
Jul 29,	1982	Jiro Watanabe w rsf 9 Gustavo Ballas	Osaka (Jap)
Nov 11,	1982	Jiro Watanabe w ret 12 Shoji Oguma (Jap)	Hamamatsu (Jap)
Feb 24,	1983	Jiro Watanabe w ko 8 Luis Ibanez (Per)	Tsu City (Jap)
Jun 23,	1983	Jiro Watanabe w pts 15 Roberto Ramirez (Mex)	Sendai (Jap)
Oct 6,	1983	Jiro Watanabe w tech dec 11 Soon-Chun Kwon (Kor)	Osaka (Jap)
Mar 15,	1984	Jiro Watanabe w rsf 15 Celso Chavez (Pan)	Osaka (Jap)
Jul 5,	1984	Jiro Watanabe w pts 12 Payao Poontarat	Osaka (Jap)
		The fight was for the WBC title. Watanabe was immediately stripped by the WBA for failing to defend against their leading contender, Kaosai Galaxy.	
Nov 21,	1984	**Kaosai Galaxy** (Thai) w ko 6 Eusebio Espinal (DR)	Bangkok (Thai)
		For vacant title	
Mar 6,	1985	Kaosai Galaxy w ko 7 Dong-Chun Lee (Kor)	Bangkok (Thai)
Jul 17,	1985	Kaosai Galaxy w rsf 5 Rafael Orono	Bangkok (Thai)
Dec 23,	1985	Kaosai Galaxy w rsf 2 Edgar Monserrat	Bangkok (Thai)
Nov 1,	1986	Kaosai Galaxy w ko 5 Israel Contreras (Ven)	Willemstad (Curacao)
Feb 28,	1987	Kaosai Galaxy w ko 13 Elly Pical (Indo)	Jakarta (Indo)
Oct 12,	1987	Kaosai Galaxy w rsf 3 Byong-Kwan Chung (Kor)	Bangkok (Thai)
Jan 26,	1988	Kaosai Galaxy w pts 12 Kongtoranee Payakarun (Thai)	Bangkok (Thai)
Oct 9,	1988	Kaosai Galaxy w ko 8 Chang-Ho Choi (Kor)	Seoul (Kor)
Jan 15,	1989	Kaosai Galaxy w ko 2 Tae-Il Chang (Kor)	Bangkok (Thai)
Apr 8,	1989	Kaosai Galaxy w pts 12 Kenji Matsumura (Jap)	Yokohama (Jap)
Jul 29,	1989	Kaosai Galaxy w rsf 10 Alberto Castro (Col)	Surin (Thai)
Oct 31,	1989	Kaosai Galaxy w ko 12 Kenji Matsumara (Jap)	Kobe (Jap)
Mar 29,	1990	Kaosai Galaxy w ko 5 Ari Blanca (Phil)	Bangkok (Thai)
Jun 30,	1990	Kaosai Galaxy w rsf 8 Schunichi Kakajima (Jap)	Chiang Mai (Thai)
Dec 9,	1990	Kaosai Galaxy w ko 6 Ernesto Ford	Petchabun (Thai)
Apr 6,	1991	Kaosai Galaxy w rsf 5 Jae-Suk Park (Kor)	Samut Songkhram (Thai)
Jul 20,	1991	Kaosai Galaxy w rsf 5 David Griman (Ven)	Bangkok (Thai)
Dec 22,	1991	Kaosai Galaxy w pts 12 Armando Castro (Mex)	Bangkok (Thai)
Jan	1992	*Galaxy retired*	
Apr 10,	1992	**Katsuya Onizuka** (Jap) w pts 12 Thalerngsak Sithbaobey (Thai)	Tokyo (Jap)
		For vacant title	
Sep 11,	1992	Katsuya Onizuka w rsf 5 Kenji Matsumara	Tokyo (Jap)
May 21,	1993	Katsuya Onizuka w pts 12 Jae-Shin Lim (Kor)	Tokyo (Jap)
Nov 5,	1993	Katsuya Onizuka w pts 12 Thalerngsak Sithbaobey	Tokyo (Jap)
Apr 3,	1994	Katsuya Onizuka w pts 12 Seungkoo Lee (Kor)	Tokyo (Jap)
Sep 18,	1994	**Hyung-Chul Lee** (Kor) w rsf 9 Katsuya Onizuka	Tokyo (Jap)

Feb 25,	1995	Hyung Chul Lee w ko 12 Tamonori Tamura (Jap)	Pusan (Kor)
Jul 22,	1995	**Alimi Goitia** (Ven) w ko 4 Hyung Chul Lee	Seoul (Kor)
Jul 22,	1995	Alimi Goitia w rsf 5 Aquiles Guzman (Ven)	Porlama (Ven)

IBF title

Dec 10,	1983	**Joo-Do Chun** (Kor) w ko 5 Ken Kasugai (Jap)	Osaka (Jap)
		For vacant title	
Jan 28,	1984	Joo-Do Chun w ko 12 Prayoonsak Muangsurin (Thai)	Seoul (Kor)
Mar 17,	1984	Joo-Do Chun w ko 1 Diego de Villa (Phil)	Kwangju (Kor)
May 26,	1984	Joo-Do Chun w rsf 6 Felix Marques (PR)	Wonju (Kor)
Jul 20,	1984	Joo-Do Chun w ko 7 William Develos (Phil)	Pusan (Kor)
Jan 6,	1985	Joo-Do Chun w ko 15 Kwang-Gu Park (Kor)	Ulsan (Kor)
May 3,	1985	**Elly Pical** w rsf 8 Joo-Do Chun	Jakarta (Indo)
Aug 25,	1985	Elly Pical w rsf 3 Wayne Mulholland (Aus)	Jakarta (Indo)
Feb 15,	1986	**Carlos Cesar Polanco** (DR) w pts 15 Elly Pical	Jakarta (Indo)
Jul 5,	1986	**Elly Pical** w ko 3 Carlos Cesar Polanco	Jakarta (Indo)
Dec 3,	1986	Elly Pical w ko 10 Dong-Chun Lee (Kor)	Jakarta (Indo)
Mar	1987	*Pical forfeited his title by challenging for the WBA version*	
May 17,	1987	**Tae-Il Chang** w pts 15 Soon-Chun Kwan (Kor)	Pusan (Kor)
		For vacant title	
Oct 17,	1987	**Elly Pical** w pts 15 Tae-Il Chang	Jakarta (Indo)
Feb 20,	1988	Elly Pical w pts 15 Raul Diaz (Col)	Pontianak (Indo)
Sep 3,	1988	Elly Pical w pts 12 Chang-Ki Kim (Kor)	Surubaya (Indo)
Feb 25,	1989	Elly Pical w pts 12 Mike Phelps (US)	Singapore
Oct 14,	1989	**Juan Polo Perez** (Col) w pts 12 Elly Pical	Roanoke, VA
Apr 21,	1990	**Robert Quiroga** (US) w pts 12 Juan Polo Perez	Sunderland (Eng)
Oct 6,	1990	Robert Quiroga w ret 3 Vuyani Nene (SA)	Benevento (Ita)
Jan 26,	1991	Robert Quiroga w pts 12 Vincenzo Belcastro (Ita)	Capo D'Orlando (Ita)
Jun 15,	1991	Robert Quiroga w pts 12 Akeem Anifowashe (Nig)	San Antonio, TX
Feb 15,	1992	Robert Quiroga w pts 12 Carlos Mercado (Col)	Salerno (Ita)
Jul 11,	1992	Robert Quiroga w pts 12 Jose Ruiz (PR)	Las Vegas, NV
Jan 16,	1993	**Julio Cesar Borboa** (Mex) w rsf 12 Robert Quiroga	San Antonio, TX
May 22,	1993	Julio Cesar Borboa w pts 12 Joel Luna Zarate (Mex)	Mexico City (Mex)
Aug 21,	1993	Julio Cesar Borboa w ko 3 Carlos Mercado	Kalispell, MT
Nov 26,	1993	Julio Cesar Borboa w rsf 5 Rolando Pascua (Phil)	Hermosillo (Mex)
Apr 25,	1994	Julio Cesar Borboa w rsf 4 Jorge Luis Roman (Mex)	Inglewood, CA
May 21,	1994	Julio Cesar Borboa w rsf 9 Jaji Sibali (SA)	Hammanskraal
Aug 29,	1994	**Harold Grey** (Col) w pts 12 Julio Cesar Borboa	Inglewood, CA
Dec 17,	1994	Harold Grey w pts 12 Vincenzo Belcastro	Cagliari (Ita)
Mar 18,	1995	Harold Grey w pts 12 Orlando Tobon (Col)	Cartagena (Col)
Jun 24,	1995	Harold Grey w pts 12 Julio Cesar Borboa	Cartagena (Col)
Oct 7,	1995	**Carlos Salazar** w pts 12 Harold Grey	Mar del Plata (Arg)

WBO title

Sep 9,	1989	**Jose Ruiz** (PR) w rsf 1 Juan Carazo (PR)	San Juan, CA
		For vacant title	
Oct 21,	1989	Jose Ruiz w rsf 12 Angel Rosario (PR)	San Juan, CA
Aug 18,	1990	Jose Ruiz w rsf 8 Wilfredo Vargas (PR)	Ponce (PR)
Nov 3,	1990	Jose Ruiz w pts 12 Armando Velasco (Mex)	Acapulco (Mex)
Feb 22,	1992	**Jose Quirino** (Mex) w pts 12 Jose Ruiz	Las Vegas, NV
Sep 4,	1992	**Johnny Bredahl** (Den) w pts 12 Jose Quirino	Copenhagen (Den)
Mar 26,	1993	Johnny Bredahl w pts 12 Rafael Caban (PR)	Copenhagen (Den)
Oct 29,	1993	Johnny Bredahl w dis 4 Eduardo Nazario (PR)	Korsör (Den)
Mar 25,	1994	Johnny Bredahl w pts 12 Eduardo Nazario	Barnholme
Aug 19,	1994	*Bredahl relinquished title*	
Oct 12,	1994	**Johnny Tapia** (USA) w rsf 11 Henry Martinez (USA)	Albuquerque, NM
		For vacant title	
Feb 10,	1995	Johnny Tapia w pts 12 Jose Rafael Sosa (Arg)	Albuquerque, NM
May 6,	1995	Johnny Tapia tech draw 8 Ricardo Vargas (Mex)	Las Vegas, NV
Jul 2,	1995	Johnny Tapia w pts 12 Arthur Johnson (USA)	Albuquerque, NM
Dec 1,	1995	Johnny Tapia w ret 9 Willy Salazar (Mex)	Indio Springs, CA

Flyweight

Flyweight (112 lb) was the last of boxing's eight "classic" divisions to become established. Until the National Sporting Club introduced it in 1909, anyone below feather-weight was regarded as a bantamweight, no matter how much weight that might force him to concede. At that time the bantamweight limit was fluctuating at anything from 105 to 118 lb, depending on which "champion" was involved, and the position clearly needed to be regularized.

The NSC, the predecessors of the modern British Boxing Board of Control, held the first British championship at the weight in 1911 and Sid Smith, the winner, went on to beat Eugene Criqui in the first international title fight in the new division. In America Johnny Coulon had been claiming the world bantamweight champion-ship at 112 lb, but he had moved up to 116 lb by the time the new category became official.

The Americans did not accept Wilde as champion until 1916, when he knocked out their representative, a New York Italian, Giuseppe di Melfi, who boxed under the name of Young Zulu Kid. Wilde did not defend his title between 1918 and his last contest in 1923, but thereafter the division became active and popular on both sides of the Atlantic – and when boxing took hold in the Orient after the Second World War, the contribution of Japanese, Filipinos and Thais was immense.

World Flyweight Championship Bouts

Apr 11,	1913	**Sid Smith** (Eng) w pts 20 Eugene Criqui (Fra) . . . . Paris (Fra)	
Jun 2,	1913	**Bill Ladbury** (Eng) w rsf 11 Sid Smith . . . . London (Eng)	
Jan 26,	1914	**Percy Jones** (Wal) w pts 20 Bill Ladbury . . . . London (Eng)	
Mar 26,	1914	Percy Jones w pts 20 Eugene Criqui . . . . Liverpool (Eng)	
May 15,	1914	**Joe Symonds** (Eng) w ko 18 Percy Jones . . . . Plymouth (Eng)	
		Jones came in overweight but Symonds claimed the title	
Nov 16,	1914	**Jimmy Wilde** (Wal) w pts 15 Joe Symonds . . . . London (Eng)	
		Billed as a title fight	
Dec 3,	1914	Jimmy Wilde w ko 9 Sid Smith . . . . Liverpool (Eng)	
		A match between Wilde and Tancy Lee, who had stopped Percy Jones, was accepted as being for the championship	
Jan 25,	1915	**Tancy Lee** (Sco) w rsf 17 Jimmy Wilde . . . . London (Eng)	
Oct 18,	1915	**Joe Symonds** w rsf 16 Tancy Lee . . . . London (Eng)	
Feb 14,	1916	**Jimmy Wilde** w rsf 12 Joe Symonds . . . . London (Eng)	
Apr 24,	1916	Jimmy Wilde w ret 11 Johnny Rosner (US) . . . . Liverpool (Eng)	
Jun 26,	1916	Jimmy Wilde w rsf 11 Tancy Lee . . . . London (Eng)	
Jul 31,	1916	Jimmy Wilde w ko 10 Johnny Hughes (Eng) . . . . London (Eng)	
Dec 18,	1916	Jimmy Wilde w ko 11 Young Zulu Kid (US) . . . . London (Eng)	
Mar 12,	1917	Jimmy Wilde w ret 4 George Clark (Eng) . . . . London (Eng)	
Apr 29,	1918	Jimmy Wilde w rsf 2 Dick Heasman (Eng) . . . . London (Eng)	
Jun 18,	1923	**Pancho Villa** (Phil) w ko 7 Jimmy Wilde . . . . New York, NY	
Oct 13,	1923	Pancho Villa w pts 15 Benny Schwartz (US) . . . . Baltimore, MD	
May 30,	1924	Pancho Villa w pts 15 Frankie Ash (Eng) . . . . New York, NY	
May 1,	1925	Pancho Villa w pts 15 Jose Senica (Phil) . . . . Manila (Phil)	
Jul 14,	1925	*Villa died, and Frankie Genaro claimed the title on the strength of his 1923 win over Villa for the US title*	
Aug 22,	1925	**Fidel LaBarba** (US) w pts 10 Frankie Genaro (US) . . . . . . Los Angeles, CA	
		For American recognition as champion	
Jul 8,	1926	Fidel LaBarba w pts 10 Georgie Rivers (US) . . . . Los Angeles, CA	

Jan 21,	1927	Fidel LaBarba w pts 12 Elky Clark (Sco) . . . . New York, NY	
		For undisputed title	
Aug 23,	1927	*LaBarba retired to enter university, and the title split*	

NBA title

Oct 22,	1927	**Pinky Silverburg** (US) w dis 7 Ruby Bradley (US) . . . . Bridgeport, CT	
		For vacant title, which Silverburg forfeited a month later for failing to meet Ernie Jarvis within the stipulated period	
Dec 19,	1927	**Albert "Frenchy" Belanger** (Can) w pts 12 Ernie Jarvis (Eng) . . . . Toronto (Can)	
		For vacant title	
Feb 6,	1928	**Frankie Genaro** w pts 10 Albert "Frenchy" Belanger . . . . . . Toronto (Can)	
Oct 15,	1928	Frankie Genaro w pts 10 Albert "Frenchy" Belanger . . . . Toronto (Can)	
Mar 2,	1929	**Emile Pladner** (Fra) w ko 1 Frankie Genaro . . . . Paris (Fra)	
		For NBA title. Pladner's win also earned him recognition by the ternational Boxing Union	

British version

Aug 29,	1928	**Johnny Hill** (Sco) w pts 15 Newsboy Brown (Rus) . . . . London (Eng)	
		Brown had been recognized as champion in California after outpointing Johnny McCoy over 10 rounds in Los Angeles on January 3, 1928	
Mar 21,	1929	Johnny Hill w pts 15 Ernie Jarvis . . . . London (Eng)	
Jun 29,	1929	Johnny Hill w dis 10 Ernie Jarvis . . . . Glasgow (Sco)	
Sep 27,	1929	*Hill died*	

NBA/IBU titles

Apr 18,	1929	**Frankie Genaro** w dis 5 Emile Pladner . . . . Paris (Fra)	
Oct 17,	1929	Frankie Genaro w pts 15 Ernie Jarvis . . . . London (Eng)	
Jan 18,	1930	Frankie Genaro w ret 12 Yvon Trevidic (Fra) . . . . Paris (Fra)	
Jun 10,	1930	Frankie Genaro w pts 10 Albert "Frenchy" Belanger . . . . Toronto (Can)	
Dec 26,	1930	Frankie Genaro drew 15 Midget Wolgast (US) . . . . New York, NY	
		For undisputed title	
Mar 25,	1931	Frankie Genaro drew 15 Victor Ferrand (Sp) . . . . Madrid (Sp)	
		Ferrand was four points ahead, but IBU rules required a challenger to have at least a five-point lead for the title to change hands	
Jul 30,	1931	Frankie Genaro w ko 6 Jackie Harmon (US) . . . . Waterbury, CT	
Oct 3,	1931	Frankie Genaro w pts 15 Valentin Angelmann (Fra) . . . . Paris (Fra)	
Oct 27,	1931	**Victor "Young" Perez** (Tun) w ko 2 Frankie Genaro . . . . Paris (Fra)	
Oct 31,	1932	**Jackie Brown** (Eng) w rsf 13 Victor "Young" Perez . . . . Manchester (Eng)	
Jun 12,	1933	Jackie Brown w pts 15 Valentin Angelmann . . . . Manchester (Eng)	
Sep 11,	1933	Jackie Brown w pts 15 Valentin Angelmann . . . . Manchester (Eng)	
Dec 11,	1933	Jackie Brown w pts 15 Ginger Foran (Eng) . . . . Manchester (Eng)	
Jun 18,	1934	Jackie Brown drew 15 Valentin Angelmann . . . . Manchester (Eng)	
Sep	1936	*Brown was stripped by the IBU for failing to give Angelmann a rematch*	

IBU title

Jan 6,	1936	**Valentin Angelmann** w ret 5 Kid David (Bel) . . . . Paris (Fra)	
		For vacant title	
Dec 12,	1936	Valentin Angelmann w pts 15 Ernst Weiss (Aut) . . . . Paris (Fra)	
Jan	1937	*The IBU withdrew recognition from Angelmann after Peter Kane had outpointed him over 12 rounds in Paris on January 18, 1937*	

NBA title

Sep 9,	1935	**Benny Lynch** (Sco) w ret 2 Jackie Brown . . . . Manchester (Eng)	
Sep 16,	1936	Benny Lynch w ko 8 Pat Palmer (Eng) . . . . Glasgow (Sco)	
Jan 19,	1937	Benny Lynch w pts 15 Small Montana (Phil) . . . . Wembley (Eng)	
		For undisputed title	

NY title

Dec 16,	1927	**Cpl Izzy Schwartz** (US) w pts 15 Newsboy Brown . . . . New York, NY	
		For vacant title	
Apr 9,	1928	Cpl Izzy Schwartz w pts 15 Routier Parra (Ch) . . . . New York, NY	
Jul 20,	1928	Cpl Izzy Schwartz w dis 4 Frisco Grande (Phil) . . . . Rockaway, NY	
Aug 3,	1928	Cpl Izzy Schwartz w ko 4 Little Jeff Smith (US) . . . . Rockaway, NY	
Mar 12,	1929	Cpl Izzy Schwartz w pts 12 Albert "Frenchy" Belanger . . . . . Toronto (Can)	
Aug 22,	1929	**Willie La Morte** (US) w pts 15 Cpl Izzy Schwartz . . . . Newark, NJ	
		New York did not recognize La Morte as champion, but withdrew recognition from Schwartz and instituted a tournament in which the finalists were Midget Wolgast and Black Bill	
Mar 21,	1930	**Midget Wolgast** w pts 15 Black Bill (Cub) . . . . New York, NY	
		For vacant title	

May 16, 1930	Midget Wolgast w ret 5 Willie La Morte	New York, NY
Dec 26, 1930	Midget Wolgast drew 15 Frankie Genaro	New York, NY
	For undisputed title	
Jul 13, 1931	Midget Wolgast (US) w pts 15 Ruby Bradley	Brooklyn, NY
Sep 16, 1935	**Small Montana** w pts 10 Midget Wolgast	Oakland, CA
Dec 16, 1935	Small Montana w pts 10 Tuffy Pierpoint (US)	Oakland, CA
Jan 19, 1937	**Benny Lynch** w pts 15 Small Montana	Wembley (Eng)
	For undisputed title	

Undisputed title

Oct 13, 1937	**Benny Lynch** w ko 13 Peter Kane (Eng)	Glasgow (Sco)
Jun 29, 1938	*Lynch forfeited the title by scaling 118½lb for a scheduled defence against Jackie Jurich*	
Sep 22, 1938	**Peter Kane** w pts 15 Jackie Jurich (US)	Liverpool (Eng)
	For vacant title	
May 1939	*Kane relinquished the title to box as a bantamweight*	

NBA title

Dec 14, 1939	*The NBA proclaimed Little Dado champion*	

Feb 21, 1941	**Little Dado** (Phil) w pts 10 Jackie Jurich	Honolulu, HI
1942	*Dado relinquished the title because of his inability to make the weight, and the NBA reinstated Kane as champion*	
Jun 19, 1943	**Jackie Paterson** (Sco) w ko 1 Peter Kane	Glasgow (Sco)
Jul 10, 1946	Jackie Paterson w pts 15 Joe Curran (Eng)	Glasgow (Sco)
Jul 31, 1947	*The NBA and BBBC stripped Paterson of the title because of his inability to make the weight for a planned defence against Dado Marino*	
Oct 20, 1947	**Rinty Monaghan** (Ire) w pts 15 Dado Marino (Haw)	London (Eng)
	For NBA and Irish Board recognition as champion. Paterson obtained a court injunction restraining the BBBC from recognizing anyone else as world champion or from recognizing as a title fight any contest not involving him	
Mar 23, 1948	Rinty Monaghan w ko 7 Jackie Paterson	Belfast (N. Ire)
	For undisputed title	

Undisputed title

Apr 5, 1949	**Rinty Monaghan** w pts 15 Maurice Sandeyron (Fra)	Belfast (N. Ire)
Sep 30, 1949	Rinty Monaghan drew 15 Terry Allen (Eng)	Belfast (N. Ire)
Mar 30, 1950	*Monaghan retired as undefeated champion*	
Apr 25, 1950	**Terry Allen** w pts 15 Honore Pratesi (Fra)	London (Eng)
	For vacant title	

YOUNG MARTIN *goes the way of most of Pascual Perez's title challengers, the Spanish flyweight knocked out in the third round in December 1957*

Aug 1,	1950	**Dado Marino** w pts 15 Terry Allen .... Honolulu, HI
Nov 1,	1951	Dado Marino w pts 15 Terry Allen .... Honolulu, HI
May 19,	1952	**Yoshio Shirai** (Jap) w pts 15 Dado Marino .... Tokyo (Jap)
Nov 15,	1952	Yoshio Shirai w pts 15 Dado Marino .... Tokyo (Jap)
May 18,	1953	Yoshio Shirai w pts 15 Tanny Campo (Phil) .... Tokyo (Jap)
Oct 27,	1953	Yoshio Shirai w pts 15 Terry Allen .... Tokyo (Jap)
May 23,	1954	Yoshio Shirai w pts 15 Leo Espinosa (Phil) .... Tokyo (Jap)
Nov 26,	1954	**Pascual Perez** (Arg) w pts 15 Yoshio Shirai .... Tokyo (Jap)
May 30,	1955	Pascual Perez w ko 5 Yoshio Shirai .... Tokyo (Jap)
Jan 11,	1956	Pascual Perez w pts 15 Leo Espinosa .... Buenos Aires (Arg)
Jun 30,	1956	Pascual Perez w ret 11 Oscar Suarez (Cub) .... Montevideo (Uru)
Mar 30,	1957	Pascual Perez w ko 1 Dai Dower (Wal) .... Buenos Aires (Arg)
Dec 7,	1957	Pascual Perez w ko 3 Young Martin (Sp) .... Buenos Aires (Arg)
Apr 19,	1958	Pascual Perez w pts 15 Ramon Arias (Ven) .... Caracas (Ven)
Dec 15,	1958	Pascual Perez w pts 15 Dommy Ursua (Phil) .... Manila (Phil)
Aug 10,	1959	Pascual Perez w pts 15 Kenji Yonekura (Jap) .... Tokyo (Jap)
Nov 5,	1959	Pascual Perez w ko 13 Sadao Yaoita (Jap) .... Osaka (Jap)
Apr 16,	1960	**Pone Kingpetch** (Thai) w pts 15 Pascual Perez .... Bangkok (Thai)
Sep 22,	1960	Pone Kingpetch w rsf 8 Pascual Perez .... Los Angeles, CA
Jun 27,	1961	Pone Kingpetch w pts 15 Mitsunori Seki (Jap) .... Tokyo (Jap)
May 30,	1962	Pone Kingpetch w pts 15 Kyo Noguchi (Jap) .... Tokyo (Jap)
Oct 10,	1962	**Masahiko "Fighting" Harada** (Jap) w ko 11 Pone Kingpetch . Tokyo (Jap)
Jan 12,	1963	**Pone Kingpetch** w pts 15 Masahiko "Fighting" Harada .... Bangkok (Thai)
Sep 18,	1963	**Hiroyuki Ebihara** (Jap) w ko 1 Pone Kingpetch .... Tokyo (Jap)
Jan 23,	1964	**Pone Kingpetch** w pts 15 Hiroyuki Ebihara .... Bangkok (Thai)
Apr 23,	1965	**Salvatore Burrini** (Ita) w pts 15 Pone Kingpetch .... Rome (Ita)
Nov	1965	*The WBA stripped Burruni for his failure to defend against Horacio Accavallo*

WBC title

Dec 2,	1965	**Salvatore Burrini** w ko 13 Rocky Gattellari (Aus) .... Sydney (Aus)
Jun 14,	1966	**Walter McGowan** (Sco) w pts 15 Salvatore Burruni ...... Wembley (Eng)
Dec 30,	1966	**Chartchai Chionoi** (Thai) w rsf 9 Walter McGowan ..... Bangkok (Thai)
Jul 26,	1967	Chartchai Chionoi w ko 3 Puntip Keosuriya (Thai) ..... Bangkok (Thai)
Sep 19,	1967	Chartchai Chionoi w rsf 7 Walter McGowan .... Wembley (Eng)
Jan 28,	1968	Chartchai Chionoi w rsf 13 Efren Torres (Mex) ..... Mexico City (Mex)
Nov 10,	1968	Chartchai Chionoi w pts 15 Bernabe Villacampo (Phil) .... Bangkok (Thai)
Feb 23,	1969	**Efren Torres** w rsf 8 Chartchai Chionoi .... Mexico City (Mex)
Nov 28,	1969	Efren Torres w pts 15 Susumu Hanagata (Jap) .... Guadalajara (Mex)
Mar 20,	1970	**Chartchai Chionoi** w pts 15 Efren Torres .... Bangkok (Thai)
Dec 7,	1970	**Erbito Salavarria** (Phil) w rsf 2 Chartchai Chionoi ..... Bangkok (Thai)
Apr 30,	1971	Erbito Salavarria w pts 15 Susumu Hanagata .... Manila (Phil)
Nov 20,	1971	Erbito Salavarria drew 15 Betulio Gonzalez (Ven) ...... Maracaibo (Ven)
		The WBC proclaimed Gonzalez champion after Salavarria was found to have used an illegal stimulant
Jun 3,	1972	**Betulio Gonzalez** w ko 4 Socrates Batoto (Phil) .... Caracas (Ven)
Sep 29,	1972	**Venice Borkorsor** (Thai) w ret 10 Betulio Gonzalez .... Bangkok (Thai)
Feb 9,	1973	Venice Borkorsor w pts 15 Erbito Salavarria .... Bangkok (Thai)
Jul 10,	1973	*Borkorsor relinquished title to box as a bantamweight*
Aug 4,	1973	**Betulio Gonzalez** w pts 15 Miguel Canto (Mex) .... Maracaibo (Ven)
		For vacant title
Nov 17,	1973	Betulio Gonzalez w rsf 11 Alberto Morales (Mex) .... Caracas (Ven)
Oct 1,	1974	**Shoji Oguma** (Jap) w pts 15 Betulio Gonzalez .... Tokyo (Jap)
Jan 8,	1975	**Miguel Canto** w pts 15 Shoji Oguma .... Sendai (Jap)
May 24,	1975	Miguel Canto w pts 15 Betulio Gonzalez .... Monterrey (Mex)
Aug 23,	1975	Miguel Canto w rsf 11 Jiro Takada (Jap) .... Merida (Mex)
Dec 13,	1975	Miguel Canto w pts 15 Ignacio Espinal (DR) .... Merida (Mex)
May 15,	1976	Miguel Canto w pts 15 Susumu Hanagata .... Merida (Mex)
Oct 3,	1976	Miguel Canto w pts 15 Betulio Gonzalez .... Caracas (Ven)
Nov 19,	1976	Miguel Canto w pts 15 Orlando Javierta (Phil) ..... Los Angeles, CA
Apr 24,	1977	Miguel Canto w pts 15 Reyes Arnal (Ven) .... Caracas (Ven)
Jun 15,	1977	Miguel Canto w pts 15 Kimio Furesawa (Jap) .... Tokyo (Jap)
Sep 17,	1977	Miguel Canto w pts 15 Martin Vargas (Ch) .... Merida (Mex)
Nov 30,	1977	Miguel Canto w pts 15 Martin Vargas .... Santiago (Ch)
Jan 4,	1978	Miguel Canto w pts 15 Shoji Oguma .... Tokyo (Jap)
Apr 18,	1978	Miguel Canto w pts 15 Shoji Oguma .... Tokyo (Jap)
Nov 20,	1978	Miguel Canto w pts 15 Tacomron Vibonchai (Thai) .... Houston, TX
Feb 10,	1979	Miguel Canto w pts 15 Antonio Avelar (Mex) .... Merida (Mex)
Mar 18,	1979	**Chan Hee Park** (Kor) w pts 15 Miguel Canto .... Pusan (Kor)
May 19,	1979	Chan Hee Park w pts 15 Tsutomo Igarishi (Jap) .... Seoul (Kor)
Sep 9,	1979	Chan Hee Park drew 15 Miguel Canto .... Seoul (Kor)
Dec 16,	1979	Chan Hee Park w ko 2 Guty Espadas .... Pusan (Kor)
Feb 9,	1980	Chan Hee Park w pts 15 Arnel Arrozal (Pan) .... Seoul (Kor)
Apr 13,	1980	Chan Hee Park w pts 15 Alberto Morales (Mex) .... Taegu (Kor)
May 18,	1980	**Shoji Oguma** w ko 9 Chan Hee Park .... Seoul (Kor)
Jul 28,	1980	Shoji Oguma w pts 15 Sung-Jun Kim (Kor) .... Tokyo (Jap)

RINGSIDE VIEW

Chartchai Chionoi
vs
Walter McGowan

BLOODY BUT UNBOWED

Scotland's Walter McGowan had won every minute of every round of his rematch with Chartchai Chionoi at Wembley on September 19, 1967, but still finished the loser as a bad cut – which had also cost him the title in their first meeting – forced the referee to stop the fight in the seventh round.

Oct 18,	1980	Shoji Oguma w pts 15 Chan Hee Park .... Sendai (Jap)
Feb 3,	1981	Shoji Oguma w pts 15 Chan Hee Park .... Tokyo (Jap)
May 12,	1981	**Antonio Avelar** w ko 7 Shoji Oguma .... Mito (Jap)
Aug 30,	1981	Antonio Avelar w ko 2 Taeshik Kim .... Seoul (Kor)
Mar 20,	1982	**Prudencio Cardona** (Col) w ko 1 Antonio Avelar .... Tampico (Mex)
Jul 24,	1982	**Freddie Castillo** (Mex) w pts 15 Prudencio Cardona ..... Merida (Mex)
Nov 6,	1982	**Eleoncio Mercedes** (DR) w pts 15 Freddie Castillo ..... Los Angeles, CA
Mar 15,	1983	**Charlie Magri** (Eng) w rsf 7 Eleoncio Mercedes .... Wembley (Eng)
Sep 27,	1983	**Frank Cedeno** (Phil) w rsf 6 Charlie Magri .... Wembley (Eng)
Jan 18,	1984	**Koji Kobayashi** (Jap) w rsf 2 Frank Cedeno .... Tokyo (Jap)
Apr 9,	1984	**Gabriel Bernal** (Mex) w ko 2 Koji Kobayashi .... Tokyo (Jap)
Jun 1,	1984	Gabriel Bernal w rsf 11 Antoine Montero (Fra) .... Nimes (Fra)
Oct 8,	1984	**Sot Chitalada** (Thai) w pts 12 Gabriel Bernal .... Bangkok (Thai)
Feb 20,	1985	Sot Chitalada w ret 4 Charlie Magri .... London (Eng)
Jun 22,	1985	Sot Chitalada drew 12 Gabriel Bernal .... Bangkok (Thai)
Feb 22,	1986	Sot Chitalada w pts 12 Freddie Castillo .... Kuwait City (Ku)
Dec 10,	1986	Sot Chitalada w pts 12 Gabriel Bernal .... Bangkok (Thai)
Sep 5,	1987	Sot Chitalada w ko 4 Rae-Ki Ahn (Kor) .... Bangkok (Thai)
Jan 31,	1988	Sot Chitalada w rsf 7 Hideaki Kamishiro (Jap) .... Osaka (Jap)
Jul 23,	1988	**Yong-Kang Kim** (Kor) w pts 12 Sot Chitalada .... Pohang (Kor)
Nov 13,	1988	Yung-Kang Kim w pts 12 Emil Romano (Phil) .... Chungju (Kor)
Mar 5,	1989	Yung-Kang Kim w pts 12 Yukhito Tamakuma (Jap) .... Aomori (Jap)
Jun 3,	1989	**Sot Chitalada** w pts 12 Yung-Kang Kim .... Trang (Thai)
Jan 30,	1990	Sot Chitalada w pts 12 Ric Siodoro (Phil) .... Bangkok (Thai)
May 1,	1990	Sot Chitalada w pts 12 Carlos Salazar (Arg) .... Bangkok (Thai)
Sep 9,	1990	Sot Chitalada w ko 1 Richard Clark (Jam) .... Kingston (Jam)
Nov 24,	1990	Sot Chitalada w pts 12 Jung-Koo Chang (Kor) .... Seoul (Kor)
Feb 15,	1991	**Muangchai Kitikasem** (Thai) w rsf 6 Sot Chitalada .... Ayuthaya (Thai)
May 18,	1991	Muangchai Kitikasem w rsf 12 Jung-Koo Chang .... Seoul (Kor)
Oct 25,	1991	Muangchai Kitikasem w pts 12 Alberto Jiminez (Mex) .... Bangkok (Thai)
Feb 28,	1992	Muangchai Kitikasem w rsf 9 Sot Chitalada .... Samut Prakan (Thai)
Jun 23,	1992	**Yuri Arbachakov** (Arm) w ko 8 Muangchai Kitikasem .... Tokyo (Jap)
Oct 20,	1992	Yuri Arbachakov w pts 12 Yun-Un Chin (Kor) .... Tokyo (Jap)
Mar 20,	1993	Yuri Arbachakov w rsf 9 Muangchai Kitikasem .... Lop Buri (Thai)
Jul 16,	1993	Yuri Arbachakov w pts 12 Ysias Zamudio (Mex) .... Kobe (Jap)
Dec 13,	1993	Yuri Arbachakov w pts 12 Nam-Hook Cha (Kor) .... Kyoto (Jap)
Aug 1,	1994	Yuri Arbachakov w ko 8 Hugo Rafael Soto (Arg) .... Tokyo (Jap)
Jan 30,	1995	Yuri Arbachakov w pts 12 Oscar Arciniega (Mex) .... Sapporo (Jap)
Sep 25,	1995	Yuri Arbachakov w pts 12 Chatchai Elite-Gym (Thai) .... Tokyo (Jap)

WBA title

Mar 1,	1966	**Horacio Accavallo** (Arg) w pts 15 Katsutoshi Takayama (Jap) . Tokyo (Jap)
		For vacant title
Jul 15,	1966	Horacio Accavallo w pts 15 Hiroyuki Ebihara .... Buenos Aires (Arg)
Dec 10,	1966	Horacio Accavallo w pts 15 Efren Torres .... Buenos Aires (Arg)
Aug 13,	1967	Horacio Accavallo w pts 15 Hiroyuki Ebihara .... Buenos Aires (Arg)
Oct 1,	1968	*Accavallo retired owing to eye injuries*
Mar 30,	1969	**Hiroyuki Ebihara** w pts 15 Jose Severino (Bra) .... Sapporo (Jap)
		For vacant title
Oct 19,	1969	**Bernabe Villacampo** w pts 15 Hiroyuki Ebihara .... Osaka (Jap)
Apr 6,	1970	**Berkrerk Chartvanchai** (Thai) w pts 15 Bernabe Villacampo . Bangkok (Thai)
Oct 21,	1970	**Masao Ohba** (Jap) w rsf 13 Berkrerk Chartvanchai .... Tokyo (Jap)
Apr 1,	1971	Masao Ohba w pts 15 Betulio Gonzalez .... Tokyo (Jap)
Oct 23,	1971	Masao Ohba w pts 15 Fernando Cabanela (Phil) .... Tokyo (Jap)
Mar 4,	1972	Masao Ohba w pts 15 Susumu Hanagata .... Tokyo (Jap)
Jun 20,	1972	Masao Ohba w ko 5 Orlando Amores (Pan) .... Tokyo (Jap)
Jan 2,	1973	Masao Ohba w rsf 12 Chartchai Chionoi .... Tokyo (Jap)
Jan 25,	1973	*Ohba was killed in a road crash*

May 17, 1973	**Chartchai Chionoi** w rsf 4 Fritz Chervet (Swi) .... Bangkok (Thai)	

For vacant title

Oct 27, 1973	Chartchai Chionoi w pts 15 Susumu Hanagata .... Bangkok (Thai)
Apr 27, 1974	Chartchai Chionoi w pts 15 Fritz Chervet .... Zurich (Swi)
Oct 18, 1974	**Susumu Hanagata** w rsf 6 Chartchai Chionoi .... Yokohama (Jap)

Chionoi forfeited the title on the scales when he weighed in 3½ lb over the limit after two attempts. Hanagata was awarded the championship when he won the fight

Apr 1, 1975	**Erbito Salavarria** w pts 15 Susumu Hanagata .... Toyama (Jap)
Oct 7, 1975	Erbito Salavarria w pts 15 Susumu Hanagata .... Yokohama (Jap)
Feb 27, 1976	**Alfonso Lopez** (Pan) w rsf 15 Erbito Salavarria .... Manila (Phil)
Apr 21, 1976	Alfonso Lopez w pts 15 Shoji Oguma .... Tokyo (Jap)
Oct 2, 1976	**Guty Espadas** w rsf 13 Alfonso Lopez .... Los Angeles, CA
Jan 1, 1977	Guty Espadas w ret 7 Jiro Takada .... Tokyo (Jap)
Apr 30, 1977	Guty Espadas w rsf 13 Alfonso Lopez .... Merida (Mex)
Nov 19, 1977	Guty Espadas w ko 8 Alex Santana (Nic) .... Los Angeles, CA
Jan 2, 1978	Guty Espadas w rsf 7 Kimio Furesawa .... Tokyo (Jap)
Aug 13, 1978	**Betulio Gonzalez** w pts 15 Guty Espadas .... Maracay (Ven)
Nov 4, 1978	Betulio Gonzalez w rsf 12 Martin Vargas .... Maracay (Ven)
Jan 29, 1979	Betulio Gonzalez drew 15 Shoji Oguma .... Hamamatsu (Jap)
Jul 6, 1979	Betulio Gonzalez w ko 12 Shoji Oguma .... Utsunomiya (Jap)
Nov 16, 1979	**Luis Ibarra** (Pan) w pts 15 Betulio Gonzalez .... Maracay (Ven)
Feb 16, 1980	**Taeshik Kim** (Kor) w ko 2 Luis Ibarra .... Seoul (Kor)
Jun 29, 1980	Taeshik Kim w pts 15 Arnel Arrozal .... Seoul (Kor)
Dec 13, 1980	**Peter Mathebula** (SA) w pts 15 Taeshik Kim ...... Los Angeles, CA
Mar 28, 1981	**Santos Laciar** (Arg) w ko 7 Peter Mathebula .... Soweto (SA)
Jun 6, 1981	**Luis Ibarra** w pts 15 Santos Laciar .... Buenos Aires (Arg)
Sep 26, 1981	**Juan Herrera** (Mex) w ko 11 Luis Ibarra .... Merida (Mex)
Dec 26, 1981	Juan Herrera w rsf 7 Betulio Gonzalez .... Maracaibo (Ven)
May 1, 1982	**Santos Laciar** w rsf 13 Juan Herrera .... Merida (Mex)
Aug 14, 1982	Santos Laciar w pts 15 Betulio Gonzalez .... Maracaibo (Ven)
Nov 5, 1982	Santos Laciar w rsf 13 Steve Muchoki (Ken) .... Copenhagen (Den)
Mar 4, 1983	Santos Laciar w ko 9 Ramon Neri (DR) .... Cordoba (Arg)
May 5, 1983	Santos Laciar w rsf 2 Suichi Hozumi (Jap) .... Shizuoka (Jap)
Jul 17, 1983	Santos Laciar w ko 1 Hi-Sup Shin (Kor) .... Cheju Do (Kor)
Jan 28, 1984	Santos Laciar w pts 15 Juan Herrera .... Marsala (Ita)
Sep 15, 1984	Santos Laciar w ko 10 Prudencio Cardona (Col) .... Cordoba (Arg)
Dec 8, 1984	Santos Laciar w pts 15 Hilario Zapata (Pan) .... Buenos Aires (Arg)
May 6, 1985	Santos Laciar w pts 15 Antoine Montero .... Grenoble (Fra)
Jul 1985	*Laciar relinquished the title to box at super-flyweight*
Oct 5, 1985	**Hilario Zapata** w pts 15 Alonzo Gonzalez (US) .... Panama City (Pan)

For vacant title

Jan 31, 1986	Hilario Zapata w pts 15 Javier Lucas (Mex) .... Panama City (Pan)
Apr 7, 1986	Hilario Zapata w pts 15 Suichi Hozumi (Jap) .... Nirasaki (Jap)
Jul 5, 1986	Hilario Zapata w pts 15 Dodie Penalosa (Phil) .... Manila (Phil)
Sep 13, 1986	Hilario Zapata w pts 15 Alberto Castro (Col) .... Panama City (Pan)
Dec 6, 1986	Hilario Zapata w pts 15 Claudemir Dias (Bra) .... Salvador (Bra)
Feb 13, 1987	**Fidel Bassa** (Col) w pts 15 Hilario Zapata ...... Barranquilla (Col)
Apr 25, 1987	Fidel Bassa w ko 13 Dave McAuley (Ire) .... Belfast (Ire)
Aug 15, 1987	Fidel Bassa drew 15 Hilario Zapata .... Panama City (Pan)
Dec 18, 1987	Fidel Bassa w pts 12 Felix Marty (DR) .... Cartagena (Col)
Mar 26, 1988	Fidel Bassa w pts 12 Dave McAuley .... Belfast (Ire)
Oct 2, 1988	Fidel Bassa w pts 12 Ray Medel (US) .... San Antonio, TX
Apr 15, 1989	Fidel Bassa w rsf 6 Julio Gudino (Pan) .... Barranquilla (Col)
Sep 30, 1989	**Jesus Rojas** (Ven) w pts 12 Fidel Bassa .... Barranquilla (Col)
Mar 10, 1990	**Yul-Woo Lee** (Kor) w pts 12 Jesus Rojas .... Taejon (Kor)
Jul 28, 1990	**Yukihito Tamakuma** (Jap) w rsf 10 Yul-Woo Lee .... Mito (Jap)
Dec 6, 1990	Yukihito Tamakuma drew 12 Jesus Rojas .... Aomori (Jap)
Mar 14, 1991	**Elvis Alvarez** (Col) w pts 12 Yukihito Tamakuma .... Tokyo (Jap)
Jun 1, 1991	**Yong-Kang Kim** (Kor) w pts 12 Elvis Alvarez .... Seoul (Kor)
Oct 5, 1991	Yong-Kang Kim w pts 12 Silvio Gamez (Ven) .... Inchon (Kor)
Mar 24, 1992	Yong-Kang Kim w ko 6 Jon Penalosa (Phil) .... Inchon (Kor)
Sep 26, 1992	**Aquiles Guzman** (Ven) w pts 12 Yong-Kang Kim .... Pohang (Kor)
Dec 15, 1992	**David Griman** (Ven) w pts 12 Aquiles Guzman .... Caracas (Ven)
Jun 21, 1993	David Griman w rsf 8 Hiroki Ioka (Jap) .... Osaka (Jap)
Oct 4, 1993	David Griman w pts 12 Alvaro Mercardo (Col) ...... Puerto La Cruz (Ven)
Feb 13, 1994	**Saensor Ploenchit** (Thai) w pts 12 David Griman .... Bangkok (Thai)
Apr 10, 1994	Saensor Ploenchit w pts 12 Jesus Rojas .... Bangkok (Thai)
Jun 12, 1994	Saensor Ploenchit w pts 12 Aquiles Guzman .... Bangkok (Thai)
Sep 25, 1994	Saensor Ploenchit w pts 12 Yong-Kang Kim (Kor) ... Kanchanaburi (Thai)
Dec 26, 1994	Saensor Ploenchit w ko 11 Danny Nunez (DR) .... Rayong (Thai)
May 7, 1995	Saensor Ploenchit w pts 12 Evangelio Perez (Pan) ..... Songkhla (Thai)
Oct 17, 1995	Saensor Ploenchit w ko 10 Hioki Ioka .... Osaka (Jap)

IBF title

Dec 24, 1983	**Soon-Chun Kwon** (Kor) w ko 5 Rene Busayong (Phil) .... Seoul (Kor)

For vacant title

Feb 25, 1984	Soon-Chun Kown w tech dec 2 Roger Castillo (Phil) .... Seoul (Kor)
May 19, 1984	Soon-Chun Kwon w pts 15 Ian Clyde (Can) .... Daejon (Kor)
Sep 7, 1984	Soon-Chun Kwon w rsf 12 Joaquin Caraballo (Phil) ...... Chungju (Kor)
Jan 25, 1985	Soon-Chun Kwon drew 15 Chong-Kwang Chung (Kor) ..... Daejon (Kor)
Apr 14, 1985	Soon-Chun Kwon w ko 3 Shinobu Kawashima (Jap) .... Pohang (Kor)
Jul 17, 1985	Soon-Chun Kwon drew 15 Chong-Kwang Chung .... Masan (Kor)
Dec 20, 1985	**Chong-Kwang Chung** w rsf 4 Soon-Chun Kwon .... Taegu (Kor)
Apr 27, 1986	**Bi-Won Chung** (Kor) w pts 15 Chong-Kwang Chung .... Pusan (Kor)
Aug 2, 1986	**Hi-Sup Shin** w rsf 15 Bi-Won Chung .... Inchon (Kor)
Nov 22, 1986	Hi-Sup Shin w rsf 13 Henry Brent (US) .... Chunchon (Kor)
Feb 22, 1987	**Dodie Penalosa** w ko 5 Hi-Sup Shin .... Inchon (Kor)
Sep 5, 1987	**Chang-Ho Choi** (Kor) w ko 11 Dodie Penalosa .... Manila (Phil)
Jan 16, 1988	**Rolando Bohol** (Phil) w pts 15 Chang-Ho Choi .... Manila (Phil)
May 6, 1988	Rolando Bohol w pts 15 Cho-Woon Park .... Manila (Phil)
Oct 5, 1988	**Duke McKenzie** (Eng) w ko 11 Rolando Bohol .... Wembley (Eng)
Mar 8, 1989	Duke McKenzie w rsf 4 Tony DeLuca (US) .... London (Eng)
Jun 7, 1989	**Dave McAuley** w pts 12 Duke McKenzie .... Wembley (Eng)
Nov 8, 1989	Dave McAuley w pts 12 Dodie Penalosa .... Wembley (Eng)
Mar 17, 1990	Dave McAuley w pts 12 Louis Curtis (US) .... Belfast (Ire)
Sep 15, 1990	Dave McAuley w pts 12 Rodolfo Blanco (Col) .... Belfast (Ire)
May 11, 1991	Dave McAuley w pts 12 Pedro Feliciano (PR) .... Belfast (Ire)
Sep 7, 1991	Dave McAuley w ko 9 Jake Matlala (SA) .... Belfast (Ire)
Jun 11, 1992	**Rodolfo Blanco** w pts 12 Dave McAuley .... Bilbao (Sp)
Nov 29, 1992	**Pichit Sitbangprachan** (Thai) w ko 3 Rodolfo Blanco ..... Bangkok (Thai)
Mar 6, 1993	**Pichit Sitbangprachan** w rsf 4 Antonio Perez (Mex) ...... Uttaradit (Thai)
Oct 3, 1993	Pichit Sitbangprachan w rsf 9 Miguel Martinez (Mex) . Chaiyaphum (Thai)
Jan 23, 1994	Pichit Sithbangprachan w pts 12 Arthur Johnson (US) . Surat Thani (Thai)
May 8, 1994	Pichit Sithbangprachan w pts 12 Jose Luis Zepeda (Mex) .... Rajaburi Province
Nov 1994	*Sithbangprachan relinquished the title rather than defend it against Jose Luis Zepeda*
Feb 18, 1995	**Francisco Tejedor** (Col) w rsf 7 Jose Luis Zepeda (Mex) .. Cartagena (Col)

For vacant title

Apr 22, 1995	**Danny Romero** (US) w pts 12 Francisco Tejedor .... Las Vegas, NV
Jul 29, 1995	Danny Romero w ko 6 Miguel Martinez .... San Antonio, TX

WBO title

Mar 3, 1989	**Elvis Alvarez** w pts 12 Miguel Mercedes (DR) .... Medellin (Col)

For vacant title

Oct 1989	*Alvarez relinquished the WBO title*
Aug 18, 1990	**Isidro Perez** (Mex) w rsf 12 Angel Rosario (PR) .... Ponce (PR)
Nov 3, 1990	Isidro Perez w pts 12 Alli Galvez (Ch) .... Acapulco (Mex)
Aug 10, 1991	Isidro Perez w pts 12 Alli Galvez .... Santiago (Ch)
Mar 18, 1992	**Pat Clinton** (Sco) w pts 12 Isidro Perez .... Glasgow (Sco)
Sep 19, 1992	Pat Clinton w pts 12 Danny Porter (Eng) .... Glasgow (Sco)
May 15, 1993	**Jake Matlala** w rsf 8 Pat Clinton .... Glasgow (Sco)
Dec 4, 1993	Jake Matlala w ret 8 Luigi Camputaro (Ita) .... Sun City (Bop)
Jun 11, 1994	Jake Matlala w ret 9 Francis Ampofo (Eng) .... London (Eng)
Oct 15, 1994	Jake Matlala w pts 12 Domingo Lucas (Phil) .... Sun City (Bop)
Feb 11, 1995	**Alberto Jimenez** (Mex) w rsf 8 Jake Matlala (SA) ...... Hammanskraal (SA)
Jun 17, 1995	Alberto Jimenez w ret 9 Robbie Regan (Wal) .... Cardiff (Wal)
Oct 9, 1995	Alberto Jimenez w rsf 2 Zolili Mbityi (SA) .... Tijuana (Mex)

DAVE McAULEY *(left) took Englishman Duke McKenzie's title to Ireland*

Light-Flyweight

The WBC introduced the light-flyweight division (weight limit 108 lb) in 1975, and must have immediately regretted it as the second fight for their championship proved an embarrassing fiasco. Rafael Lovera, a Paraguayan with an extremely persuasive manager, was installed as No. 1 contender for the title and, when the inaugural champion Franco Udella failed to defend against him, Udella forfeited the championship and Lovera faced Luis Estaba, a 34-year old grandfather from Panama, for the vacant title. Estaba won easily, prompting the WBC to investigate the impressive record which

Lovera's manager had used to manoeuvre his man into the No. 1 spot. It transpired that Lovera had never had a professional fight in his life! Despite the inauspicious start to his reign, Estaba went on to make 11 successful defences, a reign which earned the new division some degree of credibility.

The WBA crowned their first champion within four months of the WBC, and soon produced one of the outstanding champions of the decade in the Japanese Yoko Gushiken. As expected, the division has been dominated by Mexican and Oriental fighters, with the American Michael Carbajal being a notable exception.

World Light-Flyweight Championship Bouts

WBC title

Apr 4,	1975	**Franco Udella** (Ita) w dis 12 Valentin Martinez (Mex)	. . . .	Milan (Ita)
		For vacant WBC title		
Aug 1975		*The WBC withdrew recognition of Udella for failing to defend against Rafael Lovera*		
Sep 13,	1975	**Luis Estaba** (Ven) w ko 4 Rafael Lovera (Par)	. . . .	Caracas (Ven)
		For vacant title		
Dec 17,	1975	Luis Estaba w rsf 10 Takenobu Shimabakuro (Jap)	. . . . . .	Okinawa (Jap)
Feb 14,	1976	Luis Estaba w pts 15 Leo Palacios (Mex)	. . . .	Caracas (Ven)
May 2,	1976	Luis Estaba w pts 15 Juan Alvarez (Mex)	. . . .	Caracas (Ven)
Jul 17,	1976	Luis Estaba w ko 3 Franco Udella	. . . .	Maracay (Ven)
Sep 26,	1976	Luis Estaba w ret 10 Rodolfo Rodriguez (Arg)	. . . .	Caracas (Ven)
Nov 21,	1976	Luis Estaba w rsf 10 Valentin Martinez (Mex)	. . . . . .	Caracas (Ven)
May 15,	1977	Luis Estaba w pts 15 Rafael Pedroza (Pan)	. . . .	Caracas (Ven)
Jul 17,	1977	Luis Estaba w pts 15 Ricardo Estupinan (Col)	. . . . .	Puerto la Cruz (Ven)
Aug 21,	1977	Luis Estaba w rsf 11 Juan Alvarez	. . . .	Puerto la Cruz (Ven)
Sep 18,	1977	Luis Estaba w ko 15 Orlando Hernandez (CR)	. . . . . .	Caracas (Ven)
Oct 30,	1977	Luis Estaba w pts 15 Netrnoi Vorasingh (Thai)	. . . . . .	Caracas (Ven)
Feb 19,	1978	**Freddie Castillo** (Mex) w rsf 14 Luis Estaba	. . . .	Caracas (Ven)
May 6,	1978	**Netrnoi Vorasingh** w pts 15 Freddie Castillo	. . . . .	Bangkok (Thai)
Jul 29	1978	Netrnoi Vorasingh w ret 5 Luis Estaba	. . . .	Caracas (Ven)
Sep 30,	1978	**Sung-Jun Kim** (Kor) w ko 3 Netrnoi Vorasingh	. . . .	Seoul (Kor)
Mar 31,	1979	Sung-Jun Kim drew 15 Hector Melendez (DR)	. . . . . .	Seoul (Kor)
Jul 28,	1979	Sung-Jun Kim w pts 15 Stony Carupo (Phil)	. . . .	Seoul (Kor)
Oct 21,	1979	Sung-Jun Kim w pts 15 Hector Melendez	. . . .	Seoul (Kor)
Jan 3,	1980	**Shigeo Nakajima** (Jap) w pts 15 Sung-Jun Kim	. . . .	Tokyo (Jap)
Mar 24,	1980	**Hilario Zapata** (Pan) w pts 15 Shigeo Nakajima	. . . . . .	Tokyo (Jap)
Jun 7,	1980	Hilario Zapata w pts 15 Chi-Bok Kim (Kor)	. . . .	Seoul (Kor)
Aug 4,	1980	Hilario Zapata w pts 15 Hector Melendez	. . . .	Caracas (Ven)
Sep 17,	1980	Hilario Zapata w rsf 11 Shigeo Nakajima	. . . .	Gifu (Jap)
Dec 1,	1980	Hilario Zapata w pts 15 Reynaldo Becerra (Ven)	. . . . . .	Caracas (Ven)

Feb 8,	1981	Hilario Zapata w rsf 13 Joey Olivo (US)	. . . .	Panama City (Pan)
Apr 24,	1981	Hilario Zapata w pts 15 Rudy Crawford (US)	. . . .	San Francisco, CA
Aug 15,	1981	Hilario Zapata w pts 15 German Torres (Mex)	. . . . . .	Panama City (Pan)
Nov 6,	1981	Hilario Zapata w rsf 10 Netrnoi Vorasingh	. . . .	Korat (Thai)
Feb 6,	1982	**Amado Ursua** (Mex) w ko 2 Hilario Zapata	. . . .	Panama City (Pan)
Apr 13,	1982	**Tadashi Tomori** (Jap) w pts 15 Amado Ursua	. . . .	Tokyo (Jap)
Jul 20,	1982	**Hilario Zapata** w pts 15 Tadashi Tomori	. . . .	Kanazawa (Jap)
Sep 18,	1982	Hilario Zapata w pts 15 Jung-Koo Chang (Kor)	. . . . . .	Chonju (Kor)
Mar 26,	1983	**Jung Koo Chang** w ko 3 Hilario Zapata	. . . .	Daejon (Kor)

Jun 11,	1983	Jung Koo Chang w rsf 2 Masaharu Iha (Jap)	. . . .	Taegu (Kor)
Sep 10,	1983	Jung Koo Chang w pts 12 German Torres	. . . .	Daejon (Kor)
Mar 31,	1984	Jung Koo Chang w pts 15 Sot Chitalada (Thai)	. . . . . .	Pusan (Kor)
Aug 18,	1984	Jung Koo Chang w rsf 9 Katsuo Tokashiki (Jap)	. . . . .	Sapporo (Jap)
Dec 15,	1984	Jung Koo Chang w pts 12 Tadashi Kuramochi (Jap)	. . . . .	Pusan (Kor)
Aug 3,	1985	Jung Koo Chang w pts 15 Francisco Montiel (Mex)	. . . . .	Seoul (Kor)
Nov 10,	1985	Jung Koo Chang w pts 12 Jorge Cano (Mex)	. . . .	Daejon (Kor)
Apr 13,	1986	Jung Koo Chang w pts 12 German Torres	. . . .	Kwangju (Kor)
Sep 13,	1986	Jung Koo Chang w pts 12 Francisco Montiel	. . . . . .	Seoul (Kor)
Dec 14,	1986	Jung Koo Chang w rsf 5 Hideyuki Ohashi (Jap)	. . . . . .	Inchon (Kor)
Apr 19,	1987	Jung Koo Chang w rsf 6 Efren Pinto (Mex)	. . . .	Seoul (Kor)
Jun 28,	1987	Jung Koo Chang w rsf 10 Augustin Garcia (Col)	. . . . .	Seoul (Kor)
Dec 13,	1987	Jung Koo Chang w pts 12 Isidro Perez (Mex)	. . . . . .	Seoul (Kor)
Jun 27,	1988	Jung Koo Chang w rsf 8 Hideyuki Ohashi	. . . .	Tokyo (Jap)
Oct	1988	*Chang relinquished the title for health reasons*		
Dec 11,	1988	**German Torres** w pts 12 Soon-Jung Kang (Kor)	. . . . . .	Seoul (Kor)
Mar 19,	1989	**Yul-Woo Lee** (Kor) w ko 9 German Torres	. . . .	Taejon (Kor)
Jun 25,	1989	**Humberto Gonzalez** (Mex) w pts 12 Yul-Woo Lee	. . . . .	Seoul (Kor)
Dec 9,	1989	Humberto Gonzalez w pts 12 Jung Koo Chang	. . . . . .	Seoul (Kor)
Mar 24,	1990	Humberto Gonzalez w ko 3 Francisco Tejedor (Col)	. . . .	Mexico City (Mex)
Jun 4,	1990	Humberto Gonzalez w rsf 3 Luis Monzote (Cub)	. . . .	Los Angeles, CA
Jul 24,	1990	Humberto Gonzalez w rsf 5 Jung-Keun Lim (Kor)	. . . .	Los Angeles, CA
Aug 26,	1990	Humberto Gonzalez w ko 8 Jorge Rivera (Mex)	. . . . . .	Cancun (Mex)
Jun 3,	1991	Humberto Gonzalez w pts 12 Melchor Cob Castro (Mex)	. . .	Las Vegas, NV
Jan 27,	1992	Humberto Gonzalez w pts 12 Domingo Sosa (DR)	. . . . .	Los Angeles, CA
Jun 7,	1992	Humberto Gonzalez w rsf 12 Kwang-Sun Kim (Kor)	. . . . .	Seoul (Kor)
Sep 14,	1992	Humberto Gonzalez w rsf 2 Napa Kiatwanchai (Thai)	. . .	Los Angeles, CA
Dec 7,	1992	Humberto Gonzalez w pts 12 Melchor Cob Castro	. . . . .	Los Angeles, CA
Mar 13,	1993	**Michael Carbajal** w ko 7 Humberto Gonzalez	. . . . . .	Las Vegas, NV
		For WBC and IBF titles		

WBA title

Aug 23,	1975	**Jaime Rios** (Pan) w pts 15 Rigoberto Marcano (Ven)	. .	Panama City (Pan)
		For vacant title		
Jan 3,	1976	Jaime Rios w pts 15 Kazunori Tenryu (Jap)	. . . .	Kagoshima (Jap)
Jul 1,	1976	**Juan Guzman** (DR) w pts 15 Jaime Rios	. . . .	Santo Domingo (DR)
Oct 10,	1976	**Yoko Gushiken** (Jap) w ko 7 Juan Guzman	. . . .	Kofu (Jap)
Jan 30,	1977	Yoko Gushiken w pts 15 Jaime Rios	. . . .	Tokyo (Jap)
May 22,	1977	Yoko Gushiken w pts 15 Rigoberto Marcano (Ven)	. . . . .	Sapporo (Jap)
Oct 9,	1977	Yoko Gushiken w rsf 4 Montsayarm Mahachai (Thai)	. . . . .	Oita (Jap)
Jan 29,	1978	Yoko Gushiken w rsf 14 Aniceto Vargas (Phil)	. . . . . .	Nagoya (Jap)
May 7,	1978	Yoko Gushiken w rsf 13 Jaime Rios	. . . .	Hiroshima (Jap)
Oct 15,	1978	Yoko Gushiken w ko 4 Sang-Il Chung (Kor)	. . . .	Tokyo (Jap)
Jan 7,	1979	Yoko Gushiken w ko 7 Rigoberto Marcano	. . . .	Kawasaki (Jap)
Apr 8,	1979	Yoko Gushiken w rsf 7 Alfonso Lopez (Pan)	. . . .	Tokyo (Jap)
Jul 29,	1979	Yoko Gushiken w pts 15 Rafael Pedroza	. . . .	Kitakyushi (Jap)
Oct 28,	1979	Yoko Gushiken w rsf 7 Tito Abella (Phil)	. . . .	Tokyo (Jap)

Jan 27,	1980	Yoko Gushiken w pts 15 Yong-Hyun Kim (Kor) .... Osaka (Jap)
Jun 1,	1980	Yoko Gushiken w rsf 8 Martin Vargas (Ch) .... Kochi City (Jap)
Oct 12,	1980	Yoko Gushiken w pts 15 Pedro Flores (Mex) .... Kanazawa (Jap)
Mar 8,	1981	**Pedro Flores** w ret 12 Yoko Gushiken .... Okinawa (Jap)
Jul 19,	1981	**Hwan-Jin Kim** (Kor) w rsf 13 Pedro Flores .... Taegu (Kor)
Oct 11,	1981	Hwan-Jin Kim w pts 15 Alfonso Lopez .... Daejon (Kor)
Dec 16,	1981	**Katsuo Tokashiki** (Jap) w pts 15 Hwan-Jin Kim .... Sendai (Jap)
Apr 4,	1982	Katsuo Tokashiki w pts 15 Lupe Madera (Mex) .... Sendai (Jap)
Jul 7,	1982	Katsuo Tokashiki w ko 8 Masahara Inami (Jap) .... Tokyo (Jap)
Oct 10,	1982	Katsuo Tokashiki w pts 15 Sung-Nam Kim (Kor) .... Tokyo (Jap)
Jan 9,	1983	Katsuo Tokashiki w pts 15 Hwan-Jin Kim .... Kyoto (Jap)
Apr 10,	1983	Katsuo Tokashiki drew 15 Lupe Madera .... Tokyo (Jap)
Jul 10,	1983	**Lupe Madera** w tech dec 4 Katsuo Tokashiki .... Tokyo (Jap)
Oct 23,	1983	Lupe Madera w pts 12 Katsuo Tokashiki .... Sapporo (Jap)
May 19, 1984		**Francisco Quiroz** (DR) w ko 9 Lupe Madera .... Maracaibo (Ven)
Aug 18, 1984		Francisco Quiroz w ko 2 Victor Sierra (Pan) .... Panama City (Pan)
Mar 29, 1985		**Joey Olivo** (US) w pts 15 Francisco Quiroz .... Miami, FL
Jul 28,	1985	Joey Olivo w pts 15 Moon-Jin Choi (Kor) .... Seoul (Kor)
Dec 8,	1985	**Myung-Woo Yuh** (Kor) w pts 15 Joey Olivo .... Seoul (Kor)
Mar 9,	1986	Myung-Woo Yuh w pts 15 Jose De Jesus (PR) .... Suwon (Kor)
Jun 14,	1986	Myung-Woo Yuh w rsf 12 Tomohiro Kiyuna (Jap) .... Inchon (Kor)
Nov 30,	1986	Myung-Woo Yuh w pts 15 Mario de Marco (Arg) .... Seoul (Kor)
Mar 1,	1987	Myung-Woo Yuh w rsf 1 Eduardo Tunon (Pan) .... Seoul (Kor)
Jun 7,	1987	Myung-Woo Yuh w rsf 15 Benedicto Murillo (Pan) .... Pusan (Kor)
Sep 20,	1987	Myung-Woo Yuh w ko 8 Rodolfo Blanco (Col) .... Inchon (Kor)
Feb 7,	1988	Myung-Woo Yuh w pts 12 Wilibaldo Salazar (Mex) .... Seoul (Kor)
Jun 12,	1988	Myung-Woo Yuh w pts 12 Jose De Jesus .... Seoul (Kor)
Aug 28,	1988	Myung-Woo Yuh w ko 6 Putt Ohyuthanakorn (Thai) .... Pusan (Kor)
Nov 6,	1988	Myung-Woo Yuh w ko 7 Bahar Udin (Indo) .... Seoul (Kor)
Feb 12,	1989	Myung-Woo Yuh w rsf 10 Katsumi Komiyama (Jap) ...... Chongju (Kor)
Jun 11,	1989	Myung-Woo Yuh w pts 12 Mario de Marco .... Seoul (Kor)
Sep 24,	1989	Myung-Woo Yuh w ko 11 Kenbun Taiho (Jap) .... Suanbo (Kor)
Jan 14,	1990	Myung-Woo Yuh w rsf 7 Hitashi Takashima (Jap) .... Seoul (Kor)
Apr 29,	1990	Myung-Woo Yuh w pts 12 Silvio Gamez (Ven) .... Seoul (Kor)
Nov 10,	1990	Myung-Woo Yuh w pts 12 Silvio Gamez .... Seoul (Kor)
Apr 28,	1991	Myung-Woo Yuh w rsf 10 Kajkong Danphoothai (Thai) ..... Masan (Kor)
Dec 17,	1991	**Hiroki Ioka** (Jap) w pts 12 Myung-Woo Yuh .... Osaka (Jap)
Mar 31,	1992	Hiroki Ioka w pts 12 Noel Tunacao (Phil) .... Osaka (Jap)
Jun 15,	1992	Hiroki Ioka w pts 12 Bong-Jun Kim (Kor) .... Osaka (Jap)
Nov 18,	1992	**Myung-Woo Yuh** w pts 12 Hiroki Ioka .... Osaka (Jap)
Jul 25,	1993	Myung-Woo Yuh w pts 12 Yuichi Hosono (Jap) .... Seoul (Kor)
Sep	1993	*Yuh retired*
Oct 21,	1993	**Leo Gamez** (Ven) w rsf 9 Shiro Yahiro (Jap) .... Tokyo (Jap)
		For vacant title
Feb 6,	1994	Leo Gamez w rsf 7 Juan Torres (Pan) .... Panama City (Pan)
Jun 27,	1994	Leo Gamez drew 12 Kaj Ratchabandit (Thai) .... Bangkok (Thai)
Oct 9,	1994	Leo Gamez w rsf 6 Pichit Sithbangprachan (Thai) .... Bangkok (Thai)
Feb 4,	1995	**Hiyong Choi** (Kor) w pts 12 Leo Gamez .... Ulsan (Kor)
Feb 4,	1995	Hiyong Choi w pts 12 Keji Yamaguchu (Jap) .... Osaka (Jap)

IBF title

Dec 10, 1983		**Dodie Penalosa** (Phil) w rsf 11 Satoshi Shingaki (Jap) ...... Osaka (Jap)
		For vacant title
May 13, 1984		**Dodie Penalosa** w rsf 9 Jae-Hong Kim (Kor) .... Seoul (Kor)
Nov 16, 1984		Dodie Penalosa w pts 15 Jum-Hwan Choi (Kor) .... Manila (Phil)
Oct 12, 1985		Dodie Penalosa w ko 3 Yani "Hagler" Dokolamo (Indo) .... Jakarta (Indo)
July	1986	*The IBF stripped Penalosa for challenging for the WBA flyweight title*
Dec 7,	1986	**Jum-Hwan Choi** (Kor) w pts 15 Cho-Woon Park (Kor) ...... Pusan (Kor)
		For vacant title
Mar 29, 1987		Jum-Hwan Choi w pts 15 Tacy Macalos (Phil) .... Seoul (Kor)
Jul 5,	1987	Jum-Hwan Choi w rsf 4 Toshihiko Matsuta (Jap) .... Seoul (Kor)
Aug 9,	1987	Jum-Hwan Choi w rsf 3 Azadin Anhar (Indo) .... Jakarta (Indo)
Nov 5,	1988	**Tacy Macalos** w pts 12 Jum-Hwan Choi .... Manila (Phil)
May 2,	1989	**Muangchai Kitkasem** (Thai) w pts 12 Tacy Macalos ..... Bangkok (Thai)
Oct 6,	1989	Muangchai Kitkasem w rsf 7 Tacy Macalos .... Bangkok (Thai)
Jan 19,	1990	Muangchai Kitkasem w rsf 3 Chung-Jae Lee (Kor) .... Bangkok (Thai)
Apr 10,	1990	Muangchai Kitkasem w pts 12 Abdy Pohan (Indo) .... Bangkok (Thai)
Jul 29,	1990	**Michael Carbajal** (US) w rsf 7 Muangchai Kitkasem ...... Phoenix, AZ
Dec 8,	1990	Michael Carbajal w ko 4 Leon Salazar (Pan) .... Scottsdale, AZ
Feb 17,	1991	Michael Carbajal w ko 2 Nacario Santos (Mex) .... Las Vegas, NV
Mar 17,	1991	Michael Carbajal w pts 12 Javier Varquez (Mex) .... Las Vegas, NV
May 10,	1991	Michael Carbajal w pts 12 Hector Patri (Arg) .... Davenport, IA
Feb 15,	1992	Michael Carbajal w pts 12 Marcos Pancheco (Mex) .... Phoenix, AZ
Dec 12,	1992	Michael Carbajal w rsf 8 Robinson Cuestas (Pan) .... Phoenix, AZ
Mar 13,	1993	Michael Carbajal w ko 7 Humberto Gonzalez .... Las Vegas, NV
		For WBC and IBF titles

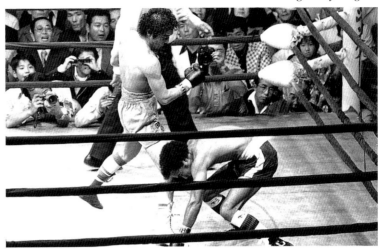

YOKO GUSHIKEN *floors Juan Guzman on his way to winning the title*

IBF/WBC titles

Jul 17,	1993	**Michael Carbajal** w ko 7 Kwang-Sun Kim .... Las Vegas, NV
Oct 30,	1993	Michael Carbajal w rsf 5 Domingo Sosa (DR) .... Phoenix, AZ
Feb 19,	1994	**Humberto Gonzalez** w pts 12 Michael Carbajal .... Inglewood, CA
Sep 10,	1994	Humberto Gonzalez w ret 7 Juan Domingo Cordoba (Arg) . Lake Tahoe, CA
Nov 12,	1994	Humberto Gonzalez w pts 12 Michael Carbajal .... Mexico City (Mex)
Mar 31,	1995	Humberto Gonzalez w ko 5 Jesus Zuniga (Col) .... Anaheim, CA
Jul 15,	1995	**Saman Sorjaturong** (Thai) w rsf 7 Humberto Gonzalez .... Inglewood, CA
Nov 12,	1995	Saman Sorjaturong w ko 4 Yuichi Hosono (Jap) .... Ratchaburi (Thai)

WBO title

May 19,	1989	**Jose de Jesus** (PR) w rsf 9 Fernando Martinez (Mex) ...... San Juan, CA
		For vacant title
Oct 21,	1989	Jose de Jesus w pts 12 Isidro Perez .... San Juan, CA
May 6,	1990	Jose de Jesus w ko 5 Alli Galvez (Ch) .... Talcahuano (Ch)
Nov 10,	1990	Jose de Jesus w rsf 7 Abdy Pohan .... Medan (Indo)
May	1992	*De Jesus stripped of the title for failure to defend it*
Jul 31,	1992	**Josue Camacho** (PR) w ko 6 Eduardo Vallejo (Mex) .... San Juan, CA
		For vacant title
Feb 2,	1994	Josue Camacho w pts 12 Paul Weir (Sco) .... Glasgow (Sco)
Jul 15,	1994	**Michael Carbajal** w pts 12 Josue Camacho .... Phoenix, AZ
Oct	1994	*Carbajal vacated the title to challenge for the IBF/WBC championships*
Nov 23,	1994	**Paul Weir** w pts 12 Paul Oulden (SA) .... Irvine, CA
		For vacant title
Apr 5,	1995	Paul Weir w pts 12 Ric Magramo (Phil) .... Irvine, CA
Jul 15,	1995	**Jake Matlala** (SA) w tech dec 5 Paul Weir .... Glasgow (Scot)

HUMBERTO GONZALEZ *(right) had epic battles with Michael Carbajal*

Strawweight

The IBF were first off the mark with the strawweight division, which is also known as the mini-flyweight (weight limit 105 lb). They crowned their inaugural champion in June 1987, and within six months there were rival champions from the WBC and WBA. The division has proved especially popular in the Orient, although the only truly outstanding champion so far produced has been the Mexican Ricardo Lopez.

World Strawweight Championship Bouts

IBF title

Jun 14,	1987	**Kyung-Yun Lee** (Kor) w ko 2 Masaharu Kawakami (Jap) . . . . . Bujok (Kor)	
Dec	1987	*Lee vacated IBF title to challenge for the WBC version*	
Mar 24,	1988	**Samuth Sithnaruepol** (Thai) w rsf 11 Domingo Lucas (Phil) Bangkok (Thai)	
		For vacant title	
Aug 29,	1988	Samuth Sithnaruepol w pts 15 In-Kyu Hwang (Kor) . . . . . . Bangkok (Thai)	
Mar 23,	1989	Samuth Sithnaruepol drew 12 Nico Thomas (Indo) . . . . Jakarta (Indo)	
Jun 17,	1989	**Nico Thomas** w pts 12 Samuth Sithnaruepol . . . . Jakarta (Indo)	
Sep 21,	1989	**Eric Chavez** (Phil) w ko 5 Nico Thomas . . . . Jakarta (Indo)	
Feb 22,	1990	**Fahlan Lukmingkwan** (Thai) w rsf 7 Eric Chavez . . . . Bangkok (Thai)	
Jun 14,	1990	Fahlan Lukmingkwan w pts 12 Joe Constantino (Phil) . . . Bangkok (Thai)	
Aug 15,	1990	Fahlan Lukmingkwan w pts 12 Eric Chavez . . . . Bangkok (Thai)	
Dec 20,	1990	Fahlan Lukmingkwan drew 12 Domingo Lucas . . . . Bangkok (Thai)	
Jul 2,	1991	Fahlan Lukmingkwan w pts 12 Abdy Pohan (Indo) . . . . . . Bangkok (Thai)	
Oct 21,	1991	Fahlan Lukmingkwan w pts 12 Andy Tabanas (Phil) . . . . . Bangkok (Thai)	
Feb 23,	1992	Fahlan Lukmingkwan w ko 2 Felix Naranjo (Col) . . . . Bangkok (Thai)	
Jun 14,	1992	Fahlan Lukmingkwan w rsf 8 Said Iskander (Indo) . . . . . . Bangkok (Thai)	
Sep 6,	1992	**Manny Melchor** (Phil) w pts 12 Fahlan Lukmingkwan . . . . Bangkok (Thai)	
Dec 10,	1992	**Ratanapol Sowvoraphin** (Thai) w pts 12 Manny Melchor . . Bangkok (Thai)	
Mar 14,	1993	Ratanapol Sowvoraphin w rsf 7 Nico Thomas . . . . Nakhon (Thai)	
Jun 27,	1993	Ratanapol Sowvoraphin w ret 7 Ala Villamor (Phil) . . . . . . Bangkok (Thai)	
Sep 26,	1993	Ratanapol Sowvoraphin w rsf 4 Dominguez Siwalette (Indo) Bangkok (Thai)	
Dec 10,	1993	Ratanapol Sowvoraphin w rsf 2 Felix Naranjo (Col) . . . Suphan Buri (Thai)	
Feb 27,	1994	Ratanapol Sowvoraphin w pts 12 Ronnie Magrama (Phil) . Bangkok (Thai)	
May 14,	1994	Ratanapol Sowvoraphin w rsf 6 Roger Espanola (Phil) . . . . Bangkok (Thai)	
Aug 13,	1994	Ratanapol Sowvoraphin w rsf 4 Marcelino Bolivar (Ven) . . . Buriram (Thai)	
Nov 12,	1994	Ratanapol Sowvoraphin w ko 3 Carlos Rodriguez (Ven) . Khon Kaen (Thai)	
Feb 25,	1995	Ratanapol Sowvoraphin w rsf 3 Jerry Pahayahay (Phil) . . . Bangkok (Thai)	
May 20,	1995	Ratanapol Sowvoraphin w rsf 2 Oscar Flores (Col) . . . . . Chiang Mai (Thai)	
Oct 29,	1995	Ratanapol Sowvoraphin w ko 2 Jack Russell (Aus) . . . . Suphan Buri (Thai)	
Dec 30,	1995	Ratanapol Sowvoraphin w rsf 26 Osvaldo Guerrero (Mex) . Bangkok (Thai)	

WBC title

Oct 18,	1987	**Hiroki Ioka** (Jap) w pts 12 Mai Thornburifarm (Thai) . . . . Osaka (Jap)	
		For vacant title	
Jan 31,	1988	**Hiroki Ioka** w rsf 12 Kyung-Yung Lee (Kor) . . . . Osaka (Jap)	
Jun 5,	1988	Hiroki Ioka drew 12 Napa Kiatwanchai (Thai) . . . . Osaka (Jap)	
Nov 13,	1988	**Napa Kiatwanchai** w pts 12 Hiroki Ioka . . . . Osaka (Jap)	
Feb 11,	1989	Napa Kiatwanchai w pts 12 John Arief (Indo) . . . . Bangkok (Thai)	
Jun 10,	1989	Napa Kiatwanchai w rsf 11 Hiroki Ioka . . . . Osaka (Jap)	
Nov 12,	1989	**Jum-Hwan Choi** (Kor) w rsf 12 Napa Kiatwanchai . . . . Seoul (Kor)	
Feb 7,	1990	**Hideyuki Ohashi** (Jap) w ko 9 Jum-Hwan Choi . . . . Tokyo (Jap)	
Jun 8,	1990	Hideyuki Ohashi w pts 12 Napa Kiatwanchai . . . . Tokyo (Jap)	
Oct 25,	1990	**Ricardo Lopez** (Mex) w rsf 5 Hideyuki Ohashi . . . . Tokyo (Jap)	
May 19,	1991	Ricardo Lopez w rsf 8 Kimio Hirano (Jap) . . . . Shizoka (Jap)	
Dec 22,	1991	Ricardo Lopez w pts 12 Kyung-Yun Lee (Kor) . . . . Inchon (Kor)	

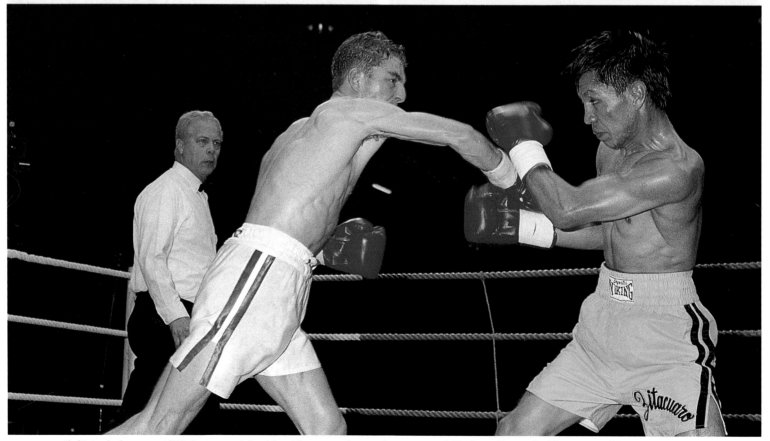

PAUL WEIR *(left) took the vacant WBO strawweight title with a seventh round stoppage of Mexican Fernando Martinez at Glasgow in May 1993*

RICARDO LOPEZ *(right) notches another inside-the-distance victory, this time over Javier Varguez in Mexico City in November 1994*

Mar 16,	1992	Ricardo Lopez w pts 21 Domingo Lucas . . . . Mexico City (Mex)
Aug 22,	1992	Ricardo Lopez w ko 5 Singpraset Kitkasem (Thai) . . Ciudad Madero (Mex)
Oct 11,	1992	Ricardo Lopez w ko 2 Rocky Lim (Jap) . . . . Tokyo (Jap)
Mar 31,	1993	Ricardo Lopez w rsf 9 Kwang-Soo Oh (Kor) . . . . Seoul (Kor)
Jul 3,	1993	Ricardo Lopez w rsf 2 Saman Sorjaturong (Thai) . . . . Nuevo Laredo (Mex)
Dec 18,	1993	Ricardo Lopez w ko 11 Manny Melchor . . . . Lake Tahoe, CA
May 7,	1994	Ricardo Lopez w pts 12 Kermin Guardia (Col) . . . . Las Vegas, NV
Sep 17,	1994	Ricardo Lopez w rsf 1 Yodsing Au Saenmorokot (Thai) . . . . Las Vegas, NV
Nov 12,	1994	Ricardo Lopez w rsf 8 Javier Varguez (Mex) . . . . Mexico City (Mex)
Dec 10,	1994	Ricardo Lopez w ko 1 Yamil Caraballo (Col) . . . . Monterrey (Mex)
Apr 1,	1995	Ricardo Lopez w rsf 12 Andy Tabanas . . . . Stateline, NV

WBA title

Jan 18,	1988	**Luis Gamez** (Ven) w pts 12 Bong-Jun Kim (Kor) . . . . Pusan (Kor)
		For vacant title
Apr 24,	1988	Luis Gamez w rsf 3 Kenji Yokozawa (Jap) . . . . Tokyo (Jap)
Feb	1989	*Gamez vacated the title to box at light-flyweight*
Apr 16,	1989	**Bong-Jun Kim** w rsf 7 Augustin Garcia (Col) . . . . Seoul (Kor)
		For vacant title
Aug 6,	1989	Bong-Jun Kim w pts 12 Sam-Jung Lee (Kor) . . . . Seoul (Kor)
Oct 22,	1989	Bong-Jun Kim w rsf 9 John Arief . . . . Pohang (Kor)
Feb 10,	1990	Bong-Jun Kim w rsf 3 Petchai Chuwatana (Thai) . . . . Seoul (Kor)
May 13,	1990	Bong-Jun Kim w tech dec 5 Silverio Barcenas (Pan) . . . . Seoul (Kor)
Nov 3,	1990	Bong-Jun Kim w pts 12 Silverio Barcenas (Pan) . . . . Seoul (Kor)
Feb 2,	1991	**Hi-Yon Choi** (Kor) w pts 12 Bong-Jun Kim . . . . Seoul (Kor)
Jun 15,	1991	Hi-Yon Choi w pts 12 Sugar Ray Mike (Phil) . . . . Seoul (Kor)
Oct 26,	1991	Hi-Yon Choi w pts 12 Bong-Jun Kim . . . . Seoul (Kor)
Feb 22,	1992	Hi-Yon Choi w rsf 10 Ryuichi Hosono (Jap) . . . . Seoul (Kor)
Jun 13,	1992	Hi-Yon Choi w ko 3 Rommel Lawas (Phil) . . . . Inchon (Kor)
Oct 14,	1992	**Hideyuki Ohashi** w pts 12 Hi-Yon Choi . . . . Tokyo (Jap)
Feb 10,	1993	**Chana Porpaoin** (Thai) w pts 12 Hideyuki Ohashi . . . . Tokyo (Jap)
May 9,	1993	Chana Porpaoin w pts 12 Carlos Murillo (Pan) . . . . Bangkok (Thai)
Aug 22,	1993	Chana Porpaoin w pts 12 Ronnie Magramo (Phil) . . . . Bangkok (Thai)
Nov 28,	1993	Chana Porpaoin w ko 4 Rafael Torres (DR) . . . . Pichit
Mar 27,	1994	Chana Porpaoin w pts 12 Carlos Murillo (Pan) . . . . Chon Buri (Thai)
Aug 27,	1994	Chana Porpaoin w pts 12 Keunyoung Kang (Kor) . . . . Petchaboon
Nov 5,	1994	Chana Porpaoin w pts 12 Manuel Herrera (DR) . . . . Hatyai
Jan 28,	1995	Chana Porpaoin w pts 12 Jiu Ho Kim (Kor) . . . . Bangkok (Thai)

Aug 5,	1995	Chana Porpaoin w ko 6 Ernesto Rubillar Jr (Phil) . . . . Bangkok (Thai)
Dec 2,	1995	**Rosendo Alvarez** (Nic) w pts 12 Chana Porpaoin . . . . Bangkok (Thai)

WBO title

Aug 31,	1989	**Rafael Torres** (DR) w pts 12 Yamil Caraballo (Col) . . Santo Domingo (Bah)
		For vacant title
Jul 31,	1990	Rafael Torres w pts 12 Husni Ray (Indo) . . . . Jakarta (Indo)
May	1992	*Torres was stripped of the title for failure to defend*
May 15,	1993	**Paul Weir** (Sco) w rsf 7 Fernando Martinez (Mex) . . . . Glasgow (Sco)
		For vacant title
Oct 25,	1993	Paul Weir w pts 12 Lindi Memani (SA) . . . . Glasgow (Sco)
Dec	1993	*Weir vacated title to box at light-flyweight*
Dec 22,	1993	**Alex Sanchez** (PR) w rsf 1 Orlando Malone (US) . . . . San Juan, CA
		For vacant title
Jan 7,	1994	Alex Sanchez w rsf 1 Arturo Garcia Mayen (USA) . . . . Palma (Sp)
Aug 13,	1994	Alex Sanchez w ko 1 Carlos Juan Rodriguez (DR) . . . . Bayamon (PR)
Sep 10,	1994	Alex Sanchez w ko 4 Oscar Andrade (Mex) . . . . Hamburg (Ger)
Jan 28,	1995	Alex Sanchez w pts 12 Rafael Orozco (Mex) . . . . Las Vegas, NV
Jul 29,	1995	Alex Sanchez w pts 12 Tomas Rivera (Mex) . . . . San Antonio, TX

RINGSIDE VIEW

Ricardo Lopez
vs
Fahlan Lukmigkwan

LOPEZ LEAVES IT LATE

Ricardo Lopez was nobody's April Fool when he stopped Andy Tabanas in the last round to retain his WBC strawweight crown at Stateline, Nevada on April 1, 1995. It was the fierce-hitting Mexican's 13th successful defence of the championship he had won in October 1990, making him the longest-serving champion in the division's brief history.

BOXING FACTS AND FEATS

Lovers of the esoteric will find much to engage and amuse them in boxing's long and colourful history. Here, to settle some arguments and start others, is an entirely random selection of Fight Game trivia.

CURIOSITIES

Largest paid attendance

132,247 to watch Julio Cesar Chavez stop Greg Haugen in five rounds at the Estadio Azteca, Mexico City on February 20, 1993.

Largest attendance (free admission)

135,132 for Tony Zale vs. Billy Pryor at Milwaukee on August 18, 1941

Boxers whose first fight was for the world title

Jack Skelly, knocked out in eight by George Dixon for the feather-weight title in New Orleans on September 6, 1992.

Pete Rademacher, knocked out in six by Floyd Patterson for the heavyweight title in Seattle on August 22, 1957.

Rafael Lovera, knocked out in four by Luis Estaba for the vacant WBC light-flyweight title in Caracas on September 13, 1975.

Longest spell between championships

George Foreman lost the heavy-weight title on October 30, 1974, knocked out by Muhammad Ali. He regained it on November 5, 1994, by knocking out Michael Moorer.

Last scheduled 20-rounds world title fight

Joe Louis' 11th round knockout of Bob Pastor in defence of the heavyweight title in Detroit on September 20, 1939. The last world title fight to go more than 15 rounds was Mike McTigue's 20-rounds points win over Battling Siki for the light-heavyweight title in Dublin on March 17, 1923.

Novice champions

Saensak Muangsurin won the WBC light-welterweight title in his third professional fight, a record. Muangsurin had considerable pre-vious experience as a kick-boxer.

Other notable novices were heavyweight Leon Spinks (champion in his eighth fight) and light-flyweight Paul Weir, who won the WBO title in his sixth fight.

Record number of world title fights

Julio Cesar Chavez (33)

Champions who had 25 or more title fights

Joe Louis (27), Henry Armstrong (26), Muhammad Ali (25)

Most championship rounds fought

Emile Griffith (339)

EMILE GRIFFITH *boxed more championship rounds than anybody else*

Famous series

Ted Kid Lewis vs. Jack Britton (20 meetings); Sam Langford vs. Sam McVey (15), Langford vs. Harry Wills (18), Joe Jeanette (14), Jeff Clark (13) and Jim Barry (12)

Most knockdowns

Sam McVey vs. Joe Jeanette, Paris, April 1909: Jeanette was floored 27 times, McVey 19. Jeanette won when McVey collapsed at the start of the 49th round, after 3 hours and 122 minutes.

Highest (verifiable) number of fights

Len Wickwar of England, who had 466 between 1928 and 1947. Americans Jack Britton (342 between 1905–30) and Johnny Dundee (337 between 1910–32) are next, and another Englishman, Billy Bird of Chelsea, is fourth with 321 between 1920 and 1948.

First southpaw champions

Heavyweight: (see over)

UNUSUAL ENDINGS

On January 13, 1995 the 12-rounder for the vacant NABF light-heavyweight title between former IBF champion Prince Charles Williams and Merqui Sosa in Atlantic City was declared a technical draw after seven rounds when the ringside doctor, Frank B. Doggett, decided they had each taken too much punishment for them safely to continue.

On the only other similar occasion, when Eddie Woods and Al Milone were too severely cut to continue their fight in Philadelphia in 1959, the result was recorded as a stoppage loss for both men.

There was a double knockout in the world lightweight title fight between champion Ad Wolgast and Mexican Joe Rivers in Los Angeles on July 4, 1912. Both were knocked down simultaneously in the 13th round, and with neither looking likely to beat the count the referee picked up the champion and, holding him under the arm, carried on counting out Rivers.

But the most peculiar ending ever to a championship fight was when challenger George Bernard of France fell asleep in his corner during the interval between the sixth and seventh rounds of his middleweight title fight with Billy Papke in Paris on December 4, 1912. He could not be woken in time for the seventh round, and the ending was recorded as a retirement. He claimed he had been drugged, and was probably right.

Michael Moorer (1992)
Cruiserweight:
Marvin Camel (1980)
Light-heavyweight:
George Nichols (1932)
Super-middleweight:
Graciano Rocchigiani (1988)
Middleweight:
Al McCoy (1914)
Light-middleweight:
Maurice Hope (1979)
Welterweight:
Young Corbett III (1933)
Light-welterweight:
Sandro Lopopolo (1966)
Lightweight:
Juan Zurita (1944)
Super-featherweight:
Flash Elorde (1960)
Featherweight:
Freddie Miller (1933)
Super-bantamweight:
Wilfredo Gomez (1977)
Bantamweight:
Jimmy Carruthers (1952)
Super-flyweight:
Jiro Watanabe (1982)
Flyweight:
Hiroyuki Eibihara (1963)
Light-flyweight:
Yoko Gushiken (1976)
Strawweight:
Ratanapol Sowvoraphin (1992).

THE BIGGEST

Heaviest men to fight for the title

1 Primo Carnera (270 lb), w pts 15 Tommy Loughran at Miami on March 1, 1934. Carnera scaled 263½ lb in his 11th round loss to Max Baer at Long Island, NY, on June 14, 1934, 260½ lb when knocking out Jack Sharkey in six at Long Island on June 29, 1933 and 259½ lb when out-pointing Paulino Uzcudun in Rome on October 22, 1933.

2 George Foreman (257 lb), l pts 12 Evander Holyfield in Atlantic City on April 19, 1991. Foreman was a pound lighter for his 12 rounds points win over Axel Schulz in Las Vegas on April 22, 1995.

3 Abe Simon (255 lb), l ko 6 Joe Louis in New York on March 27, 1942. Simon was half a pound lighter when he faced Louis for the first time, losing on a 13th round stoppage in Detroit on March 21, 1941.

4 Leroy Jones (254½), l bl rsf 8 Larry Holmes in Las Vegas on March 31, 1980.

5 Buddy Baer (250 lb), l ko 1 Joe Louis in New York on January 9, 1942. George Foreman weighed the same when he knocked out Michael Moorer in 10 in Las Vegas on November 5, 1994.

THE BEST

The multiple champions

Five weights: Thomas Hearns and Sugar Ray Leonard
Four weights: Roberto Duran and Pernell Whitaker
Three weights: Bob Fitzsimmons, Tony Canzoneri, Barney Ross, Henry Armstrong, Wilfred Benitez, Alexis Arguello, Wilfredo Gomez, Jeff Fenech, Julio Cesar Chavez, Mike McCallum.

Only Fitzsimmons, Canzoneri, Ross and Armstrong were undisputed champions of three divisions, Armstrong being the only man to hold three titles simultaneously. Emile Griffith won a version of the light-middleweight title, recognized only in Austria, to go with his welterweight and middleweight titles. Leonard's claim to five titles does not satisfy all the purists since he won two of them in the same fight, against Donny Lalonde, under artificial conditions which compelled Lalonde, the defending WBC light-heavyweight champion, to come in under the super-middleweight limit so that the vacant WBC version of that title could also be at stake.

WINNERS ...

Famous come-from-behind victories in world title fights

Julio Cesar Chavez w rsf 12 (2 min 58 sec) Meldrick Taylor to retain the WBC and win the IBF light-welterweight titles in Las Vegas on March 17, 1990.

Jake LaMotta w ko 15 (2:47) Laurent Dauthuille to retain the middleweight title in Detroit, September 13, 1950.

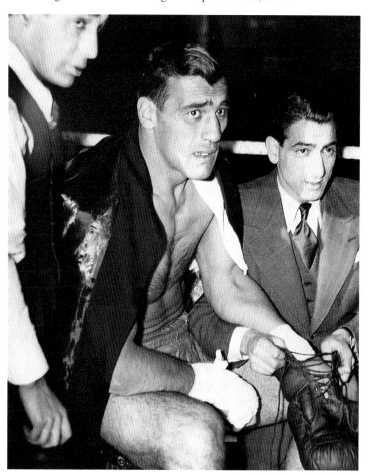

MAN MOUNTAIN *Primo Carnera was the heaviest man to fight for a title*

Paul Vaden w ko 12 Vince Pettway (2:33) to win the IBF light-middleweight title in Las Vegas on August 12, 1995.

Mike Weaver w ko 15 (2:15) John Tate to win the WBA heavyweight title in Knoxville, Tennessee on March 31, 1980.

Oscar Albarado w ko 15 (1:57) Koichi Wajima to win the WBA light-middleweight title in Tokyo on June 4, 1974.

Jeff Harding w rsf 12 (1:23) Dennis Andries to win the WBC light-heavyweight title in Atlantic City on June 24, 1989.

Humberto Gonzalez w rsf 12 (55 sec) Kwang-Sun Kim to retain the WBC light-flyweight title in Seoul on June 7, 1992.

Highest number of inside-schedule wins

Archie Moore, with 145 between 1936 and 1963. Young Stribling is second with 126 (1921–33) and Billy Bird third with 125 (1920–48).

Most consecutive quick wins

Heavyweight Lamar Clark, who scored 44 (mostly against very poor opposition) between 1958 and 1960. Blackjack Billy Fox is second with 43 between 1943 and 1946, but at least one – the notorious stoppage of Jake LaMotta – was fixed, and it may safely be assumed that this was not the first time it had happened in his career. No such suspicion attaches to the third-highest, Ghanaian bantamweight Bob Allotey, who scored 33 between 1957 and 1963, or to the brilliant Wilfredo Gomez, who had 32 between 1974 and 1981.

Longest unbeaten streak

Hal Bagwell (183, 1938–48)
Packey McFarland (97, 1905–15)
Fred Dyer (94, 1908–12)
Pedro Carrasco (93, 1964–71)
Ray Robinson (91, 1943–51)
Julio Cesar Chavez (90, 1980–94)

Olympic champions who won professional world titles

1920 Frankie Genaro (flyweight);
1924 Jackie Fields (featherweight); Willie Smith (bantamweight); Fidel LaBarba (flyweight);
1948 Pascual Perez (flyweight);
1952 Floyd Patterson (middleweight);
1960 Cassius Clay (light-heavy); Nino Benvenuti (welterweight);
1964 Joe Frazier (heavyweight);
1968 George Foreman (heavyweight);
1972 Mate Parlov (light-heavy);
1976 Leon Spinks (light-heavy); Mike Spinks (middleweight); Ray Leonard (light-welter); Leo Randolph (flyweight);
1980 Slobodan Kacar (light-heavy); Patrizio Oliva (light-welter);
1984 Frank Tate (light-middle); Mark Breland (welterweight); Pernell Whitaker (lightweight); Meldrick Taylor (featherweight); Maurizio Stecca (bantamweight);
1988 Lennox Lewis (super-heavy); Ray Mercer (heavyweight); Henry Maske (middleweight); Giovanni Parisi (featherweight); Kennedy McKinney (bantamweight);
1992 Oscar De La Hoya (lightweight).

... AND LOSERS

World champions who were unsuccessful in five or more world title fights (losses, unless otherwise specified)

10 Tony Canzoneri (9 losses, 1 draw)

9 Betulio Gonzalez (7 losses, 2 draws)

8 Emile Griffith, Shoji Oguma (7 losses, 1 draw), Sugar Ray Robinson (7 losses, 1 draw)

7 Susumu Hanagata, Juan LaPorte, Daniel Zaragoza (4 losses, 3 draws)

6 Iran Barkley, Carmen Basilio, Rocky Lockridge, Jersey Joe Walcott, Jack Britton (4 losses, 2 draws), Gene Fullmer (3 losses, 3 draws), Leo Gamez (5 losses, 1 draw), Hiroki Ioka (5 losses, 1 draw), Luis Mendoza (5 losses, 1 draw), Jorge Paez (4 losses, 2 draws), Hilario Zapata (5 losses, 1 draw),

5 Fabrice Benichou, Don Curry, Albert Davila, Roberto Duran, Larry Holmes, Thierry Jacob, Roger Mayweather, Ruben Olivares, Floyd Patterson, Jose Luis Ramirez, Sugar Baby Rojas, German Torres, Terry Allen (4 losses, 1 draw), Sot Chitalada (4 losses, 1 draw), Carlos De Leon (4 losses, 1 draw), Harry Forbes (4 losses, 1 draw), Frankie Genaro (3 losses, 2 draws), Thomas Hearns (4 losses, 1 draw), Soo-Chun Kwon (3 losses, 2 draws), Tony Lopez (4 losses, 1 draw), Freddie Miller (4 losses, 1 No Contest), Azumah Nelson (3 losses, 2 draws), Raul Perez (3 losses, 1 draw, 1 technical draw), Lou Salica (4 losses, 1 draw), Marlon Starling (3 losses, 1 draw, 1 No Contest), Ishimatsu Susuki (4 losses, 1 draw), Ben Villamor (2 losses, 3 draws,) Marcos Villasana (4 losses, 1 draw), Koichi Wajima (4 losses, 1 draw)

World champions with more than 50 defeats

65 Fritzie Zivic
52 Lauro Salas
51 Johnny Jadick

Statistics can be misleading: Zivic was a famously tough and durable fighter who beat many outstanding performers, including Henry Armstrong, in a 232-fight career.

Most knockdowns suffered in a title challenge

Fourteen, by English bantamweight Danny O'Sullivan against South African champion Vic Toweel in Johannesburg on December 2, 1950. O'Sullivan was down eight times in the fifth round, but somehow kept going until the 10th, when he retired.

THE LONGEST

Longest fight

110 rounds (7 hours 19 minutes) Andy Bowen drew with Jack Burke, New Orleans, April 6, 1893.

Longest bare-knuckle fight

6 hours 15 minutes, James Kelly vs. Jack Smith at Melbourne, Australia, October 19, 1856.

Longest title reigns in each division

Heavyweight: Joe Louis (11 years, eight months, 18 days)
Cruiser: Anaclet Wamba (4 years 5 months to end of 1995)
Light-heavyweight: Archie Moore (9 years 2 months)
Super-middleweight: Chong Pal Park (3 years 6 months)
Middleweight: Carlos Monzon (6 years 9 months)
Light-middleweight:: Gianfranco Rosi (5 years 2 months)
Welterweight: Freddie Cochrane (4 years, 6 months, 3 days, one day longer than Jose Napoles managed)
Light-welterweight: Julio Cesar Chavez (4 years 8 months)
Lightweight: Roberto Duran (6 years 7 months)
Super-featherweight: Flash Elorde (7 years 3 months)
Featherweight: Eusebio Pedroza (7 years 2 months)
Super-bantamweight: Wilfredo Gomez (5 years 10 months)
Bantamweight: Orlando Canizales (6 years 5 months)
Super-flyweight: Kaosai Galaxy (7 years 1 month)
Flyweight: Jimmy Wilde (7 years 4 months)
Light-flyweight: Myung Woo Yuh (6 years)
Strawweight: Ricardo Lopez (5 years 2 months to end of 1995)

THE SHORTEST

Shortest fight on record

Ever Beleno vs. Alfredo Lugo, April 21, 1995, five seconds.

Shortest world championship reign

Technically the distinction belongs to Pernell Whitaker, who relinquished

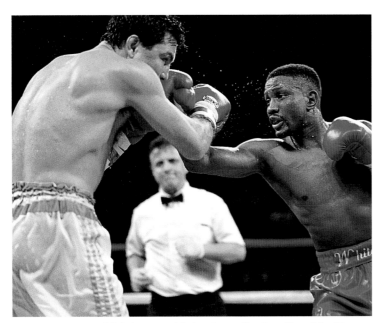

PERNELL WHITAKER *(right) won a title but immediately relinquished it*

the WBA light-middleweight title immediately after winning it from Julio Cesar Vasquez in Atlantic City on March 4, 1995. There have also been cases where a man has won a title but then been stripped of it after failing a drugs test, but flyweight Emile Pladner, whose 47-day reign extended from March 2, 1929 to April 18, 1929, was the quickest to lose it in the ring.

Shortest-reigning European champion

Featherweight Ernst Weiss of Austria, whose 31-day reign lasted from May 30 to June 30, 1941.

Shortest-reigning British champion

Frank Goddard, who was heavyweight champion for just 24 days from May 25 to June 17, 1919.

Shortest-reigning Commonwealth champion

Heavyweight Richard Dunn, who won the title on September 30, 1975 and lost it 36 days later, on November 4.

NOTABLE FIRSTS

First Lonsdale Belt outright winners

Heavyweight: Billy Wells (1916).
Cruiserweight: Johnny Nelson (1991).
Light-heavyweight: Dick Smith (1918).
Super-middle: Sam Storey (1995).
Middleweight: Len Harvey (1930).
Light-middleweight: Maurice Hope (1976).
Welterweight: Johnny Basham (1916).
Light-welterweight: Joey Singleton (1975).
Lightweight: Freddie Welsh (1912).
Junior-light/Super-featherweight: Jimmy Anderson (1969).
Featherweight: Jim Driscoll (1911).
Bantamweight: Digger Stanley (1913).
Flyweight: Jimmy Wilde (1917).

First to win three world titles

Bob Fitzsimmons – middleweight 1891, heavyweight 1897 and light-heavyweight 1903.

First (and only man) to hold three titles simultaneously

Henry Armstrong – featherweight 1937, welterweight 1938, and lightweight 1938.

First world heavyweight title fight outside America

Tommy Burns vs. Gunner Moir in London on December 2, 1907.

First judges in a world heavyweight title bout

Tex Rickard and Anthony Drexel Biddle, for the Jack Dempsey vs. Jess Willard fight on July 4, 1919.

First woman to judge a title fight

Eva Shain (Muhammad Ali vs. Earnie Shavers in New York on September 29, 1977).

First to win a world title on disqualification

Pedlar Palmer, against Billy Plimmer in London on November 25, 1895.

First black referee in a world title bout

Zack Clayton, who handled Jersey Joe Walcott vs. Ezzard Charles on June 5, 1952.

First million-dollar gate

Jack Dempsey vs. Georges Carpentier, at Rickard's Oval, Jersey City on July 2, 1921. 80,183 fans paid $1,789,238. It was the first of the five million-dollar gates Dempsey drew, the others being against Luis Firpo, Gene Tunney (twice) and Jack Sharkey.

First brothers to retain world titles on the same show

Rafael and Gabriel Ruelas, in Las Vegas on January 28, 1995. Rafael stopped Billy Schwer in eight rounds to retain the IBF lightweight title, and Gabriel kept his WBC super-featherweight crown by stopping Fred Liberatore in the second round.

First use of a motion picture camera

Exhibition between James J. Corbett and Peter Courtney over six rounds at Edison Laboratories, Llewellyn, NJ, in 1897. Corbett knocked him out in the final round.

First movie of a fight

Bob Fitzsimmons vs. James J. Corbett, Carson City, Nevada, March 17, 1897.

First movie of a fight in Britain

Jack Johnson vs. Ben Taylor at the Cosmopolitan Gymnasium, Plymouth on July 31, 1908

First radio transmisson of a fight result

Jack Dempsey vs. Jess Willard at Toledo, Ohio on July 4, 1919.

First radio commentary

Packey O'Gatty vs. Frankie Burns at Boyle's Thirty Acres, Jersey City on July 2, 1921, a preliminary on the Dempsey vs. Carpentier card. This was also the fight in which, for the first time, the ring MC used a microphone.

First radio commentary in Britain

Johnny Curley vs. Harry Corbett at the National Sporting Club, London on March 29, 1926

First televised boxing

Exhibition between Archie Sexton and Laurie Raiteri at Broadcasting House, London on August 22, 1933.

First televised fight

Len Harvey vs. Jock McAvoy at Harringay Arena, April 4, 1938.

First televised fight to be publicly screened

Eric Boon vs. Arthur Danahar at Harringay Arena, February 23, 1939.

First closed-circuit screening

Joe Louis vs. Lee Savold in New York on June 15, 1951.

First British closed-circuit screening

Willie Pastrano vs. Terry Downes for the world light-heavyweight title in Manchester on November 30, 1964. It was shown in the Phoenix Theatre, London.

First million-dollar purse

Sonny Liston and Floyd Patterson were each paid $1,434,000 for their heavyweight title rematch in Las Vegas on July 22, 1963.

First use of a four-roped ring in title fight

Emile Griffith vs. Luis Rodriguez for the welterweight title in New York on June 8, 1963. The fourth rope was introduced as a safety measure following Benny Paret's death in a fight with Griffith the previous year, when he became entangled in the ropes and was unable to avoid Griffith's punches.

First champion from each country

Algeria – Marcel Cerdan (1948)
America – Paddy Duffy (1888)
Antigua – Maurice Hope (1979)
Argentina – Pascual Perez (1954)
Australia – Jimmy Carruthers (1952)
Austria – Jack Root (1903)
Bahamas – Elisha Obed (1975)
Barbados – Joe Walcott (1901)
Belgium – Gustav Roth (1936)
Brazil – Eder Jofre (1960)
Canada – George Dixon (1890)
Colombia – Antonio Cervantes (1972)
Cuba – Kid Chocolate (1931)

MIKE McCALLUM *Jamaica's first*

Congo – Anaclet Wamba (1991)
Denmark – Battling Nelson (1905)
Dominican Republic – Carlos Teo Cruz (1968)
France – Charles Ledoux (1912)
England – Bob Fitzsimmons (1891)
Germany – Frank Mantell (1907)
Ghana – David Kotey (1975)
Greece – Anton Christoforidis (1941)
Guadaloupe – Gilbert Dele (1991)
Guyana – Dennis Andries (1986)
Hawaii – Dado Marino (1952)
Indonesia – Elly Pical (1985)
Ireland – "Nonpareil" Jack Dempsey (1884)
Italy – Frankie Conley (1910)
Jamaica – Mike McCallum (1984)
Japan – Yoshio Shirai (1952)
Korea – Kim Ki-Soo (1966)
Kyrgyzstan – Orzubek Nazarov (1993)
Martinique – Daniel Londas (1992)
Mauritania – Taoufik Belbouli (1989)
Mexico – Battling Shaw (1933)
New Zealand – Billy Murphy (1890)
Nicaragua – Alexis Arguello (1974)
Nigeria – Hogan Bassey (1957)
Norway – Pete Sanstol (1931)
Panama – Panama Al Brown (1929)
Philippines – Pancho Villa (1923)
Puerto Rico – Sixto Escobar (1934)
Russia – Louis Kid Kaplan (1925)
Scotland – Tancy Lee (1915)
Senegal – Battling Siki (1922)
South Africa – Willie Smith (1927)
Spain – Baltazar Sangchilli (1935)
Sweden – Ingemar Johansson (1959)

CHARLES LEDOUX *first French champ*

Switzerland – Frank Erne (1899)
Thailand – Pone Kingpetch (1960)
Trinidad – Claude Noel (1981)
Tunisia – Victor Young Perez (1931)
Uganda – Ayub Kalule (1979)
Venezuela – Carlos Hernandez (1965)
Virgin Islands – Emile Griffith (1961)
Wales – Jim Driscoll (1912)
Yugoslavia – Mate Parlov (1978)
Zaire – Sumbu Kalambay (1987)

THE FASTEST

Fastest one-round finish to a title fight in each division (winner named first)

Heavyweight: James J. Jeffries vs. Jack Finnegan, 55 seconds, April 6, 1900.
Cruiserweight: James Warring vs. James Pritchard, 24 seconds, September 6, 1991.
Light-heavyweight: Bobby Czyz vs. David Sears, 61 seconds, December 12, 1986.
Super-middleweight: Roy Jones vs. Antoine Byrd, 126 seconds, March 18, 1995.
Middleweight: Bernard Hopkin vs. Steve Frank, 24 seconds, January 27, 1996.
Light-middleweight: Julio Cesar Vasquez vs. Aquilino Asprilla, 47 seconds, February 22, 1993.
Welterweight: Lloyd Honeyghan vs. Gene Hatcher, 45 seconds, August 30, 1987.
Light-welterweight: Akinobu Hiranaka vs. Edwin Rosario, 92 seconds, April 10, 1992.
Lightweight: Tony Canzoneri vs. Al Singer, 66 seconds, November 14, 1930.
Super-featherweight: Genaro Hernandez vs. Raul Perez (technical draw) 28 seconds, April 26, 1993.
Featherweight: Kuniaki Shibata vs. Raul Cruz, 124 seconds, June 3, 1971.
Super-bantamweight: Daniel Jiminez vs. Harold Geier, 19 seconds, September 3, 1994.
Bantamweight: Sixto Escobar vs. Indian Quintana, 109 seconds, October 13, 1936.
Super-flyweight: Joo-Do Chun vs. Diego del Valle, 155 seconds, March 17, 1984.
Flyweight: Emile Pladner vs. Frankie Genaro, 58 seconds, March 2, 1929.
Light-flyweight: Myung-Woo Yuh vs. Eduardo Tunon, 166 seconds, March 1, 1987.
Strawweight: Ricardo Lopez vs. Yamil Caraballo, 70 seconds, December 10, 1994.

Fastest world title fight

Daniel Jiminez's 19-second knockout of Harold Geier of Austria to retain the WBO super-bantamweight title at Wreiner Neustadt on September 3, 1994.

Fastest British title fight

Dave Charnley w ko 1 Darkie Hughes for the European, British and Empire lightweight title in 40 seconds at Nottingham on November 20, 1961. This fight also holds the record for the quickest finish to both a British and Empire (later Commonwealth) championship.

THE OLDEST

Oldest men to win titles

Heavyweight: George Foreman (45 years, 10 months, 25 days)
Cruiserweight: James Warring (33 years, 9 months, 11 days)
Light-heavyweight: Bob Fitzsimmons (40 years, 5 months, 30 days)
Super-middleweight: Sugarboy Malinga (36 years, 2 months, 20 days)
Middleweight: Roberto Duran (37 years, 8 months, 8 days)
Light-middleweight: Gianfranco Rosi (38 years, 9 months, 9 days)
Welterweight: Jack Britton (33 years, 5 months, 3 days)
Light-welterweight: Juan M. Coggi (34 years, 24 days)
Lightweight: Claude Noel (33 years, 1 month, 18 days)
Super-featherweight: Azumah Nelson (37 years, 2 months, 12 days)

GRANDAD GEORGE *Champion at 45*

Featherweight: Eder Jofre (37 years, 1 month, 10 days)
Super-bantamweight: Daniel Zaragoza (37 years, 5 months, 26 days)
Bantamweight: Johnny Buff (33 years, 3 months, 11 days)
Super-flyweight: Santos Laciar (28 years, 3 months, 16 days)
Flyweight: Dado Marino (33 years, 11 months, 6 days)
Light-flyweight: Luis Estaba (34 years, 1 month)
Strawweight: Samuth Sithnaruepol (28 years, 10 months, 7 days)

THE YOUNGEST

Youngest men to win titles

Heavyweight: Mike Tyson (20 years, four months, 22 days)
Cruiserweight: Carlos DeLeon (21 years, 6 months, 20 days)
Light-heavyweight: Michael Moorer (21 years, 21 days)
Super-middleweight: Darrin Van Horn (22 years, 8 months, 11 days)
Middleweight: Al McCoy (19 years, 5 months, 14 days)
Light-middleweight: Darrin Van Horn (20 years, 4 months, 28 days)
Welterweight: Pipino Cuevas (18 years, 6 months, 20 days)
Light-welterweight: Wilfred Benitez (17 years, 5 months, 24 days)
Lightweight: Edwin Rosario (20 years, 1 month, 17 days)
Super-featherweight: Ben Villaflor (19 years, 5 months, 15 days)
Featherweight: Tony Canzoneri (18 years, 11 months, 18 days)
Super-bantamweight: Julio Gervacio (20 years, 1 month, 11 days)
Bantamweight: Teddy Baldock (18 years, 11 months, 15 days)
Super-flyweight: Cesar Polanco (18 years, 2 months, 17 days)
Flyweight: Joe Symonds (19 years, 4 months, 18 days)
Light-flyweight: Netrnoi Vorasingh (19 years, 14 days)
Strawweight: Hiroki Ioka (18 years, 9 months, 10 days)

THE HEAVYWEIGHTS

Shortest-reigning heavyweight champion

Tony Tucker (two months, one day).

Longest unbeaten run en route to the heavyweight title

Rocky Marciano (43)
George Foreman (38)
Tony Tucker (35, including one No Contest)
Riddick Bowe (32)
Mike Tyson (31).

Heavyweight champion with the fewest fights when winning title

Leon Spinks (8).

Heavyweight champion with the most fights

Ezzard Charles (122). Charles also had the most defeats (25), although many of those occured after he had lost the title.

Smallest attendance at a heavyweight title fight

2,434 to watch the rematch between Muhammad Ali and Sonny Liston at a High School arena in Lewiston, Maine on May 25, 1965.

Greatest combined weight in a title fight

488 ¾ lb, when Primo Carnera (259½ lb) outpointed Paulino Uzcudun (229 ¼ lb) in Rome on October 22, 1933. This was also the only occasion when two Europeans contested the world heavyweight title. (Lennox Lewis's meeting with Frank Bruno involved only the WBC version of the title.)

BAD STARTS

World champions who lost professional debut

Bruno Arcari, Henry Armstrong, Rodolfo Blanco, Jack Britton, Joe Brown, Victor Callejas, Miguel Canto, Freddie Castillo, Jesus Castillo, Frank Cedeno, Chang-Ho Choi, Billy Conn, Roberto Cruz, Carlos Teo Cruz, Pipino Cuevas, Joe Dundee, Harry Forbes, Nestor Giovanni, S.T. Gordon, Bernard Hopkins, Daniel Jiminez, Sung Jun Kim, Tae-Shik Kim, Pone Kingpetch, Tippy Larkin, Alfredo Layne, Benny Leonard, Benny Lynch, Tacy Macalos, Eddie Martin, Manny Melchor, Manuel Ortiz, Freddie Pendleton, Eddie Perkins, Bonecrusher Smith, Seung-Il Suk, Wilfredo Vasquez, Mike Weaver, Prince Charles Williams

World champions held to a draw on debut

Pedro Adigue, Rolando Bohol, Jeff Chandler, Tae-Il Chung, Victor Cordoba, Jack Dempsey, Jack Dillon, Ralph Dupas, Angel Espada, Johnny Famechon, Perico Fernandez, Ceferino Garcia, Wilfredo Gomez, Pete Herman, Soo Hwan Hong, Beau Jack, Matty Matthews, Dave McAuley, Tod Morgan, Billy Papke, Young Perez, Bernardo Pinango, Dwight Muhammad Qawi, Rigoberto Riasco, Arnold Taylor, Aquiles Guzman, Buddy McGirt, Jake Rodriguez, Gabriel Ruelas, Johnny Tapia

KINGS OF THE DRAW

World champions who fought 10 or more draws

41	George Dixon
37	Young Griffo
31	Tod Morgan
30	Joe Walcott
28	Mysterious Billy Smith
23	Harry Forbes
22	Maxie Rosenbloom
20	Jack Britton, Bob Godwin, Jimmy Goodrich, Solly Smith, Johnny Thompson
19	Torpedo Billy Murphy, Battling Nelson
18	Abe Attell ,Johnny Dundee, Matty Matthews, Jimmy Walsh
16	Philadelphia Jack O'Brien, Midget Wolgast
15	Perico Fernandez, Ceferino Garcia, Benny Lynch, Young Perez, Dave Sullivan, Chalky Wright
14	Mike Ballarino, Jack Dillon, Dixie Kid, Nicolino Locche, Honey Mellody, Marcel Thil, Ad Wolgast
13	Baby Arizmendi, Joe Brown, Young Corbett III, Vince Dundee, Gorilla Jones, Battling Levinsky, Ted Kid Lewis, Joe Lynch
12	Miguel Angel Castellini, Frank Erne, Tommy Freeman, Louis Kid Kaplan, Frankie Klick, Al McCoy, Willie Ritchie, Lauro Salas, Lou Salica, Cpl. Izzy Schwartz, Young Jack Thompson
11	Panama Al Brown, Jackie Callura, Paddy Duffy, Jack Johnson, Santos Laciar, Leo Rodak, Phil Terranova
10	Tony Canzoneri, Young Corbett II, Eugene Criqui, Joe Dundee, George Gardner, Al Hostak, George Lavigne, Small Montana, George Nichols, Emile Pladner, Ed Babe Risko, Petey Sarron

BOXING CHRONOLOGY

Who, what, where and when ... an at-a-glance guide to some of the pivotal events in boxing history.

1681 (January) First known newspaper report of a prize-fight appears in the *Protestant Mercury*.

1743 Jack Broughton introduces the first set of formal rules to govern prize-fights.

1810 (December 18) Tom Cribb beats Tom Molineaux, a former slave, in the first major international match.

1838 London Prize Ring Rules are established.

1860 (April 17) Tom Sayers fights a 42-round draw with John Carmel Heenan of America in the last great prize-fight to be staged in England.

1867 The Queensberry Rules are published by John Graham Chambers.

1882 (February 7) John L. Sullivan beats Paddy Ryan in nine rounds to become the last bare-knuckle heavyweight champion.

1889 (July 8) Sullivan stops Jake Kilrain in 75 rounds in the last bare-knuckle title fight.

1891 The National Sporting Club is formed in London: it will administer the sport in Britain until 1929.

1892 (September 7) James J. Corbett knocks out Sullivan in 21 rounds in the first gloved heavyweight title fight.

1897 (March 17) Bob Fitzsimmons becomes the only English-born world heavyweight champion by knocking out James J. Corbett in the 14th round. The fight also marks the birth of the movie age, as it is the first to be filmed.

1907 (December 2) The world heavyweight title is contested outside America for the first time as Tommy Burns beats Gunner Moir in London.

1908 (December 26) Jack Johnson, the first black heavyweight champion, takes the title from Tommy Burns in Sydney. Race riots ensue across America, and the hunt begins for a Great White Hope to beat him.

1909 (September) *Boxing*, a weekly paper, makes its first appearance. It survives today as *Boxing News*, the oldest publication in the world devoted exclusively to the sport.

1910 (July 4) Jack Johnson stops James J. Jeffries in a much-publicized "black vs. white" battle.
(December 26) Jimmy Wilde, the first great flyweight champion, makes his pro debut.

1911 The Frawley Law legalizes boxing in New York. The International Boxing Union (IBU) is formed.

1913 (October 6) Ted "Kid" Lewis wins the first of his many titles, beating Alec Lambert for the British featherweight championship.

1920 The New York State Athletic Commission takes over the running of boxing in the state, and will become the most influential governing body in the world. The National Boxing Association is formed at a meeting in New York.

1921 (July 2) Jack Dempsey knocks out Georges Carpentier in the first fight to draw a million dollars.

1923 (March 17) Mike McTigue outpoints Battling Siki over 20 rounds to win the world light-heavyweight title in the last world title bout to go more than 15 rounds.

1926 (October 22) Harry Greb, former middleweight champion and veteran of 299 fights, dies following an eye operation.

1927 (September 22) Jack Dempsey fails to regain the heavyweight title from Gene Tunney in the famous "Battle Of The Long Count".

1929 The British Boxing Board of Control is formed.

1931 (April 24) Tony Canzoneri wins his third world title by knocking out light-welterweight champion Jack Kid" Berg.

Jack Solomons, the most flamboyant and successful British promoter, stages his first show. He loses £275.

1933 (June 23) Barney Ross wins the first of his three world titles (lightweight, light-welterweight and welter-weight).
(June 29) The Mob's proudest achievement: Primo Carnera takes the heavyweight title from Jack Sharkey.

1935 (June 13) James J. Braddock wins the heavy-weight title in a huge upset, outpointing Max Baer.

1937 (August 30) Tommy Farr of Wales, whom the Americans considered a no-hoper, defies Joe Louis for the full 15 rounds in Louis' first defence of the heavy-weight title.
(October 13) Scottish fly-weight Benny Lynch retains the world title in a thriller against Peter Kane.

1938 (April 4) Television comes to boxing as the Len Harvey vs. Jock McAvoy fight becomes the first to be shown on TV.
(August 17) Henry Arm-strong beats Lou Ambers to become the only man in his-tory to hold three titles simultaneously: feather-weight, lightweight and welterweight.

1939 (September 30) The last scheduled 20-rounds world title fight takes place: Joe Louis knocks out Bob Pastor in the 11th round.

1941 (June 18) Joe Louis scores his finest victory when, trailing on points, he knocks out Billy Conn in the 13th round to retain the heavyweight title.

1948 (July 26) Freddie Mills ends Gus Lesnevich's long spell as light-heavyweight champion, in London.
(October 29) Willie Pep's fabulous reign as featherweight champion is ended by Sandy Saddler.
The European Boxing Union is formed.

1949 (October 27) Marcel Cerdan, the best and most popular European fighter since Georges Carpentier, dies in a plane crash on his way to America for a middleweight title rematch with Jake LaMotta.

1951 (February 14) Ray Robinson wins the first of his five middleweight titles, stopping Jake LaMotta in 14 rounds.
(July 10) Randolph Turpin scores a famous victory by dethroning Robinson in London. He reigns for just 64 days, losing the title back to Robinson in September.

1952 (September 23) Rocky Marciano wins the heavyweight title from Jersey Joe Walcott.
(November 15) Australia's first undisputed world champion, Jimmy Carruthers, knocks out Vic Toweel in the first round to win the bantamweight title.

1956 (April 27) Rocky Marciano retires as heavyweight champion, the only one to remain undefeated throughout his entire career.

1959 (June 26) Ingemar Johanason brings the heavyweight title back to Europe by stopping Floyd Patterson in New York.

1960 (March 16) Gabriel "Flash" Elorde wins the recently revived 130 lb title. He will retain it 10 times, and earn the division general acceptance.
(April 16) Thailand's first champion, Pone Kingpetch, takes the flyweight title from long-reigning Pascual Perez.
(June 20) Floyd Patterson becomes the first to regain the heavyweight title, knocking out Ingemar Johansson in five rounds.

1961 (October 28) Joe Brown sets a lightweight record by retaining the title for the 11th and final time, beating Bert Somodio on points.

1962 (April 2) Benny Paret dies after being stopped in a welterweight title defence by Emile Griffith.
(August) The National Boxing Association changes its name to the World Boxing Association: the Alphabet Boys are born.

1963 (February 14) The World Boxing Council is formed in Mexico City.
(July 22) Sonny Liston and Floyd Patterson become the first to earn over $1m when they each get $1,434,000 for their heavyweight title rematch.

1964 (February 25) Cassius Clay (Muhammad Ali) shocks the world by beating Sonny Liston for the heavyweight title.

1971 (March 8) Muhammad Ali loses for the first time as Joe Frazier retains the heavyweight title in New York.
(March 16) Henry Cooper, Britain's longest-serving heavyweight champion and the only boxer to win three Lonsdale Belts outright, retires after a controversial loss to Joe Bugner.

1972 (June 26) Roberto Duran wins his first world title, beating lightweight champion Ken Buchanan in 13 rounds in New York.

1976 (March 6) Wilfred Benitez of Puerto Rico becomes the youngest world champion in history when, aged 17 years and six months, he takes the WBA light-welterweight title from Antonio Cervantes.

1977 (August 29) Carlos Monzon, the most successful middleweight champion in history with 14 defences, retires as undefeated champion

1978 (June 9) Larry Holmes launches one of the great championship reigns by beating Ken Norton for the WBC heavyweight title.

1981 (June 20) Nicaraguan Alexis Arguello wins his third world title, outpointing Scotland's Jim Watt for the WBC lightweight title.

1982 (August 12) Featherweight champion Salvador Sanchez, a brilliant Mexican, dies in a car crash just weeks after retaining his WBC title against future champion Azumah Nelson.

1983 The International Boxing Federation is formed by a breakaway group from the WBA.
(April) Wilfredo Gomez relinquishes the WBC super-bantamweight title after a record 17 defences, all inside the distance.

1985 (June 8) Ireland's most successful fighter, Barry McGuigan, wins the WBA featherweight title from Eusebio Pedroza, making his 20th defence.

1986 (November 22) Mike Tyson becomes the youngest heavyweight champion by taking the WBC title from Trevor Berbick at the age of 20 years and five months.

1987 (April 6) Ray Leonard ends Marvin Hagler's reign as middleweight champion after 12 successful defences.

1988 (April 9) Evander Holyfield unifies the cruiserweight titles for the only time in the division's history.

(November 4) Thomas Hearns becomes the first to win titles in five divisions, beating his arch-rival Ray Leonard to the record by three days.

1990 (February 11) Buster Douglas knocks out Mike Tyson in the biggest shock in boxing history.
(July 28) Dennis Andries makes British boxing history by winning the WBC light-heavyweight title for the third time, knocking out Jeff Harding in seven rounds.

1992 (October 15) Duke McKenzie takes the WBO super-bantamweight title from Jesse Benavides to become the first British boxer to claim world titles in three divisions.

1993 (November 6) Evander Holyfield regains the heavyweight title from Riddick Bowe, in an epic fight interrupted by the arrival in the ring of a para-glider.

1994 (January 29) Julio Cesar Chavez, world champion at three weights and the greatest fighter of his time, loses the WBC light-welterweight title to Frankie Randall. It is his first defeat in 91 fights.
(November 5) George Foreman becomes the oldest-ever world champion at any weight when, aged 45 years and 10 months, he takes the heavyweight title from Michael Moorer.

1995 (March 18) Steve Collins wins his second WBO title, and ends Chris Eubank's 43-fight unbeaten record, to become super-middleweight champion.
(September 2) Frank Bruno wins a version of the heavyweight title at the fourth attempt, outpointing Oliver McCall to become WBC champion.

1996 (March 16) Mike Tyson regains the WBC title by stopping Frank Bruno in the third round in Las Vegas.

INDEX

The publishers would like to thank the following sources for
their kind permission to reproduce the pictures in this book:

Action Images; Allsport Al Bello, Simon Bruty, David Cannon,
Chris Cole, Phil Cole, Robert Dibue, Stephen Dunn, John
Gichigi, Jed Jacobsohn, David Leah, Ken Levine, Bob Martin,
Marc Morrisson, Mike Powell, Steve Powell, Holly Stein, Patty
Wood; **Allsport Historical/Hulton Getty Collection; Allsport
Historical/MSI; Associated Press; Boxing News; Corbis-
Bettmann**/UPI; **Mary Evans Picture Library; Popperfoto.**

Special thanks are due to Daffydd Bynon at Allsport and Boxing
News for allowing us to decimate their photographic archive.

*Every effort has been made to acknowledge correctly and
contact the source and/or copyright holder of each picture, and
Carlton Books Ltd apologises for any unintentional errors or
omissions which will be corrected in future editions of this book.*